Hiking the Sierra Nevada

A Guide to the Area's Greatest
Hiking Adventures

Third Edition

Barry Parr

FALCONGUIDES

GUILFORD, CONNECTICUT
HELENA, MONTANA
AN IMPRINT OF GLOBE PEQUOT PRESS

To my brother, Doug, a longtime mountaineer.
"The clearest way into the Universe is through a forest wilderness." —John Muir

To buy books in quantity for corporate use
or incentives, call **(800) 962-0973**
or e-mail **premiums@GlobePequot.com.**

FALCONGUIDES®

All interior photographs are by the author unless otherwise noted.

Layout: Mary Ballachino
Maps by Daniel Lloyd © Morris Book Publishing, LLC

Library of Congress Cataloging-in-Publication data is available on file.

ISSN 1555-4945
ISBN 978-0-7627-8237-6

Printed in the United States of America
10 9 8 7 6 5 4 3 2 1

Contents

The Hikes

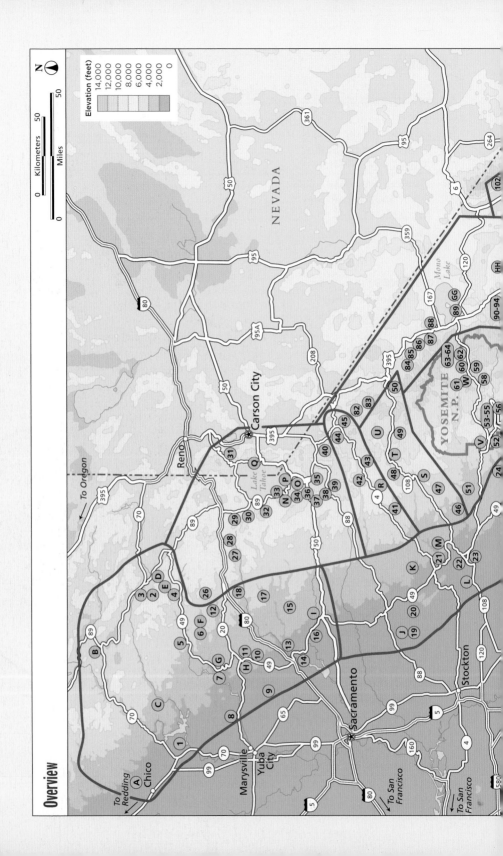

Overview

Elevation (feet)
14,000
12,000
10,000
8,000
6,000
4,000
2,000
0

Kilometers

Miles

NEVADA

Carson City

Reno

Lake Tahoe

To Oregon

To Redding

Chico

Marysville
Yuba City

Sacramento

Stockton

YOSEMITE N.P.

Mono Lake

To San Francisco

To San Francisco

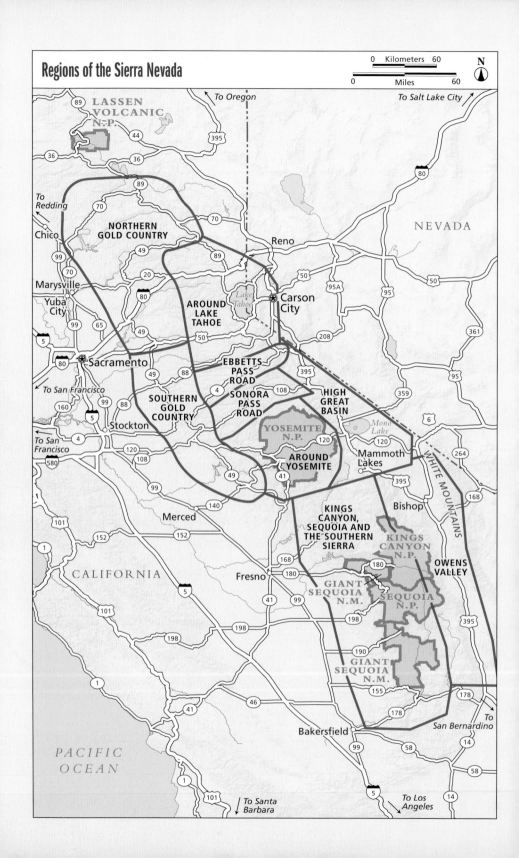

Acknowledgments

I greatly appreciate the time and effort that many people took to read and comment on parts of this book over different editions, including Forest Service rangers and personnel Susan Burkindine, Larry Randall, Jeff Weise, Terry Martin Austin, Jon Jue, Lester Lubetkin, Joy Barney, Dean Lutz, David E. Michael, and Don Lane. A special shout out to seasonal rangers Lauren Hollen and Angela Tomczik of the White Mountain Ranger District of Inyo National Forest for their generous time; to Alexandria Williams, who runs their Junior Ranger Program; and to their Area Manager, John Louth, who produced the highly informative video on Bristlecone Pines for the Schulman Grove Visitor Center. Thanks also to Matt Green of Empire Mine State Park, Wendy Harrison of Calaveras Big Trees State Park, Mark Fincher of Yosemite, Dayna Higgins of the Sequoia Natural History Association, and Mary Cole, Carol Hallacy, and Denise Alonzo of Sequoia National Forest and Sequoia National Monument. A special thanks to Steve Diers of the East Bay Municipal Utilities District, not only for his kindly advice, but for his dedication to the construction of the Mokelumne Coast to Crest Trail. Last but not least, I would like to express my deep appreciation to Bill Schneider for signing me on with Falcon Guides in the beginning, and to my editors Imee Curiel, Marianne Steiger, and Roberta Monaco.

Mule Ears, the backpacker's best friend, has been known for centuries to make excellent "mountain money."

Introduction

The Sierra Nevada is a superlative range. Roughly 400 miles long from Tehachapi Pass to where it fades into the Cascade Range just north of the Feather River, and from 50 to 80 miles wide, it is the longest single mountain range (as opposed to a mountain system like the Rockies) in the continental United States. Within that purview you will find the largest and oldest trees, the most temperate summer climate, the greatest snow depths, the mightiest escarpment, the deepest canyon (arguably), and the highest waterfalls in the United States. Its rivers water the richest agricultural region, and its placers and quartz veins produced and still hoard the richest gold deposits. The highest US mountain outside of Alaska is a Sierra summit, Mount Whitney. The oldest large-scale public park to be established by the federal government—the nation's first "national" park, if you will—is the combined parcels of Yosemite Valley and the Wawona Grove of giant sequoias, signed over to the state of California by President Abraham Lincoln in 1864, eight years before Congress created Yellowstone National Park.

What sets the Sierra Nevada apart from other landscapes, however, owes more to the testimony of the senses than to factual assessments. For anyone even moderately receptive to the beauty of mountain landscapes, the Sierra Nevada offers a lifetime of enthralling study, pleasure, and recreation. No matter where you go, there is always something extraordinary to experience. The scent of pungent mountain misery is every bit as heady as the aroma of deep pine forests or sagebrush basins. The dazzling wildflower pastures of Butte County in spring or of Carson Pass in summer give way to the dazzling autumnal leaf displays of the eastern canyons of Mono, Alpine, and Inyo Counties. The widest, most sublime of Sierra vistas evokes a sense of wonder no less engaging than the most exquisite details that lie immediately under our noses: a trailside rock garden, that delicious scent of sun-warmed Jeffrey pine, bumblebees sheltering from rain under the umbels of a blooming flower stalk, the fat marmot who lives atop Mount Whitney . . .

The Sierra Nevada is much, much more than a sum of its peaks. When you stand before the majesty of a soaring alpine summit, spare some thought for the broad belts of desert, forest, and foothill that cushion your solitude; the lower canyons that carry the streams and their sediments away from the highlands; the boreal larders of food and shelter for wildlife. The western foothills and forests are a prelude to the High Sierra, the east-side deserts its grand finale. Without the lowlands, the high country would be immeasurably less sublime. By extension, the degradation of the foothills also degrades the High Sierra, for the failing health of one zone infringes upon the next and weakens the whole.

The great national parks, truly wonderful though they are, fall far short of representing and preserving the complexity, depth, and diversity of the Sierra Nevada. Yosemite's park boundaries were originally drawn up to fence in natural curiosities—Yosemite Valley and the giant sequoias. Although later expanded to the crest of the range, the boundaries still stop short of preserving enough of the lower lands to protect the park's wildlife, water and air quality, and uncluttered vistas from encroachment. The Wilderness Act of 1964 attempted to amend this oversight of nineteenth-century Congresses, and the additions are heartily appreciated. But still, the designated wilderness areas in the Sierra Nevada remain primarily high-altitude tracts, places far more easily protected by the severity of winter than the foothills and farmlands ever will be either by nature or by government fiat. Burgeoning development in the lowlands gravely affects the High Sierra, not only in the impact of view-spoiling, tree-killing smog, but also in the intrusion of city mentality on areas that were so recently remote, resulting at best in crowded trails and at worst in more pavement and houses, motorized intrusions on the trails, and even crime and vandalism, like the graffiti occasionally found on rocks at Lake Tahoe, Yosemite, the lower Kern Canyon, and Bishop Canyon.

For such reasons, I hope this guidebook encourages hikers to explore the Sierra Nevada more widely, to realize that hiking in the Sierra means far more than hiking the high country or the national parks or a specific wilderness area. To really know the Sierra Nevada, you should also know its foothills, the Gold Country canyons, the sage flats of the eastern escarpment, the deep forests, and the neighboring ranges. My hope is that as more hikers embrace these "peripheral" areas as an integral part of the Sierra Nevada, they will also deem them worthy of greater protection.

Naturalist John Muir extolled this extraordinary richness of the Sierra Nevada in his writings. He recognized the rare magic of these mountains at his first glimpse, as he crossed the Coast Ranges en route from San Francisco to Yosemite, and the Sierra never disappointed him:

> *At my feet lay the Great Central Valley of California, level and flowery, like a lake of pure sunshine, forty or fifty miles wide, five hundred miles long, one rich furred garden of yellow Compositae. And from the eastern boundary of this vast golden flower-bed rose the mighty Sierra, miles in height, and so gloriously colored and so radiant it seemed not clothed with light, but wholly composed of it, like the wall of some celestial city. Along the top and extending a good way down, was a rich pearl-gray belt of snow; below it a belt of blue and dark purple, marking the extension of the forests; and stretching along the base of the range a broad belt of rose purple; all these colors, from the blue sky to the yellow valley smoothly blending as they do in a rainbow, making a wall of light ineffably fine. Then it seemed to me that the Sierra should be called, not the Nevada or Snowy Range, but the Range of Light. And after ten years of wandering and wondering in the heart of it, rejoicing in its glorious floods of light, the white beams of the morning streaming through the passes, the noonday radiance on the crystal rocks, the flush of the alpenglow, and the irised spray of countless waterfalls, it still seems above all others the Range of Light.*

The mountains have a way of kneading and slapping life back into an existence wearied and dulled by too much city living. Who needs a personal trainer when you can hike a Sierra peak? Who needs a stiff belt down at Joe's when the stinging shock of a cold wind off a high snowbank, or even a damp grass stain on the seat of your britches, bellows out that you are a vibrant part of the planet? Hiking the Sierra Nevada is not always a romp through posy fields. The mountains can parch you, exhaust you, freeze you, drench you, wear holes in the knees of your trousers, or break your bones with complete indifference, though never with malice. A week on its trails has a wondrous way of shifting priorities back into their proper places, of reminding us of the preeminent excellence of simple things—dry clothes, rest, food, water, camaraderie, a campfire. Our ancient ancestors ranked such basic commodities highest among life's happiest and most precious attainments. Bring along a good book or a guitar, and we can add to that state of natural bliss a touch of high culture too.

Overview of the Range

The Sierra Nevada runs some 400 miles northwest to southeast in a diagonal that roughly parallels the eastern border of California, though Nevada does stake claim to part of Lake Tahoe and the Carson Range. The mountains tend to grow higher and more rugged the farther south you go, until you pass the cluster of 14,000-foot peaks around the Whitney Crest, whereupon the elevations begin a slow decline across the Kern Plateau and southward to the dry Tehachapi Mountains and the Mojave Desert. Consequently, all but two of the road passes in the Sierra Nevada are north of Yosemite Valley. No road crosses the range for 160 miles in a straight line between Yosemite's Tioga Pass Road (CA 120) and the Sherman Pass Road (J-41 and FR 22S05) over the Kern Plateau.

The eastern slope of the range is very abrupt, reaching gradients of 25 percent from the floor of the Owens Valley to the crest. For miles along this magnificent escarpment, the rocky walls are too steep to support thick forests, though woodlands of cottonwood, aspen, and assorted pines thrive in lateral canyons. The Sierra Crest blocks the clouds blowing in from the Pacific, leaving the eastern side in a rain shadow, where sagebrush and other high-desert plants of the Great Basin predominate. Because their catchment areas are so dry and narrow, the streams of the east side are relatively small, and all that are not tapped for water supplies sink into the Great Basin. Foremost among the eastern rivers are the Truckee (which flows into and out of Lake Tahoe), the Carson, and the Walker. There's also the Owens River, which was commandeered and is annually drunk dry by the city of Los Angeles.

The rise of the western slope is far more gradual than the eastern, averaging a gradient of about 2 percent from the Central Valley to the crest. This broad western band begins in grassy foothills, climbing into woodlands of oak, gray pine, and chaparral. Growing more rugged as it mounts to the east, it is cut by rivers into a series of eastwest-running canyons and ridges, making something of a roller-coaster ride for travelers driving north or south along the Gold Country's Highway 49. Broad belts of coniferous forest start at elevations between 2,000 and 3,000 feet, thickly covering the lands up to about 8,000 or 9,000 feet, depending on the latitude.

The Feather, Yuba, and American River systems, the largest of the Sierra Nevada, flow into the northern Sacramento River. The smaller Cosumnes and Mokelumne Rivers join the Sacramento farther downstream. Moving south, the major rivers—Stanislaus, Tuolumne, Merced, and San Joaquin—all join in the San Joaquin Valley, flowing north to meet the Sacramento River in the Sacramento–San Joaquin Delta, where, after running the gauntlet of siphons devised to quench a thirsty state, the remaining blend of "Sierra Champaign" flows west into the Pacific Ocean through San Francisco Bay and the Golden Gate. The largest southern Sierra rivers—the Kings, Kaweah, Tule, and Kern—are mostly consumed by agriculture en route to their natural sinks in the southern San Joaquin Valley.

The Story in the Stone

Although most people think of granite when they think of the Sierra Nevada, the particular beauty and character of the range turns on a much more complex interplay of granitic, volcanic, and ancient metamorphic rock. That sounds like a dry subject, but it's not. Telling the difference between these three basic categories of rock is actually very interesting and will greatly boost your enjoyment of any Sierra hike.

Granite is indeed the hallmark of the Sierra Nevada. The Sierra's most monumental landscapes are wrought in clean, ice-sculptured granite. The enormous cliffs, domes, spires, sawtooth ridges, and sharp peaks of glistening gray, white, and even pink and orange rock, as well as the basins that hold most of the range's lakes and lush meadows, are granitic landscapes. Granite is a plutonic rock, meaning that it solidified from magma underground, cooling so slowly that quartz crystals were able to grow large enough to be seen by the naked eye. Granite forms the core of the Sierra Nevada, even when it is covered with dirt and other rock. The dividing line between the Cascades and the Sierra Nevada in the forested highlands north of the Feather River is hard to identify on the ground, but a geologic map readily depicts where the Cascades (volcanic to the core) end and the Sierra Nevada (with granitic core and volcanic and metamorphic rock riding atop) begins.

Though found throughout the Sierra, volcanic rock dominates the landscapes around Mammoth Mountain and Mono Lake and over much of the northern third of the range. Volcanic rock differs from plutonic rock (like granite) because it forms aboveground, cooling quickly in the air and thereby developing a much finer grain—that is to say, the crystals are not visible to the naked eye. Characterized by reddish or ochre, dry, crumbly ground, highly porous volcanic landscapes do not retain lakes very well but do support some of the most prolific wildflower gardens. (Anglers and mosquito haters can benefit from this lesson when planning a trip.) Ancient volcanoes account for most of the bizarre hoodoos, palisades, plugs, and mesas of the Gold Country and the landscapes around Sonora, Ebbetts, and Carson Passes.

One of the great monuments to the heroic age of trail building is Forester Pass on the John Muir Trail. PHOTO BY IVAN PARR

The metamorphic rocks of the Sierra Nevada might be less familiar to the casual observer, but they carry a particularly fascinating story. Metamorphic rock comprises most of the native bedrock where gold is found, and it is most spectacularly exposed in many places atop the highest Sierra crest. Hikers climbing east-side canyons readily recognize it in many of the hulking, shattered massifs that rise to the very crest of the range, typically more ragged and darker in color than the surrounding peaks and slopes of granite, and draped with gargantuan talus fields that clink musically underfoot. Metamorphic rocks are the oldest of the Sierra.

To glimpse a notion of the ancient age of the metamorphic rocks, you need first to realize that the Sierra Nevada that we see today is only about 5 million years old, and it is the second mountain range to occupy this address, replacing an "ancestral Sierra Nevada" that rose millions of years before it. The ancestral Sierra Nevada arose from a geologically cataclysmic process called subduction, itself caused by continental drift. The present site of the Sierra Nevada was long covered by ocean, while the shore of North America lay far to the east, part of the supercontinent, Pangaea. Current geologic theories propose that when Pangaea broke up about 185 million years ago, the North American plate drifted westward, crashing into a series of island arcs carried on two other suboceanic plates, the Angayucham and the Mezcalera Plates, which overrode the North American plate. While the tremendous heat and pressure created by this continental collision transformed older volcanic and sedimentary rocks into metamorphic rock, these islands added land to North America's western shore, and raised mountain ranges. Traces of the ancient range, including the Sierra's famous gold deposits, remain in the metamorphic rock. These oldest rocks in the Sierra Nevada are about 500 million years old and were formed under the sea.

Even as volcanic eruptions continued to add new rock to the ancestral Sierra Nevada, erosion was also relentlessly wearing it down. Far older than the current Sierra Nevada, in fact, is the Central Valley, whose ancient ground was washed down over millennia as silt from the ancestral Sierra Nevada. As a third oceanic plate, the Farallon Plate, collided with and was subducted beneath the North American plate, it began uplifting the present Sierra Nevada and forced rifting of the Basin and Range Province, a process still happening today.

The granitic core of the Sierra Nevada formed underground about 60 million years ago, after the heat from subduction melted great quantities of rock into vast subterranean seas of magma, which cooled over millennia to form solid masses of new granitic rock called plutons. About 5 million years ago, a massive block of extremely dense rock broke off from the underside of the western part of the Sierra Nevada and sank into the earth's mantle, causing the lighter granitic plutons to buoy upward on the east side of the range. Breaking loose along fault lines in a process called fault blocking, the eastern face of the Sierra Nevada upraised into a long escarpment that gives the range its characteristic westward tilt. At the same time, blocks of land east of the crest subsided, creating the Basin and Range Province and forming the Owens Valley, the Tahoe Basin, and other sunken valleys of the Great Basin. The Sierra's eastern escarpment reaches its zenith at the Whitney Crest, which soars more than 2 miles above the floor of the Owens Valley, making this the deepest valley in the United States. Residents of that valley witnessed one staggering installment of this mountain-building process in the earthquake of 1872, when the Sierra jumped 13 to 20 feet upward and about 35 to 40 feet horizontally in a matter of seconds. The jolt destroyed the town of Lone Pine and killed twenty-seven residents. Some geologists surmise that the Sierra Crest is growing at a rate of about 26 feet per millennium. Not all scientists agree.

As the granitic Sierra uplifted, it pushed some of the old metamorphic range aside and carried other fragments upward on its back. The western foothills were shunted aside and still retain their ancient metamorphic bedrock, readily visible in Gold Country mines, the great slate canyons of the Yuba and American Rivers, the cave-bearing rocks of Calaveras County, and a multitude of serpentine outcrops, like the Red Hills. (All of these can be seen on hikes described in this book.) Although most of the old metamorphic pieces of the ancestral Sierra Nevada that were stranded atop the "new" granite range eroded away, we still find large chunks of it sitting like dark islands, often red or black, atop the lighter granitic rock. Geologists call them roof pendants. Along the Sierra Crest the Ritter Range and the mountains around Tioga Pass, Saddlebag Lake, Lundy Canyon, and Virginia Lakes are roof pendants visited by trails described herein. The caves of western Sequoia and Kings Canyon delve through roof pendants of ancient marble.

Volcanoes have continued to erupt in many far-flung regions of the Sierra Nevada during its 5-million-year uplift, covering large areas of granitic, metamorphic, and older volcanic rock with layers of dark basalt lava flows, yellowish rhyolite, reddish andesite, and deposits of pumice, obsidian, and tuff. Lake Tahoe was formed when a volcanic eruption dammed the Truckee River. When the Long Valley Caldera, current home of Mammoth Lakes, blew up about 760,000 years ago, fragments of rock landed in Kansas and Nebraska. The youngest mountains in North America are the Mono Craters, overlooking Mono Lake, of which Panum Crater erupted as recently as 600 years ago. Scattered hot springs and the ominous rumblings that occasionally shake the Mammoth Lakes region show that volcanism is not a spent force in the Sierra Nevada. See for yourself on hikes described in this book.

The abrupt lifting and tilting of the range accelerated riverine erosion toward the west. Rivers running down from the Sierra Crest have gouged some of the deepest canyons in North America. Ice age glaciers moving down these same canyons recarved them into some of the most celebrated features of the Sierra Nevada. Starting some 3 million years ago and disappearing only 20,000 years ago, these recurring glacier systems, some more than 2,000 feet thick, carved the V-shaped riverine gorges into U-shaped valleys, creating such features as hanging valleys, plunging waterfalls, moraines, tarns, paternoster lakes, and horn-shaped peaks. Since the climate began warming after 1800, only a few small glaciers still cling to Sierra peaks, the largest grouped among the Palisades.

Weathering accounts for many other characteristic features of the Sierra Nevada. The famous granite domes were shaped by exfoliation, or a peeling away of the layers of rock like the layers of an onion. While erosion and frost action slowly flake away rock, avalanches and landslides transform other landscapes yearly. Though wind-carved arches are rare in the range, there are epic examples in the Alabama Hills.

A Brief Human History

This abbreviated history provides only the most meager gloss of the Sierra Nevada's Native American history, its commercial exploitation in the nineteenth century, and the resultant conservation movement that such rampant development sparked. For more detailed historical information, visit some of the museums in the towns and cities around the Sierra Nevada or refer to books such as Francis Farquhar's *History of the Sierra Nevada* or Clarence King's *Mountaineering in the Sierra Nevada.*

The Native American populations of the Sierra Nevada dwelled primarily in the foothills and valleys east and west of the High Sierra. Indians from both sides frequented the higher mountains for trade, hunting, and relief from summer heat. We know little about their cultures because they disappeared so quickly at the onset of the Spanish and American eras, decimated by disease and killed outright by settlers. Existing records are based on relatively meager sources, artifacts, and oral histories.

Even the names by which we know them are rarely the names they called themselves. The names that we use, such as Miwok, Mono, and Piute, refer very broadly to peoples loosely linked by language and culture but who lived in hundreds of distinct groups and called themselves by distinct names. In recent years historians working with the park and forest services have made greater efforts to present their stories in public exhibits, so that we now distinguish some specific bands or tribes, though the general names are still useful to distinguish broader cultural regions.

The native residents along the Eastern Sierra—around Mono Lake and the Owens Valley—were Piute. They subsisted on nuts from the piñon pines, supplemented by game, rodents, insects, roots, and seeds. Among the Piute peoples were the Tubatulabal of the upper Kern River, and the Kuzedika, who were noted for harvesting the larvae of a brine fly found in Mono Lake, where they lived. So popular a delicacy was this larvae that it formed a primary item of trade with the Yokuts and others who lived on the west side of the Sierra. Other items of trade were obsidian, pine nuts, mineral paints, and salt. Farther north, around Lake Tahoe, the Washoe were known for some of the finest basketry ever created.

Among the major culture groupings of the west side were the Foothill Yokuts and Monache in the south, the Mono and Miwok in the central region, and the Maidu in the north. Acorns provided the staple of their diets, supplemented by hunting, fishing, and gathering. Among the items sent for trade with the Piute were seashells and freshwater shells, bear skins, manzanita berries, elderberries, beads, and acorns. Their acorn-grinding rocks are a familiar feature in many parts of the western and southern Sierra. Although archaeologists have yet to formally survey the 350 massive rock

Though it is not enshrined in the Constitution, the freedom to hike is a precious one.
PHOTO BY IVAN PARR

basins cut into granite slabs of the Mokelumne River canyon, apparently the indigenous people who cut them were also manufacturing and trading salt, an economic venture far more socially complex than mere hunting and gathering.

Among the best places to glean a picture of the Native American cultures of the Sierra Nevada are Indian Grinding Rock State Park near Jackson, the Yosemite Museum, the Sierra Mono Museum in Northfork, the Piute Cultural Center in Bishop, the Mono Basin Scenic Area Visitor Center near Lee Vining, the California Indian Museum in Sacramento, the Nevada State Museum in Carson City, and Wassama Round House State Historic Park near Oakhurst.

The Spanish did not venture far into the Sierra Nevada, though Pedro Font did sight the range in 1776 and inadvertently bestowed its name of "Snowy Range" when he described it as "*una gran sierra nevada.*" A few Americans—notably the mountain men and explorers Jedediah Smith, Joe Walker, Kit Carson, John Fremont, and Jim Beckwourth—crossed the range in search of furs or routes to the fertile country of California. Not until gold was discovered by James Marshall at Coloma on the American River in 1848, however, did large numbers of people begin to migrate to the Sierra Nevada, a catastrophe for the Native American population. Mining camps and larger towns sprouted overnight in the foothills and canyons from the Feather River south to the Merced. Ghost towns and camps abound. Among the gold rush towns

Lonely Basque sheepherders have left their marks on the bark of many an aspen in the Eastern Sierra grazing country.

preserved as state parks are Columbia, Coloma, Johnsville, and North Bloomfield, but many more live on as vibrant towns, like Nevada City, Grass Valley, Auburn, Placerville, Jackson, Sonora, and Mariposa.

The Sierra Nevada was a major obstacle to the settlement of California. Residents of the Gold Country pushed trails, and later roads, over the passes, but even still these were difficult and exhausting. The discovery of silver at the Comstock Lode in western Nevada forced the improvement of trans-Sierra highways, like Hawley Grade, which in turn spurred development of the region around Lake Tahoe. When the first transcontinental railroad was built through Donner Pass, north of Lake Tahoe, it ensured that this northern corridor of the Sierra Nevada would become its most heavily traveled trans-section of the range.

The timber, mining, and grazing industries throughout the nineteenth and early twentieth centuries continued to treat the Sierra Nevada as a treasure chest of free, or dirt-cheap, resources. Gold and silver booms brought small rushes to ephemeral settlements along the eastern side of the range at Mammoth and around Mono Lake, and on the south end in the Kern River drainage. Mining companies replaced the lone prospectors of an earlier era, raising capital to sink huge hard-rock mines, like the Empire Mine, and washing away tons of debris in devastating hydraulic mines. Lumber companies began the systematic destruction of the groves of giant sequoias along the western slopes. Homesteaders and landholders platted the shores of Lake Tahoe and divided up Yosemite Valley. Sheepherders and cattle ranchers penetrated the deep canyons and meadows of the High Sierra. Unregulated hunting drove the California grizzly bear to extinction. Dams flooded river canyons, even drowning the magnificent valley of Hetch Hetchy.

In light of the more devastating excesses of these commercial enterprises, many people began to recognize that the resources of the Sierra Nevada were not inexhaustible, and that unchecked exploitation was fouling the rivers and threatening the forests. The backlash to the wholesale ravishment of the Sierra Nevada sparked probably the most important conservation movement of the nineteenth century. Farmers in 1884 successfully lobbied the state to curtail hydraulic mining, which was wreaking havoc not only on the range but in the Central Valley and even as far downstream as San Francisco Bay.

Foremost among the voices of preservation was John Muir, who arrived in the Sierra Nevada in 1868. Muir also deserves a lot of credit for winning President Theodore Roosevelt over to the idea of establishing the national forests. Led by George Stewart, editor of the *Visalia Delta,* citizens of Visalia also lobbied successfully for the creation of Sequoia National Park in 1890. The twentieth century saw an expansion of federally protected lands in the Sierra Nevada, particularly with the passage of the Wilderness Act of 1964. California took a new tack in 2004 with the creation of the Sierra Nevada Conservancy, a state agency mandated with assisting local Sierra counties and communities in efforts to preserve and restore lands, regulate development, and promote sustainable economic activities like recreation, regulated timber harvesting, and family ranches.

You will discover the marks, both subtle and profound, of all these peoples along trails described in this book.

Planning Your Hike

When to Go

The Sierra Nevada enjoys a reputation for sunny weather, but hikers also need to be prepared for bad or even dangerous weather on any day. This book's recommendation of the best season for any given hike neither fixes the weather for your comfort nor overrules the basic law of common sense. Use your own good judgment when planning a hike, and always take local conditions and your own abilities into account.

The Sierra Nevada has a four-season year that only loosely corresponds with the calendar year and can vary a good deal from one year to the next. Generally speaking, winter is the wet season in lowland California, including the Sierra Nevada foothills, and summer is typically dry. In the higher mountains, winters have spells alternately clear and snowy, and summers are alternately clear and rainy.

High summer, from July to early September, is the most popular time for mountain vacations, though it can be uncomfortably hot and dry below 4,000 feet—not the time to hike most foothill trails. Many waterfalls begin to dry up, but the creeks and passes are easier to cross. Snow can remain in the highest passes, especially if they face north or are shaded by outcrops. This is the best time for high-country wildflowers, though the mosquitoes are at their worst at 8,000 feet and above through August. Weather is generally fine at high elevations, but short, intense afternoon thundershowers are common in the high country above 8,000 feet (though not so common as in the Rockies). In some weeks the rain can fall for several days, while in other weeks it does not rain at all. Snow can also fall at high elevations in summer, but generally it is light. In late July and August, "monsoon" storms blow up the east side of the Sierra Nevada from the Gulf of California and hit mainly along the Sierra Crest. High-country trails are at their most crowded during summer, reaching their peak over Fourth of July and Labor Day weekends, when I recommend avoiding the most popular areas.

Beginning after Labor Day and running to early November, fall offers arguably the best season for backpacking or hiking in much of the Sierra Nevada. The trails are less crowded, and the weather by day is typically warm, clear, and dry, growing crisp at night. After the first cold snap in September, mosquitoes usually are not a problem. Many of the waterfalls have disappeared and the cascades are diminished in grandeur, but the creeks and passes are easiest to cross. If you backpack in the high country in October or later, make sure you are prepared for snow, which can fall at any time. Many roads—such as the Tioga Pass Road (CA 120) in Yosemite and the streets of Mammoth Lakes—do not allow overnight parking after designated dates, when snowfall can close the roads.

Most hunting seasons arrive in autumn, though how you reckon with that is up to you. Certainly some people don't mind sharing the forests with hunters, while others feel uneasy. If you hike in the national forests in October and November, wear bright colors. If you want to avoid hunters, save your autumn hikes for the national parks, where hunting is illegal.

Among the highlights of fall are the spectacular leaf colors. These start about mid-September to early October in the higher elevations and are particularly beautiful in Alpine County around Markleeville, Carson Pass, Lake Tahoe, and Ebbetts Pass. As September and October progress, the yellowing foliage moves down to lower elevations, turning the canyons of the eastern slope into rivers of blazing color. The Gold Country foothills and other low places on the west side, including Yosemite Valley, reach their stunning peak of fall color around the end of October. Another colorful hallmark of fall is the annual salmon run on some east-side streams. One of the best places to see the salmon migration is Taylor Creek at the Lake Tahoe Visitor Center near South Lake Tahoe.

Winter begins not necessarily with the first snow but rather with the first snow that does not melt after a couple of days. Ebbetts Pass (CA 4), Tioga Pass (CA 120), Sherman Pass, and Sonora Pass (CA 108) will close and reopen typically more than once in autumn before they finally close for the winter, usually by mid-November. Carson Pass (CA 88), Donner Pass (I-80), Echo Summit (US 50), and CA 70 along the Feather River are kept open by snowplows throughout the winter.

The Sierra gets the greatest snowfall and deepest drifts of any range in the United States. The heaviest snows fall in the Carson Pass area, a boon for skiers but a job for the ski patrols who scout potential avalanches and dislodge the most dangerous with charges. Despite the cold, blizzards, and avalanches, winter days in the Sierra are often brilliant and clear—ideal skiing or snowshoeing weather, providing winter exercise for hikers who enjoy those sports.

Those who detest snow, however, can still hike trails in the western foothills and Inyo Valley, lands generally 4,000 feet and below. This is not to say that an altitude of 4,000 feet does not receive snow—it can, but it usually doesn't stick long. By keeping tabs on the weather reports, and by being prepared to survive in freak blizzard conditions, hikers can enjoy altitudes that would offer only arctic conditions in, for instance, the northern Appalachians.

When snow blankets the upper elevations, the lower elevations are subject to rain. California weather patterns usually bring storms of two or three days' duration, which then blow away until the next storm cycle, leaving a period of typically clear skies—ideal hiking weather in the foothills. The foothill grasses in winter are green and lush. One real problem during winter is slippery mud on steep paths, and this is something that you must check out with the local ranger before driving to the trailhead. Winter landslides also close trails. Still, a determined and properly prepared backpacker can plan and execute a real mountain trip during winter along the Yuba, American, and Kaweah canyons and in many other places.

Spring creeps up the mountains from about March at the lower elevations, reaching Yosemite Valley generally by April, Lake Tahoe by early May, and the high country by the end of June, when summer has unmistakably taken hold everywhere else. Aside from the extraordinary releafing of deciduous trees and the bursting forth of wildflowers, it brings longer stretches of good weather between the rainstorms. Waterfalls and creeks swell impressively with snowmelt, one of the most spectacular sights of the Sierra Nevada but also the most dangerous, for drowning causes more deaths there than any other cause. Another unpleasant side of spring is mosquitoes.

Public Land Jurisdiction

Much of the Sierra Nevada above 5,000 feet is public land. The differing government agencies that administer these lands each post different rules and regulations regarding recreational use.

National Park Service

National parks provide the greatest measure of protection, permitting fishing with a license but no hunting or collecting of any kind. There are three national parks in the Sierra Nevada: Yosemite, Kings Canyon, and Sequoia, the latter two administered by the same office. Although the developed areas of the parks contain stores, lodging, restaurants, visitor centers, and other amenities, large sections are designated wilderness areas, which are closed to all vehicles and motorized equipment. Wilderness areas cannot be developed with any facilities, aside from trails, signs, bridges, or other features deemed necessary to administer the area. Dogs are typically restricted from trails, but leashed dogs may use roads and campgrounds.

USDA Forest Service

The Forest Service, run by the US Department of Agriculture, oversees the most extensive areas of public land in the Sierra Nevada. The eight national forests of the Sierra Nevada are Plumas, Tahoe, Eldorado, Humboldt-Toiyabe (known by many simply as Toiyabe), Stanislaus, Sierra, Inyo, and Sequoia. A newer ninth division is the Lake Tahoe Basin Management Unit, formed from sections of Tahoe, Eldorado, and Toiyabe National Forests and charged with the special mandate of caring for Lake Tahoe. Each national forest is subdivided into different ranger districts, each with a main office and many smaller substations.

The Forest Service is the most complex of any government agency in the Sierra, because its mandate must satisfy the demands of multiple uses, not just recreation and preservation. Forestry, mining, grazing, wood gathering, and collecting are all permitted (with regulations) on national forest land, as are hunting and fishing during appropriate seasons and with appropriate permits. Complicating matters are the many private inholdings and long-term leases in some national forests. National forests allow for a wide array of recreation. The Forest Service issues special-use permits for privately operated ski resorts, stables, and even private cabins. The Forest Service builds trails, regulates off-road vehicle use, publishes maps, and maintains many designated campgrounds. They also permit free-range camping outside of developed campgrounds over much, though not all, of their land. If you build a campfire or use a camp stove on national forest land, you will need a campfire permit, which is issued free, usually for the year. Dogs typically are allowed to use national forest trails if they are under control of the owner, although some locales specifically require leashes.

The Forest Service also administrates designated wilderness areas, established by the Wilderness Act of 1964. Congress passed this act "to assure that an increasing population, accompanied by expanding settlement and growing mechanization, does not occupy and modify all areas within the United States." No roads or mechanized gear are allowed in designated wildernesses, though hunting and grazing are permitted in some. The only modifications allowed are bridges, trails, directional signs, established campfire rings, occasional drift fences, and other features deemed necessary to administer the area. There are seventeen designated wilderness areas within Sierra Nevada national forests.

National Monuments

These are usually run like national parks, the main difference being that monuments are created by presidents, and parks by Congress. Devils Postpile National Monument, near Mammoth Lakes, follows this model. When Giant Sequoia National Monument was created in 2000, however, management policies allowed most traditional Forest Service uses to continue, including hunting and grazing. Giant Sequoia National Monument is managed by Sequoia National Forest.

Bureau of Land Management (BLM)

With mandates similar to the Forest Service, the areas administered by the BLM in the Sierra Nevada are minor compared to their jurisdiction over the US desert lands. The BLM lands are concentrated on the dry eastern and southern edges of the range, and in the more rugged parts of the western foothills. Although traditionally geared to serve mainly mining, timber, and ranching concerns, in recent years the BLM has taken a stronger interest in recreational users of its land. Dogs typically are allowed to use BLM lands if under control of the owner.

State Parks

California has a long history of managing parks in the Sierra Nevada. Yosemite was run as a state preserve before it became a national park. Hunting is prohibited in California designated state parks, but some allow fishing and gold panning. Dogs are typically restricted from trails. On the eastern shore of Lake Tahoe, the state of Nevada runs the splendid Lake Tahoe State Park on land leased in large part from the Forest Service.

Other Government Agencies

Reservoirs managed by the US Army Corps of Engineers, the US Bureau of Reclamation, and the East Bay Municipal Utilities District preserve land from sprawling development in the western foothills. Lake Camanche, Pardee Reservoir, and New Melones Reservoir are open to the public and post their own specific rules. The California Department of Fish and Game manages some choice parcels, among them Table Mountain near Oroville and the Spenceville Wildlife Refuge. Municipal agencies also preserve many important historical and scenic sites, including the city of Chico's magnificent Bidwell Park.

Mountain Hazards

Although the Sierra Nevada has been called a "gentle wilderness," all mountains can be dangerous if you do not exercise common sense and good judgment. The following pointers are rudimentary.

High Water

In nearly every year that passes, people drown in the Sierra Nevada. Rushing water has a power that's easy to misjudge, even for experienced hikers. A stream no deeper than your ankles can knock you down. If you are not sure of yourself in a creek crossing, look for an easier crossing, wait for competent assistance, or turn around. Do not tie anyone to a rope when crossing, for it is as likely to hinder as to help a person thrashing through cold water. Using a walking stick helps you keep your balance in creek crossings. Carry creek-crossing shoes or sandals to protect your feet from sharp rocks. You can reduce the danger of stream crossings by planning trips later in summer; be extremely wary of the snowmelt seasons of late spring and early summer. Do not swim in rivers above waterfalls. That may sound obvious, but a surprising number of swimmers have been swept to their deaths over waterfalls.

Wildlife

Do not feed any wild animals. Not only is it unhealthy for the animal and illegal for the transgressor, but even "cute" wild animal can prove dangerous. Deer have sharp hooves and strong legs. Raccoons can be very nasty-tempered, and they carry diseases.

The only bear of the Sierra Nevada is the **black bear,** though it may come in brown, blond, and cinnamon as well as black. Black bears are the most unfairly maligned of all Sierra wildlife. I have often overheard people seriously speculating on whether a missing hiker might have been carried off by a hungry bear. Sierra bears can be pests—and a 350-pound pest with claws, sharp teeth, and a determination to eat your food can also be dangerous. But black bears do not hunt people down to eat them. Grizzly bears are altogether a different kind of beast, but they are extinct in California.

Aggressive behavior by black bears is almost always caused by human interference. Bears who view human food as an easy and tasty meal cause great property damage by breaking into vehicles, cabins, tents, and backpacker food caches. Not only is human food unhealthy for bears, but dependence upon it causes them to abandon their natural food-gathering techniques, making them more dependent on begging, scavenging, and aggression. If a bear comes into camp, yell and bang pots to drive it away; but if it manages to seize your food, the game is over—it's the bear's food now. Rangers sometimes track down, tranquilize, and remove an aggressive bear to a more remote location, but a hopelessly corrupted bear will be killed. Feeding bears, or taking insufficient measures to secure your food from them, thereby threatens the very existence of bears in the Sierra. It is also a felony. Wilderness rangers routinely give tickets to backpackers who have not properly stored or guarded their food.

Many drive-in campgrounds in the Sierra have installed bear-proof metal boxes at each site. Sequoia and Kings Canyon National Parks have even installed them at popular backcountry camping sites. Where they do not exist, backpackers have traditionally tied their food into a tree by the counterbalance method, described in leaflets at almost every ranger station in the Sierra. Since clever bears in many places have figured out how to overcome backpackers' ropes, rangers in some areas now require that backpackers carry portable bear-proof food canisters, which can be purchased or rented from many ranger stations and mountain stores. The bear canister is by far the most convenient method of protecting your food—and thereby of protecting bears— in the Sierra Nevada. You can learn more tips in *Bear Aware* (FalconGuides, 2012).

Mountain lions are typically shy, and many a lifelong hiker in the Sierra has never seen one. They are most common in the lower-elevation foothills, canyons, and forests. Apparently emboldened or made desperate by the stress of encroaching civilization, mountain lion attacks have increased in recent years. Some people have been killed, including a runner in the Auburn State Recreation Area. At greatest risk are children walking alone. A mountain lion seems to be incited to attack when the object that it is investigating bolts and runs, so in the unlikely event that you are confronted, stand your ground, shout, and make yourself look large (by opening your jacket, for instance). If attacked, fight back with all your strength. Refer to *Lion Sense* (FalconGuides, 2005) for more tips.

The Sierra's only venomous snake, the **rattlesnake,** is common in the foothills and along canyon floors up to 8,000 feet, but they have been reported at higher altitudes. Be especially wary among rocks and tall grasses near streams and in chaparral. If possible, the rattler gives fair warning of its presence by shaking its tail to produce a buzzing sound. Your best defense is to give them enough warning of your approach, so that they return the favor with their rattle. Walking with a stick, and using it to sweep suspect areas ahead of you as you walk, can help. Many hikers carry venom extractors in their first-aid kits, but their effectiveness is marginal. Immobilize, calm, and evacuate a bite victim. Never cut the wound or apply a tourniquet. Fatalities from rattlesnake bites are rare, and snakes are essential for keeping down the rodent population. Killing a rattlesnake that gives fair warning is bad policy, for it favors the propagation of snakes disinclined to give a warning rattle.

Vermin

Bane of the Sierra spring and summer, clouds of **mosquitoes** rise from wet meadows and dank woods, driving campers crazy, especially just before dusk and just after dawn. Some now carry West Nile fever, which has caused illness and even death in some parts of the country. Mosquito repellent provides short-term relief, but mosquito head nets are more effective. Choose dry campsites. **Biting flies** also live in the Sierra Nevada. **Ticks** live in the grasses and chaparral of the lower Sierra. Check your clothes and body for ticks after walking through brush. If bitten, save the extracted body to test for diseases. Although some cases of Lyme disease have been reported in the Sierra, tick-borne disease seems rarer in the Sierra Nevada than in the Rockies or on the East Coast.

   Squirrels, chipmunks, mice, marmots, and **wood rats** can be carriers of flea-borne bubonic plague. Don't feed them. **Deer mice** spread the virus that causes the potentially deadly hantavirus pulmonary syndrome, which humans contract from inhaling, usually by kicking up dust mixed with mice droppings or urine. Do not camp or rest near animal burrows. Beware of inhaling dust in cabins and confined areas that might be infested with mice.

Poison Oak

Learn to recognize this common plant. Contact with its leaves, berries, bare twigs, or even smoke from burning bushes can impart an oil that causes a severe allergic rash in many people. The shrub, which can be a climbing vine or a freestanding bush, grows most heavily in the western foothills, thriving in road- or trail-cuts up to about 5,000 feet. Its leaves grow in groupings of three, turn red in late summer, and drop off before winter. Poison oak stems are smooth and waxy. If you come in contact with poison oak, washing the affected area with cold water helps. If the rash breaks out, doctors can prescribe treatments for relief.

Learn to recognize poison oak's "leaves of three" when you hike in the foothills.

Lightning

Lightning storms are common in the Sierra during summer. Do not climb up high, exposed ridges and peaks when a storm threatens. Plan to descend from peaks, ridges, and passes before midafternoon, the most likely time for thunderheads to build.

If you are caught in a lightning storm, shun the temptation to seek "shelter" in a rocky recess or cave on a slope highly exposed to lightning. Lightning strikes in confined areas are catastrophic. A tourist was killed on Moro Rock in a lightning storm in 1976 after retreating into a rock recess. Others have been killed in a rock shelter atop Half Dome, and in the stone hut atop Mount Whitney when lightning struck in the doorway.

The best policy when caught in a storm is to squat low on your boot soles and, if possible, some other insulating material (like a coiled rope or a sleeping pad), in a place where you are neither the highest object around nor in the bottom of a confined recess. Do not lean against rock walls or trees, but allow a buffer zone of a few feet from other objects. If you are part of a group, spread out; if lightning does strike, you will need survivors to tend the injured.

Dehydration

Many cases of headache and fatigue are directly related to not drinking enough water. This is particularly true at higher elevations. Even if you are not feeling thirsty, keep drinking as you hike. When a dehydrated hiker neglects to drink liquids, heat exhaustion may set in, with cramping, exhaustion, lightheadedness, and nausea. You can treat heat exhaustion by getting out of the sun and drinking liquids. Sipping an electrolyte solution helps; make it with one teaspoon of salt and one tablespoon of sugar dissolved in a liter of water. Some commercial drinks, like Gatorade, also replace electrolytes.

Sunburn

Radiation from the sun at higher altitudes is more intense than at sea level, even when the air temperature is cool. Wear sunblock on the trail, and a hat with a brim. Be especially careful to not let your feet get sunburned. Wear dark glasses that cut ultraviolet light to protect your eyes, especially in places where light-colored rock or patches of snow reflect light up in your face.

Hypothermia

The primary cause of weather-related deaths on the trail is hypothermia, a severe drop in the body's temperature. Even when the air temperature is well above freezing, wet clothing clinging to the body, exhaustion piqued by chill wind, or even insufficient food can all reduce the body's ability to manufacture heat. Symptoms of hypothermia—severe shivering, lethargy, and loss of judgment—start when the body's core temperature drops to 90°F from a normal range of 99°F to 100°F. If steps are not taken to warm the victim by replacing wet clothes with dry ones and guiding him or her to shelter in a warm place, the body temperature can drop low enough to kill. Common sense and appropriate clothing can prevent hypothermia. By dressing in layers, you can more easily regulate body temperature. Bring an outer shell (waterproof jacket or poncho) to repel water, and wear a hat. If bad weather threatens and you still intend to hike, bring dry clothes in a waterproof bag.

Altitude Sickness

Many hikers experience headache and nausea during the first day or two at elevations above 7,000 feet. The best treatment for mild altitude sickness is to rest and to keep drinking liquids. When planning a long trip at elevation, plan an extra day or two of low exertion to accustom yourself to the altitude. Acute mountain sickness (AMS), though much rarer, requires the immediate evacuation of the patient to lower elevations. Symptoms are more severe, with a dry cough developing into a wet cough, gurgling sounds, flulike or bronchitis symptoms, and lack of muscle coordination.

Giardia

Giardia lamblia is a protozoan parasite that lives part of its life cycle as a cyst in water sources. Giardia can induce cramping, diarrhea, vomiting, and fatigue within two days to two weeks after ingestion. The parasite spreads when infected mammals defecate in water sources. Giardiasis is treatable with prescription drugs. If you believe you've contracted giardiasis, see a doctor as soon as possible. Giardia can be present in any Sierra Nevada stream or lake but is especially prevalent in grazing country.

Filtering creek water with a pump is probably the best way to ensure your water is free from giardia and chemical flavors.

There are five main methods of treating water to remove the threat of giardiasis: boiling, chemical treatment, mechanical filtering, gravity filtering, and ultraviolet treatment. If you boil water, keep a rolling boil for 10 to 15 minutes. Chemical treatment may kill giardia without affecting other pollutants, and it can taste unpleasant. Filters (mechanical and gravity) and ultraviolet devices are more expensive but are preferred because they remove giardia and other contaminants, and they don't leave an aftertaste.

Mine Hazards and Claims

Mines are dangerous. There are countless mines throughout the Sierra, and many are not mapped or sealed. Miners still work existing claims, especially in the foothills. Respect all existing claims, all mining encampments, and all private property. Miners typically do not welcome trespassers, and they can be very cantankerous. Do not drink water flowing from a mine, as it may be toxic.

Knowing Where You Are

Trails can be like train tracks: You set your mind on "daydream" while your feet follow the route without close attention. But trails can also be concealed under snow or disappear on unyielding granite that doesn't register a tread. They can be unclear, unmaintained, unmapped, devoid of signage, or *braided* (e.g., cut with so many in-roads and use-trails as to confuse the main trail). Use-trails are unofficial, unplanned paths cut by the feet of passing hikers, and include anglers' trails, climbers' trails, miners' trails, etc.

When trails cross slickrock they are usually marked with *ducks,* which are small piles of rocks. Some trails through forests are marked with blazes, which are slashes cut in trees, usually I-shaped or T-shaped. Ideally, the next blaze or duck should always be visible from the one before, so that hikers can follow a route from point to point. Don't follow blazes and ducks unquestioningly, however. Trails are always being realigned while tree blazes aren't. Ducks can tumble or be plunked down capriciously by ignorant, careless, or mischievous persons.

The main point here is that you need to pay attention to keep from getting lost. Carry a good topographic map and know how to read it, keeping in mind that trails get realigned and that maps fall out of date. Stop frequently to identify your position, making sure that you know where you are. Look behind you from time to time if you are going to return along the same route. By making a mental note of the scene behind you, you may be able to recognize it later. A compass is helpful if you know how to use it, especially in landscapes with low horizons. GPS devices are likewise helpful—again, if you know how to use it and pay heed to your battery supply before setting out. I sometimes see hikers depending on GPS devices to "show them the way," without mastering the GPS device beforehand—a mistake. You need to be the master of your GPS, not a trusting dependent.

If you do become lost, don't panic. Try to identify your position. If you can, retrace your steps. If darkness is coming, make immediate plans to spend the night. The first priority is shelter and warmth, not food. A fire might help guide the rescue party.

Preventative measures are always best. Don't hike alone. Notify someone of your intended route. Carry a small bundle of emergency supplies, including matches, a whistle, high-energy food, a knife, and a sweater or jacket.

Mountain Etiquette

There is no law against obnoxious behavior, but there are long-standing traditions among Sierra Nevada hikers that should be observed. One fine old custom on Sierra trails is to greet the people you meet. If you find someone in need of help, stop and lend assistance. Respect private property. Keep noise levels down in camp, especially at night. Please do not foist upon us that incessant ringing, tweeting, beeping clamor of electronic devices and toys. The out-of-doors should be a haven from city life, not only from honking traffic, urban noise, television, radio, and telephones, but also the whole mentality of tightly scheduled days and the ill-natured attitudes that rise from living in the rat race. Incessant bellyaching and abusive, sewer-mouthed language are abominations. Most of us come to the mountains to escape that.

Of course, a bit of grousing about the trail, food, weather, rangers, guidebook writers, etc., is a time-honored birthright of hikers. Likewise, a well-rounded cuss directed toward deer flies, backpacking stoves, mosquitoes, barked shins, and other maladies can be a colorful and satisfying part of the western experience. My point is this: Use common sense and courtesy, be thoughtful toward others, and have a care for the land and its resident beasts and plant life.

A Note on Cell Phones

Many hikers now carry cell phones into the backcountry. Cell phones can be handy in some emergencies, but they are frequently unreliable because signal reception is so hard to find in the mountains. For most hikers, cell phones provide a misleading sense of safety. Do not let a cell phone be an excuse to forgo the forethought, common sense, and basic skill that mountaineers have relied on for centuries to find their way and to deal with emergencies. The ease of a cell phone to summon assistance seemingly enables hikers to forgo the mountaineers' first and fundamental duty, *to come prepared for emergencies with skills and gear,* as well their second duty, to methodically explore all possibilities for helping themselves and their group before summoning a rescue party. You will pay dearly for the privilege of being rescued by someone else. If you carry a phone, do not think that it renders traditional mountaineering skill and caution superfluous.

Unfortunately, most cell phones in the mountains are used for frivolous reasons. That is a citizen's right, of course, but please, do not confuse one's rights with a sense of entitlement to intrude on other mountaineers' precious, hard-earned, time-honored right to cut ties (however fleetingly) with civilization. It is aggravating to be taking a breather atop a remote mountaintop or pass, enjoying the vast, sublime views and awe-inspiring solitude, only to be overtaken by a party of fresh arrivals who immediately start dialing out and crowing, "Guess where I'm calling from!"

Leave No Trace

Always leave an area just like you found it, if not cleaner. Camp no closer than 100 feet away from water or the trail. Avoid camping in fragile alpine meadows and along the banks of streams and lakes. Do not modify a campsite. Build fires, where they are permitted, only in existing campfire rings. Use only dead wood from the ground if it is abundant. Remember that plants and animals depend on downed and decomposing logs and forest duff for food, shelter, or nutrients. Do not break branches from standing bushes or trees, even if they are dead. Be aware where and when fires are restricted. Better yet, forgo the fire and use a camp stove.

Pack up all of your trash and extra food. Bury human waste at least 100 feet from water sources under 6 to 8 inches of topsoil. In some overused areas you will be asked to pack out human waste. Never put any soap in a lake or stream. It is illegal to remove flowers, rocks, pinecones, or anything else from any national park. Although this rule is amended in some areas of national forests, check the policy in a particular area before doing so. Shortcuts on switchbacks cause erosion. Don't add to the burgeoning maze of use-trails in some areas. If you fish, practice catch-and-release methods with barbless hooks; but if you do fish for your dinner, make sure you have a license and don't overfish your limit. By the same token, tasting a thimbleberry or wild strawberry is a fine part of the mountain experience, but remember that wildlife depends on that fruit and you do not.

Permits

Wilderness permits are required in national parks and designated wilderness areas for overnight use. In some places (like Desolation Wilderness) they are required even for day hikers. Backcountry rangers ask to see these permits and enforce the law with fines. Most are free, though the three national parks charge fees to issue them in advance.

Group Size

To preserve the integrity of wilderness, different agencies put restrictions on the size of overnight parties entering at specific trailheads. In Yosemite, for instance, the limit is eight people if you are leaving the trail, and fifteen if you are staying on it. Some national forests mandate groups of fifteen people or fewer. Crowds diminish the wilderness experience. If you are part of a group, keep noise levels down and do not intrude on others' solitude.

Trail Stock

Equestrians and pack trains have the right-of-way on the trail. When you encounter stock animals, step off the trail on the downhill side but remain in full view, and offer a friendly greeting to reassure the animal that you pose no threat. Cattle graze in many parts of the range in summer, and their presence indicates a need to be especially vigilant in purifying water.

A refreshing Sierra tradition: Trailside snowcones, made from real snow and a strong shot of powered drink mix.

Dogs

Keep your dog under control. Know the rules of the land administrators. Obey leash laws, where they exist. Bury your dog's waste or pack it out in resealable plastic bags.

Sharing the Mountains

Although this book is intended for hikers and backpackers, other groups also claim use of public lands—recreational vehicles, mechanized campers, mountain bikers, equestrians, packers, ATV users, hunters, anglers, cattlemen, loggers, and miners. Respect their rights, and most will respect yours. True, most hikers have short tolerances for motorized recreational trail users, who have the greatest capacity for wreaking havoc through carelessness. But remember that civil discourse with responsible user groups and rangers will do more to curb the renegades than any other means.

Compromise is the key. Many conservationists oppose commercial and mechanized activities on public lands—as indeed there are equestrians and hikers who would exclude mountain bikers, and miners who would exclude hikers from the vicinity of their mineral claims. As appealing as one group might find the utter exclusion of another, in light of the fact that we all must share the public lands, it seems reasonable to try to find some common ground. The array of government agencies provides for compromise. For example, some timber harvesting is permitted in national forests in exchange for complete protection in the national parks and designated wilderness areas (a protection that has not always been respected). If hikers want to keep mountain bikers out of the wilderness areas, they need to accede some places where they can ride. New mines and mining roads are excluded from wilderness areas, but we still honor existing claims.

Common ground that most users of the mountains share is a desire to preserve them from urbanized development. No hunter would rather see a meadow filled with strip malls. Conservationists and hunters sometimes forget that they are natural allies; many of our greatest conservationists in fact were hunters. Lumberjacks and cowpunchers likewise don't want to demolish forests and meadows. If they wanted to work among pavement and buildings, they could find easier, safer jobs in town. Rather, they would prefer to perpetuate their ways of life, which depend on the meadows and forests. Certainly, we must enforce regulations to prevent harmful clear-cutting or overgrazing and must support private and government agencies that encourage good land management. For the same reason, backpackers—who likewise bear some responsibility for fouling creeks and spoiling meadows—must accept the regulations of wilderness permits.

As a hiker and backpacker, I savor the wildest parts of the Sierra Nevada and would like to see greater areas preserved from development. More foothill tracts, especially, should be purchased and preserved as parks and reserves. Realistically, I recognize that much of the land in greatest threat of development is privately owned and is not going to be returned to wilderness or sold to the lowest bidder. If ranchers and farmers cannot turn a profit from their lands, they are going to sell to developers. Conservation groups ought to recognize that profitable agriculture is probably the strongest, most practical check that we have against the creeping development of the Sierra Nevada foothills, and that ranchers and farmers, like packers and hunters, should be cultivated as allies, not antagonists. That is one reason why I tend to view grazing cattle on a national forest with tolerance, not ire. Yes, I know that bovine-trammeled meadows and streams are ugly and detrimental to wilderness. Good grazing practices should be enforced on public land. My argument is that conservationists do not hold all the cards and should broaden their appeal in the lowlands, where ranches are headquartered, by a willingness to listen and compromise. The bottom line is, I'd rather see a ranch than a thousand ranchettes.

How to Use This Guide

The Sierra Nevada offers thousands of miles of trails, and no single hiking guide can be both comprehensive and portable. Many excellent hiking guidebooks explore specific parks or regions, but this guide attempts to provide an overview of the entire range.

Yes, it's a fleeting overview. After all, the area covered is vast. Consider that if laid out on the Eastern Seaboard, the Sierra Nevada would reach from Boston to Washington; if in the Rockies, from Wyoming to Santa Fe. These mountains also embrace an extraordinary variety of landscapes, elevations, biological zones, and histories. To convey a portrait of such a vast region, I had to be selective.

I want readers to glean a fuller appreciation for the whole Sierra Nevada, with hopes that you too will grow to love the rich and ever-beguiling beauty and variety of all its landscapes, not just the ones that most please the hasty tourist. Consequently, I've gathered together an admittedly motley grab bag of superlative hikes from all around the range—foothill, canyon, forest, alpine rock garden, desert edges, and even the neighboring Mono Basin, Owens Valley, and White Mountains, which frame the Sierra Nevada so majestically. Some of these hikes are actually set in the gold rush towns of Coloma, Nevada City, Placerville, Columbia, and Grass Valley. All these regions and places are integral to the vibrant health and character of the Sierra Nevada, and each hike, moreover, helps build a transcendent appreciation for the whole shebang.

So how do I choose which hikes to include? Most hikes highlight stupendous scenery, the Sierra Nevada's hallmark waterfalls, cliffs, domes, trees, glaciers, limestone caverns, etc. Others draw attention to the fascinating panoply of passing peoples who left their mark on these mountains, such as the ingenious engineers who built their incredible waterworks, mines, trails, roads, and railroads. Places utterly unique to the Sierra Nevada feature in many of my choices, wonderful oddities found nowhere else, such as the Smith Cabin Tree, the Black Point Fissures, the beehive hut atop Muir Pass, the tunnels and snowsheds of the First Transcontinental Railroad, the sight of Black Bart's first robbery site, and the catfish pond atop Donner Pass, just to name a few.

I likewise aim to describe hikes for all four seasons; many worthy Sierra trails don't get covered by winter snows. Although I include a handful of challenging backpacking trips, the book emphasizes day hiking rather than backpacking (though many day hikes make wonderful overnighters). I cater to hikers of different abilities. Some offer easy rambles suitable for families with young children. Other routes delve off cross-country, guiding experienced hikers through a route without benefit of trail. There are even trails or trail sections suitable for wheelchairs.

A dilemma for writers of hiking guides is that we put high value on uncrowded trails, while encouraging people to hike them. Granted that the chance to earn my bread in part by hiking tempted me to take this project on, but there's also strong moral justification for hiking guides. The more people who know and love the Sierra Nevada, the more who will want to preserve it. If there were no backpackers, there would be no designated wilderness areas. If no one appreciated how lovely the sagebrush frames a peak, or how hauntingly a cicada's strange whine complements the hot, still stretches of foothill wood and canyon floor, then no one would care if these more "marginal" landscapes disappeared under development. If no one were interested in hiking, it's only a matter of time before the trails would be turned into roads.

There have always been people who prefer the city to the wilds. Fair enough. Yet I worry to see how many of our younger generation have grown to prefer electronic "adventures" over real, physical ones. As fewer and fewer American children camp, hike, or even play in the backyard, and more and more reach for electronics to fire up their social lives and stir their natural sense of adventure, how can we expect future generations to care about Sierra Nevada wild lands? To promote the perpetuation of wild, open, public land, we have to encourage new generations to know, love, and care for the wild Sierra Nevada. The best way for that is to take kids hiking. Responsible hikers are the least intrusive of all people in the mountains. Certainly, many stunning roads and vistas are accessible by car, but the finest way to experience the Sierra Nevada, to cultivate adventures and fine fellowship, is afoot.

How the Hikes Are Organized

I divide the Sierra Nevada into nine geographical regions, each a chapter. Each chapter begins with a regional introduction, giving a sweeping look at the land and historical setting. I then follow with anywhere from five to twenty detailed hikes and end each chapter with **Honorable Mentions**—worthy hikes that are mainly too short and simple (like self-guided nature trails) or too "loose" (more suitable for wandering at your will than needful of purposeful guidance) to describe in more detail, but which you should not miss.

For each detailed hike in the book, I begin with a hike summary—a brief taste of the adventure to follow. Next you'll find the quick, nitty-gritty details of the hike: where the trailhead is located, hike length, approximate hiking time, difficulty rating, type of trail terrain, best hiking season, what other trail users you may encounter, land status, the nearest town, usage fees, pertinent maps, and trail contacts (for updates on trail conditions), etc.

My comments on **trail difficulty** are necessarily subjective—obviously, an "easy" hike for a seasoned hiker can be "strenuous" for a couch potato. I love to encourage couch potatoes to get out on trails. But they should understand up front that by "easy," I mean that someone in fair physical condition should be able to do it easily. When I say a trail is "strenuous," recognize that someone who is not acclimated to the elevation or who is not in good condition, might find it brutal. The rating is based on the length of the hike, the condition of the trail, and the elevation gain and loss. Note that when I mention "overall elevation gain," I mean the approximate total rise in feet that a hiker walks uphill, even if these rises are interspersed with downhill sections. I call this a "gain and loss" of elevation on out-and-back hikes, because you return to the same spot.

In the category of **Trail condition**, I call a conventional footpath a "singletrack," while an old dirt road with a vegetated crown down the middle is a "doubletrack."

The **Finding the trailhead** section gives directions from a nearby city or town to the trailhead parking area.

The **Hike** section provides my impression of the trail. To keep that section livelier, I save some of the boring but necessary details for the **Miles and Directions** section that follows the hike description.

A Note on Maps

The maps in this book use elevation tints to portray relief and give you a good idea of elevation gain and loss. The selected route is highlighted and directional arrows, when needed, point the way. Access roads, landmarks, water, points of interest, and geographical features are marked.

On extended hikes in wild areas, you should be carrying a good topographic map. For that reason, for every hike I list what I think to be the best available topographic maps for each hike. The basis of all these topographical maps are the 15-minute and even more detailed 7.5-minute maps published by the United States Geological Survey (USGS). Aside from recording all the old trails and mines and other such fascinating ephemeral information that gets dropped from newer maps, these splendid sheet maps still form the basis for all other commercial maps and mapping software. I list the USGS 7-minute quadrants (known as quads) by name for each hike because they are the most detailed and complete topographical rendering of any map available, though they are *not* the most up-to-date in terms of trails or developed features. Topographic maps are available to view for free or for downloading directly from the US Geological Survey map store website, on the Map Locator & Downloader page: http://store.usgs.gov.

Probably more useful to most hikers are the regional topographic maps published on paper by the US Forest Service and private publishers like Tom Harrison, National Geographic Trails Illustrated, and Fine Edge Productions. Other government agencies (e.g., the BLM, state parks, and the like) provide decent trail maps on-site. I also list these for different hikes. Hikers nowadays can also print out good trail (and off-trail) map sections from commercial topographic mapping software websites or apps (e.g., National Geographic TOPO, Backpacker Map Maker, Trails.com, and others).

GPS devices made for outdoor enthusiasts also sell downloadable topographical maps, though a GPS still cannot replace a real map, and real experience in using it, in serious cross-country travel. GPS devices are useful, but a paper map and traditional compass are easier to comprehend *spatially* and are more reliable (they don't run low on batteries, for example). GPS devices prove particularly troublesome when hikers use them without studying a map, set them to beep at a particular destination, and then fail to pay careful attention to the surrounding landscape en route. True, a GPS also proves useful in retracing one's steps, thereby reducing a hiker's chance to getting lost. They are also convenient in navigating through forests off-trail, or through a fog, provided you don't lose the signal. Consequently, they are wonderful to carry with you, but they do not replace a map and good navigational sense and experience.

Map Legend

Municipal

≡⟨80⟩≡ Interstate Highway

≡⟨50⟩≡ US Highway

≡⟨137⟩≡ State Road

≡⟨CR 12⟩≡ Local/County Road

= = = = Unpaved Road

⊢—+—+ Railroad

⊢———⊣ Tunnel

– – – – State Boundary

━━━━ National/Wilderness

———— State Park

Trails

– – – – – Featured Trail

- - - - - Trail

·········· Off-Route Hike

Water Features

Body of Water

Glacier

Marsh

River/Creek

Intermittent Stream

Waterfall

Spring

Symbols

〜 Bridge

■ Building/Point of Interest

▲ Campground

∧ Cave/Cavern

⊔⊔⊔⊔ Cliff

— Dam

⟊ Gate

🅿 Parking

✕ Pass

▲ Peak/Elevation

🛉 Picnic Area

▲ Primitive Campsite

🏠 Ranger Station/Park Office

🚻 Restroom

Scenic View

•—•—| Ski Lift

Tower

○ Town

⟨20⟩ Trailhead

? Visitor/Information Center

Land Features

•—•—•—• Powerline

⊢—+—⊣ Fence/Wall

Northern Gold Country

The gold-bearing region from Mariposa north to Oroville is known as the Gold Country. The forty-niners didn't call it that. They referred to the Gold Country as "the Mines." They knew the large region drained by the Feather, Yuba, and American Rivers as "the Northern Mines"—the purview of this chapter. (The Southern Mines region is the subject of the next chapter.) The principle gold rush towns of the Northern Mines are Auburn, Grass Valley, Nevada City, and Downieville, all linked along Highway 49, and Oroville, in the Feather River country farther north along CA 70.

The Northern Mines embraces much of the high country of the Feather and Yuba Rivers, where snow falls and sticks all winter long. Summer is the best time for hikers to visit the scenic Gold Lakes Basin in the shadow of the spectacular Sierra Buttes, Plumas-Eureka State Park, and the lake country of Nevada County. The Northern Mines area also encompasses an expanse of western foothills and wild canyons that provide snow-free hiking all year round. These foothill hikes are at their best in spring, when the flowers bloom, and autumn, when the leaves turn, but winter can also bring clear skies and ideal hiking weather. Summer temperatures in the foothills routinely reach the 90s and above, but morning and evening temperatures can be very comfortable, and a dunk in the river can bring perfection to even the hottest hike.

Despite a population boom in foothill towns, most of the backcountry remains less heavily populated today than it was a century and a half ago. Many local trails were originally forged by miners and later abandoned, only to be revived in recent years by hardworking volunteer organizations like Sequoya Challenge, the Forest Trails Alliance, Pony Express Association, the Bear Yuba Aland Trust, and the Western States Trail Foundation. Most of these trails follow rivers or climb between ridges and canyon bottoms, typically in the Yuba and American River drainages. Not only are they scenic, but most contain a good deal of historical interest, such as old bridges, mines, water ditches, and rock walls. Even if it's nothing more substantial than the story behind a place name, a little of the history of a place makes the hike all the more interesting.

Many contemporary mining claims still dot the Gold Country. Most of them are on public land, but they are private claims nonetheless. Respect those claims. Never disturb or even investigate a contemporary mining camp or its equipment, and do not remove any rocks or minerals from any claim. Miners are notoriously proprietary about their claims. If you want to pan for gold, find a stretch of claim-free public land. The Auburn State Recreation Area and Malakoff Diggins State Historic Park, for instance, both encourage claim-free recreational panning.

1 Oroville's North Table Mountain

A massive lava flow of olivine basalt rock, ending on the west in a palisade of cliffs above the Sacramento Valley, North Table Mountain offers some of the most brilliant wildflower displays in the Sierra Nevada. A ramble over its broad volcanic plateau also turns up many other surprises, including vernal pools, ephemeral waterfalls, box canyons, and a strangely beautiful, moor-like terrain.

Start: Table Mountain parking area on Chero-kee Road, north of Oroville

Distance: 7.5-mile lollipop loop

Hiking time: About 4–5 hours

Difficulty: Moderate, with only about 500 feet of elevation lost and regained

Trail condition: There are no established trails here. You are free to ramble at will. The cross-country route described here traverses open rock and grass, employing fences, trees, a faint doubletrack, and a canyon rim as landmarks. Watch for poison oak, ticks, and rattlesnakes.

Seasons: The best time to see blooming wildflowers in a year of average rainfall and temperatures is mid-Mar through mid-Apr. Colder temperatures will delay the blooms. The reserve is open throughout the year and makes very pleasant walking in winter months, the best time to view the vernal pools and falls. Summer can be scorching.

Other trail users: Grazing herds of timid cattle flee ahead of hikers and are not aggressive. Dogs must be leashed. Bikes, equestrians, and campers forbidden. Seasonal hunting permitted. Tours available.

Land status: North Table Mountain Ecological Reserve, California Department of Fish and Wildlife

Nearest town: Oroville

Fees and permits: None

Map: USGS 7.5-minute quad: Oroville

Trail contacts: North Table Mountain Ecological Reserve, California Department of Fish and Wildlife, 1812 19th St., Sacramento, CA 95811; (916) 358-2869; www.dfg.ca.gov/lands/er/region2/northtable.html

Special considerations: With no trails and rolling, wide-open terrain, Table Mountain can be disorienting, especially in a winter fog. A compass or GPS device is handy. The boundaries of the reserve are irregular but mostly defined by sturdy, well-maintained barbed-wire fences marked with yellow signs. Private property lies beyond. (If you look west from the parking area, you can see an example of a marked boundary fence.) Be aware that the "faint doubletrack" described below and shown on the map is very faint indeed and sometimes hard to see, so pay attention to the other landmarks mentioned herein: fence lines, trees, watercourses, canyons, and compass directions. Look behind you as you walk in order to recognize your return route. Hikers uncomfortable with cross-country travel certainly can stay within sight of the car and still enjoy the flower display, or they can take an organized tour.

Finding the trailhead: From CA 70 in Oroville, take the CA 162 exit east 1.7 miles to the intersection where 162 splits to the right (south), but we head left (north) on Washington Avenue, driving 0.8 mile to a traffic roundabout, where you take Table Mountain Boulevard north across the Feather River 0.8 mile to Cherokee Road. Turn right (northeast) onto Cherokee Road. Drive up this narrow, winding, paved road, leveling out on the flat top of Table Mountain. At 6.2 miles from Table Mountain Boulevard, look for a gravel parking area on the left (west), next to a cattle chute (N39 35.713' / W121 32.489'). There is no identifying sign, water, or amenities. Trailhead GPS: N39 35.757' / W121 32.483'

Steep-sided Coal Canyon, which cuts deeply into North Table Mountain, is thickly covered in woods along its bottomlands.

The Hike

When gold rush chronicler Dame Shirley passed by in 1851, she observed that Table Mountain was "extended like an immense dining board for the giants, its summit, a perfectly straight line penciled for more than a league against the flowing sky." This Victorian lady aptly described the distant view of a volcanic plateau, but a walk around North Table Mountain quickly dispels the notion that it's "flat as a pencil line."

Managed by the Department of Fish and Game, this 3,315-acre preserve was established largely to protect the northern basalt-flow vernal pools, a natural feature that is rapidly being destroyed by development over much of California. Vernal pools are intermittent puddles, filling in the rainy season and drying up later in the year. Table Mountain is an ideal spot for vernal pools because it's composed of hard, non-porous basalt rock that does not readily absorb water. Freshwater shrimp live in vernal pools, and these in turn attract hungry birds.

Winter is a good time to hike North Table Mountain, not only to see the vernal pools and intermittent waterfalls that drain the swales, but also just to relish the bleakly beautiful rolling landscapes. The greatest glories of Table Mountain come in spring, however, when the flowers bloom and transform the plateau from grassy green or dark basalt brown to patches and carpets of gold, blue, red, white, and lavender. Among the scores of species are goldfields, yellowcarpet, monkeyflowers of different varieties, pussy paws, yellow violets, golden poppies, pinkish owl's clover, baby blue eyes, and white meadow foam. A newly described flower species found in vernal swales, the Butte County golden clover, is known to exist only on Table Mountain and along nearby Cottonwood Road.

From a gate on the north side of the parking area (elevation 1,320 feet), strike north toward the wreck of a large, fallen oak tree. Watch the ground for signs of a faint doubletrack, which can serve as a path over the open grassy terrain and through a dilapidated barbed-wire fence. Passing just to the left (west) of the fallen oak, we follow the doubletrack northwest clear to a well-maintained barbed-wire fence line that marks the northern boundary of the state reserve.

Now the fence line west to corner post #1, where the fence bends north in a right angle. Standing at this corner post, look west to Coal Canyon, at the edge of Table Mountain, and continue walking west toward its rim. As you stroll westward down a rolling grassy incline, you will shortly intercept a ravine. Follow its watercourse (typically dry) downstream. After passing a clump of willows, the watercourse arcs northward to the abrupt edge of Coal Canyon. In a wet season, this streamlet forms an ephemeral waterfall, pouring straight over the volcanic brink and dropping about 40 feet into Coal Canyon. From our vantage point at the lip of the falls, we can look down upon the wooded floor of Coal Canyon, hemmed in by rugged basalt bluffs.

From the ephemeral falls, climb westward to a grove of oak trees on the hill above, passing through a dilapidated fence. Following the wooded south rim of Coal Canyon westward, the Sacramento Valley and the Coast Ranges are in distant view. As a northern branch of Coal Canyon becomes visible, wet-season hikers might catch a glimpse of another ephemeral waterfall, Ghost Falls, in delicate free-fall from the farthest bluffs.

After a mile's amble down the rim of Coal Canyon, you will meet another well-maintained fence line that marks the preserve's western boundary. Strike south, following the fence line. You will pass a small reservoir. At corner post #2, where the boundary fence makes a sharp right-angle turn to the west, pass through a gap in an abandoned fence line, and walk a hundred yards south to another faint set of doubletracks. Turn right (west) and follow the tracks to the edge of the state's property, a ridge swathed in oaks where you can look down from fissured volcanic cliffs into Beatson Hollow and the Sacramento Valley. At an elevation of about 890 feet, this is the lowest point of the hike. The rail line bound for the Feather River passes just below the cliffs. Rising sheer from the low Sacramento plains in the middle distance, the fantastic Sutter Buttes punch upward well over 2,000 feet, a confined, rugged cluster of 3-million-year-old volcanoes known hereabouts as the world's smallest mountain range.

Oroville's North Table Mountain

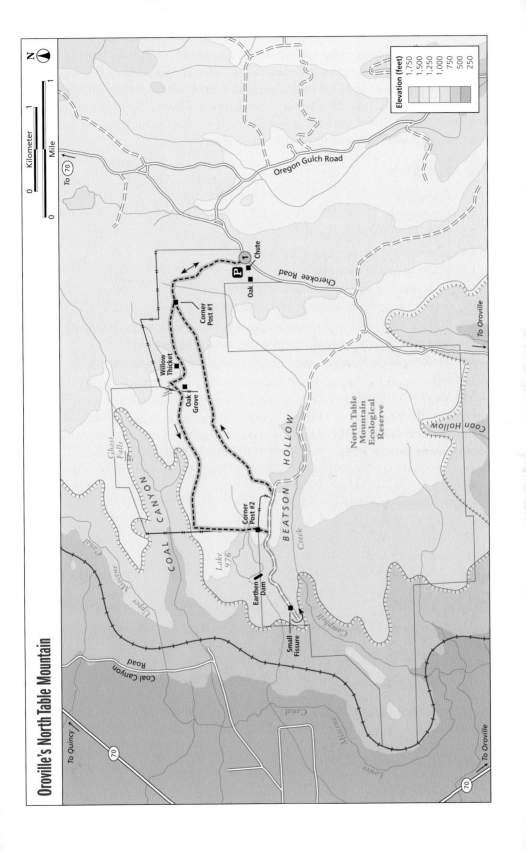

When ready to return, you can follow the doubletrack all the way back to the trailhead. Paralleling the northern rim of Beatson Hollow, walk east until you cross through an abandoned fence line, where you will find a fork in the well-trampled gap between fence posts. Take the left (northeast) fork, and follow it back over the rolling, open countryside. As you near its northernmost reaches, you will begin to notice familiar countryside that you passed through on your way out.

Miles and Directions

0.0 Parking area.

0.4 Lone blue oak.

0.7 Meet northern boundary (barbed-wire fence); turn left (west).

0.9 Corner post #1; walk west toward Coal Canyon.

1.2 Watercourse; follow downstream.

1.5 Top of ephemeral waterfall; continue west on canyon rim.

2.7 Arrive at western boundary (barbed-wire fence); turn left (south).

3.3 Corner post #2; pass through dilapidated gate to faint doubletrack and turn right (west).

4.0 Arrive at Beatson Hollow overlook; turn back and follow doubletrack east.

4.9 Gap in dilapidated fence; turn north on faint doubletrack and follow it back to parking area.

6.6 Meet northern boundary fence.

7.1 Lone blue oak.

7.5 Arrive back at the parking area.

2 Jamison Lake

Of many possible hikes into the Lakes Basin Recreation Area, this one offers mining history, mountain vistas, a waterfall, and lakes.

Start: Jamison Mine parking area
Distance: 6.4 miles out and back
Hiking time: About 3 hours
Difficulty: Moderate, with an overall elevation gain and loss of about 1,000 feet
Trail condition: Good, well-signed, singletrack trail
Seasons: June–Oct
Other trail users: No dogs or bikes permitted on the state park trail, but equestrians are. Dogs under control are allowed to use national forest trails.
Land status: Plumas-Eureka State Park; Lakes Basin Recreation Area, Plumas National Forest

Nearest towns: Mohawk, Graeagle, and Blairsden have stores and cafes, but Quincy is the nearest large town.
Fees and permits: Campfire permit required if using a stove or campfire
Maps: Forest Service: *Lakes Basin, Sierra Buttes, and Plumas-Eureka State Park*. USGS 7.5-minute quad: *Gold Lake*.
Trail contacts: Plumas-Eureka State Park, 310 Johnsville Rd., Blairsden, CA 96103; (530) 836-2380; www.parks.ca.gov/?page_id=507. Plumas-Eureka State Park Association, www .parks.ca.gov/?page_id=26306

Finding the trailhead: Plumas-Eureka State Park headquarters lie 4.7 miles southwest of CA 70 at the Mohawk exit. From the park museum, drive back toward Mohawk 0.5 mile to a junction (GPS: N39 45.530' / W120 41.467') with the unpaved Jamison Mine Road. Turn to the right (south) and drive 1.3 miles to the parking area. The trail starts at the metal gate and trail signage on the southeast side of the parking area. Trailhead GPS: N39 44.533' / W120 42.079'

The Hike

The lakes of Plumas and Sierra Counties occupy a special place in the annals of gold rush lore. The story goes that an eccentric miner, Thomas Stoddard, while being chased westward across the Sierra by hostile Piutes in the fall of 1850, ran past a lake whose shores were littered with gold nuggets. Reaching safety, he wintered in Nevada City, taking pains to repeat his story to everyone who asked. An army of argonauts intent on helping him pick up those loose nuggets soon gathered in town. When Stoddard set out in spring to find his lake, he also found himself unwittingly leading a company of hundreds and unable to shake them off. They followed him for miles over the mountains, supposedly to the Lakes Basin region, where he went from lake to lake on a fruitless hunt for free gold nuggets. After three months of misadventuring, when it became apparent that Stoddard was delusional, some of his irate followers threatened to lynch him, but they were stopped by calmer heads who were better able to appreciate a cosmic joke at their own expense. All was not a total loss, since parties breaking up from what is now known as the Gold Lake Stampede prospected other Plumas County creeks, many of which proved rich in gold for those willing to work.

The forest has reclaimed most of the dooryards of the old buildings scattered around the Jamison Mine, in Plumas-Eureka State Park.

We begin our hike above the banks of Little Jamison Creek, at the Jamison Mine, an area prospected by Gold Lake Stampeders. Pictures of the Jamison Mine from the early twentieth century show a neighborhood largely denuded of forest, and a development even more extensive than what now appears from the road and trail. Though several mining buildings still stand in excellent condition, the invigorated forest that surrounds them must surely conceal many other ruined structures, tailings, excavations, and rusty pieces of mining equipment.

The steepest part of our entire trail climbs the hillside beyond the mine, sometimes by aid of stone steps. Just as the gradient begins to lessen, we pass the signposted junction with the Smith Lake Trail (keep right), and shortly thereafter cross the state park boundary into the Lakes Basin Recreation Area of Plumas National Forest. Reaching our first mile, we come to a little spur fork that leads back to the banks of Little Jamison Creek, whose pretty waterfall splashes some 30 feet down through a ravine.

Just beyond we enter the valley where Grass Lake lies, ringed by greensward, with Mount Washington looming above and behind. As we advance alongside the lake, trickling seeps muddy the tread and cause the trailside shrubbery to thrive and crowd

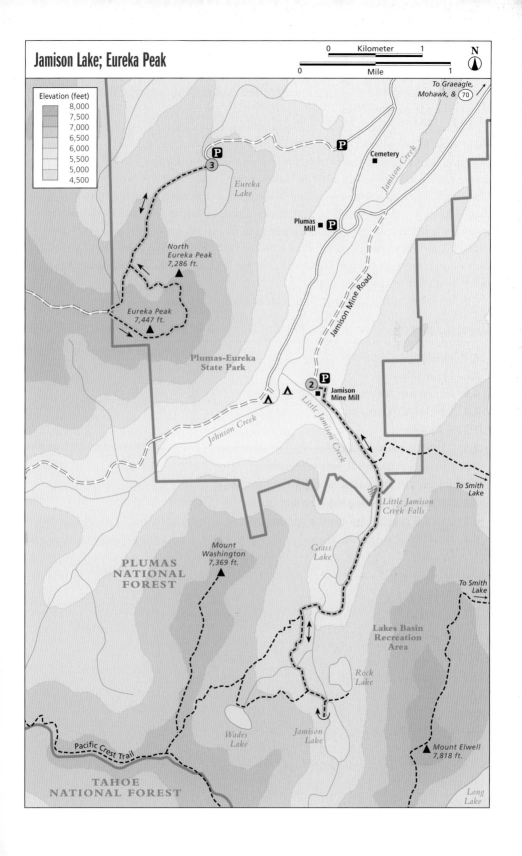

Jamison Lake; Eureka Peak

Elevation (feet)
8,000
7,500
7,000
6,500
6,000
5,500
5,000
4,500

To Graeagle,
Mohawk, & 70

Cemetery

Eureka
Lake

Plumas
Mill

North
Eureka Peak
7,286 ft.

Jamison Creek

Jamison Mine Road

Eureka Peak
7,447 ft.

Plumas-Eureka
State Park

Johnson Creek

Little Jamison Creek

2 Jamison
Mine Mill

Little Jamison
Creek Falls

To Smith
Lake

Mount
Washington
7,369 ft.

Grass
Lake

PLUMAS
NATIONAL
FOREST

Lakes Basin
Recreation
Area

To Smith
Lake

Rock
Lake

Pacific Crest Trail

Wades
Lake

Jamison
Lake

Mount Elwell
7,818 ft.

TAHOE
NATIONAL FOREST

Long
Lake

our path. The entire valley seems verdant, even at the full height of summer, when flowers already withered down along the Feather River are still blooming here. Little Jamison Creek emerges from its tunnel of foliage just long enough for us to hop across on some handy stones.

Passing the junction with the trail that leads up to the Pacific Crest Trail (PCT), a route of favor to backpackers, we opt for the left-hand fork instead and again begin to climb. The terrain becomes drier and more open, permitting views of the ridges that define the valley's headwalls. The highest point is the 7,818-foot hump of Mount Elwell, which stands above as-yet-unseen Jamison Lake. Passing some boulders bigger than elephants and the cutoff trail to Wades Lake, we swing eastward to the outlet stream of Jamison Lake, where another junction asks us to choose between Rock and Jamison Lakes. Both are close. Jamison is on the right, an old reservoir behind a rock dam overgrown with foliage. The best views are from the rocky heights around the right (west) side of the dam.

When ready to leave, retrace your steps to the parking area.

Miles and Directions

0.0 Parking area.

0.1 Jamison Mine mill.

0.8 Junction with Smith Lake Trail; keep right (south).

1.0 Little Jamison Creek Falls.

1.2 Grass Lake.

2.0 Ford of Little Jamison Creek.

2.2 Junction with trail to PCT; keep left (southeast).

2.8 Junction with Wades Lake cutoff; bear left (southeast).

3.0 Junction with Rock Lake Trail; keep right (south).

3.2 View over Jamison Lake from the western side.

6.4 Arrive back at the parking area.

3 Eureka Peak

One of the renowned treasure mountains of the Gold Country, Eureka Peak surrendered millions of dollars of gold-bearing ore from more than 60 miles of tunnels before its mines closed down in 1943. Now preserved in the 5,500-acre Plumas-Eureka State Park, Eureka's 7,447-foot summit is celebrated today for wide-ranging views over the northeastern Sierra Nevada.

Start: Eureka Lake
Distance: 3.7-mile lollipop loop
Hiking time: About 2 hours
Difficulty: Moderate, with an overall elevation gain and loss of about 1,200 feet
Trail condition: Good singletrack trail, with some dirt road

Seasons: May–Oct
Other trail users: No dogs allowed. Vehicles may be present on the dirt road just west of Eureka Peak.
Land status: Plumas-Eureka State Park
For additional information, see Hike 2.

Finding the trailhead: Plumas-Eureka State Park headquarters lie 4.7 miles southwest of CA 70 at the Mohawk exit. From the park museum, drive north through Johnsville 1.4 miles to the Eureka Bowl parking lot. From a metal gate (GPS: N39 45.878' / W120 41.857'), a narrow, rough dirt road continues uphill 1.2 miles to the shore of Eureka Lake, 660 feet higher in elevation than Eureka Bowl. If your vehicle has low clearance, consider parking at Eureka Bowl and walking this road to Eureka Lake. Eureka Lake trailhead GPS: N39 45.808' / W120 42.784'

The Hike

Our trail starts beside Eureka Lake (6,180 feet), a reservoir dammed to supply power for the mines, particularly for the stamp mills, on the east side of Eureka Peak. Beginning in the 1850s, when Eureka Peak was known as Gold Mountain, lode mining reached its apex in the 1880s when 173 miners (and a contingent of mules to pull the mining skips) were working the tunnels of the Plumas-Eureka Mine. A tram carried ore down the mountain to the sixty-stamp Mohawk Mill, still standing near the park museum, and now-sleepy Johnsville was a very lively town. But don't think that life on Eureka Peak was all work and no play: Eureka Peak is also famed as the birthplace of organized downhill ski racing. Starting in the 1860s, Johnsville was sponsoring winter competitions between ski teams from other Gold Country settlements as far away as La Porte, Onion Valley, and Poker Flat. Near Eureka Bowl, the small ski area that you pass on the road to Eureka Lake, competitors set early records with feats of downhill skiing at speeds approaching 80 mph.

The blasting and hammering in the mines has now ceased, and the pounding stamp mills are quiet. We walk across the dam on Eureka Lake's west side, admiring the handsome profile and reflection of North Eureka Peak. Hiking uphill on a trail

The Mohawk Mill used to process gold ore mined from Eureka Peak, behind it.

through evergreen woods, it's interesting to note that photographs taken during the mining heyday show the mountain denuded of forest.

After climbing 1 mile and nearly 700 feet of elevation, we reach an unsigned junction and take the right-hand fork. (We will loop back on the left-hand trail.) Another climb of about 375 feet in 0.4 mile brings us to a more open ridge, where we meet a dirt road coming into the state park from the Plumas National Forest, immediately to the west. You may see vehicles on this road. Turn left and follow this road up the ridge toward the summit of Eureka Peak. The road peters out to become a singletrack trail before we get there.

The mountain tops out somewhat indecisively at 7,447 feet amid outcrops of quartz porphyry entangled in montane chaparral. Two separate boulder piles are marked with posts, and both seem to have equal claim as the actual summit. Gazing south across the rugged canyons and ridges toward the saddle-shaped Sierra Buttes, 11 miles away, our simple admiration for grand mountain scenery is enhanced by a geological fact of enormous interest to gold miners: We are standing near the northern limit of a major belt of mineralization—specifically, veins of gold-bearing quartz—that stretches like a miniature Mother Lode from Eureka Peak southward to the opposite side of the Sierra Buttes, where the rich mines of Sierra City burrow and delve.

Our trail now hooks north on a ridge toward North Eureka Peak (7,286 feet), with views eastward into the vast Sierra Valley, the largest subalpine valley in the United States. The trail veers left (west) before reaching this second and more pointed, though lower, summit of Eureka Peak. Anyone who wants to bag it can leave the trail at this point and will find it a more challenging scramble than the main peak. The path, however, descends abruptly into thicker forest and rejoins the original trail that takes us back to Eureka Lake.

Miles and Directions

0.0 Parking area at Eureka Lake.

1.0 Junction (no signpost) with return loop; stay right (south).

1.4 Junction with dirt road; turn left (east).

1.7 Summit of Eureka Peak.

2.2 Closest trail point to North Eureka Peak.

2.7 Junction (no signpost) with return trail; turn right (north).

3.7 Arrive back at the parking area.

4 Sierra Buttes

With vast views and a spectacularly exposed stairway climb to the very pinnacle of this jagged 8,857-foot summit, the lookout tower on Sierra Buttes is a popular destination for hikers.

Start: Packer Lake Saddle parking area
Distance: 4.8 miles out and back
Hiking time: About 4 hours
Difficulty: Moderate, despite a 1,500-foot elevation gain
Trail condition: A combination of dirt road and singletrack trail, with metal steps and catwalk at the lookout
Seasons: June–Oct
Other trail users: Dogs are welcome. Four-wheel-drive vehicles can drive to a point 1.6 miles from the trailhead, beyond which the path is typically more crowded.
Land status: Tahoe National Forest
Nearest towns: Sierra City, Downieville
Fees and permits: None
Maps: Forest Service: *Lakes Basin, Sierra Buttes, and Plumas-Eureka State Park.* National Geographic: *Tahoe National Forest.* USGS 7.5-minute quad: Sierra City.
Trail contacts: Tahoe National Forest, 15924 Highway 49, Camptonville, CA 95922; (530) 288-3231; www.fs.usda.gov/tahoe

Finding the trailhead: From its junction with Highway 49, drive 1.4 miles north on Gold Lake Highway to the Sardine Lake turnoff (GPS: N39 37.264' / W120 36.645'). Turn left (west) and drive 0.3 mile to another fork (GPS: N39 37.320' / W120 36.933'), where you turn right (north). After 2.7 miles you will reach a junction beside Packer Lake (GPS: N39 37.420' / W120 39.217'). Turn left (south) and drive up this road 1.5 miles to Packer Lake Saddle (GPS: N39 37.167' / W120 40.034'), a four-way junction on top of the ridge. Turn left (south) and drive 0.5 mile down the spine of the ridge to a turnoff marked with a Forest Service bulletin board. Our trail begins at the locked gate adjacent. Trailhead GPS: N39 36.686' / W120 39.917'

The Hike

There are many routes to the top of the Sierra Buttes. The hardest trails climb from near Lower Sardine Lake (elevation 5,750 feet) or from Highway 49 at the Pacific Crest Trail (PCT) crossing (elevation 4,580 feet). The easiest starts from the four-wheel-drive parking area on the mountain's shoulder, at just under 8,000 feet.

Our trail starts at 7,000 feet, on the PCT. Walk around the metal gate that blocks vehicular traffic, and ascend the ridgeback southward on a dirt road. The views are rendered wide-open by low-growing montane foliage, flowery alpine meadow, and a sparse forest cover. The Sierra Buttes themselves are an obvious presence, and westward we look out over the heavily forested maze of drainages (Butcher Creek, Ladies Canyon, Hog and Pig Canyons, etc.) that feed the Yuba River near Downieville.

Although we pass several spur tracks and the PCT itself splits off at 1 mile, our mandate is simple: Always take the fork that climbs. After entering dense forest on

The lookout tower atop the Sierra Buttes is reached by an exciting climb up a steep metal stairway.

singletrack switchbacks, we pass some large photogenic boulders with fine views of the Buttes in profile and of Young America and Sardine Lakes. After crossing the parking area for four-wheel-drive vehicles (which have come by another route), our singletrack trail climbs steeply to a dirt road, by which Forest Service vehicles reach the lookout tower. Although closed to other motorized traffic, it also serves as our path.

Steep, narrow, open, and lofty, the road grows more exposed and dramatic as we climb toward the enormous summit block. Composed of ancient metamorphic rock

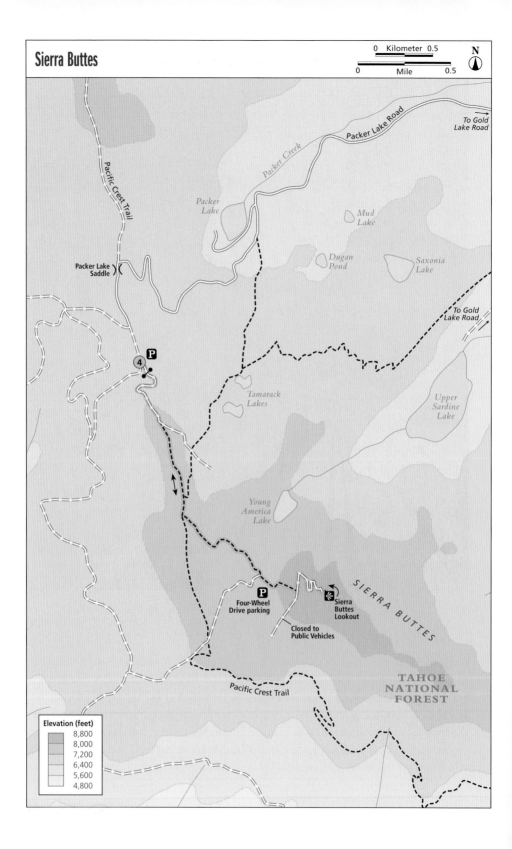

Sierra Buttes

Packer Lake Road
To Gold Lake Road
Packer Creek
Pacific Crest Trail
Packer Lake
Mud Lake
Packer Lake Saddle
Dugan Pond
Saxonia Lake
To Gold Lake Road
4 🅿
Tamarack Lakes
Upper Sardine Lake
Young America Lake
🅿 Four-Wheel Drive parking
SIERRA BUTTES
Sierra Buttes Lookout
Closed to Public Vehicles
Pacific Crest Trail
TAHOE NATIONAL FOREST

Elevation (feet)
8,800
8,000
7,200
6,400
5,600
4,800

0   Kilometer   0.5
0   Mile   0.5

N

borne from an undersea volcano, the hard sheer walls and towers of the summit block crown the peak like a mountaintop castle.

The final assault is made by sturdy metal stairways anchored to the rock, the highlight of the hike. Arriving at the narrow top, look for the nineteenth-century graffiti scratched by neat-handed visitors before the stairway was installed. From the catwalk surrounding the tower, you can read the ridges and valleys of the Yuba watershed like a map. In one panoramic glance you can embrace the 110-mile sweep from Mount Lassen to the ranges above the shore of Lake Tahoe.

Miles and Directions

0.0 Parking area.

0.9 Junction with Tamarack Lakes Trail; keep right (south).

1.0 Junction with PCT; turn left (southeast).

1.6 Parking area for four-wheel-drive vehicles.

1.8 Singletrack trail joins unpaved road.

2.3 Base of lookout stairway.

2.4 Sierra Buttes Lookout.

4.8 Arrive back at the parking area.

Historic visitors who scratched their names at the summit of the Sierra Buttes would have climbed there without benefit of the metal stairway.

5 Halls Ranch Trail to Fiddle Creek

Fit for an off-season hike or a summer day's soak, this historic trail leads to a mountain creek in a valley above the North Yuba River.

Start: Highway 49 turnout west of Goodyears Bar

Distance: 5.4 miles out and back

Hiking time: About 2-3 hours

Difficulty: Moderate, with an overall elevation gain and loss of 2,300 feet

Trail condition: Good singletrack trail

Seasons: All year, weather permitting. Snow does fall here in winter.

Other trail users: Dogs, equestrians, and mountain bikes are permitted.

Land status: Tahoe National Forest

Nearest town: Downieville

Fees and permits: None

Map: USGS 7.5-minute quad: Goodyears Bar

Trail contacts: Tahoe National Forest, 15924 Highway 49, Camptonville, CA 95922; (530) 288-3231; www.fs.usda.gov/tahoe

Finding the trailhead: The signposted parking area for Halls Ranch Trail is on the south side of Highway 49, about 6 miles west of Downieville and 37.5 miles north of Nevada City. The elevation is about 2,600 feet. The trail starts at a steep, unpaved driveway to a summer-home tract across the highway. Trailhead GPS: N39 32.292' / W120 54.921'

The Hike

The country north of the North Yuba River is some of the most primitive of the Gold Country. Paved roads and settlements are very few and far between in the high mountains and deep canyons from Highway 49 clear to Lake Almanor, 50 miles to the north. Some people call this region the "Lost Sierra." But it isn't lost to gold miners. Most of the dirt tracks and trails there were first built to serve the mines and were maintained for practical use long after the rest of the state was linked by vehicular roads. As late as the "second gold rush" of the Great Depression, mule trains were still the main means of supplying many of the remote settlements in these mountains. In recent years mountain bikers and four-wheeling enthusiasts have "discovered" these dusty old dirt tracks and trails, and are making them work harder than ever before.

The trail to Halls Ranch was built as a working trail. It connected the mining settlement of Saint Joe's Bar, at the nearby confluence of Ramshorn Creek and the North Yuba, with Halls Ranch, on the road between the now-vanished mining towns of Brandy City and Eureka City.

Cross Highway 49 and walk up the dirt road toward the summer-home tract, but swerve left at the first opportunity onto the signposted singletrack trail. Climbing on switchbacks through conifer forest, our trail ascends almost 1,200 feet to a ridge, where it slips into a westbound contour along the high hillside. The views of the heavily forested North Yuba canyon extend down to the river and upstream some

Halls Ranch Trail to Fiddle Creek

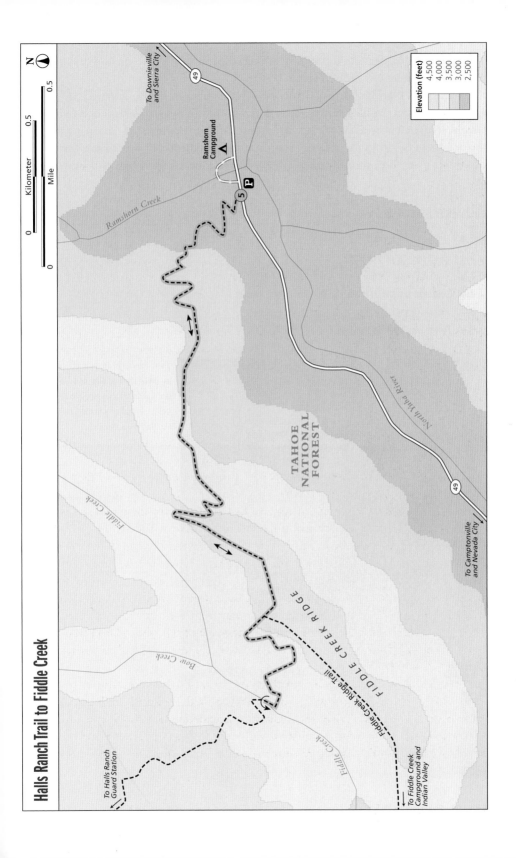

Elevation (feet)
4,500
4,000
3,500
3,000
2,500

To Downieville
and Sierra City

49

Ramshorn Campground

Ramshorn Creek

P

5

TAHOE
NATIONAL
FOREST

North Yuba River

49

To Camptonville
and Nevada City

Fiddle Creek

Bow Creek

Fiddle Creek

FIDDLE CREEK RIDGE

Fiddle Creek Ridge Trail

To Halls Ranch
Guard Station

To Fiddle Creek
Campground and
Indian Valley

N

Kilometer
0   0.5   0.5
Mile
0   0.5

15 miles to the rugged Sierra Buttes. More switchbacks bring us to the top of Fiddle Creek Ridge, at an elevation of about 4,000 feet.

Fiddle Creek Ridge forms a narrow hogback, its steep flanks dropping on the east and west. On the west side we look down to the confluence of Bow and Fiddle Creeks, separated by a denuded ridge. Our route drops down into that canyon, passing the trail that goes to Indian Valley. A couple of steep, well-shaded switchbacks suffice to deposit us on the wooded banks of Fiddle Creek, an excellent spot to soak your feet.

Miles and Directions

0.0 Highway 49 turnoff.

0.1 Start of singletrack trail.

1.6 Fiddle Creek Ridge.

2.0 Junction of trail to Indian Valley; keep right (west).

2.7 Fiddle Creek.

5.4 Arrive back at the trailhead.

The Halls Ranch Trail looks as well-trod today as when the Gold Rush prospectors first started exploring the northern mountains.

6 Humbug Trail to the Yuba River

Dropping into the steep, heavily forested canyon of the South Yuba River, the Humbug Trail is historically linked to the heyday of the hydraulic mining era. It still serves modern gold panners who want to try their luck on the wild banks of the South Yuba. Shady in summer but accessible on most winter days, the Humbug makes an equally good day hike or backpacking overnighter.

Start: Humbug Trailhead on North Bloomfield Road, Malakoff Diggins

Distance: 5.4 miles out and back

Hiking time: About 5 hours

Difficulty: Moderate, despite a 900-foot climb back out of the canyon

Trail condition: A clear path, though occasionally steep and narrow. Watch for poison oak and rattlesnakes.

Seasons: Year-round, depending on the local weather. The trailhead may be briefly inaccessible when rare winter snowstorms temporarily close Malakoff Diggins State Historic Park.

Other trail users: No bikes or dogs allowed. Equestrians are rare.

Land status: Malakoff Diggins State Historic Park. The BLM manages some of the land along the river.

Nearest towns: Nevada City, though there's a store at North San Juan

Fees and permits: Drivers to the park need to pay a day-use fee at the park visitor center in North Bloomfield and display a pass on the windshield. If camping at the South Yuba Primitive Camp, obtain a fire permit from the Tahoe National Forest office in Nevada City if you intend to use a stove.

Maps: Forest Service: *South Yuba River Recreation Guide.* USGS 7.5-minute quad: North Bloomfield.

Trail contacts: Malakoff Diggins State Historic Park, 23579 N. Bloomfield Park Rd., Nevada City, CA 95959; (530) 265-2740; www.parks .ca.gov/?page_id=494

Option: The South Yuba River hosts an extensive trail network, the main stem being the South Yuba River Trail (see Hike 12).

Backpackers and ambitious day hikers might enjoy an excellent 11.5-mile loop trip incorporating the Humbug Trail. From the bridge near the mouth of Humbug Creek, hike upstream (east) on the South Yuba Trail some 3.5 miles to the Missouri Bar Trail. That trail climbs about 1,200 feet in 1.8 miles to the unpaved Relief Hill Road. Turn left (west) and hike the unpaved road 0.8 mile to North Bloomfield, and 2.7 miles farther on North Bloomfield Road to your vehicle at the Humbug Trailhead.

Finding the trailhead: From Nevada City, drive 10 miles west and north on Highway 49 to Tyler Foote Crossing Road. Turn right (east) and drive 16.4 miles through the hamlet of North Columbia, staying on the paved road and following the signs to Malakoff Diggins State Historic Park. The road changes names a few times, but the signs are clear. From the park boundary, continue down past Chute Hill Campground to the preserved "ghost town" of North Bloomfield, where you can find the park museum and visitor center. (Park Headquarters GPS: N39 22.097' / W120 53.970') Stop there to buy a state park pass, to be displayed on your car's windshield. Then drive the last 2.7 miles on the North Bloomfield Road, past the Malakoff Diggins Overlook parking area (where the pavement ends) and the Hiller Tunnel, to the trailhead, which is marked by a small sign on the left (south). Park on either side of the road. Trailhead GPS: N39 21.917' / W120 55.404'

Humbug Creek drains the Malakoff Diggins, the world's largest hydraulic mining pit. Between 1852 and 1884 miners wielding high-power hose nozzles, called monitors, eroded this 600-foot-deep basin from San Juan Ridge. You can see this man-made canyon on the north side of the road near the trailhead, hedged in by eroded dirt cliffs the color of a inconsistently licked orange cream bar. The basin was drained into Humbug Creek initially by the Hiller Tunnel (see "Honorable Mention" hike F), which you can see on the north side of the road from North Bloomfield, about 0.2 mile east of the Humbug Trailhead. When hydraulic operations expanded in 1870, engineer Hamilton Smith Jr. designed a second drain tunnel, nearly 8,000 feet long and some 200 feet beneath the Hiller Tunnel, that also drained into Humbug Canyon. So great was the runoff from the Malakoff Diggins that silt accumulated in lower Humbug Canyon to the depth of 60 feet. The silt also raised riverbeds in the Sacramento Valley, flooding farms and cities, and even filled in vast areas of marshy shoreline along San Francisco Bay. Farmers fought back with a lawsuit principally against the North Bloomfield Gravel Mining Company, which mined the Malakoff Diggins. They won in 1884, forcing the largest hydraulic mines to close.

Vast amounts of gold remain in San Juan Ridge and elsewhere, commercially impractical to mine. Low-impact mining is still allowed in the South Yuba River, however, and the state park museum at North Bloomfield will even provide gold pans and instruction before sending you down the Humbug Trail.

Our hike begins at an elevation of 3,050 feet, following an easy gradient down a minor tributary to Humbug Creek. Knowing this canyon served as a drain for that gaping scar of Malakoff Diggins, we half expect to find a wasteland. The canyon, in fact, shows off nature's great powers of recovery. Thickly overgrown with Douglas fir and cedar, as well as maple, alder, and dogwood along the creek, the trail is well cushioned with fallen leaves and needles.

On our right (west) at about 0.3 mile, we pass a round "coyote hole"—a shaft dug during excavation of the great drain—now fenced and filled with rainwater, the first of three along our trail. Wooden platforms carry us over a seep, and shortly before the first mile, we meet and briefly follow a dirt track once used for tunnel maintenance.

Leaving the dirt track at another coyote hole, we cross a tributary creek and make a slight ascent. Sporadic poison oak shrubs crop up next to the trail. Humbug Creek and Trail now begin to drop more steeply. Where the creek rushes down a sheer granite pitch, we scramble down the waterfall's side over rocky outcrops. In the narrowing canyon, we pass a rock tower rising dramatically from the middle of the gorge, and cross a short gap bridged by a wooden trestle. The lower reaches of Humbug Creek's canyon are about 1,000 feet deep and half a mile from rim to rim. Its tapered walls and woods cast shadows on the trail even at midday. You can see why you want to return before dusk: A slip from this sheer path could dump you down a very steep slope. Though not likely to be lethal, it would be a painful climb out even with only a sprained ankle.

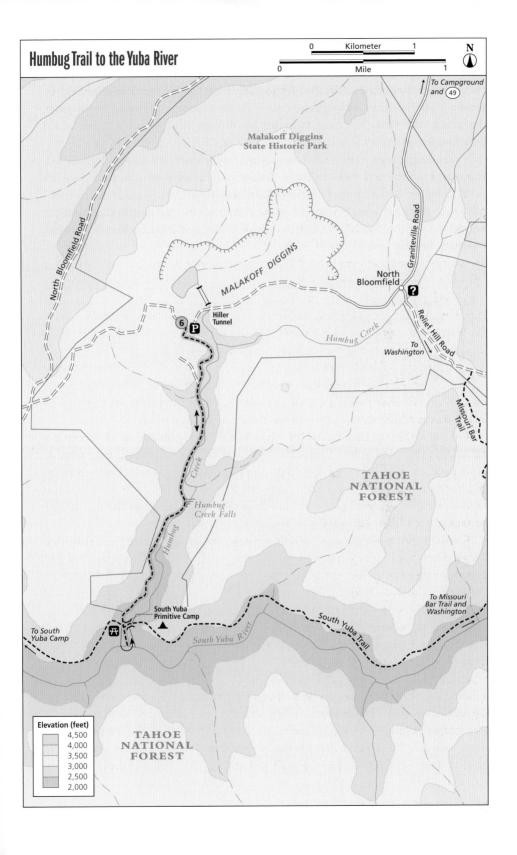

To Campground
and (49)

Malakoff Diggins
State Historic Park

North Bloomfield Road

MALAKOFF DIGGINS

Graniteville Road

North
Bloomfield

Hiller
Tunnel

6 P

Humbug Creek

To
Washington

Relief Hill Road

Missouri Bar Trail

TAHOE
NATIONAL
FOREST

Creek

Humbug
Creek Falls

Humbug

South Yuba
Primitive Camp

To South
Yuba Camp

South Yuba River

South Yuba Trail

To Missouri
Bar Trail and
Washington

Elevation (feet)
4,500
4,000
3,500
3,000
2,500
2,000

TAHOE
NATIONAL
FOREST

As we near the bottom of the Humbug's canyon, searching through the trees for a clear sight of the Yuba River and its lateral canyon, we hit the steepest section of trail—a short stretch of about 200 feet, where many hikers check their sliding by grabbing onto the trees and shrubbery. Landing on a flat, wide, wooded bench above the South Yuba River, we meet the wide South Yuba Trail. A trail sign marks this junction, along with a handful of picnic tables.

Hikers have worn more than one use-trail to the river, where we can pick our way over boulders and rocks to the water's edge. The most obvious path goes left (east) and down to the bridged crossing of Humbug Creek, where a sign directs back-packers to the South Yuba Primitive Camp, 0.3 mile on the trail upstream. Swimming holes await on the Yuba River, but beware of cold water and treacherous currents, especially in early season.

Miles and Directions

0.0 Humbug Trailhead.

1.1 Unnamed creek crossing.

1.5 Humbug Creek waterfall.

2.6 South Yuba Trail.

2.7 South Yuba River.

5.4 Arrive back at the trailhead.

7 Jones Bar Loop

Although known today mainly as a swimming hole, Jones Bar was once the largest mining camp on a 25-mile stretch of the South Yuba River. The highlight of this day hike is the section known as the Independence Trail West, which follows a reconstructed mining flume along the upper canyon wall.

Start: Independence Trailhead on Highway 49, south of the South Yuba River bridge
Distance: 4.1-mile loop
Hiking time: About 2 hours
Difficulty: Moderate, with a loss and gain of 450 feet in elevation
Trail condition: The first 1.5 miles is an excellent level trail suitable for wheelchairs. Beyond, the trail is excellent for hikers, though occasionally steep. Watch for rattlesnakes and poison oak.
Seasons: All year, local weather conditions permitting
Other trail users: The Independence Trail West section was designed to handle wheelchairs. Bikes, dogs, horses excluded.

Land status: South Yuba River State Park. The Independence Trail section was built and is maintained by the nonprofit Sequoya Challenge.
Nearest town: Nevada City
Fees and permits: None, though there is a sign-in board at 0.4 mile
Maps: *South Yuba River State Park* map. USGS 7.5-minute quad: Nevada City.
Trail contacts: South Yuba River State Park, 17660 Pleasant Valley Rd., Penn Valley, CA 95946; (530) 432-2546; www.parks.ca .gov/?page_id=496. Bear Yuba Land Trust, 12183 Auburn Rd., Grass Valley, CA 95949; (530) 272-5994; bylt.org.

Finding the trailhead: Drive a little over 6 miles northwest of downtown Nevada City on Highway 49 to the signed parking area for the Independence Trail on the right (east) side of the road. There is room for several cars, but on weekends the lot can fill up early. Trailhead GPS: N39 17.504' / W121 05.839'

The Hike

Of all the works left by the miners, few are more dramatic than the ditches and flumes built to transport water to power hydraulic mining operations or stamp mills. Hung precipitously from canyon walls, the most magnificent of these waterworks rounded mountainsides like reckless juggernauts, rushing in and out of steep ravines, leaping over gorges on wooden flumes, bearing river waters hundreds of feet above their natural channels. The Independence Trail follows just such a canal, the Excelsior Ditch, built in 1856 to transport South Yuba River water 25 miles to the hydraulic monitors at Smartsville.

The first 1.5 miles of this hike follow the western branch of the Independence Trail (see Hike G for the eastern branch), most of it accessible to wheelchairs. Beyond that point hikers can descend to the South Yuba River site of the Jones Bar, once the most populous mining encampment on the river between Bridgeport and Washington.

Flume 28 on the Independence Trail West, a part of the Jones Bar Loop, makes a big horseshoe around Rush Creek's ravine.

From the parking area (elevation 1,500 feet), we join the trail behind the sign and turn right, ducking to go under Highway 49. Wheelchair-bound travelers and pedestrians alike can use the dirt-floored bottom of the ditch, though hikers might prefer the ditch-tender's path on its right bank.

Bypassing the shortcut to Jones Bar, stay on the ditch trail, stopping at the Yuba Rim Overlook to sign the board and admire the view. Following the contours as it weaves in and out of a ravine, we pass an outhouse dubbed "Diamond Head" and wrap around a ridge to a striking view of Flume 28, the most remarkable piece of engineering on this trail. This 550-foot wooden trestle crosses Rush Creek, the largest tributary of the South Yuba along the Independence Trail. Beyond and beneath, a fascinating ramp of wooden switchbacks zigzags down to Rush Creek through natural oak landscaping. The top of the switchbacks offers a view of a small waterfall on Rush Creek, which dries out toward the end of July.

After investigating the switchback ramp and its intriguing views of Rush Creek's riparian woodlands and Flume 28, we continue west on the ditch trail, at 1.2 miles passing a wooden platform that serves as a campsite accessible to wheelchairs. The site has an outhouse. Beyond the campsite the trail narrows, grows rougher, and is not suitable for wheelchairs.

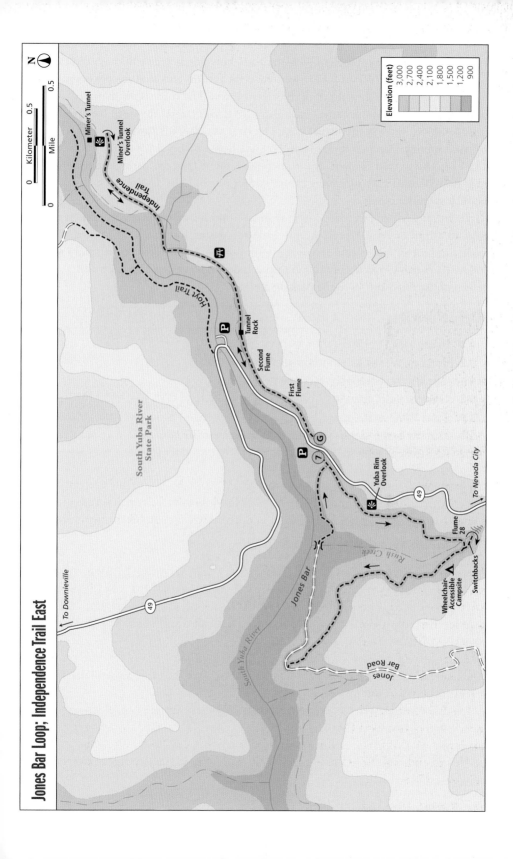

Jones Bar Loop; Independence Trail East

Hikers will have no problem with the path, however. It winds through the trees to unpaved Jones Bar Road, where we turn right (north) and drop steeply downhill for a mile, enjoying views ahead of the river canyon. The road meets the river on a wide, relatively level bank above Jones Bar. Use-trails descend the steep bank to the parklike shores, shady with mature oaks. The river at this point flows through a series of pools among bleached rocks. Jones Bar was home to hundreds of miners in the 1850s and has served likewise as the anchorage for at least four bridges on the old road from Nevada City to mining camps farther north. Today it's known mainly as a popular swimming hole.

Returning to the dirt road, continue in an upstream direction (east) through the trees to a ford of Rush Creek. A nifty little suspension footbridge of wooden slats hung from cables crosses just downstream from the ford. Once across, turn right and follow the narrow trail steeply uphill to the Independence Trail. Turn left (east) and return under Highway 49 to the parking area.

Miles and Directions

0.0 Parking area.

0.2 Junction with Jones Bar shortcut; stay left on flume trail.

0.4 Yuba Rim Overlook and sign-in clipboard.

0.5 "Diamond Head" outhouse.

0.9 Flume 28 over Rush Creek.

1.0 Rush Creek ramp; detour to Rush Creek, then return to main trail.

1.2 Rush Creek campsite and outhouse.

2.2 Jones Bar Road; go downhill (right).

3.2 Jones Bar.

3.3 Suspension bridge across Rush Creek.

3.9 Rejoin Independence Trail; turn left.

4.1 Arrive back at the parking area.

8 Point Defiance Loop

This short loop hike through the foothills starts at a historic covered bridge and visits the drowned confluence of the main Yuba and South Yuba Rivers.

Start: North side of the highway bridge at Bridgeport, South Yuba River State Park
Distance: 2.6-mile loop
Hiking time: About 1.5 hours
Difficulty: Moderate, with an elevation gain and loss of about 540 feet
Trail condition: Occasionally steep trail, partly on dirt roads, with some poison oak. Watch for rattlesnakes.
Seasons: All year, local weather conditions permitting. Mar–June is best for wildflowers. June–Aug can be uncomfortably hot.

Other trail users: Dogs must be on a 6-foot leash. No bikers or equestrians.
Land status: South Yuba River State Park
Nearest towns: Grass Valley and Nevada City
Fees and permits: Parking fee in state park
Maps: *South Yuba River State Park* map. USGS 7.5-minute quad: French Corral.
Trail contacts: South Yuba River State Park, 17660 Pleasant Valley Rd., Penn Valley, CA 95946; (530) 432-2546; southyubariverstate park.org

Finding the trailhead: Start at the visitor center at the hamlet of Bridgeport, headquarters of South Yuba River State Park. To get there from Marysville, drive 25.5 miles east on CA 20 from its junction with CA 70 to Pleasant Valley Road. This same junction is 8 miles east of Grass Valley on CA 20. Turn north onto Pleasant Valley Road and drive 8 miles to Bridgeport. Park in one of two parking areas on either side of the vehicular bridge. The south-side lot is adjacent to the visitor center (GPS: N39 17.508' / W121 11.733'), but the Point Defiance Trailhead starts across the street from the north-side lot. Trailhead GPS: N39 17.625' / W121 11.590'

The Hike

As a mining camp, Bridgeport had a very short run of two years before the placer gold ran out. Where it made a lasting mark was as a bridge crossing on a river where bridges were few and far between. Built in 1862 by David Isaac Wood, the 229-foot Bridgeport Bridge was and remains the longest single-span wooden covered bridge in the United States. The covered bridge at Knights Ferry ("Honorable Mention" hike L) is longer, but is not a single span.

Unfortunately the park service has closed the bridge to foot traffic till funds can be raised for restoration. So, before starting the Point Defiance Trail, spend a few minutes around the visitor center on the south side of the bridge, trying to glean some sense of the tumult of teamster traffic converging on this crucial bottleneck on the road from Marysville to the booming Comstock silver mines of Virginia City, Nevada. Inspecting the approach road to the bridge—the Virginia Turnpike—imagine how much work (and even stress) a nineteenth-century bridge toll collector had to invest in the job. The turnpike is lined by long, parallel walls of gargantuan,

The huge stone walls that line Bridgeport's Virginia Turnpike were built to keep the anxious teamsters in line.

dry-piled boulders, built to prevent wagons from jumping the traffic line and, especially, sneaking past the toll booth. Considering the backbreaking labor and expense invested here to encourage good behavior among nineteenth-century drivers, road rage in the age of the wagon must have been as real—and maybe even more "hands-on" and "in your face"—than it is in the age of the automobile. Before leaving, take a look also at the tiny Kneebone family cemetery, still maintained by the descendents of the operators of this property when it was a private, working concern.

Having gleaned some tangible historical sense of the once vital life of the Bridgeport covered bridge, start the Point Defiance hike at the trailhead on the north side of the river. Walk down the dirt road, the Virginia Turnpike, into the trees toward the river. At the north portal of the covered bridge, framed by large trees and smelling of musty timbers, a sign there promises to deliver us to Lake Englebright in 1 mile. As our foot trail bobs and weaves a bit through the oak and madrone woodlands along the bank of the South Yuba, we look down on the final set of ripples in the river before it is swallowed by reservoir. Glancing backward from an open vantage point, we can see the shingled covered bridge set amid green Pleasant Valley like a Currier and Ives print. The newer auto bridge is hidden behind the wooden bridge and does

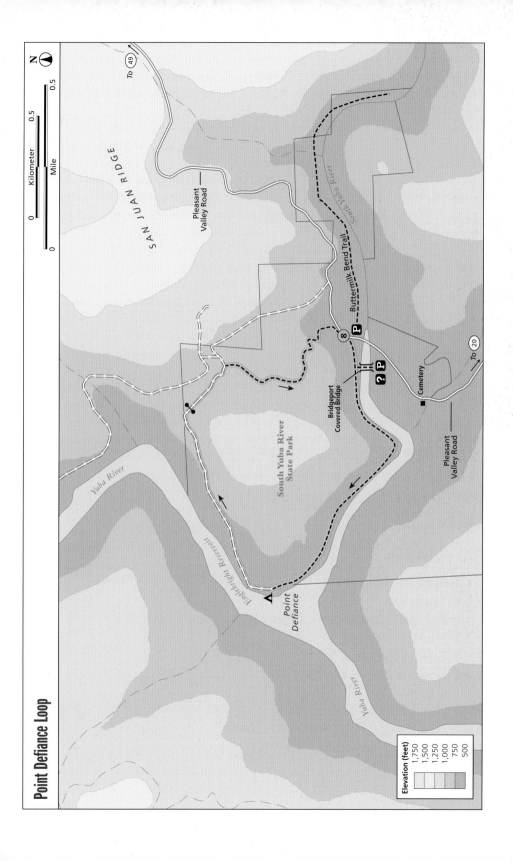

Point Defiance Loop

Elevation (feet)
1,750
1,500
1,250
1,000
750
500

SAN JUAN RIDGE

Pleasant Valley Road

To 49

South Yuba River

Buttermilk Bend Trail

P

8

P

? P

Bridgeport Covered Bridge

Cemetery

To 20

Pleasant Valley Road

South Yuba River State Park

Yuba River

Englebright Reservoir

Point Defiance

Yuba River

N

0   0.5   Kilometer

0   0.5   Mile

not intrude on the scene, except for one curious optical illusion at a certain point along the trail where the roof of the covered bridge just conceals the top of the highway span. When cars drive across the highway bridge, they appear to be driving on the roof of the covered bridge.

Walking onward, the river begins to clog up behind the reservoir, turning an unnatural bluish-green tinge—a sight not without beauty but certainly lacking the dynamism of a river, and biologically poorer too.

Point Defiance juts out at the confluence of the South Yuba and the main branch of the Yuba River, itself formed not far upstream by the joining of the Yuba's northern and middle forks. Today the point merely juts into Englebright Reservoir. A huge berry patch sprawls over the point between the trail and the shore.

Our singletrack trail ends at a dirt road and a boat- or hike-in campground operated by the Army Corps of Engineers. Turn right and start climbing the biggest hill on the hike. The road is washed out in places, preventing vehicle access but presenting no problems for hikers. As we climb, the narrow reservoir, laid out between rounded, thickly wooded mountainsides, begins to resemble a broad midwestern river more than a lake. The original dam at Englebright was built to prevent the muck running down from the hydraulic mines at Malakoff Diggins (see hikes 6 and F) and San Juan Ridge from flooding Sacramento Valley farms downstream.

Near the top of the hill, we pass around a metal gate, crossing a ridge through chaparral to a new landscape of rolling grasslands studded with stout, old blue oaks—classic California savanna country. In a few yards, make a sharp right onto a faint dirt road. A few yards beyond that junction, a sign points left to a singletrack trail that crosses a gulch on a small wooden bridge, and then switchbacks down a steep slope into Pleasant Valley. As we near the bottom, we can see the tops of the large stone embankments that the bridge tender piled alongside the roadway to control gate-crashers. Passing the driveway to the state park residence, drop down to the old dirt road where we started.

Miles and Directions

0.0 Trailhead on Virginia Turnpike.
0.1 Covered bridge.
1.1 Point Defiance campground/picnic area.
1.8 Metal gate on BLM land.
2.0 Beginning of singletrack trail.
2.6 Arrive back at the Virginia Turnpike.

9 Spenceville to Shingle Falls

Shingle Falls (also known as Fairy Falls) is an unexpected oasis, a swimming hole popular with locals but little known among the broader hiking fraternity. The surrounding Spenceville Wildlife Area is a foothill sanctuary that preserves acres of classic pastoral Sierra foothill landscape, green in winter, gold in summer.

Start: Trailhead at the end of the Old Spenceville Road

Distance: 5.2-mile lollipop loop

Hiking time: About 3 hours

Difficulty: A moderate ramble, with about 580 feet of elevation gained and lost

Trail condition: Dirt road and singletrack path, almost none of which labeled with signs

Seasons: All year, but summer can be hot. The falls are best Dec through mid-May.

Other trail users: Hunting season for turkey, pig, and other game runs Sept to end of Jan; turkey hunters have a second season from late Mar to early May. Equestrians, leashed dogs, and bike riders may use the Old Spenceville Road and Fairy Falls Trail, but singletrack trails are for pedestrians only.

Land status: California Department of Fish and Wildlife

Nearest town: Lincoln

Fees and permits: None

Map: USGS 7.5-minute quads: Camp Far West, Wolf (**Note:** Not all trails are marked on maps.)

Trail contacts: Spenceville Wildlife Management Area, Department of Fish and Wildlife, Lands and Facilities Branch, 1812 Ninth St., Sacramento, CA 95811; (916) 445-0411; www.dfg.ca.gov/lands/wa/region2/spenceville .html

Finding the trailhead: From I-80 east of Roseville, take the Roseville Bypass (Highway 65) north about 22 miles to the small town of Wheatland. Turn right (east) onto the two-lane Camp Beale Highway. Drive 5.5 miles east and make a very sharp right turn on Camp Far West Road. To avoid the irregular edge of Beale Air Force Base, Camp Far West Road wanders in a seemingly random fashion for 8.2 miles, during the course of which it narrows to one paved lane and later turns to gravel after entering the Spenceville Wildlife Refuge. It ends at the junction of unpaved Spenceville Road. Turn right and drive 2.3 miles to where Spenceville Road ends at Dry Creek, parking on the north side of the road next to a concrete bridge that's closed to vehicles. That bridge is our trailhead. Trailhead GPS: N39 06.838' / W121 16.251'

The Hike

Spenceville sprouted to life after copper was discovered along Dry Creek in the mid–nineteenth century. At its height it had a school, post office, hotel, and stores, but the copper gave out shortly before the First World War, and Spenceville hit a dead end. During World War II the US military fitted Spenceville's abandoned buildings and streets with German signs and props and conducted war games there. Today only vacant land and the concrete bridge across Dry Creek remain to mark the site.

At an elevation of 350 feet above sea level, we now cross that bridge and turn right onto the unpaved Old Spenceville Road. The old copper mine was located on

Spenceville Wildlife Area's rolling landscapes are classic examples of California pastoral foothill scenery.

the hillside above the bridge and is fenced off. After crossing the scraggly flats where the town once sat, Old Spenceville Road turns uphill, temporarily leaving Dry Creek behind. Our road goes up a tributary ravine through pretty pastoral scenes of oak woodland and grassy hills. This must have been a land of milk and honey to the Ninsenan people, who lived here before the gold rush, for the abundant acorns scattered beneath the blue and interior live oaks were their primary staple.

As Old Spenceville Road nears the top of this first gentle hill, the North Valley Trail (closed to bikes) branches left (north) through a narrow gate into a broad valley. We continue straight on the Old Spenceville Road another 0.1 mile to the next junction. Here we turn hard right (south), crossing through a gate hedged in by some soggy ground in winter and spring, and which in the drier seasons still sports a lush growth of trees and shrubs. The rough dirt road beyond the gate is called the Fairy Falls Trail, though there's no sign to tell you so. (Fairy Falls was the original name of Shingle Falls, and some locals still use the old name.) The dirt road climbs to the top of a slight grassy knoll, where it forks again. We take the left (east) fork, walking over a barred cattle guard.

As Fairy Falls Trail curves down into a ravine, two singletrack footpaths break away from it on the left. There is no sign posted, but they are known as the Upper

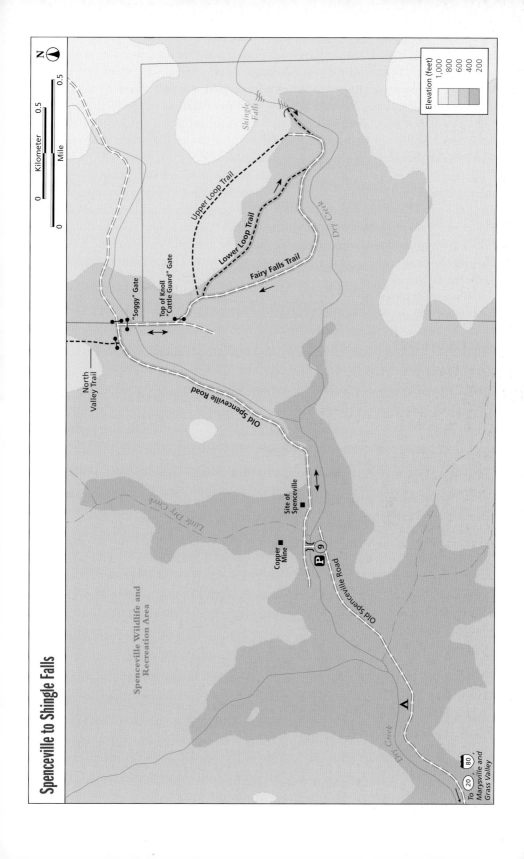

Spenceville to Shingle Falls

Spenceville Wildlife and Recreation Area

N

Elevation (feet)
1,000
800
600
400
200

Kilometer
0   0.5

Mile
0   0.5

Shingle Falls

Upper Loop Trail

Lower Loop Trail

Fairy Falls Trail

Dry Creek

Top of Knoll
"Cattle Guard" Gate

"Soggy" Gate

North Valley Trail

Old Spenceville Road

Little Dry Creek

Copper Mine

Site of Spenceville

P 9

Old Spenceville Road

Dry Creek

To 20 80
Marysville and Grass Valley

and Lower Loop Trails. The second footpath (Lower Loop Trail) is the one we want. It takes us into an oak forest and down a ravine, crossing a (usually dry) creek bed, and over a low ridge rife in spring with buttercups and golden poppies. Soon we spy Dry Creek again and promptly descend to rejoin the Fairy Falls Trail on the creek's north bank. Dry Creek now appears rockier than when we last saw it at the Spenceville site. There are many inviting pools for soaking on warm spring days, and sharp-eyed searchers can find acorn-grinding holes among the rocks.

To get to Shingle Falls, turn left (east) onto the dirt road and walk upstream. After making a hard turn uphill to the left, walk about 50 yards to a pair of use-trails that peel off to the right. The lower one leads to a swimming hole on Dry Creek. The higher trail leads to another swimming hole, but this one has a view of lower Shingle Falls, which drops about 30 feet in an awkward twist through a rocky gap. By scrambling up the rocks upstream, you can follow the cascades to a second waterfall, known as the upper Shingle Falls.

When ready to return to the parking area, you can backtrack or, for a slightly different view, stay on the Fairy Falls Trail all the way to the Spenceville Road.

Miles and Directions

- **0.0** Parking area.
- **0.2** Site of Spenceville; stay on road at the singletrack junction.
- **1.2** North Valley Trail junction (closed to bikes).
- **1.3** "Soggy" gate.
- **1.5** Cattle guard gate atop grassy knoll.
- **1.6** Lower Loop Trail junction.
- **2.2** Rejoin road (Fairy Falls Trail) at Dry Creek.
- **2.6** Shingle Falls.
- **5.2** Arrive back at the parking area.

10 Empire Mine Loop

Once the largest, richest, deepest hard-rock gold mine in California, the Empire Mine is now owned by California, which preserves it as the centerpiece of a woodsy, semiwild, 805-acre state park on the edge of Grass Valley. Our route explores a shady network of old roads surrounding the old mine, visiting a trove of historical mining ruins and well-preserved buildings.

Start: Empire Mine State Historic Park, outside visitor center
Distance: 4.0-mile loop, plus an optional additional 1.0-mile tour of the Empire Mine yard and mansion grounds
Hiking time: About 2–3 hours for the hike, plus an optional additional hour for the park and grounds immediately surrounding the mine
Difficulty: Moderate, with an elevation gain and loss of about 450 feet
Trail condition: This route follows two established loops—the Hardrock Trail and the Osborn Hill Loop Trail—to make a larger loop, mostly on good dirt roads with excellent signage.
Seasons: Year-round, but mid-May through June is best for wildflowers

Other trail users: Dogs on leash, equestrians, mountain bikers
Land status: Empire Mine State Historic Park
Nearest town: Grass Valley
Fees and permits: The hike described costs nothing, but the state park charges visitors to enter the visitor center, mine yard, and mansion grounds—a very worthwhile expense.
Maps: California State Parks: *Empire Mine State Historic Park* brochure. USGS 7.5-minute quad: Grass Valley.
Trail contacts: Empire Mine State Historic Park, 10791 E. Empire St., Grass Valley, CA 95945; (530) 273-8522; www.parks.ca .gov/?page_id=499. Empire Mine Park Association; www.empiremine.org.

Finding the trailhead: From Highway 49 in Grass Valley, drive east on East Empire Street 1.3 miles to the Empire Mine's main parking area in front of the visitor center. The loop starts outside the visitor center. Trailhead GPS: N39 12.428' / W121 02.815'

The Hike

The independent forty-niner with his gold-pan and hand tools cleaned out most of the "easy" placer gold deposits from Gold Country riverbanks and streams by the early 1850s. Much more gold was locked in Gold Country rock. By the late 1850s the independent, small-time miner was being marginalized by a new breed of industrialist miner, usually a man with the business acumen to finagle the San Francisco or East Coast investor backing needed to acquire the necessary machinery and materials, and to hire the engineers and labor crews required to sink big mines deep into hard rock. The Empire Mine was just such a massive industrial operation, reaching far and wide beneath the streets of Grass Valley. During its 106-year working life, miners dug 5.8 million ounces of gold from the Empire. Tons of ore brought to the surface were crushed in the Empire's gargantuan stamp mill of sixteen batteries—an awesome total of eighty stamps, each weighing 1,750 pounds. The Empire stamp mill worked continually, 24 hours a day, 365 days a year. The constant hammering roar could be heard 2 miles away in downtown Grass Valley, where townsfolk grew so used to it that they paid it no heed, unless it stopped. On such occasions the sudden silence would rouse them from their sleep, and the Empire's switchboard operator would be swamped with worried calls.

After closing in 1956 the Empire's tunnels flooded with groundwater, and woods overgrew the once heavily industrialized landscape. Today it is serene, a fascinating, even downright charming spot for a hike.

Leaving the front of the visitor center, our singletrack Hardrock Trail leads northwest, amiably sandwiched between shady Empire Street and the handsome rock wall that encloses the 13-acre gardens of the Bourn family mansion, Empire Cottage, designed by illustrious San Francisco architect Willis Polk in 1897. The Bourn family owned controlling interest in the Empire Mine from 1869 until 1929, living in this "cottage" when they came to Grass Valley on mining business. If you are tall enough to peek over the wall, you will see that they lived in a style befitting California gentry—and if you are not tall enough, tour it at the end of this hike.

Reaching Penn Gate—named for the Pennsylvania Mine, one of the many neighboring mining operations swallowed up by the giant Empire—head left (south) on the Hardrock Trail, now a dirt road. Almost immediately we pass the signposted sites of the Pennsylvania and WYOD Mines, the latter an acronym for Work Your Own Diggins. The owners of the WYOD leased portions of the mine to individual miners, hence the name. Despite the forest cover, the ground everywhere around here shows signs of having been turned upside down, leaving a shell-shocked landscape of rocky piles of mine tailings, hunks of rusty machinery, and derelict ruins.

Atop an earthen berm built of waste rock dumped from the Pennsylvania Mine, the Hardrock Trail crosses Little Wolf Creek and begins to ascend a slope with views over the central area of the park, a recovering wasteland of mine tailings and ponds currently closed to the public. The forest has taken it back.

Turning right at the Osborne Hill Crosscut, we shortly join the Osborne Hill Loop, which climbs about 400 vertical feet up the slope of Osborne Hill and then back down again on a counterclockwise loop. Several independent mines operated on Osborne Hill during the latter nineteenth and early twentieth centuries, none with anywhere near the spectacular good fortune of the Empire Mine. Spur paths spin off to the Daisy Hill, Conlon, and Betsy Mines, all marked by large tailing piles, although the Conlon Mine (near the top of the hill) and the trailside Prescott Hill Mine still preserve their stamp mill foundations. Somewhere on the slopes of Osborne Hill in the mid-1850s occurred a local miners' feud known as the Osborne Hill War. Its origins are murky, but it reached its climax when an armed gang attempted to seize a claim worked by two brothers named McMurty. They dropped one of the brothers, a dentist, with a shotgun blast, but he still managed to draw his navy revolver and fire six times, killing five of his attackers and wounding a sixth. If the report is accurate, it's a feat more lethal than the gunfight at the OK Corral.

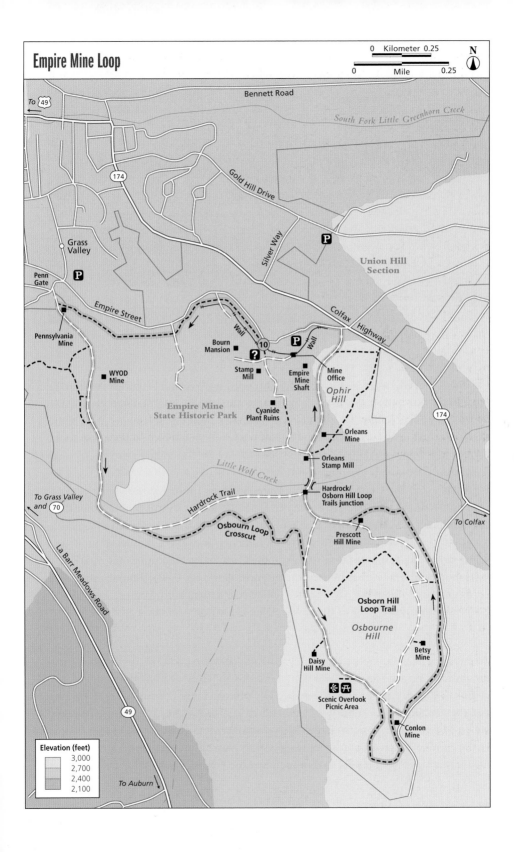

Empire Mine Loop

Bennett Road

To 49

South Fork Little Greenhorn Creek

174

Gold Hill Drive

Silver Way

P

Union Hill Section

Grass Valley

P

Penn Gate

Empire Street

Colfax Highway

Wall

Pennsylvania Mine

Bourn Mansion

10

P

Wall

?

WYOD Mine

Stamp Mill

Empire Mine Shaft

Mine Office

Ophir Hill

Empire Mine State Historic Park

Cyanide Plant Ruins

174

Orleans Mine

Little Wolf Creek

Orleans Stamp Mill

To Grass Valley and 70

Hardrock Trail

Hardrock/ Osborn Hill Loop Trails junction

To Colfax

Osbourn Loop Crosscut

Prescott Hill Mine

La Barr Meadows Road

Osborn Hill Loop Trail

Osbourne Hill

Betsy Mine

Daisy Hill Mine

49

Scenic Overlook Picnic Area

Conlon Mine

Elevation (feet)

3,000
2,700
2,400
2,100

To Auburn

The Bourn Cottage at the Empire Mine is surrounded by formal gardens.

When you reach the three-way junction with the Hardrock Trail at the bottom of the Osborne Hill Loop, turn right (north) on the Hardrock Trail to cross Little Wolf Creek on a footbridge. As you start climbing Ophir Hill back to the Empire Mine, you will pass the ruins of the Orleans stamp mill, which served another once-independent mine bought out by the Empire, whose encircling fences and walls come into view as you top the knoll.

Gazing over the stone wall into the Empire Mine's historic yard—directly accessible only to those who pay their entrance fee at the nearby visitor center—mechanically enthused observers should be excused for drooling at the trove of rusty mining cars, Pelton wheels, boilers, hoists, motors, winches, and other "historical junk" salvaged from this vast operation and set down amid the handsome industrial-scale workshops and offices that housed the essential workings of the Empire Mine. You could end your visit at the parking area where you started, but if you've never taken a closer look at ground zero of the Empire Mine, don't pass up that option.

Option

After paying the admission fee, an easy mile of wandering around the Empire's mining yard and Bourn "cottage" will impress upon you the wealth and dynamics of successful Gold Country industrial mining. The visitor center contains one of the best museums of the Gold Country, packed with informative historical exhibits, including samples of gold ore in their vaults. Most fantastic of all is the massive scale model of the Empire ordered built by its managers to map all its adits, drifts, and stopes—*tunnels* to a layman—a model so thorough that the company kept it locked in a secret room so that no outsiders could fathom the intricate twists and turns of the Empire's complex network of rich quartz veins. Offices and workshops stand open to view, as if managers, engineers, and craftsmen have just gone out to lunch en masse, leaving the switchboard unattended, huge map rolls and surveying equipment still spread over backroom tables, the workmen's tools abandoned on workshop benches. The manicured gardens and walks surrounding the Bourn family's Empire Cottage display both their enormous wealth and their excellent taste.

Miles and Directions

0.0 Visitor center.

0.6 Penn Gate.

1.3 Junction with Osborne Hill Crosscut; go right (east).

1.8 Junction with Osborne Hill Loop; turn right (south).

2.1 Daisy Hill Mine.

2.6 Conlon Mine.

3.2 Prescott Hill Mine stamp mill foundation.

3.5 Junction with Hardrock Trail; turn right (north) and cross Little Wolf Creek.

3.7 Orleans stamp mill site.

4.0 Arrive back at the visitor center.

11 Cascade Canal

Aside from a loyal dog, there's no better companion for a long, relaxing hike than a miner's flume. This burbling, splashing, gentle, handcrafted creek will keep constant company with you on this virtually flat, completely shaded pathway through the forest outside Nevada City.

Start: Red Dog Road, Nevada City
Distance: 4.4 miles one-way
Hiking time: About 2 hours
Difficulty: Easy
Trail condition: Wide, flat, unpaved path with some narrow metal catwalks
Seasons: Year-round
Other trail users: Dogs, joggers, mountain bikers

Land status: Nevada Irrigation District, Bear Yuba Land Trust
Nearest towns: Nevada City, Grass Valley
Fees and permits: None
Maps: USGS 7.5-minute quads: North Bloomfield, Chicago Park
Trail contacts: Bear Yuba Land Trust, 12183 Auburn Rd., Grass Valley CA 95949; (530) 272-5994; bylt.org

Finding the trailhead: From Highway 49 in downtown Nevada City, drive east about half a mile on Boulder Street to Red Dog Road. Turn right on Red Dog and drive almost 2 miles to the Cascade Canal. Park on the shoulder. The canal path starts by the gate on the south side of the road. Trailhead GPS: N39 15.551' / W120 58.508'

To place a shuttle car at the end of the hike from downtown Nevada City, drive 0.2 mile east on Boulder Street where it crosses Highway 49. Turn right on Park Avenue and almost immediately right again onto Nimrod Street. Drive south about half a mile on Nimrod, past Pioneer Park, to Gracie Road. Turn left on Gracie and drive 1.6 miles southeast to the junction of Banner Lava Cap Road, where you can park on the small, unpaved corner lot next to the flume. Ending trailhead GPS: N39 14.406' / W120 59.774'

The Hike

Gold Country remnants can be unlovely things—piles of industrial junk, scarred hillsides, dangerous mines. But the Gold Country also preserves a goodly number of the loveliest of all historical remnants in the working flumes and ditches that still carry water from high-country reservoirs to foothill towns below. Cascade Canal is a fine example of this. To walk along it doesn't require undue mental or physical exertion. Set your feet going at the start on Red Dog Road, and just follow it to the end on Banner Lava Cap Road. Walk back again if you can't arrange a shuttle. Heck, walk it in either direction. There's no advantage to one way over the other.

On the way you will see a lot of piney forest. You will cross two metal catwalks where the canal is carried across creeks in enclosed pipes. You will occasionally see some distant, forested ridges to the northwest. Along the latter half of the hike, you will pass numerous pleasant-looking homes built on the hillside above the canal,

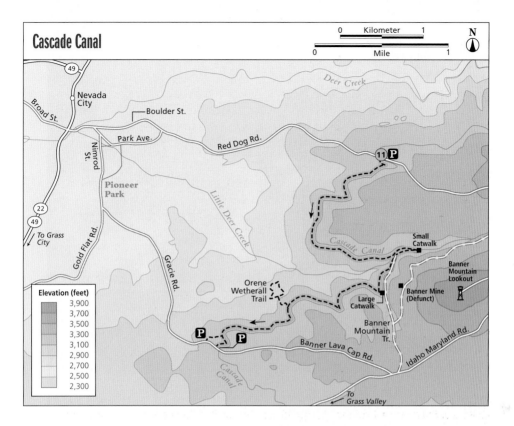

Cascade Canal

Nevada City
Boulder St.
Broad St.
Park Ave.
Nimrod St.
Red Dog Rd.
Deer Creek
Pioneer Park
Little Deer Creek
Gracie Rd.
Gold Flat Rd.
To Grass City
Orene Wetherall Trail
Cascade Canal
Large Catwalk
Small Catwalk
Banner Mountain Lookout
Banner Mine (Defunct)
Banner Mountain Tr.
Idaho Maryland Rd.
Banner Lava Cap Rd.
Cascade Canal
To Grass Valley

Elevation (feet)
3,900
3,700
3,500
3,300
3,100
2,900
2,700
2,500
2,300

many of them sporting jerry-rigged drawbridges so that the homeowners, too, can get to the canal path. If you are feeling frisky, take a detour around the 0.6-mile Orene Wetherall Trail loop through the Woodpecker Wildlife Preserve on the hillside below the canal. This is a leisurely, linear (but hardly straight) stroll, lulled by the sound of the canal, as comforting as the sound of rain on a roof.

Of course, Cascade Canal was not built as a mesmerizing diversion. It was and remains a working canal. Originally dug in 1860 to supply miners and townsfolk in Nevada City and Grass Valley, Cascade Canal carried water from the South Yuba River by way of Fordyce Reservoir. Upgraded in the 1880s, its waters were tapped to run machinery at Grass Valley's mighty Idaho-Maryland Mine, as well as the brawny North Star, later acquired by the Empire Mine. The mines are gone, but the water today is used by the Nevada Irrigation District. The canal continues on to either end of this described hike, but the pathways beside those outlying stretches are nowhere near so nicely maintained as the one along this particular stretch of Cascade Canal.

Miles and Directions

0.0   Red Dog Road trailhead.

2.0   Small catwalk over Little Deer Creek.

A walk along the Cascade Canal always brings peace of mind.

2.6 Banner Mountain Trail; continue right (west) over large catwalk, following the canal to the right on the opposite side.

3.6 Orene Wetherall Trail junction; stay with the canal.

4.1 Unmarked trail to Gracie Road parking area; stay on canal.

4.4 Arrive at the Banner Lava Cap Road parking area.

12 South Yuba River Trail

One of the longest, wildest footpaths of the Gold Country follows the South Yuba River. Spring brings profuse wildflower displays, but the trail is best in fall, when the dark-green forests give grudging way to patches of yellows and reds, and a sense of impending seasonal change descends upon the canyon.

Start: Poorman Creek trailhead
Distance: 19.8 miles one-way/shuttle
Hiking time: 2 days overnight recommended, with a camp at Humbug Creek or Illinois Crossing, but a strong hiker could do it in 10–12 hours
Difficulty: A moderately demanding overnighter or daunting day hike with more than 6,400 feet of elevation gained and more than 7,300 feet lost along the entire length
Trail condition: Excellent singletrack trail, with some dirt roads
Seasons: Spring and autumn are best, though winter brings many highly suitable days, and summer is fine if you can stand the heat
Other trail users: Equestrians, mountain bikers, and hikers with dogs all use this trail.
Land status: Tahoe National Forest, BLM, and Malakoff Diggins State Historic Park. Pay attention to Private Property signs.

Nearest towns: Washington has a store, hotel, and restaurant. Nevada City has all amenities.
Fees and permits: None
Maps: Forest Service: *South Yuba River Recreation Guide. South Yuba River State Park* brochure map. USGS 7.5-minute quads: Washington, North Bloomfield, Nevada City.
Trail contacts: BLM Mother Lode Field Office, 5152 Hillsdale Circle, El Dorado Hills, CA 95762; (916) 941-3101; www.blm.gov. Tahoe National Forest, Yuba River Ranger District, 601 Coyote St., Nevada City, CA 95959; (530) 265-4531; www.fs.usda.gov.
Special considerations: Water flow on the South Yuba River is regulated by a dam above Washington and cannot be predicted by season. Since a road and other trails intersect with the South Yuba Trail, hikers have many options to shorten their journey.

Finding the trailhead: A car shuttle is required for this hike. To get to Poorman Creek from Nevada City, drive about 13.5 miles east on CA 20 to the Washington Road junction; turn left (north) and drive 5.5 miles down to Washington; then cross the bridge and drive 2.5 miles up Relief Hill Road to the Poorman Creek parking area. Trailhead GPS: N39 21.553' / W120 48.609'. The trail ends near Purdon Crossing, about 7 miles north of Nevada City on Purdon Road. Purdon Crossing GPS: N39 19.655' / W121 02.791'.

The Hike

At an elevation of about 2,600 feet, the Poorman Creek trailhead is about 1,000 feet higher than Purdon Crossing, some 20 miles downstream. Since our trail rises and falls in deference to ridges, not the river, don't expect this downstream hike to translate into a downhill hike.

Mounds of river-rounded cobbles heaped along Poorman Creek attest to the intense history of mining here. Far from being a poor claim, it yielded a million dollars in gold over the years. A century and a half ago, hundreds of miners combed this part of the Yuba canyon. A newspaper reported in April 1854 that a miner took out 47 ounces of gold in a week from a claim at Jefferson City, a mile downstream from Washington. Like Brandy City, Banjo Bar, and a dozen other settlements along this stretch of the river, Jefferson City now exists only in name, a place haunted by half-forgotten lore. Today you can walk for miles without meeting another soul.

From the confluence of Poorman Creek and the South Yuba River, the trail quickly climbs to a contour high above the Yuba and does not descend to the river again until Missouri Bar. Cedar, Douglas fir, and yellow pine duff cushion our tread. We pass metamorphic outcroppings of slate and greenstone; thickets of maple, hazelnut, alder, and black oak; and patches of poison oak. Occasionally the foliage opens up to grand vistas down the main South Yuba canyon, cutting its deep, steep-sided boulevard through the mountains.

To maintain its contour, our trail makes a series of detours up into side canyons—McKilligan, Logan, Union, and Eastern—fleetingly intruding upon small tributary creeks rife with ferns, sycamores, and wild grapes. In October the little bridges on these creeks, covered in fallen yellow leaves, make a scene as pretty as a Japanese woodblock print.

Signs of human intervention are surprisingly rare above Illinois Crossing. Miners may mark their claims and reach them by steep use-trails dropping to the river. At the historic river crossing of Missouri Bar, passersby have piled up white and black rocks to create a kind of sculpture garden on the riverbank. (You have an "escape" option on the Missouri Bar Trail, which climbs from the north bank about 1,200 feet in 3.2 miles to Malakoff Diggins State Historic Park. Another old road climbs from the south bank to the ridge at Central House, near CA 20.)

Heading downstream again, the trail (after climbing along the canyon wall for another 3-mile stretch) again descends to the river at the South Yuba Primitive Camp, run by the BLM and accessible only to foot travelers. It has tables and a chemical toilet, but you'll have to purify your drinking water from the Yuba River.

Heading downstream from the camp on river-washed bedrock, the trail again climbs to a shelf after crossing Humbug Creek. (The Humbug Trail—Hike 6—ascends from here to the Malakoff Diggins, gaining about 850 feet in 2.3 miles.) The 5.6-mile stretch of trail from the Humbug junction to Edwards Crossing mainly follows a contour some 250 feet above the river. Overlook Point offers a stately view of a grand oxbow on the South Yuba River. On the ridge above, prominent scars mark the old hydraulic mining operations at Sailor Flat and Blue Tent Diggins.

At Kennebec Creek an old stage road cuts down to the South Yuba at Illinois Crossing, a steep detour from our trail. (Robbers murdered the two toll collectors at the crossing in 1866. The murderers were never caught. The following year one Thomas Holden, with a team of six horses and 8,000 pounds of freight, drove his rig into the Yuba there and drowned. A row of BLM campsites occupies a terrace above the river, a pleasant enough site if its forlorn history doesn't spook you.) Skipping this

South Yuba River Trail

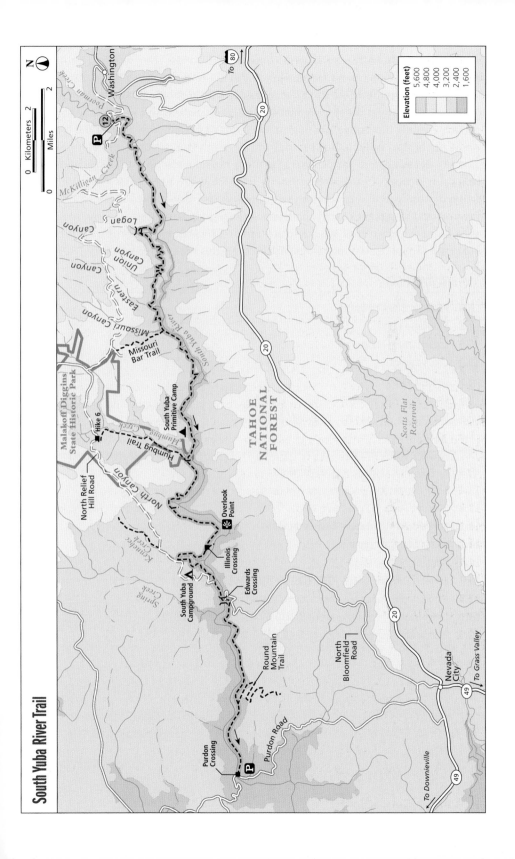

Elevation (feet)
| 5,600 |
| 4,800 |
| 4,000 |
| 3,200 |
| 2,400 |
| 1,600 |

detour, the South Yuba Trail sticks to its contour far above the river, wending through the South Yuba Campground (accessible to vehicles) to the unpaved North Bloomfield Road. A dusty downhill stroll (made dustier if a car should pass) then brings us to Edwards Crossing, a deceptively frail-looking metal arch with a wooden bed.

After crossing the bridge, the singletrack South Yuba Trail turns right at the south end of the bridge, heading downstream on the south bank initially through heavy forest. A treat is in store for us when the forest cover opens up into a dramatically stark, open section of canyon. For about a mile the pathway traverses a precipitous section of canyon wall on a foundation of meticulously dry-stacked masonry, a most attention-grabbing piece of trail construction. Then the forest closes in again, screening us from the river until we arrive at Purdon Crossing, where a rusty cantilever bridge still carries the old road from Malakoff Diggins back to Nevada City.

Miles and Directions

0.0 Poorman Creek trailhead.

1.1 McKilligan Creek.

3.5 Logan Canyon bridge.

5.0 Union Canyon.

5.7 Eastern Canyon.

6.3 Missouri Canyon Creek crossing.

6.4 Missouri Bar Trail junction; go straight (west).

9.4 South Yuba Primitive Camp.

9.7 Humbug Creek crossing.

9.8 Humbug Trail junction; go straight (west).

11.2 North Canyon Trail junction; bear right (west).

12.8 Overlook Point.

13.7 Illinois Crossing junction; bear right (north).

14.2 South Yuba Campground.

14.4 North Bloomfield Road.

15.4 Edwards Crossing bridge (GPS: N39 19.766' / W120 58.950').

17.5 Junction with Round Mountain Trail; go straight (west).

19.7 Lower trailhead parking area (GPS: N39 19.610' / W121 02.679').

19.8 Purdon Crossing bridge (GPS: N39 19.655' / W121 02.791').

13 The Quarry Trail Loop

The lower American River Middle Fork's canyon has a rough-and-tumble kind of charisma borne of a gold rush legacy full of violence and greed but also charm and grandeur.

Start: Quarry Road Trail parking area, next to the bridge over the American River on Highway 49, near Auburn
Distance: 9.3-mile lollypop loop
Hiking time: About 4–5 hours
Difficulty: With nearly 900 feet of elevation gained in the middle, this trail is moderately difficult.
Trail condition: This mixture of dirt road and singletrack trail is not always clearly marked, especially as it passes through the old quarry.
Seasons: Year-round, though June–Aug can be hot. Apr–June is best for wildflowers.

Other trail users: Mountain bikers, equestrians, dog walkers
Land status: Auburn State Recreation Area
Nearest town: Auburn
Fees and permits: The state charges a day-use fee for every car parked in the parking area.
Maps: *Auburn State Recreation Area* brochure trail map. USGS 7.5-minute quad: Auburn.
Trail contacts: Auburn State Recreation Area, 501 El Dorado St., Auburn, CA 95603; (530) 885-4527; www.parks.ca.gov

Finding the trailhead: From I-80 in Auburn, drive 3.6 miles south on Highway 49 and turn right across the American River toward Cool. The dirt parking area is 0.25 mile south of the bridge on the left. Trailhead GPS: N38 54.698' / W121 02.073'

The Hike

Preserved today as part of the Auburn State Recreation Area, the Middle Fork of the American River's lower canyon is undergoing a transformation nearly as dramatic as the changes brought by the forty-niners, but this time in reverse. In the 1850s thousands of gold miners worked rich placers along this river, building flumes and diverting channels. Into the twentieth century, hundreds of quarrymen worked the canyon, gouging out a mountainside and trucking out the rocks along what now serves as the Quarry Road Trail. The forty-niners are long gone, their encampments existing only as names to mark a particular bend or shoal in the river. The quarrymen have also departed—moved farther up the hill, actually—leaving the scarred mountainside and our trail.

From the gate in the Quarry Road Trail parking area, at an elevation of about 600 feet, walk downhill on a road that was once paved but is rapidly deteriorating to gravel. The canyon is a gaping slash in the landscape, barely softened with forests. Precipitous highways climb both canyon walls. As our track meanders in leisurely fashion about 100 feet above the river, decent paths leading down to the shores are very few and far between. As we move upstream, the roar of the river begins to drown out the vehicular noise from the highway. The canyon has a rough grandeur.

We are restricted from crossing through the quarry near the river level. Instead, we follow a directional sign uphill for a short climb above the ruined foundations of dismantled quarry hoppers. Likely looking side paths climb up and down from the main track, but we stay at a steady contour, maintaining a generally even distance above the river. Keep an eye open for Hawver Mine (N38 54.971' / W121 00.879'), a natural cavern once home to prehistoric mammals, who left their bones inside. Reamed out for its valuable limestone and renamed Mountain Quarries Mine, its rusty, metal-gated mouth makes it look more mine than cave. On hot days the cool air that still pours from its inner sanctums is mightily refreshing.

Passing through a metal gate, we leave the quarry on its eastern side. As we turn the corner, we pass above Murderers Bar, which supported a population of hundreds of miners in the early 1850s. It took its name as the scene of a spate of gold rush killings sparked by lust and vengeance, though accounts vary greatly. One version claims that miners from Oregon attempted rape of some local Native American women, shot the men who tried to rescue them, and were in turn killed in revenge. The Oregonian accounts painted the Indians as the aggressors in league with Californians based at Sutter's Mill, Coloma—men who wanted the Oregonians out of "their" goldfields. When John Sutter attempted to defend the native captives detained by the Oregonians in Coloma, the Oregon crew sent him fleeing back to Sacramento in fear for his life and then massacred their native prisoners when they tried to escape.

We meet the Western States Trail cutoff—our return route—as it descends from the upper quarry. Less than 100 yards after this junction, an obvious but unmarked, eroded path goes steeply down to Mammoth Bar. The north side of the river here is sometimes crowded and noisy with the roar of off-highway vehicles, but fewer people will be on our side of the river.

Continuing upstream on the Quarry Road Trail past Texas Bar, we welcome the ever-increasing shade from oak, yellow pine, and madrone, a sign of the canyon's recovery from the upheaval of the gold rush. We are also enjoying increasing peace and quiet. The Auburn State Recreation Area permits gold panning, and both Texas and Browns Bars offer good river access.

Beyond cobbled Browns Bar we reach a junction of the Browns Bar and Western States Trails, where we leave the easy-rambling Quarry Road Trail and turn uphill. Gaining nearly 900 feet of elevation in the next mile, we cross Browns Bar Canyon Creek four times in step-across fords, taking frequent rest stops to admire the ferns and (if you come in spring) a profusion of butterflies and wildflowers.

At a three-way junction, before reaching the top of the hill, we follow the Western States Trail right, into the steepest section of our trail. Arriving on a wooded ridge, our singletrack trail soon settles into an easier contour, sauntering sometimes up and sometimes down, through alternating pasture and oak woodland. We enjoy the distant views west across the American River Canyon to Auburn, but some large modern houses on the ridge to the south briefly mar the prospect.

The Quarry Trail Loop; The Cool to Canyon Loop

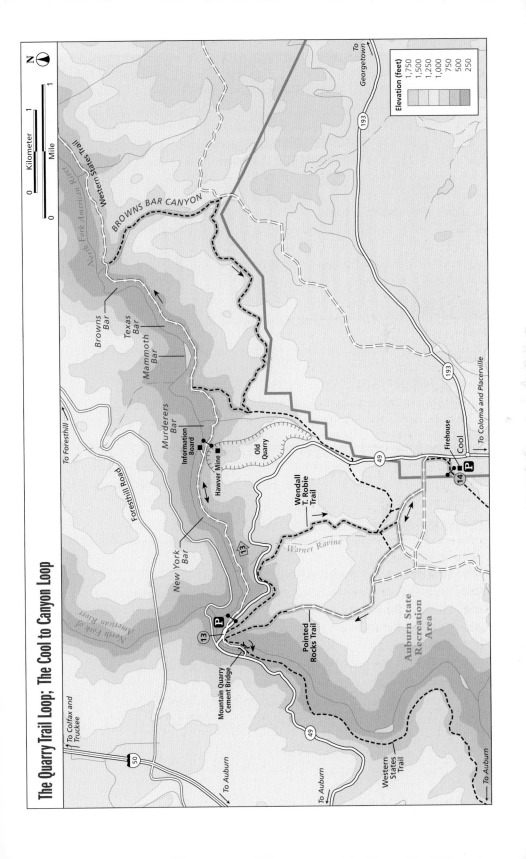

Once home to prehistoric mammals, Hawver Cave became a mine in the 19th century.

At about 6 miles we begin a steep descent back toward the river, joining first with the Western States cutoff, where a wide path leads steeply down to the Quarry Road Trail near Mammoth Bar. From there, we can backtrack along the Quarry Trail to the parking area.

Miles and Directions

0.0 Parking area.

1.3 Uphill detour through quarry, past Hawver Mine.

2.0 Junction with Western States Trail cutoff; go left (east) on Quarry Road Trail.

2.2 Use-trail to Mammoth Bar.

2.6 Texas Bar.

3.2 Browns Bar.

3.4 Junction of Browns Bar and Western States Trails; go right (southeast), uphill.

4.5 Three-way junction; go right (west) on Western States Trail.

6.8 Junction with Western States Trail cutoff; go right (north), downhill.

7.3 Junction with Quarry Road Trail; go left (west).

9.3 Arrive back at the parking area.

14 The Cool to Canyon Loop

Linking rolling, pastoral grasslands with the raw, rugged American River Canyon, this loop trail embraces two very different but very classic faces of Gold Country foothill scenery.

Start: Cool Firehouse
Distance: 6.2-mile lollipop loop
Hiking time: About 3 hours
Difficulty: Moderate, with a total of about 1,380 feet in elevation gained and lost
Trail condition: Part dirt road and part single-track. There is one very steep hill, slippery

when wet. Watch for rattlesnakes and poison oak.
Seasons: All year, but summers can be very hot, and rainy days very muddy
For more information, see Hike 13

Finding the trailhead: The trail starts from the parking lot behind the fire station on the north end of the small town of Cool. You get there by driving about 18.5 miles north on Highway 49 from Placerville and turning left into the lot, or by driving about 6.7 miles southbound on Highway 49 from downtown Auburn and turning right. Trailhead GPS: N38 53.379' / W121 01.035'

The Hike

As more and more of California's classic foothill scenery falls to development, the portions already preserved in the 35,000-acre Auburn State Recreation Area grow all the more special. Of its more than 100 miles of hiking, biking, and equestrian paths, this challenging loop on the Pointed Rocks, Western States, and Wendall T. Robie Trails traverses a rich range of foothill scenery—rolling oak savanna, chaparral, and rugged river canyon.

From the parking area behind the Cool Firehouse, at an elevation of about 1,520 feet, our path departs through a gate on the north side, rounding a fenced field in a counterclockwise direction. On the north side of the field, we meet a wider dirt track coming in from Highway 49 and turn left (west). For the sake of simplicity, stick diligently to this wide track clear to the three-way junction at 1.5 miles, ignoring all narrower side paths.

Rising and falling with easy gait through rolling grassland luxuriously dotted with blue oak, interior live oak, forked gray pine, and seasonal wildflowers, we pass our trail's namesake, the Pointed Rocks, commonly called "tombstone rocks" by the early miners. These splintery outcrops of metamorphic stone are the remains of ancient seabeds, snapped and upended in the Sierra upheaval and exposed by weathering.

At the three-way junction, take the right-hand (west) track, passing a sign restricting bicycles. Dropping briefly and then rising to a ridge choked with manzanita, chamise, toyon, and other scrub, we obtain our first view of the American River Canyon and the soaring green Foresthill Road bridge, propped up between the high walls of the North Fork. As we begin our precipitous descent, our easy saunter abruptly changes into a staggering lope—and a treacherous one too, if the trail is wet, in which case a hiking stick may brake your slipping. (The gradient of our return route is much gentler.) Dropping rapidly to midslope, we reach a level ridge spur where our dirt track ends at a pylon. Passing under its power lines, we resume our plunge on a narrower footpath, slamming into the comparatively horizontal Wendall T. Robie Trail at 2.8 miles. Turning left (west), we follow its much more gradual decline down to the Mountain Quarry Cement Bridge, which crosses the American River immediately below the confluence of its north and middle forks. Dubbed by equestrians as "No Hands Bridge," this sturdy viaduct was the largest concrete-arch railroad bridge in the world when completed in 1912. Today it handles hikers and dismounted equestrians only. It is the Western States Trail's last river crossing before its final 4.2-mile mount to Auburn.

To complete the loop back to Cool, return the way you came as far as the junction of the Wendall T. Robie and Pointed Rocks Trails, 0.3 mile above the bridge. At this fork bear left (east) onto the Robie Trail, which parallels Highway 49 on a higher contour, sometimes in trees and sometimes opening to unusual views of the converging roads, streams, canyons, and bridges. Rising steadily but easily to the mouth of Warner Ravine, which our path ascends, we turn south and climb through pasture and oak woodland to emerge on our original track, just south of Cool. Turn left and follow our now-familiar trail 0.8 mile back around the field to the firehouse.

Miles and Directions

- **0.0** Cool Firehouse.
- **0.2** Footpath joins wider track; bear left (west).
- **0.8** Upper junction with Wendall T. Robie Trail; go straight (west) on Pointed Rocks Trail.
- **1.5** Three-way junction; bear right (west).
- **2.8** Lower junction of Robie and Pointed Rocks Trails; bear left (west).
- **3.1** Mountain Quarry Cement Bridge.
- **3.4** Return to lower junction of Robie and Pointed Rocks Trails; bear left (east).
- **4.5** Beginning of Warner Ravine.
- **5.4** Junction with Pointed Rocks Trail; bear left (east).
- **6.2** Arrive back at the Cool Firehouse.

15 Otter Creek Trail to Volcanoville

This steep miners' trail is a shorter, tamer version of the Last Chance Trail (see Hike 17). Descending steeply into a thickly wooded canyon, site of a gold scramble in 1851, the trail climbs to the old mining camp of Volcanoville.

Start: Eldorado National FR 13N60
Distance: 5.8 miles out and back
Hiking time: About 3 hours
Difficulty: With 1,800 feet of elevation lost and gained overall, expect some vigorous effort.
Trail condition: The trailhead is not clearly marked, but once found the trail is obvious, though steep. Watch for poison oak and rattlesnakes. The segment into Volcanoville follows the unpaved Paymaster Road.
Seasons: Mar through early June is the best time for water displays and wildflowers, but Otter Creek might be hard to cross. June–Nov promises easier fording. Oct–Nov is best for fall colors. Hiking can be good Dec–Feb if the trail is not too slippery from storms.
Other trail users: Hikers with their dogs, hunters, and equestrians all use this trail. Vehicles use the Paymaster Road.
Land status: Eldorado National Forest
Nearest town: Georgetown
Fees and permits: None
Map: USGS 7.5-minute quad: Georgetown
Trail contacts: Eldorado National Forest, Georgetown Ranger District, 7600 Wentworth Springs Rd., Georgetown, CA 95634; (530) 333-4312; www.fs.usda.gov

Finding the trailhead: From Georgetown, drive 2.7 miles east on the Wentworth Springs Road to Breedlove Road. Turn left onto Breedlove Road (CR 112) and drive 2.5 miles over rough dirt to a skewed four-way intersection (GPS: N38 56.794' / W120 46.941'). Take the road numbered 13N60 (GPS: N38 56.793' / W120 46.929') and drive 0.3 mile to where the larger road bends left (a private drive), and a smaller, unsigned dirt road forks right—this is our trailhead. (Trailhead GPS: N38 57.031' / W120 46.834') You could park on the shoulder at this intersection, taking care not to obstruct traffic. Alternatively, about 500 feet down, our trail (a rough, narrow dirt road) widens enough for a couple cars on the shoulder.

The Hike

From the intersection of dirt roads atop a ridge, at an elevation of about 3,050 feet, take the dirt road on the right that drops steeply downhill to a junction where a sign points left (northwest) to Otter Creek. Another junction with another sign follows fast upon the first, again pointing us to the left (northwest).

Now on a singletrack trail, we walk through what appears to be an old mining ditch and round the hill through thick forests of Douglas fir, mossy tan oak, toyon, and madrone, a broadleaf tree with very hard yellowish wood and reddish peeling bark. From time to time we catch views through the trees of the ridge between Otter Creek and Missouri Canyon, jutting like a ship's prow into the canyon where their waters join.

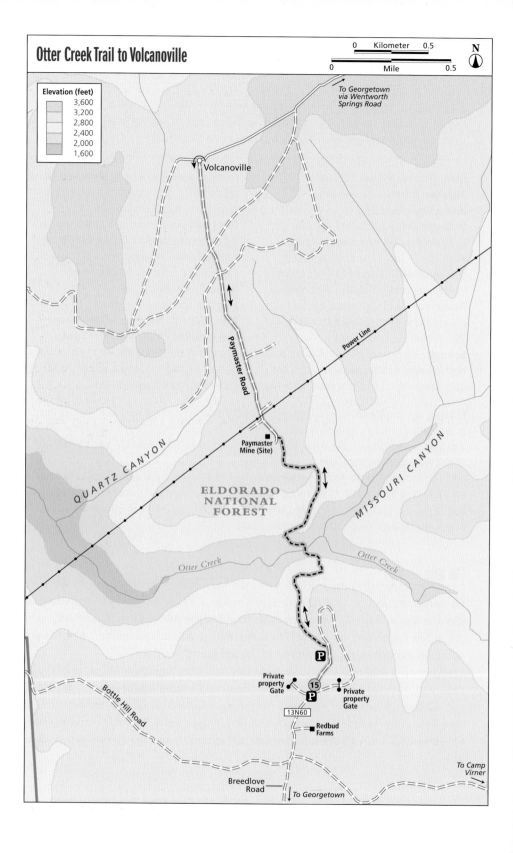

Otter Creek Trail to Volcanoville

Elevation (feet)
- 3,600
- 3,200
- 2,800
- 2,400
- 2,000
- 1,600

0   Kilometer   0.5

0   Mile   0.5

N

To Georgetown via Wentworth Springs Road

Volcanoville

Paymaster Road

Power Line

Paymaster Mine (Site)

QUARTZ CANYON

ELDORADO NATIONAL FOREST

MISSOURI CANYON

Otter Creek

Otter Creek

P

Private property Gate

15

Private property Gate

P

Bottle Hill Road

13N60

Redbud Farms

To Camp Virner

Breedlove Road

↓ *To Georgetown*

A couple of switchbacks finish our descent to Otter Creek, where clumps of poison oak grow close to the trail. There are no vistas. The narrow canyon presses in, a riot of riparian growth—close, cool, dank, somewhat claustrophobic. The ground near the river shows evidence of having been dug up by miners, exposing gray bedrock for a distance from the water, but there's no obvious sign of the six-stamp ore mill that once stood here.

Crossing Otter Creek might be difficult, even impossible, during high water. Even if the water is low enough to keep your feet dry, be wary of the slippery slate bedrock. On the north bank our singletrack trail launches uphill with a vengeance, plowing over bedrock and through mud like a crazed miner bound for town on a Saturday night. Take heed of the dry leaves, slippery on such steep slopes (especially when descending!), and beware the steep drop into Missouri Canyon. Mounting to a spur ridge of the Hornblende Mountains, you pass some barriers placed to deter vehicles, emerging at the cleared site of the Paymaster Mine. There our trail meets the unpaved Paymaster Road, where we turn right (north) to follow it uphill, passing under some power lines and ignoring the many Forest Service roads and little tracks that branch off to the left and right. Stick to the main road, which follows the ridge in a mostly level, fairly straight line, and it will lead you to Volcanoville, about 1 mile beyond the power lines. Your arrival will probably be heralded by a chorus of unseen barking hounds. Aside from a scattering of houses and the paved dead-end road from Georgetown, there's not much left of Volcanoville. Its moment of glory hit in 1856 with the discovery of a 42.8-ounce nugget here. The town burned long ago, and its post office closed in 1953.

Miles and Directions

0.0 Parking area.

0.2 First Otter Creek Trail sign (N38 57.176/W120 46.700).

0.3 Second Otter Creek Trail sign.

0.9 Otter Creek.

1.8 Site of Paymaster Mine; turn right onto unpaved Paymaster Road.

1.9 Pass under power lines.

2.9 Volcanoville.

5.8 Arrive back at your vehicle.

16 Coloma Loop

The gold rush of 1849 began with James Marshall's fateful find at Sutter's Saw Mill in Coloma. The valley was inundated with argonauts, and the gold was quickly depleted. The boom quickly passed, leaving Coloma to fade quietly into a peaceful, half-abandoned village. This hike visits several historic sites around town, as well as the pastoral hillsides and woodlands above Coloma Valley.

Start: Coloma visitor center
Distance: 3.5-mile loop
Hiking time: About 2 hours
Difficulty: Moderate, with 750 feet of elevation gained and lost
Trail condition: Partly quiet, paved road; partly singletrack path. Watch for poison oak and rattlesnakes.
Seasons: Year-round, though May through Sept afternoons may be hot.
Other trail users: No dogs or bikes allowed on Monroe Ridge Trail. Watch for vehicles on the road portion of this hike.
Land status: Marshall Gold Discovery State Historic Park
Nearest towns: There are stores at Coloma, and more at nearby Lotus, as well as gas and restaurants. Placerville and Auburn are the nearest large towns with all amenities.
Fees and permits: Small per-vehicle fee
Maps: *Marshall Gold Discovery State Historic Park Map.* USGS 7.5-minute quad: Coloma.
Trail contacts: Marshall Gold Discovery State Historic Park, 310 Back St., Coloma, CA 95613; (530) 622-3470; www.parks.ca .gov/?page_id=484
Special considerations: The Coloma Loop incorporates town streets and three separate trails: the Monument Trail, the Monroe Ridge Trail, and the Gold Discovery Trail. Consequently, walkers can easily shorten the distance of this hike if so inclined.

Finding the trailhead: Marshall Gold Discovery State Historic Park straddles Highway 49 (Main Street) about 7.5 miles northwest from Placerville and 16 miles southeast from Auburn. Signs point out the visitor center on a side street. Visitor center GPS: N38 48.017' / W120 53.533'

The Hike

Starting at the visitor center parking area, where a historic foundation now serves as the Beer Garden picnic area, walk southeast up shady Back Street. Like Main Street (Highway 49), the next parallel block, Back Street used to be more thickly platted and crowded with buildings, but the largest structure left is the ruins of the El Dorado County Jail, standing forlorn in a broad pasture. Built ambitiously of stone in 1852, it saw its fortunes flee with the county seat to Placerville in 1857, shortly after which it was sold for building materials. Enough materials remain in the walls to suggest that the buyer didn't take his money's worth.

Turning right up residential High Street, we walk uphill past some historic old homes toward the simple St. John's Catholic Church, built in 1856, its bell hung in a

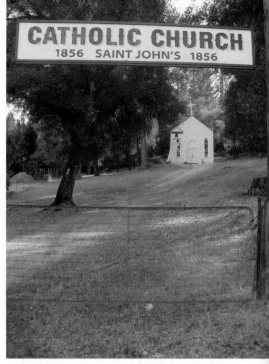

separate wooden frame in front. Passing under the high entrance gate, climb the dirt track in front for a peek inside its open doors. This is an enchanting, quiet spot, redolent of rural villages across America during the nineteenth century. Looking left (east) through a line of trees and a wire fence, you can see the white belfry and roof of Emmanuel Church, built in 1856, rising with peaceful beauty above the fields and trees.

Cross the tiny footbridge over the miners' ditch behind St. John's to the tranquil Catholic cemetery. The oldest graves date from the early 1850s, but surviving headstones, inscribed with mostly Irish names, are newer. Immediately across the narrow paved road stands the restored cabin built in 1862 by James Marshall, where he dwelled until the late 1870s. Surrounded by

Built in 1856, Saint John's Church stands peacefully today amidst fields and woods on the edge of once-hectic Coloma.

cedar and oak, adjacent to the miners' ditch that he probably helped dig, the cabin is furnished with period furniture, which is visible through windows.

Continue up the tight, shaded curves of Monument Road to the top of the knoll, capped by the Marshall Monument, beneath which James Marshall lies buried. Five years after his death in 1885, the state legislature dedicated this 31-foot-tall granite monument, capped with a 10.5-foot bronzed zinc statue of James Marshall pointing down toward the site of the mill on the river where he picked up the first nuggets in 1848.

Our route continues across the monument parking area to the southwest, where the signed MONROE RIDGE TRAIL begins on a dirt road that leads to a decaying spring house. A singletrack path now launches up a series of easy switchbacks through woodlands of live oak, buckeye, bull pine, ponderosa, and toyon, whose red berries cheer up the scenery in fall and winter. Crossing a dry mining ditch about midway up the hill, the trail crests near a sign that directs you right, to the first vista point, where the views, in fact, are mostly blocked by trees. The vistas improve sporadically as you continue along Monroe Ridge, granting fleeting glances north to Lotus Valley and east to where Mount Murphy rises across Coloma Valley.

Monroe Ridge is named after the family who owned this land before selling it to the state for a park in the 1940s. The Monroes trace their roots in Coloma back to 1849, when the matriarch, Nancy Gooch, arrived as a slave but was freed under

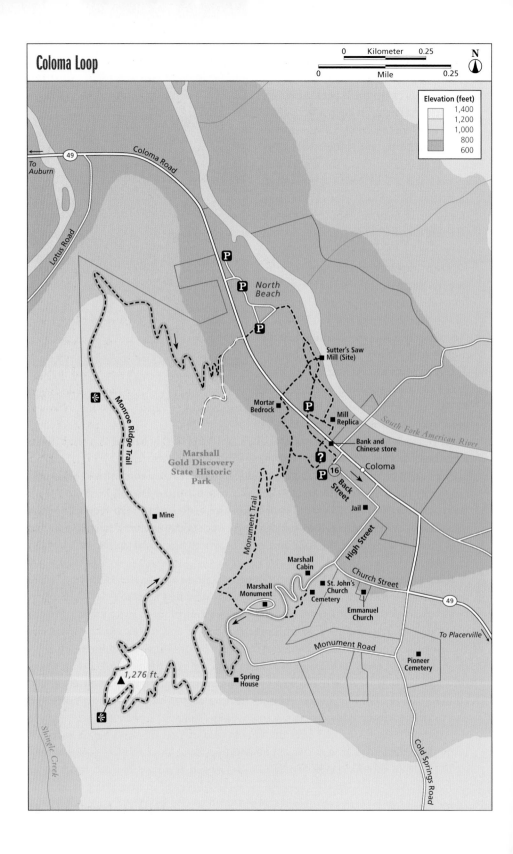

Coloma Loop

Kilometer 0.25
Mile 0.25

N

Elevation (feet)
1,400
1,200
1,000
800
600

To Auburn

49

Coloma Road

Lotus Road

North Beach

P

P

P

Sutter's Saw Mill (Site)

Mortar Bedrock

P

Mill Replica

South Fork American River

Bank and Chinese store

Monroe Ridge Trail

Marshall Gold Discovery State Historic Park

Mine

Monument Trail

Coloma

16

P

Back Street

Jail

High Street

Marshall Cabin

Church Street

Marshall Monument

St. John's Church

Cemetery

Emmanuel Church

49

To Placerville

1,276 ft.

Spring House

Monument Road

Pioneer Cemetery

Cold Springs Road

Shingle Creek

mining laws that did not tolerate slavery (or rather, the use of slaves to work mining claims). By doing household chores and laundry work, Nancy earned the money to buy freedom for her son, Jim Monroe, who joined her from Missouri with his wife, Sara. The Monroes prospered by planting orchards and selling fruit, eventually owning about 80 acres around Coloma, including the site of Sutter's Saw Mill.

At about the middle of the ridge, the trail passes a fenced mine shaft that Jim's son, Andrew, dug during the second gold rush in the 1930s. He found scant pay dirt, for Coloma's famous golden hoard came principally from river placers washed down from the Mother Lode, which crosses the river near Chili Bar, about 5 miles upstream from Coloma.

After passing a second vista point at 1,150 feet, where a picnic table offers the clearest views of Coloma Valley along the entire trail, our route descends on switchbacks through Jim Monroe's overgrown orchards to Highway 49. Crossing the road and through the gap in a rail fence, pick up the footpath again on the river side of the North Beach parking area.

A short walk upstream from here takes you to the Gold Discovery Site, where you can still see the original tailrace where the momentous first nugget of the gold rush was found on the morning of January 24, 1848. One of the most historic sites in the West, the exact location of Sutter's Saw Mill was positively identified in 1947 by archaeologists, who unearthed pieces of timber, bolts, and tools, now on display at the visitor center. Beyond, on slightly higher ground, the replica of Sutter's Mill was built with hand tools in 1968.

Cross back over Highway 49 to two stone buildings that served as a bank and a store, both run by Chinese businessmen. The bank now contains a mining exhibit, and the other building a period store display. The flat picnic area adjacent to the visitor center is the likely site of the Nisenan village of Kullo-ma, origin of Coloma's name. The Nisenan were a southern Maidu people. Marshall hired several Nisenan men to help dig his tailrace. A large boulder on the northwest end of the flats contains the mortar holes where village women used to grind seeds and acorns into meal with stone metates.

Miles and Directions

0.0 Visitor center.

0.3 St. John's Catholic Church.

0.4 Marshall Cabin.

0.6 Marshall Monument.

1.6 First vista point.

2.3 Second vista point.

3.0 Cross Highway 49 to North Beach parking area.

3.3 Sutter's Saw Mill site.

3.5 Arrive back at the visitor center.

17 The Last Chance Trail to Swinging Bridge

This rugged trail to a remote crossing of the North Fork of the Middle Fork of the American River traverses some of the wildest "foothill" country of the Gold Country, a region well settled a century ago with mining settlements but today virtually deserted of all but hikers, anglers, horseback riders, and subsistence or hobby miners.

Start: Michigan Bluff

Distance: 17.4 miles out and back

Hiking time: A 2- or 3-day trip is recommended.

Difficulty: With more than 7,000 feet of elevation lost and gained, this is a formidable hike.

Trail condition: Excellent, well-signed, but often very steep singletrack trail, sometimes on precipitous slopes. Parts of the route near Deadwood follow dirt roads. The trail is marked by flexible fiberglass slats by the Western States Trail Association, labeled with a round horseback-rider symbol and the letters ws.

Seasons: Fall and spring. Dry days in winter can be good, despite occasional snow on the higher ridges. Avoid wet weather. Summer is hot. Avoid the annual Western States Endurance Run, held the last weekend in June, and the Tevis Cup long-distance horseback trail ride, held in late July or early Aug.

Other trail users: Equestrians, mountain bikers, motorized bikers, hunters, and dog owners all use this trail. Sections near Deadwood are open to ATVs.

Land status: Tahoe National Forest. Pay attention to signs that mark adjacent private property.

Nearest town: Foresthill

Fees and permits: Campfire permit required if using a stove or campfire

Maps: Trails Illustrated: *Tahoe National Forest.* USGS 7.5-minute quads: Michigan Bluff, Greek Store.

Trail contacts: Tahoe National Forest, American River Ranger District, 22830 Foresthill Rd., Foresthill, CA 95631; (530) 367-2224; www.fs .usda.gov/tahoe

Finding the trailhead: From I-80 on the eastern edge of Auburn, take the Foresthill exit and drive on Foresthill Road about 18 miles east to the town of Foresthill. Continuing east on Foresthill Road for 4 miles, turn right (south) at the sign toward Michigan Bluff. Follow the wide paved road 3 miles to Michigan Bluff, a village perched on a ridge overlooking the forested drainage of the American River. The main road ends near a small stone monument and interpretive sign commemorating the Western States Trail. These mark our trailhead. Beside them is a narrow gravel lane, Turkey Hill Road. Across the street stands a memorial water spigot and trough maintained by the Western States Trail Association. Park along a street curb in town, clear of any drive, and respecting any No Parking signs and the wishes of local residents. Trailhead GPS: N39 02.458' / W120 44.091'

The Hike

A part of the Western States Trail, the Michigan Bluff to Last Chance Trail was built as a toll road in the early 1850s, enabling mule skinners to drive pack trains from Michigan City (the old name of Michigan Bluff) to Last Chance and back, in one day.

Before the mines declined at the end of the nineteenth century, millions of dollars in gold were packed out along the trail.

Carved out with a single-minded purpose of expediting business, this trail courts no truck with mollycoddling gradients but drives relentlessly down thousands of feet of canyon wall and up the other side—not once but twice. And if that seems like a lot of work today just to see an old graveyard, or a rotting pile of timbers that was once a building, or the railed graves of abandoned mines, or empty stretches of wild river canyons where forty-niners once toiled, then you're starting to get an accurate picture of the Last Chance Trail. No picnic jaunt, it is nonetheless a beautiful, historic, fascinating journey to places settled in a whirlwind during the nineteenth century and forsaken in the twentieth.

Our Turkey Hill Road trailhead heads northeast between private homes, through a gate, to a prominent brown sign that announces the Western States Trail at an elevation of about 3,500 feet. We begin descending immediately through sturdy manzanita chaparral that has overgrown the barrens gouged by hydraulic mining before it was banned in 1883. Forests of oak and ponderosa pine close in as you drop farther into Poor Mans Canyon, where the penniless Leland Stanford started his mining career, earning the nest egg that he used to set up shop in Michigan City, and later to beget his fabulous fortune from the first transcontinental railroad. Just before passing your first trail mile, you will step across Poor Mans Canyon Creek, where you will not find sufficient flat ground even for pitching a pup tent.

As you round the ridge out of Poor Mans Canyon, the roar of the American River, less than a mile down-canyon, reaches your ears. Above its southern banks you will see the road cut of the Mosquito Ridge Road. The trail steepens, though its precipitous drop is well screened by ever-present foliage. After crossing three separate doubletracks, unmarked on the USGS topo maps, you will reach some flat, spacious, undeveloped campsites near the bridged crossing of El Dorado Canyon's stream, a drop from the Michigan Bluff trailhead of more than 1,700 feet in 2.3 miles, to an elevation of 1,800 feet.

Your climb out of El Dorado Canyon begins immediately. Turning left (north) at the signed junction (the right fork goes 2 miles to the abandoned mining settlement of Bake Oven), you will pass the worked-over site of the Rainbow Land Mine, sealed, railed off, and overgrown with forest and poison oak. Another switchback aligns the trail onto its steady northwest diagonal up the side of El Dorado Canyon, rising by degree to impressive views of stony Codfish Point, above the confluence of the West and East Branch streams. After a climb of slightly more than 1.5 miles and 1,000 feet, refresh yourself at a trailside spring, gushing through a black pipe amid a melee of ferns; filter it before drinking. After another climb of near equal length and elevation gain, the path rounds the forehead of the ridge, crosses a Forest Service trail-bike route, and follows the Western States Trail sign to the site of Deadwood.

Though Deadwood once boasted a hotel, mines, and houses, nothing remains today except a wide dirt road in the forest, some foundation excavations, a handful

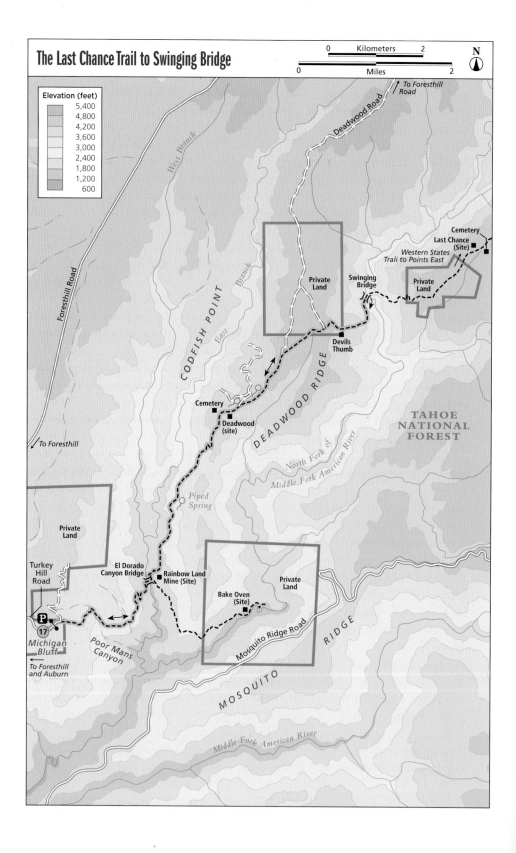

The Last Chance Trail to Swinging Bridge

of posted mining claims, and a cemetery behind an ornamental gateway on a hilltop at the west end of "town." Although no old tombstones remain, the graves are still planted with irises, and their occupants are commemorated on a modern monument of black marble. At an elevation of 3,800 feet, "downtown" Deadwood has no obvious water sources, but you can find some springs along the four-wheel-drive double-tracks that run down the north side of the ridge.

The trail climbs gently now along the ridge eastward, paralleling and occasionally joining a dirt road through forests of incense cedar and ponderosa pine. Forestry tracks intersect the main path; ignore them and keep moving east, following the Western States Trail signs. Dipping slightly to cross a small streamlet, you can find some potential campsites on national forest land to the right (south), but stay off the private property immediately to the left (north) side of the trail. The path then rises to a railed view point overlooking the spectacular canyon of the North Fork of the Middle Fork of the American River, at another Forest Service trail-bike crossing. The ridge falls abruptly away into hydraulically ravaged Devils Basin, wherein stands a lava pinnacle known as Devils Thumb. At 4,350 feet, this is the high point of our trail.

Now begins the descent into our second canyon, shorter but steeper than our first descent into El Dorado Canyon. At first winding down the edge of a hillside, the trail drops suddenly in a regimen of knee-jarring switchbacks through evergreen forests. As you near the bottom, the trail meets a creek dashing in from the left (north) and fords it after one more switchback, immediately above its confluence with the American River. This ford is a particularly pretty spot, with a white-foaming waterfall pouring through thick greenery.

Immediately beyond, the Swinging Bridge crosses the American River below a roaring cascade at an elevation of 2,750 feet. Large trout visible in the water promise good fishing. Though the canyon bottom is narrow, many small level areas on either bank make fine campsites.

Options

A good day hike from your American River campsite goes up the east side of the canyon to the site of Last Chance. Although large enough in 1852 to support a post office, today nothing remains of Last Chance except a cemetery. The trail is arduous, climbing 1,800 feet in 2.6 miles to an elevation of 4,550 feet. Beyond Last Chance the Western States Trail continues eastward to Robinson Flat, Squaw Valley, and Robie Park, with connections to the Lake Tahoe trail system and the Pacific Crest Trail.

Miles and Directions

0.0 Michigan Bluff, corner of Turkey Hill Road.

0.1 Metal gate.

0.2 Western States Trail sign; turn right, downhill.

1.0 Poor Mans Canyon Creek.

2.5 El Dorado Canyon bridge.

2.6 Bake Oven Trail junction; bear left (north).

4.0 Piped spring.

5.6 Deadwood cemetery.

7.5 Ridge above Devils Thumb.

8.7 Swinging Bridge.

17.4 Arrive back at the parking area.

18 American River Canyon Trek

Miles of trails explore the deep, remote canyon of the North Fork of the American River, but the effort required to get there keeps the crowds away. With the help of a car shuttle, this hike descends to the American River Trail via the Mumford Bar Trail and climbs back out on the Beacroft Trail. It's worth the effort not only for its pristine beauty and old mining history, but for its challenging late-season backpacking possibilities.

Start: Mumford Bar Trailhead
Distance: 9.2 miles one-way/shuttle
Hiking time: About 7 hours but better to allow 2 days
Difficulty: A grueling day hike or strenuous overnighter, with an overall loss and gain in elevation of more than 3,300 feet
Trail condition: Clear but often steep single-track trail. Beware rattlers, poison oak.
Seasons: Mar through mid-Nov. During winter the American River Trail itself should be free of snow, but the road heads can be closed by snow.

Other trail users: Dogs, equestrians, and mountain bikes are permitted.
Land status: Tahoe National Forest
Nearest town: Foresthill
Fees and permits: Campfire permit required if using a stove or campfire
Maps: Trails Illustrated: *Tahoe National Forest.* USGS 7.5-minute quad: Duncan Peak.
Trail contacts: Tahoe National Forest, American River Ranger District, 22830 Foresthill Rd., Foresthill, CA 95631; (530) 367-2224; www.fs.usda.gov/tahoe

Finding the trailhead: From I-80 on the eastern edge of Auburn, take the Foresthill exit and drive on Foresthill Road about 18 miles east to the town of Foresthill. Continue east on paved Foresthill Road for 15 miles to the signposted Mumford Bar Trailhead (elevation 5,370 feet) on the left. Trailhead GPS: N39 10.725' / W120 38.442'

If you are shuttling, park the second vehicle at the Beacroft Trail road head (elevation 5,460 feet), 4.5 miles farther. Ending trailhead GPS: N39 11.618' / W120 34.045'

The Hike

From the parking area, a rough dirt road leads north through thick forest, cresting the rim of the canyon, where a singletrack trail takes over. (Some vehicles park at this point.) From here on to the river, basically, the Mumford Bar Trail constitutes a long, downhill, forest hike that tantalizes us mildly, on occasion, with glimpses through the trees of the North Fork canyon (itself heavily forested). Although considered the easiest route into the canyon, some hikers may consider the descent of nearly 2,700 feet in 3.6 miles to be steep. Take comfort (or not!) in the thought that hikers who know the Beacroft Trail (our return route) generally praise the Mumford Bar Trail for the pains its builders took to ease the gradient by routing it across a longer swath of ridge and hillside and making switchbacks only on the steepest slopes.

Reaching the American River, the USGS map shows the Mumford Bar Trail crossing the river and continuing up to the north rim. You will find no bridge at Mumford Bar, however, and the ford may not be possible until late summer. Fortunately for us, the American River Trail starts here and goes upstream on the southern bank. Maidu tribes had fishing camps at Mumford Bar in spring and fall, and would catch the prolific salmon with their bare hands. The banks and bars were later mined for placer gold, which drifted down over millennia from rich deposits on the Foresthill Divide, where our trail started. A snug cabin built by miner John Mumford still stands at Mumford Bar.

The American River Trail is a pleasure to walk. The gradient is pretty even and the scenery agreeable, though heavily forested with Douglas firs, maples, oaks, and ponderosa pines. Watch out for poison oak. Although most of the trail is contoured high above the water, there is a very convenient access point at the 5-mile mark, near a distinctive conical hill that rises from the river. A half mile farther stands a tiny log cabin, a miner's shelter designated as the Hope Placer Claim.

As we approach Beacroft Bar, the river cascades through an inner gorge of dark rock. We pass more good campsites beyond, shortly before hitting the junction of the Beacroft Trail, marked by a small sign and huge black oak. The American River Trail continues upstream from here, after crossing nearby Tadpole Creek on a bridge; but we turn right (south) to climb the Beacroft Trail back up to the Foresthill Divide.

The Beacroft Trail climbs 2,570 feet in about 2 miles. Steep and relentless, it was clearly "surveyed" by the soles of the boots of miners anxious to reach the river. We take some heart initially from splashing Tadpole Creek. Other small encouragements come from a sweet little spring encircled by ferns, and by slowly emerging views over the American River Canyon. But mostly, this trail is a slog. Try, however, to derive some pleasure from it in considering that *you* are not carrying 140 pounds of shovels, picks, pans, blankets, cooking gear, canvas tent, rifle and hunting kit, harmonica, and two weeks' worth of weevil-infested supplies. Likewise, the prospects of a cold one awaiting in Foresthill before nightfall are better today than in 1849. So take heart, and enjoy your slog.

At long last we reach an obvious dirt track that contours along the hill, perpendicular to our path. Our trail steps right across that track and cranks out another couple of switchbacks before meeting the entrenched Iowa Hill Mining Ditch, which used to carry water some 40 miles to mines on the Iowa Hill Divide. Clamber over the berm and into the ditch (which is dry), turn left, and walk about 200 feet to where our trail climbs out the other side. Continuing briefly up the hill, we level out on an unpaved road. Other tracks diverge from this road, but it leads us unmistakably, in short order, to the road head at Foresthill Road. This area, known as Whisky Hill, was famous in the late nineteenth century for its rich drift mines.

Options

From the Beacroft Trail junction, the American River Trail plows up-canyon another 3.2 miles to an old ford that crosses to the Big Granite Trail from Loch Leven Lakes

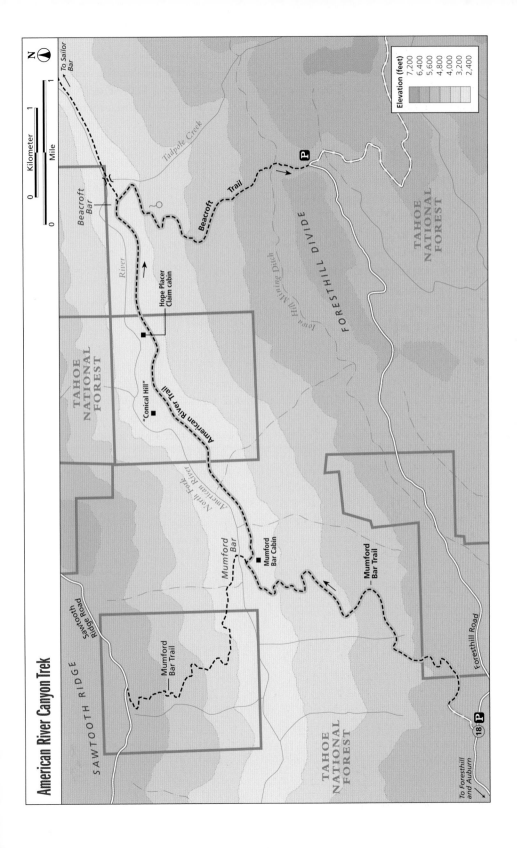

American River Canyon Trek

To Sailor Bar

Beacroft Bar

Tadpole Creek

Elevation (feet)
7,200
6,400
5,600
4,800
4,000
3,200
2,400

N

Kilometer
0   1

Mile
0   1

Beacroft Trail

P

Hope Placer Claim cabin

River

"Conical Hill"

American River Trail

North Fork American River

Mumford Bar

Mumford Bar Cabin

FORESTHILL DIVIDE

Iowa Hill Mining Ditch

TAHOE NATIONAL FOREST

TAHOE NATIONAL FOREST

SAWTOOTH RIDGE

Sawtooth Ridge Road

Mumford Bar Trail

Mumford Bar Trail

Foresthill Road

TAHOE NATIONAL FOREST

18 P

To Foresthill and Auburn

(Hike 27); the ford may be too dangerous until late summer. Continuing 1.2 miles farther up the south bank, the American River Trail ends at Sailor Bar, where adventurous backpackers can work their way upstream (cross-country) to the Royal Gorge. From Sailor Bar a maintained trail climbs about 4 miles to Sailor Flat on Foresthill Road.

Miles and Directions

0.0   Mumford Bar Trailhead.

0.3   Dirt road ends and singletrack begins.

3.7   American River.

3.8   Mumford Bar cabin.

5.6   Hope Placer Claim cabin.

6.7   Beacroft Trail junction; turn right (south).

7.5   Spring with ferns.

8.7   Dirt track.

8.8   Iowa Hill Mining Ditch.

9.2   Beacroft Trail road head.

Honorable Mentions

A Big Chico Creek

The city of Chico's Bidwell Park takes in a variety of foothill scenery, from grassland to woodland to craggy volcanic ridges spiked with spectacular basalt palisades. Its most unusual feature, however, is the entrenched inner box canyon of Big Chico Creek, which cuts down the middle of the much larger box canyon, a U-shaped coulee with intermittently sheer walls and two distinct plateaus on the north and south rims. The surprisingly narrow inner gorge of Big Chico Creek offers many surprising views along its cliff-top brink. You can go at any time of year, but try to go on a weekday, when the Upper Park Road is closed to vehicles and the park is less crowded. Park at Area E and walk up Upper Park Road from the vehicular gate (trailhead GPS: N39 46.323' / W121 46.746'). Big Chico Creek runs parallel to the road, mostly out of sight. Look for the entrance to the Yahi Trail at about 0.5 mile (GPS: N39 46.318' / W121 46.345'), where you can cut down to a dirt path that follows Big Chico Creek nearly 2 miles upstream through riparian woodland thick with sycamores, alders, shrubby willows, wild grape vines, cottonwoods, and box elders to Bear Hole, a popular skinny-dipping spot known to locals as Bare Hole. At this point, return to Upper Park Road (near Parking Area K), and continue upstream for highlight views into the fascinating inner canyon. You will need to detour from the road to see them. The vantage point at Parking Area P offers a fine view of Big Chico Creek pouring down through its sheer-walled box canyon. At Parking Area Q, you can stand atop a basalt lava flow similar to Devils Postpile, where blocks of lava split off from the wall form deep fissures in the rock. The vantage point at Devils Kitchen (Parking Area R), 3.7 miles from the starting gate, is particularly intriguing because it lets you look straight down about 10 feet to the top of a dense forest of large, mature trees growing on a shelf of the inner canyon wall, an unusual perspective on nature that could occupy a birder or painter for hours. For more information, contact Friends of Bidwell Park, PO Box 4837, Chico, CA 95927; friendsofbidwellpark.org.

B Yellow Creek Trail

Active mining claims still work the banks and bars of Yellow Creek, giving this undemanding trail something of an air of living history. It is also a pleasant walk, especially on warm days when the canyon's depth, heavy forest, and roaring water together provide natural, shady air-conditioning. Starting at the confluence of Yellow Creek and the Feather River, at the Beldon Powerhouse, this sometimes narrow and steep trail was hacked with pick-and-shovel from the basalt rocks. Miners' use-trails periodically lurch off from the main trail toward the rocky riverbanks, and we pass a continuous stream of posted mining claims with interesting monikers. Since this is public land, we have a right to pass through, to soak our feet in the creek, and to fish (with a license); but the claimants have the sole right to mine it. The maintained trail peters out at about 1.6 miles. To get there, drive to Eby Stamp Mill Rest Area on the Feather River National Scenic Byway (CA 70), across the river from Belden, itself about 25 miles west from the Plumas National Forest ranger station west of Quincy. Contact: Plumas National Forest, 39696 CA 70, Quincy, CA 95971; (530) 283-0555; www.fs.usda.gov/plumas. Trailhead GPS: N40 00.434' / W121 15.040'

C Bald Rock

The native Maidu believed this granite dome to be the home of a powerful spirit who guarded the lower Feather River Canyon. Hikers who explore its easily accessible summit find a bizarre landscape of unearthly charisma. The surface is heavily weathered. Many cabin-size boulders scattered about the surface look like glacial erratics, but (amazingly!) they were actually weathered in place. Splendid views reach to the Central Valley and Coast Ranges. To get there from CA 70 in Oroville, drive east on CA 162 (the Oroville-Quincy Highway) 19.3 miles to Bald Rock Road. Turn right and drive 7.3 miles farther to the Bald Rock parking area entrance (GPS: N39 38.715' / W121 20.433') on the left (north), marked by a Plumas National Forest sign. Contact: Feather River Ranger District, 875 Mitchell Ave., Oroville, CA 95965; (530) 534-6500; www.fs.fed.us/r5/plumas. Trailhead GPS: N39 38.769' / W121 20.458'

D Frazier Falls

This easy paved path winds through the forest and across a bridge to a view point overlooking this unexpectedly impressive 176-foot cascade. Though easy and short (1 mile round-trip), the route is scenic. The boulders and trees display a character that seems almost cultivated, like an exquisite garden. From Graeagle, drive 1.3 miles south on CA 89 to the Gold Lake Highway. Turn right and drive 1.7 miles to the signposted Frazier Falls turnoff. The parking area is 4.2 miles up this narrow paved road. Contact: Plumas National Forest, 39696 CA 70, Quincy, CA 95971; (530) 283-0555; www.fs .usda.gov/plumas. Trailhead GPS: N39 42.500' / W120 38.763'

With benches and well-graded pavement, the Frazier Falls Trail is suitable for wheelchairs.

E Sand Pond Trail

The Sierra Buttes are the most splendidly jagged peaks of the northern Sierra, every bit as stunning as the mountains on a carton of Challenge Butter. This short (0.8 mile), easy loop trail provides striking, picturesque vistas of the Buttes, especially in spring when the snow still clings to them. One highlight of the trail is a boardwalk through a forest and meadow flooded by a beaver dam. Beavers are nocturnal, so dusk is the best time to see one. From Bassetts Station on CA 49, drive 1.4 miles up the Gold Lake Highway to the Sardine Lakes junction (N39 37.264' /W120 36.645'), where you turn left (west). The Sand Pond parking area is 0.6 mile up this road. Contact: Tahoe National Forest; 15924 Highway 49, Camptonville, CA 95922; (530) 288-3231; www.fs.usda.gov/recarea/tahoe. Trailhead GPS: N39 37.136' / W120 37.099'

F Malakoff Diggins

Preserving the largest hydraulic mining excavation in the United States, this state park is crisscrossed by trails, including the Humbug Trail (Hike 6). The most interesting shorter trails are the 3.0-mile Rim Trail, which follows the edge of the pit, and the 3.0-mile Diggins Loop Trail. The latter wanders around the once desolate but slowly recovering basin that was gouged out of San Juan Ridge by miners wielding powerful hose nozzles, called monitors. To drain the basin, engineers constructed the 556-foot Hiller Tunnel, which hikers can walk through when the water level is low enough; bring

North Bloomfield doesn't have much going on around town, aside from just sitting pretty.

water shoes and flashlights. The park headquarters at North Bloomfield, a perfectly charming gold country hamlet, is about 26 miles northeast of Nevada City via Highway 49 and Tyler Foote Crossing Road. Contact: Malakoff Diggins State Historic Park, 23579 N. Bloomfield Park Rd., Nevada City, CA 95959; (530) 265-2740; www .parks.ca.gov/?page_id=494. Park headquarters GPS: N39 22.097' / W120 53.970'

G Independence Trail East

The first path through a roadless area in the United States built expressly for wheelchairs, the Independence Trail starts at the same trailhead as the Jones Bar Loop (Hike 7). Instead of going west to Jones Bar, however, we take the eastern branch, a wide, nearly level path within a now-dry mining canal, beautifully engineered along a high contour on a canyon wall high above the South Yuba River. This north-facing mountainside is shady with dense foliage of tan oak, manzanita, live oak, madrone, toyon, wild grape vines, and clumps of poison oak. In spots where the mountainside falls away too steeply for an earthen canal, we cross those gaps on spectacular wooden flumes, rebuilt for hikers like railed catwalks over thin air, with fine views into the canyon. Sometimes we cross creeks on trestles, ideal platforms for gazing down on beautiful forest scenes of dashing water, mossy rocks, and gnarled oaks. The turn-around point at 2.2 miles is not marked by a sign, but we can recognize it by its broad view over the Yuba River, swirling through its rocky pools above the Miner's Tunnel. Cut 600 feet through hard rock in the early 1870s, the Miner's Tunnel diverted the river around a channel rich in placer gold. Beyond this point the maintained trail stops, but a use-trail continues up-canyon through Devils Slide. Contact: Bear Yuba Land Trust, 12183 Auburn Rd., Grass Valley, CA 95949; (530) 272-5994; bylt.org. Trailhead GPS: N39 17.504' / W121 05.839'. (See map 7, Jones Bar Loop.)

⊢ Nevada City Trails

Many folks claim that Nevada City is the prettiest large town of the northern Gold Country, especially in fall when the leaves turn red and yellow. Its hilly streets make for pleasant walking, but even more special are the footpaths that crisscross it, many of them orignally built by miners. Among the trails maintained by the Bear Yuba Land Trust are the 1.5-mile Deer Creek Environs Trail, Cascade Canal (see Hike 11), the 2.4-mile Hirshman Trail, and the cross-town Deer Creek Tribute Trail. For more information, contact Bear Yuba Land Trust, 12183 Auburn Rd., Grass Valley, CA 95949; (530) 272-5994; bylt.org. You can also find maps and information at the Nevada City Chamber of Commerce. GPS: N39 15.782' / W121 01.018'

⊦ Gold Bug Park, Placerville

This small park in a ravine north of Placerville contains a stamp mill, mining museum, two mines that you can tour, and some short trails. This ravine was a virtual "neighborhood" of miners during the second gold rush of the 1930s, when a community of independent miners settled and scratched out meager livings. The 0.5-mile Priest Trail passes two mines open for visits (on weekends, weather permitting, or by arrangement; call first). Said to take its name from a Catholic service held in a side chamber, the Priest Mine is unusual for being carved from sandstone. The more successful Gold Bug Mine was worked between 1888 and World War II. Contact: Gold Bug Park, 2635 Gold Bug Ln., Placerville, CA 95667; (530) 642-5207; goldbugpark .org. GPS of park entry gate: N38 44.552' / W120 48.063'

Southern Gold Country

The area covered by this chapter was known to the forty-niners as "the Southern Mines," a foothill stretch of the Gold Country drained by the Cosumnes, Mokelumne, Stanislaus, Tuolumne, and Merced Rivers. The Southern Gold Country is drier and generally lower in elevation than the Northern Gold Country, and all the hikes here are well suited for winter, spring, and fall.

The greatest of all Sierra Nevada gold-bearing quartz veins, the Mother Lode, runs north and south through this region, closely traced by Highway 49, which links the five principal gold rush towns of Jackson, Angels Camp, Sonora, Jamestown, and Mariposa. Jamestown still supports the largest operating gold mine in the Sierra today, the open-pit Harvard Mine on Table Mountain. The Southern Gold Country embraces the Calaveras Formation, one of the largest cave-bearing regions west of the Rockies.

Indian Grinding Rock State Park gives a visitor a solid idea of Native American life in the Sierra foothills before the Gold Rush.

19 The Mokelumne River Trail to Middle Bar

Traversing a remote section of the Mokelumne Coast to Crest Trail (MCCT), this long but leisurely shuttle hike starts out on a historic stage road through Gold Country grasslands before traversing the steep-walled, rugged confines of the lower Mokelumne canyon.

Start: Campo Seco Staging Area, near Pardee Reservoir

Distance: 13.3 miles one-way/shuttle

Hiking time: About 6 hours

Difficulty: Strenuous, mainly for length; net elevation gain of about 600 feet. You can shave 2.3 miles off total by exiting at Rich Gulch (see "Finding the trailhead").

Trail condition: Excellent dirt or gravel roads on the first 9 miles, with the remainder mostly on superb singletrack trail, all well marked with signposts

Seasons: Early spring or fall are best. Summer is hot. Winter is the season to see bald eagles above Pardee Reservoir.

Other trail users: Equestrians are permitted but no bikes or dogs. Livestock graze along the trail.

Land status: East Bay Municipal Utility District (EBMUD)

Nearest town: Valley Springs

Fees and permits: A hiking permit (fee) from the EBMUD is required, available on line at www.ebmud.com/recreation/trail-use-permit/sierra-foothills-trails or from the entrance kiosks at Pardee Recreation Area (the closest to this trailhead) and Lake Camanche. Hikers must sign in at the trailhead and abide by the EBMUD's rules and regulations.

Maps: EBMUD: Trails of the Pardee & Comanche Watersheds (www. ebmud.com/recreation/trail-use-permit/sierra-foothills-trails). USGS 7.5-minute quads: Valley Springs, Jackson, Mokelumne Hill.

Trail contacts: EBMUD, (209) 772-8204. Pardee Recreation Area, (209) 772-1472. EBMUD Foothill Trails, www.ebmud.com/recreation/trail-use-permit/sierra-foothills-trails. Mokelumne Coast to Crest Trail, http://mc2ct.org.

Finding the trailhead: You can reach the Campo Seco Staging Area from CA 99 in Stockton by taking the Jackson/88/Waterloo Road exit. Drive east on CA 88 for nearly 20 miles, through Clements, to the intersection with CA 12. Go straight and proceed through the intersection on CA 12. Follow CA 12 for about 15 miles to a four-way stop in Valley Springs. Make a left at the four-way stop and go 1 block. Turn right onto Daphne Street (Daphne Street becomes Paloma Road). Drive 2.5 miles and turn left onto Campo Seco Road. Drive 0.7 mile to the Campo Seco Staging Area, on the right. Trailhead GPS: N38 13.308' / W120 49.852'

To find the Middle Bar Takeout parking lot from Valley Springs, stay on the above-mentioned Paloma Road clear to the hamlet of Paloma, where you turn left (north) on the Gwin Mine Road. This narrow, paved road drops rapidly down Rich Gulch, past the mine ruins, to Rich Gulch, where a very small parking area on the right marks where the MCCT crosses Gwin Mine Road (Rich Gulch Trail Access Point trailhead GPS: N38 17.145' / W120 45.446'), handy if you want to shave a couple miles off the hike. If going the entire distance, drive 1.25 miles farther, crossing the Mokelumne on the iron Middle Bar Bridge, and park in the lot on the north side. Middle Bar Trail Access parking GPS: N38 17.916' / W120 45.015'

Special considerations: Because trail markers demark the entire route, providing direction at every spur and fork, to list every junction in this hike description would be tedious and confusing.

Suffice it to say that the route on the ground is obvious. There is no potable water available along the trail. There are outhouses at Lawry Flat, the Lower Log Boom, and the Middle Bar Takeout parking area. You pass through many gates; if you find them closed, leave them closed behind you. Make sure that you have your permit before you arrive at the staging area. The trail closes at sunset.

The Hike

The Campo Seco Staging Area (about 740 feet elevation) lies near the head of Salt Gulch, down which our road descends on a mild gradient, between grassy hills dotted with oaks. After hitting bottom at 0.5 mile, we barely begin to rise up the other side when we arrive at Wildermuth House, one of the best-preserved stone houses of the Gold Country. A stone granary and other structures cluster about the grounds, at the heart of which stands the handsome house itself, built in 1861 of sandstone blocks quarried from a nearby hillside and shaped by hand with a stone adze. A stone wall encloses house and garden, with fruit trees, a grape arbor, and a large cactus. Our route was the main highway between Campo Seco and Paloma, headquarters of the booming Gwin Mine. Countless wagons, stages, freighters, and other travelers passed this way between the 1860s and the first decade of the twentieth century.

Continuing up the road through classic California pastoral scenery, we climb by gentle degrees to a large grassy valley, Lawry Flat. Just beyond the sturdy corral at the eastern side of the flats, we turn north and begin a mile's descent into McAfee Gulch. This ravine sports a healthy growth of chaparral, but an enterprising homesteader also cultivated an olive orchard here. We get some good views of Pardee Reservoir on the downhill stretch, where winter hikers should keep watch for bald eagles. At the bottom of McAfee, we briefly contour eastward above the lakeshore to Shad Gulch, where we cross a muddy seep and begin a gentle ascent via an intermittent tributary called Peon Gulch. Once again in rolling oak savannah, we pass an old kiln.

The 3-mile stretch of rolling road from the kiln to Gales Ridge passes through an idyllic countryside of pasture, chapparal, and oak woodland. After climbing to Gales Ridge, the sharp descent to Fletcher Gulch is a wake-up call that things are about to change. Climbing steeply out of Fletcher Gulch, our dirt road becomes a singletrack, our pastures turn to canyon walls, gray pines invade the oaks, and we cross from cowboy country to miners' hardscrabble. This is the canyon of the Mokelumne River, with the long, narrow arm of Pardee Reservoir far below, flooding the bottom of its V.

As we contour eastward on this well-engineered path, we gain some good views of conical Jackson Butte, a landmark hill near the town of Jackson up on Highway 49, a Mother Lode landmark. The most encompassing view of the reservoir is from Patti's Point, where we cross through a gate and begin what is by far the most attention-grabbing stretch of this trail, and indeed one of the best examples of trail building in the Sierra. Known to the volunteers who built it as "the longest mile," it was carved and cobbled into the steep canyon wall over a period of ten years and descends 550

Pardee Reservoir, as seen from the Mokelumne Coast to Crest Trail, enjoys a quiet dawn.

feet in elevation, in part on steps and in part on a trail bed of carefully stacked rocks. Bottoming out on a footbridge across Spanish Gulch, the trail makes a short hump around the next ridge and comes down to land at a pastoral cove alongside the fenced-off reservoir. Before the river was flooded, miners knew this area as James Bar. Just to the east, a log boom is stretched across the lake to catch debris washed down the Mokelumne River.

Around the corner on a doubletrack, we pass through a gate and cross the narrow, quiet, paved Gwin Mine Road to a small parking lot at Rich Gulch. The remains of the Gwin Mine lie hidden up the gulch. Acquired in the 1860s by US Senator William Gwin, the mine at its height of operations in 1903 kept a hundred-battery stamp mill working constantly, a racket that would have flooded this area with noise. Today, silence reigns supreme.

From Rich Gulch our singletrack winds up and down its final 2-mile stretch of woodland and chaparral, ridge and gulch, plunking down to the shaded flats of Jackass Gulch. At this junction the MCCT turns right, but we turn left to meet the Gwin Mine Road as it crosses the Mokelumne on the steel Middle Bar Bridge to the parking area on the north side of the river.

Miles and Directions

- **0.0** Campo Seco Staging Area.
- **0.6** Wildermuth House.
- **2.5** Lawry Flat corral (outhouse).
- **3.1** Olive orchard.

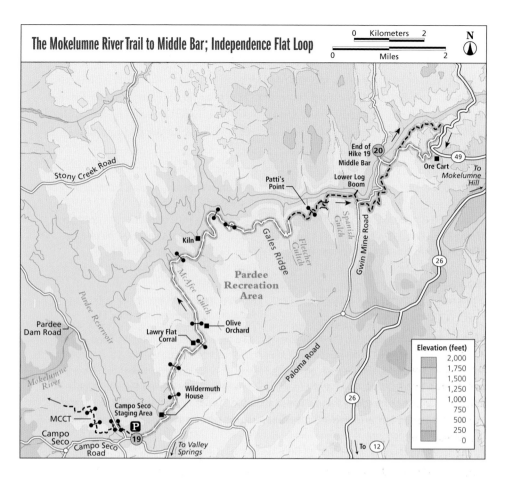

The Mokelumne River Trail to Middle Bar; Independence Flat Loop

4.1 McAfee Gulch.

5.1 Kiln.

8.1 Gales Ridge.

8.7 Fletcher Gulch.

8.9 Start of singletrack trail.

9.6 Patti's Point.

10.1 Spanish Gulch.

10.8 James Bar (outhouse).

11.0 Gwin Mine Road crossing.

12.3 Poorman's Gulch (footbridge and dirt road).

13.1 Junction with Independence Loop trail; turn left (west).

13.2 Middle Bar Bridge.

13.3 Middle Bar Trail Access parking (outhouse).

20 Independence Flat Loop

Starting where Hike 19 ends, this trail carries the next leg of the Mokelumne Coast to Crest Trail (MCCT) eastward, almost to Highway 49. A pretty ramble through woodland and rolling foothill rangeland, passing the lonely sites of many vanished gold miners' camps, this loop presents a shorter alternative to the previous hike, with no need for a shuttle.

Start: Middle Bar Takeout staging area, elevation 590 feet
Distance: 4.3 miles lollipop loop
Hiking time: About 2–3 hours
Trail condition: Excellent, sometimes very steep dirt road and superb singletrack trail, all well marked with signposts
Seasons: Early spring or fall are best. Summer is hot. Winter can be fine.

Difficulty: Moderate, with an ascent and descent of about 750 feet
Other trail users: Equestrians are permitted (except on the single track) but no bikes or dogs. Cattle graze along the trail.
Land status: East Bay Municipal Utilities District (EBMUD)
Nearest town: Mokelumne Hill
For more information, see Hike 19

Finding the trailhead: From CA 99 in Stockton, take the Jackson/88/Waterloo Road exit. Drive east on CA 88 for nearly 20 miles, through Clements, to the intersection with CA 12. Go straight and proceed through the intersection on CA 12. Follow CA 12 for about 15 miles to a four-way stop in Valley Springs. Make a left at the four-way stop and go 1 block. Turn right onto Daphne Street (Daphne Street becomes Paloma Road) and drive 7 miles to the hamlet of Paloma, where you turn left (north) on the Gwin Mine Road. This narrow, paved road drops rapidly down to the Mokelumne River, crossing on the iron Middle Bar Bridge, 2.3 miles from Paloma. Park in the lot on the north side. Middle Bar parking lot GPS: N38 17.916' / W120 45.015'

The Hike

Starting on the north side of the Mokelumne River at an elevation of around 650 feet, step down to paved Gwin Mine Road and walk across the old metal bridge. Cars are uncommon hereabouts, lending an almost folksy feel to the scene of bridge, river, and canyon. At the south end, turn left onto the dirt road beyond the gate, signing in your name and permit number at the board and walking just a jot farther to the first junction of our hike. This is where MCCT drops down from the hills on the west; we follow it straight as it begins its next climb east-bound. The flat ground around the junction, now lushly overgrown, is where the business end of Middle Bar once served as a supply hub for the local mines.

Although we initially follow the MCCT uphill on the dirt road, out of the trees and through a cattle gate, we are destined to leave it barely 300 feet beyond at another signed junction. Here, the MCCT heads right, up a very steep hill that happens to be our return route—but we go left, and soon find our doubletrack reduced to a singletrack trail.

Although the entire hike is full of pleasant scenery, the following 1.5-mile passage of woodsy singletrack pathway is the most pleasing of the entire trail. Partly following old ditches that carried water to the diggings, we climb easily though the trees on a hillside above the Mokelumne River, sometimes catching sight of the water, sometimes hearing it. We pass places with names, gulches mostly, but nothing to be seen to show that they were once populated neighborhoods of miners, clustered down-slope from the ridgetop settlement of Independence Flat, itself now only a ghost. Look for evidence of placer mining in the stacked rocks downstream of some of the gulches.

Reaching the end of our singletrack trail, we encounter another dirt road and a sign that strongly advises us not to proceed farther upstream to Big Bar, where Highway 49 crosses the Mokelumne River. The MCCT will one day continue up this canyon but has not yet been built. Consequently we follow the dirt road as it swings sharply right, climbing steadily and (judging by the sound of the cars above) parallel with Highway 49. At the top of the hill, at an elevation of 1,160 feet, we actually come to a locked gate set right on Highway 49. Beyond we can see an ore cart filled with rock and painted with the notice for south-bound travelers on Highway 49 that they just entered Calaveras County.

At this point we start back down the return of our loop. Although our dirt road cuts down through ground that is occasionally level enough to have once hosted the town of Independence "Flat," nothing around here is particularly flat, and in fact the road at one point drops so steeply that you will be glad for going down it rather than up. At the bottom of this hill, you will close the loop and find yourself on trail that you've already met. At that point it's an easy half-mile walk back to the car.

Miles and Directions

0.0 Middle Bar Staging Area. Start by crossing bridge.
0.1 Turn left (east) off Gwin Mine Road, through gate.
0.2 Junction with MCCT; go straight (east).
0.3 Cattle gate; go through and turn left.
0.4 Junction; go left to leave the MCCT.
0.5 Cattle gate; start singletrack trail.
0.7 Garavanta Gulch.
2.0 End singletrack trail at EBMUD gate; continue up road to right.
2.7 Cattle gate.
2.8 Site of Independence Flat.
3.0 Junction; note Highway 49 and the ore cart to the left, but turn right (west).
4.3 Arrive back at the Middle Bar Staging Area.

21 The Upper Natural Bridge of Calaveras County

One of the wonders of the Gold Country, this remarkable cave on Coyote Creek cuts clear through a limestone ridge, permitting people to swim or float through the heart of the rock.

Start: Natural Bridges parking area, on Parrotts Ferry Road

Distance: 2.0 miles out and back

Hiking time: About 1 hour, but allow more time to explore the cave

Difficulty: The trail is easy, but exploring the cave requires scrambling, wading, or swimming.

Trail condition: Wide, well-marked trail to the bridge; some steps. Watch for poison oak and rattlesnakes.

Seasons: All year. If you're swimming, pick a hot day, typically May–Sept.

Other trail users: Some visitors bring dogs.

Land status: New Melones Reservoir, Bureau of Reclamation, Department of the Interior

Nearest towns: Angels Camp, Colombia

Fees and permits: None

Map: USGS 7.5-minute quad: Columbia (**Note:** The trail is not marked.)

Trail contacts: New Melones Lake Recreation Area Office, 6850 Studhorse Flat Rd., Sonora, CA 95370; (209) 536-9094; www.recreation .gov

Finding the trailhead: From Angels Camp on Highway 49, drive nearly 5 miles east on CA 4 to the settlement of Vallecito. Turn right onto Parrotts Ferry Road. Drive nearly 4 miles southward (passing the turnoff to Moaning Caverns) and make a very tight right turn after the Natural Bridges sign into a small, signed parking area made from a section of the old highway. The trail starts at a narrow gate in the fence at an elevation of 1,500 feet. Trailhead GPS: N38 03.124' / W120 28 285'

The Hike

The extensive karst region of Calaveras County, in the Sierra foothills, is famed for its caves, of which the commercially operated Moaning Caverns lies close to our hike. Although highly celebrated among nineteenth-century tourists, the Natural Bridges today are visited mostly by locals, who enjoy their exquisite coolness on hot days.

Our red-earth footpath descends the east side of a ravine bedecked with wild oats, chamise, poison oak, gray pine, toyon, buckeye, and other shrubs and scrubby trees typical of the lower foothills. Crossing its intermittent creek on a wooden plank, we climb a couple of railroad ties to meet an old stagecoach spur road descending the opposite bank through chaparral and oak woodland toward the larger canyon of Coyote Creek. As we enter this larger canyon, the old road hooks sharply right, upstream, embanked upon well-fitted stone embankments. Through sparse foliage we can see Coyote Creek below us, alternately flowing and pooling in the gray bedrock at the canyon bottom.

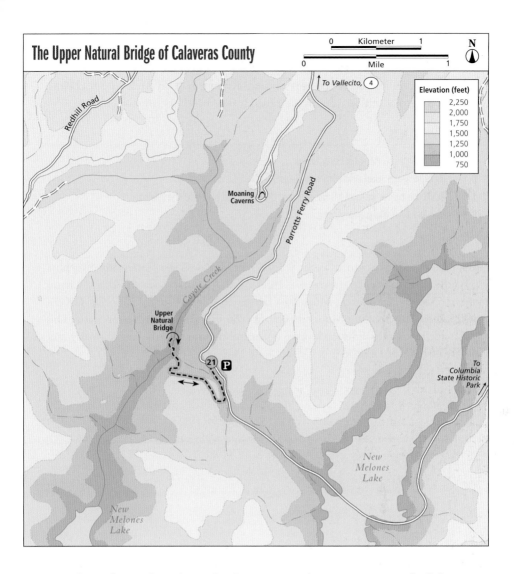

Where the track makes a hard turn onto the overgrown roof of the upper bridge—you'll know it by the stone monument and plaque—take the steep steps on the left down past some picnic tables to the downstream entrance of the upper cave, an enchanting limestone grotto framed by ferns and foliage. Curtains of water trickle like rain from the flowstone ceiling into the wide, cool pool of dark water. At the back of the cavern, Coyote Creek flows from the dark interior, where the water is much deeper. Springs trickle from the side of the cave. Swimmers who brave the initial cold shock of water can swim through that cave about 250 feet to the upstream entrance, an equilateral arch about 50 feet wide, with round-leafed ferns hanging sparsely from the sides and ceiling. Shallow pothole "bathtubs" in the smooth bedrock by the upper entrance are considerably warmer than the water in the cave.

This cave and its sister about a half mile downstream, the Lower Natural Bridge, were developed as tourist attractions in the 1880s by a man named L. A. Barnes, who lived in a cabin on the top of the upper bridge. Known as "Old Bach" (for bachelor), he gave names to all the features in the caves, as was the Victorian custom.

Miles and Directions

0.0   Parking area on Parrotts Ferry Road.
0.1   Meet old stage road and turn right (east).
1.0   Reach the upper natural bridge plaque; descend the steps to the grotto.
2.0   Arrive back at the parking area.

Local Attractions

If you prefer guided cave tours in the region, visit Mercer Caverns in nearby Murphys (209-728-2101; mercercaverns.com). Other nearby natural caves are Black Chasm National Natural Landmark, Moaning Caverns in Vallecito, and California Cavern State Historic Landmark in Mountain Ranch (866-762-2837; caverntours.com). This same company offers a different kind of underground tour into the operational Sutter Gold Mine in Sutter Creek.

22 Tuolumne Table Mountain

Travelers in the 1800s went out of their way to see it, as attested by the many references in travelogues and even fiction. When nineteenth-century miners cracked its geological mystery, they drove hundreds of tunnels beneath it. Bypassed by twentieth-century tourism, though still a magnet for twenty-first-century mining, Tuolumne County's Table Mountain is a remarkable sight that grows even more amazing when you know its story. Vernal pools and unique plant species make it even more fascinating to biologists.

Start: Shell Road, New Melones Reservoir
Distance: 2.7-mile lollipop loop
Hiking time: About 1 hour
Difficulty: Moderate, with an overall ascent and descent of about 680 feet
Trail condition: Mainly singletrack trail, though exploring the table-top involves some cross-country walking on open, level ground
Seasons: All year, weather permitting. Summer can be very hot.
Other trail users: Climbers practice on the wall. Some hikers bring dogs.
Land status: New Melones Reservoir, Bureau of Reclamation, Department of the Interior

Nearest town: Jamestown
Fees and permits: None
Maps: Tuolumne County Transport Council: online map of Table Mountain Trail (http://tuolumnecountytransportationcouncil.org/pdfs/map_table_mountain.pdf). USGS 7.5-minute quad: Jamestown.
Trail contacts: New Melones Lake Recreation Area Office, 6850 Studhorse Flat Rd., Sonora, CA 95370; (209) 536-9094; www.usbr.gov/mp/ccao/newmelones
Special considerations: Consider taking the guided walk offered by the New Melones Lake Recreation Area Office.

Finding the trailhead: From Highway 49 in Jamestown, drive north on Rawhide Road 2.2 miles, over Table Mountain, to the junction of Shell Road. Turn left onto Shell Road and drive 1.2 miles to the junction of Old Melones Dam Road, where you turn left to stay on Shell Road. Drive 0.5 mile to a closed gate. (GPS at closed gate: N37 56.632' / W120 27.727') From this point onward, unpaved Shell Road is very rough. If you are driving a low-clearance vehicle, or if the road is wet and you don't have four-wheel drive, park on the side of the paved road outside the gate and clear of the road. (Parking here will add another 1.8 miles onto your hike, out and back along the dirt road, or via the signposted trail that starts at this first gate. The road crosses private property but passage is permitted as long as you stay on the road or trail.)

If your car has high clearance and you are a patient, careful driver, open the gate, drive through, and close it behind you. You are now on private property. Drive 0.9 mile to a second gate with a cattle guard; close it behind you. You are now on land owned by the New Melones Lake Recreation Area. Slightly downhill stands an outhouse on the right. Our dirt trail starts at the sign on the left (east) side of the road. Park to one side of the road. Trailhead GPS: N37 55.926' / W120 27.739'

The Hike

The geological story of Table Mountain is fascinating, even if you don't give a hoot for geology. Table Mountain is the fossil of an ancient river, formed by lava pouring

Looking west from Table Mountain, hikers can see beyond New Melones Lake to Funk Hill, where Black Bart made his name, and lost his hanky.

out from a volcano near Sonora Pass. As the lava flowed down-country, it sought (like any other fluid substance) the lowest available channel—in this case, the channel of the ancestral Stanislaus River. Hardened in place, this flat-topped frozen river of solidified andesite still follows the ancient river channel as it winds across the lowlands of Tuolumne County. The softer rock around it has long since eroded, leaving Table Mountain's characteristic sheer-walled sides.

When geologists figured out this geological mystery, they realized that the ancient Stanislaus River (like the contemporary Stanislaus, now dammed as New Melones Lake) must contain rich, untouched gold placers in its riverbed, hidden under Table Mountain. The resulting rush to dig beneath the formation resulted in a few lucky strikes, like the nearby Rawhide Mine, but Table Mountain is huge, hard, and much wider than the ancient Stanislaus riverbed, reducing the odds that any random tunnel will hit pay dirt. Looking for golden needles under this gargantuan haystack has exhausted the capital of many mining companies, leaving most of the speculative treasure of the ancient Stanislaus River still untouched, locked in its bed hundreds of feet beneath the surface of Table Mountain. The Gold Country's largest operating

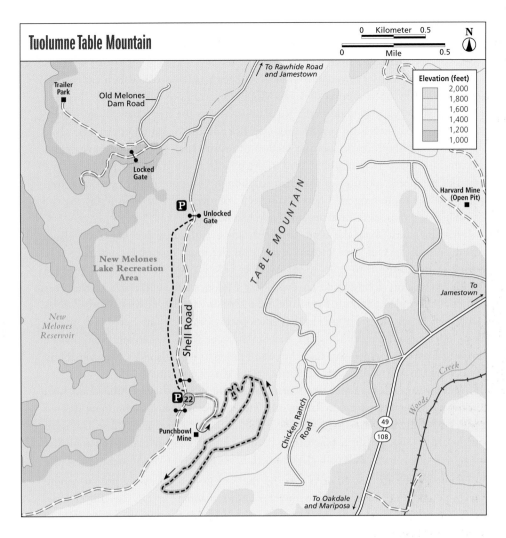

0   Kilometer   0.5

0   Mile   0.5

N

Elevation (feet)
2,000
1,800
1,600
1,400
1,200
1,000

To Rawhide Road
and Jamestown

Trailer
Park

Old Melones
Dam Road

Locked
Gate

Harvard Mine
(Open Pit)

P

Unlocked
Gate

TABLE MOUNTAIN

New Melones
Lake Recreation
Area

New
Melones
Reservoir

Shell Road

To
Jamestown

P 22

Punchbowl
Mine

Chicken Ranch Road

Woods   Creek

49

108

To Oakdale
and Mariposa

mine today is the Harvard, on Table Mountain. The Harvard dodged some risk and expense associated with classic tunneling by developing an open-pit mine.

Leaving vehicles on Shell Road, we walk up the rutty dirt track under some power poles to a junction marked by a flexible fiberglass column.

Detour: Before going left (northeast) to the top of Table Mountain, take a detour to the right (south) for a peek into two mining adits from the defunct Punchbowl Mine. A bushwhacking climber's trail pushes up beyond to the steep wall of Table Mountain, atop a shifting pile of talus boulders. It's an interesting perspective to look up to the cliffs where you shall shortly be standing.

Returning to the aforementioned junction: Our maintained trail pushes through chaparral and oak woodland, ducking under a flourishing clump of spice-bush. Then we begin an ascent of the steep, wooded, western face of Table Mountain on a trail sometimes lined with rock and sometimes cobbled into crude steps and some twenty-five tight switchbacks that grow tighter toward the top. The thick woods of oak, manzanita, and buckeye are picturesque.

Nearing the top, views open up over New Melones Reservoir. When we emerge on the broad, flat open summit of Table Mountain, take note where you are, because you will return via this same path. Note the fence to the left (north) and a house visible beyond, which is on private property. Keep in mind that another fence some 0.7 mile to the south marks another section of private land, so that our explorations are confined to this strip of public land in the middle. A use-trail wanders around the edges of the public portion of this plateau, though you don't really need it to find your way. The route suggested here is simple: a counterclockwise loop following the two edges and two fence lines around Table Mountain.

Heading south along the bluff, the west-facing cliffs are sheer. There are places where sections of cliff have broken away from the main mountain and hang as if poised to fall to the talus piles about 250 feet below. Climbers sometimes practice on the walls. Our views stretch far over New Melones Lake and north to the Bear Mountains. Strong updrafts roll up from the reservoir, carrying raptors. About 7 miles northwest, above the reservoir, history aficionados can pick out Funk Hill, where Black Bart carried out both his first and his last stage robberies. It was there that he dropped his hanky, which was traced to San Francisco by its laundry mark, enabling Wells Fargo to put paid to Bart's colorful career as a highwayman.

When you reach the fence that marks the southern boundary of public land, turn left (southeast) and cross to the other side. This east-facing bluff looks down upon a gentler ranching landscape, with the Red Hills in the near distance. Follow this edge northward to the northern fence line. Before cutting west to regain the trail that leads back down to Shell Road, glance north toward Jamestown for a glimpse of the open-pit Harvard Mine.

Miles and Directions

0.0 Shell Road.
0.2 Start of singletrack trail.
0.6 Top of Table Mountain.
2.7 Arrive back at Shell Road.

23 Red Hills Loop

The hard-bitten, scruffy, gain-forsaken landscapes of the Red Hills appeal to cooler-season hikers who can appreciate how their unique geology, vegetation and history have set them apart from the surrounding ranchlands.

Start: Red Hills Staging Area
Distance: 8.4-mile loop
Hiking time: About 4-5 hours
Difficulty: Moderate, with an overall elevation gain and loss of about 1,300 feet
Trail condition: Dirt road and rocky singletrack trail. Novice hikers who are uncomfortable walking trails that are not clearly marked may find the profusion of unmarked use-trails confusing. Be aware that many unmarked use-trails diverge only to rejoin the main path ahead. Stay oriented by relying on topographical clues and compass directions as well as the occasional junction signs, which are written on pipes hammered into the ground. A compass or GPS device will be helpful.
Seasons: Spring is best, especially during the Mar–Apr wildflower bloom. Birders may prefer winter, when bald eagles come to hunt and roost near Don Pedro Reservoir. Autumn

is pleasant, but avoid the scorching days of summer.
Other trail users: Equestrians and leashed dogs are welcome. Mountain bikers also use the trails.
Land status: Red Hills Area of Critical Environmental Concern (ACEC), BLM
Nearest towns: Chinese Camp has a store. Jamestown, Sonora, and Oakdale have more amenities.
Fees and permits: None
Maps: Tuolumne County Transport Council: online map of the Red Hills (http://tuolumne countytransportationcouncil.org/pdfs/Red Hills_map_complete.pdf). USGS 7.5-minute quad: Chinese Camp.
Trail contacts: BLM Mother Lode Field Office, 5152 Hillsdale Circle, El Dorado Hills, CA 95762; (916) 941-3101; www.blm.gov/ca/st/en/fo/folsom/redhills.html

Finding the trailhead: From downtown Sonora, drive 6.5 miles south on Highway 49 to Chinese Camp Road. Turn left (southeast) and drive 3.6 miles to the village of Chinese Camp. Turn right onto Red Hills Road and drive 3.6 miles south to the Red Hills Staging Area. Trailhead GPS: N37 50.288' / W120 28.158'

The Hike

Covered in chaparral, the Red Hills stand in stark contrast to the thriving ranchlands that surround them. From a distance they look to be upholstered in threadbare corduroy. The hills are composed of serpentine, the California state mineral, a rock (and soil) that is toxic to most plants, save for a few specially evolved species. Because of its inhospitable soil, the Red Hills have always been considered marginal land. To the Miwok they were desolate of the oaks and game that supplied their food. Gold miners found but paltry pickings here, leaving behind disgruntled names like Sixbit Gulch, Hungry Hill, and Poor Mans Gulch. Homesteaders found the prospects even worse. This is hard country.

The Red Hills therefore come down to us today as unclaimed federal land managed by the BLM. In the late twentieth century, the BLM established the 7,100-acre

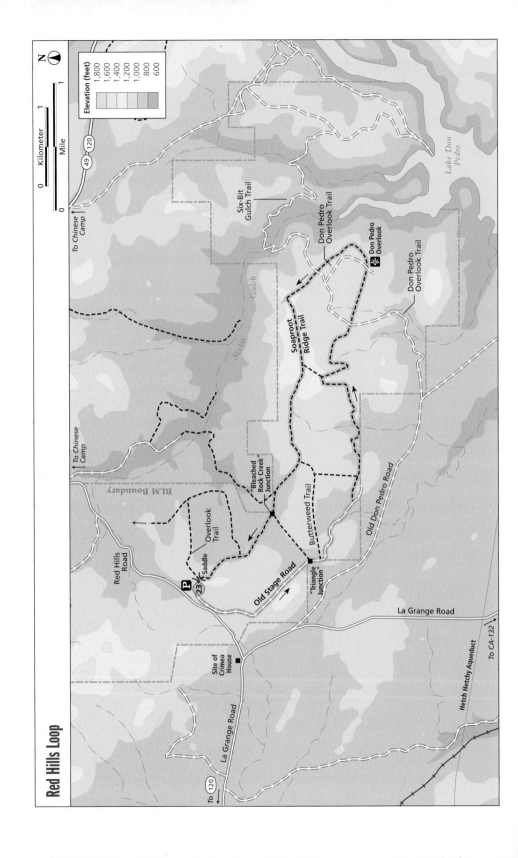

Red Hills Loop

Elevation (feet)
- 1,800
- 1,600
- 1,400
- 1,200
- 1,000
- 800
- 600

N

0   1   Kilometer
0   1   Mile

To Chinese Camp

49 120

To Chinese Camp

Red Hills Road

BLM Boundary

Saddle

P 23

Overlook Trail

Old Stage Road

"Bleached Rock Creek" Junction

Butterweed Trail

"Triangle Junction"

Old Don Pedro Road

Soaproot Ridge Trail

Six-Bit Gulch Trail

Sabir Gulch

Don Pedro Overlook Trail

Don Pedro Overlook

Don Pedro Overlook Trail

Lake Don Pedro

Site of Crimea House

La Grange Road

La Grange Road

Hetch Hetchy Aqueduct

To CA-132

To 120

Red Hills Management Area, a refuge for several unique and rare plants and animals. Volunteers have since developed more than 17 miles of trails. Our own route makes a loop by traveling east via the Old Stage Road and returning on the Soaproot Ridge Trail.

Starting from the signed trailhead on the south side of the Red Hills Road parking area, the Old Stage Road immediately meets a fork with the Soaproot Ridge Trail. Keep straight (south) on the Old Stage Road, which once carried passengers to La Grange and the San Joaquin Valley. Cresting a hill, the dirt track descends slightly to a fence line on the edge of the Red Hills, a distinct breach between the stark Red Hills and the scattered oak trees and

The Red Hills presents a stark aspect that only the most die-hard Sierra enthusiasts find beautiful, although it is noted for spring wildflower displays.

flourishing nonnative grasses that provide pasturage for livestock. Such pasture grasses and oaks do not thrive in serpentine soil, however, leaving the Red Hills a distinct stronghold of native grasses and shrubs and foothill pine.

Upon these fertile flatlands just beyond the hills stood the crossroads way station known as Crimea House, which burned in 1949. The vicinity is thought to be the site of a pitched battle between two parties of Cantonese miners in 1856, in which 900 men faced off against 1,200 protagonists, armed with guns and an assortment of pikes, spears, swords, tiger forks, and other weaponry forged locally to Chinese specifications. The fight was supposedly triggered by a mining accident involving rival parties at Two-Mile Bar, 10 miles west on the Stanislaus River, but it was almost certainly exacerbated by regional, ethnic, and political rivalries that were then rampant in the Pearl River Delta of Guangdong Province, the Cantonese homeland. The battle was well advertised, attracting curious crowds and rabble-rousers who egged them on. Before the law finally put a stop to it, four men were killed, four were wounded, and 250 were arrested.

The Old Stage Road turns east, jouncing down a typically dry ravine to what I call "Triangle Junction" on the map. The junction post lies just beyond three stout wooden fence posts that mark the corner of private property. At the junction sign, turn right to stay on the Old Stage road, walking uphill. Passing a signed junction with the Butterweed Trail, we reach the top of the next ridge at 1.5 miles.

From here the trail plows steadily eastward over stony ridge and dry ravine, sometimes on singletrack and sometimes on doubletrack. Despite the flurry of use-trails leading right and left, just keep pushing eastward, keeping right at two signed trails junctions (both of which lead north to the Soaproot Ridge Trail). At nearly 4 miles we meet a gravel road, labeled the Don Pedro Overlook Trail. Cross it and continue eastward on the dirt track. A half mile later we meet the same gravel road, the Don Pedro Overlook Trail, as it loops back to its namesake vista point. Cross this road again; the Soaproot Ridge Trail starts on the opposite (east) side.

Our trail (now the Soaproot Ridge Trail) contours northward along the rim of the flooded canyon where Sixbit Gulch joins the Tuolumne River. With views over Lake Don Pedro, some 550 feet below us, this is a good spot to look for bald eagles in winter. As it curves west, we meet a rough dirt road that drops steeply into Sixbit Gulch, marked by a signed junction. Stay on the Soaproot Ridge Trail, sticking to the ridge for the next 2 miles, and ignoring any spur trails that try to tempt us from our westward course.

As our trail descends from Soaproot Ridge into a valley, we meet a signed junction at a creek that drains into Sixbit Gulch. I call this junction "Bleached Rock Creek" on the map. Stay right on the Soaproot Ridge Trail, crossing the creek bed and skirting the edge of a relatively lush, fenced, privately owned meadow. Crossing through this stony, scrub-covered, and publicly owned part of this Sixbit Gulch, we mount a low saddle between two hills and drop back to the staging area.

Miles and Directions

0.0 Red Hills Staging Area (toilet).

0.1 Junction with Soaproot Ridge Trail; keep right (south).

1.2 "Triangle Junction" (GPS: N37 49.546' / W120 27.792'); follow Old Stage "road" right, uphill (south).

1.3 Signed junction with Butterweed Trail; go right (south).

1.5 Top of second ridge (GPS: N37 49.371' / W120 27.738').

2.4 Signed junction to Butterweed Trail; stay right on Old Stage Road (east).

3.2 Signed junction to Soaproot Ridge Trail; stay right on Old Stage Road (east).

3.9 First crossing of Don Pedro Overlook Trail (gravel road).

4.4 Second crossing of Don Pedro Overlook Trail.

4.5 Turn left (north) onto Soaproot Ridge Trail.

5.0 Signed junction with dirt road into Sixbit Gulch (GPS: N37 49.747' / W120 27.537'); go left (west).

6.0 Signed junction to Old Stage Road (GPS: N37 49.580' / W120 26.231'); stay right on Soaproot Ridge Trail (west).

6.8 Signed junction with Butterweed Trail (GPS: N37 49.539' / W120 26.992'); stay right on Soaproot Ridge Trail (northwest).

7.3 Junction at "Bleached Rock Creek" (GPS: N37 49.747' / W120 27.537'); keep right (north) on Soaproot Ridge Trail (northwest).

7.8 First junction with Overlook Trail loop; keep left (northwest).

8.0 Saddle above parking area. Second junction with the Overlook Trail; keep left (west).

8.4 Arrive back at the staging area.

24 Merced River Trail

Walking down the lower gorge of the wild Merced River, hikers along the abandoned Yosemite Valley Railroad bed can explore the remnants of a gold rush encampment clustered around the mouth of the North Fork.

Start: Railroad Flat Campground
Distance: 6.0 miles out and back
Hiking time: About 2–3 hours
Difficulty: Moderate, with virtually no elevation gain or loss
Trail condition: Good flat trail, though occasionally rocky
Seasons: Apr–June is best for wildflowers and water displays, though high water might prevent crossing of the Merced River's north fork (which is not necessary for the hike described here). Oct–Mar is pleasant, local weather conditions permitting. The hot days of July–Sept should be avoided, unless you plan for a dip.

Other trail users: Some hikers bring dogs, but bikes and horses are blocked by a gate.
Land status: BLM
Nearest town: Mariposa
Fees and permits: None for day trip. Campfire permit required for stove or campfire.
Maps: USGS 7.5-minute quads: Bear Valley, Buckhorn Peak
Trail contacts: BLM Mother Lode Field Office, Briceburg Visitor Center, Highway 140, Mariposa, CA 95338; (209) 379-9414; www.blm.gov/ca/st/en/fo/folsom/mercedriverrec.html

Finding the trailhead: This trail starts from the Railroad Flat Campground, on BLM land. To get there from Mariposa, drive about 12 miles north on CA 140 to Briceburg, at the bottom of the Merced River Canyon, where a fine stone building housing the Merced River Canyon Visitor Information Center stands on the left (west) side of the road. A sign adjacent to the building points down an unpaved road toward some campgrounds. Take that well-graded gravel road, which directly crosses the Merced River on a single-lane bridge and continues downstream on the north bank, passing McCabe Flat and Willow Placer Campgrounds before arriving at Railroad Flat Campground, 5.3 miles from CA 140. A gate blocks vehicular entry. Park on the side of the wide road clear of the gate. Trailhead GPS: N37 37.150' / W120 01.195'

The Hike

The Merced is the southernmost major river of California's Gold Country. The Merced Canyon below Briceburg reached its climax of commercial importance after 1907, when the Yosemite Valley Railroad completed a 78-mile line up the river's northern bank from Merced to El Portal, just below Yosemite Valley. Carrying mainly passengers and timber, the line closed in 1945, severing the lower canyon's material links with civilization. The Merced River Trail follows the old railroad bed for some 28 miles, from El Portal to Highway 49 near Bagby, and the Merced itself here is designated a National Wild and Scenic River.

Our section of the trail begins at the end of the public road at Railroad Flat Campground, at an elevation of about 1,050 feet. Beyond the gate we cross Halls

Merced River Trail

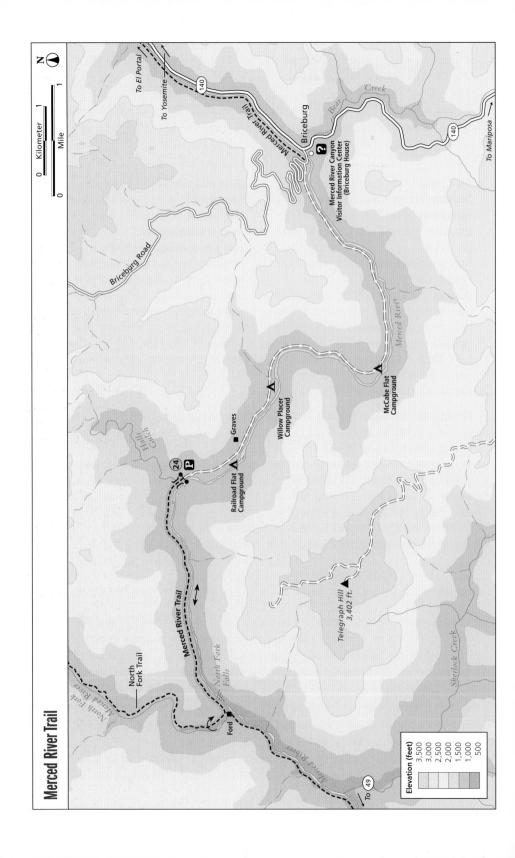

Gulch, a narrow creek, on a wooden bridge fitted with a metal gate that allows entry to hikers, though it's too narrow for horses or bicycles. We cross a stretch of private property with a house. Beyond, the old railroad bed becomes rockier, especially along a quarter-mile stretch where landslides force us to maneuver around boulders and step over some unsteady rocks.

At a depth of about 1,300 feet, the canyon harbors few large plants on its dry walls, aside from gray pines on the higher elevations. In spring I have seen these walls aflame with golden poppies, rolling upward along the river to heights 2,000 feet above, and more. Rocky bluffs sometimes echo the roar of the river, startling us with a stereophonic effect. The riverbed keeps a fairly consistent distance below our virtually level railroad bed.

Passing the wreckage of an old diversion dam, we notice the remains of rock walls and a flume on the opposite bank. As we approach the rapids known as North Fork Falls, we pass a portage frame built of galvanized pipes that stretch down to the river, allowing rafters to pull out before the wild water. The river roars briefly over and around a stack of boulders, sometimes too rough to run at that point, before resuming its steadier course below, where we find the second portage frame used to reenter the river.

Arriving at the North Fork of the Merced, we find the pier of the old railroad bridge, the trestle long since washed away. Our path swerves right, going up the canyon of the North Fork as it pours over its rocky bed. Watch out for poison oak. Along the banks are strewn the ruins of rock walls and ditches built by miners. The most intriguing is about 0.2 mile upstream, where the trail passes a large boulder that serves as a roof on an underground chamber, walled off in the front with rocks.

Options

If you don't mind sharing the canyon with the ghosts of California's history, there are many good camping sites along the banks of the North Fork, many of them well shaded with toyons, oaks, buckeyes, and pines. The confluence of the North Fork and the main stem of the Merced River makes a convenient base camp for further exploration of the region. You could try to trace the unmaintained North Fork Trail some 3 miles up the canyon to Shilling Road. If you can ford the North Fork, the Merced River Trail continues downstream toward Highway 49.

Miles and Directions

- **0.0** Railroad Flat Campground.
- **0.1** Halls Gulch.
- **2.6** North Fork Falls portage.
- **2.8** North Fork of the Merced River.
- **3.0** Ruins of old mining settlement.
- **6.0** Arrive back at the campground.

25 Hite Cove

Revered by the Miwok and later developed as Mariposa County's richest gold mine, historic Hite Cove today sits in splendid isolation along its lonesome trail. This out-and-back hike follows the wild South Fork of the Merced River through the rugged foothills below Yosemite.

Start: CA 140
Distance: 7.2 miles out and back
Hiking time: About 4 hours
Trail condition: Good, occasionally exposed singletrack trail. Watch for poison oak.
Seasons: The trail closes in summer and is open in seasons of low fire danger, typically Nov–May. This makes a good winter hike but is at its best when the flowers bloom in spring.
Other trail users: Dogs must be under firm control.
Difficulty: Moderate, with scant gain or loss in elevation

Land status: Mostly Sierra National Forest, though it starts and ends on private property
Nearest town: El Portal
Fees and permits: Overnight campers on national forest land must obtain a fire permit from the Mariposa Interagency Office
Maps: USGS 7.5-minute quads: Kinsley, El Portal
Trail contacts: Mariposa Interagency Visitor Center, 5158 Highway 140, Mariposa, CA 95338; (209) 966-7081; www.fs.usda.gov/main/sierra/home

Finding the trailhead: From downtown Mariposa, drive 22 miles north on CA 140 toward Yosemite, or about 11 miles west of the Arch Rock Entrance to Yosemite National Park. You will see a historical sign for Savage's Trading Post. Park on the north shoulder of the road, clear of the highway. Parking GPS: N37 39.269' / W119 53.263'. The trailhead is across the highway on private property, the site of Savage's Trading Post. Walk uphill to the left on the paved driveway, and turn right on the unpaved spur road, where a brown Forest Service sign points the way toward Hite Cove through a metal gate. Trailhead GPS: N37 39.271' / W119 53.236'

The Hike

Lower than Yosemite Valley, Hite Cove was a wintering ground for local Miwok people, who came and went via a historic trail that ran up the South Fork of the Merced River between the Yosemite region and the confluence of the Merced River's main fork and South Fork. Unaware of Yosemite, James Savage built his trading post at that river confluence in 1850, employing scores of native Miwok laborers to mine gold from Merced River placers. When the Miwok rebelled, killing miners and burning Savage's trading post, he retaliated with a state-sponsored militia known as the Mariposa Battalion. Led by "Major" Savage, the battalion pursued the Indians up the South Fork of the Merced and into the mountains, where they stumbled upon Yosemite Valley, thereby bringing it to the attention of a wider world.

Hite Cove itself, a small valley along the South Fork, proved to be the richest gold mine in Mariposa County. The mine owner, John Hite, built a small town on the site, complete with a twenty-stamp mill, hotel, suspension bridge, roads, and two saloons. Rusting machinery and stone walls mark the spot.

The South Fork Trail starts at an elevation of 1,450 feet, on the site of Savage's Trading Post, which today is private property marked NO TRESPASSING. In fact, the first 0.75 mile of this hike crosses private land. The Forest Service maintains a right-of-way along the trail, but keep moving and do not stray from the path. After passing around the metal vehicular gate at the trailhead sign, the singletrack trail climbs above the buildings past two water tanks. The path contours upstream above the eastern bank of the South Fork on the side of a very steep hill between 100 and 200 feet above the river. Though safe, the trail is exposed in places, occasionally cutting through rock outcroppings on rough steps. Other sections are built atop dry stone embankments. A parched but handsome chaparral covering of chamise, manzanita, buckeye, and canyon live oak softens the steep V-shaped cut of the gorge, interspersed with gray pine and laurel. The redbuds put on a magnificent Easter show on the lower Merced River, blooming with masses of magenta flowers. In autumn the turning leaves of the wild grape vines, alders, willows, and maples tint the canyon bottom with splashes of yellow. Also beautiful for its red fall colors is poison oak, which grows in patches along the trail.

Crossing a couple of seasonal creeklets within the first 2 miles, the trail descends to a sandy bar beside the river, following the water more closely for the next mile. At about 2.6 miles we pass a startling sight: an extraordinary rock ledge immediately between the trail and the river. The swirling patterns in the rock indicate its sedimentary origins, but it has been so bent and folded by metamorphic processes that it appears almost like a paisley print in black and white. The rocks along the bottom of the lower Merced canyons are the oldest in the Yosemite region.

Continuing along the shore, we watch the canyon ahead for the telltale sign of widening that might indicate a "cove," or valley. We know we are close when we enter thicker woods, encountering a broad, flat stretch of sandy ground. Some rusty pieces of mining equipment are laid out neatly on the left (north) side of the trail: large cone grinders, arrastras, and a broken Pelton wheel. Dating from 1899, these were used to grind up the tailings from the Hite Mine for extracting any overlooked bits of ore—the last hurrah of the Hite Cove mine. The crushed gravel is spread over a wide area.

As we walk farther, we begin to pass dry rock walls and building foundations, many thickly overgrown. Some are the remains of Hite Cove's Chinatown; Chinese comprised a large percentage of the workforce in many nineteenth-century mining communities of the American West.

Entering Hite Cove proper, we must cross a ragged ravine. Near the river lies the wreckage of the stamp mill, while above us the old hotel site is now occupied by a framed plywood shack—the private property of the current claim-holder. The grove of black locust trees at the far end of the cove was planted when the town was in full swing.

Hite Cove is full of stories. One says that John Hite found the gold vein in 1861. After nearly dying in an early snowstorm and being rescued by local Indians, he fell in

Hite Cove

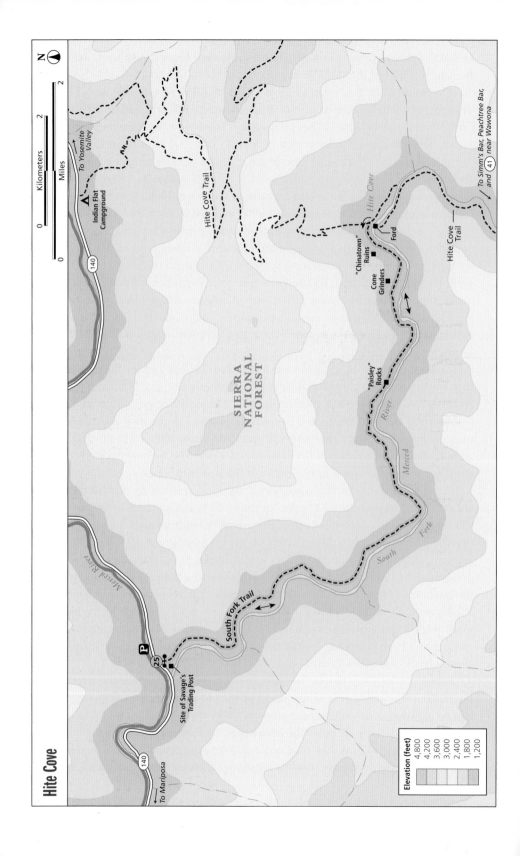

Elevation (feet)

4,800
4,200
3,600
3,000
2,400
1,800
1,200

love with his Miwok nurse, who led him to this valley. When she died, he married her sister, Lucy, and they set up home in Hite Cove. Hite's mine made him a millionaire, but he later abandoned Lucy and lost a big chunk of his wealth to divorce lawyers.

Another intriguing legend claims that Chief Tenaya's ashes were taken to Hite Cove after he was killed at Tenaya Lake by irate Mono warriors, whom his party had robbed of horses.

Miles and Directions

0.0 Highway 140 at site of Savage's Trading Post.

2.6 "Paisley" rocks.

3.3 Cone grinders.

3.6 "Downtown" Hite Cove.

7.2 Arrive back at the trailhead.

Honorable Mentions

⌄ Lake Camanche Trails

For some serious, snow-free winter hiking, Lake Camanche offers a 14.3-mile stretch of the Mokelumne Coast to Crest Trail (MCCT), connecting at Lake Pardee's Campo Seco Staging area with another 14.9-mile section of the MCCT, described in this book under Hikes 19 and 20. Taken all together or broken into shorter jaunts, the MCCT provides hiking options for any ambition, from easy stroll to ultra-marathon. This section of the MCCT passes through classic California oak woodlands, rolling hills, grassy oak savannah, and historic gold-mining sites. On Lake Camanche's north shore, the China Gulch Trail offers yet another Gold Country option, a 10.2-mile round-trip through open, rolling countryside redolent of old California, visiting now-vanished mining settlements of China Gulch and Lancha Plana. Hikers can opt to take a shorter 3-mile loop that starts from the same trailhead, the China Gulch Staging Area. The East Bay Municipal Utility District (East Bay MUD) requires a hiking permit for these trails. Obtain it online or from the East Bay MUD Moke-lumne Watershed Headquarters at 15083 Camanche Parkway South, Valley Springs, CA 95252 (GPS: N38 13.148' / W120 53.131'). Contact: (209) 772-8204; www .ebmud.com/recreation/trail-use-permit/sierra-foothills-trails.

The trails of Lake Comanche make for pleasant winter walking.

K Indian Grinding Rock State Park

Most people come to this small park to visit the excellent museum of Miwok culture and to see the reconstructed Miwok village and the colossal grinding rock. Less well known but well worth noting are its two short trails. The 0.5-mile South Trail is a self-guided nature walk that identifies the native plants that the Miwok used for food and other purposes. This trail offers probably the best introduction to native plant use in the Sierra Nevada, and will leave you with a surprising sense of how rich the foothill forests and meadows were (and are) as larders and storehouses for practical human use. Test your newfound knowledge on the 1.0-mile North Trail, and you'll find yourself looking at the profuse foliage with an entirely new eye. The park lies about midway between Pine Grove and Volcano on the Pine Grove–Volcano Road, just north of CA 88. Contact: Indian Grinding Rock State Park, 14881 Pine Grove–Volcano Rd., Pine Grove, CA 95665; (209) 296-7488; www.parks.ca.gov/default.asp?page_id=553. Indian Grinding Rock Museum GPS: N38 25.480' / W120 38.481'

L Knights Ferry

Famed for its sturdy covered bridge, the tiny gold rush settlement of Knights Ferry offers gentle walking along the banks of the Stanislaus River. Open now only for pedestrians, the massive bridge was built of heavy timbers in 1863, replacing an earlier span designed (as rumor has it) by temporary resident Ulysses S. Grant. At 330 feet, it is the longest wooden covered bridge in California. On the north bank stands the impressive ruins of a gristmill built in 1856. From there a dirt track above the river follows the shallow canyon upstream about 0.7 mile, whence you can walk down to the river and return on braided trails closer to the rocky shore. Another 0.4-mile trail starts on the south bank of the vehicular bridge across the Stanislaus and leads downstream, past prolific blackberry bushes to a cobble flat at Russian Rapid, across the river from Table Mountain. A stroll through the quiet streets of downtown Knights Ferry is also rewarding. For more information, visit the Stanislaus River Parks Information Center, adjacent to the covered bridge in Knight's Ferry; (209) 881-3203; www.spk.usace.army.mil/Locations/SacramentoDistrictParks/StanislausRiverParks .aspx. Headquarters GPS: N37 49.198' / W120 39.972'

M Columbia State Historic Park

The self-guided Karen Bakerville Smith Memorial Trail loops through a half mile of native woodland and meadow on the edge of Columbia State Historic Park, near the town cemetery and the picturesque two-story schoolhouse. The trail brochure gives insight into the life of the native Miwok people and the cataclysmic changes that the gold rush brought. Walk this trail as part of a larger stroll around Columbia, whose historic downtown streets are often closed to vehicular traffic, and whose state-preserved buildings are still operated as independent businesses. Combined with

The two-story Columbia Schoolhouse stands on a hill beside the Karen Bakerville Smith Memorial Trail.

the town, cemetery, schoolhouse, a mine tour, and mining displays of Matelot Gulch, the nature trail gives a deeper, richer understanding of the color, import, triumphs, and tragedy of gold rush history. Columbia can be a hauntingly beautiful place to walk in the quieter times of winter, spring, and especially fall, when the leaves turn. Contact: Columbia State Historic Park, 22708 Broadway, Columbia, CA 95310; (209) 588-9128; www.parks.ca.gov/default.asp?page_id=552. Smith Memorial Trailhead GPS: N38 02.283' / W120 23.881'

Around Lake Tahoe

S pectacularly deep and clear, Lake Tahoe fills a basin that dropped between two fault block ridges—the Sierra Crest on the west, and the Carson Range on the east—during the Sierra Nevada uplift, about 5 million years ago. Subsequent volcanic eruptions poured lava into the Truckee River Valley, forming a natural dam. The Truckee River has since cut partly through this dam and still drains the waters of Lake Tahoe into the Great Basin.

History threw Lake Tahoe into the path of American progress before the conservation movement had a chance to take root. Lumber from Tahoe's forests was being cut to supply the gold and silver settlements of western Nevada by the 1860s, when Mark Twain paid a visit. (Although awestruck by "the fairest picture the whole earth affords," he laid claim to his own "timber ranch" and promptly burned it down with an errant campfire.) The lake was opened to further development by ease of access to early trans-Sierra roads. By the late nineteenth century, when conservationists were beginning to champion the preservation of public lands farther south in the Sierra Nevada, much of Lake Tahoe was already in private hands. Despite more-stringent building regulations imposed in the twentieth century, much of the Lake Tahoe basin today is developed with homes and businesses. Lake Tahoe is the Sierra's most popular tourism destination, catering to a wide array of recreational interests, in both summer and winter.

Although haphazard planning, unsightly development, and heavy traffic have blighted the Tahoe Basin, public and private agencies are attempting to slow and even reverse some of the damage. California and Nevada made early efforts by preserving shoreline with Emerald Bay, D. L. Bliss, Sugar Pine Point, and Lake Tahoe State Parks. The USDA Forest Service more recently took the lead by establishing the Lake Tahoe Basin Management Unit (LTBMU). Created from parts of Tahoe, Eldorado, and Humboldt-Toiyabe National Forests, the LTBMU's primary mission is the preservation of Lake Tahoe, a departure from the traditional Forest Service mandate of balancing commercial and recreational uses of forests.

Tahoe is a great destination for day hikers who enjoy returning to urbane comforts after a day on the trail. Some of these day hikes serve well as backpack trips, or can be incorporated into longer journeys along the Tahoe Rim Trail, Western States Trail, Pacific Crest Trail, and Tahoe-Yosemite Trail. Because of their popularity, Tahoe's wilderness areas are among the most strictly controlled in the Sierra Nevada, especially the heavily used Desolation Wilderness, which has sign-in boards for day hikers, entrance quotas, and overnight user fees for some trails.

26 Glacier Lake

The high country of Nevada County is locally famous for its many lakes, of which Glacier is one of the prettiest and most remote.

Start: Grouse Ridge trailhead
Distance: 7.2 miles out and back
Hiking time: About 3-4 hours
Difficulty: Moderate, with about 1,300 feet of elevation lost and regained overall
Trail condition: Good singletrack trail
Seasons: June–Oct
Other trail users: Horses, bikes, and walkers with dogs all use the trail.
Land status: Grouse Lakes Vehicle Control Area, Tahoe National Forest

Nearest town: Nevada City
Fees and permits: No wilderness permit required. Campfire permit required if using a stove or campfire.
Maps: USGS 7.5-minute quad: English Mountain (**Note:** The trail is not entirely shown.)
Trail contacts: Tahoe National Forest, 15924 Highway 49, Camptonville, CA 95922; (530) 288-3231; www.fs.usda.gov/tahoe

Finding the trailhead: Drive to Bowman Lake Road on CA 20; the junction is 3.9 miles west of I-80 at Yuba Pass and 23 miles east of Highway 49 in Nevada City. Turn north onto Bowman Lake Road and drive 6.3 miles to the Grouse Ridge Road junction. Turn right (east) and drive 5 miles over this unpaved road to Grouse Ridge, then continue another 0.2 mile to the campground area. There, at a fork, a trailhead sign directs you left (north) another 0.1 mile to an unpaved parking area. Trailhead GPS: N39 23.469' / W120 36.534'

The Hike

From our trailhead on Grouse Ridge, at an elevation of about 7,400 feet, we enjoy unobstructed views of the high lakes basin at the headwaters of Canyon and Lake Creeks, tributaries of the South Yuba River. Below us lie Island, Feely, and Hidden Lakes, with the reddish cone of Fall Creek Mountain immediately behind them. On a clear day the 10,457-foot dome of Mount Lassen is visible 90 miles to the northwest. The distinctive Sierra Buttes (8,587 feet) punctuate the northern horizon at 14 miles.

A couple of use-trails head down the ridge toward the Forest Service bulletin board, where they merge into a singletrack near the boundary of the Grouse Lakes Vehicle Control Area. Descending through conifers, we enjoy excellent views to our right (east) of Downy Lake at the head of deep Granite Creek Canyon, and to our left (west) of Milk Lake.

Reaching the heavily forested floor of the basin, we bear right at the next three junctions, whereupon the trail begins a more varied eastward march through a mixture of meadows and woodland. The scenery grows more dramatic as we turn southward to face the volcanic plugs of the Black Buttes, especially when we clamber over a rocky outcrop. This is particularly true in October, when low-growing herbs turn bright red and the meadows of stunted willow turn yellow.

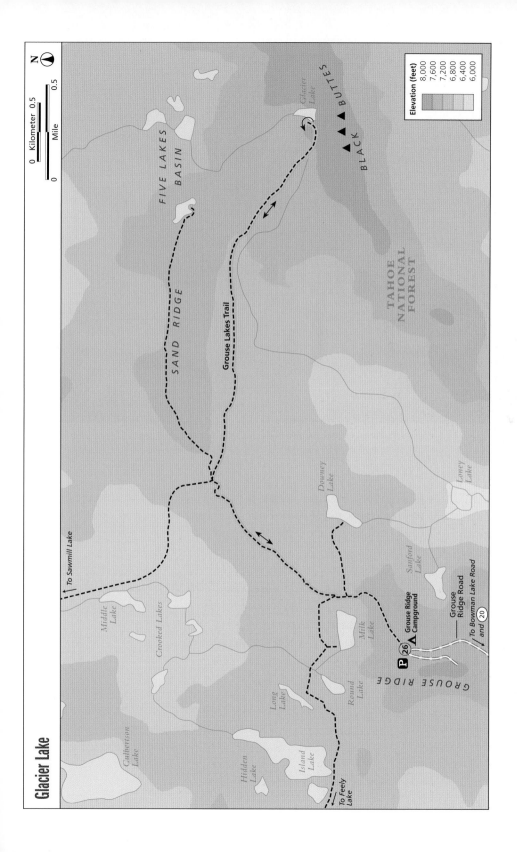

Glacier Lake

N

Elevation (feet)
8,000
7,600
7,200
6,800
6,400
6,000

0   Kilometer   0.5

0   Mile   0.5

Middle Lake

Culbertson Lake

Crooked Lakes

Hidden Lake

Island Lake

Long Lake

To Feely Lake

To Sawmill Lake

SAND RIDGE

FIVE LAKES BASIN

Glacier Lake

Grouse Lakes Trail

BLACK BUTTES

Round Lake

Milk Lake

P **26** ▲ Grouse Ridge Campground

GROUSE RIDGE

Grouse Ridge Road

To Bowman Lake Road and (20)

Sanford Lake

Downey Lake

Loney Lake

TAHOE NATIONAL FOREST

The trail to Glacier Lake enjoys some rousing views of Nevada County's high country lakes and canyons, and puts on a colorful display in fall.

The forest closes in again as we approach the lake, which lies in a deep cirque beneath the north-facing slope of Black Buttes, requiring a short drop down to the shore. Rocks and trees around the north shore provide shade and seating sufficient for a regimental picnic.

Miles and Directions

0.0 Parking area.

0.4 Downey Lake junction; bear left (north).

0.5 Junction with trail to Milk Lake; bear right (northeast).

1.4 Junction to Sawmill Lake; bear right (east).

1.5 Junction with Sand Ridge Trail; bear right (east).

3.6 Glacier Lake.

7.2 Arrive back at the parking area.

27 Loch Leven Lakes

A handy out-and-back day hike from hectic I-80, Loch Leven Lakes provide a dose of classic Sierra beauty—flowers, forest, granite, and water—without a lot of preparation or strain. For backpackers, the trail also connects with very ambitious routes into the wild American River backcountry.

Start: Loch Leven Lakes trailhead, near Big Bend Visitor Center
Distance: 5.6 miles out and back
Hiking time: About 4 hours
Difficulty: Moderate; elevation gain and loss of nearly 1,200 feet
Trail condition: Easy to follow, despite some ducked stretches near the beginning of the hike
Seasons: May through late Oct
Other trail users: Bikes, dogs under firm control (leash or voice), and equestrians are permitted.
Land status: Tahoe National Forest

Nearest towns: Truckee, though Cisco Grove has some basic services
Fees and permits: None for day trip. Fire and wilderness permits needed for overnighter.
Maps: USGS 7.5-minute quads: Cisco Grove, Soda Springs (*Note:* The current trail route is not accurately depicted on USGS quads.)
Trail contacts: Tahoe National Forest, Big Bend Visitor Center, 49685 Hampshire Rocks Rd. (old CA 40) near the Rainbow Lodge; (530) 426-3609. Tahoe National Forest, Nevada City Ranger District, 631 Coyote St., Nevada City, CA 95959; (530) 265-4531; www.fs.usda .gov/recmain/tahoe/recreation.

Finding the trailhead: The trailhead parking lot lies on the north side of Hampshire Rocks Road (also called Rainbow Road), a frontage road off I-80. Coming from the east, take the Big Bend exit (about 18 miles west of the Truckee Ranger District Station), drive under the freeway, and continue 1 mile west to the trailhead (0.2 mile farther to the Big Bend Visitor Center). Coming from the west, exit at Cisco Grove (about 52 miles from Auburn) and drive eastward 2 miles to the visitor center, then 0.2 mile farther to the trailhead. The parking area has an outhouse but no potable water. The trailhead lies on the south side of Rainbow Road, across the street and about 200 feet east of the trailhead parking area. Trailhead GPS: N39 18.553' / W120 30.963'

The Hike

From the signed trailhead, at an elevation of 5,800 feet, you start out on a rock-lined path over granite that leads 0.3 mile south to a junction. Turn left (east) and ascend the granite slabs, keeping track of your faint path by means of ducks and worn, gravelly tread. Profuse displays of early-season wildflowers somewhat compensate for the distracting roar of the freeway. Looking down-canyon you can also see the railroad grade.

After rounding a granite-rimmed pond, we descend slightly to a snowmelt creek, cross it on a wooden bridge, and scramble up the berm to the railroad bed, where we find two sets of tracks, a rack of signal lights, and a green water tank. Realigned and modernized, this is none other than the nation's first transcontinental railroad,

PUBLIC TRANSPORT AT LAKE TAHOE

The road around Lake Tahoe is narrow and busy, especially on the California side, and parking at trailheads during weekends in summer may be tricky. Consider using public transport, which is also useful for point-to-point hikes.

Serving the north side of Lake Tahoe, Tahoe Area Regional Transit (TART) runs shuttle buses from Truckee on Highway 80 down to Tahoe City, Squaw Valley and Crystal Bay. From there, another route runs along the north and west shore from Incline Village south to Sugar Pine Point. Visit TART at www.placer.ca.gov/works/tart/tart.htm.

North Lake Tahoe Water Shuttle offers a ride on the lake between four docks on the north shore. www.northlaketahoewatershuttle.com/lake-tahoe-water-shuttle

On the south shore, The South Lake Tahoe area's coordinated transit system includes South Shore fixed-route service, the seasonal Nifty 50 Trolley, seasonal ski shuttles and commuter bus service to Carson City and the Carson Valley. There is a line that goes from South Lake around the west side of the lake to the US Forest Service Visitor Center, Emerald Bay Vikingsholm parking lot, D.L. Bliss State Park, Meeks Bay, Sugar Pine Point and other stops in between there and the South Y Transit Center in South Lake Tahoe. Go to http://tahoetransportation.org/transit-and-shuttles/bluego.

South Tahoe Express, providing shuttle service between Reno-Tahoe International Airport and South Lake Tahoe Resorts. www.southtahoeexpress.com

driven eastward over this spot in 1867 by teams of mostly Chinese laborers directed by Charles Crocker. Freight and passenger trains speed past at all hours of day and night, so look before crossing to the other side.

Our path next climbs into a forest of fir trees, rising nearly 800 feet on switchbacks over the next 1.3 miles. Approaching the ridge, the trees thin out and the tight hairpins begin to slacken and roll with the terrain. As we round the granite ridgeline, scattered with boulders and solitary trees, we cross from the Yuba to the American River drainage, and catch our first view of Lower Loch Leven. Descending to its shore, at about 6,790 feet, you might well be satisfied to bide your time between its ample shade and sunny rocks.

The middle lake, an easy 0.4 mile ahead, is larger and prettier. To get there, continue along the Lower Loch's shore, taking the middle (south) fork at the Salmon Lake Trail junction and crossing Lower Loch Leven's outlet steam. Topping the next low ridge, you will find yourself nearing island-studded Middle Loch Leven.

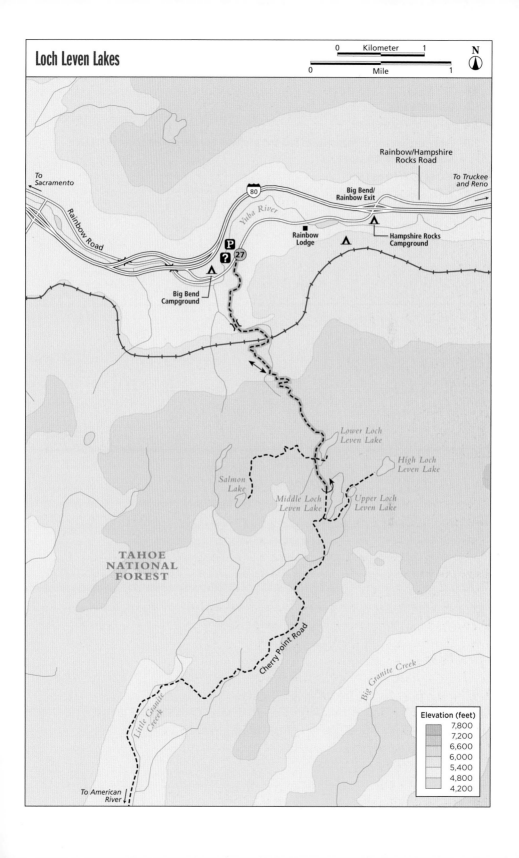

Loch Leven Lakes

To Sacramento

Rainbow Road

Yuba River

80

Big Bend/
Rainbow Exit

Rainbow/Hampshire
Rocks Road

To Truckee
and Reno

Rainbow
Lodge

Hampshire Rocks
Campground

P
? 27

Big Bend
Campground

Lower Loch
Leven Lake

High Loch
Leven Lake

Salmon
Lake

Middle Loch
Leven Lake

Upper Loch
Leven Lake

TAHOE
NATIONAL
FOREST

Cherry Point Road

Big Granite Creek

Little Granite Creek

To American
River

0   Kilometer   1

0   Mile   1

N

Elevation (feet)	
	7,800
	7,200
	6,600
	6,000
	5,400
	4,800
	4,200

Miles and Directions

0.0 Trailhead.

1.0 Railroad tracks.

2.4 Lower Loch Leven Lake.

2.5 Three-way junction of Salmon Lake Trail and unofficial use-trail around Lower Loch Leven; take the middle fork (south).

2.8 Middle Loch Leven Lake.

5.6 Arrive back at the trailhead.

28 Historic Donner Pass

There are more majestic and pristine Sierra passes, but none packs in more hands-on history with scenic views. Explore old pioneer roads, the original Lincoln Highway, and the celebrated summit tunnels and snowsheds of the First Transcontinental Railroad.

Start: Parking area near Lake Mary on Old Donner Pass Rd.
Distance: 4.2 miles out and back, easily shortened or extended to suit your preferences
Hiking time: About 4 hours
Difficulty: Easy
Trail condition: Varied: old roads, old railroad bed, wet tunnels, some rock scrambling. There are no trail signs to point out our route.
Seasons: Spring–Nov; some go in winter with snowshoes
Other trail users: Bikes, dogs
Land status: Tahoe National Forest
Nearest towns: Truckee, though Soda Springs has some basic services

Fees and permits: None
Maps: USGS 7.5-minute quads: Norden
Trail contacts: Tahoe National Forest, Truckee Ranger District, 10811 Stockrest Springs Rd., Truckee, CA 96161; (530) 587-3558; www.fs .usda.gov/tahoe
Note: Bring a flashlight for the tunnels if you dread stepping into puddles. Read more background information on Donner Pass, and consider joining an organized tour with the Donner Pass Historical Society, donnersummit historicalsociety.org.

Finding the trailhead: From Truckee, go to the west end of Donner Lake and take Donner Pass Road, also known as Donner Summit Road, up and over Donner Pass, after which you will take the first south (left) turn on to Sugar Bowl Road. Turn left at first chance onto Old Donner Pass Road, and park perpendicular to the shoulder on the north side of the road, across from Lake Mary.

From the west on I-80 near Donner Summit, take the Norden and Soda Springs exit on to Donner Summit Road, also known as Donner Pass Road. Drive east toward the pass. You will pass some ski areas; watch for Sugar Bowl. Turn south (right) on Sugar Bowl Road, and almost immediately left onto the one-lane Old Donner Pass Road. Park across the road from Lake Mary, perpendicular to the shoulder. Parking area GPS: N39 18.867' / W120 19.695'

The Hike

No other pass in California is more crucial to the nation, historically and presently, than Donner Pass. The main transcontinental freeway, I-80, funnels more cars into the state than any other route from the east. Following Native American routes, the first American pioneer wagons of the Stephens-Townsend-Murphy party crossed here in 1844. The pass acquired its infamous name two years later when the Donner party failed to cross before winter, and thirty-six died of cold and starvation on the eastern side before rescue came; survivors resorted to cannibalism of the dead. Although not the easiest

Cutting under the train tracks near Donner Pass, the underpass of the old Lincoln Highway frames the Rainbow Bridge on Highway 40, the road that replaced it.

of the Sierra passes, this pioneer route became the route of choice after the gold rush, when the northern Sierra became a national target of westward migration. The Big Four of the Central Pacific Railroad (Leland Stanford, Collis Huntington, Mark Hopkins, and Charles Crocker) and their chief engineer Theodore Judah, chose this pass for the First Continental Railroad, as the most logical to link their Sacramento-based business empires (and California) to the rest of the country. That precedent set, Donner Pass in 1913 became the target of the first transcontinental highway, the Lincoln Highway, which stretched more than 3,000 miles between San Francisco's Lincoln Park and Times Square, New York City. Beacons for the first transcontinental flight path were built in the pass. Highway 40 followed in 1926 and was the primary east–west roadway through the Sierra until it was supplanted by I-80 in 1964.

That massive freeway, I-80, funnels cars through the north side of this broad gap above Donner Lake at a point called Donner Summit (7,240 feet), leaving the earlier historical route through Donner Pass (7,056 feet) relatively quiet on the south side, along Highway 40. This is an important winter ski area, but in summer most visitors come to rock-climb or hike in search of history.

From the parking area, walk east on Old Donner Pass Road a couple hundred feet to where a dirt road meets the single lane of pavement. This dirt road is the old

Lincoln Highway. At this spot you will see signage for the Pacific Crest Trail (PCT), arriving from the south, yet another transport artery to make use of Donner Pass. Instead of taking the PCT, however, turn east onto a narrow, unmarked dirt path partially blocked by small boulders, which is the overgrown bed of both the old Lincoln Highway and earlier pioneer routes. As you walk down this old road, look for the sign that commemorates the first pioneer crossing.

Arriving at the high berm of the First Transcontinental Railroad, the old Lincoln Highway passes beneath it through an underpass, a landmark for your return. Just to the east of the underpass, the rail bed passes over the famous China Wall, a massive, 75-foot foundation of dry-stacked gravity-fixed boulders built by Chinese railroad workers in the 1860s to fill a ravine between Tunnels #7 and #8. From this spot you have a clear view just north to the "new" Donner Pass road and the famous Rainbow Bridge just below. Much farther, you can see the twin-barreled freeway of I-80 curving up the opposite canyon wall. In the valley below lies Donner Lake, delightfully blue but more grimly remembered as the bitter winter campsite of some of the Donner party. You will likely be able to see climbers on the surrounding rocks.

At this juncture—the underpass—you have three recommended spur routes for exploring this area before returning from here to your vehicle.

The first is to follow the old Lincoln Highway down to the rock slabs below the pass. Look for an old highway advertisement for the New Whitney Hotel, in Truckee, painted on the slab and surrounded by a circle of rocks. If you pick your own way over the slab down to Highway 40, you can see petrographs made by the earliest visitors.

The second option is to walk westward on the railroad bed, through Tunnel #7 to the eastern portal of Tunnel #6, the Summit Tunnel. Construction, mainly by Chinese crews working from both ends and outward from a vertical shaft in the middle, took two years. (Chinese crews reportedly left writing on the rock in that vertical shaft.) Completed in 1867, the 1,659-foot Summit Tunnel was the single most ambitious undertaking of the entire transcontinental railway. It served as the sole cross-Donner tunnel until 1925, when a 10,322-foot tunnel under Mount Judah—the Big Hole—was drilled a mile to the south for a second track. Trains then used both tunnels, one for each direction, until 1993, when the Big Hole was expanded, and the tracks through the Summit Tunnel were removed. On the north (right) side of the eastern portal, you can see the curve of the first pioneer highway across the pass, a toll route known as the Dutch Flat Donner Lake Wagon Road, built in 1864. To avoid holding up railroad construction eastward from Truckee while the Summit Tunnel was under construction, the Central Pacific in 1866 hauled four locomotives over this roadway to crews in Truckee. The first automobile to cross the pass also used this road in 1901.

The third option from the Lincoln Highway underpass is to walk eastward, over the China Wall and through the series of tunnels (#8 through #12) and snowsheds. The tunnels have rock walls. The massive snowsheds were originally built of wood, but the present ones are concrete, though a lot of the original stonework built by

Historic Donner Pass

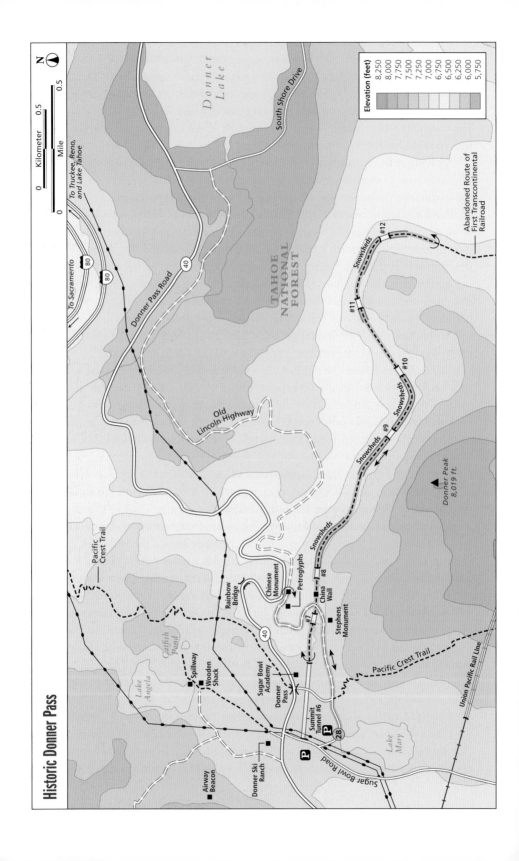

Chinese crews survives on the south wall, against Donner Peak. Periodic gaps in the snowsheds allow you to step out into the light for stupendous views over Donner Lake. Dripping water creates puddles and curious percussion noises, and the dungeon-like atmosphere is lightened considerably by the parties of weekend hikers (including many excited children) and the artistic graffiti on snowshed walls, which, despite being an abomination anywhere in the Sierra Nevada, in all honesty shows a higher degree of imagination than most. I can't deny that visitors seem to enjoy it.

Option

Supplied under "Miles and Directions" below are specific directions to the Catfish Pond, a very curious historical oddity. The difficulty in getting there is that this area has a maze of roads and unmarked use-trails, hence the need to take note of landmarks and use the map and a compass or GPS. Whether to even bother going there, a nondescript and unnamed pond, depends on your interest in the following story. The pond is home to a school of hungry catfish, who will come to the surface if you chum it with pieces of bread. They ought not be there, naturally, because catfish are a warm-water fish, yet here they survive at 7,200 feet, thriving in a pond that freezes over in winter. How they got there is the historical mystery. The most intriguing notion is that the Chinese railroad builders, encamped near Donner Pass for two years while building the Summit Tunnel, planted them to supplement their meals with fresh fish. If so, these catfish are living history, captive descendents of direct witnesses to the building of the First Transcontinental Railroad over Donner Pass.

Miles and Directions

- **0.0** Old Donner Pass Road parking (GPS: N39 18.867' / W120 19.695').
- **0.1** Junction at southbound PCT sign (GPS: N39 18.879' / W120 19.634'); turn left (east) onto unmarked Lincoln Highway between small boulders.
- **0.5** Underpass (GPS: N39 18.941' / W120 19.256'); walk through and down old Lincoln Highway.
- **0.6** Granite slabs below railroad line. Explore, then return to rail bed and walk west.
- **0.7** Eastern Portal of Summit Tunnel #6. Explore, then turn around and walk eastward on tracks.
- **0.8** Western Portal of Tunnel #8, near China Wall. Walk eastward through snowsheds.
- **1.2** Gap between tunnels #10 and #11.
- **1.8** End of tunnel #12 view point (GPS: N39 18.685' / W120 17.711'); turn around.
- **3.8** Return to old Lincoln Highway underpass.
- **4.2** Arrive back at the parking area.

Option to Catfish Pond

- **0.0** Old Donner Pass Road parking. Walk west on road.
- **0.2** Junction with Sugar Bowl Road; turn right.
- **0.3** Cross Donner Summit Road (Highway 40) and walk up Donner Ski Ranch driveway.

Hikers can't ignore the graffiti that covers the snow shed walls on the old Union Pacific line through Donner Pass.

0.5 Leave pavement under power lines (GPS: N39 19.128' / W120 19.738') and follow likely use-trail that leads overall (despite turns) in a direction of roughly 30 degrees toward Lake Angela's dam.

0.4 Spillway of Lake Angela (GPS: N39 19.337' / W120 19.545'); shoot compass bearing of roughly 80 degrees, start walking, and look for likely use-trail.

0.5 Catfish Pond (GPS: N39 19.360' / W120 19.413').

1.0 Arrive back at the parking area.

29 Tinker Knob

One of the most delightful, rewarding day-hike destinations in the Tahoe region, this high volcanic ridge between Donner Pass and Squaw Valley stands center stage to splendid views of the northern Sierra, Lake Tahoe, the mountains and high desert of western Nevada, and miles and miles of wide-open wildflower pastures.

Start: The former Squaw Valley Fire Station, now a maintenance building

Distance: 11.8 miles out and back

Hiking time: About 7–8 hours

Difficulty: Strenuous, with an overall elevation gain and loss of nearly 4,000 feet

Trail condition: Well-marked singletrack trail in good condition, except for the last scramble up Tinker Knob

Seasons: Late June through Oct

Other trail users: Equestrians and dogs under firm control (leash or voice). Bikes are not permitted on the Pacific Crest Trail (PCT).

Land status: Tahoe National Forest and land leased by the Squaw Valley Resort

Nearest towns: Tahoe City or Truckee

Fees and permits: None for day hikers. Campfire permit required for stove or fire.

Maps: Tom Harrison: *Lake Tahoe & Tahoe Rim Trail.* Trails Illustrated: *Lake Tahoe Basin.* USGS 7.5-minute quads: Tahoe City, Granite Chief.

Trail contacts: Tahoe National Forest, Truckee Ranger District, 10811 Stockrest Springs Rd., Truckee, CA 96161; (530) 587-3558; www.fs .usda.gov/tahoe

Finding the trailhead: For public transport, see sidebar on p. 136. If driving from I-80 in the north, take the South Lake Tahoe exit, west of Truckee, and drive 8.4 miles south on CA 89 to the entrance of Squaw Valley. From the south, drive from the South Lake Tahoe Y intersection nearly 27 miles on CA 89 to Tahoe City, where you turn left after the Truckee River Bridge and drive 5.6 miles to the Squaw Valley turnoff. The large parking area lies near the end of the road on the right (north) side of Squaw Valley, 2.3 miles west of the Squaw Valley entrance. Park near a maintenance building that used to be a firehouse (recognizable by its large fire-truck doors) on the right (north) side of lot. The trail starts exactly at the eastern wall of this defunct firehouse building. Trailhead GPS: N39 11.943' / W120 14.152'

The Hike

At an elevation of about 6,220 feet, the Granite Chief Trail starts up an embankment behind the former Squaw Valley fire station, breaking into several use-paths. Contour left (west) above the parking lot toward the head of Shirley Canyon, passing a ropes course and the Olympic Village Inn complex, before starting to rise on a dry, gravelly slope through Jeffrey pine, mule's ears, manzanita, thimbleberry, and red fir. We soon hear Squaw Creek splashing on our left; continue upstream on a course parallel to a small unnamed tributary that flows down from Silver Peak. After stepping across this tributary, look for an important junction marked by a sign nailed to a tree. The left-hand fork will cross Squaw Creek and continue upstream on the Shirley Lake Trail, but our route—the Granite Chief Trail—goes to the right (north).

A troop of backpackers heads south from Tinker Knob saddle.

Now we begin our 1,750-foot climb up the north wall of Shirley Canyon in earnest, recrossing the unnamed tributary creek twice and climbing gradually through alternating forests of pine, sunny montane chaparral, and dry flowery meadows. We can measure our vertical progress against the Squaw Valley cable car on the south side of the canyon. (Its upper terminus at High Camp sits at about 8,125 feet in elevation, only slightly higher than the ridge we are currently seeking to surmount, but well short of our final destination.)

The prettiest section of the Granite Chief Trail starts about midway up Shirley Canyon, where we emerge from woods into a steep hillside basin rife with mule's ears. After stepping across a lively creek that bisects this meadow, we climb a rocky path through waist-high shrubbery to a series of wildflower gardens that cling to the foot of a granite cliff. Surmounting to a sloping granite slab, our rock-lined trail meets and fords another unnamed creek, shaded by a stout pine. After a step-across ford, a handful of abrupt switchbacks carry us up the west bank of the creek (which in spring overflows its bed to flood the trail) and back into forest.

At just over 3 miles, the Granite Chief Trail hits the top of the ridge to meet the Pacific Crest Trail (PCT) amid forest. Turning right (north) onto the PCT, we soon spot Tinker Knob, the prominent tip at the distant end of the curving ridge on which we now stand. For a moment one hopes that the PCT will simply follow that ridge to the summit, but no such luck. Instead it dips some 400 feet down into the basin that drains Mountain Meadow Lake, well below the ridge on its western side, before climbing back up to the shoulder of Tinker Knob. Although this entails more work for the hiker, the apparent disadvantage is quickly dispelled by the magnificent views that open up along this rocky stretch. To the south rises the ridge defined by Granite Chief (9,006 feet) and knobby Needle Peak (8,971 feet), a north-facing slope that retains its enchantingly beautiful mantle of snow well into summer. The network of forested canyons and valleys below, to the west, give rise to the headwaters of the North Fork of the American River. To the north and east we are treated to a panoply of ranked palisades and fluted protuberances that indicate volcanic origins. One thing that map readers might expect to see, but which we hikers do not see, is Mountain Meadow Lake, the source of the North Fork of the American River. It lies concealed off-trail in woods on land owned by the University of California, which manages it as an ecological study area.

Before hitting the bottom of the basin, we pass the junction to Painted Rock, named such for the (probably Maidu) pictographs carved thereon. We stick to the PCT, which drops on switchbacks to Mountain Meadow Lake's outlet stream, a step-across ford in a willowy meadow, quickly followed by a second stream crossing, before beginning the ascent back up to the ridge. Splendid wildflower meadows watered by small seasonal creeks abound here, garlanded with evergreen copses and overwhelmingly dominated by furry mule's ears, that stalwart friend of all forgetful mountaineers. The dazzling views along here only improve as you assault the base of Tinker Knob on two large switchbacks, climbing to the saddle between Tinker Knob and Peak 8761, where the trail to Coldstream Canyon departs for Donner Lake. Even if you don't intend to finish the final stretch to the top of Tinker Knob, the vista here is worth the hike, with dazzling Lake Tahoe in the distance, framed by the sharp-spurred volcanic ridge.

For those who do want to finish the job right, Tinker Knob is that somewhat-forbidding, steep-walled volcanic vent on the left (west) of our trail. We pass first a wooden sign identifying it and then meet the use-trail junction to the top. To call it a

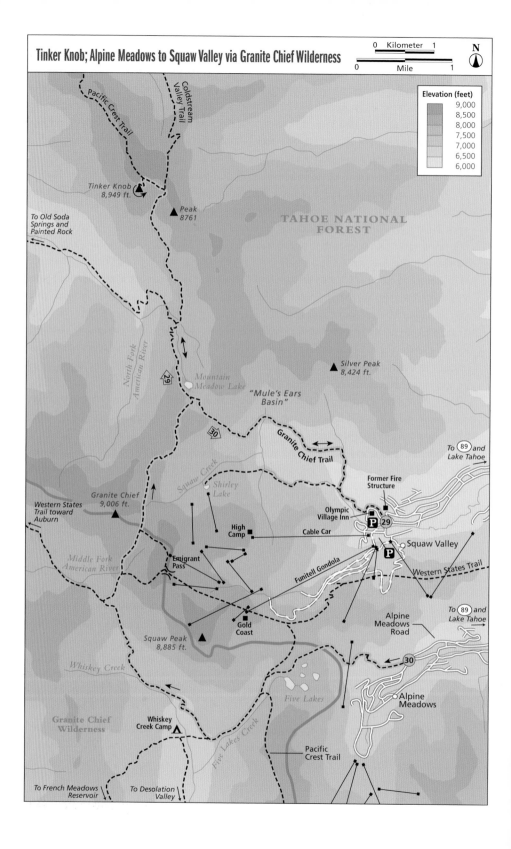

Tinker Knob; Alpine Meadows to Squaw Valley via Granite Chief Wilderness

0   Kilometer   1

0   Mile   1

N

Elevation (feet)
9,000
8,500
8,000
7,500
7,000
6,500
6,000

Pacific Crest Trail

Coldstream Valley Trail

Tinker Knob
8,949 ft.

Peak
8761

To Old Soda
Springs and
Painted Rock

TAHOE NATIONAL
FOREST

North Fork American River

29

Mountain
Meadow Lake

Silver Peak
8,424 ft.

"Mule's Ears
Basin"

30

Granite Chief Trail

To 89 and
Lake Tahoe

Squaw Creek

Shirley
Lake

Former Fire
Structure

Granite Chief
9,006 ft.

Olympic
Village Inn

29

Western States
Trail toward
Auburn

High
Camp

Cable Car

Squaw Valley

Middle Fork
American River

Emigrant
Pass

Funitell Gondola

P

Western States Trail

Gold
Coast

Alpine
Meadows
Road

To 89 and
Lake Tahoe

Squaw Peak
8,885 ft.

30

Whiskey Creek

Five Lakes

Alpine
Meadows

Granite Chief
Wilderness

Whiskey
Creek Camp

Five Lakes Creek

Pacific
Crest Trail

To French Meadows
Reservoir

To Desolation
Valley

trail is an exaggeration. This is a real climb up none-too-stable rocks, using both hands and feet. Although exposed to drop-offs that would render you very sore (or worse) if you slip, it is not a difficult climb for anyone who can remember how much fun it was scrambling up rocks as a kid. The reward of standing on its 8,949-foot summit is consequently greater for your effort—a 360-degree view that stretches eastward over the Truckee basin far into Nevada, and west into the gaping upper basin of the North Fork of the American River, flowing 5,500 feet below us, unseen, at the foot of prominent Snow Mountain. The star attraction to the southeast, of course, is the gigantic blue expanse of Lake Tahoe itself. Even farther south we can pick out peaks in the Carson and Crystal ranges, while to the north the Sierra Buttes are distinct. Closer at hand the PCT cuts a distinct gash along the ridge through the dry volcanic meadows toward Donner Pass, 7 miles north, and onward to Canada. Before leaving, sign the register and add a stone to the cairn.

Tinker Knob was named in honor of the red-veined schnozzle of A. J. Tinker, a blasphemous, hard-drinking teamster who used to drive freight between the old Central Pacific depot at Tinkers Station (now known as Soda Springs) and the mines of Foresthill Divide. His road passed through the wild basin of the American North Fork, below us to the west. I find it pleasant to think that this well-liked roughneck would find the North Fork country even less populated today than when he hauled his last payload through it a century and a half ago.

Miles and Directions

0.0 Former Squaw Valley fire station.

0.7 Junction of Granite Chief Trail and Shirley Lake Trail; turn right (north).

2.0 "Mule's ears basin" creek crossing.

3.0 Junction with PCT; turn right (north).

3.9 Junction with Painted Rock Trail; turn right (northeast).

4.0 Mountain Meadow Lake creek crossings.

5.5 Junction with Coldstream Valley Trail on Tinker Knob saddle; go left (northwest).

5.7 Junction of spur to Tinker Knob; turn left (southwest).

5.9 Summit of Tinker Knob.

11.8 Arrive back at the former fire station at Squaw Valley.

30 Alpine Meadows to Squaw Valley

Delving into the isolated headwaters canyon of the American River's middle fork, this ambitious day hike through the Granite Chief Wilderness offers alpine scenery, lofty views of Lake Tahoe, and forest solitude. With a campsite at Whiskey Creek, it also makes a good overnighter.

Start: Five Lakes Basin trailhead, Alpine Valley Road

Distance: 10.6 miles one-way shuttle

Hiking time: About 7 hours

Difficulty: With an overall gain of nearly 2,900 feet in elevation, and an even larger loss, this is a strenuous hike.

Trail condition: Well-marked singletrack

For more information, see Hike 29

Finding the trailhead: If driving from I-80 in the north, take the South Lake Tahoe exit, west of Truckee, and drive 10.2 miles south on CA 89 to the entrance of Squaw Valley. From the south, drive from the South Lake Tahoe Y intersection nearly 27 miles on CA 89 to Tahoe City, where you turn left after the Truckee River Bridge and drive 3.8 miles to the Alpine Meadows turnoff. The trailhead is 2.1 miles up Alpine Meadows Road, on the right (north). Alpine Road trailhead GPS: N39 10.755' / W120 13.778'

To find end of the trail in Squaw Valley, see "Finding the trailhead" in the Tinker Knob hike (Hike 29). Trailhead end GPS: N39 11.943' / W120 14.152'

The Hike

From a starting elevation of 6,350 feet, the trail to Five Lakes Basin departs steeply and steadily from the road, cutting westward up dry, south-facing slopes clothed alternately with chaparral and clumps of trees that are refreshingly cool on a hot day. After passing under a ski lift at 7,185 feet, we enter a more barren zone where granite hoodoos stick up sharply above the sandy slope that carries our trail across private land. On the ridge to the north, the ski lifts of Squaw Valley top out on the ridge, while views to the south take in the basin of the Alpine Valley Ski Resort. Crossing the boundary of Granite Chief, we enter the thicker forests of the Five Lakes Basin good and ready to see some of these lakes, but they are elusive. You'll catch glimpses of blue lake through the green trees on the left, but if you actually want to sit down and rest by one, you will have to take one of the side trails.

When you meet a junction with the PCT at the top of our first rise, ignore the northbound trail that goes to the high southern boundary of Squaw Valley. Our route follows the PCT left (southeast), following the drainage of the Five Lakes Basin downhill on well-graded switchbacks through increasingly open country, with views of a volcanic ridge to the south and of Squaw Peak to the north. Reaching a junction in the forest, a fork drops down to rejoin the creek at Whiskey Creek Camp, about 0.25 mile west, but we day hikers again stick with the PCT, taking the right (northern) fork.

Now comes a steep climb on a dry slope into the upper drainage of Whiskey Creek. We meet the young Whiskey Creek himself where our path levels out in a forest, a nice breather. Passing some nice campsites on flat ground, our respite quickly ends as we launch into the final steep climb to the heavily forested divide between Whiskey Creek and the headwaters of the Middle Fork of the American River.

Although our initial view of the Middle Fork's headwaters basin is concealed by forest, its historical heft should be noted before we take another step. This high and historic mountain basin once served as a major pioneer conduit into California on the Placer County Emigrant Road. Blazed in 1855, this route conducted travelers over the Sierra Crest from Squaw Valley in the Tahoe Basin over Emigrant Pass into the American River drainage, and thence to the Gold Country via the Foresthill Divide. The road is still there, but today it is a footpath known to hikers as the Western States Trail.

Our first marked junction with the Western States Trail pops up almost immediately after crossing the divide, with the westbound branch leading west toward Auburn, but we stick to the northbound PCT toward the Granite Chief saddle, crossing and recrossing the diminutive headwaters creek of the Middle Fork of the American River, gaining increasingly alpine views of the upper basin. Although Squaw Valley ski resort structures intrude upon the views, none can conceal the rocky saddle of historic Emigrant Pass on the eastern ridge. At least three trails (only one legitimate) descend from Emigrant Pass to meet the PCT; ignore them all and stick with the PCT clear to the top of 8,550-foot Granite Chief saddle, which marks the boundary of the Granite Chief Wilderness, whose namesake rises immediately to the west. This 9,006-foot mountain of granite has so far outlasted the forces of erosion that stripped the softer volcanic rock that once covered it. Granite Chief's saddle is part of the Great Western Divide, parting the waters of Squaw Creek, which flows into the Truckee, from the American River drainage.

Descending from Granite Chief saddle, we dip cross the headwaters of Squaw Creek and climb through forest to another high ridge, where we leave the PCT behind at a junction at an elevation of 8,000 feet. Turning right (east) on the Granite Chief Trail, we begin our great descent of the hike—1,750 in elevation lost down Shirley Canyon into Squaw Valley.

A set of short switchbacks through thick forest drops us on some granite slabs, which we cross on a stone-lined path through beautiful, rocky wildflower gardens set beneath a granite cliff. After stepping across a pretty creek, we traverse the loveliest section of Shirley Canyon through a steep hillside basin of mule's ears. Dropping gradually through an ever-changing panoply of forest, meadow, rock garden, and montane chaparral, we catch frequent sight of the Squaw Valley cable car as it passes to and from its upper terminus at High Camp. As the Squaw Valley parking lot grows closer, ignore the many use-trails that spring up from Squaw Creek, descending through gravelly terrain sporadically wooded with fir, pine, and montane chaparral. Passing a ropes course, the trail plunks us down at the former fire station in Squaw Valley.

Miles and Directions

0.0 Alpine Valley Road trailhead.

1.1 Pass under ski lift.

1.6 Enter Granite Chief Wilderness at Five Lakes Basin.

1.7 Unsigned junction to the lakes; keep right (southwest).

1.9 Junction with PCT; bear left (southwest) on northbound PCT.

2.9 Junction with trail to Whiskey Creek Camp; bear right (north) on PCT.

4.9 Junction with west-bound Western States (Tevis Cup) Trail; go right on northbound PCT.

5.3 Junction with east-bound Western States (Tevis Cup) Trail; go left on northbound PCT.

5.8 Granite Chief saddle.

7.6 Junction with trail to Squaw Valley. Leave PCT; turn right (east).

8.4 "Mule's ears basin" creek crossing.

9.9 Junction with Shirley Lake Trail; turn left (southeast).

10.6 Former Squaw Valley fire station.

Alpine Valley is famous for winter skiing, but makes way for hikers from late spring through fall.

31 The Ophir Creek Trail from Tahoe Meadows

Plunging steeply down from lush alpine meadows to Great Basin desert, Ophir Creek Canyon's barren, crumbling mountainsides, pungent sagebrush, nagging winds, and gulches choked with cottonwoods and aspens evoke a powerful, colorful, wonderful sense of old-time Washoe, as Nevada once was called. You could make an easier and absolutely lovely loop by staying entirely in Tahoe Meadows, of course, but the full descent to Upper Price Lake adds challenge, charm, and interest to this out-and-back lollipop-loop hike.

Start: Tahoe Meadows, on NV 431
Distance: 6.4-mile lollipop loop
Hiking time: About 3–4 hours
Difficulty: The elevation loss and gain of 1,400 feet makes a difficult hike. For easier options, just explore the boardwalk loops through Tahoe Meadows.
Trail condition: Good, though the trail below the meadow on the banks of Ophir Creek is overgrown for want of wear
Seasons: Usually open June–Oct; late Sept through early Oct is best for fall colors.
Other trail users: Bikes, equestrians, and dogs under firm control (leash or voice). The Tahoe

Rim Trail (TRT) in this section is closed to bikes on odd dates.
Land status: Humboldt-Toiyabe National Forest
Nearest town: Incline Village, Nevada
Fees and permits: Campfire permit required for fire or stove
Maps: Fine Edge Productions: *North Lake Tahoe Basin.* USGS 7.5-minute quads: Mt. Rose, Washoe City.
Trail contacts: Humboldt-Toiyabe National Forest, Carson Ranger District Office, 1536 S. Carson St., Carson City, NV 89701; (775) 882-2766; www.fs.usda.gov/htnf

Finding the trailhead: The trail starts on the south end of Tahoe Meadows, on the eastern side of NV 431, at an elevation of 8,550 feet. Park on either shoulder of the highway. From the junction of NV 28 and NV 431 in Incline Village, drive 6.8 miles north on the Mount Rose Highway (NV 431). From Reno, the trailhead is 18 miles south of the junction of US 395 and NV 431. Trailhead GPS: N39 18.059' / W119 55.181'

Note that the northern end of Tahoe Meadows has a large parking area and trailhead for Tahoe Meadows (northern trailhead GPS: N39 18.448' / W119 54.482'), with vault toilets. This lot is about 0.8 mile north of our trailhead, so add the extra distance if starting there.

The Hike

From the highway, a dirt road heads southeast through a lodgepole wood, with glimpses through the trees of Tahoe Meadows to the left. It looks inviting, but if you are going to Upper Price Lake, save the meadows for the return trip. We stay in the woods, following Ophir Creek Trail through the first two junctions (the first where Tahoe Rim Trail joins us from the north, and the second where it leaves us heading south). The Ophir Creek Trail—still a dirt road—cuts downhill through a forest logged more than a century past. Meeting a battery of signs, we learn that those logs were "floated to market" via a hair-raising logging flume (now gone) fed by Ophir Creek, sweeping down this precipitous canyon to the mill on the flats of Washoe Valley, a distance of some 4 miles in a drop of 3,000 feet. There they were milled for use in the mines at Virginia City, where no suitable timber grew. What a spectacular one-way downhill roller-coaster ride it must have been in that wooden flume! I wonder whether any foolhardy daredevil ever took that ride on the back of a log, as some dared to do in logging flumes on the west side of the Sierra.

Another sign takes note of Slide Mountain (9,700 feet), that crumbly-looking hulk to the north, looming above Ophir Creek's canyon. It takes its name from a propensity to shed both its rocks and winter snows in massive slides at inopportune moments, which we hope to avoid on this hike.

Dropping now steeply on our dirt road, passing up two junctions that lead back to Tahoe Meadows, take note of the lower one, the Lower Tahoe Meadows Loop, which we will take on our return trip. For now, we continue to drop until we swing down into a meadow near the banks of Ophir Creek itself, flowing through an embankment of shrubby willows. From here the trail grows less trodden as we follow the creek downstream. Hopping over a muddy trickle, we pass through a willow thicket and launch into another long, steep downhill session. We have some good views along this stretch. Four miles and nearly 3,000 feet below us, where our V-shaped canyon spills into wide Washoe Valley, we can see the waters of Washoe Lake. Beyond that rises the parched Virginia Range, where Virginia City and the fabulous Comstock Lode lie 13 miles due east from where we stand, on the far slopes of Mount Davidson, the high point on the ridge at 7,864 feet and the richest treasure mountain in American history.

Steady and steep, our trail crosses two more rills that feed into Ophir Creek, which flows unseen to the left (north) of the trail. We cross the largest tributary yet and arrive at a signed trail junction amid a thick grove of conifers. Take the left-hand fork to Upper Price Lake. Narrow and steep, the trail plunges in a beeline down to the water; it bears the hallmarks of a fishermen's trail, for an engineer would have used switchbacks on such a steep mountainside. As we drop, we hear and catch glimpses of Ophir Creek crashing down its ravine through the forest. The trees open further to reveal Upper Price Lake, surrounded by willows and aspens that turn yellow in autumn, and backed by the shattered, steep eastern face of Slide Mountain. Upper Price is an old reservoir. A large, flat boulder beside its outlet provides a fine picnic spot with views over the reflective little lake. There we can watch the quaking aspens shimmy in the breezes and listen to the outlet creek rushing through its narrow concrete canal. It is very peaceful.

To return, retrace your steps up the steep canyon trail to the Lower Meadow Loop junction, where we turn right (north), soon crossing a creeklet on large stepping stones. The trail climbs very gradually through aspens and conifers to the edge of Tahoe Meadows, the kind of pasture landscape that romantic bovines dream of while chewing their cud in a wintry paddock—acres and acres of juicy green grass watered

The Ophir Creek Trail from Tahoe Meadows

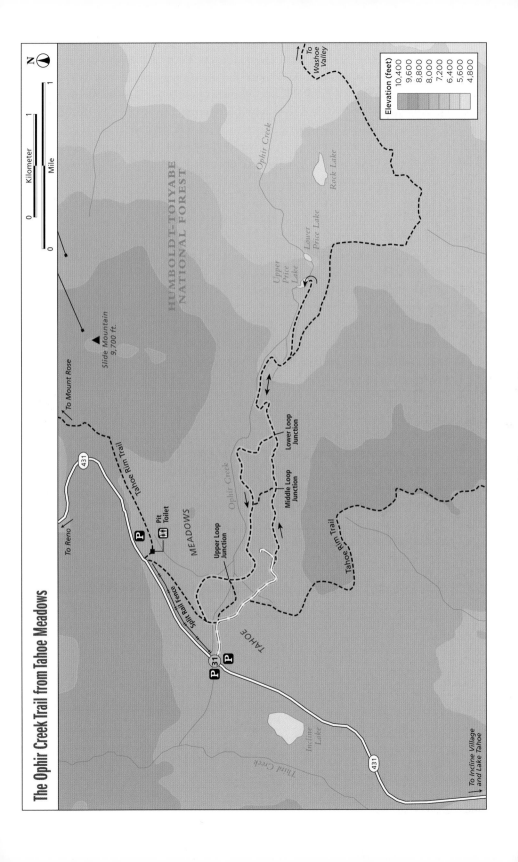

by a lackadaisical stream. Stay on the Lower Meadow Loop at the next two junctions. After the latter the trail pushes out into the often soggy meadow on wooden boardwalks to protect the fragile, pretty embankments from erosion. Raised above the little rills of newborn Ophir Creek, leisurely meandering, the boardwalks are, quite simply, delightful. Toddlers love them as much as older folk dependent on canes, for Tahoe Meadows is a gentle landscape easily reached from the trailhead, without that steep climb down to, and then back up from, Upper Price Lake. Tahoe Meadows is a worthy destination in its own right.

Miles and Directions

0.0 Trailhead south of Tahoe Meadows.

0.3 Junction with northbound TRT (aka Upper Meadow Loop); continue straight (east) on Ophir Creek Trail (OCT).

0.4 Junction with southbound TRT; bear left (southeast) on OCT.

0.5 Battery of signs.

0.6 Minor creek crossing.

1.2 Junction with Middle Meadow Loop; keep right (east), downhill.

1.5 Junction with Lower Meadow Loop; keep right (east), downhill.

1.9 Enter meadow near Ophir Creek.

2.4 Larger creek crossing.

2.5 Junction with Upper Price Lake Trail; bear left (east).

3.0 Arrive at Upper Price Lake. To return, retrace trail uphill to Lower Meadow Loop junction.

4.5 Lower Meadow Loop Junction; turn right on Lower Meadow Loop (north).

4.8 "Stepping stone creeklet."

5.3 Junction with Middle Meadow Loop; keep right.

5.8 Junction with upper Meadow Loop; keep right onto boardwalk.

6.1 Junction with TRT; turn left (south) to cross bridge across headwaters of Ophir Creek to junction with Ophir Creek Trail, where you turn right (west).

6.4 Arrive back at your parked car.

32 Meeks Bay to Crag Lake

This quiet backdoor entry to Desolation Wilderness receives far less traffic than the southern trailheads (like Emerald Bay), where the granite high country looms in plain view. This unhurried path along Meeks Creek, the start of the Tahoe–Yosemite Trail, builds to its climax by more leisurely degrees, padding through meadowland and deep forest for miles before reaching the first of its many beautiful lakes.

Start: CA 89 at Meeks Bay
Distance: 10.0 miles out and back
Hiking time: About 6 hours
Difficulty: Moderate, with an elevation gain of about 1,270 feet
Trail condition: Excellent well-graded trail
Seasons: May–Oct
Other trail users: Equestrians and dogs under firm control (leash or voice). Bikes are not permitted in the Desolation Wilderness but are common in the first 2 miles, outside the wilderness area.
Land status: Lake Tahoe Basin Management Unit (LTBMU); Desolation Wilderness
Nearest towns: South Lake Tahoe or Tahoe City
Fees and permits: Permit required if you enter Desolation Wilderness, even for day hikes. Day users can self-register at the trailhead. Overnight users obtain permits (fee) at the Taylor Creek Visitor Center or LTBMU office.
Maps: Fine Edge Productions: *South Lake Tahoe Basin*. USGS 7.5-minute quads: Meeks Bay, Homewood, Rockbound Valley.
Trail contacts: Taylor Creek Visitor Center (open Memorial Day–October), on CA 89 about 3.2 miles north of its junction with US 50 (the South Lake Tahoe Y intersection); (530) 543-2674; www.fs.usda.gov/recarea/ltbmu/recarea/?recid=11785. Lake Tahoe Basin Management Unit, 35 College Dr., South Lake Tahoe, CA 96150-4500; (530) 543-2600; www.fs.fed.us/r5/ltbmu/contact.

Finding the trailhead: The Meeks Bay parking area is on CA 89, about 16 miles north of the South Lake Tahoe Y intersection, or 11 miles south of the Truckee River Bridge in Tahoe City, on the west side. Park on the dirt shoulder, well off the road. The trailhead is on the north side of the parking area, beside a log cabin. Fill out your permit at the trailhead before leaving. Trailhead GPS: N39 02.241' / W120 07.594'

The Hike

From the sign-in board in the broad valley of Meeks Creek (elevation 6,250 feet), walk through the gate and along a flat dirt road edged by meadows on one side and conifer forest on the other, both shoulders rife with chinquapin, bitterbrush, Indian cornflower, bracken, willow, alder, and seasonal wildflowers. Across the meadows the symmetrical northern face of Rubicon Peak rises to 9,183 feet.

After 1.3 miles of easy strolling, the road veers left at a junction signpost, while we take the dusty singletrack footpath (the Tahoe–Yosemite Trail) uphill to the right. As we climb through mixed woods of pine and fir, refreshed by the sounds of splashing Meeks Creek, backward glances eventually reward us with glimpses of Lake Tahoe as

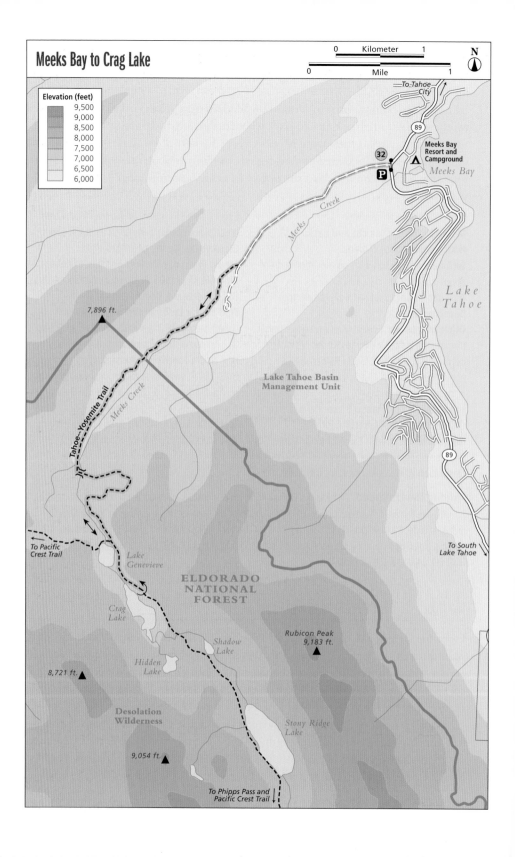

Meeks Bay to Crag Lake

0   Kilometer   1

0   Mile   1

N

Elevation (feet)
9,500
9,000
8,500
8,000
7,500
7,000
6,500
6,000

To Tahoe City

89

Meeks Bay Resort and Campground

32

P

Meeks Bay

Lake Tahoe

Meeks Creek

Lake Tahoe Basin Management Unit

7,896 ft.

Tahoe–Yosemite Trail

Meeks Creek

89

To Pacific Crest Trail

To South Lake Tahoe

Lake Genevieve

ELDORADO NATIONAL FOREST

Crag Lake

Shadow Lake

Rubicon Peak
9,183 ft.

8,721 ft.

Hidden Lake

Desolation Wilderness

Stony Ridge Lake

9,054 ft.

To Phipps Pass and Pacific Crest Trail

we top the rocky rise at a little over 2 miles. Leveling out on the north bank of Meeks Creek, we plod comfortably onward over alternating level and uphill gradients, passing the signposted boundary of Desolation Wilderness at 2.4 miles. Another mile of easy walking through heavy forest cover brings us to a wooden bridge that crosses Meeks Creek.

Now our path makes a sharp turn eastward, rising on sunny slopes above the granite-walled basin, where creeks tumble unseen but loudly heard. Entering dense forest again, we climb first to the outlet creek and then the shady shoreline of Lake Genevieve, whose waters reflect two prominent unnamed mountains, the farther slightly over 9,000 feet. From a signposted junction on the shore, the poorly maintained General Creek Trail splits off to the right (west) across a logjam at the lake's outlet, but we continue south, following the forested shoreline of Lake Genevieve. There are many fine picnic spots along Genevieve's shore, but even prettier sites abound just 0.3 mile ahead, where Crag Lake's outlet stream comes rushing out, framed by conifers against rugged mountains. Backpackers will find many fine campsites nearby.

Options

Immediately south from Crag Lake, the Tahoe-Yosemite Trail passes Shadow, Stony Ridge, and Rubicon Lakes on its way over Phipps Pass to the Rubicon River watershed, the heart of Desolation Wilderness. Continuing to Yosemite is a 175-mile possibility, but there are many splendid loop trips closer at hand. With connections to the Pacific Crest Trail (PCT), hiking opportunities from this trailhead are unlimited.

Miles and Directions

0.0   Meeks Bay parking area.

1.3   Junction of dirt road and Tahoe-Yosemite Trail; bear right (west).

2.4   Desolation Wilderness boundary.

3.4   Wooden bridge over Meeks Creek.

4.7   Lake Genevieve.

5.0   Crag Lake.

10.0   Arrive back at the parking area.

33 Rubicon Trail from Emerald Bay to Lester Beach

Lake Tahoe's span of brilliant-blue hues ranges from green-turquoise near the shore to a deepwater blue of such intensity that the sky pales in comparison. This panoramic hike to a historic mansion on Emerald Bay is the finest footpath of its length along Lake Tahoe's California shoreline.

Start: Vikingsholm parking area on CA 89 above Emerald Bay
Distance: 5.0 miles one-way to Lester Beach in D. L. Bliss State Park, or 10.0 miles out and back. Consider taking public transport.
Hiking time: About 3 hours one-way
Difficulty: A fairly relaxed hike
Trail condition: Excellent singletrack trail
Seasons: May through mid-Nov
Other trail users: No dogs, equestrians, or bikes allowed
Land status: D. L. Bliss and Emerald Bay State Parks
Nearest towns: South Lake Tahoe or Tahoe City

Fees and permits: Motorists are charged a day-use fee at D. L. Bliss State Park.
Maps: Fine Edge Productions: *South Lake Tahoe Basin*. Tom Harrison: *Lake Tahoe*. USGS 7.5-minute quad: Emerald Bay.
Trail contacts: Emerald Bay State Park; (530) 541-3030; www.parks.ca.gov/?page_id=506. D. L. Bliss State Park Visitor Center; (530) 525-7277; www.parks.ca.gov/?page_id=505. Taylor Creek Visitor Center (open Memorial Day – Oct), on CA 89 about 3.2 miles north of its junction with US 50 (the South Lake Tahoe Y intersection); (530) 543-2674; www.fs.usda .gov/recarea/ltbmu/recarea/?recid=11785.

Finding the trailhead: You can hike the Rubicon Trail in either direction, but by starting at Vikingsholm parking area and hiking north to end at Lester Beach, you avoid a steep uphill climb at the end. The Vikingsholm parking area is on CA 89, about 8.8 miles north of the South Lake Tahoe Y intersection, and about 18.8 miles south of the Truckee River Bridge in Tahoe City, on the east side of the road. Vikingsholm trailhead GPS: N38 57.261' / W120 06.605'

To reach the end trailhead at Lester Beach, drive to the D. L. Bliss State Park entrance on CA 89, nearly 2.5 miles north of the Vikingsholm parking area, on the right. Pass the visitor center and continue downhill on the paved road to the entry station, where you pay the day-use fee. At a stop sign 2 miles from CA 89, turn right and drive 0.3 mile to the end of the road above Lester Beach. Arrive early because the small parking lot fills up fast. Ending trailhead GPS: N38 59.916' / W120 05.848'

The Hike

Our trailhead served as the top of the driveway to Vikingsholm, a Viking-inspired "castle" built in 1929 on the shore of Emerald Bay by wealthy doyenne of the National Biscuit Corporation, Lora Josephine Knight. The driveway is closed to public vehicles. From the rocky overlooks adjacent to the trailhead, 400 vertical feet above Lake Tahoe, plenty of nonhikers gather to enjoy the dramatic views over Emerald Bay and up the granite canyon of Eagle Creek into the mountains of Desolation Wilderness. Fewer—but still many—walk down that steep, narrow lane to see the

Tahoe's famous blue hue really shows from the Rubicon Trail.

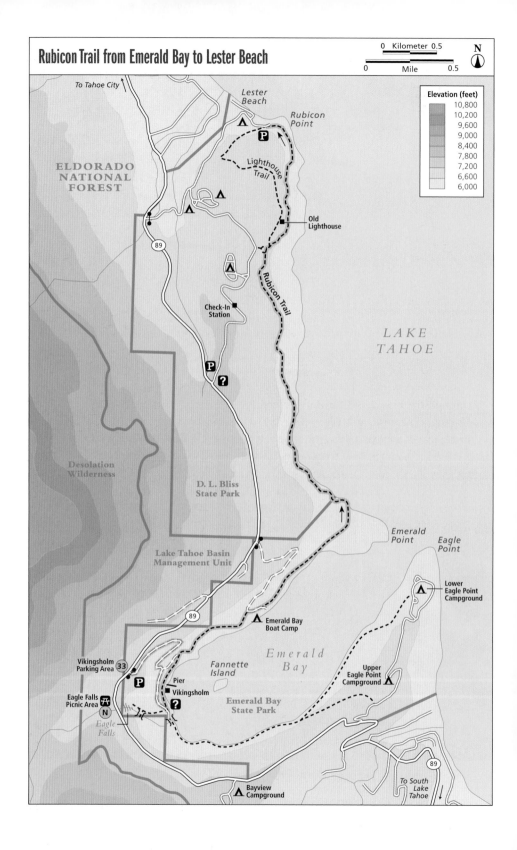

Rubicon Trail from Emerald Bay to Lester Beach

To Tahoe City

Lester Beach

Rubicon Point

0 Kilometer 0.5

0 Mile 0.5

N

Elevation (feet)

10,800
10,200
9,600
9,000
8,400
7,800
7,200
6,600
6,000

ELDORADO NATIONAL FOREST

Lighthouse Trail

Old Lighthouse

89

Rubicon Trail

Check-In Station

P

?

LAKE TAHOE

Desolation Wilderness

D. L. Bliss State Park

Lake Tahoe Basin Management Unit

Emerald Point

Eagle Point

Lower Eagle Point Campground

89

Emerald Bay Boat Camp

Vikingsholm Parking Area

33

P

Pier

Vikingsholm

?

Fannette Island

Emerald Bay

Upper Eagle Point Campground

Eagle Falls Picnic Area

N

Eagle Falls

Emerald Bay State Park

Bayview Campground

To South Lake Tahoe

89

castle. Embanked with solid stone walls, this steep lane to Vikingsholm bends through three hairpin turns amid piney scents and the refreshing splash of little streams that dash down the slope.

Leveling near the bottom amid large cedars and pines, we pass a gardener's cottage and other outbuildings before hauling up at the courtyard entrance of Vikingsholm itself. Mrs. Knight employed a crew of 200 workmen to fashion this timber and stone mansion, largely by hand. She used it for a summer home. During summer you can tour the house, but even if you don't go inside, take a moment to wander around the grounds and building, look into the courtyard, and admire the hand-hewn timbers, dragon roof ridges, hand-planed wall boards, and even the hardware, forged on-site. The house faces the beach on Emerald Bay, where a dock points out to Fannette Island. There, Mrs. Knight kept a stone teahouse, visible from many points on our route.

Continuing our hike, the Rubicon Trail hugs the shore of Emerald Bay around to the left (north), passing the boaters' camp (water and toilets). Look back frequently, as the granite backdrop of Desolation Wilderness rises into view over fjord-like Emerald Bay, presenting an enchanting picture of blue waters, green forests, and the white streak of Eagle Falls. A passing parade of small boats enters the bay to pay homage, including sightseeing stern-wheelers.

Turning north at Rubicon Point, our trail climbs to slopes higher above Lake Tahoe through forest so thick that the great lake is reduced to slivers of blue glimpsed through the branches. Our duff-hushed footfalls are disturbed only by the *ch-ch-ch-* chiding of inquisitive Steller's jays. As we pass through patches of mixed chaparral, our lake views expand. Pesky motorboats zoom by offshore and quiet kayakers probe the inlets. The water's extraordinary clarity reveals individual boulders on the floor of the lake, 100 feet below the surface. Gazing east across the lake, we can see the distant towers of Stateline casinos.

After entering Bliss State Park, the trail cuts a precipitous contour above Lake Tahoe on little cliffs fenced with chains, a scene rich in charm, like a Japanese woodblock print where each branch, each rock, each pine and manzanita seem sculpted by design and boldly outlined against the aquamarine colors of the lake beyond. We near the end as Lester Beach pulls into sight, its white sands set in brilliant contrast against Lake Tahoe's blue, and all colorfully speckled with brave swimmers, sunbathers, picnickers, and sailboats.

Miles and Directions

0.0 Vikingsholm parking area on CA 89.

0.6 Paved fork; turn right.

0.9 Vikingsholm (water fountain, toilets).

1.8 Emerald Bay Boat Camp.

4.3 First junction with Lighthouse Trail; go left (south).

4.7 Rocky ledge.

5.0 Lester Beach trailhead and Lighthouse Trail junction.

34 Mount Tallac

The sheer face of Mount Tallac, with its celebrated crucifix of snow, looms formidably above Lake Tahoe, a worthy notch in any mountaineer's belt. This summit hike presents a near-continuous panoply of changing vistas over Lake Tahoe, Fallen Leaf Lake, Emerald Bay, and Desolation Wilderness, all leading to an extraordinary grand finale. Mile for mile, it's one of the premier hikes of the Tahoe Sierra.

Start: Mount Tallac trailhead
Distance: 9.6 miles out and back
Hiking time: About 7 hours
Difficulty: Strenuous, with an overall elevation gain and loss of nearly 3,300 feet
Trail condition: Generally good, occasionally steep singletrack trail
Seasons: Late June through Oct
Other trail users: No bikes permitted. Equestrians and dogs under firm control allowed.
Land status: Lake Tahoe Basin Management Unit; Desolation Wilderness

Nearest town: South Lake Tahoe
Fees and permits: Obtain a free permit for day hikers at the trailhead. Overnighters need to get a wilderness permit (fee) from the Taylor Creek Visitor Center.
Maps: Fine Edge Productions: *South Lake Tahoe Basin*. Tom Harrison: *Lake Tahoe*. USGS 7.5-minute quad: Emerald Bay.
Trail contacts: See Hike 32

Finding the trailhead: Drive 3.9 miles northwest on CA 89 from its junction with US 50 (the South Lake Tahoe Y). Opposite the Baldwin Beach turnoff, a Forest Service sign for the Mount Tallac trailhead directs you left (south) on unpaved Mount Tallac Road. Follow the narrow road 1.1 miles to the parking area. Trailhead GPS: N38 55.282' / W120 04.095'

The Hike

Our trail starts at about 6,440 feet on an old forest road, behind the bulletin board where day-use wilderness permits are available. Gently ascending through a brushy landscape of sage, huckleberry oak, and conifer, we obtain our first really great view a little more than half a mile into the walk, when the trail mounts to a hogback ridge high above Fallen Leaf Lake. Languorous, long, and blue in its glacial valley, Fallen Leaf Lake is a textbook example of a moraine-dammed lake. Beyond the moraine at the lake's north end sprawls Lake Tahoe, larger than life and bluer than blue. Views of Mount Tallac meanwhile open between the thick-trunked junipers, silver pines, and Jeffrey pines that give majesty and shade to this surprisingly narrow ridge spine. Even if you go no farther than this magnificent ridge, this hike is already worth the price of admission.

But let us continue. The trail makes a short descent westward into the shallow valley of Spring Creek and then starts up again on short switchbacks, past the signposted boundary of Desolation Wilderness, to the heavily wooded shore of Floating Island

In addition to a steep climb, the trail to Mount Tallac offers inspiring views of Fallen Leaf Lake and Lake Tahoe's south shore for much of the way.

Lake, whose quiet waters take their name from the mats of pond weeds floating on the surface. It's a very popular picnic spot for mosquitoes.

We find some relief from the bloodsuckers by climbing upward into the drier forest, brush, and granite landscape. After stepping across Cathedral Creek, we meet a junction with the steep path that descends to Fallen Leaf Lake; go right (south). Meager of size and hemmed in by boulders, Cathedral Lake floods the bottom of a narrow cirque just beyond.

Now we begin a steeper ascent into upper Cathedral Basin, switchbacking on a handsome trail through alternating tracts of rocks, brush, and woods. Rambunctious Cathedral Creek crosses the trail in slapdash fashion, the trail and creek actually sharing the same bed briefly as they cut capers through a forest glen where corn lilies and willows grow rampant.

Emerging from the woods into a cirque choked with rocks and willows, we come face-to-face with the headwall of Cathedral Basin, an intimidating barricade of scree. This section proves the steepest and most pigheaded of the entire trail, even as the lofty views grow ever more sublime. Initially cutting a diagonal northward up the scree, the official trail makes a sharp switchback south about a third of the way up. Because snowfields sometimes linger on the trail ahead until well into July, many

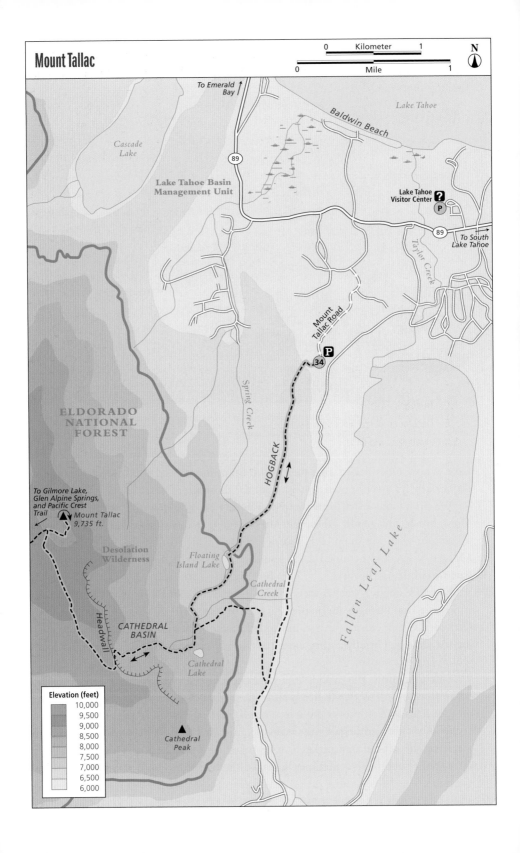

hikers seeking to avoid snow have worn a sheer use-trail straight-on through the scree from this switchback. Both trails meet atop the headwall, but for the record, I find the official trail easier.

Atop the headwall you will find yourself in a vast, rocky, open, rolling meadow, with fine views of the Crystal Range along the western horizon. To the north rises the rather uncharismatic backside of Mount Tallac. It is now just a matter of steady walking uphill through meadow and copse, approaching ever closer to the rocky summit. Immediately below the summit block, we meet the junction to Gilmore Lake. Turn right (east) and climb to the edge of the windy northern cliffs that overlook Lake Tahoe. Taking care not to get blown over, we make a brief and airy scramble to the metamorphic summit, at 9,735 feet.

Mount Tallac offers a front-row seat on a real-life, full-scale relief map of the Tahoe Basin. You can pick out scores of defining points, the most obvious being Emerald Bay, Cascade Lake, Fallen Leaf Lake, Mount Rose (10,776 feet), and Freel Peak (10,887 feet). To the southwest rolls Desolation Wilderness beneath the point of Pyramid Peak (9,983 feet); to the southeast, the high country around Carson and Ebbetts Passes.

Miles and Directions

- **0.0** Parking area.
- **0.5** Hogback ridge.
- **1.5** Desolation Wilderness boundary.
- **1.6** Floating Island Lake.
- **2.1** Lower Cathedral Creek crossing.
- **2.2** Junction with trail to Fallen Leaf Lake; keep right (south).
- **2.3** Cathedral Lake.
- **2.5** Upper Cathedral Creek crossing.
- **2.9** Foot of scree wall in upper Cathedral Basin.
- **4.5** Gilmore Lake junction; go right (east).
- **4.8** Summit of Mount Tallac.
- **9.6** Arrive back at the parking area.

35 Hawley Grade

This short hike goes up and down an intact stretch of a historic trans-Sierra highway, one of the most visually attractive sections of the old Pony Express route.

Start: South Upper Truckee Road in Christmas Valley
Distance: 4.2 miles out and back
Hiking time: About 2 hours
Difficulty: Moderate, with nearly 900 feet in elevation gained and lost
Trail condition: This obvious, well-graded route has one tricky early-season stream crossing.
Seasons: May–Oct. Best as a morning hike.
Other trail users: Dogs under firm control (leash or voice), equestrians, bikes

Land status: Lake Tahoe Basin Management Unit
Nearest town: Meyers
Fees and permits: None
Maps: Fine Edge Productions: *South Lake Tahoe Basin*. Tom Harrison: *Lake Tahoe*. USGS 7.5-minute quad: Echo Lake.
Trail contacts: See Hike 28

Finding the trailhead: From the South Lake Tahoe Y (where CA 89 and US 50 join), drive south 5.3 miles through Meyers to South Upper Truckee Road. Turn left (south) onto this two-lane paved road and continue through Christmas Valley, lined with meadows, woods, and summer homes. After 3.2 miles the road narrows to one paved lane. At 3.5 miles from CA 89, the rough, well-marked Hawley Grade departs on the right. Do not drive onto it; instead park on the wide shoulder of South Upper Truckee Road, well off the pavement. Trailhead GPS: N38 47.838' / W120 01.214'

The Hike

Built by Asa Hawley in 1857, Hawley Grade was the first properly graded wagon road to cross the central Sierra Nevada. From then until the improvement of the Johnson Pass Grade in 1861, most trans-Sierra traffic used this route, jamming it by day with wagons, Concord coaches, freight schooners, peddlers, and mule trains. The short-lived Pony Express used Hawley Grade. It was along this route, too, that stagecoach driver Hank Monk carried Horace Greeley on his wild ride to Placerville, so picturesquely recounted by Mark Twain in *Roughing It*. In Twain's words, the coach "bounced up and down in such a terrific way that it jolted the buttons all off Horace's coat, and finally shot his head clean through the roof of the stage." Whereupon Monk bellowed down to him, "Keep your seat, Horace, and I'll get you there on time!" Whether you believe this is your own business.

Hawley Grade strikes south from South Upper Truckee Road on a gravel lane (elevation 6,500 feet), following the Truckee River upstream through bouldered meadows and groves of aspen and fir, past several old summer houses. By the side of the last house stands a wooden post labeled HAWLEY GRADE. At this point the wide dirt road dwindles to a rocky track inundated in early season by snowmelt and narrowed even further by erosion and encroaching shrubbery.

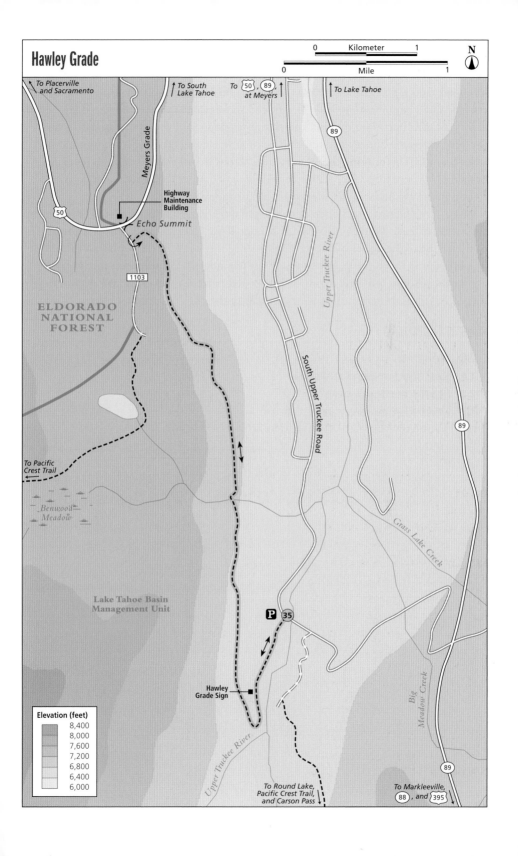

Making a sharp U-turn, our track proceeds askance up the steep east-facing flank of the Upper Truckee canyon. Bitter cherry, buckthorn, manzanita, wild currant, scrub oak, and red fir crowd the path, but occasional sections still retain the original cobbles and stone retaining walls. Bright-red snow plants sprout from the shade in early season. At one point the trail cuts sharply upslope to circumvent a landslide and at 1 mile meets the outlet stream from Benwood Meadow and its adjacent pond, atop Echo Summit. This crossing can be very treacherous in early season, though there are boulders sufficient for a hiker with a decent sense of balance (and maybe a good stick) to hop across. By midsummer the stream can disappear.

As you rise higher, views open downhill to homes along the Upper Truckee River and north to Lake Tahoe and Nevada's Mount Rose (10,776 feet). After you begin to notice the traffic noises of Meyers Grade, our route turns steeply uphill to the left in a final climb to FR 1103, at Echo Summit (elevation 7,370 feet). You might catch a glimpse of some old "trail signs"—dabs of red paint on the rocks and diamond-shaped XP markers nailed to trees—that indicate the old Pony Express route.

Miles and Directions

0.0 Parking area.

1.0 Cross creek from Benwood Meadow.

2.1 FR 1103, near Echo Summit.

4.2 Arrive back at the parking area.

36 Lake Aloha

Bespattered across the floor of Desolation Valley, stark alpine centerpiece of Lake Tahoe's Desolation Wilderness, Lake Aloha takes on different appearances depending on the season. Choked blue with ice in early spring, it can shrink drastically by autumn, but throughout the summer it provides an extensive, irregular, stunning shoreline to explore.

Start: Upper Echo Lake boat dock
Distance: With the water taxi (fee), 6.8 miles out and back (see "Options" for an 11.8-mile hike without it)
Hiking time: About 5–6 hours, including the water taxi
Difficulty: Moderate with the water taxi
Trail condition: Excellent singletrack trail over dirt, stone, and duff
Seasons: June through mid-Sept. Oct usually has pleasant daytime temperatures but shorter days and a longer hike without the water taxi service.
Land status: Eldorado National Forest and Desolation Wilderness
Other trail users: No bikes. Dogs under firm control (leash or voice) and equestrians.

Nearest town: Meyers, though Echo Lakes has a small general store and lunch counter
Fees and permits: For day use, obtain a free permit at the Echo Lakes trailhead sign-in board, next to the market. For overnight use, obtain a wilderness permit (fee) from the Pacific Ranger District. No campfires in Desolation Valley. The water taxi charges a fare.
Maps: Fine Edge Productions: *South Lake Tahoe Basin.* Tom Harrison: *Lake Tahoe.* USGS 7.5-minute quad: Echo Lake.
Trail contacts: Eldorado National Forest, Pacific Ranger District, 7887 US 50, Pollock Pines, Camino, CA 95726; (530) 644-2349; www.fs.usda.gov/eldorado. Echo Chalet, 9900 Echo Lakes Rd., Echo Lake, CA 95721; (530) 659-7207 (summer only); echochalet.com.

Finding the trailhead: The Echo Lakes parking lot lies 2 miles from US 50, near Echo Summit. Coming from Lake Tahoe, turn right onto Johnson Pass Road, 4.8 miles from the bridge over the Truckee River in Meyers. Coming from the west, turn left onto Johnson Pass Road, about 46 miles from Placerville. Once on Johnson Pass Road, drive 0.9 mile to the first junction and turn left onto Echo Lakes Road. The road narrows but remains paved. Passing summer homes and the Berkeley camp, after 0.8 mile we come to backpacker parking lot, with a view over Lower Echo Lake. Park there (backpacker parking lot GPS: N38 50.012' / W120 02.5576') and walk down to Echo Chalet, which sits adjacent to the Echo Lakes dam and has a market, lunch counter, ice cream, phone, boat rentals, and a dock where you catch the water taxi. Water taxi dock GPS: N38 50.093' / W120 02.657'

From this dock, take the water taxi to our trailhead at the dock on the western end of Upper Echo Lake (elevation 7,400 feet). Passengers will enjoy the views of the glaciated canyon walls from the boat, and the tight passage through the narrows between Lower and Upper Echo Lakes. Trailhead GPS at Upper Echo Lake dock: N38 50.800' / W120 04.718'

The Hike

As you step off the water taxi, you will find a telephone beside the dock for calling the boat back when you are ready to return. On the right (east) side of the dock, a

Lake Aloha fills a rocky granite basin in the Desolation Wilderness.

short spur trail leads uphill through lodgepole pines to our main path, which does triple duty also as the Pacific Crest Trail (PCT) and the Tahoe-Yosemite Trail. We head up-canyon on a moderately rising gradient through lodgepole pines, which give way grudgingly to patches of scrub and isolated junipers, which themselves surrender in time to expanses of granite, parts of which have been dynamited to give us easier passage. So sharp are some pieces of shattered granite in the trail that they can bruise your heels if you don't have proper boots.

Our ascent opens wide vistas up the glaciated canyon to pyramidal Ralston Peak (9,235 feet). At 0.7 mile we pass the official wilderness boundary, followed immediately by a fork to Triangle Lake. After gaining about 400 feet in elevation above Echo Lakes, we reach the broad granite shelf where Tamarack Lake lies off to the south, unseen as yet but reached by a ducked spur path. As we continue up the mountainside on our trail, aiming toward an obvious, low, wide, and forested saddle at the canyon's head, we catch a backward glance of Tamarack Lake and of Echo Lakes. Mounting two long switchbacks through rocky, open country, we meet the Lily Lake Trail junction near the top, where we follow the PCT northwest into thick woods of lodgepole and fir.

Crossing easily over the shady divide, a pass so broad and flat that its curvature is not immediately apparent, we enter Haypress Meadow (8,300 feet), ignoring four

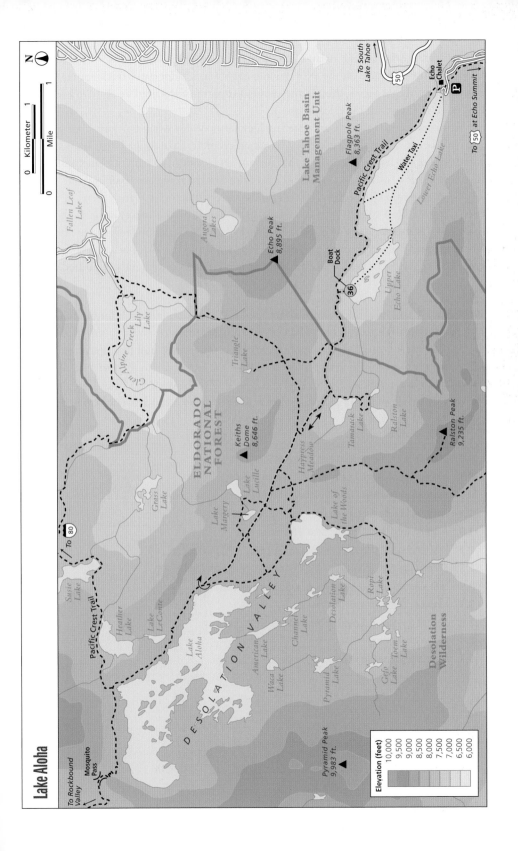

Lake Aloha

Elevation (feet)
10,000
9,500
9,000
8,500
8,000
7,500
7,000
6,500
6,000

N

0   Kilometer   1

0   Mile   1

To Rockbound Valley

Mosquito Pass

Pacific Crest Trail

Susie Lake

To 80

Heather Lake

Lake LeConte

Lake Aloha

DESOLATION VALLEY

Waca Lake

American Lake

Pyramid Lake

Channel Lake

Desolation Lake

Ropi Lake

Cefo Lake

Toem Lake

Desolation Wilderness

Pyramid Peak 9,983 ft.

Grass Lake

Lake Margery

Lake Lucille

Lake of the Woods

Ralston Lake

Tamarack Lake

Haypress Meadow

Ralston Peak 9,235 ft.

Keiths Dome 8,646 ft.

ELDORADO NATIONAL FOREST

Glen Alpine Creek

Lily Lake

Triangle Lake

Angora Lakes

Echo Peak 8,895 ft.

Fallen Leaf Lake

Boat Dock

36

Upper Echo Lake

Pacific Crest Trail

Water Taxi

Lower Echo Lake

Flagpole Peak 8,363 ft.

Lake Tahoe Basin Management Unit

To South Lake Tahoe

50

Echo Chalet

P

To 50 at Echo Summit

side trails that offer to take us away to the north and south. Instead, we maintain a steady northwest course on the PCT, staying mostly in a forest cover thick enough to obstruct our distant views, though the pointed summit of Pyramid Peak (9,983 feet) hovers on the west-southwest horizon.

We know for sure that we are entering Desolation Valley when our trail drops into a sharp descent. From the thick cover of mixed conifers, Lake Aloha bursts upon the scene only at the last moment as we hit bottom, encountering a truly sublime, almost surreal scene. It is, indeed, as desolate as a Salvador Dali painting, sans melting watches: a forlorn migration of turtle-backed islands receding across a watery plain (Lake Aloha, in this case) spiked with dead trees and backed by the inhospitable ridge of the Crystal Range to the south and west, and by Jacks Peak (9,856 feet) to the north. There are many places to camp on granite shelves around the lake, but the best forest cover is along the southeast shoreline, where our trail has conveniently deposited us.

Options

If the Echo Lakes water taxi is not running—or if you simply want a longer trail—start from the dam next to Echo Chalet. This adds 2.5 miles one-way to the route to the dock at the western end of Upper Echo Lake, where this trail description starts. After mid-September, falling water levels confine the water taxi to the first lake, forcing riders to disembark at the dock on the west side of Lower Echo Lake. This alternative adds a walk of only 0.8 mile one-way to the Upper Echo Lake dock trailhead.

Miles and Directions

- **0.0** Boat dock on the western end of Upper Echo Lake.
- **0.1** Junction of dock spur path with PCT; bear left (west).
- **0.7** Junction with Triangle Lake Trail; bear left (west).
- **1.1** Junction with Tamarack Lake Trail; bear right (northwest).
- **1.8** Junction with Lily Lake Trail; bear left (northwest).
- **2.1** First junction with Lake of the Woods Trail; bear right (northwest).
- **2.3** Second junction with Lake of the Woods Trail; bear right (northwest).
- **2.5** First junction to Lake Margery; go straight (northwest).
- **2.7** Junction; take right fork (northwest).
- **2.8** Second junction to Lake Margery; go straight (northwest).
- **3.4** Lake Aloha's shore.
- **6.8** Arrive back at the boat dock.

37 Lovers Leap

The sheer face of Lovers Leap looms above the American River valley like a bantamweight Gibraltar, a familiar landmark to Tahoe-bound travelers on US 50. Rock climbers know the face more intimately as the Tahoe region's premier climbing wall. The trail to the 6,944-foot summit, however, is easy enough for children.

Start: Camp Sacramento on US 50 near Twin Bridges
Distance: 2.2 miles out and back
Hiking time: About 1–2 hours
Difficulty: Easy, despite a 540-foot gain in elevation
Trail condition: Good
Seasons: May through late Oct
Other trail users: Dogs under firm control (leash or voice). Equestrians and bikes are not permitted on this route, though they may ascend Lovers Leap from other trails. Climbers ascend the sheer face, so do not throw anything over the cliff.

Land status: Eldorado National Forest. Camp Sacramento permits hikers to pass through.
Nearest towns: Camp Sacramento has a small store. Strawberry has food and lodging.
Fees and permits: None
Maps: Fine Edge Productions: *South Lake Tahoe Basin.* Tom Harrison: *Lake Tahoe.* USGS 7.5-minute quads: Echo Lake, Pyramid Peak.
Trail contacts: Eldorado National Forest, Pacific Ranger District, 7887 US 50, Pollock Pines, Camino, CA 95726; (530) 644-2349; www.fs.usda.gov/eldorado

Finding the trailhead: Park in the small, designated lot on Camp Sacramento property, just off US 50. Coming from Lake Tahoe, this Camp Sacramento gate is on the left (south) side of US 50, about 9.5 miles from the bridge over the Truckee River in Meyers. Coming from the west, the driveway is on the right (south) side of the road, about 43.5 miles from Placerville (Camp Sacramento gate GPS: N38 48.198' / W120 07.074'). A short, unpaved, narrow driveway crosses the American River on a bridge. Park immediately beyond the bridge on the left, by the Lovers Leap Parking sign. An archery range stands across the driveway. Parking GPS: N38 48.178' / W120 06.965'

The Hike

Walk up the driveway to Camp Sacramento. There is a small store with patio tables selling refreshments on the right, and customers are welcome to stop. Walk past it to the right (west) on a rutty dirt road, passing several cabins, to the edge of camp at Cabin 53. There you will find the trailhead sign directing you toward Lovers Leap (trailhead GPS: N38 48.081' / W120 07.062'). If you have trouble finding it, the camp staff can direct you.

As we climb moderately through the forest on singletrack, the broad, white twist of Horsetail Falls comes into view on the opposite mountainside, framed by red columns of lichen-covered firs. These long views soon withdraw behind trees and an intervening granite knoll. We briefly join with the Pony Express route (marked XP)

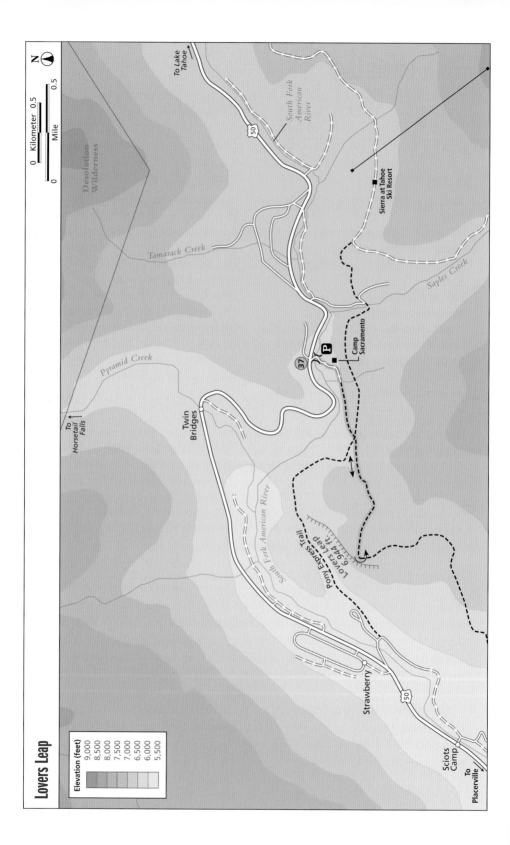

Lovers Leap

Elevation (feet)
- 9,000
- 8,500
- 8,000
- 7,500
- 7,000
- 6,500
- 6,000
- 5,500

N

0 Kilometer 0.5

0 Mile 0.5

Desolation Wilderness

To Lake Tahoe

South Fork American River

50

Tamarack Creek

Sayles Creek

Sierra at Tahoe Ski Resort

Pyramid Creek

To Horsetail Falls

Twin Bridges

37

P

Camp Sacramento

Pond Express Trail

Lovers Leap 6,944 ft.

South Fork American River

Strawberry

50

Sciots Camp

To Placerville

as it comes down from Echo Summit before forking off steeply downhill toward the old Strawberry station at the bottom of the canyon. We keep climbing.

Near where the forest draws back to reveal the weathered granite hindquarters of Lovers Leap, overeager hikers have blazed a flurry of unofficial trails in search of the cliff. Stick to the obvious main trail, which ascends the back of the dome on an open switchback. At the high point you will see a large Jeffrey pine on your right (northwest) with a sign warning against throwing anything over the cliff, for fear of hitting climbers on the wall. The edge is obvious from here, though masked by masses of scrub oak and Jeffrey pine. Approach with caution as the cliff-side footing is gravelly. The highest edge of the precipice stands about 600 feet above the hamlet of Strawberry, hugging the American River like a toy-train village. Looming above all to the north is Pyramid Peak (9,983 feet), which, like Lovers Leap itself, was carved by glaciers some 200,000 years ago.

Miles and Directions

0.0 Parking area.

0.1 Camp Sacramento center (store, toilet, drinking water).

0.2 Trailhead sign at Cabin 53.

0.3 Junction of XP trail from Echo Summit; go straight (west).

0.4 Junction; XP trail veers right (downhill) toward Strawberry; we go straight to Lovers Leap.

1.1 Lovers Leap.

2.2 Arrive back at the parking area.

38 Round Lake

Its dramatic volcanic backdrop lends outstanding panache to Round Lake, already rich in wildflower gardens and historic connections to the first trans-Sierra expedition of explorers Kit Carson and John C. Fremont.

Start: Meiss Lake parking area, just west of Carson Pass on CA 88

Distance: 10.6 miles out and back

Hiking time: About 6 hours

Difficulty: Mild gradients make this a moderate hike.

Trail condition: A good, singletrack, dirt trail most of the way, though the last quarter mile follows an unmarked use-trail

Seasons: June–Oct

Other trail users: No bikes are allowed on the Pacific Crest Trail (PCT), but bikes do approach Round Lake from the north. Dogs under firm control (leash or voice) and equestrians are permitted.

Land status: Lake Tahoe Basin Management Unit

Nearest towns: Woodfords has some amenities, Markleeville more.

Fees and permits: No wilderness permit required. Campfire permit required for stove or fire. Parking fee required during summer at the Meiss Lake and Carson Pass parking areas.

Maps: Fine Edge Productions: *South Lake Tahoe Basin*. USGS 7.5-minute quad: Carson Pass.

Trail contacts: Carson Pass Visitor Center is seasonally open. Lake Tahoe Basin Management Unit, 35 College Dr., South Lake Tahoe, CA 96150-4500; (530) 543-2600; www.fs .usda.gov/ltbmu

Finding the trailhead: From Carson Pass, drive west about 0.2 mile to a large parking area (fee) on the north side of CA 88, the Meiss Lake trailhead. Trailhead GPS: N38 41.805' / W119 59.522'

The Hike

Setting out on the high-flying Pacific Crest Trail northbound from the Meiss Lake parking area (elevation 8,550 feet), our first mile follows a nearly level contour above CA 88. Although the Sierra juniper, lodgepole, manzanita, willow, and some well-weathered granite boulders are handsome enough all year round, this stretch in midsummer explodes into one of the loveliest flower gardens on the face of the planet.

Crossing a fledgling tributary of Woods Creek, which flows south and west into the American River drainage, we mount a handful of switchbacks up 300 feet of waterless ridge to an unnamed pass—at 8,800 feet, the high point of this hike. This gentle divide, where we pass through a gate beside a large pond, separates the American River drainage from that of the Truckee River, which flows north into Lake Tahoe and thence into its Great Basin sink. In other words, we are standing on a rather unprepossessing, though

The spectacular cliffs above Round Lake steal the show, but the lake plays a nice second fiddle. ▶

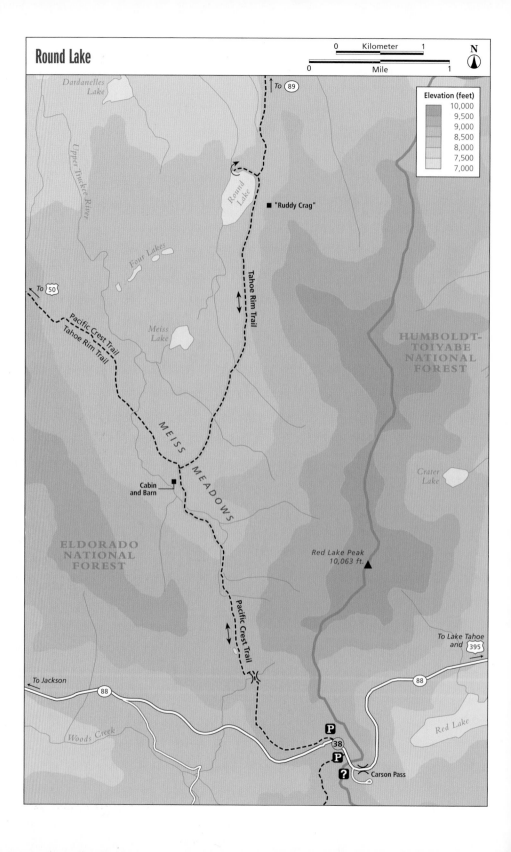

Round Lake

0   Kilometer   1

0   Mile   1

N

Elevation (feet)
10,000
9,500
9,000
8,500
8,000
7,500
7,000

Dardanelles Lake

To 89

Upper Truckee River

Round Lake

■ "Ruddy Crag"

Four Lakes

To 50

Pacific Crest Trail
Tahoe Rim Trail

Meiss Lake

Tahoe Rim Trail

HUMBOLDT-
TOIYABE
NATIONAL
FOREST

M E I S S   M E A D O W S

Crater Lake

Cabin
and Barn

ELDORADO
NATIONAL
FOREST

*Red Lake Peak
10,063 ft.* ▲

Pacific Crest Trail

*To Lake Tahoe
and* 395

To Jackson

88

88

Woods Creek

P
38

P
?

Carson Pass

Red Lake

very pretty, outpost of the Sierra Crest. There is a fine view south to Round Top (10,381 feet) and its ridge, ramparts of the Mokelumne Wilderness. Looking east we can see the raw flank of Red Lake Peak (10,063 feet). When the party of American explorers led by Kit Carson and John C. Fremont crossed the Sierra in February of 1844, deep snows, scant food, and rugged unfamiliar terrain slowed them to a miserable slog. To get their bearings, they climbed at least partway up Red Lake Peak, where they became the first non–Native Americans to glimpse Lake Tahoe.

Although Lake Tahoe lies well hidden beyond the horizon from our trail, we soon are keeping good company with its largest tributary, the Truckee, as it splashes down from its headwaters neighborhood. As we descend northward toward the broad flats of the Upper Truckee Basin on an old doubletrack, we may pass some patches of snow clinging to north-facing pockets clear through summer; but just ahead, spring seems to linger long into fall on the 12,000-acre expanse of Meiss Meadows. After crossing the meandering Truckee twice by easy fords, we reach a signposted junction in the middle of the meadows, near a cabin and barn still used during winter by an outfitter guide with a Forest Service permit. (The cowboys who used to bunk in summer no longer come, since their herds were banned from these meadows in 2002, a Forest Service mandate to improve water quality in the Upper Truckee Basin.)

We part company with the PCT at the Meiss Meadows junction, turning right (northeast) toward Round Lake. We now find ourselves on the Tahoe Rim Trail. After a comfortable walk through open forest and meadowland, and then a steeper descent darkened by conifers, we level out on the wooded shore of Round Lake, about 2 miles from the Meiss Meadows junction. Although pretty enough in its forest setting, Round Lake from this angle seems nothing special. Keep walking, however, to the point where the main trail leaves the lakeshore. Take a look at the unusual volcanic mudflows around us, a natural "concrete" of sculpted aggregate. Then continue around the lake, counter-clockwise, on the use-trail to a little peninsula near Round Lake's outlet stream.

By now it should be obvious why Round Lake is a special place. A mammoth, ruddy, volcanic cliff hems in the east side, rent by rain furrows and buttressed with a colossal crag that soars above the rest. Whoever named this lake merely "Round" clearly suffered from a paltry imagination.

Miles and Directions

0.0 Parking area.
0.9 Cross small tributary of Woods Creek.
1.4 Gate and pond at unnamed pass.
2.9 Meiss Meadows junction; turn right (northeast).
5.0 Arrive at Round Lake's shoreline.
5.1 Aggregate rock formations; leave main trail for use-trail around lake.
5.3 Outlet creek peninsula.
10.6 Arrive back at the parking area.

39 Carson Pass to Winnemucca, Round Top, and Fourth of July Lakes

This sturdy day hike calls upon Winnemucca Lake and Round Top Lake en route to a large, handsome lake plunked down on a high shelf above the deep canyon of the Mokelumne River drainage. Covered-wagon pioneers knew this country well, and their venerable lore still hangs heroically from these mountains and valleys.

Start: Behind visitor center at Carson Pass, CA 88

Distance: 11.8 miles out and back

Hiking time: About 6–7 hours

Difficulty: Strenuous: You will gain and lose about 2,450 feet of elevation.

Trail condition: Good, singletrack, dirt trail

Seasons: June–Oct

Other trail users: No bikes. Dogs under firm control (leash or voice) and equestrians are permitted.

Land status: Eldorado National Forest, Mokelumne Wilderness

Nearest towns: Woodfords has some amenities, Markleeville more.

Fees and permits: Parking fee required. No permit needed for day hikers; wilderness permits for overnighters. Campfire permit required for stove or fire.

Maps: Forest Service: *Mokelumne Wilderness*. USGS 7.5-minute quads: Carson Pass; Caples Lake.

Trail contacts: Carson Pass Visitor Center is seasonally open. Amador Ranger District, Eldorado National Forest, 26820 Silver Dr., Pioneer, CA 95666; (209) 295-4251; www.fs.usda.gov/eldorado.

Finding the trailhead: Day hikers park at Carson Pass (fee); overflow can drive west about 0.2 mile to a large parking area (fee) on the north side of CA 88, the Meiss Lake trailhead. Trailhead GPS: N38 41.682' / W119 59.360'

The Hike

From the parking lot atop 8,600-foot Carson Pass, the highest point on CA 88, we strike south on the Pacific Crest Trail (PCT) into a forest of fir and lodgepole pine, then climb through dry meadows of mule's ears, sage, currant, and seasonal wildflowers to the ridge above Carson Pass, where a little spur path goes to nearby Frog Lake.

Look around and consider the historical import of this ridge, which separates the American River drainage from the Great Basin. Thousands of pioneers crossed near here en route to California in the mid-1800s. Looming above us now is the Elephants Back (9,585 feet), a volcanic bluff that so vividly symbolized their experience that to "see the elephant" became a catchphrase for going to California (at least that's one story of that phrase origin). From this spot, the elephant's back is obvious but not the actual view that inspired its name. ("Elephant's Back" was coined by pioneers approaching from Hope Valley on the eastern side, where the elephant shape is enhanced by a long crevasse of snow, suggesting a tusk.) From Carson Pass, emigrant

The long day hike to Fourth of July Lake will provide enough exercise for most hikers.

wagons dropped to a low point in the large valley to the west, now under Caples Lake. From there they had to climb again to West Pass (9,550 feet), about 4 miles to the southwest from here. For them, West Pass was the highest point on the Carson Emigrant Route. (The reason why Carson Pass can be the high point of our modern road crossing today is because CA 88 engineers avoided West Pass by dynamiting a ledge through the rock just west of Kirkwood Ski Resort.)

From the Frog Lake spur trail, we continue up the PCT to a major junction, where the PCT turns left (east) and we continue south, straight past Elephants Back toward snow-spackled Round Top (10,381 feet), whose old glacial cirque played nursemaid to Winnemucca Lake. Climbing smoothly through gravelly meadows and sparse trees, passing labeled campsites, we cross a well-watered meadow to the edge of Winnemucca Lake, sparkling in the high-altitude glare of its rocky bowl.

From the unbridged outlet of Winnemucca Lake, we next climb up to the ridge that separates Winnemucca's cirque from the cirque that birthed Round Top Lake. It's a mixed triumph: On one hand, this is the high point of our trail at 9,373 feet; on the other, the lowest point is still 1,168 feet below us, and you have to climb back over this hump when you return.

Descending slightly to the shores of Round Top Lake, we meet a four-way junction. The route to the right goes downhill to Woods Lake. To the left is an unofficial trail to the summit of Round Top. We go straight, along the piney shore of Round Top Lake, past signposted backpacker campsites, and jumping the outlet creek.

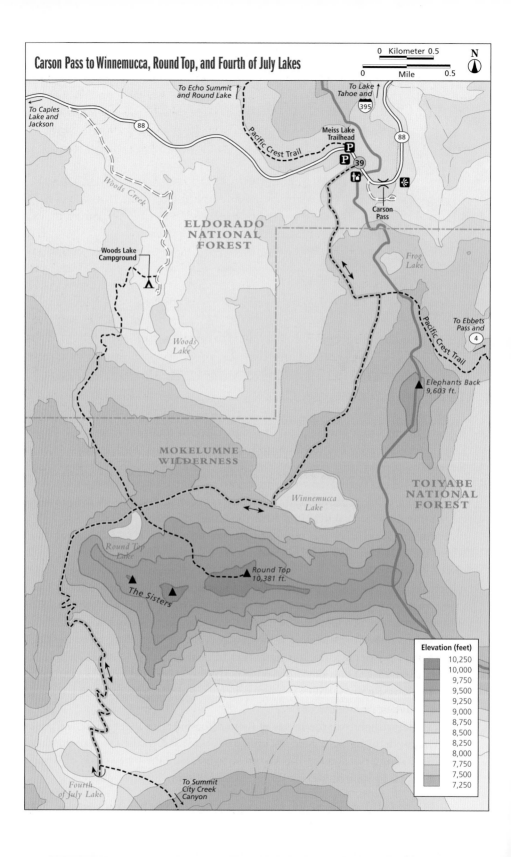

Carson Pass to Winnemucca, Round Top, and Fourth of July Lakes

0 Kilometer 0.5
0 Mile 0.5

N

To Echo Summit
and Round Lake

To Lake
Tahoe and
395

To Caples
Lake and
Jackson

88

88

Pacific Crest Trail

Meiss Lake
Trailhead

P
P
39

Carson
Pass

Woods Creek

ELDORADO
NATIONAL
FOREST

Woods Lake
Campground

Frog
Lake

Pacific Crest Trail

To Ebbets
Pass and
4

Woods
Lake

Elephants Back
9,603 ft.

MOKELUMNE
WILDERNESS

TOIYABE
NATIONAL
FOREST

Winnemucca
Lake

Round Top
Lake

Round Top
10,381 ft.

The Sisters

Fourth
of July Lake

To Summit
City Creek
Canyon

Elevation (feet)

10,250
10,000
9,750
9,500
9,250
9,000
8,750
8,500
8,250
8,000
7,750
7,500
7,250

And now as our trail curves around the high, open shoulder of Round Top, a rocky prominence called the Sisters, we enjoy the unobstructed views westward toward Kirkwood Ski Resort and the high ridge that curves above and behind it, a ridge anchored in the foreground by Fourth of July Peak (9,536 feet). West Pass, the target of the pioneers, lies hidden behind, but the surrounding countryside provides plenty of testament to the hardships our stalwart ancestors had to put up with, like hauling wagons up crumbling slopes with insufficient water.

Our view shed changes abruptly as we cross our own unnamed saddle through this ridge, leaving behind the American River drainage, and giving us a sudden view down into the canyons of the Mokelumne drainage. We can also see Fourth of July Lake midway down our steep feeder canyon wall, on a shelf decorated with trees. An old miners' trail is likewise clearly visible, cutting in no-nonsense fashion straight down our feeder canyon toward Summit City Creek Canyon, at the bottom. Avoid that direct trail, and take the newer one that contours more intelligently down the steep slope in a few sweeping switchbacks, dropping 1,100 feet in elevation in less than 2 miles. With the trail edged in wildflowers and short-cropped foliage and dotted only sparsely with large, impressive trees, the views are stupendous. The gradient lessens as we pull into the shelf where Fourth of July Lake lies, coddled in a narrow forest belt that harbors pleasant campsites on the west and south sides.

Option

A sweet option here for the experienced backpacker would be to drop from the junction near the lake's south side outlet into Summit City Creek Canyon, perhaps to the old silver ghost town of Summit City. Be aware that the trails in the upper canyons of the Mokelumne drainage are not known for being well marked or heavily traveled.

Miles and Directions

0.0 Carson Pass parking area.

0.5 Enter Mokelumne Wilderness.

1.1 Frog Lake fork; continue south on PCT.

1.3 Junction with PCT: head right (south).

2.5 Winnemucca Lake.

2.6 Four-way junction; go straight (west).

2.7 Cross Winnemucca's outlet stream.

3.4 High point of trail.

3.5 Round Top Lake: four-way junction with trail to Woods Lake and unofficial trail to summit of Round Top; keep straight (west).

3.6 Outlet stream from Round Top Lake.

4.1 Saddle between American and Mokelumne River drainages.

5.9 Fourth of July Lake.

11.8 Arrive back at Carson Pass.

40 Charity Valley to Hot Springs Valley

Succulent green meadows rife with wildflowers, brilliant autumnal displays of yellow leaves, dark red-hued mountains patched with white snow, and typically blue skies provide the Carson River drainage with some of the Sierra's most colorful hikes. This point-to-point hike, which requires a car shuttle, drops from subalpine meadow to a sheltered, forested valley, where you can take a dip in the hot springs.

Start: Charity Valley on the Blue Lakes Road
Distance: 7.0 miles one-way/shuttle
Hiking time: About 4–5 hours
Difficulty: Moderate, with some bushwhacking on the middle section of the trail
Trail condition: Good for the first third; mediocre for the middle third; excellent for the last third. The problem with the middle section is overgrown chaparral, so wear long pants for more comfortable bushwhacking.
Seasons: June for wildflowers; Sept–Oct for fall colors. July–Aug can be pleasant in the morning but hot in the afternoon.
Other trail users: Bikes, equestrians, and dogs under firm control (leash or voice) are permitted.

Land status: Humboldt-Toiyabe National Forest
Nearest town: Markleeville
Fees and permits: None for day hike. Campfire permit required for stove or fire. Grover Hot Springs State Park charges a fee to use the hot springs pools.
Maps: Forest Service: *Mokelumne Wilderness*. Fine Edge Productions: *South Lake Tahoe Basin*. USGS 7.5-minute quads: Carson Pass, Markleeville.
Trail contacts: Humboldt-Toiyabe National Forest, Carson Ranger District Office, 1536 S. Carson St., Carson City, NV 89701; (775) 882-2766; www.fs.usda.gov/htnf

Finding the trailhead: This hike starts at the Charity Valley trailhead and ends near Grover Hot Springs. The two trailheads, both on land managed by Humboldt-Toiyabe National Forest, are 17.5 miles apart by road.

To reach the eastern terminus near Grover Hot Springs State Park, drive east on CA 89 from Picketts Junction (with CA 88) in Hope Valley. At Woodfords turn right and drive to the Alpine County town of Markleeville. From the center of town, turn right (west) at a signed junction indicating Grover Hot Springs, and drive 2.8 miles to a pullout on the right side of the road, just before the bridge across Hot Springs Creek. End trailhead GPS: N38 41.958' / W119 49.433'

To reach the Charity Valley trailhead from South Lake Tahoe, drive south on CA 89 over Luther Pass to Hope Valley. At the junction with CA 88—known as Picketts Junction—turn right (west) and drive 4 miles to Blue Lakes Road (paved), where you turn left (south), passing Hope Valley Campground and Faith Valley. At 6.1 miles from the last junction, we arrive at the Charity Valley trailhead on the east side of Blue Lakes Road; the trailhead was not signposted at press time. Park on the paved turnout on the west side of the road. Trailhead GPS: N38 40.332' / W119 55.053'

The Hike

The hike divides into three roughly equal sections: an easy amble through the flowery hillsides above lush Charity Valley; a steep, bushwhacking descent into Hot Springs Valley; and a plod through the dry piney woods along the valley bottom.

From the east side of Blue Lakes Road (elevation 7,850 feet), our unsigned trail passes through a rustic gate, rolling easily onto high ground above Charity Valley. Though dry and rocky, it thrives with pungent sagebrush, rabbitbrush, currant, lodgepole pine, juniper, and a myriad of early-season wildflowers, such as paintbrush, pussy paws, mariposa lily, phlox, and furry mule's ears, the hiker's good friend. With fine views west to the reddish-brown, lava-buttressed summits of the Carson Range and south to Markleeville Peak (9,417 feet), the trail rises ever so gently above well-watered Charity Valley, where cattle graze behind fences. By slow degree we then descend through lodgepole woods, stepping over some trickling seasonal creeklets, until we join Charity Valley Creek near the start of its wild descent into Hot Springs Valley.

Confined in a narrowing valley, our path now pushes through alternating stretches of meadow and woods, occasionally dropping down over low granite benches. On the flat sections, where the creek turns aside for a slow mosey among thickets of willow and alder, we find ourselves increasingly having to elbow through bushes and step over downed timber. Curiously weathered granite walls close in. At nearly 3 miles into the hike, we pass through a particularly pretty dell bedecked with some giant Jeffrey pines and a granite-rimmed pond filled with lily pads, before coming to an abrupt view point on a granite notch above the 2,000-plus-foot-deep gorge of Hot Springs Valley.

Now begins a rocky descent down dry switchbacks choked with huckleberry oak, manzanita, and other scrub—a steep, shadeless, often hot stretch further encumbered with loose cobbles. As we reach a wooded bench, our route becomes somewhat confused by well-worn use-trails (some with ducks) spinning off into the brush. Keep to the main path closest to the creek. After rock-hopping across two streams—the second being Hot Springs Creek from Burnside Lake—we meet a signed trail junction. Heading right (east), our trail hereafter proves to be excellent, wide, and clear of brush. It is interesting to note that Kit Carson and John C. Fremont ascended this canyon in February of 1844 on their landmark expedition across the Sierra Nevada. (They did not ascend Charity Creek, however, but continued up Hot Springs Creek.)

Within earshot of crashing Hot Springs Creek, unseen in the ravine to our right (south), we continue our switchback descent into the valley, losing nearly 1,200 feet in 1.5 miles, while enjoying views through scrub and pine to the large green meadow at Grover Hot Springs. Carved by glaciers, Hot Springs Valley is U-shaped, with walls rising more than 2,000 feet above the meadow. Rocks heated by mountain-building pressures still underlie the region, heating the snowmelt that trickles down. Percolating to the surface as Grover Hot Springs, the water emerges at 148°F. on the hillside across the meadow and is used to heat the adjacent swimming pools.

Reaching the heavily forested valley floor, we proceed on a shaded, sandy, duff-covered track, going straight (east) at the signed turnoff to Hot Springs Creek Waterfall and passing through a wooden gate. Through sugar pine forest near the beautiful meadow, we pad softly onward to a gated road that leads to the Quaking Aspen

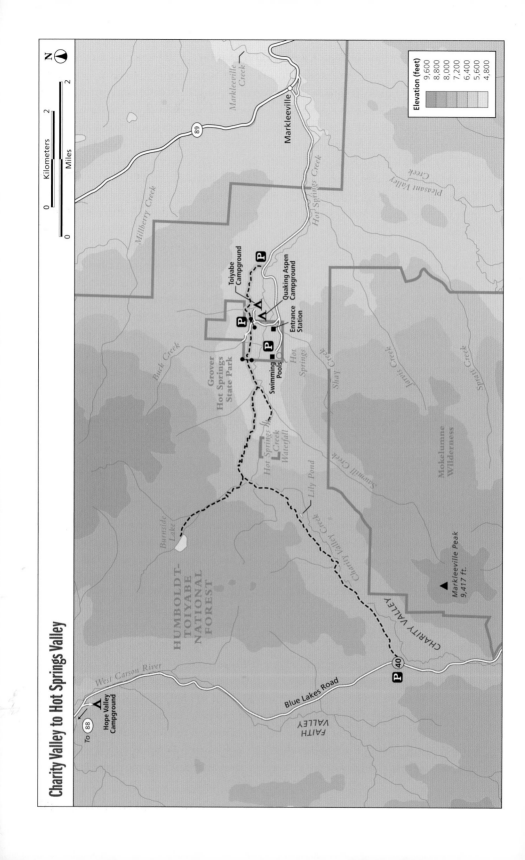

Charity Valley to Hot Springs Valley

N

Elevation (feet)

9,600
8,800
8,000
7,200
6,400
5,600
4,800

Markleeville Creek

89

Markleeville

Millberry Creek

Hot Springs Creek

Pleasant Valley Creek

Toiyabe Campground

P

Quaking Aspen Campground

P

Entrance Station

Buck Creek

Grover Hot Springs State Park

P

Swimming Pools

P

Hot Springs

Shay Creek

Jaunis Creek

Spratt Creek

Hot Springs Creek Waterfall

Lily Pond

Sawmill Creek

Mokelumne Wilderness

Burnside Lake

HUMBOLDT-TOIYABE NATIONAL FOREST

Cherry Valley Creek

Markleeville Peak 9,417 ft.

CHARITY VALLEY

West Carson River

Hope Valley Campground

To 88

Blue Lakes Road

FAITH VALLEY

P 40

Kilometers

Miles

Campground in Grover Hot Springs State Park. Don't go through that gate. Instead, veer uphill to the left (east) on our trail, contouring for 0.8 mile along the hillside above the campsites, until we descend to our parking spot on Grover Hot Springs Road.

Options

On any hot day take a detour to Hot Springs Creek Waterfall, where you can soak in cool pools of splashing water. The falls are about half a mile beyond the Hot Springs Creek Waterfall trail junction, adding another mile—and a world of refreshment—to your hike. Alternatively, you can end your hike with a dip in the hot springs pools, operated by Grover Hot Springs State Park (fee); (530) 694-2248; www.parks .ca.gov/?page_id=508.

Miles and Directions

0.0   Charity Valley trailhead.

2.8   Top of switchback descent.

3.6   Hot Springs Creek crossing.

3.7   Junction with trail to Burnside Lake; bear right (east).

5.3   Hot Springs Creek Waterfall trail junction; stay straight (east).

6.2   Quaking Aspen Campground gate, Grover Hot Springs State Park.

7.0   Hot Springs Road trailhead.

Honorable Mentions

N Eagle Lake

This popular and easy 1.8-mile round-trip hike climbs to a subalpine lake in a verdant pocket of a granite basin. Go early in the day to avoid crowds, preferably on a weekday and as close to the beginning of June as you can. Within the first 0.2 mile, Eagle Creek comes thundering through its narrow granite gorge beneath a footbridge. (By midsummer the roar becomes a burble.) Climbing to the bridge on some fancy stonework steps, we cross the creek and mount briskly through alternating sectors of shady woods and rock-lined granite slabs. The views behind us reach down the glaciated canyon to Emerald Bay and Lake Tahoe. The trailhead parking area (fee) is on CA 89 at the head of Emerald Bay. Contact: Taylor Creek Visitor Center (open Memorial Day–Oct.), (530) 543-2674; www.fs.usda.gov/recarea/ltbmu/recarea/?recid=11785. Trailhead GPS: N38 57.119' / W120 06.816'

O Cascade Falls

This short round-trip stroll of 1.4 miles leads to delightful Cascade Creek, which plunges 200 feet down a granite incline on the flanks of Mount Tallac into Cascade Lake. Go on a warm spring day, and you can easily make a full day of it, basking on sun-warmed granite slabs, listening to the soothing sounds of flowing water, soaking your feet, watching other hikers come and go, snoozing in the shade, searching for water ouzels. If you go after midsummer, however, you'll find the water has receded to a trickle. The trail follows a rocky ledge with fine views down to Cascade Lake, a mile-long oval of blue separated by its glacial moraine from the far larger body of Lake Tahoe. After a final scramble over broken granite slabs, you'll find plenty of room for staking out a peaceful picnic spot along the creek frontage. The Cascade Falls parking area is at the west end of Bayview Campground, on the ridge south of Emerald Bay. Contact: Taylor Creek Visitor Center (open Memorial Day–Oct), (530) 543-2674; www.fs.usda.gov/recarea/ltbmu/recarea/?recid=11785. Trailhead GPS: N38 56.612' / W120 06.001'

P Rainbow Trail

One of five short nature trails starting at the Taylor Creek Visitor Center, the 0.5-mile Rainbow Trail is unique. Much of the path is on a wheelchair-accessible boardwalk through a meadow (very marshy in spring) to the banks of Taylor Creek, where it descends underground to the Stream Profile Chamber. There, a large glass window provides a fish's-eye view of a living Sierra stream. Do not miss this walk in early October, when the kokanee salmon spawn sends thousands of blood-red fish swarming through Taylor Creek—an awesome sight. Contact: Taylor Creek

Colors of sand and water at Sand Point are downright tropical.

Visitor Center (open Memorial Day–Oct), (530) 543-2674; www.fs.usda.gov/rec area/ltbmu/recarea/?recid=11785. Visitor center GPS: N38 56.140' / W120 03.236'

Q Sand Point Nature Trail

Scenic centerpiece of Nevada's Tahoe shoreline, Sand Harbor on warm summer days is packed with swimmers, boats, kayaks, and beachgoers parked under colorful umbrellas. The half-mile-long, wheelchair-accessible Nature Trail around Sand Point is likewise popular, and for good reason. This stretch of Lake Tahoe shoreline is one you might see on calendars and postcards, with translucent coves and white beaches framed by wind-sculpted trees, granite boulders and rock formations jutting up before an intensely blue expanse of water, and distant views of mountains, snowcapped in spring and later fall, the best times to visit if you prefer the views to the crowds. Five miles south of Incline Village on the eastern shore of the lake, Lake Tahoe State Park charges an entrance fee. Contact: Nevada State Parks: (775) 831-2514; parks.nv.gov/parks/sand-harbor. Trailhead GPS: N39 11.879' / W119 55.918'

Along the Ebbetts Pass Road

The Ebbetts Pass Road (CA 4) crosses the Sierra Nevada between the Gold Country town of Angels Camp (famed for Mark Twain's "Celebrated Jumping Frog of Calaveras County") and sparsely populated Alpine County. Along the way a driver passes the famed Calaveras redwoods and extensive volcanic high country punctuated by hoodoos and crenellated ridgelines. Named for Major John Ebbetts, who scouted the 8,731-foot pass in 1850, it was later rejected as a route for the first transcontinental railroad. To this day, it remains one of the lesser-traveled trans-Sierra highways, and long sections near the summit have a single lane, though it is a well-paved, decent road. Ebbetts Pass closes during winter. The road passes through Stanislaus National Forest on the west side of the pass, Humboldt-Toiyabe National Forest on the east. To its north lies the Mokelumne Wilderness, a region of rugged canyons and crumbly, dark, volcanic peaks. Also heavily volcanic, Carson-Iceberg Wilderness lies to the south of the road.

"The Notch," on the trail to Wheeler Lake, is the sign that you are about to start your big descent (Hike 42).

41 Calaveras South Grove

This large and wild grove of giant sequoias can be visited only on foot, a boon to solitude. The Palace Hotel Tree, gargantuan Agassiz Tree, and Smith Cabin Tree (see "Option") are three particularly intriguing features of this relatively remote Big Tree grove.

Start: South Grove parking lot
Distance: 5.3 miles round-trip to Agassiz Tree
Hiking time: About 3 hours; allow at least an hour more for the Smith Cabin Tree
Difficulty: Rather easy, with scant elevation gained or lost. The optional walk to the Smith Cabin Tree is not easy, however, because it is off-trail, and recommended only for people who can route-find with compass or GPS.
Trail surface: A well-marked route on clear tread nearly all the way to the Agassiz Tree. There is no trail to the Smith Cabin Tree, and the route is heavily overgrown.

Seasons: May through late Oct
Other trail users: Dogs and bikes not allowed
Land status: Calaveras Big Trees State Park
Nearest towns: Arnold and Dorrington
Fees and permits: None, though the park charges an entrance fee.
Maps: California State Parks: *Calaveras Big Trees State Park*. USGS 7.5-minute quads: Dorrington, Stanislaus, Crandall Peak, Boards Crossing.
Trail contacts: Calaveras Big Trees State Park, 1170 Highway 4, Arnold, CA 95223; (209) 795-2334; www.parks.ca.gov/?page_id=551

Finding the trailhead: From the entrance to Calaveras Big Trees State Park on CA 4, drive 8.2 miles down the Walter Smith Memorial Parkway to the South Grove parking lot. The road is paved but narrows and loses the painted meridian line after crossing the Stanislaus River. The parking lot has pit toilets, picnic tables, and refuse bins, but no potable water. Trailhead GPS: N38 14.810' / W120 16.068'

The Hike

While chasing a wounded grizzly, professional hunter A. T. Dowd first stumbled upon Calaveras County's giant sequoias in the spring of 1852. Flabbergasted but unable to convince anyone of their existence, Dowd resorted to a ruse, pleading for help to drag a grizzly carcass back to the community stew pot. Raising a party in the gold rush camp of Murphys, he led them to what is now Calaveras Big Trees State Park and spectacularly proved his veracity at the foot of the massive Grizzly Giant, now renamed the Discovery Tree. From that day onward, the Big Trees of Calaveras County have been one of California's most enduring tourist attractions. Thousands of visitors yearly stroll the well-groomed North Grove trails, but only a small percentage ever stray to the less developed South Grove, although it is ten times as large and harbors the park's largest trees.

The well-marked South Grove Trail departs a woodsy picnic area (elevation 4,400 feet), and almost immediately intercepts a well-engineered, wheelchair-accessible loop called the Beaver Creek Trail. Winding through a tall-grass meadow to the Beaver Creek Bridge, we depart the Beaver Creek Trail to cross the bridge. On hot days

Even the big toe of the Agassiz Tree dwarfs awestruck visitors.

kids and other people splash around in the polished bedrock pools below. Passing the Bradley Grove junction, we rise very easily through thick forests of incense cedar, white fir, yellow pine, and white-blooming dogwood. Within earshot of unseen Big Trees Creek, we cross a dirt fire road, jogging slightly left to continue on the signed trail.

At 1.4 miles we bear left at a signed trail junction and pad silently onward, expectantly scanning left and right for a reclusive Big Tree. The forest hush is deep and pervasive, broken mainly by the incessant insect hum of the summery air. Trailside thickets of azalea from time to time stop us in our tracks with an unexpected waft of heady, sweet scent.

Then, one by one, almost reluctantly, the first sequoias begin to appear. Their lone, ruddy, massive columns stand aloof, as if in vain attempt to blend in with the well-proportioned, far more numerous columns of fir and sugar pine. Soon we begin to notice more sociable groupings of two, three, or more sequoias. At 1.8 miles we pass another signed junction, bearing left (northeast) into forest more thickly seeded with Big Trees. Devoid of fencing and other crowd-control measures, the South Grove's untrammeled understory grows rank with deer brush, dogwood, and chinquapin. The trail passes between two imposing sequoias growing so closely together that

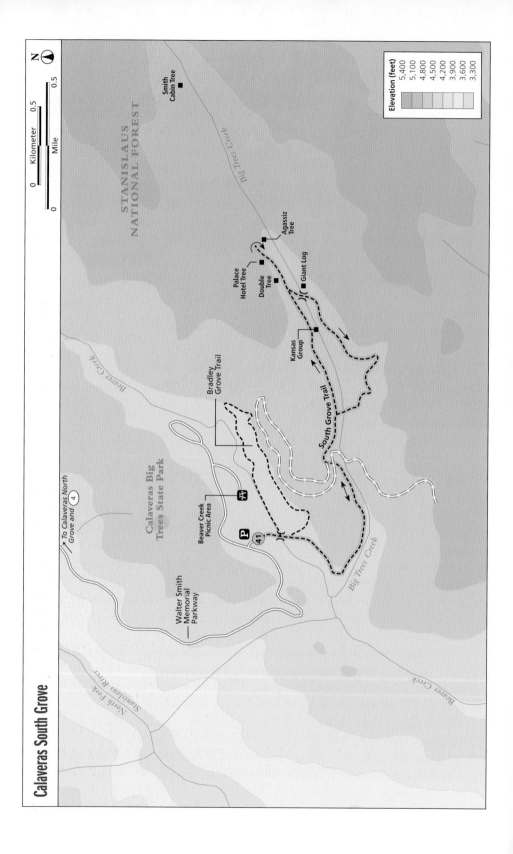

Calaveras South Grove

Smith
Cabin Tree ■

STANISLAUS
NATIONAL FOREST

Big Trees Creek

Agassiz
Tree ■

Palace
Hotel Tree ■
Double
Tree ■
■ Giant Log

■ Kansas
Group

South Grove Trail

Bradley
Grove Trail

Beaver Creek

Calaveras Big
Trees State Park

Beaver Creek
Picnic Area

🅿
🔢 41

Walter Smith
Memorial
Parkway

To Calaveras North
Grove and ④

North Fork
Stanislaus River

Beaver Creek

Big Trees Creek

N

0   Kilometer   0.5
0   Mile   0.5

Elevation (feet)
5,400
5,100
4,800
4,500
4,200
3,900
3,600
3,300

they appear from some angles to form a single gargantuan trunk. More impressive yet is the signposted Palace Hotel Tree, whose gaping entrance, burned-out interior, window-like vents, and domed "ceiling" reminded overly romantic early visitors of the grand carriage entrance of San Francisco's most celebrated nineteenth-century hotel.

Nothing yet seen on this trail prepares us for the ponderous bulk of the Agassiz Tree, believed by some to be one of the Sierra's ten largest sequoias, measuring nearly 250 feet tall and 97 feet in circumference. Visitors tracing circuits round it have worn a path to the back side, where you can contemplate the massive cavity burned into this healthy tree's living girth. More than likely you can enjoy this spectacle alone and in silence.

The officially maintained trail ends at the Agassiz Tree, our turnaround point. (Hikers seeking the Smith Cabin Tree, if they are comfortable hiking off-trail in dense forest, should see "Option" below.)

We return to the parking area by a slightly different route. Backtracking to our last junction, this time we turn left (south) to duck under the cave-like buttress of a fallen sequoia to emerge in a bosky forest garden on the banks of Big Trees Creek. After crossing on a little bridge, our path winds in leisurely fashion over the hillside above the creek's southern bank, passing several giant sequoias, especially enchanting when they catch late afternoon light. After bridging back over the creek to rejoin our original trail, turn left (west) at the signed junction and backtrack to the parking area, perhaps with a stop to cool off in Beaver Creek.

Option

The Smith Cabin Tree is renowned for the historical anecdote that surrounds it. The magic is largely maintained by the fact that Smith's tree is not marked by sign or by trail. It just stands surrounded by the thick forest, blending in much better than one might expect from a giant sequoia. Do not attempt to find it if you are not at home with route finding in a thick forest. And don't go if you cannot tread lightly on this special stretch of land.

Alexander Jackson "Trapper" Smith was the South Grove's first guardian, and it was in this cozy hollow tree that he lived, and very nearly died on a stormy night in December 1861. As Smith cowered in abject terror in the hollow of his tree, winds toppled a neighboring behemoth, Old Goliath. The awful crash of Old Goliath's grand finale nonetheless shook the grove guardian's den like a craps game croupier shakes his dice cup, whereupon old Smith up and departed to seek employment and more conventional quarters elsewhere.

Start your search for the Smith Cabin Tree from the end of the South Grove Trail, by the Agassiz Tree (Smith Cabin Tree "trailhead" GPS: N38 14.914' / W120 14.508'). The tree lies at a distance of about 1.0 mile northeast and above the north bank of Big Trees Creek. You will not be able to walk in a straight line to get there. You will bushwhack, weave through low branches of trees that want to knock your hat off, climb around big trees that want to send you sprawling, and break a mess of webbing from spiders who don't mean you any harm at all—and all for no guarantee that you will find Smith's tree, or indeed, that you can find your way back.

What you are looking for are two giant sequoias, one standing and one prone. Old Goliath lies just as Smith left him more than a century and a half ago, hardly aged at all. Inspecting Smith's old quarters, you have to marvel firstly at how pleasantly snug a home it must have been, and secondly, at how close he came to a uniquely splendid demise. With this story in mind, you may agree that the world does not hold a more dramatic pair of vegetables than the Smith Cabin Tree and Old Goliath.

Miles and Directions

0.0 South Grove parking lot. Immediately beyond, go right at the trail fork.

0.3 Beaver Creek Memorial Bridge.

0.4 Junction with Bradley Grove Trail loop; bear right (south) toward South Grove.

1.2 Cross dirt fire road.

1.4 Junction; bear left (east).

1.8 Junction; bear left (northeast).

2.5 Palace Hotel Tree.

2.6 Agassiz Tree; turn around here. (See "Option" for off-trail visit to Smith Cabin Tree.)

3.6 Junction; bear left (south).

4.4 Junction; bear left (west) and return the way you came.

5.3 Arrive back at the parking lot.

42 Wheeler Lake

The scenic highlight of this hike is not so much the lake itself, quiet and pleasant as it is, but the magnificent trailside view of wildflower gardens, distant peaks, and the gargantuan Mokelumne River canyon.

Start: Woodchuck Basin trailhead, Ebbetts Pass Road
Distance: 6.8 miles round-trip
Hiking time: About 4–5 hours
Difficulty: With about 1,000 feet gained and lost in each direction (2,000 feet overall), this is a moderately difficult day hike or a comfortable overnighter.
Trail condition: Decent singletrack mainly; a use-trail surrounds lake
Seasons: June–Oct
Other trail users: Dogs under control permitted. No bikes.
Land status: Stanislaus National Forest, Mokelumne Wilderness

Nearest town: Lake Alpine has a store, restaurant, and lodging.
Fees and permits: None for day hikers. Campfire permit for stove or fire. Overnighters can obtain wilderness permit from the small ranger station on CA 4 on the east side of Bear Valley (Ranger Station GPS: N38 28.410' / W120 01.562'). Spots along the lake's north shore are marked No CAMPING.
Maps: Forest Service: *Mokelumne Wilderness*. USGS 7.5-minute quad: Spicer Meadow Reservoir, Pacific Valley.
Trail contacts: Stanislaus National Forest, Calaveras Ranger District, PO Box 500 (CA 4), Hathaway Pines, CA 95233; (209) 795-1381; www.fs.usda.gov/stanislaus

Finding the trailhead: Woodchuck Basin trailhead lies on the north side of the Ebbetts Pass Road (CA 4), 12.7 miles west of Ebbetts Pass and 52.2 miles east of Angels Camp. It has a large dirt parking area. Trailhead GPS: N38 29.614' / W119 58.851'

The Hike

Wheeler Lake (about 7,860 feet) and its Woodchuck Basin trailhead (about 7,800 feet) lie at roughly the same altitude, with an interposing 8,800-foot ridge between them. The lake basin's surrounding meadow and forest offer a pretty sight and pleasant camping, but it's that intervening ridge—hung between Mount Reba (8,755 feet) on the west and a peak just called Wheeler (8,977 feet) on the east—that provides the stunning highlight of this hike.

Begin in forest, rising steadily out of Woodchuck Basin above Silver Creek, the main feeder stream of Lake Alpine. After the trail hops across that creek, you may anticipate an immediate enlargement of scenic offerings. Larger meadows make inroads into patchier forest, while a backdrop of ruddy, fluted, volcanic cliffs rises into view as we cross into Mokelumne Wilderness. Climbing ever higher, the wetter meadows of mule's ears give way to drier wildflower slopes. Acres of stalks and splotches of brilliant flowery colors play through summer among the trailside rock

The trail to Wheeler is the highlight of the hike.

gardens under the watch of massive, solitary junipers. Views open to the south, the broad granitic basin of the North Fork of the Stanislaus, of forest green, stippled with blue lakes. With foreknowledge, or a map, you can pick out Inspiration Point (Hike R), Lake Alpine, and the distant Dardanelles.

Reaching the westernmost prow of our ridge, the trail turns abruptly north, contouring high above wild Underwood Valley, itself sweeping downward into the gaping maw of the Mokelumne River canyon. Above all frowns Mount Reba, infested with ski lifts. The view changes abruptly again as we reach the north edge of the ridge, where a notched monument of volcanic aggregate rock (marked "The Notch" on the map) frames northward views to the mountains around Carson Pass, and to the east around Ebbetts Pass, staking out the immense headwaters basin of the Mokelumne. Meanwhile, somewhere down in that forest, unseen, Wheeler Lake bides her sweet time.

The trail now drops like a trap door into that basin on a series of steep zigzags, first down a rocky slope and then more mercifully through forest, before easing gradually into the long bend of Avalanche Meadow, whose edge we follow. Near the meadow's bottom we are supposed to meet a trail coming from the east, according to the map,

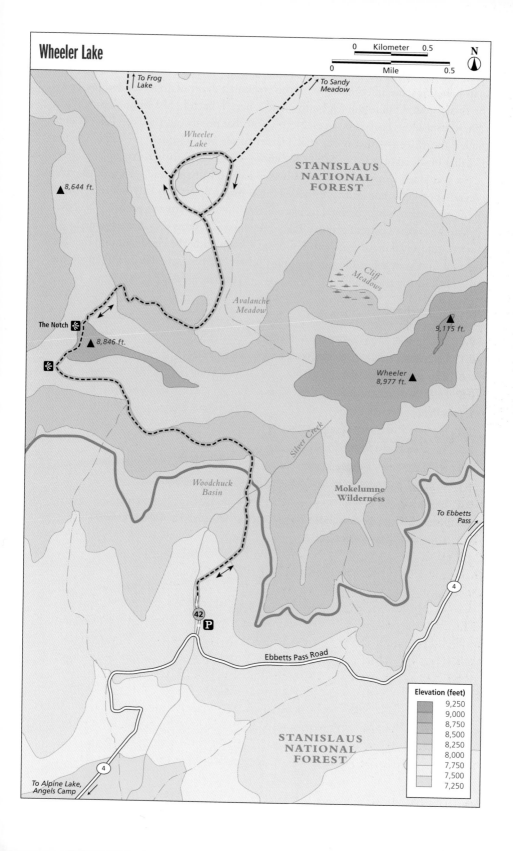

Wheeler Lake

To Frog Lake

To Sandy Meadow

Wheeler Lake

STANISLAUS NATIONAL FOREST

8,644 ft.

Cliff Meadows

Avalanche Meadow

9,115 ft.

The Notch

8,846 ft.

Wheeler 8,977 ft.

Silver Creek

Woodchuck Basin

Mokelumne Wilderness

To Ebbetts Pass

42 P

Ebbetts Pass Road

4

STANISLAUS NATIONAL FOREST

To Alpine Lake, Angels Camp

4

| Kilometer | 0 | 0.5 |
| Mile | 0 | 0.5 |

N

Elevation (feet)	
	9,250
	9,000
	8,750
	8,500
	8,250
	8,000
	7,750
	7,500
	7,250

but the junction apparently has gone rogue, and the willow thickets that conceal it aren't talking. No problem—our own trail is clear enough. We depart the meadow at its lowest reaches in company with the creek that drains it, together dashing down the final forested hill to the flat bottomland where Wheeler Lake languishes behind a rich, wet meadow, backed by trees. Note a post that points out the Frog Lake Trail to the left (northwest)—that is our trail. Harder to see but definitely present is another trail that heads right (east) to Sandy Meadow—that one is our return trail.

As you stroll clockwise around Wheeler Lake on its use-trail, you will discover a secret apparently not known to desk-bound mapmakers: This lady is a reservoir. A rough, rock dam was cemented in place across the outlet stream, probably by cowboys in the early twentieth century. Take care when you cross it, because the decaying mortar on top makes for treacherous footing. Completing the circuit around the lake, you will find yourself at the junction post where we first saw the lake. Retrace the route back to the trailhead.

Miles and Directions

- **0.0** Parking area; follow doubletrack northward.
- **0.1** Doubletrack ends at signboard; continue uphill on singletrack.
- **0.6** Step across Silver Creek.
- **0.8** Enter Mokelumne Wilderness.
- **1.7** Arrive at point with view.
- **1.8** The "notch" at the top of switchbacks.
- **2.3** Top of Avalanche Meadow.
- **2.9** Frog Lake–Sandy Meadow junction post; go left (northwest).
- **3.1** No CAMPING post junction: go right (following lakeshore) on use-trail.
- **3.3** Dam and outlet creek.
- **3.9** Return to Frog Lake–Sandy Meadow junction; turn left (south) to return to trailhead.
- **6.8** Arrive back at the parking lot.

43 Bull Run Lake

Ascending a tributary ravine of the upper Stanislaus River, fording streams, traversing deep forest and lush meadow, the Bull Run Lake Trail passes through such varied and beautiful terrain that the journey is the highlight of the trip. Bull Run makes a splendid day hike, but backpackers also enjoy its pretty forest solitude.

Start: Stanislaus Meadows, Ebbetts Pass Road
Distance: 7.2 miles out and back
Hiking time: About 3-4 hours
Difficulty: Moderate, with an overall elevation gain exceeding 1,000 feet.
Trail condition: Clear, well-graded, popular trail requiring several creek crossings, potentially wet in early season
Seasons: June through mid-Oct
Other trail users: Equestrians and dogs are permitted. Bikes are excluded from Carson-Iceberg Wilderness. Hunters use the trail in fall.
Land status: Stanislaus National Forest, Carson-Iceberg Wilderness
Nearest towns: Lake Alpine has a store, restaurant, and lodging. Arnold has other services.

Fees and permits: None for day hikers. Campfire permit for stove or fire. Overnighters can obtain wilderness permit from the small ranger station on CA 4 on the east side of Bear Valley (Ranger Station GPS: N38 28.410' / W120 01.562').
Maps: Forest Service: *Carson-Iceberg Wilderness.* USGS 7.5-minute quads: Pacific Valley, Spicer Meadow.
Trail contacts: Stanislaus National Forest, Calaveras Ranger District, 5519 Highway 4, Hathaway Pines, CA 95233; (209) 795-1381; www.fs.usda.gov/stanislaus

Finding the trailhead: Park in a large, dirt parking area on the south side of CA 4, about 53 miles east of Angels Camp and 10 miles west of Ebbetts Pass. You can drive a half mile farther on FR 8N13, but the road is very rough. Trailhead GPS: N38 30.376' / W119 56/617'

The Hike

Our trail starts out on the dirt road (FR 8N13) that heads south from the parking area, at 7,900 feet. At the first turn, you pass a signed junction pointing out the Emigrant Trail, a narrow, unmaintained footpath. Stick with the road. Tracing the boundary of fenced Stanislaus Meadow but keeping mostly within the forest's edge, our first mile of road, and then trail, is gentle but very muddy in early season. After passing a sign demarking the boundary of the Carson-Iceberg Wilderness, watch for a junction where an unofficial pathway leads left (east) around the foot of Stanislaus Meadow. We, however, take the official trail, bearing right (south) to begin a 0.5-mile descent beside the cavorting young Stanislaus River.

Leveling out at the bottom of a forested valley, we now cross the Stanislaus, a wet ford in early season, and then immediately ford its tributary, the outlet stream from Bull Run Lake. Swinging eastward now, alternating through meadow and woods, our

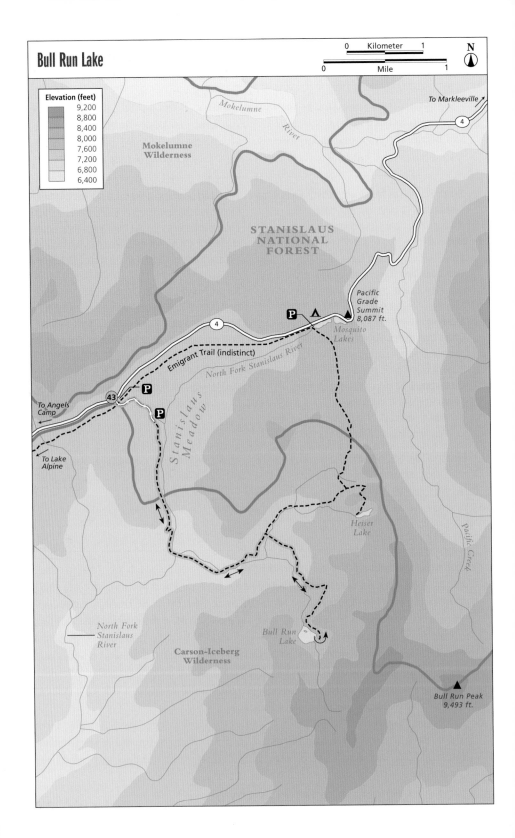

Bull Run Lake

0   Kilometer   1

0   Mile   1

N

Elevation (feet)
9,200
8,800
8,400
8,000
7,600
7,200
6,800
6,400

Mokelumne

River

To Markleeville

4

**Mokelumne
Wilderness**

**STANISLAUS
NATIONAL
FOREST**

*Pacific
Grade
Summit
8,087 ft.*

P

4

*Mosquito
Lakes*

Emigrant Trail (indistinct)

North Fork Stanislaus River

P

43

*Stanislaus
Meadow*

To Angels
Camp

P

To Lake
Alpine

*Heiser
Lake*

Pacific Creek

*North Fork
Stanislaus
River*

*Bull Run
Lake*

**Carson-Iceberg
Wilderness**

▲
*Bull Run Peak
9,493 ft.*

path recrosses the outlet stream and begins to ascend its sun-blanched canyon. Rising little more than 300 feet in 0.6 mile, this stretch of canyon trail tantalizes the ear with the splashing creek entrenched at the bottom of a ravine, close at hand but hard to reach, while our granite-bound trail straggles upward over gravelly tread, past tufts of grass, huckleberry oaks, and dazzling patches of dry-slope wildflowers.

Leveling briefly into a forest, we come to a signed junction. The left (east) route climbs steeply up to Heiser Lake, and eventually to Mosquito Lakes, on a poorly maintained trail, but we head right (south), rock-hopping across Heiser's lively outlet stream. Winding through the woods, crossing and recrossing early-season tributaries, we begin our second 300-foot climb of the hike, this time with ready access to shade and water. The trail fades from time to time, forcing us to keep an eye open for i-blazes and ducks. Rounding the top of the ridge, we arrive at the shore of Bull Run Lake near a small granite island. Forested campsites abound.

Miles and Directions

- **0.0** Parking area.
- **0.1** Junction with Emigrant Trail; stay on road.
- **0.9** Enter Carson-Iceberg Wilderness.
- **1.6** Ford of North Fork of Stanislaus River.
- **2.6** Junction to Mosquito Lakes; bear right (south).
- **3.6** Bull Run Lake.
- **7.2** Arrive back at the parking area.

44 Ebbetts Pass to the Hoodoos above Eagle Creek

Although it can be reached on a day hike, Eagle Creek serves best as a backpackers' base camp for exploring the bizarre, jumbled, fascinating rock wonderland around the slopes of Raymond Peak and Reynolds Peak. This ramble along the Pacific Crest Trail (PCT) ranks among the Sierra's finest wildflower hikes.

Start: Ebbetts Pass
Distance: 12.0 miles out and back
Hiking time: About 6 hours with a businesslike pace, but if you want to explore, allow all day or more
Difficulty: A moderate overnighter or vigorous day hike
Trail condition: Obvious singletrack trail
Seasons: June–Oct; June–July best for wildflowers
Other trail users: Equestrians and dogs permitted. Bikes excluded from the PCT. Hunters use trail in fall.
Land status: Humboldt-Toiyabe National Forest, Mokelumne Wilderness

Nearest towns: Markleeville has food and supplies. Gas available at Woodfords.
Fees and permits: Day hikers should register at the trailhead. Overnighters require wilderness permits in the Mokelumne Wilderness. Campfire permit required for stove or fire.
Maps: Forest Service: *Mokelumne Wilderness*. USGS 7.5-minute quad: Ebbetts Pass.
Trail contacts: Humboldt-Toiyabe National Forest, Carson Ranger District Office, 1536 S. Carson St., Carson City, NV 89701; (775) 882-2766; www.fs.usda.gov/htnf

Finding the trailhead: Park at Ebbetts Pass (CA 4), on either side of the cattle guard at the pass. Walk on the road 0.1 mile eastward (toward Nevada) and look for the trailhead on the left (northwest) side of the road. Ebbetts Pass is 125 miles east of Stockton and nearly 13 miles west of CA 89. Trailhead GPS: N38 32.745' / W119 48.673'

The Hike

From our trailhead our path (the PCT) hooks right (east) across an old doubletrack, over orange-tinged gravelly ground, and past worn granite boulders and scattered pines toward some dry volcanic bluffs, where a spur trail leads to an overlook. (Take that short detour for the view over the dry valleys and mountains toward Nevada.) Returning to the junction post, we resume the Canada-bound direction of the PCT, with views west to Ebbetts Peak. Profusions of flowery tufts sprout from the sandy soil and rocky clefts, sweetening the sagebrush-scented breezes. The abundance and variety of wildflowers that bloom on this poor soil testify to the urgency of attracting pollinators in the short alpine summer.

From our trail's high point—a rocky saddle festooned with lupine, gooseberry, mariposa lilies, phlox, and wild currant—we are struck by a mid-distant view north to an astoundingly snarled ridgeline, dark and volcanic. Formidable armories of stone

Raymond Meadows lies beneath the craggy volcanic ridge that runs south from Reynolds Peak.

chimneys, pinnacles, spurs, and protrusions arch skyward from the backs and ridges of Reynolds Peak (9,679 feet), on the left, and wickedly jumbled Raymond Peak (10,014 feet), on the right.

Our trail drops down around the northern side of Ebbetts Peak, skirting a medley of ponds amid a wood of stunted aspen. The largest pond, Sherrold Lake, is pretty but hardly worthy of being called "lake." Rising gently past cinnamon-plated silver pines and gardens of Indian paintbrush, mule's ears, forget-me-not, wallflower, and buckwheat, we traverse a meadow drained by a seasonal creek and briefly descend beneath some tortuously folded rock benches, bulwarks of the Sierra Crest, which parallels our route just to the west.

At 1.5 miles we arrive at a junction, where a spur trail wends in somewhat feeble fashion downward toward Upper Kinney Lake, a reservoir, while we continue northward on higher ground through thick forest. Rounding the rim of the Upper Kinney Lake basin, our trail moves progressively north across a parched, wide-open hillside with long views northeast to Nevada's Pine Nut Mountains and southeast to the high ridge above Noble Canyon. Staying high, we cross three low spur ridges that divide Kinney Lakes from the headwater valleys of Silver and Raymond Meadows Creeks. The last spur ridge before Raymond Meadows marks the boundary of Mokelumne Wilderness.

Though lush in spring, Raymond Meadows has more scrub than succulent grass. Skirting its western edge, we find ourselves moving through an increasingly fantastic,

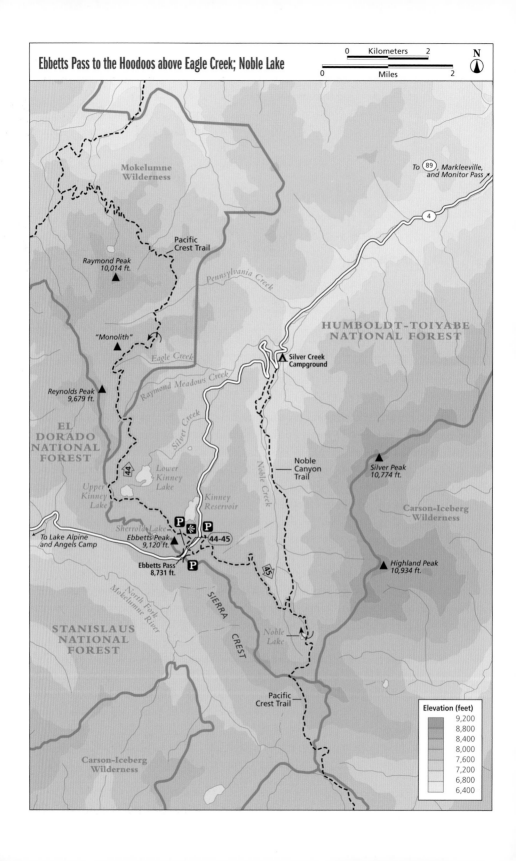

Ebbetts Pass to the Hoodoos above Eagle Creek; Noble Lake

Mokelumne
Wilderness

Pacific
Crest Trail

To 89, Markleeville,
and Monitor Pass

4

Pennsylvania Creek

Raymond Peak
10,014 ft.

HUMBOLDT-TOIYABE
NATIONAL FOREST

"Monolith"

Eagle Creek

Silver Creek
Campground

Reynolds Peak
9,679 ft.

Raymond Meadows Creek

EL
DORADO
NATIONAL
FOREST

Silver Creek

Noble
Canyon
Trail

Silver Peak
10,774 ft.

44

Lower
Kinney
Lake

Noble Creek

Upper
Kinney
Lake

Kinney
Reservoir

Carson-Iceberg
Wilderness

Sherrold Lake

To Lake Alpine
and Angels Camp

P

P

Ebbetts Peak
9,120 ft.

44-45

Highland Peak
10,934 ft.

Ebbetts Pass
8,731 ft.

P

45

North Fork
Mokelumne River

SIERRA

CREST

Noble
Lake

STANISLAUS
NATIONAL
FOREST

Pacific
Crest Trail

CARSON-ICEBERG
Wilderness

Elevation (feet)
9,200
8,800
8,400
8,000
7,600
7,200
6,800
6,400

rocky landscape, rife with sage, locoweed, phlox, paintbrush, asters, daisies, gillia, and mule's ears. Reynolds Peak and its spur ridges are strewn across the landscape in gargantuan jumbles, like three-dimensional rock mazes. As we cross the next low divide into the Eagle Creek valley, the more scenically susceptible among us are momentarily struck dumb by a towering, ruddy-colored monolith that would not be out of place in Zion itself, encircled by a phalanx of savage-looking pinnacles. It's hard to believe that such a stunning monument has not been baptized with some rumbling Gothic appellation, like the Barbican or Gargoyles Roost, but on further consideration, its anonymity has probably saved it from becoming the focus of a New Age cult.

Eagle Creek has plenty of room for camping, and the countryside can certainly absorb your time and attention. But even day hikers short on time should walk a little farther on the trail to see a bit more of these fantastic rock gardens. By continuing 1.3 miles farther to the divide between the Eagle Creek and Pennsylvania Creek drainages, you will see some gnarly specimens of weather-beaten juniper and pass close below a particularly fine stretch of petrified hoodoos. I once met a distracted PCT through-hiker on this stretch. He was looking for a rock that, he claimed, had saved his life some years before. He had been caught ill-prepared in a sudden snowstorm and survived by taking shelter for three days in one of its cozy recesses.

Miles and Directions

0.0 Ebbetts Pass trailhead.

0.6 Sherrold Lake.

1.5 Signed junction to Upper Kinney Lake; go left (west).

3.5 Entrance to Mokelumne Wilderness.

3.7 South end of Raymond Meadows.

4.7 Eagle Creek.

5.0 Hoodoos.

6.0 Divide between Eagle and Pennsylvania Creeks.

12.0 Arrive back at the trailhead at Ebbetts Pass.

45 Noble Lake

Although Noble Lake lacks the pristine splendor of many High Sierra lakes, the hike to it offers sensational views of the volcanic Sierra Crest, glaciated Noble Canyon, and rugged alpine summits. Part of the Pacific Crest Trail (PCT), it is also an exceptionally well-engineered route, providing striking views along its entire length, with a minimum of ups and downs.

Start: Ebbetts Pass
Distance: 7.4 miles out and back
Hiking time: About 5 hours
Difficulty: A moderate hike, despite a 1,350-foot elevation gain overall
Trail condition: A well-graded trail—occasionally narrow, slippery, and exposed—with 2 tricky creek crossings in early season
Seasons: June-Oct
Other trail users: Equestrians and dogs permitted. Bikes are excluded from the PCT. Hunters may use the trail in fall.
Land status: Humboldt-Toiyabe National Forest.

Nearest towns: Markleeville has food and supplies. Gas available at Woodfords.
Fees and permits: Day hikers register at trailhead. Overnighters require wilderness permits only if camping overnight in the Carson-Iceberg Wilderness, which lies beyond Noble Lake. Campfire permit required for fires or stoves.
Maps: Forest Service: *Carson-Iceberg Wilderness.* USGS 7.5-minute quad: Ebbetts Pass.
Trail contacts: Humboldt-Toiyabe National Forest, Carson Ranger District Office, 1536 S. Carson St., Carson City, NV 89701; (775) 882-2766; www.fs.usda.gov/htnf

Finding the trailhead: Park at Ebbetts Pass (CA 4), on either side of the cattle guard at the pass. Walk on the road 0.1 mile eastward (toward Nevada) and take the trailhead on the right (southeast) side of the road. Ebbetts Pass is about 125 miles east of Stockton and nearly 13 miles west of CA 89. Trailhead GPS: N38 32.743' / W119 48. 672'

The Hike

From an elevation of 8,700 feet just east of Ebbetts Pass, the signposted trail delves southbound for 0.3 mile through a forest of pine, fir, and hemlock to a junction, where we head right (east). (The left-hand trail descends 0.3 mile to another parking area on CA 4.) Climbing slightly, we emerge into more-open country, enjoying views north to bulbous Ebbetts Peak, Reynolds Peak (9,679 feet), and Raymond Peak (10,014 feet). The distant, rolling, mountainous landscape—splotched with struggling clumps of hemlock, pine, and juniper, and tawny-colored patches of sage and grass—somewhat resembles a mangy, well-gnawed hound-dog hide stretched taut over bony ribs.

Rounding the first low ridge, we come face-to-face with the strikingly dramatic Sierra Crest, composed here of reddish-brown volcanic mudflow and so convoluted with rock spires, snow-choked crevices, solidified mudflows, and volcanic plugs that it brings to mind a massive, old, brick apartment block whose facade has collapsed in an earthquake, leaving a background network of corroded pipes, plumbing fixtures, window frames, and half-toppled chimneys, with a pile of dusty red rubble in the foreground.

For the next 2.8 miles, our trail roughly parallels this crest at elevations some 600 to 1,400 feet beneath it, in the course losing 500 feet in elevation, but so judiciously that it barely fatigues a hiker in reasonable condition, either coming or going. It is an inspiring walk, frequently wooded but sustaining grand views down Noble Canyon and up its far wall to the summits of Silver (10,774 feet) and Highland (10,934 feet) peaks. As we approach the barren semicircular basin at the head of Noble Canyon, looking up to views of Tryon Peak, we begin a series of delightful creek crossings, more numerous when early-season snowmelt comes cascading down chutes through the volcanic mudflow. A curious pile of boulders composed of aggregate stuck with shards of rock congregates at one intermittent crossing. After crossing the largest creek, an unnamed stream draining the flanks of Tryon Peak, we round the canyon head and climb a dry ridge past a stand of grotesque juniper trees.

Passing into the next ravine, once again in heavy forest, we meet the Noble Canyon Trail coming up from the left. We bear right (south) at this fork, hiking to our second-largest creek crossing, the outlet of Noble Lake. Now we commence a series of switchbacks up steep and largely barren slopes of natural aggregate, the surface mostly broken into scree. Volcanic hoodoos and crags lined by eroded gullies thrust upward on both sides, while the outlet stream from Noble Lake gouges noisily through its ravine below. Despite the sound of water, the alpine coolness, and the natural flower gardens of paintbrush and mariposa tulip, the ground immediately beneath our feet is so dry and rocky, and the long views so rugged and arid, that anyone with a love for desert hiking will feel exhilarated.

Cresting the hill, we find ourselves on a spacious, rolling shelf beneath the Sierra Crest, with views north to distant mountains. Small, greenish Noble Lake, crowded by willow, offers scant shelter to campers, with only one decent campsite on the shore, next to the outlet stream, and another in a clump of trees on a hilltop to the north. Raked by winds blowing up from the canyons, it's a site better suited for a day hike than a backpacker's destination, though it is convenient for climbing the surrounding mountains or as a one-night stand en route to the adjacent Carson-Iceberg Wilderness. The carousing frogs and the bees droning in the hillside flower gardens seem to like it well enough.

Miles and Directions

- **0.0**   Ebbetts Pass trailhead.
- **0.3**   Junction with spur route to CA 4; bear right (east).
- **2.9**   Junction with Noble Canyon Trail; bear right (south).
- **3.2**   Step across Noble Lake outlet stream.
- **3.8**   Noble Lake.
- **7.4**   Arrive back at the trailhead at Ebbetts Pass.

Honorable Mention

R Inspiration Point

This 2.6-mile out-and-back scramble to the flat summit of a volcanic mesa above Lake Alpine affords maplike views over the Stanislaus River's north fork basin. Leaving from a gated dirt road at the edge of Pine Martin Campground on the eastern end of Alpine Lake, our signed trail quickly forks to a singletrack through forest of red fir to the foot of a nearly 600-foot-high volcanic rock, deeply fluted on the sides. We climb it via a rocky contour on the mesa's north side, steadying ourselves with our hands in the final chute on slippery volcanic aggregate. Surrounded by bluffs on nearly all sides, this 7,900-foot-high plateau is open and flat enough to explore safely at will, taking in views of Utica and Union reservoirs, bright blue against the darker green forest, and Duck Lake in its dazzling green meadow. Although our panorama extends north to Mount Reba (8,755 feet), northeast to the peaks above Ebbetts Pass, and southeast to the Dardanelles and the peaks around Sonora Pass, the most popular inspiration on Inspiration Point seems to entail something altogether separate from the views. Scores of visitors, maybe even hundreds, have been inspired to record their visits, and their sweethearts' names, by setting down stones to form letters that spell out messages like "Luann-baby and Steve" and "Kyle loves Lisa." Trailhead GPS: N38 28.817' / W119 59.372'

A hiker ponders the meaning of LOVE on Inspiration Point.

Along the Sonora Pass Road

The Sonora Pass Road (CA 108) runs east–west through the Sierra Nevada between the Gold Country town of Sonora, in the western foothills, and Mono County. Not the most sensible of Sierra passes, the route was hyped into existence by nineteenth-century Sonora boosters, who advertised an "emigrant route" that ran 8 miles south of the present pass, but it was too rugged to be practical. The present route was completed in 1864 as a toll road and received a lot of use during the heyday of the silver and gold booms on the east side of the Sierra Nevada in the 1870s. Rising to 9,643 feet, second highest of Sierra road crossings, Sonora Pass is also one of the steepest and most twisting. By the same token, it is exceptionally beautiful. Heavy snows keep it closed all winter.

The highway passes through Stanislaus National Forest on the west side and Humboldt-Toiyabe National Forest on the east. Much of the higher country on the north side of the road is protected in the Carson-Iceberg Wilderness, a heavily volcanic region with many buttes and few lakes. To the south, Emigrant Wilderness and Hoover Wilderness run clear to the borders of Yosemite National Park and are popularly vaunted as the northern end of the "High Sierra." Being largely granitic, they are also famed for their lakes. The principal summer resort is at Pinecrest Lake, while Strawberry, Dardanelles, Kennedy Meadows, and Leavitt Meadow are much smaller.

46 West Side Railroad Trail to the Tuolumne North Fork

Cherished birthright of the great American hobo, the uncommon pleasure of walking a railroad track is known to few kids nowadays, to their loss. This trail, descending on a long, steady, abandoned railroad grade into the North Fork Tuolumne River Canyon, provides happy salvation for the soul beset by too many video games. The trains are gone, the engineers, firemen, and railroad bulls lie in their graves, but the abandoned tracks and rustic canyon scenery remain, preserved in a time warp.

Start: Staging area at corner of Buchanan and Miramonte Roads, Tuolumne

Distance: 5.4 miles one-way shuttle

Hiking time: About 3 hours

Difficulty: Moderate, with an overall loss of only about 430 feet

Trail condition: A gentle-graded railroad bed, much still with track. Some singletrack trail. Minor bushwhacking. Beware of rattlers and poison oak.

Seasons: All year, weather permitting, but summer can be hot

Other trail users: Dogs, equestrians, bikes

Land status: Tuolumne Park and Recreation District, BLM and Stanislaus National Forest. Private property adjacent to start of hike.

Nearest towns: Tuolumne, though Sonora has more amenities

Fees and permits: None

Map: USGS 7.5-minute quad: Tuolumne

Trail contacts: Stanislaus National Forest, Mi-Wok Ranger District, 24695 Highway 108, Mi-Wuk Village, CA 95346; (209) 586-3234; www.fs.usda.gov/stanislaus

Finding the trailhead: To reach the staging area in Tuolumne City from Sonora, take the Mono Way exit from eastbound CA 108. Turn right on Mono Way and drive 0.5 mile to Tuolumne Road. Turn right and drive Tuolumne Road nearly 7 miles to the little town of Tuolumne, where you turn left on Carter Street. Drive 0.3 mile up Carter Street and turn right on Buchanan Road. After about 0.5 mile look for a small parking lot on the left at the intersection of Buchanan and Miramonte Roads. Tuolumne City trailhead GPS: N37 58.391' / W120 13.637'

If doing a shuttle, park a car near the lower trailhead along the Tuolumne River. From the staging area in Tuolumne City, drive 4.2 miles farther down Buchanan Road (FR 1N04) into the canyon to the unmarked ending trailhead, on the left (north) side of the road (ending trailhead GPS: N37 59.819' / W120 10.926'). If you miss it, you will almost immediately pass the back entrance gate of the River Ranch Campground on the right (south) side of the road (camp back entrance GPS: N37 59.830' / W120 10.909'). If the campground gate is open, park in there; if it is closed, go to the main entrance, 0.5 mile farther, around the bend on the south side of the Tuolumne River. River Ranch Campground has public and private sites, potable water, and vault toilets. You can also park on the shoulder, clear of the road.

The Hike

Tuolumne City was a mill town, the mountain terminus of the Sierra Railway. More than 3 billion board feet of red and white fir, ponderosa, sugar pine, and incense cedar cut from logs in the West Side Lumber Company mill at Tuolumne City rode that

Hikers lounging at the Canyon View Rest Area along the old West Side Railroad cut have a shaded view into the Tuolumne canyon.

lonesome railroad down to the Southern Pacific railhead at Oakdale, where they were reloaded for shipment to markets across country. To supply itself with these logs, the West Side Lumber Company built a narrow-gauge railroad line in the other direction, higher into the Sierra forest belt above Tuolumne City. In its heyday year of 1949, the narrow-gauge West Side Railroad snaked through 72 miles of track to remote lumber camps like Niagara and Buffalo Landing, hauling timber back down for milling in Tuolumne City. (See one of the little engines that used to pull these trains in a park in the middle of Tuolumne City.) Replaced by logging trucks, the last logging train ran in 1961. The narrow-gauge tracks were abandoned. Forest and scrub were reclaiming them until public land managers and volunteers began clearing it for a hiking trail. Though far from complete, this rail-trail may one day again reach from the Gold Country to the Sierra forest belt as a historic, colorful, well-graded hiker's thoroughfare.

For now though, this short section from Tuolumne City to the North Fork of the Tuolumne River is open for business. We start the trail in a dry flume cut at 2,850 feet elevation, amid oaks and scattered houses, at the site of the vanished Friedenberg Station. Walking eastward, we pass under a wet flume, encounter some trail signage, and achieve our first view into the North Fork Canyon at half a mile. Now the real fun starts.

Like all well-graded railroad right-of-ways, this one keeps an even keel, contouring like a Disneyland train ride along the canyon wall, delving into side gulches and back out to ridges bulging over steep canyon drop-offs, continuously rendering enjoyable passage through otherwise rough, steep, rocky terrain.

After the first mile the tracks appear, like congenial sidekicks from an old Western. The railroad bed's downward trend is at any given point imperceptible underfoot, but whenever a distant slope pops into view, you can clearly see that the track is losing elevation steadily. The rails are in good shape, some clearly stamped with record of their Buffalo, New York, casting in 1907. We pass other mementos of the old economy, based on timber and gold: signal posts, painted mile markers, a steep dirt road leading up to the once-rich Buchanan Mine, the overgrown site of a watering station, a loose pile of stacked rails, a railway switch.

Although volunteers have cleared back the montane chaparral from the higher reaches of this trail, temporarily staving off that vanishing act that nature mandates for humankind's abandoned works, the farther you go from Tuolumne City, the more the right-of-way begins to resemble a Mayan precinct engulfed by jungle. Not only do you see but you also smell and brush against a panoply of leathery, spiky, stickery shrubs and trees, including scrub oak, deer brush, buckeye, gray pine (the source of those big, heavy, prickly cones), and manzanita, not to mention that vile, nonnative weed, yellow star thistle, which sometimes crowds our path and painfully pokes at the wearer of short pants. At one spot grows a bank of wild grape, producing small but tasty fruit in September, but with enormous seeds, so that you eat them like sunflower seeds, gumming them to extract the tart-sweet flesh and spitting the pith out, an enormously engaging activity for those who can walk and chew grapes at the same time.

We pass through road cuts hacked and blasted by Chinese labor crews through shiny schistoid rock, that metamorphic calling card of Gold Country geology. The camps of Soulsbyville, Confidence, Arastraville, and Sugar Pine all sprang up along the quartz veins not 4 miles from our path, grouped along a vein of gold known as the East Belt, which runs parallel and east of the true Mother Lode at Sonora.

At just over 5 miles, you will encounter a clear but unmarked singletrack trail that parts from the railroad bed on the right, leading by easy gradient (though the steepest on our hike) down to paved Buchanan Road at the bottom of the canyon. River Ranch Campground (elevation 2,550 feet) sits across the road, equipped with pit toilets and piped water. The North Fork Tuolumne River itself flows through, rather lackadaisical and gentle during summer and fall, perfect for children who like to search for trout and crawdads in the shallow pools.

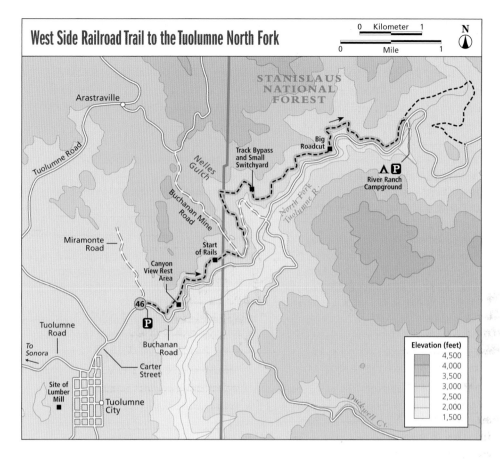

West Side Railroad Trail to the Tuolumne North Fork

0 Kilometer 1

0 Mile 1

N

STANISLAUS NATIONAL FOREST

Arastraville

Tuolumne Road

Nelles Gulch

Track Bypass and Small Switchyard

Big Roadcut

Buchanan Mine Road

River Ranch Campground

North Fork Tuolumne R.

Miramonte Road

Start of Rails

Canyon View Rest Area

46

Tuolumne Road

To Sonora

Buchanan Road

Carter Street

Site of Lumber Mill

Tuolumne City

Duckwell Ct.

Elevation (feet)
4,500
4,000
3,500
3,000
2,500
2,000
1,500

Miles and Directions

0.0 Tuolumne City staging area.

0.1 Water spigot.

0.3 Signage.

0.5 First Bench; canyon view.

1.1 Tracks start.

1.4 Buchanan Mine Road crossing.

2.5 Doubletrack and switch.

4.0 Big rock cut.

5.1 Junction of trail to Tuolumne River; turn right (downhill).

5.4 Lower trailhead on Buchanan Road, near back gate to River Ranch Campground.

47 Burst Rock Trail to Chewing Gum Lake

One of the shortest routes into spectacular Emigrant Wilderness, the Burst Rock Trail puts the steepest climb at its beginning. Historic and scenic, the trail offers magnificent vistas far south into Yosemite and north to the jumbled volcanic peaks of the Sonora Pass country.

Start: Gianelli Cabin trailhead
Distance: 8.0 miles out and back
Hiking time: About 6 hours
Difficulty: Moderate, with an overall elevation gain of about 2,000 feet
Trail condition: Excellent (and popular)
Seasons: June to avoid the cattle, though you may hit snow and *will* hit mosquitoes. July–Sept has fewer mosquitoes, more cattle. Oct typically fine, though you may encounter hunters.
Other trail users: Dogs must be leashed. Equestrians and hunters welcome. Bikes are not allowed in Emigrant Wilderness.

Land status: Emigrant Wilderness, Stanislaus National Forest
Nearest towns: Sonora, though Pinecrest has amenities
Fees and permits: None for day hikes. Overnighters need a wilderness permit.
Maps: Forest Service: *Emigrant Wilderness.* USGS 7.5-minute quads: Pinecrest, Cooper Peak. (**Note:** The trail has been realigned since maps were updated.)
Trail contacts: Stanislaus National Forest, Summit Ranger Station, 1 Pinecrest Lake Rd., Pinecrest, CA 95364; (209) 965-3434; www .fs.usda.gov/stanislaus

Finding the trailhead: From the Summit Ranger Station at the junction of CA 108 and Pinecrest Lake Road, drive 0.3 mile up Pinecrest Lake Road to the first right-hand turn on a public road. Turn right and drive nearly 3 miles to the entrance of the Dodge Ridge ski resort. Turn right and drive 0.5 mile to the next junction, Crabtree Road. Turn left (southeast) and drive 1.6 miles to yet another signed junction, where you turn on FR 4N47, immediately passing Aspen Meadow Pack Station. The Gianelli Cabin parking area is 6.8 miles farther on a road that changes from pavement to well-graded gravel to rocky dirt. The trail begins on the left (north) side of the parking area at an elevation of 8,600 feet. Trailhead GPS: N38 11.900' / W119 53.037'

The Hike

Crossing between the sawn logs, the trail crosses a poor dirt road and climbs moderately uphill through a red fir forest. Bending into switchbacks, we climb to an exposed rock outcrop with views north over the canyon of the South Fork of the Stanislaus to the reddish volcanic ridge that defines the northern boundary of Emigrant Wilderness, including the Three Chimneys, Castle Rock, and Cooper Peak. Continuing uphill, the gradient decreases as the forest clears, and we find ourselves rounding to the top of a dry, rocky ridge.

A sign atop the ridge marks the boundary of the Emigrant Wilderness and recalls the history of the Sonora Pass Route, which passed this spot in the early 1850s and was probably the most onerous emigrant trail over the Sierra Nevada. Burst Rock is

Burst Rock Trail to Chewing Gum Lake

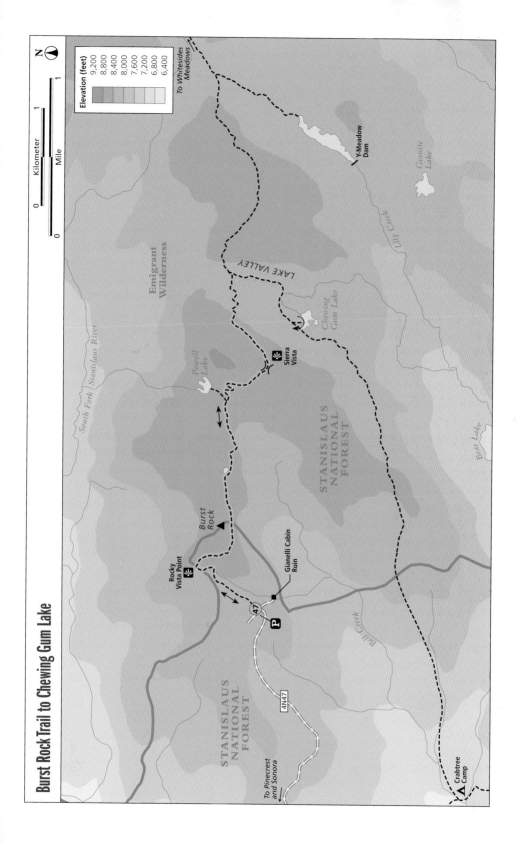

not a saddle pass but the 9,161-foot crown of a ridge. This ridge proved more readily accessible to wagons than the surrounding canyons. Its name is supposedly a corruption of "Birth Rock," alluding to a story that claims a pioneer woman gave birth in a rock shelter near here.

Our trail slips down the east side, back into the trees over a couple of rocky switchbacks. Passing a granite-bound pond, we descend smoothly to a saddle in the divide between the Stanislaus drainage to the north and the Tuolumne drainage to the south. An unsigned spur trail from this saddle leads left (north) to nearby Powell Lake, which shortly appears below in its handsome granite basin as we zigzag up the saddle's east side.

The forest thins as we cross a section of gravel and granite slabs on the second ridge of our trail, at about 9,150 feet. From a jumble of granite boulders on the east side of this ridge, a place I call "Sierra vista" on the map, a startling view of the Sierra spreads before us. This is a wonderful spot to sit with a large map, a compass, and a pair of binoculars. More than 8 miles due south, we can see the massive cliffs of the Cherry Creek canyon, beyond which lies Yosemite National Park. Prominent among the southern summits is Haystack Peak (10,015 feet), which looks like it was cut from granite with a hatchet. On the east-southeastern horizon, Mount Conness (12,590 feet) marks both the Sierra Crest and the eastern boundary of Yosemite, 35 air miles away but closer to 100 by trail. Near at hand, Lake Valley spreads out before us, luxuriant and green beneath the unnamed granite ridge that forms its eastern edge. We can even pick out glimpses of blue Chewing Gum Lake down there, through the forest.

We contour around the northern ridge of Lake Valley, enjoying the view. Crossing an open granite slab, we begin to drop gradually into the valley, with views opening north to the reddish volcanic plugs of the Three Chimneys. These predominantly lava landscapes of the Stanislaus drainage seem to merge at our ridge with the mostly granitic landscape of the Tuolumne drainage to the south, for we can find both granitic and lava rocks along our trail.

As we level out among conifers on the floor of Lake Valley, we arrive at a junction in the woods. We turn right (south) and step from the woods into the long, wet meadows of Lake Valley, where we find traces of the old emigrant route, now blocked with logs. Intensely green, Lake Valley is a pleasure to look at, but a haven for mosquitoes. Slogging through muddy spots and past islands of granite boulders in the meadows, we hike a half mile before the trail makes a sharp right turn into the trees to avoid a brook. Passing through an even soggier meadow, we branch left (southeast) on a use-trail that leads to the granite shores of Chewing Gum Lake. Although its rocky benches are ideal for picnics and loafing, early-season campers will want to retreat up the forested slopes for some relief from mosquitoes.

Miles and Directions

0.0 Signed trailhead

1.2 Burst Rock (first ridge).

1.9 Junction with trail to Powell Lake; go straight (east).

2.4 Second ridge (Sierra vista).

3.3 Lake Valley junction; go straight down Lake Valley (south).

4.0 Chewing Gum Lake.

8.0 Arrive back at the parking area.

48 Disaster Creek Trail

Seekers of solitude will appreciate this up-canyon hike, a steady panoply of forest, ridge, meadow, and distant peak.

Start: Iceberg Meadow
Distance: 11.6 miles out and back
Hiking time: About 6–7 hours
Difficulty: Moderately strenuous, with an overall (but very gradual) elevation gain of more than 2,000 feet
Trail condition: Good singletrack trail
Seasons: June–Oct
Other trail users: No bikes allowed. Dogs under control and equestrians are permitted.
Land status: Carson-Iceberg Wilderness, Stanislaus National Forest

Nearest towns: Strawberry and Pinecrest have stores and cafes, but Sonora is the nearest large town with all amenities.
Fees and permits: Wilderness permit required for overnight use. Campfire permit required with stove or campfire.
Maps: Forest Service: *Carson-Iceberg Wilderness.* USGS 7.5-minute quads: Dardanelles Cone, Disaster Peak.
Trail contacts: Stanislaus National Forest, Summit Ranger Station, 1 Pinecrest Lake Rd., Pinecrest, CA 95364; (209) 965-3434; www.fs.usda.gov/stanislaus

Finding the trailhead: From the Summit Ranger Station, drive 19.4 miles up CA 108 to the Clark Fork Road. Turn left onto it, drive 9.2 miles to Iceberg Meadow at the end of the road, and park on the shoulder. The trailhead is on the north side of the road, at an elevation of about 6,480 feet. Trailhead GPS: N38 25.070' / W119 45.040'

The Hike

We start right off with the steepest rise of the entire trail, switchbacking up about 330 feet in the first half mile—a trivial climb by Sierra standards. Disaster Creek flows through its deep channel, unseen to the west, while the crumbly monolith known as the Iceberg rises behind the forest on the east. At the top of the switchbacks, we settle into a straightforward walk up the bottom of Disaster Creek's canyon, alternately wooded and meadowed, on an easy gradient that sets the pace for the remainder of the hike. Our trail is well engineered and well maintained.

Hopping across two unnamed tributary creeks, we catch intermittent glimpses of the mostly bare, rounded ridges that cradle this valley: Lightning Mountain on the west and the slopes of Disaster Peak on the east. Like Disaster Creek, the latter takes its name from an accident that befell a topographer named Cowells while surveying this canyon on September 6, 1877. "We had finished a very successful day's work, and were completing our labors by putting up the usual monument," wrote Lieutenant Montgomery Macomb of the *Wheeler Survey.* "Mr. Cowles loosened a heavy mass, which, slipping from its bearings, precipitated him some 15 feet upon the jagged rocks below, passing over his legs as it rolled on. Mr. Vail and myself, on hastening to his assistance, were inexpressibly shocked to find that both legs had been broken."

Half Moon Lake makes a better marsh than it does a fishing hole for Sierra anglers, but it's pretty nonetheless.

Rock-hopping across the creek from Paradise Valley, we meet a trail junction just beyond the northern bank. This trail climbs very steeply to the right (east) toward the PCT, but we continue straight (north) up the Disaster Creek Trail, enjoying much the same kind of scenery, gradient, and solitude that has so far characterized our route, although some truly large junipers lend more charisma to the forest. As we near the headwaters of Disaster Creek, a barbed-wire fence line appears on the left (west), evidence of recent cattle grazing in these mountains. Passing through a stock gate, we leave the Disaster Creek watershed behind and enter the drainage of Arnot Creek on a fading, old doubletrack.

Glimpsing some mountaintops to the west, you might want to make a slight detour from the trail for a view down the Arnot Creek canyon against the backdrop of Hiram, Airola, and Iceberg peaks. (You'll pass an obvious and convenient knoll that suits this purpose nicely, immediately to the side of the path.)

Our trail continues north to a meadow beneath the volcanic palisades of 10,054-foot Arnot Peak's western face. In the middle of the meadow on the banks of juvenile Arnot Creek, we find a signposted junction with the barely distinct Arnot Creek Trail, which pushes downstream to the Clark Fork Road. Our own route follows

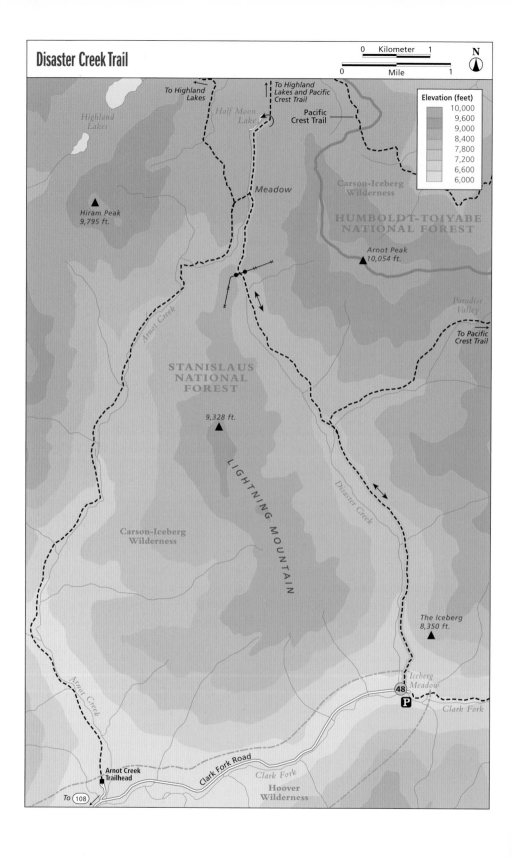

Disaster Creek Trail

0 Kilometer 1
0 Mile 1

N

Elevation (feet)
10,000
9,600
9,000
8,400
7,800
7,200
6,600
6,000

To Highland Lakes

To Highland Lakes and Pacific Crest Trail

Half Moon Lake

Pacific Crest Trail

Meadow

Highland Lakes

▲ Hiram Peak
9,795 ft.

Carson-Iceberg Wilderness

HUMBOLDT-TOIYABE NATIONAL FOREST

Arnot Peak
▲ 10,054 ft.

Arnot Creek

STANISLAUS NATIONAL FOREST

Paradise Valley

To Pacific Crest Trail

9,328 ft.
▲

Carson-Iceberg Wilderness

L I G H T N I N G   M O U N T A I N

Disaster Creek

The Iceberg
8,350 ft.
▲

Iceberg Meadow

48

P

Clark Fork

Arnot Creek

Clark Fork Road

Clark Fork

▲ Arnot Creek Trailhead

To 108

Hoover Wilderness

dwindling Arnot Creek upstream to its source, placid Half Moon Lake, at an elevation of about 8,560 feet, held in thrall by its watery fringe of electric-green marsh grasses. It's too marshy to approach, but our view point is pretty and makes a good turnaround point.

Miles and Directions

0.0 Parking area.

1.3 Unnamed creek crossing.

2.9 Junction with Paradise Valley Trail; keep left (northwest).

4.4 Stock gate.

5.2 Junction with Arnot Creek Trail; bear right (north).

5.8 Hillside above Half Moon Lake.

11.6 Arrive back at the parking area.

49 Sonora Pass to Latopie Lake

The country around and above Sonora Pass is sublime. Few other Sierra trailheads along the Pacific Crest Trail (PCT) launch the hiker into such vast, wild grandeur within so short a walking distance from the road head.

Start: Sonora Pass
Distance: 10.0 miles out and back
Hiking time: About 6-7 hours
Difficulty: A strenuous day hike, with a gain and loss of nearly 5,500 feet overall
Trail condition: Excellent singletrack trail
Seasons: June-Oct
Other trail users: Equestrians and dogs under control are allowed but no bikes.
Land status: Stanislaus and Humboldt-Toiyabe National Forests
Nearest town: Bridgeport

Fees and permits: None required for day use. Wilderness permit for overnighters.
Maps: Tom Harrison: *Hoover Wilderness*. USGS 7.5-minute quads: Sonora Pass.
Trail contacts: Stanislaus National Forest, Summit Ranger Station, 1 Pinecrest Lake Rd., Pinecrest, CA 95364; (209) 965-3434; www .fs.usda.gov/stanislaus. Humboldt-Toiyabe National Forest, Bridgeport Ranger District, HC 62 Box 1000, Bridgeport, CA 93517; (760) 932-7070; www.fs.usda.gov/htnf.

Finding the trailhead: Drive to Sonora Pass on CA 108. The parking area is about 100 yards west of the pass. To reach the proper trailhead on CA 108, find the unmarked path at the east end of the parking area (unmarked trailhead GPS: N38 19.741' /W119 38.104'), and follow it about 50 yards to the signed trailhead on the main highway. Signed trailhead GPS: N38 19.683' / W119 38.236'

The Hike

The views from Sonora Pass (9,643 feet) are extensive and wide-open. Our trail, the PCT, offers more of the same but amplified on a scale increasingly more grand. To be sure, when the skies glower and cold winds blow, these high mountain ramparts strike the mind unfamiliar with them as intensely raw and stark, desolate and forbidding—and yet, with a brilliant-blue sky, some early-season snow patches, and a profusion of flowers, there's nothing at all grim about them.

Striking southward from the highway at Sonora Pass, we climb a disarmingly easy gradient into the basin of the infant, hop-across Sardine Creek. Looking at our map, we see that Sardine Creek drops to a waterfall a mere 250 yards below, but it's totally invisible from our trail (and not to be confused with Sardine Falls on nearby McKay Creek, visible from cars climbing the eastern side of the Sonora Pass road).

Our route climbs smoothly around Sardine's back basin, a perfect half-circle rise, hitting the actual Sierra crest on a north-facing prominence. Views reach out for miles above timberline. Hikers accustomed to the granitic High Sierra may find these volcanic peaks somber, dark, and crumbly—some would say almost a moonscape—and

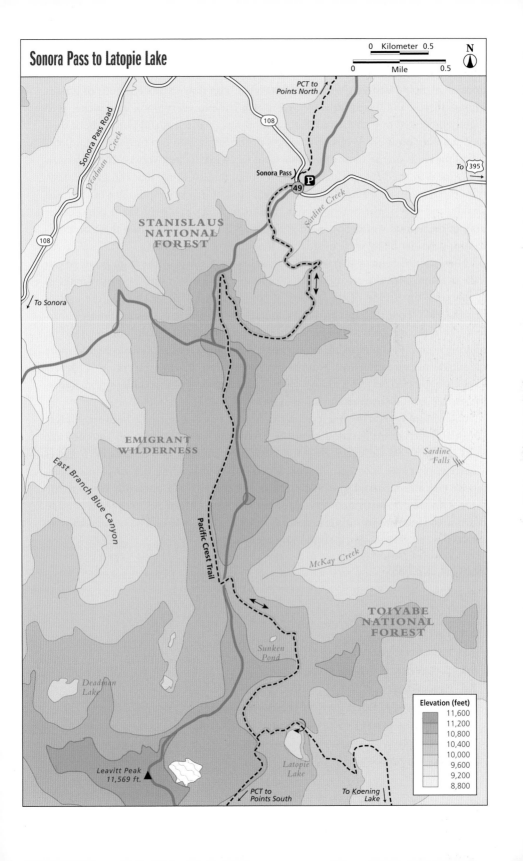

Sonora Pass to Latopie Lake

0   Kilometer   0.5

0   Mile   0.5

N

PCT to
Points North

108

Sonora Pass Road

Deadman Creek

108

To Sonora

Sonora Pass

P

49

Sardine Creek

To 395

STANISLAUS
NATIONAL
FOREST

EMIGRANT
WILDERNESS

East Branch Blue Canyon

Pacific Crest Trail

Sardine
Falls

McKay Creek

TOIYABE
NATIONAL
FOREST

Sunken
Pond

Deadman
Lake

Latopie
Lake

Leavitt Peak
11,569 ft.

PCT to
Points South

To Koening
Lake

Elevation (feet)	
	11,600
	11,200
	10,800
	10,400
	10,000
	9,600
	9,200
	8,800

yet, as you can see all around you, up close and personal, this "moonscape" is teeming with hardy life, even if on a diminished scale, stunted by wind and the arctic conditions of an alpine winter. Our path is festooned with flowers, lichens, tufts of grasses, stunted shrubs, and tough little evergreens that cling to every nook and pocket even slightly protected from the wind. Fat marmots sun themselves and putter about their seed-nibbling business. As always throughout the Sierra, you can find their scatological calling cards on the most prominent boulders with the best views—the same seats that appeal to tired hikers, incidentally. It's tempting to think that the grand views from these marmot "outhouses" constitute a kind of marmot equivalent of the Sears catalog, and that a marmot in repose atop its rock appears very like a philosopher king of the animal world. Sober-sided biologists, however, tell us that these boulder-bathrooms more likely serve as strategic lookouts for predators.

Now the PCT turns sharply south, climbing the ridge to the high point of our trail, at about 10,930 feet, amid a landscape so vast that it dwarfs and exhilarates us at the same time. One of the aspects of engineering a trail so close to the crest is that the PCT now takes on an almost leisurely, level gradient, passing almost effortlessly from the east side to the west, and then back to the east at an unnamed saddle, offering continuous unbroken, astoundingly sweeping views of mountains and more mountains in every direction. From this saddle we descend into the cirque of McKay Creek, stopping to inspect a strange sunken lake with no possible outlet stream, unless the surface level were to rise a hundred feet.

Once more we rise to cross a ridge, this time the east–west saddle between McKay Creek and the Leavitt Meadow drainage. From here we look down on Latopie Lake in its cirque below Leavitt Peak (11,569) with its remnant glacier. The PCT makes a descending curve into Latopie Lake's cirque before heading out to points south, but we take an unmarked spur that picks its way somewhat haphazardly down to the shore. This trail down is not very clear, but neither is it difficult to choose a route down to the windswept, meadowed north shore of Latopie Lake. The better campsites are on the east side, scattered amid some rocky copses.

Miles and Directions

0.0	Trailhead.
0.6	Sardine Creek crossing.
1.8	Point of ridge.
2.2	High point of trail.
3.4	Saddle; cross to east side of ridge.
3.8	Sunken Pond.
4.1	Saddle between McKay Creek and Leavitt Creek Drainage.
4.6	Trail down to Latopie Lake; turn left (east).
5.0	Latopie Lake.
10.0	Arrive back at the trailhead.

50 Leavitt Meadow to Fremont Lake

The most majestic scene on the ever-scenic Sonora Pass Road is Leavitt Meadow—spacious, lush, and enfolded in mountains, of which the stately Tower Peak stands tallest. This out-and-back trail shadows the old, historic Sonora Pass Route to the shores of three forest-ringed lakes.

Start: CA 108 near Leavitt Meadow Campground
Distance: 17.4 miles out and back
Hiking time: About 9-10 hours
Difficulty: An extremely strenuous day hike but a moderate backpack trip of 3 nights
Trail condition: Good but dusty singletrack trail; you need to ford the West Walker River to get to Fremont Lake, which can be difficult in early summer
Seasons: June-Oct
Other trail users: You will meet lots of pack trains, and many hikers bring their dogs.

Land status: Humboldt-Toiyabe National Forest
Nearest town: Bridgeport
Fees and permits: None for day use. Campfire permit required for campfire or stove. Overnight groups limited to 15.
Maps: Tom Harrison: *Hoover Wilderness*. USGS 7.5-minute quad: Pickell Meadow, Tower Peak.
Trail contacts: Humboldt-Toiyabe National Forest, Bridgeport Ranger District, HCR 1, Box 1000, Bridgeport, CA 93517; (760) 932-7070; www.fs.usda.gov/htnf

Finding the trailhead: The overnight parking area is on the south side of the Sonora Pass Road (CA 108), just west of Leavitt Meadow Campground, about 8 miles east of Sonora Pass and 7 miles west of US 395 at Sonora Junction. (Overnight parking GPS: N38 19.913' / W119 33.206') Day hikers can park in designated sites in Leavitt Meadow Campground, where you will find the actual signed trailhead. Trailhead GPS: N38 20.039' / W119 33.117'

The Hike

Broad Leavitt Meadow seemed to be a natural gateway into the Sierra Nevada for pioneers in 1852, when the seventy-five-member Clark-Skidmore party managed to drag their wagons through here clear to the Gold Country. Ecstatic visions of new customers pouring into Sonora stirred town boosters to send out a delegation to drum up more emigrants. The following year, when the Duckwall party attempted to traverse what the Sonorans brightly dubbed the "Sonora Pass Route," their wagons bogged down in the rugged mountains and they had to be rescued. A few other wagon parties attempted the crossing, but the Sonora Pass Route quickly earned a reputation as being too rugged for wheels. Pack trains continued to use the route, and another famous traveler here was Grizzly Adams, who crossed on foot in April 1854 in company with his two tame grizzly bears, Ben Franklin and Lady Washington. The Sonora Pass Route was later realigned northward along present CA 108, leaving the old route still traceable across the Sierra through the Hoover Wilderness on the east side of the crest, and Emigrant Wilderness on the west, a boon to hikers and backpackers.

Start by walking up the shoulder of the highway about 50 yards east to the Leavitt Meadow Campground. From there, walk the campground road left until you get to the bridge crossing the West Walker River. The trail on the opposite bank climbs a dry knoll to a signed fork, where we turn right (southwest) onto the West Walker Trail.

Descending to Leavitt Meadow, follow the river upstream through a sagebrush plain, bypassing the network of unsigned stock paths that split right (west) from the main trail toward the Leavitt Meadow Pack Station, which presently appears on the edge of the meadow. The spectacular panorama southward, down the stately sage and river flats of Leavitt Meadow to Tower Peak (11,755 feet), on Yosemite's northern boundary, is as fine a picture of mountain majesty as the Sierra holds, most dramatic (and cooler) in the early morning or late afternoon, when a lower sun casts long shadows. The striking view stays with us for nearly the next 1.5 miles, while we trace the meadow's edge along a rolling contour low on a sandy ridge.

Then the trail cuts steeply up the forested ridge, leveling out at a junction with the Secret Lake Trail. We turn right (south), presently passing the boundary of Hoover Wilderness, marked by a signboards containing, among other information, the history of the Sonora Pass Route. Descending to the north shore of Roosevelt Lake, backed to the east by dry, rounded mountains, we skirt its western shore before climbing a little above Lane Lake, which is joined to Roosevelt by a narrow channel. Unmarked spur paths drop down to Lane Lake, which offers some pleasant campsites. Both lakes are pleasant but so languid that they seem perfect candidates to transmogrify into meadows over the next century or two.

Passing Lane Lake's sluggish outlet stream, we begin a sustained uphill stretch with west-facing views over the West Walker River canyon, a welcome change to the dry meadows and woods that opened the hike. Steadily climbing 650 feet in elevation, we cross two creeks that send their bubbly water down into the West Walker's canyon. We hit the top of a ridge at just under 8,000 feet, thinking we've got this trail licked, when the trail gods send us suddenly careening downhill again—it seems like such a waste to lose elevation having worked so hard to gain it! But their plans all work out for the best, plunking down at a junction in a meadow. The left-hand spur trail fords the river and climbs 0.2 mile to stagnant, sulfurous Hidden Lake, definitely not a pleasant campsite. Fortunately, there's a good campsite right on the river next to the junction.

Continuing toward Fremont Lake from the junction, we continue south, following the eastern bank of the West Walker, a narrow, rocky passage cut at times through granite. Heads up for the next junction, where horses ford the river, and a hard-to-see sign points hikers toward a ford farther upstream. Although you can shave 0.4 mile from the trip by fording with the horses, their ford is deeper than the hiker ford. Continue upriver on the eastern bank, therefore, and take the shallower crossing.

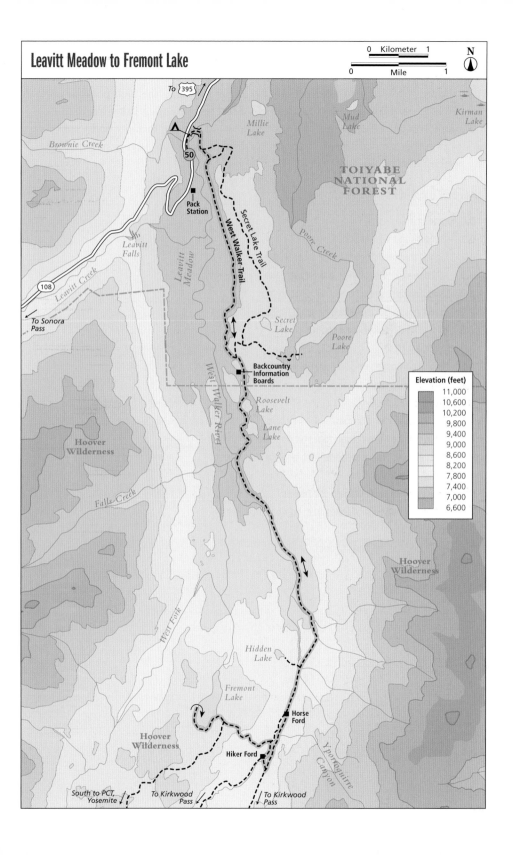

Leavitt Meadow to Fremont Lake

0   Kilometer   1

0   Mile   1

N

To 395

Brownie Creek

Millie Lake

Mud Lake

Kirman Lake

50

Pack Station

Leavitt Falls

108   Leavitt Creek

To Sonora Pass

Leavitt Meadow

Secret Lake Trail

West Walker Trail

Secret Lake

Poore Creek

Poore Lake

TOIYABE NATIONAL FOREST

Backcountry Information Boards

Roosevelt Lake

Lane Lake

Hoover Wilderness

West Walker River

Falls Creek

West Fork

Hoover Wilderness

Hidden Lake

Fremont Lake

Horse Ford

Hoover Wilderness

Hiker Ford

Ypoqoquirre Canyon

South to PCT, Yosemite

To Kirkwood Pass

To Kirkwood Pass

Elevation (feet)

11,000
10,600
10,200
9,800
9,400
9,000
8,600
8,200
7,800
7,400
7,000
6,600

Once on the west bank of the West Walker River, we rendezvous with the horse cutoff and together begin a steep climb up a rocky hillside. Tower Peak comes into view, always a handsome mountain from any angle. Reaching the high point of our trail at a ridge at 8,300 feet, we take the right-hand fork. Fremont Lakes lies beyond, in a granite-bound valley. With a nice little rock island to swim to and woodsy campsites on the south end, Fremont Lake (8,221 feet) is by far the largest, most robust, and prettiest lake of our hike.

Miles and Directions

0.0   Parking area.

0.1   Campground sign-in board.

0.2   Signed trailhead above Walker River Bridge.

0.5   Junction with West Walker and Secret Lake Trails; go right (south).

2.5   Junction with signed horse trail; stay on foot trail.

2.7   Junction with Secret Lake Trail; go right (south).

2.8   Hoover Wilderness boundary.

3.3   Roosevelt Lake.

3.8   Path to campsites on south end of Lane Lake.

4.8   Small creek crossing.

6.0   Larger creek crossing.

6.5   Hidden Lake Trail junction.

7.0   Horse ford of Walker River; foot trail does not ford here.

7.7   Junction with Paiute Meadow Trail; go right (northwest).

7.8   Ford Walker River.

7.9   Junction with horse trail; go left (west).

8.5   Junction with Chain of Lakes trail; go right (northwest).

8.7   Fremont Lake.

17.4   Arrive back at the parking area.

Honorable Mentions

S Trail of the Gargoyles

Two easy, self-guided trails trace the crumbling edge of a dramatic volcanic cliff over-looking a deep, broad, forested canyon. The 1.1-mile trail on the left (south) side of the parking area leads to curious volcanic formations like the Wall of Noses and the Maze. The 0.4-mile trail on the right (north) side crosses above the small waterfall of Cow Creek (dry by midsummer) and ends at the foot of Gargoyle Ridge. Also known as Bull Run Rock, Gargoyle Ridge is a fantastic conglomeration of volcanic knobs, pinnacles, fissures, and even windows. The trail brochure available from the Summit Ranger Station is keyed to numbered posts and provides an interesting geologic overview of volcanism in this part of the Sierra Nevada. From Summit Ranger Station (GPS: N38 11.270' / W120 00.466') on CA 108 at the junction of Pinecrest Lake Road, drive east 3.6 miles to the turnoff of Herring Creek Road (GPS: N38 12.601' / W120 00.991'), where a sign points to the Gargoyles. Turn east and drive 6.8 miles (the last part on well-maintained unpaved road) to the signposted Gargoyles turnoff. Drive 0.25 mile and park clear of the road. Trailhead parking GPS: N38 14.958' / W119 56.603'

T Columns of the Giants

This mile-long (round-trip) wheelchair-accessible trail visits a rock formation similar to Devils Postpile—dramatic cliffs of basalt lava solidified into regular columns. Crossing the Stanislaus River on a sturdy bridge, we pass through forests of cottonwood, quaking aspen, and pine to a looming mountain of talus. The angular columns, solidified from a 150,000-year-old lava flow, are splayed across the cliffs above like a row of pickets. Beneath the talus an ice field lies hidden, remnant of the glacier that swiped the face of this cliff during the last ice age, exposing the lava flow. You can climb to holes dug into the talus to feel the chill of prehistoric ice on breezes blowing through the rocks. The signposted parking area is on CA 108, about 53 miles east of Pinecrest and 11.5 miles west of Sonora Pass. Trailhead GPS: N38 20.389' / W119 48.338'

U Sonora Pass Vista

For a less strenuous high-altitude jaunt than Hike 49 to the south of the pass, head north on the PCT from the Sonora Pass. Climbing with only moderate tenacity, we are treated to magnificent views out over the strikingly barren-looking (though hardly barren!) country around Sonora Pass. The high, jagged, barren-looking mountain to the south is Leavitt Peak (11,569 feet), whose left (eastern) shoulder serves to carry the PCT southward through an apparent moonscape of mountains. (We

The vast alpine panorama around Sonora Pass opens outward even wider as you climb the Pacific Crest Trail northward from the pass.

ourselves are climbing on the flank of 11,459-foot Sonora Peak, a summit not much shorter than Leavitt's.) As we rise higher, ruddy-colored volcanic outcrops close in on the trail, and the slope on the downhill side steepens dramatically, even dangerously. The slope is crumbly; you can see that you don't want to slip. There is no clear-cut turnaround spot on this hike, though a good target (if you can read your maps and landscapes closely enough) is a rocky outcrop on a ridge dividing the Sardine Creek drainage from the Wolf Creek drainage, 2.7 miles from the parking area. You can recognize it because the trail makes a 90-degree turn to the north, and the stupendous views reach far east into the Great Basin and south to Tower Peak, on the northern boundary of Yosemite. Trailhead GPS: N38 19.787' / W119 38.116'

Around Yosemite

The enormous granite walls of Yosemite Valley tower above meadow, river, and forest, and are hung with the continent's greatest collection of waterfalls. The valley lies at the heart of a far larger park that spans from chaparral to Sierra Crest and anchors the second-largest roadless area in the Sierra Nevada. The Tioga Pass Road (CA 120) links the lowlands with the highlands, cresting at 9,943-foot Tioga Pass before dropping down spectacular Lee Vining Canyon to the high-desert floor of the Mono Lake Basin. Park highways, commercial centers, and roadside scenic attractions teem with car-bound visitors, but hikers can escape the hubbub if they are willing to work for it.

51 Preston Falls

The big rocks and wild Tuolumne River scenery give a higher-country feel to this canyon, but its low-altitude location welcomes hikers long after the real high country is under snow. This trail makes a pleasant day hike or off-season overnighter.

Start: Kirkwood Powerhouse, on the Tuolumne River

Distance: 8.8 miles out and back

Hiking time: About 4 hours

Difficulty: Moderate, with an elevation gain and loss of about 300 feet

Trail condition: Good singletrack

Seasons: May through mid-Nov is best. Winter can be good, depending on local weather.

Other trail users: Leashed dogs and equestrians are welcome.

Land status: Stanislaus National Forest

Nearest town: Groveland

Fees and permits: No wilderness permit required. Campfire permit required if using a stove or campfire.

Map: USGS 7.5-minute quad: Cherry Lake South

Trail contacts: Stanislaus National Forest, Groveland Ranger Station, 24545 Highway 120, Groveland, CA 95321; (209) 962-7825; www.fs.usda.gov/stanislaus

Finding the trailhead: From Groveland, drive about 14 miles east on CA 120. Just after the Tuolumne River South Fork bridge, turn north on the Cherry Lake Road (GPS: N37 49.476' / W120 00.724'). Drive about 9 miles down the Cherry Lake Road to the main Tuolumne River, cross the bridge, and turn right into the Robert C. Kirkwood Powerhouse compound, owned by San Francisco as part of their Hetch Hetchy waterworks. Drive to the end and park in the designated lot, at an elevation of about 2,450 feet. Trailhead GPS: N37 52.722' / W119 57.021'

Note: The massive Rim Fire of 2013 swept over 400 square miles of forest west of Yosemite, including the lower Tuolumne River Canyon. At press time the Preston Falls Trail remains closed, but should reopen in 2015.

The Hike

Our path starts as dirt road, soon narrowing to a singletrack after passing a hand-pulled cable car (chained and locked), which crosses the Tuolumne River to a gauging station. Hiking up-canyon through alternating stretches of meadow, scrub, and mixed forests of oak, laurel, buckeye, and conifer, an overriding scent of mountain misery fills the air.

Tumbled-down boulders litter the forest floor, so it seems only fair that a heavy growth of trees and shrubs has taken root in the crannies of the canyon walls. No glaciers buffed these walls to a monumental surface, as they did the rock walls of Hetch Hetchy, less than 12 miles up-canyon. Our trail follows the river, keeping a fairly even gradient, until we meet a large granitic slab that constricts the river in a narrow gorge. Climb up and around this minor impediment, enjoying the view of the white cascade and green pools below. Less than a mile later, we surmount a second rocky knoll by means of a couple of scrubby switchbacks.

Preston Falls

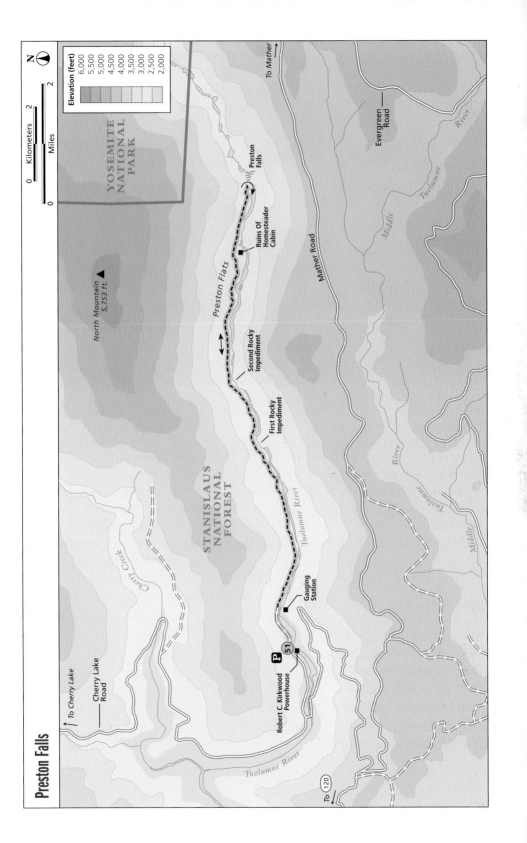

Elevation (feet)
6,000
5,500
5,000
4,500
4,000
3,500
3,000
2,500
2,000

YOSEMITE NATIONAL PARK

N

Kilometers
0   2

Miles
0   2

To Mather

Evergreen Road

Tuolumne River

Middle

Tuolumne

Middle River

Mather Road

Preston Falls

Ruins Of Homesteader Cabin

Preston Flats

North Mountain
5,753 ft.

Second Rocky Impediment

First Rocky Impediment

STANISLAUS NATIONAL FOREST

Cherry Creek

To Cherry Lake

Cherry Lake Road

Tuolumne River

Gauging Station

51

Robert C. Kirkwood Powerhouse

Tuolumne River

To (120)

Sugar Pine Cones are the longest in the Sierra Nevada.

Beyond, the trail levels again, the valley grows parklike, and many good campsites appear along the broad, sandy riverbanks, well shaded and covered in pine needles. Preston Flats lies at the eastern end of this parklike stretch. You will recognize it by the big meadow, thick with sedges and soggy in spring. Twentieth-century homesteaders built a cabin in the woods between the trail and the river. Their rock fireplace and concrete floor remain.

Our trail ends on a large granite slab below Preston Falls, where the Tuolumne drops 15 feet into a large green pool. The sunny rocks are perfect for lounging, and the swimming is delightful if the current is not too strong.

Miles and Directions

- **0.0** Kirkwood Powerhouse parking area (toilet).
- **0.3** Gauging station; start of singletrack trail.
- **1.8** First granite slab.
- **2.5** Second rocky impediment.
- **3.8** Homesteader cabin ruin.
- **4.4** Preston Falls.
- **8.8** Arrive back at the parking area.

52 Little Nellie Falls

The dry chaparral growing along most of this trail does not stir great interest among hikers who like their trails "pretty," and serves thereby as a kind of buffer against crowding at this exquisite forest oasis. All the better for those of us to enjoy a peaceful, off-season, out-and-back jaunt on a historic, old-time country road.

Start: Foresta, in Yosemite
Distance: 5.6 miles out and back
Hiking time: About 2-3 hours
Difficulty: A rather laid-back hike, unless you've got a hot day
Trail condition: Well-graded dirt road with no directional signage
Seasons: Apr through early June is best for water and wildflowers. Mid-June through Sept is fine, though often hot. Oct-Nov typically has good weather.
Other trail users: Since this is a public road, leashed dogs, bikes, and motorists are allowed, though vehicles (and other users in general) are few.

Land status: Yosemite National Park and Stanislaus National Forest. Foresta is a private residential inholding within the national park boundaries.
Nearest town: Yosemite Village
Fees and permits: None needed for day hike. A Forest Service campfire permit is required for campfire or stove use. Yosemite charges an entrance fee.
Maps: USGS 7.5-minute quads: El Capitan, El Portal
Trail contacts: Big Oak Flat Entrance Station, Yosemite National Park; or Yosemite Valley Visitor Center, Yosemite Village, CA 95389; (209) 372-0200; www.nps.gov/yose

Finding the trailhead: From the Big Oak Flat Road in Yosemite, turn south onto Foresta Road, nearly 7 miles down from the junction with CA 120 at Crane Flat, or 3.5 miles up from the junction with CA 140 at the west end of Yosemite Valley. Drive 1.8 miles down paved Foresta Road, dropping steeply into a broad valley burned in a 1990 forest fire, to a wooded junction with the unpaved Old Coulterville Road. Park there. The walk begins at the vehicular gate on Coulterville Road. Trailhead GPS: N37 42.161' / W119 45.047'

The Hike

Dr. John Taylor McLean, builder of the Coulterville Road, named Little Nellie Falls after his daughter, Mary Helen. With dreams of opening a lucrative stage route into Yosemite Valley, Dr. McLean invested his personal fortune to build this road after contracting with Mariposa County in exchange for a fifty-year franchise to all tolls. To his dismay, the state legislature then granted a rival company rights to build the nearby Big Oak Flat Road, destroying his monopoly. Both roads opened in the summer of 1874, but the popularity of the Big Oak Flat Road soon drove the Coulterville Road into a forlorn state of disuse. Dr. McLean went bankrupt. When he died in 1907, all rights to the toll road, as well as all litigation attempting to recover his investments, were inherited by "Little Nellie," who likewise failed to recoup the family fortune. When the family's fifty-year franchise expired in 1920, the Coulterville Road passed

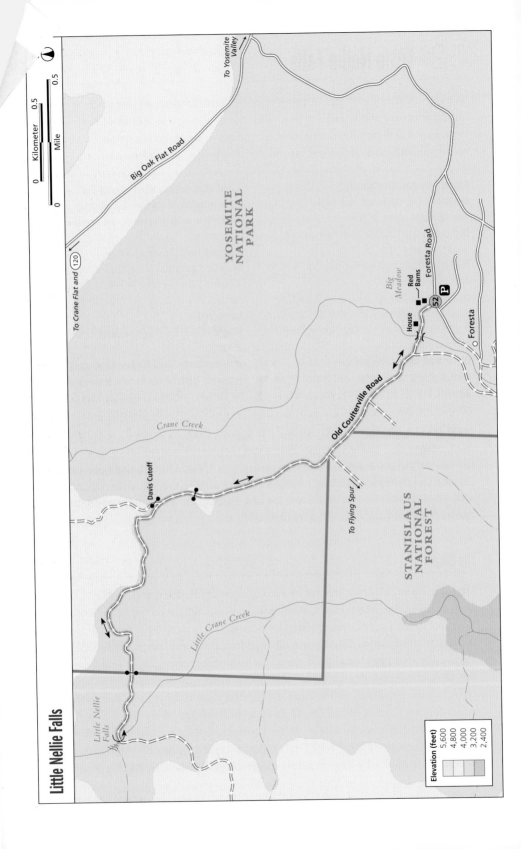

Little Nellie Falls

Elevation (feet)
5,600
4,800
4,000
3,200
2,400

Big Oak Flat Road

To Yosemite Valley

To Crane Flat and (120)

YOSEMITE NATIONAL PARK

Crane Creek

Davis Cutoff

Old Coulterville Road

Big Meadow

Red Barns

House

52

P

Foresta Road

Foresta

To Flying Spur

STANISLAUS NATIONAL FOREST

Little Crane Creek

Little Nellie Falls

Kilometer

Mile

0   0.5

0   0.5

into public domain. The portion of the Old Coulterville Road running west from Little Nellie Falls to Bower Cave, passable to high-clearance vehicles with four-wheel drive, receives scant use.

From your car, follow the dirt Coulterville Road past two red barns and a blue-green house with a rusty metal roof on the edge of Big Meadow, to dilapidated, wooden Crane Creek Bridge. Vehicles are prohibited. Cross to the opposite bank and bear right (north) to ascend the gentle gradient through acres of tall burned pines standing like totem poles amid spicy-scented groundcovers of mountain misery, manzanita, lupine, nightshade, ceanothus, and other low-growing shrubs and herbs. Lizards, bumblebees, and numerous bird species thrive in the flowering chaparral, and the footprints of bears, deer, and mountain lions further attest to a rich food supply.

As you rise in elevation, El Capitan and Half Dome slide into view eastward above Big Meadow. When the dirt road cuts momentarily through a corner of Stanislaus National Forest, note the thicket of pines reseeded by the Forest Service, which does not follow the National Park Service mandate to let nature take its course. Keeping right at the next two dirt-track forks, you quickly surmount the low ridge between Crane and Little Crane Creeks, leaving the burned zone near the Davis Cutoff, a dirt track that ascends to Crane Flat.

Now the road meanders easily along contours through wide-open foothill terrain, where vistas roll down against the rugged 2,000-foot-high south wall of the Merced River's lower canyon. Dropping more steeply into thicker woodlands of mixed California black oak, ponderosa pine, and Douglas fir, you begin to hear the muffled roar of Little Crane Creek. After passing through a metal gate at the boundary between Yosemite National Park and Stanislaus National Forest (close the gate behind you), follow the road around two more bends to the wet ford of Little Crane Creek. On your right, Little Nellie Falls rushes down its 25-foot wall of granite into a sandy pool. On your left a shady campsite (with picnic table and fire pit) overlooks the lower cascades.

Miles and Directions

- **0.0** Parking area.
- **0.2** Crane Creek Bridge. Cross and go right (north) on Coulterville Road.
- **0.6** Unnamed junction; keep straight (northwest).
- **0.9** Flying Spur junction; go right on dirt road (northwest).
- **1.5** Davis Cutoff; bear left (west).
- **2.8** Little Nellie Falls.
- **5.6** Arrive back at the parking area.

53 Yosemite Falls

A chance to stand at the lip of this grand force of nature is a thrill matched by few hikes anywhere in the world. You'll pay your dues with a steep climb, but the ever-changing views over Yosemite Valley afford a terrific tonic for fatigue along nearly every stretch of this spectacular out-and-back route.

Start: Camp 4 in Yosemite Valley

Distance: 6.4 miles out and back

Hiking time: About 5–6 hours

Difficulty: Strenuous because of the 2,600-foot elevation gain and loss

Trail condition: Occasionally steep and rocky, sometimes slippery, often crowded. The last section is exposed to sheer cliffs.

Seasons: Mid-May through June is best for water display. The falls typically dry up from mid-July through Oct, but the trail is passable.

Other trail users: No dogs or bikes

Land status: Yosemite National Park

Nearest town: Yosemite Village

Fees and permits: None for day trip. Wilderness permit required for overnighter. Yosemite charges an entrance fee.

Maps: Tom Harrison: *Yosemite High Country*. USGS: Map of Yosemite Valley. USGS 7.5-minute quads: Half Dome, Yosemite Falls.

Trail contacts: Yosemite Valley Visitor Center, Yosemite Village, CA 95389; (209) 372-0200; www.nps.gov/yose

Finding the trailhead: This trail description starts at the northwest corner of the Camp 4 parking area in Yosemite Valley. Since only registered campers may park at Camp 4, ride the free shuttle bus to Stop 8 at the front door of Yosemite Lodge. The front desk staff can point you toward Camp 4, about 0.2 mile northwest across the parking lots. Camp 4 parking area trailhead GPS: N37 44.557' / W119 36.143'

Note: If you approach on the trail from Lower Yosemite Falls, you will bypass Camp 4 altogether, in which case you will encounter the official, signposted junction at GPS N37 44.563' / W119 36.190'.

The Hike

Be forewarned: This hike takes stamina and perseverance. The long switchbacks, climbing 2,600 feet in fewer than 3 miles, dampen the enthusiasm of many hikers. In the end the reward for your endurance will be nothing more, or less, than to stand at the brink of North America's highest waterfall.

From the northwest corner of the Camp 4 parking area (elevation 3,950 feet), find a worn path that leads straight toward the north wall of Yosemite Valley. You will quickly encounter a major trail running in an east–west direction. Go left (west), and within a few yards you will see the official, signed junction of the Yosemite Falls Trail.

Our first series of some fifty switchbacks now begins among oak-shaded boulders, where Camp 4 climbers practice their moves before tackling the big walls. Built in the 1870s, these foreshortened switchbacks zigzag upward within such a narrow, steep corridor that we can keep close tabs on our fellow hikers ahead and behind us, chugging back and forth up the mountainside with mantra-like monotony. Reaching

Looking down Yosemite Creek's hanging valley from the Yosemite Falls Trail offers a good view of the glacier-polished apron of Glacier Point, in the middle ground on the left.

the climax of the first batch of switchbacks, we contour right (eastward) along a wide, wooded shelf, stepping across a seasonal creek and conquering a couple more exposed switchbacks to Columbia Rock, with its railed, intimate view of the valley from about 1,000 feet above the floor.

From there, our trail darts up a slope so sandy and steep that it is held in place by metal braces, wire, and rocks. We are then treated to a brief but welcome respite from relentless climbing as we follow a wooded ledge across some seasonal creeklets, dropping once to avoid a granite bulge, and so by degree working our way around the north-wall buttress to a sudden, startling view of Upper Yosemite Fall, blowing like a streamer in a stiff spring wind. So grandiose is its 1,430-foot free-fall leap that the cascades below it—675 feet of booming, churning, raging power that in any other setting would constitute a paragon of nature—are quite diminished in stature. Yosemite search-and-rescue teams routinely climb down to the cascades to rescue hikers who stray down there, beyond their abilities.

As we traverse along the rim of the cascades' side canyon, we can just pick out the ant-like people at the rails atop the bulge of Yosemite Point, to the right of Upper Yosemite Fall. The thumb-like pinnacle of the Lost Arrow rises majestically from its

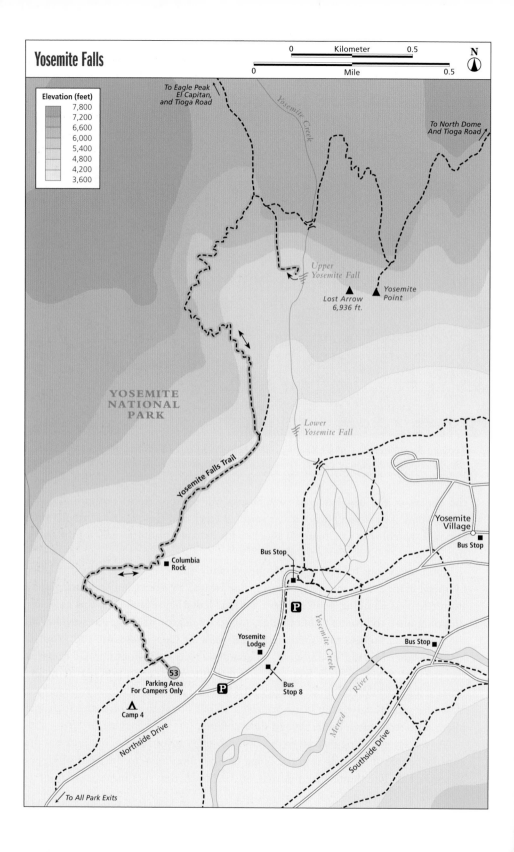

Yosemite Falls

Elevation (feet)
7,800
7,200
6,600
6,000
5,400
4,800
4,200
3,600

Kilometer
0   0.5

Mile
0   0.5

N

To Eagle Peak
El Capitan,
and Tioga Road

To North Dome
And Tioga Road

Yosemite Creek

Upper
Yosemite Fall

Lost Arrow
6,936 ft.

Yosemite
Point

YOSEMITE
NATIONAL
PARK

Lower
Yosemite Fall

Yosemite Falls Trail

Columbia
Rock

Bus Stop

Yosemite
Village

Bus Stop

P

Yosemite Creek

Yosemite
Lodge

Bus Stop

53

Parking Area
For Campers Only

P

Bus
Stop 8

Camp 4

Merced River

Northside Drive

Southside Drive

To All Park Exits

anchorage. Another curious sight on the wall behind the Upper Fall is a large horizontal ledge about one-third up from the base of the waterfall. John Muir brushed close to death one moonlit night as he inched out upon this ledge behind the falling water, exhilarating briefly "in fairyland between the dark wall and the wild throng of illuminated waters," until the wind abruptly shifted, sending the flood crashing down upon him and nearly sweeping him into the chasm. Fortunately, another shift in the wind pushed the waterfall outward, and Muir was able to scoot to safety. Do not try this yourself.

Drawing nearer to the great wall itself, we enter a small evergreen wood, watered by the mist from the falls, and begin our next set of switchbacks. Our route ascends a rocky ravine to the left of the falls, accompanied by a seasonal creek. Great labor went into making this trail, especially the long stretches of cobbled steps. Dry manzanita, ceanothus, and occasional pines crowd the trail, further hedged in by sheer granite walls on either side. As we climb we watch with fascination as Yosemite Falls, in profile, disappears behind one granite wall, which then eclipses Half Dome, like a moonrise played backwards.

This battery of switchbacks tops out at a junction in the shallow hanging valley of Yosemite Creek, atop the Yosemite Valley's north wall. Turning right toward the bridged crossing of Yosemite Creek, we approach but do not quite reach it before meeting another signed junction to the top of the falls. Turning right, we advance toward the cliff over granite slabs scattered with trees and boulders.

Reaching the edge, and a heart-pounding view, search for the rock steps leading downward to the left (east), only marginally sheltered from the yawning chasm by strategically located rocks. Descending, we follow a ledge to a sloping granite bench above rushing Yosemite Creek. Again beware: You will not survive a slip into that maelstrom.

For its grand finale, our trail now turns cliff-ward through a low notch in the granite and descends a flight of narrow steps affixed to the cliff, with a metal rail to hang on to, the valley floor agape beneath your feet. Landing on a railed ledge about 15 feet wide and 50 feet long, walk to the end and look over. The lip of Upper Yosemite Fall hangs in its trough just beyond the edge of the ledge, roaring over the brink of its 2,425-foot plunge to the floor of Yosemite Valley.

Miles and Directions

- **0.0** Camp 4 trailhead.
- **0.1** Intersect main east-west-running trail and go left (west). Soon after, reach the signed junction with Yosemite Falls Trail and bear right (north).
- **1.0** Columbia Rock.
- **2.9** Top of Yosemite Falls Trail; bear right (east).
- **3.0** Junction of spur trail to brink of Upper Yosemite Fall; bear right (south).
- **3.2** Brink of falls.
- **6.4** Arrive back at Camp 4.

54 Finding Solitude, Scenery, and Lore in Eastern Yosemite Valley

Private cars are restricted from the eastern margin of Yosemite Valley, so this point-to-point route offers some of your best chances for serenity on the valley floor—though it cannot evade all the crowds. While enjoying sublime vistas of Half Dome, Glacier Point, and other great walls, hikers can explore the lore of Indian Caves, Tenaya Canyon, Happy Isles, Elmer, and the once-wondrous firefall.

Start: Ahwahnee Hotel shuttle stop, Yosemite Valley

Distance: 8.0 miles one-way/shuttle

Hiking time: About 5 hours, with stops to explore

Difficulty: Moderate because of the distance

Trail condition: Mostly wide, unpaved singletrack, some of it terribly dusty, worn, and heavily fertilized by livestock. Because of the countless divergent paths, pay close attention to the map and signage.

Seasons: Mar-Nov. Apr-June best for water displays, Oct for fall colors.

Other trail users: Crowds flock to Mirror Lake, Happy Isles, and Camp Curry. Equestrian trains make heavy use of trails around Mirror Lake.

For more information, see Hike 53

Finding the trailhead: Ride the free Yosemite Valley Shuttle Bus to the Ahwahnee Hotel. The trail starts on the left (north) end of the hotel parking lot. Trailhead GPS: N37 44.841' / W119 34.400'. You will be able to catch the shuttle bus again from Camp Curry.

The Hike

From the Ahwahnee Hotel shuttle bus stop (elevation 4,000 feet), walk toward the northeast end of the parking lot, toward the nearest valley wall. There, near an Indian grinding rock, an old trail sign points us to Mirror Lake. Following an old road that was once paved but is now worn down to a patchy, potholed surface, we pass through an extraordinarily beautiful, rich woodland of California laurel, incense cedar, ponderosa pine, oak, and dogwood. It is especially colorful in autumn, when the dogwood leaves turn red and the oaks' foliage a brilliant yellow. Almost immediately we step across two rambunctious (in spring and early summer) branches of Royal Arches Creek, fresh from their thousand-foot streak down the cliff as Royal Arch Cascade.

Across the valley (southeast) the glacier-polished apron of Glacier Point comes into view through the trees. Old-timers can point out the route of the abandoned Ledge Trail, which started in the talus above Camp Curry and ascended a very steep, narrow ledge that climbs diagonally up the left-hand side of Glacier Point. About two-thirds of the way up, it cut sharply left into a southeast-climbing gully. Hikers mounted 3,800 feet in 1.5 miles, but that route was always a killer—perilous, exposed, plagued by unstable footing, prone to rockslides. Deaths and injuries haunted the Ledge Trail since the beginning, when James Hutchings first started leading tourists

A woman's visage, roughly drawn in profile by colored lichens, is said to mark the face of Half Dome.

up it in 1871; his own 17-year-old daughter, Florence, whom even the peerless mountaineer John Muir admired as an accomplished mountain guide, was crushed by a loosened boulder while guiding a party up the Ledge Trail in 1881. The Park Service closed it altogether in the 1960s, and stretches of the "trail" (and the ledge itself!) have since been swept away by rock fall. Still, Yosemite's search-and-rescue squads mount expeditions to bring down wannabe hikers from the old Ledge Trail, dead and alive.

Closer at hand on our left (north), we catch some fine views of the Royal Arches, a series of great stone arcs formed by exfoliation in a 1,500-foot-high wall. Bacon-colored streaks on the wall are water stains. Boulders fallen in rockslides have built up a talus skirt along the base of the cliffs, overgrown with old, twisting oak trees. Somewhere along this stretch of wall, the native Ahwahneechee people knew a curious route from the valley floor to the north rim, according to Lafayette Bunnell of the Mariposa Battalion, who was conducted by Chief Tenaya from a ledge high alongside the Royal Arches, down through rocks, and finally to the base of the cliff by climbing down through the branches and trunk of a stout oak tree that is probably long gone.

Meeting a paved bicycle path, keep left on the dirt path, which winds among some elephantine gray boulders. The Royal Arches now give way to Washington Column, a turret of stone rising 1,900 feet above the valley floor. Even more impressive is the great, sheer face of Half Dome (8,842 feet), looming above the east end of the valley. Many people have observed the visage of an old woman, limned by lichens on the right face of the dome. Her profile faces up Tenaya Canyon, thick eyelashes closed blissfully. Faintly, she seems to be smiling. Why? One clue seems to be the black stains dribbling down her chin, which experts believe to be a chaw of tobaccy.

The largest boulder pile yet seen on this hike, Indian Caves, soon appears on the left (north), below the prow of Washington Column in a level, wooded area blanketed with pine needles. Near the site is a flat boulder pocked with mortar holes for grinding acorns into meal. When the Mariposa Battalion arrived in the valley in 1851, an Ahwahneechee village stood here, one of twenty-two such villages in Yosemite Valley, which Yosemite Museum staff speculate was home to probably around 3,000 people. The Ahwahneechee used the caves for storage and took shelter in them during warfare or bad weather, though under ordinary circumstances they preferred dwelling in teepee-shaped houses of incense cedar bark. I don't blame them, though climbing through the dark talus "caves" is great fun, especially for kids.

Rounding the talus buttress below Washington Column, we turn northward and begin to climb into Tenaya Canyon on a dusty, rough trail worn thin by horses' hooves. Tenaya is one of three main canyons that feed into the eastern end of Yosemite Valley (the others being Merced and Illilouette Canyons), each of which was carved by separate glaciers. Our trail soon meets the Mirror Lake Trail on the "shore" of Mirror Lake, where we will turn left (north). Unless there's an unusually heavy spring snowmelt, you won't actually find Mirror Lake but rather a widening of Tenaya Creek as it flows through a sandy, willowy meadow. Mirror Lake of old fame drew so many tourists by the 1890s that Yosemite boosters sought to maintain its water level by constructing a small check dam. Park officials in later years abetted this scheme by dredging. Not until the 1960s did park policies finally change to allow nature to do what comes naturally to silty lakes. The dredging stopped, the check dam was dismantled, and Mirror Lake soon morphed into a willow-fringed marsh and meadow called (with more regard for legacy than logic) Mirror Meadow.

Padding north through thick forests of incense cedar, Douglas fir, ponderosa pine, and white fir, our trail parallels Tenaya Creek upstream. We enjoy the up-canyon view of bulbous Mount Watkins (8,500 feet) and Clouds Rest (9,926 feet), as well as more intimate views of Half Dome, lofting nearly a mile above us. The farther you get from Mirror Meadow, the fewer hikers you will encounter, enabling one of the most peaceful of hikes on the floor of the valley. Passing the junction of the Snow Creek Trail, we cross a small bridge over a runoff channel of Snow Creek, before coming to the larger, arched footbridge over Tenaya Creek, where waders splash and sunbathe on hot days. No official trails ascend farther up Tenaya Canyon, which quickly narrows to a gorge impassable except by skilled rock climbers with full climbing regalia.

As we double-back down the east bank of Tenaya Creek through thick forest and marshy ground, the forest opens suddenly where a rockslide poured granite slabs and boulders 1,800 feet down from Ahwiyah Point in March 2009, covering hundreds of feet of trail. Crews reopened the trail in October 2012, providing easy and beautiful access to spectacular "new" views of the canyon walls. The sight of "fresh" talus is sobering, especially when considering how much talus we have already passed on this hike, most of it "softened" with forest. The truth is, rock fall and high water make Yosemite one of the more lethal places in the national park system—though the odds of us surviving this hike on any particular day are rather favorable, I think.

As we again pass the sandy remnants of Mirror Lake, still popular as a streambed watering hole, we descend back into the main Yosemite Valley on a trail so dusty and worn by horse hooves that by the time we reach the road at Tenaya Creek, we may be tempted to walk to Happy Isles on the paved shuttle road—a fair alternative to the trail, which closely parallels the road anyway. Both trail and road climb over the Medial Moraine, a low, thickly wooded ridge of dirt and rock deposited by ice age glaciers from debris scraped from Tenaya and Merced Canyons. The trail improves thereafter, a serene path handsomely landscaped with grand boulder piles.

We rejoin the crowds near the road bridge that spans the Merced River at Happy Isles. Cross that bridge and turn left (south) up the wide, paved path parallel to the river toward the Happy Isles. Named after two small islands in the Merced River, Happy Isles is one of the most mesmerizing and exhilarating spots in Yosemite Valley. You can cross to these namesake "happy isles" on a signposted, narrow, wooden footbridge. This short, dead-end detour is spectacular in spring, when the isles are engulfed around their rocky edges by the roaring, boiling white cascades of the Merced. Beware of these spectacularly violent rapids in spring, for they have swept many hikers to their deaths.

Upon recrossing the bridges back to the "mainland," visit the adjacent Nature Center if you wish, and take a look behind the building at the flattened forest of fir and cedar trees, leveled by a 1996 rock fall from Glacier Point—though the rocks never touched them. It was the blast of wind created by this rock fall that knocked the trees down, crushing one man. Compare the advanced state of forest recovery with the more recent Ahwiyah slide.

From the Nature Center, head back downstream along the Merced, briefly, watching out to turn left when you see the sign to the Happy Isles fen. We cross the fen, a shallow marsh, on a wooden boardwalk. Right beneath our feet, the clear, broad, ankle-deep sheet of fen water flows enchantingly through bending reeds and grasses. Lying belly-down on the dry boardwalk, you can watch for water boatmen, tiny frogs, and caddis fly larvae encased in "shells" cemented together from grains of sand. On summery days winged brigades of darting dragonflies, birds, and butterflies make the air hum. The crowds seem to avoid the fen, probably not knowing what a fen is. Their absence is our gain.

After crossing the fen, we enter drier woods, bearing right (north) to meet the shuttle bus road, where we turn left (west) on a paved path for the final stroll to the edge of Curry Village, a flurry of white canvas tent cabins that house temporary guests and employees. Founded in 1899 as Camp Curry, and still known by that name by old-timers, the commercial center of the resort was declared a National Historical District in 1979. A rockfall from Glacier Point in 2008 injured three visitors and hastened closure of nearly 280 cabins deemed particularly vulnerable to rockfall. After walking past the wooden decks and larger buildings of Curry Village's busy commercial center, we enter the campfire circle—which is not a circle, but a rustic stage with bench seating. This historic spot has a clear view of Glacier Point's cliff edge, 3,200 feet above. With a pair of binoculars, you can see people looking down at you.

It was between these two distant points—Glacier Point and the Camp Curry campfire circle—that one of Yosemite's most fondly remembered rituals used to play out nightly in summers through most of the first six decades of the twentieth century. Crowds would assemble nightly at both spots for campfire programs that ended invariably with a man at Camp Curry, hands cupped around his mouth, throwing his head back and roaring upward, "Let the fire fall!" And fall it would. As men with rakes atop Glacier Point pushed their cliff-side campfire over the brink, the crowds in the valley would behold a searing orange streak of fire crawling with almost slug-like deliberation over the lip and down the face of the vertical wall. It seemed to hang a few moments only, and then to fade into blackness. Like Mirror Lake's dredging, the firefall was curtailed in the 1960s as an artificial intrusion on a natural wonder that truly has no equal in the world.

Back then, however, as the firefall watchers in the meadows and clearings began heading back to their campfires and tents, summer evenings would end with a unconnected chorus of voices calling out, "Elmer! Elmerrrrr!" Their cries would be answered by yet more voices, distant and near, also shouting, "Elmer! Elll-merrrr!"

Finding Solitude, Scenery, and Lore in Eastern Yosemite Valley

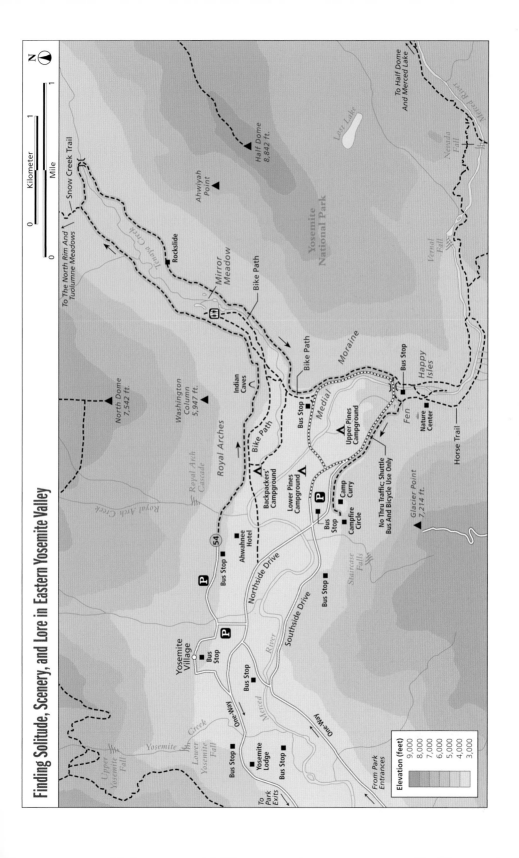

Who Elmer was, and why we strangers would shout his name, has not been definitively explained, despite some old-timers' theories that you can dredge up on the Internet. The custom of shouting "Elmer" seems also to have disappeared in recent years.

Miles and Directions

0.0 Ahwahnee Hotel.

0.1 Royal Arches Creek.

1.1 Indian Caves (GPS: N37 44.638' / W119 33.550').

1.8 Junction with Mirror Lake Trail (GPS: N37 44.992' / W119 33.030'); turn left (north).

2.8 Snow Creek Trail junction; bear right (northeast).

3.0 Small bridge.

3.2 Tenaya Creek footbridge (GPS: N37 45.557' / W119 32.068').

3.9 Ahwiyah Point rockslide.

4.7 Site of Mirror Lake.

5.4 Trail meets Tenaya Creek vehicular bridge.

6.3 Happy Isles vehicular bridge; cross and turn left (south).

6.5 Wooden footbridge to the namesake islets of Happy Isles.

6.6 Nature Center.

6.9 The fen.

8.0 Camp Curry campfire circle.

55 Vernal and Nevada Falls

Probably the single-most amazing short hike in the Sierra Nevada, this wildly popular lollipop loop gets awfully crowded on summer days. But don't miss it—for the sake of the superlative scenery, the cliffs and rocks, the distant vistas of leaping waterfalls, the in-your-face proximity of Vernal Fall on the Mist Trail, the power of the rampaging Merced River. This hike is a classic.

Start: Happy Isles Bridge in Yosemite Valley
Distance: 5.2-mile lollipop loop
Hiking time: About 5 hours, allowing extra time to enjoy the views
Difficulty: Strenuous, with an overall elevation gain and loss of more than 2,300 feet
Trail condition: This well-signed and well-maintained trail can be very crowded. The Mist Trail portion has more than 300 slippery rock steps. At several points the trail skirts some lethal drop-offs, but it is walled or railed. A patch of ice might jam the narrow John Muir Trail section on the cliff above Nevada Fall in early season, but hikers can scramble over it with caution.
Seasons: Late May through early July is best for water volume, but the trail is typically open through the end of Oct.

Other trail users: No dogs or bikes. Horses use the John Muir Trail (JMT) above Vernal Fall.
Land status: Yosemite National Park
Nearest town: Yosemite Village
Fees and permits: None needed for day hike. Yosemite charges an entrance fee.
Maps: Tom Harrison: *Yosemite High Country*. USGS 7.5-minute quad: Half Dome.
Trail contacts: Yosemite Valley Visitor Center, Yosemite Village, CA 95389; (209) 372-0200; www.nps.gov/yose
Special considerations: Bring appropriate clothing for a drenching on the Mist Trail. Restrain children at the water's edge. Many swimmers have been swept to their deaths over the falls. The steps can be treacherous; it is far easier to ascend the Mist Trail and descend on the JMT than to descend the Mist Trail.

Finding the trailhead: Take the free Yosemite Valley Shuttle Bus (see sidebar p. 284) to the Happy Isles shuttle bus stop #16. The trail starts on the far side (east) of the large road bridge. Trailhead GPS: N37 43.960' / W119 33.477'

The Hike

Tourists in the 1800s called the Merced Canyon above Yosemite Valley "the Giant Stairway," because the Merced River drops from Little Yosemite to the main valley floor—a horizontal distance of about 1.5 miles with a vertical drop of 2,000 feet—over two large steps. The lower step is Vernal Fall (317 feet); the higher one is Nevada Fall (594 feet). Clearly seen from Glacier Point, these two giant steps stand at right angles to each other, half a mile apart.

Start the hike on the east end of the Happy Isles road bridge, at an elevation of 4,050 feet. Gigantic boulders, fallen from the cliffs, decorate the trail. Passing above Happy Isles, you look down upon a lovely, dense woodland of white alder, dogwood, Douglas fir, cedar, ponderosa pine, white fir, laurel, and bigleaf maple, which coddles

The trail to Vernal Falls is the most popular in the park.

the namesake "happy" islets in a canopy of green. Just as the trail begins to steepen, a prolific little spring pours out from the rocks and is briefly impounded in a stonework basin, before darting off to find the Merced.

Our wide path now climbs high above the thundering gorge on a shelf edged by well-dressed masonry walls, the granite contrasting beautifully with the writhed limbs of the canyon live oak. When the trail rounds an exposed buttress of granite, glance back for an extraordinary view of Yosemite Falls, leaping in two steps down Yosemite Valley's northern wall. Then look south across the Merced Canyon to where Illilouette Creek, largest of the Merced River's many tributary streams, pours 370 feet down into the gorge from its hanging valley.

After traversing a landslide of large talus blocks, a short downhill brings us to the Vernal Fall Bridge, where we get our first, famous view of Vernal Fall, a white curtain of water framed by trees and canyon walls. Lest anyone forget who is boss here, the river thunders beneath our feet.

Across the bridge we begin a fresh uphill climb through conifers. The John Muir Trail splits off to the right—a wide switchback trail suitable for horses—but we head straight up-canyon on the Mist Trail, the more exciting route for hikers. Breaking from the trees, now in full view of Vernal Fall, we pick our way up an even steeper path of slippery stone steps and short switchbacks through talus. Crowds of hikers take turns on narrower stretches of stairway, so be patient and enjoy the scenery. The Ahwahneechee knew Vernal as *Yan o-pah,* or Cloud of Water, a particularly apt name when the river runs high and swirling clouds of mist roll up from the gorge, drenching us.

From a stand of trees that hugs Vernal's head wall, a flight of steps brings us to the cliff face, dripping with ferns, where we snatch a stunning view of the falls in profile. Scrambling up this chiseled ledge, fenced on the outside, brings us to granite slabs above the falls. Walk down to the railed brink, where the green sheet of water glides over the broad, keen edge of the cliff, free-falling into misty oblivion. It's absolutely awesome.

When ready to set off for Nevada Fall, walk up the river's south bank to placid-looking Emerald Pool. Its cool, green waters may look tempting, but swimmers and waders have been swept from there to their deaths on the rocks below Vernal Fall. The pool is fed by the Silver Apron, a sheet cascade that throws the Merced River into a "waterwheel" during heavy spring runoff. Mounting to a granite terrace, we cross the river on a bridge above a narrow chute known as Diamond Cascade.

Now on the north bank, we near the water-streaked cliff whereupon hangs Nevada Fall, visible through the trees. It is a much more concentrated waterfall than Vernal. Shot through a narrow notch near the top of the cliff, it free-falls briefly before striking the cliff's apron, broadening toward one side. This off-kilter shape inspired the Ahwahneechee name of *Yo-wiye,* or Twisted Fall.

After a series of dry switchbacks up the talus slopes to the north of Nevada Fall, encouraged by frequent stops to admire Nevada's profile, we crest the ridge and

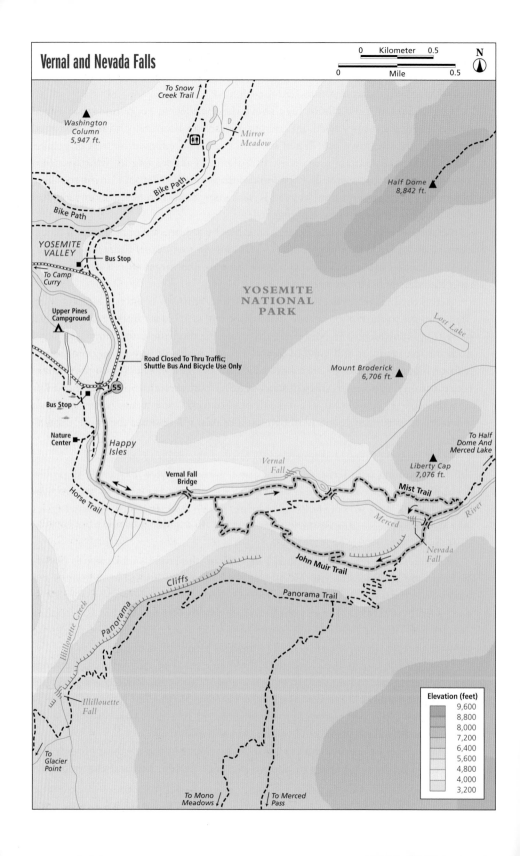

Vernal and Nevada Falls

0 — Kilometer — 0.5
0 — Mile — 0.5

N

Washington
Column
5,947 ft.

To Snow
Creek Trail

Mirror
Meadow

Half Dome
8,842 ft.

Bike Path

Bike Path

YOSEMITE
VALLEY

Bus Stop

To Camp
Curry

YOSEMITE
NATIONAL
PARK

Upper Pines
Campground

Lost Lake

Road Closed To Thru Traffic;
Shuttle Bus And Bicycle Use Only

155

Mount Broderick
6,706 ft.

Bus Stop

Nature
Center

Happy
Isles

Horse Trail

Vernal Fall
Bridge

Vernal
Fall

Liberty Cap
7,076 ft.

To Half
Dome And
Merced Lake

Mist Trail

Merced

River

John Muir Trail

Nevada
Fall

Cliffs

Panorama Trail

Panorama

Illilouette Creek

Illilouette
Fall

To Glacier
Point

To Mono
Meadows

To Merced
Pass

Elevation (feet)

9,600
8,800
8,000
7,200
6,400
5,600
4,800
4,000
3,200

double-back downstream toward the lip of the falls. Just before the bridge (north side), leave the beaten path to pick your way carefully across the granite slabs toward the cliff; near the high point you will see some rough railed steps that drop to a railed ledge a bit above the chute that conducts the Merced River over the brink. Compressed by this narrow channel, the river explodes to freedom, roaring over the drop and pulverizing into a torrential mist on the sheer rock face.

Climbing back to the main trail, we turn right (south) to cross the Merced River on a bridge above the waterfall's chute. Our return route to Happy Isles now follows the John Muir Trail down the south wall of the Merced gorge. Passing the junction with the Panorama Trail to Glacier Point, we traverse a cliff on a 1,000-foot shelf blasted from the Panorama Cliff and walled off to prevent skittish horses from shying at the brink. Water trickling down the cliff cuts loose above the trail cut, raining down on our ledge in mellow curtains, cooling us on hot afternoons but making treacherous ice in early and late season. From this ledge we nab a classic view of Nevada Fall, hanging crooked on its high wall and backed by a progression of monolithic rocks: Liberty Cap (7,076 feet), Mount Broderick (6,706 feet), and the rounded back of Half Dome (8,842 feet).

The remainder of our trail back to Vernal Fall Bridge follows a series of steep, wide switchbacks below the Panorama Cliffs, which can be grueling on the knees. The gnarly oaks and scrub that grow among the boulders, stone walls, and granite cliffs are as exquisitely arranged as bonsai gardens, on an epic scale. At the Mist Trail junction, turn left (west) to backtrack to the Vernal Fall Bridge and onward to Happy Isles.

Option

Many of the hikers you will see on this trail are bound to or coming from the summit of Half Dome, Yosemite's most beloved mountain and an icon of American mountaineering. This is an exceptionally strenuous day hike, adding 9 miles and nearly 3,000 feet of elevation gain and loss to the present hike, all from the junction above Nevada Fall. Hikers aiming for Half Dome need to start from Happy Isles early, certainly not later than 6 a.m. The final push to the summit is up the famously intimidating, spectacularly exposed apex of the dome by the aid of metal cables fastened to the granite. Because of Half Dome's popularity, permits are required and issued daily for only 300 hikers. For information, visit www.nps.gov/yose/planyourvisit/hdpermits.htm.

Miles and Directions

0.0 Happy Isles Bridge.

0.4 View of Yosemite and Illilouette Falls.

0.8 Vernal Fall Bridge. Toilets and water fountain on south side of bridge.

1.0 Junction of Mist Trail and John Muir Trail; continue straight up the Mist Trail.

1.3 Top of Vernal Fall.

1.4 Emerald Pool on left; junction to toilet on right.

1.5 Junction to JMT; bear left (north).

1.6 Bridge above Diamond Cascade.

2.3 Junction with trail to Half Dome and Little Yosemite; bear right (southwest). Toilet.

2.5 Top of Nevada Fall.

2.8 Junction with Panorama Trail to Glacier Point; bear right (west) toward Happy Isles.

3.6 Junction with trail to Vernal Fall; bear left (west) to Happy Isles.

4.2 Junction with Mist Trail; bear left (west).

4.4 Vernal Fall Bridge.

5.2 Happy Isles Bridge.

56 Sentinel Dome, the Fissures, and Taft Point

Any one of these three natural wonders would stand central in its own national monument, but in Yosemite, where wonders accrue without stint, you can visit these towering, knife-edge cliffs and the summit of this illustrious dome all in one moderate loop hike.

Start: Sentinel Dome parking area, Glacier Point Road
Distance: 5.6-mile lollipop loop
Hiking time: About 3 hours
Difficulty: Moderate, with an overall gain and loss of about 1,200 feet
Trail condition: Worn but well-marked dirt trail and easily navigated open granite slabs
Seasons: Late May through late Oct
Other trail users: No dogs or bikes
Land status: Yosemite National Park

Nearest town: Yosemite Village
Fees and permits: None, but Yosemite levies an entrance fee
Maps: Trails Illustrated: *Yosemite Valley & Wawona*. USGS 7.5-minute quad: Half Dome.
Trail contacts: Yosemite Valley Visitor Center, Yosemite Village, CA 95389; (209) 372-0200; www.nps.gov/yose
Special considerations: The Fissures and Taft Point are not fenced. Use caution.

Finding the trailhead: From Chinquapin, on CA 41 between Yosemite Valley and Wawona, drive east on the Glacier Point Road a bit more than 13.5 miles. Park in the lot on the left (north) side of the road, at the trailhead for Sentinel Dome. Consider riding the bus from Yosemite Valley. Trailhead GPS: N37 42.755' / W119 35.181'

The Hike

From the trailhead (elevation 7,750 feet), walk northeast on a dusty trail through a rocky, dry forest of red fir and lodgepole interspersed with manzanita, chinquapin, huckleberry oak, and bracken. As the steep south face of rounded Sentinel Dome looms closer, our route intercepts and follows an abandoned roadway that used to allow cars to drive to granite slabs on the north side. From there, the route is obvious: straight up the rock slope, steep and steady but not scary, to the broad summit. The highest point on the south rim of Yosemite Valley at 8,122 feet, Sentinel Dome sponsors a magnificent 360-degree vista, with a classic view of Half Dome in profile, looking somewhat like a hooded monk, or maybe the ghost of Christmas-Yet-to-Come with shrouded arm pointing eternally up Tenaya Canyon. Scattered about us, scores of other iconic features rise as if from a gargantuan map—Yosemite Falls, the Lost Arrow, Little Yosemite Valley, El Capitan, North and Basket Domes, the Clark and Cathedral ranges, Mount Hoffman, and much more that could happily absorb hours of contemplative gazing from a thoughtful geographer, glaciologist, backpacker, poet, or geologist. Ah heck, even Bozo the Clown digs this view.

Sentinel Dome is the easiest to climb of the Valley's big domes.

But onward: Descend the dome the way you came up, but at the granite "parking lot" landing, keep descending on the marked trail toward Glacier Point and Taft Point. Turn left (west) when you meet the Pohono Trail, continuing to descend, with ever-intriguing views of Yosemite Valley through the trees, passing behind Sentinel Rock and crossing Sentinel Creek before climbing again 0.5 mile to a junction labeled "Return Junction" on the map. To see the Fissures, turn right (west).

After crossing a marshy meadow to a jumble of large boulders in the trees, we descend to an open sandy area overgrown with scrub, which lies close to the obvious

Sentinel Dome, the Fissures, and Taft Point

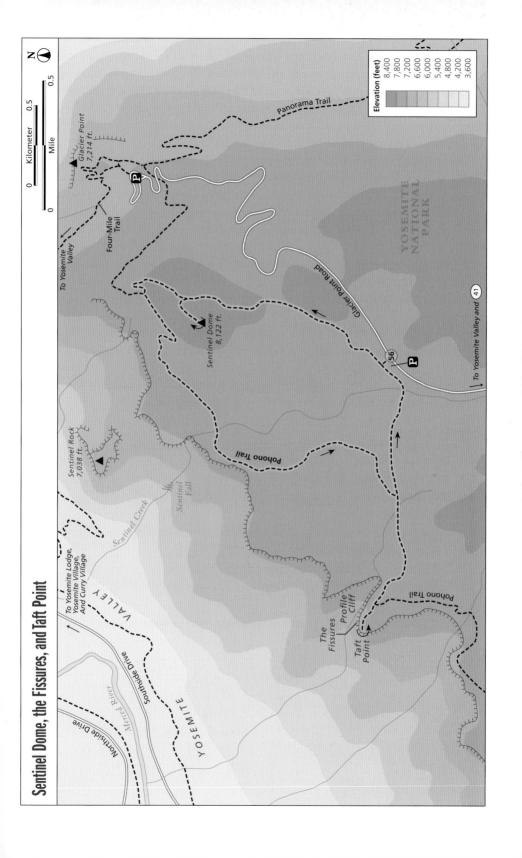

rim of Yosemite Valley. The eager feet of anxious hikers have obliterated any single trail, so choose one that heads toward the valley rim. The Fissures are great clefts in the granite, a few feet across and hundreds of feet deep. Tucked almost unobtrusively among the rocks and bushes, they gape like missing pieces of an enormous stone cake, neatly sliced and the pieces spirited away, leaving five telltale gaps. Formed over centuries by weathering, some are jammed with fallen boulders.

Beyond the Fissures we can see the fenced railing of overhanging Profile Cliff. Climbing to the bars, we have a tremendous view of nearby Taft Point on our immediate left. Across the valley the old Big Oak Flat Road climbs through the rockslides to the left of monolithic El Capitan. Yosemite Falls hangs from its wall about 5 air miles distant, while the Merced River twines along the valley floor, nearly 3,500 feet below us.

No railing surrounds Taft Point, which we gingerly approach over bare granite. If it increases your confidence and stability, there's no dishonor in dropping to your belly and inching forward to the verge. Peering down into that gargantuan abyss, you may well find your scalp and toes tingling. Few sights in the world can rival this thrill. True enough, one of them is nearby Glacier Point, but heavily walled-off Glacier Point is reached by road and unrailed Taft Point only by trail—and therein lies a big difference.

The shortest route back to the parking area retraces our trail back to "Return Junction," where we walk straight (east) 0.6 mile back to the trailhead.

Miles and Directions

0.0 Parking area. Turn right (northeast) at trailhead sign.

0.8 Trail junction to Glacier Point; go left.

1.0 Base of dome.

1.1 Summit of Sentinel Dome.

1.2 Return to base of dome; at trail junction sign, head downhill toward Glacier Point.

1.6 Turn left at junction onto Pohono Trail.

3.6 Turn right (west) at "Return Junction," staying on the Pohono Trail.

4.0 The Fissures.

4.3 Taft Point.

5.0 Junction with Pohono Trail to Glacier Point; go straight (east) toward parking area.

5.6 Arrive back at the parking area.

57 Chilnualna Falls

Of Yosemite's highest waterfalls, Chilnualna is the most reclusive, showing itself only to hikers willing to toil up a trail too homely and switchbacked ever to be called a crowd-pleaser. The Chilnualna Trail offers many pleasures of a more subtle hue, not the least of which is solitude. To tackle it on a hot summer's afternoon takes a bit of fortitude and a couple quarts of water, but the trail makes an invigorating muscle-stretcher in spring or fall, when high-country routes are under snow.

Start: End of Chilnualna Road in Wawona, southern Yosemite
Distance: 7.4 miles out and back
Hiking time: About 4 hours
Difficulty: Strenuous because of an elevation gain and loss of more than 2,300 feet
Trail condition: Steep trail with many duff-covered switchbacks
Seasons: Late Apr through mid-June is best for water displays. Mid-June through Aug can be hot. Sept through early Nov is very pleasant.
Other trail users: No dogs, horses, or bikes allowed
Land status: Yosemite National Park. Wawona is a private residential inholding within the national park.

Nearest towns: Wawona has groceries and gas, Fish Camp has most other amenities.
Fees and permits: None for day hike. For overnighters, obtain a wilderness permit from the Information Station in Hill's Studio, next to the Wawona Hotel. Yosemite charges an entrance fee.
Maps: Tom Harrison: *Yosemite High Country.* USGS 7.5-minute quads: Wawona, Mariposa Grove.
Trail contacts: Wawona Visitor Center at Hill's Studio, adjacent to the Wawona Hotel; (209) 375-9501, www.nps.gov/yose/planyourvisit/permitstations.htm

Finding the trailhead: A private inholding in southern Yosemite, Wawona straddles Chilnualna Road east of CA 41, 60 miles north of Fresno, and 32 miles south of Yosemite Valley. The Chilnualna Road turnoff is immediately north of the bridge over the South Fork of the Merced River. Bear left (north) at the first fork, winding for 2 more miles on Chilnualna Road, past the Wawona school, library, a small grocery store, and scores of cabins and houses until you reach the dirt parking lot for Chilnualna Falls on the right (south), marked by a signpost. (Parking area GPS: N37 32.889' / W119 38.081') To find the trailhead, walk 0.1 mile east to the end of Chilnualna Road. Trailhead GPS: N37 32.914' / W119 38.019'

The Hike

From the dusty trailhead on the edge of Wawona (elevation 4,200 feet), the well-worn path strikes steeply through forests of black and canyon live oak, pine, and incense cedar, and up stone steps above cascading Chilnualna Creek. Picnickers scrambling off-trail have scuffed steep treads down to creek-side slabs and boulders. (Racing waters are dangerous during spring runoff.) Near the top of the cascade, the

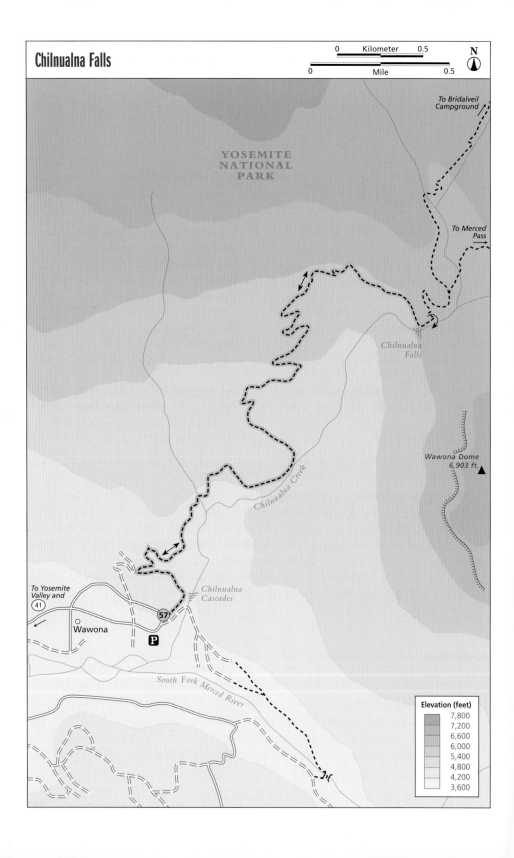

Chilnualna Falls

0   Kilometer   0.5
0   Mile   0.5

N

YOSEMITE NATIONAL PARK

To Bridalveil Campground

To Merced Pass

Chilnualna Falls

Wawona Dome 6,903 ft.

Chilnualna Creek

Chilnualna Cascades

To Yosemite Valley and (41)

Wawona

57

P

South Fork Merced River

Elevation (feet)

	7,800
	7,200
	6,600
	6,000
	5,400
	4,800
	4,200
	3,600

trail makes an abrupt hairpin turn, climbing to a paved dead-end road, which marks the end of the hikers' steepest stretch.

Switching directions yet again, ascend through boulders and manzanita to a sandy flat surrounded by cedar, red fir, and black oak clumped sporadically among pungent carpets of kit-kit-dizze—better known as mountain misery—a medicinal herb valued by the Miwok, who drank an infusion of its steeped leaves. Next you embark on a new set of switchbacks, which—though never particularly steep—stick doggedly to the task for the next 2.5 miles and 1,300 vertical feet. As you climb, the broken face of Wawona Dome rises into view across the deep ravine where unseen Chilnualna Creek splashes. A vista unfolds over Wawona Valley, a choice encampment favored by the Miwok for its game meadows, which has since been converted into a golf course. The Mariposa Grove of giant sequoias crowns the ridge directly to the south. *Wawona* was the Miwok word for "big tree" and is said to imitate the hoot of an owl, Miwok guardian deity of the giant sequoia.

Soon after turning east on the highest switchback, you will catch a fleeting glimpse of Chilnualna Falls, falling with a peculiar twist 240 feet down the back of its narrow, shadowy gorge. Take a good look, for no other angle from the trail offers so complete a view of the falls.

After a short stretch blasted through granite, the trail emerges above the brink of the falls. Be careful if you walk down for a closer look, for there are no railings. Excellent campsites abound 0.5 mile above the main falls, near some upper cascades and splendid pools.

Miles and Directions

0.0 Parking area.

0.1 Lower cascade of Chilnualna Creek.

0.5 Paved road; stay on trail.

3.5 View of Chilnualna Falls.

3.7 Brink of Chilnualna Falls.

7.4 Arrive back at the parking area.

58 Clouds Rest

A gargantuan presence looming in the background of countless Yosemite Valley views, Clouds Rest is both the highest point on the valley rim and the largest continuous rock slope in the Sierra Nevada. Its 9,926-foot summit provides sublime vistas in all directions, especially down.

Start: Sunrise Trailhead, southwest end of Tenaya Lake

Distance: 13.2 miles out and back

Hiking time: About 7–8 hours

Difficulty: Strenuous, with an overall elevation gain and loss of more than 2,450 feet

Trail condition: Excellent, well-marked dirt trail, but narrow and exposed for the last few hundred feet

Seasons: June–Oct

Other trail users: Equestrians and pack trains use the trails, except for the final scramble to the summit. No dogs or bikes allowed.

Land status: Yosemite National Park

Nearest town: Tuolumne Meadows or Yosemite Village

Fees and permits: None for day trip. For overnighter, obtain a wilderness permit from the Yosemite Wilderness Office. Yosemite charges an entrance fee.

Maps: Tom Harrison: *Yosemite High Country.* USGS 7.5-minute quad: Tenaya Lake.

Trail contacts: Tuolumne Meadows Visitor Center, open seasonally; Yosemite Valley Visitor Center, Yosemite Village, CA 95389; both at (209) 372-0200; www.nps.gov/yose

Finding the trailhead: The trailhead parking lot is on the east side of CA 120 (Tioga Pass Road), 0.2 mile south of Tenaya Lake. To get there from Tuolumne Meadows, drive nearly 9 miles south on CA 120 from the bridge over the Tuolumne River. From the Crane Flat junction, drive about 31 miles north. Ride there (stop #10) from Tuolumne Meadows on the free shuttle (see sidebar on p. 284). Trailhead GPS: N37 49.545' / W119 28.193'

The Hike

Signs on the east side of the parking lot (elevation 8,150 feet) point out two trails. We want the path toward Sunrise High Sierra Camp, which strikes east through lodgepoles, fording Tenaya Creek, a very wet crossing in early season. Turning right (south) at the signed junction on the opposite bank, we follow the creek downstream for a spell before veering away, climbing a low ridge, and dropping to a small outlet brook from Mildred Lake, tucked out of sight on her shelf about 1,400 feet above us. After plodding along a level stretch, crossing two seasonal creeks and the wreckage of some past winter's avalanche, we begin to climb again on a diagonal line through forests of pine and fir that partially block our westward views of Mount Hoffmann and Tuolumne Peak. We meet the steepening gradient with a series of more than fifteen switchbacks that carry us to the ridgetop junction with the Sunrise Trail, having climbed a tad more than 1,000 vertical feet above our trailhead.

Turning right (south) at the fork, we cross the ridge and make a steep but short descent on switchbacks into a forested valley. Passing a wet meadow, we veer over a low shoal of jumbled rocks, touching down again near a small, tranquil, unnamed lake. A nice, flat stretch of forest walking follows, entailing at one point the potentially muddy rock-hopping of an unnamed tributary of Tenaya Creek. After easily clambering up to our next ridge, we meet another signed junction with a shortcut to Yosemite Valley.

Clouds Rest lies to the right (west). Having left the valleys behind, our dry and dusty path undulates over a forested ridge, bringing Clouds Rest finally into proximate view. This eastern face appears nowhere near as expansive and formidable as its western face. Rather, it puts one in mind of a giant granite helmet placed atop a knoll amid the forest.

We now approach the ridge on switchbacks, eager to commence the best part of the hike. The forest peters out as we gain the granite shoulder, where views westward across Tenaya Canyon hint at the majesty to come. (If you suffer from vertigo, this might be the view point where you turn around.) Mounting now upon the granite "helmet," our clear-cut path crosses to the east side of the ridge, insulated from the sheer western face by a high granite bench. We know it is time to leave the main trail when masses of bushy chinquapins crowd in, with a handful of pines, and we find ourselves staring up at the final 0.2-mile stretch of rocky ridge leading to the summit. Where the main trail veers left through the chinquapin bushes, we climb up the granite blocks to the right, toward the ridge.

We crest on a backbone of disconnected rocks, a ridge spine averaging between some 5 and 10 feet in width. To the right (west), the formidable western face of Clouds Rest drops almost 5,000 feet in 1.5 miles to the glades and forests on the floor of Tenaya Canyon. By comparison, the 1,700-foot drop eastward to Sunrise Creek seems a pussycat, though it would kill you just the same. Walking up this ridge can be scary, especially if it is windy, though technically it is not much more difficult than walking on a typical sidewalk. What gives us hesitation, what makes us so acutely conscious of every ripple on the rock and worn spot on the soles of our boots, is the perception, however unlikely, that a faltering step might send us plummeting headlong into oblivion. Exercise reasonable caution, and you will be standing on Clouds Rest's spacious summit within a couple of minutes. And having made the passage once, you will find the return trip along this ridge to be much less frightening.

From the summit we survey the park in all its glory, from the northern boundary along Sawtooth Ridge southward to the Clark Range; from the eastern mounts of Lyell and Dana to El Capitan and the rolling forestlands of the west. Tenaya and Merced Canyons (including Merced Lake) spread open on either side. Most intriguing of all is Half Dome, looking very trim from this side angle. With binoculars, we can clearly see the line of people trudging up its shoulder switchbacks. Putting down the binoculars and looking around, chances are fair that you will be alone on Clouds Rest's summit for at least part of your time.

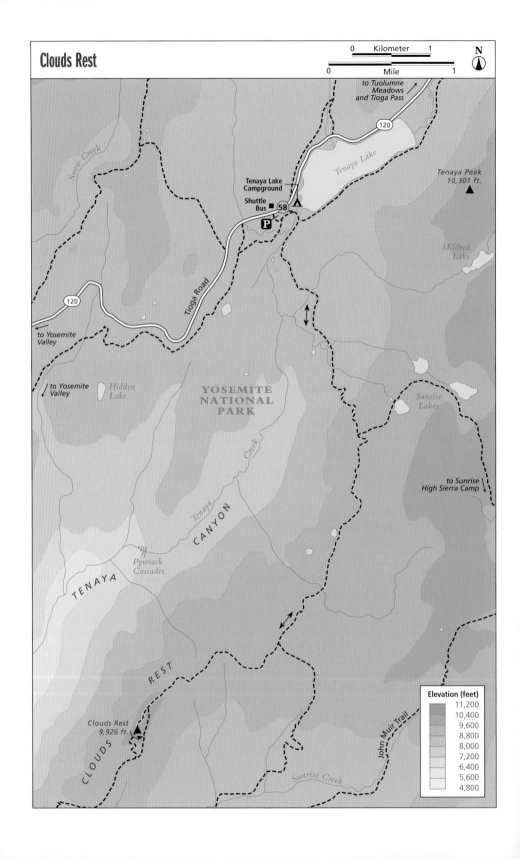

Clouds Rest

0   Kilometer   1
0   Mile   1

N

to Tuolumne
Meadows
and Tioga Pass

120

Snow Creek

Tenaya Lake

Tenaya Lake
Campground

Shuttle
Bus   58

P

Tioga Road

120

to Yosemite
Valley

to Yosemite
Valley

Hidden
Lake

YOSEMITE
NATIONAL
PARK

Tenaya Peak
10,301 ft.

Mildred
Lake

Sunrise
Lakes

to Sunrise
High Sierra Camp

Creek

Tenaya

CANYON

Pywiack
Cascades

TENAYA

REST

Clouds Rest
9,926 ft.

CLOUDS

Sunrise Creek

John Muir Trail

Elevation (feet)

11,200
10,400
9,600
8,800
8,000
7,200
6,400
5,600
4,800

Miles and Directions

0.0 Trailhead parking lot.

0.1 Ford Tenaya Creek.

0.2 Junction with trail that leads to Tenaya Lake's northeast shore; bear right (south).

2.4 Junction with Sunrise Trail; bear right (south).

4.6 Junction with shortcut trail toward Yosemite Valley; bear right (southwest).

6.4 Leave the main trail for the final scramble up the summit ridge.

6.6 Summit of Clouds Rest.

13.2 Arrive back at the trailhead parking lot.

59 Cathedral Lakes

Set in a high mountain valley between stream-braided meadow, forest, and glacier-polished slabs of granite, the Cathedral sisters are two of Yosemite's prettiest lakes. The trail is popular with backpackers, but both lakes are close enough for an out-and-back day hike.

Start: Cathedral Lakes trailhead on the Tioga Pass Road, near Tuolumne Meadows
Distance: 9.2 miles out and back
Hiking time: About 5-6 hours, allowing time to explore the lakeshore
Difficulty: Moderate, with an overall elevation gain and loss of about 1,350 feet
Trail condition: Although an excellent tread through the forests, the path is wet and sloppy in early-season meadows, especially near Cathedral Lake.
Seasons: Late June through Sept
Other trail users: Equestrians and pack trains are common. Dogs and bikes prohibited.

Land status: Yosemite National Park
Nearest town: Tuolumne Meadows
Fees and permits: None for day trips, but a wilderness permit and bear-proof food canister are required of overnighters. No campfires allowed at Cathedral Lakes. Yosemite charges an entrance fee.
Maps: Tom Harrison: *Yosemite High Country*. USGS 7.5-minute quad: Tenaya Lake.
Trail contacts: Tuolumne Meadows Visitor Center, Yosemite National Park; (209) 372-0200; www.nps.gov/yose

Finding the trailhead: In Yosemite National Park, drive 1.6 miles westerly on CA 120 from the bridge over the Tuolumne River and park on the wide shoulder on either side of the road. Ride there (stop #7) from Tuolumne Meadows on the free shuttle (see sidebar p. 284). Trailhead GPS: N37 52.378' / W119 22.981'

The Hike

Following an ancient Indian path and the John Muir Trail (JMT), the Cathedral Lakes trail has long served as the primary foot trail between Yosemite Valley, Tuolumne Meadows, and the Great Basin. From the south side of the Tioga Pass Road (CA 120) adjacent to the trailhead sign (elevation 8,550 feet), our path heads into the dense forest on the west bank of Budd Creek. Almost immediately we meet a junction with the Tuolumne Meadows–Tenaya Lake trail; go straight (southwest), climbing on stony soil through a dry forest of lodgepole pine and red fir. Likewise, stay the course (southwest) when you pass the narrow, unsigned, unofficial trail to Budd Lake, which spurs off from the left (east) at roughly 0.5 mile.

Our trail levels out at about 0.7 mile, and we stroll on sandy soil through a pleasing forest interspersed with wet meadows. For the first time on this trail, you start to see mountains beyond the trees. The great, rounded buttress of Cathedral Peak appears, dome-like, just ahead. Passing beneath it, we dip into another forest and then cross a meadow watered by Cathedral Creek and its small, seasonal tributaries—a muddy passage in early season.

After crossing the last of the streamlets, our path turns south, tracing the course of Cathedral Creek upstream within earshot of its tantalizing babble, cutting switchbacks through the forest. About halfway up the hill, a prolific spring comes welling out from the dry hillside, the surprising fountainhead of Cathedral Creek (for Cathedral Creek does not issue from Cathedral Lakes). At this point a fine view corridor sweeps down through the red fir–lined meadow to ice-sculptured Fairview Dome. On the horizon to the left, we can see Matterhorn Peak (12,264 feet) and the jagged Sawtooth Ridge, the northern boundary of Yosemite. As we climb the hill, bulky Mount Conness (12,590 feet) appears to the northeast. At roughly 2 miles the trail begins to level out again on gravelly tread through the pines. Medlicott Dome appears on the right (west), while the continuous wall of Cathedral Peak, capped by spindly pinnacles, rises on the left (east).

The Cathedral Lakes junction presents you with a choice of two very different, very scenic lakes. Most backpackers continue left (south) to Upper Cathedral Lake, since it lies beside the main trail and does not require a detour. But heck, let's do both, starting with lower Cathedral Lake: Take the right (west) fork, stumbling downhill on a shabby trail over rocks and roots, through woods, and across the outlet stream from Upper Cathedral Lake. A confusing clutch of use-trails branches from the opposite bank. By turning downstream, we quickly identify the main trail and follow it through a meadow being reclaimed by young forest. The passage of thousands of feet have cut the path deep into the earth.

Emerging from the wooded hillside, we arrive on the verge of a magnificent meadow. In early season it is also one of the muddiest. The creek, arriving with us, makes a last dash onto the flats over rust-colored granite slabs, where the water spreads into a wide, ankle-deep sheet, as if being emptied down an angled driveway from a bottomless water bucket. As the creek commences a slow dillydally through the broad, potholed meadow, our trail debauches into several parallel tracks cut by hikers seeking new routes around puddles that invariably fill the old ones.

Despite the muck, these miniature plains are enchanting. When the sun shines, the meadows saturate the landscape with a radiant green, and each deep pool of water stands so clear in its turfy basin that we can count individual grains of sand on the bottom, and watch as darting fish decimate the mosquito egg rafts. You will have to cross the creek at least three times to get across this meadow, and in early season even experienced broad jumpers will get wet feet.

The west side of the meadow laps up against the rim of the irregular granite bowl that encases lower Cathedral Lake (9,288 feet), a cold, blue, sparkling expanse of water, one of the most intriguing in the entire Sierra. A big part of its fascination stems from the fact that a peninsula cuts off views of its farther shore, so that we are not even sure of its shape without making an effort to explore (or consulting a map). You can spend an agreeable day lounging on the granite slabs and following the shore around to the west side, through forest and over rock and meadows. From the outlet stream, which drains into Tenaya Canyon and thence into Yosemite Valley, you can

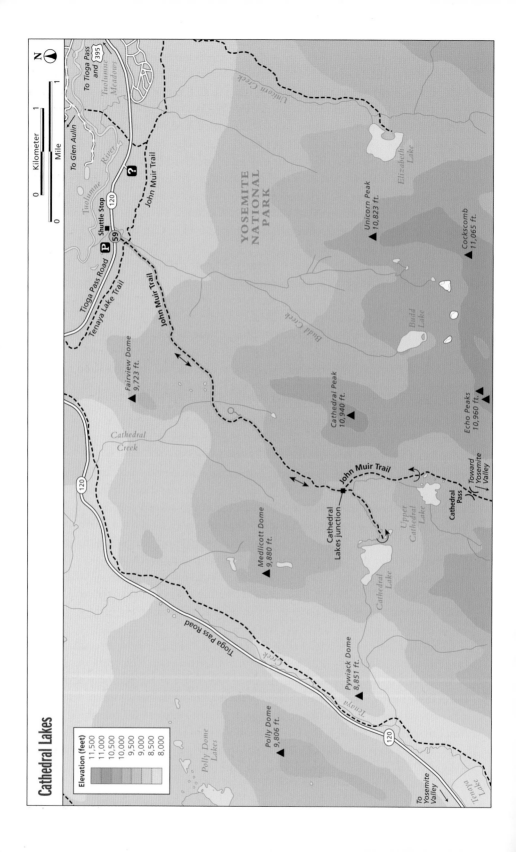

Cathedral Lakes

Elevation (feet)
11,500
11,000
10,500
10,000
9,500
9,000
8,500
8,000

N

0   Kilometer   1
0   Mile   1

To Tioga Pass
and 395

To Glen Aulin

Tuolumne
Meadows

Unicorn Creek

Tuolumne River

Shuttle Stop

Tioga Pass Road

Tenaya Lake Trail

John Muir Trail

120

59

P

?

YOSEMITE
NATIONAL
PARK

Elizabeth
Lake

Unicorn Peak
10,823 ft.

Cockscomb
11,065 ft.

Budd Lake

Budd Creek

Fairview Dome
9,723 ft.

John Muir Trail

Cathedral
Creek

Cathedral Peak
10,940 ft.

Echo Peaks
10,960 ft.

Medlicott Dome
9,880 ft.

John Muir Trail

Cathedral
Lakes junction

Upper
Cathedral
Lake

Cathedral
Lake

Cathedral Pass

Toward
Yosemite
Valley

120

Tioga Pass Road

Tenaya Creek

Pywiack Dome
8,851 ft.

Polly Dome
9,806 ft.

Polly Dome
Lakes

120

To Yosemite
Valley

Tenaya
Lake

look northwest to Polly Dome (9,806 feet) and Tuolumne Peak (10,845 feet), and due west to Mount Hoffmann (10,850 feet). Behind us (east) Cathedral Peak (10,940 feet) protrudes above the horizontal bands of granite, meadow, and forest. From this angle it appears spindling, almost decrepit, hardly recognizable as the same elegant mountain that lords so majestically over Tuolumne Meadows.

Upper Cathedral Lake, the smaller of the pair, lies at an elevation of 9,600 feet, 0.6 mile above the Cathedral Lakes junction on the John Muir Trail. Upper Cathedral Lake fills a shallow basin ringed by granite ridges, with a curious view of Cathedral Peak, looking very gaunt and undernourished. Its shores seem more open to the sky than its forest-girdled sister downstream.

Miles and Directions

0.0 Cathedral Lakes trailhead.

0.1 Tenaya Lake Trail; continue straight (southwest).

0.5 Junction with unofficial Budd Lake trail; continue straight (southwest).

1.5 Cross Cathedral Creek.

1.8 Cathedral Creek spring.

2.8 Cathedral Lakes junction; bear right (west) for the lower Cathedral Lake.

3.2 Lower Cathedral Lake.

4.0 Return to Cathedral Lakes junction; turn right (south) toward Upper Cathedral Lake.

4.6 Upper Cathedral Lake.

9.2 Arrive back at the trailhead.

60 Lembert Dome

Anchored high above Tuolumne Meadows on the polished granite apex of Lembert, hikers on this adventurous out-and-back climb are treated to a real-scale map of northern Yosemite.

Start: Dog Lake trailhead, Tuolumne Meadows
Distance: 2.2 miles out and back
Hiking time: About 3 hours, with time to explore the summit
Difficulty: A short, steep climb with an overall elevation gain of about 850 feet. To reach the top, you will need to scramble over steep rock.
Trail condition: Decent, well-marked trail in the forest, but the dome's summit is smooth granite slab without tread or markers
Seasons: June-Oct
Other trail users: Equestrians and pack trains may use the forest trail but do not ascend the dome's summit. No dogs or bikes.

Land status: Yosemite National Park
Nearest town: Tuolumne Meadows
Fees and permits: None for day trip. Yosemite charges an entrance fee.
Maps: Tom Harrison: *Yosemite High Country.* National Geographic Trails Illustrated: *Yosemite NE.* USGS 7.5-minute quad: Tioga Pass.
Trail contact: Tuolumne Meadows Visitor Center, Yosemite National Park; (209) 372-0263; www.nps.gov/yose

Finding the trailhead: The Dog Lake parking area is at the base of Lembert Dome on the Tuolumne Lodge Road, 0.5 mile from the Tioga Pass Road (CA 120) and about 0.4 mile from the Tuolumne Meadows Lodge. Ride there (stop #2) on the free Tuolumne Meadows shuttle. (**Note:** There is another prominently signposted Lembert Dome trailhead on the north side of the Tuolumne Meadows vehicular bridge, but our trailhead is different.) Trailhead GPS: N37 52.703' / W119 20.341'

The Hike

Of the many heavily glaciated, monolithic granite peaks that rise so abruptly above the green flats of Tuolumne Meadows, Lembert Dome is the easiest to climb. A type of mountain known to geologists as a *roches moutonnee,* or "rock sheep," Lembert was carved by glaciers riding roughshod over its back, grinding, rounding, polishing, and plucking away the rock to leave a cliff at the "downstream" end. The Tuolumne Glacier also left behind many large boulders, called "erratics," on Lembert's slopes, including one right at the very summit. Sheer on the north and west but with gradually steepening inclines along its broad southern flank, this granite dome attracts both scramblers and experienced rock climbers. It's fun to just start climbing up any likely looking slope on your own, and many people do—just make sure you know your abilities and use good judgment because a slip could prove fatal.

This trail bypasses Lembert's exposed lower slopes with a safe and sure-footed alternative. Starting on the road to Tuolumne Meadows Lodge, the trail crosses Tioga

The iconic, glacier sculpted hump of Lembert Dome rises above Tuolumne Meadows.

Pass Road and muscles its way uphill through the lodgepole forest just to the east of the rock itself. This steep, shady climb is an admittedly workaday affair, but bear with it because, after reaching the Dog Lake junction, things quickly get interesting.

Reaching the shoulder of the rock itself, you leave the dirt path and step onto the granite itself. Suddenly the exposure is obvious. To one side is a stubby cliff, to the other, Lembert's southern flank sliding steadily downward to the distant meadows. Just ahead of you (west) rises the summit knob, glistening with glacial polish. Climbing that knob directly from this angle would be foolhardy without rock-climbing gear and experience, but there is an easier way for ordinary hikers to walk to the summit: Contour left (south) onto the sloping granite south face. Pick your way across these leaning slabs of granite to the opposite (western) side of the summit knob, and then make your ascent. Some hikers may feel intimidated by walking over such a lofty, steeply angled pitch of rock, yet it's a very large, rough-textured slope, and with ordinary caution you should have no trouble sticking to it merely by the friction of

Lembert Dome

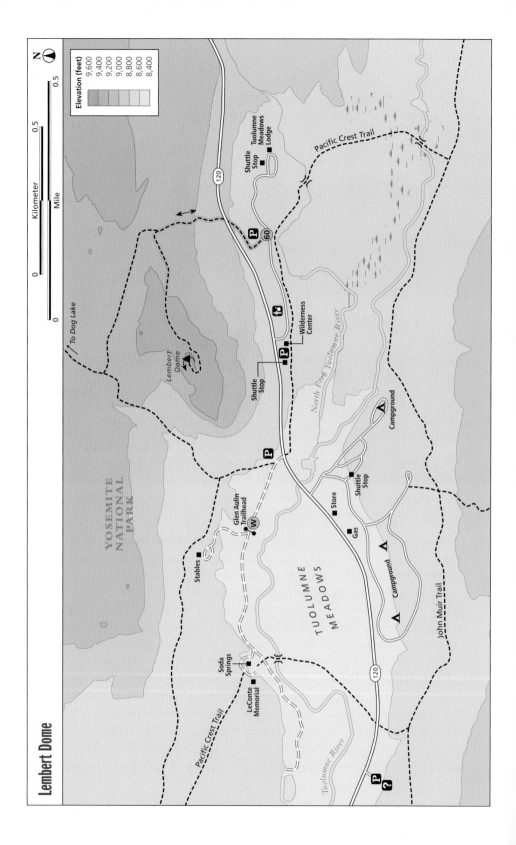

your boot soles. Most hikers quickly get comfortable with it, and after visiting the summit are ready to explore more of Lembert's ridgeline, even scrambling (with caution) clear to the cliffs on the far western side.

Enjoy the glorious views of the Tuolumne region: the streams and rivers meandering through green meadows; the glacier-gouged canyons of the Lyell Fork and Mono Pass; the maplike lines of campground, lodge, and road. To the southwest juts Cathedral Peak (10,940 feet) and other horned summits of the Cathedral Range. Northward looms Ragged Peak (10,912 feet) and Mount Conness (12,590 feet), while on the far southern horizon, Banner Peak (12,945 feet) and Mounts Ritter (13,157 feet) and Lyell (13,114 feet) rear up like the kind of mountains children draw with crayons. Reddish Mount Dana (13,053 feet) and gray Mammoth Peak (12,117 feet) anchor the eastern skyline. Close at hand, stunted pines and purple penstemon grow out of narrow clefts in the rock.

Miles and Directions

0.0 Dog Lake trailhead.

0.1 Cross Tioga Pass Road.

0.5 Dog Lake junction; go left (west).

0.9 Granite shoulder; head onto the rock.

1.1 Summit.

2.2 Arrive back at the parking area.

61 Glen Aulin and Waterwheel Falls

Waterwheel Falls is the culmination of a string of cascades that electrify the Tuolumne River's frenzied descent from Tuolumne Meadows into the Grand Canyon of the Tuolumne via Glen Aulin. When running at full speed, these spectacular waterworks stand out as remarkable, even in a park famous for its waterfalls.

Start: The gravel road to Soda Springs, Tuolumne Meadows

Distance: Glen Aulin: 11.2 miles out and back; Waterwheel Falls: 17.2 miles out and back

Hiking time: About 6 hours to Glen Aulin and back; 10–12 hours for Waterwheel. A 2-night backpack trip is worth the extra time.

Difficulty: As a day hike, challenging to Glen Aulin and strenuous to Waterwheel Falls, which demands an overall elevation loss and gain of more than 2,550 feet. By backpacking for 2 nights in Glen Aulin, hikers can visit Waterwheel on a moderate day hike.

Trail condition: Excellent pack trail with lots of granite slabs

Seasons: June–July is best to see the "waterwheels." The trail is passable usually through Oct.

Other trail users: Pack trains are common. Dogs and bikes are prohibited.

Land status: Yosemite National Park

Nearest town: Tuolumne Meadows

Fees and permits: None for day hike. Overnighters require a wilderness permit. Yosemite charges an entrance fee.

Maps: Tom Harrison: *Yosemite High Country, Yosemite National Park*. USGS 7.5-minute quads: Tioga Pass, Falls Ridge.

Trail contact: Tuolumne Meadows Visitor Center, Yosemite National Park; (209) 372-0263; www.nps.gov/yose

Finding the trailhead: Just north of the bridge where the Tioga Pass Road (CA 120) crosses the Tuolumne River in Tuolumne Meadows, turn west on a gravel road toward the stables. Day hikers can park along the left (south) side of the road. Overnight hikers must use the Wilderness Center parking lot. Our trail starts at the metal gate 0.3 mile from CA 120, where that road makes a sharp 90-degree turn to the right. (Trailhead GPS: N37 52.734' / W119 21.503') Ride there (stop #4) from Tuolumne Meadows on the free shuttle.

The Hike

Between Tuolumne Meadows and Hetch Hetchy Reservoir, the Tuolumne River descends 4,800 feet of elevation in about 20 miles by means of a sensational string of cascades and waterfalls. This marvelous trail accompanies it as far as Waterwheel Falls, the highlight of the Grand Canyon of the Tuolumne River.

Starting at the metal gate that blocks public traffic on the old road to Soda Springs, we walk west on that old doubletrack road through the stateliest of Sierra landscapes, admiring the broad meadows along the Tuolumne River and the sharp, monumental peaks of the Cathedral Range along the southern horizon. As the old road approaches Soda Springs (see Hike W), it curves around the high side of the hillock to avoid the muddy ground. As the road comes down out of that curve toward a stone chalet, you

Tuolumne Meadows has some of the most sublime scenery in the Yosemite high country.

will meet a signposted singletrack trail junction that marks the start of the Glen Aulin trail (GPS: N37 52.740' / W119 22.021'). That's our trail.

After an uneventful mile's walk through lodgepole forest, we cross Delaney Creek on an upstream log. Our trail soon leaves the trees and again enters the meadows. Appreciative of our restored views of the river and Cathedral Range, we march onward over nearly level stretches of meadow, sometimes lightly forested. We cross some extensive slabs of granite with the aid of stone ducks, though with the river always at our left, we need not fear getting lost.

By the time we ford the shallow branches of Dingley Creek, we are aware of changes coming over the river. After its long, mostly placid stretch, the Tuolumne is now flowing more vigorously through a narrowing valley, rushing toward a defile in an obvious granite bench ahead of us. Climbing over it, we get our first view into the upper Grand Canyon of the Tuolumne and begin our descent toward its first bridge crossing, from which we clinch a stirring view down steep cascades toward Tuolumne Falls.

Dropping through mixed forests, ducked granite slabs, and pocket meadows lodged among the rocky shelves, we descend along the southern bank with the river crashing in our ears—raging white cataracts, one after another. Just as we approach the Glen Aulin High Sierra Camp, the river plunges down the White Cascade, foaming over high rocks into a deep, green pool. We cross below the pool on a metal bridge to meet a major junction: We continue downriver, but the Pacific Crest Trail (PCT) takes off up Cold Creek for points north. Before continuing, make a short detour across the Conness Creek bridge to see the Glen Aulin High Sierra Camp, a sandy, cheerful encampment of canvas tent cabins. Camping is allowed in this immediate area only in the nearby backpackers' camp.

From the aforementioned bridge below White Cascade, we continue downstream, hiking over a granite dike that separates us from Glen Aulin proper—a long, verdant, U-shaped valley. Upon descending the granite on a couple of switchbacks, we enjoy some easy hiking for more than a mile down the soft-floored glen. The bears in Glen Aulin are famous for their sense of entitlement toward backpacker's food caches, so be prepared if you are camping.

After flowing calmly through much of Glen Aulin, breaking occasionally into ripples and small rapids, the Tuolumne River resumes its downward calling with a vengeance at the western end of the glen. We know we are nearing the end of the glen when we cross the outlet stream of Mattie Lake, a tricky ford in early season, when it comes noisily cascading down from the side of Wildcat Point. From here on down to Waterwheel Falls, the canyon takes the form of a giant stairway—a stairway, however, built without level, square, or plumb bob. In its first giant step, the river lurches down a mighty set of cascades known as California Falls. The trail tags along at its side, zigzagging down through a surprisingly drier landscape. We watch the schizophrenic river rampage and foam through its steepest pitches, white and violent, only to pull up short in an intervening forest, where we find it biding time quietly in a still, green pool.

Glen Aulin and Waterwheel Falls

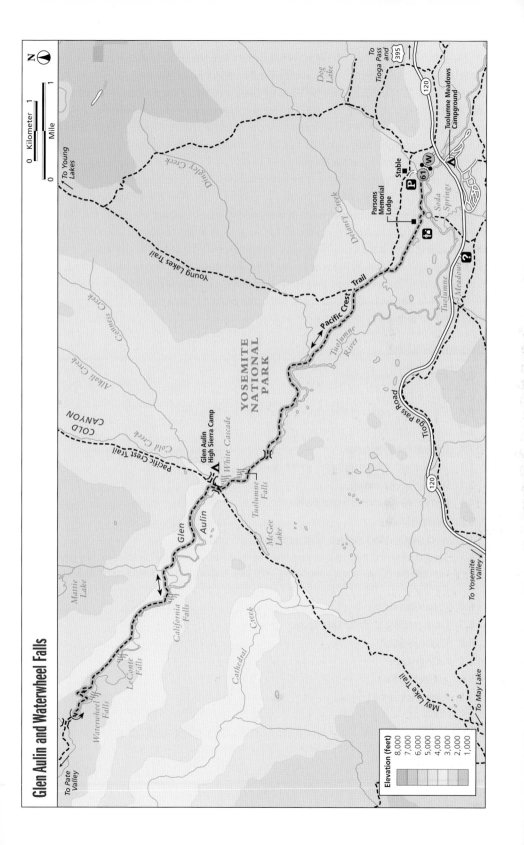

Even as we savor this serene interlude, the river abruptly launches into its next pitch, followed again by another spell of doldrums. The sequence is repeated again at LeConte Falls. Despite the repetition of these cascading sequences, they are never monotonous. On the contrary, like the rocks that they crash through, the cascades are infinitely varied, always fascinating, and intensely exciting to watch from the trail. When the river runs full, some of LeConte's hydro-technics are so spectacular that some hikers mistake them for Waterwheel Falls.

Beware: These cascades are extremely treacherous.

The final pitch is Waterwheel Falls. The river rolls over the brink and down a long, steady, steep granite incline that is relatively free of major obstructions. Building momentum, it suddenly strikes a submerged rock and is thrown violently into the air, arcing backward onto itself in a "waterwheel." Pleased with this trick, it then does it again and again. Waterwheels are common enough in the granitic Sierra, but nowhere else in the range can you find so many waterwheels in a single cascade. The incline is not so steep that you can't walk out on it for a close look, but beware: A slip could be lethal.

Miles and Directions

0.0   Trailhead at metal gate.

0.5   Soda Springs.

0.6   Signposted junction of Soda Springs road and Glen Aulin trail.

1.3   Junction with trail back to stables; go straight (northwest).

1.4   Delaney Creek crossing.

1.7   Junction with Young Lakes Trail; go left (west).

2.7   Dingley Creek crossing.

4.1   First bridge crossing of Tuolumne River.

4.8   Tuolumne Falls.

5.1   Junction with May Lake Trail; bear right (north).

5.2   Second bridge crossing of Tuolumne River, below White Cascade. At the adjacent trail junction with the PCT, continue downstream (left) after a short detour to Glen Aulin High Sierra Camp.

5.6   Upper Glen Aulin.

6.7   Creek crossing of Mattie Lake outlet.

6.9   California Falls.

8.0   LeConte Falls.

8.6   Waterwheel Falls.

17.2   Arrive back at the trailhead.

62 Gaylor Lakes and the Great Sierra Mine

One of the most godforsaken sights you will ever see—and also one of the most starkly beautiful—is the view of Gaylor Lakes from the old silver-mining camp of Dana. This out-and-back day hike offers history and spectacular scenery.

Start: Tioga Pass
Distance: 3.6 miles out and back
Hiking time: About 3 hours
Difficulty: Moderate, with an elevation gain and loss of about 1,000 feet
Trail condition: Good dirt tread. Use caution around mine shafts.
Seasons: July–Sept
Other trail users: Dogs and bikes prohibited. Equestrians unlikely. No camping is allowed in this drainage.

Land status: Yosemite National Park
Nearest towns: Tuolumne Meadows or Lee Vining
Fees and permits: None, but Yosemite charges an entrance fee
Maps: National Geographic Trails Illustrated: *Yosemite NE.* USGS 7.5-minute quad: Tioga Pass.
Trail contact: Tuolumne Meadows Visitor Center, Yosemite National Park; (209) 372-0263; www.nps.gov/yose

Finding the trailhead: Park in the lot on the west side of CA 120 immediately west of the Tioga Pass entrance station to Yosemite. Tioga Pass is a little less than 12 miles west of CA 120's junction with US 395, near Lee Vining, and about 6.75 miles east of the bridge over the Tuolumne River at Tuolumne Meadows. Ride there from Tuolumne Meadows Lodge on the free shuttle. Trailhead GPS: N37 54.614' / W119 15.500'

The Hike

From a bracing elevation only 50 short of 10,000 feet, this hard-rock miners' trail charges hot up the chilly ridge, gaining 600 feet of elevation within the first 0.5 mile. We rise steeply through scattered trees and boulders, stopping frequently to enjoy over-the-shoulder views of Dana Meadows, Mount Dana (13,053 feet), and Mammoth Peak (12,117 feet). After a couple of switchbacks, we contour over the hump and find ourselves standing above a broad, desolate valley seemingly barren of life, save for a few tough pines and some low-growing alpine vegetation. Immediately below us lies oblong Middle Gaylor Lake.

Cutting diagonally down the slope, we crop the northeastern end of the lake, enjoying views across to distant peaks of the Cathedral Range. We hop across the inlet creek, entrenched in the meadow like a monastic turf maze, and swing right (north) under a wide sky, driving up the broad, open valley toward Upper Gaylor Lake. Up ahead, we can see the trail scar and a building on a ridge to the left—the remains of the nineteenth-century silver-mining settlement of Dana. Our approach trail edges around the northern shore of Upper Gaylor Lake on hard, clinking chunks of rock.

The declivitous path to the mines climbs from the lake's north shore through reddish metamorphic rocks and gray granite. Arriving at the first and most "sophisticated"

PUBLIC TRANSPORT IN YOSEMITE

Yosemite Valley is served during summer by the Yosemite Area Regional Transportation System (YARTS) from Merced along Highway 140 and Sonora along Highway 120, with many stops en route. Another YARTS bus runs between Yosemite Valley and Mammoth Lakes, with stops at Tuolumne Meadows, Lee Vining, and other points along the Tioga Road (Highway 120). During fall, winter and spring, only the Merced-Yosemite Valley route operates. For more information contact YARTS at www.yarts.com/.

Yosemite Valley has extensive, free shuttle services that runs at regular intervals along prescribed routes. For a Yosemite Valley shuttle map, see www.nps.gov/yose/planyourvisit/upload/valleyshuttle.pdf.

During summer months, a free shuttle runs daily every half hour from stops at Tuolumne Meadows Lodge (stop #1), wilderness office (stop #3), store (stop #5), campground (stop #5) and visitor center (stop #6) to trailheads along the Tioga Road as far west as Olmstead Point (stop #12). Free shuttles also connect Tuolumne Meadows Lodge and Tioga Pass, four times daily, with a stop at Mono Pass trailhead at Dana Meadows. Information: www.nps.gov/yose/planyourvisit/tmbus.htm.

Delaware North Companies runs a bus route (fee) between Yosemite Valley and Glacier Point, and another to Tuolumne Meadows. Information: www.nps.gov/yose/planyourvisit/publictransportation.htm.

---

cabin—a structure built of stacked stone, with wood-framed door and window, chimney, and collapsed timber roof—we turn to survey the stark scene below. Pyramidal Gaylor Peak, slightly higher than 11,000 feet, wears a small glacier on its lower slopes, poised as if ready to slip into already-frigid Upper Gaylor Lake. Though lovers of wildlands will thrill at the vistas, give some thought to the gloom this same scene must have inspired among the miners who had to live and work here in the 1880s.

You can get an idea of their dismal conditions by continuing up the hill to the low-rent district, where a handful of remaining "cabins" built of piled stones still stand in various states of disrepair among the wind-stunted, nourishment-starved pines. Crudely roofed to deter rain, snow, and incessant wind, some are barely big enough to accommodate a man lying on his back—that is to say, they are proportionately smaller, and undoubtedly less snug, than a rodent's nest.

Exploring the mountainside immediately to the south, you can still find at least one flooded vertical shaft and one closed horizontal adit of the Great Sierra Mine, the justification behind this "town." (Use care—mine shafts are dangerous.) The quantities of ore extracted could not balance the expense of hauling equipment and supplies

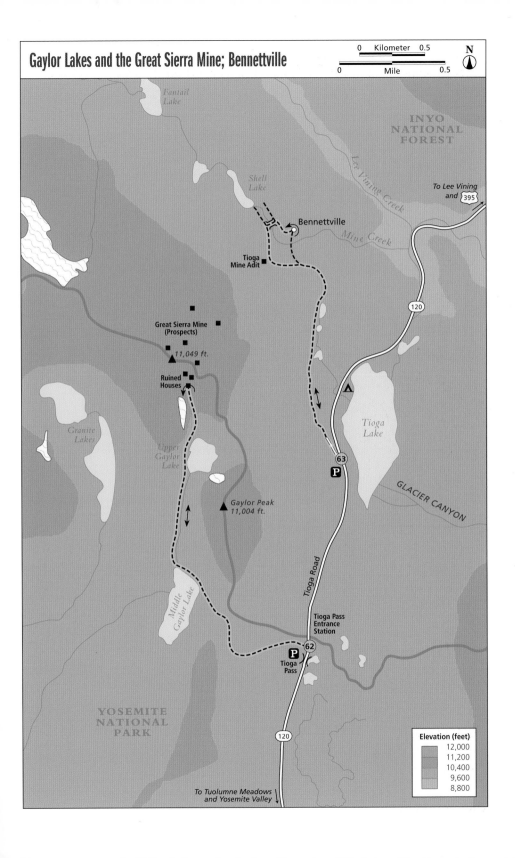

Gaylor Lakes and the Great Sierra Mine; Bennettville

0   Kilometer   0.5

0   Mile   0.5

N

Fantail Lake

INYO NATIONAL FOREST

Shell Lake

Lee Vining Creek

To Lee Vining and 395

Bennettville

Mine Creek

Tioga Mine Adit

120

Great Sierra Mine (Prospects)

11,049 ft.

Ruined Houses

Tioga Lake

Granite Lakes

Upper Gaylor Lake

63

P

GLACIER CANYON

▲ Gaylor Peak 11,004 ft.

Middle Gaylor Lake

Tioga Road

Tioga Pass Entrance Station

62

P

Tioga Pass

YOSEMITE NATIONAL PARK

120

Elevation (feet)
12,000
11,200
10,400
9,600
8,800

To Tuolumne Meadows and Yosemite Valley

to such a remote location, however, and the Great Sierra Consolidated Silver Mining Company, which also operated the mine at nearby Bennettville, went bankrupt in 1884.

Miles and Directions

0.0 Trailhead.

0.6 Trail crest.

0.7 Middle Gaylor Lake.

1.4 Upper Gaylor Lake.

1.8 Great Sierra Mine settlement.

3.6 Arrive back at the trailhead.

63 Bennettville

A historic miner's road, remains of a mining ghost town, stark mountain scenery, and a gaping silver mine all collude to make this one of the most engaging easy hikes in the Tioga Pass region.

Start: Bennettville trailhead parking area, on CA 120 east of Tioga Pass
Distance: 2.8 miles out and back
Hiking time: About 2 hours, with time to explore the town site
Difficulty: Easy, with scant elevation gain or loss

Trail condition: Excellent
Seasons: June through early Oct
Other trail users: Dogs, bikes, and equestrians allowed
Land status: Inyo National Forest
For more information, see Hike 62

Finding the trailhead: From the entrance station to Yosemite at Tioga Pass, drive 0.9 mile east (away from Yosemite) on CA 120. You will see an outhouse and a battery of signs depicting the local history on the right (southeast) side of the highway, overlooking Tioga Lake. You could park in this paved parking area. (Information parking area GPS: N37 55.260' / W119 15.147') A couple of cars can also fit right at the trailhead itself, a smaller, unmarked, unpaved wide shoulder of CA 120 a few hundred feet downhill from the informational signs on the left (northwest) side of the road. Trailhead GPS: N37 55.382' / W119 15.346'

The Hike

Our route lies entirely along the well-graded Great Sierra Wagon Road, forerunner of the now realigned, paved, and very busy Tioga Pass Road (CA 120). And thereby hangs a tale.

While exploring the eastern flanks of the Sierra Nevada near Tioga Pass in 1874, a prospector named William Brusky stumbled upon a silver mine, a rusting pick and shovel, and a weather-worn notice of 1860 staking claim to the Sheepherder Mine. The claimants themselves had vanished. Brusky's discovery touched off a small silver rush to this remote part of the range, giving birth to the boomtown of Bennettville.

Hard-rock mining required more capital than what lone prospectors could command, however. Enter the Great Sierra Consolidated Silver Mining Company, which took over the Sheepherder claim and renamed it the Tioga Mine. Throughout the snowy spring of 1882, twelve company men and a pair of mules hauled eight tons of mining equipment on sleds up Lake Canyon, lowering it over the Tioga Crest to Bennettville by block and tackle. So difficult was this operation that company executives agreed to build a roadway from the west to get their silver out. Although they completed the Great Sierra Wagon Road as far as Bennettville, these heavy investments exhausted the company before the Tioga Mine could pay a return. The company went bankrupt in 1884, and Bennettville was abandoned.

From the unmarked trailhead (elevation 9,750 feet) just above Tioga Lake and below Mount Dana (13,053 feet), our trail—the unpaved remnant of the Great Sierra Wagon Road—rolls easily away through meadow and lodgepole woods, past three blue tarns coddled in the red metamorphic rock of the region. After the last tarn the trail humps a slight crest into the canyon of Mine Creek, where the remains of Bennettville suddenly appear on a low ridge to the right (east), backed by the dry mountains of Lee Vining Canyon.

To avoid a wet ford of Mine Creek, our path does not lead directly to Bennettville but continues along the west side of the canyon, approaching the Tioga Mine adit, a horizontal tunnel belching out rusted pieces of track and machinery and a heap of tailings. The Forest Service has thrown up a strong gate inside the adit, but a quick duck into the sunlit entrance—walking on the wooden track ties if the creek is running high—reveals more pieces of mining junk, including an engine block.

From the entrance, continue along the hillside before hooking right (east) to cross Mine Creek on a log bridge. Across the creek, turn right (south) and walk to what's left of Bennettville, on its low, open ridge. Of the town's original fourteen structures, only two remain, both reconstructed in 1993 and open for viewing. The larger building served as bunkhouse (upstairs) and stable, the smaller as an assay office. Glass and metal shards litter the ground.

Miles and Directions

0.0 Trailhead.

1.1 Tioga Mine adit.

1.4 Bennettville.

2.8 Arrive back at the trailhead.

64 Twenty Lakes Basin

This alpine basin studded with lakes and ringed by spectacular mountains appeals to hikers seeking exceptional scenery without the stiff elevation gains required of most lakes in northern Yosemite. Even small children can enjoy a short segment of the route as far as Greenstone Lake, especially with the boat taxi ride across Saddlebag Lake.

Start: Boat landing on north shore of Saddlebag Lake

Distance: 4.3 miles round-trip. (Without the water taxi, hiking the trail along Saddlebag Lake's western shore from the parking area will add 3 miles, making a total loop hike of 7.3 miles.)

Hiking time: About 4 hours should suffice, but you'll want to cushion your pickup time for the boat taxi.

Difficulty: Comparatively level terrain makes a fairly easy hike.

Trail condition: Mostly good, but the section of trail between Shamrock Lake and Lake Helen is often covered with snow into late season. Be prepared to climb down a steep rock near the lower crossing of Mill Creek.

Seasons: Late June through early Oct. The Saddlebag Lake Resort boat taxi operates July through early Sept.

Other trail users: Dogs are welcome. Equestrians and bikes are allowed but seldom met.

Land status: Hoover Wilderness, Inyo National Forest

Nearest towns: Saddlebag Lake resort runs a cozy cafe and anglers' store. Lee Vining has more amenities.

Fees and permits: None for a day hike. Overnighters need a wilderness permit from the Mono Basin Scenic Area Visitor Center. No campfires allowed. The boat taxi charges a fare.

Maps: National Geographic Trails Illustrated: *Yosemite NE.* USGS 7.5-minute quads: Tioga Pass, Dunderberg Peak.

Trail contacts: Mono Basin Scenic Area Visitor Center, Inyo National Forest, US 395, Lee Vining, CA 93541; (760) 647-3044; www.fs.usda .gov/inyo

Special considerations: Before starting the hike, arrange your pickup time with the boat-taxi skipper. Walking the trail back from the north shore dock will add 2 miles along Saddlebag Lake's western shore and 2.4 miles along the eastern shore.

Finding the trailhead: The signed Saddlebag Lake Road forks north from the Tioga Pass Road (CA 120), 2.2 miles east of the Yosemite Park boundary at Tioga Pass and 10 miles west of CA 120's junction with US 395 near Lee Vining. Drive 2.5 miles up the well-graded gravel (with occasional short stretches of pavement) of Saddlebag Lake Road. At that point you will see the Saddlebag Lake dam on your left and Saddlebag Lake Resort just ahead. Take the first right turn (south) onto a short road, passing a group campsite, to the parking lot. Go to the Saddlebag Lake Resort to arrange the boat-taxi ride to the north shore, where the hike begins. Saddlebag Lake Resort GPS: N37 57.971' / W119 16.268'

The Hike

After riding the water taxi to the boat landing on the north shore of Saddlebag Lake (10,066 feet), walk up the use-trail to the broader main trail and turn left (west). Meandering through a pretty meadow, we pass a sign-in board for the Hoover

Wilderness. A use-trail wanders off to the left, but we bear right on a defunct mining road, following it over flat ground to the edge of Greenstone Lake. A turf meadow lines the shore, with plenty of boulders for picnics and stupendous views southwest to majestic Mount Conness (12,590 feet) and its glacier, and west to a far-off but clamorous cataract pouring down from the Conness Lakes basin, below North Peak (12,242 feet).

Departing from Greenstone's northern shore, we head uphill to a low ridge, where we cross quietly from the Lee Vining Canyon watershed into the Lundy Canyon watershed. Passing Z Lake, tucked out of sight on the right, our old road drops down to the outlet creek of Wasco Lake, which we follow downstream to Steelhead Lake. Surrounded by high granite benches, the setting is starkly beautiful. After jogging around a rocky area, we run into Steelhead Lake's outlet stream, Mill Creek. Here a signed junction points the old road left (west), toward the Hess Tungsten Mine, while we rock-hop with some care straight across Mill Creek, a tricky crossing in early season.

No longer a dirt road, our poorly graded footpath (which evolved as a use-trail) clambers very steeply up a rocky hill. The trail improves once we top the hogback, sauntering through meadow and talus to a high point above island-studded Shamrock Lake. There we behold a classically majestic vision of glacier-scoured ridges and summits, mounting to glorious culmination atop North Peak, and all reflected again on the surface of Shamrock Lake—an alpine scene to rival even the most exaggerated oil-on-black-velvet landscape painting displayed at the flea market.

Pressing onward over a minor granite ridge, we pass some stunted whitebark pines and descend steeply, looking down rugged Lundy Canyon toward the arid Great Basin. We already feel its relentless winds blowing. A patch of snow lingers here until late season, but push through resolutely and you will recover the trail in the meadow at the bottom. Traversing above Lake Helen, we cross another lingering snow patch and emerge from the talus on solid granite above Lake Helen's outlet stream, our old friend, Mill Creek.

At this point you must literally climb down about 10 feet of the rock face and hop across Mill Creek. At the signed junction on the opposite bank, turn right (south) on a trail that hugs Lake Helen's shore before ducking up a narrow ravine shared with the outlet stream from Odell Lake. After passing that large lake on a high granite bench, we roll right over the high-sounding but thoroughly painless Lundy Pass to find ourselves back in the watershed of Lee Vining Canyon. Passing through the meadows and boulders near Hummingbird Lake, we exit Hoover Wilderness and find ourselves approaching Saddlebag Lake. A Forest Service wilderness ranger's cabin stands in the trees on the left (east). Find the use-trail that returns to the boat landing.

Miles and Directions

0.0 Boat landing on north shore of Saddlebag Lake.

0.1 Junction; bear left (west).

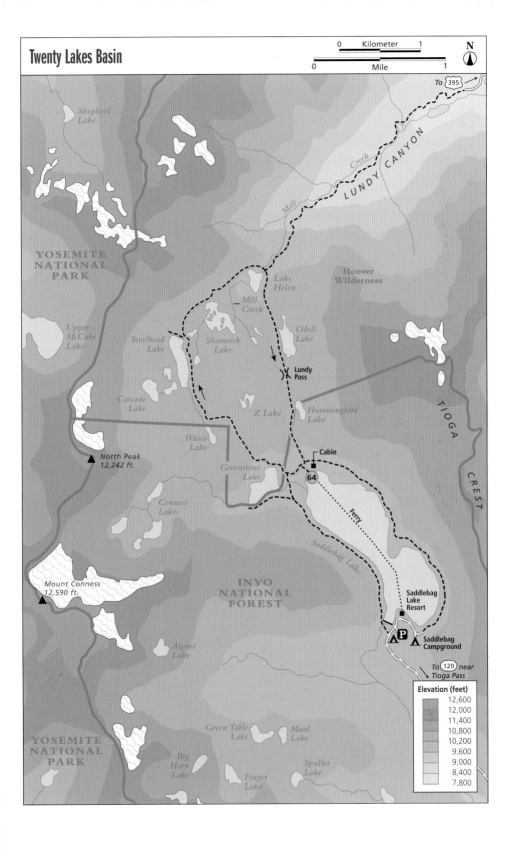

Twenty Lakes Basin

To 395

LUNDY CANYON

Mill Creek

Creek

Shepherd Lake

YOSEMITE NATIONAL PARK

Hoover Wilderness

Lake Helen

Mill Creek

Odell Lake

Upper McCabe Lake

Steelhead Lake

Shamrock Lake

Lundy Pass

TIOGA

Cascade Lake

Z Lake

Hummingbird Lake

▲ North Peak 12,242 ft.

Wasco Lake

Cabin

64

CREST

Greenstone Lake

Ferry

Conness Lakes

Saddlebag Lake

INYO NATIONAL FOREST

Mount Conness 12,590 ft. ▲

Saddlebag Lake Resort

Alpine Lake

Saddlebag Campground

P

To 120 near Tioga Pass

YOSEMITE NATIONAL PARK

Green Table Lake

Maul Lake

Big Horn Lake

Spuller Lake

Finger Lake

Elevation (feet)	
	12,600
	12,000
	11,400
	10,800
	10,200
	9,600
	9,000
	8,400
	7,800

0.3 Sign-in at Hoover Wilderness; bear right (north) on main trail.

0.4 North shore of Greenstone Lake.

1.1 Wasco Lake outlet stream.

1.4 Steelhead Lake.

1.9 Mill Creek crossing.

2.2 Northwest corner of Shamrock Lake.

2.8 Cross Lake Helen's outlet stream and bear right (south) at junction.

3.2 Odell Lake.

3.6 Lundy Pass.

4.2 Junction; bear right (west) and cross inlet creek.

4.3 Arrive back at the boat landing.

Honorable Mentions

V   Rockefeller Grove of Sugar Pines

John Muir's favorite pine was the sugar pine. Largest of any pine species, and with the longest cones of any pine, they grow in this grove up to several feet thick. This gentle forest path follows an abandoned railroad grade through a forest of pine, incense cedar, black oak, manzanita, and mountain misery, and is usually free of snow from May through mid-November. Snowshoers can also enjoy it in winter, and the path is marked for winter with orange metal rectangles nailed to trees. The Rockefeller Grove starts about 2.3 miles from the trailhead (around GPS N37 45.981' / W119 49.703'). There are no signs, so you must recognize it by the massive trees, their needles grouped five to a bundle, and their spectacular litter of long, sticky cones. Longest of all pinecones, some reach 20 inches in length. The trailhead lies across the road from the small parking area for the Merced Grove of giant sequoias, on CA 120, 4 miles east from the Big Oak Flat Road and 3.75 miles west from the Crane Flat junction. Park there, cross the Big Oak Flat Road, and walk about 50 yards left (west) to a dirt road, closed to cars by a metal gate. This is your trail. Trailhead GPS: N37. 45.810' / W119 50.569'. Contact: www.nps.gov/yose.

W   Tuolumne Meadows Stroll

No visit to Tuolumne Meadows is complete without a walk on the meadows, prefer- ably in the peaceful evening light when the deer come out to graze. Start anywhere and go anywhere. One option is Pothole Dome, on the west end of the meadow beside the Tioga Pass Road (GPS: N37 52.627' / W119 23.701'); see Glen Aulin and Waterwheel Falls map. A short use-trail leads to the base of the granite hump, which you can safely climb at may points to splendid views across the northern meadows and west toward the walls of Tuolumne's big downstream canyon. Another great option is historic, orange-tinged Soda Springs, bubbling up within its ruined log cabin (see Lembert Dome map, Hike 60). Charged with carbonic acid, the water is better loved as a curiosity than a beverage. Nearby stands the Parsons Memorial, a stone chalet built by the Sierra Club in 1915; a cozy ranger's house; and a footbridge across the Tuolumne River with stirring views of Lembert Dome and Unicorn and Cathedral peaks. Soda Springs is a half-mile (one-way) walk from the start of Hike 61 (Glen Aulin and Waterwheel Falls; Trailhead GPS: N37 52.734' / W119 21/503'.) Contact: www.nps.gov/yose.

Kings Canyon, Sequoia, and the Southern Sierra

Lying south of Yosemite on the western side of the range, this rugged region contains the largest forests of giant sequoias, the deepest canyons, and the longest caves of the Sierra Nevada, as well as many of its highest interior mountain ridges. The twin national parks of Sequoia and Kings Canyon comprise the centerpiece of the southern Sierra. Giant Sequoia National Monument sprawls across the Great Western Divide, embracing mountains, foothills, and extensive forests, including many groves of giant sequoias. Well buffered on almost all sides by wilderness, these parks embrace the heart of the largest roadless area in the Sierra Nevada. Since no road crosses this part of the Sierra Nevada, the hikes in this chapter all start on the west side. (For hikes into this region from the east, see the chapter "Eastern Sierra: Owens Valley.")

At the southern end of the Sierra Nevada, the mountains do not peter out into flatlands. Rather, they collide with the Transverse Ranges and the mountainous Mojave Desert, breaking into a complex system of dry spur ranges—the Piutes, the Tehachapis, and the Scodies. This is the most biologically diverse quarter of the Sierra Nevada, the meeting point of five different biozones—the Mojave Desert, Great Basin, Sierra Nevada, Central Valley, and Transverse Ranges. Within a very short radius, a fortunate hiker could find oaks and sagebrush, pines and cacti, condors and bears, Joshua trees and giant sequoias, wolverines (very rare!) and navel oranges. Walker Pass (CA 178) is the most southerly crossing of the range and remains open year-round. The Sherman Pass Road (J-41 and FR 22SO5) closes for winter.

◀ *The Boole Tree is thought to be the eighth largest tree on earth (Hike 68).*

65 San Joaquin River Gorge

The easy trail to a bridge crossing of a wild gorge is a blessing in disguise for hikers who need a quick winter fix of mountain and river scenery. The trail is particularly rewarding for children, who love the bridge.

Start: Trailhead campground
Distance: 2.2 miles out and back
Hiking time: About 1 hour
Difficulty: Easy
Trail condition: Good singletrack trail
Seasons: Spring is best. Summer can be very hot. Fall and winter are good.
Other trail users: Equestrians, dogs under control, mountain bikes
Land status: San Joaquin River Gorge Management Area, BLM

Nearest town: Auberry
Fees and permits: Drivers pay an entrance fee to the park.
Maps: BLM: *San Joaquin River Gorge Management Area.* USGS 7.5-minute quad: Millerton Lake east.
Trail contacts: Park office: (559) 855-3492. BLM, 3801 Pegasus Dr., Bakersfield, CA 93308; (661) 391-6000; www.blm.gov

Finding the trailhead: From CA 168 at Prather, head east 1 mile to Auberry Road. Turn left (north) and drive 2.9 miles to the junction of Powerhouse Road in the small town of Auberry. Turn left (northwest) on Powerhouse Road, and drive 1.9 miles to the junction of Smalley Road, just beyond the north end of New Auberry. Turn left (west) and drive about 4.6 miles down to the BLM park. Pay your entrance fee at the visitor center. Park at the trailhead campground. Trailhead GPS: N37 04.977' / W119 33.257'

The Hike

If ever there was a sweet, young trail with promise to grow into a truly vast, hairy-chested Paul Bunyan of a trail, this is it. Although short, it is the nugget of a grand scheme to cross the Sierra Nevada within the broad and relatively low, but extremely rugged, San Joaquin River drainage. That feat used to be done in the form of the French Trail, which itself followed venerable routes of the Mono people, but so many miles of those historic trails have vanished into nature that the concept needs to be heralded anew to Sierra Nevada hikers. Proponents of the San Joaquin River Trail envision a 73-mile trail from Friant Dam to the Pacific Crest Trail (PCT) near Devils Postpile. Much work is to be done. This short trail provides a very picturesque, sturdy, key crossing of the San Joaquin River.

In sight of the flat-topped mesas that define the gorge, the trail sets off through oak savannah on a gentle downhill gradient. Curving into a parallel track with the river, hikers hear the water long before they see it. The dry, grassy hillside is perfect habitat for rattlesnakes and poison oak, and take special care if you have young kids that they don't slip and slide down the steep bank on the river side.

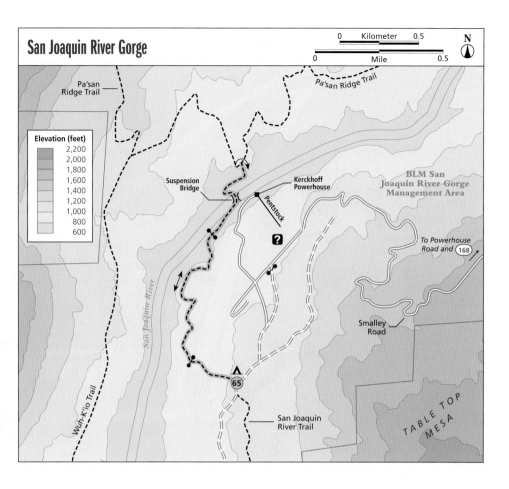

San Joaquin River Gorge

Elevation (feet)
2,200
2,000
1,800
1,600
1,400
1,200
1,000
800
600

Pa'san Ridge Trail

Pa'san Ridge Trail

Suspension Bridge

Kerckhoff Powerhouse

Penstock

BLM San Joaquin River Gorge Management Area

To Powerhouse Road and (168)

Smalley Road

San Joaquin River

Wuh-K'io Trail

65

San Joaquin River Trail

TABLE TOP MESA

The green, arched, metal bridge above the granite gorge seems built for a thousand-year flood. Even in late season, you can spend an enjoyable hour on the deck of the bridge and the banks, watching the green waters swirl and pool about the rocks, but in spring the flood can be electrifying. This is not a particularly easy river to access, but some people work their way down to it on the north, downstream bank. Otherwise, hike as far as the junction with the Pa'san loop trail, above the north bank, before turning around. Just upstream from the bridge stands a power plant fed by penstocks from reservoirs higher upriver.

Options

On the north side of the bridge, the 6-mile loop on the Pa'san Ridge Trail will bring a sweat to hikers who didn't find the Gorge Trail to be enough of a physical challenge. If you want to sample another segment of the SJRT, the 3-mile downstream stretch to Millerton Lake State Recreation Area starts just across the park road from campground trailhead and connects with other trails.

The big arch bridge across the San Joaquin Gorge will outlast the ages.

Miles and Directions

0.0 Trailhead campground.

0.1 First gate.

0.7 Second gate.

0.8 Junction with spur to powerhouse road; go left.

0.9 Bridge.

1.1 Junction with Pa'san Trail loop; turn back here.

2.2 Arrive back at the trailhead.

66 George Lake

From its vantage on the shoulder of 10,320-foot Kaiser Peak, the shelf around George Lake commands views over the broad, rolling watershed of the San Joaquin River. This forested route through Kaiser Wilderness also visits two other lakes and enjoys a distant vista of the High Sierra.

Start: Potter Pass trailhead on Kaiser Pass Road

Distance: 9.4 miles out and back

Hiking time: About 6 hours

Difficulty: A rigorous day hike or a more relaxed overnighter, with an overall elevation gain of nearly 1,500 feet

Trail condition: Good singletrack trail

Seasons: June–Sept. Weekdays are less crowded than weekends.

Other trail users: Equestrians and dogs under control are permitted. Bikes are prohibited in Kaiser Wilderness.

Land status: Kaiser Wilderness, Sierra National Forest

Nearest town: Huntington Lake

Fees and permits: None for day trip. Overnighters require wilderness permit (fee), obtainable from the Eastwood Visitor Center.

Maps: USGS 7.5-minute quads: Mount Givens, Kaiser Peak

Trail contacts: Sierra National Forest, 1600 Tollhouse Rd., Clovis, CA 93611; (559) 297-0706; www.fs.usda.gov/sierra. Eastwood Visitor Center, Highway 168, Huntington Lake, CA 93634; (559) 893-6611.

Finding the trailhead: From Fresno, drive 50 miles north from central Clovis on CA 168 to the east shore of Huntington Lake. Turn right (east) onto the Kaiser Pass Road (FR 80). The Eastwood Visitor Center is at this junction. Drive nearly 5 miles east on the highway, and look for the hikers' parking area on the right (south) side of the road, with a prominent sign that says CALIF. RIDING-HIKING TRAIL 24E03. The Potter Pass trailhead is across the road. Trailhead GPS: N37 16.170' / W119 07.283'

The Hike

From the parking area on the south side of the Kaiser Pass Road, at an elevation of about 8,250 feet, cross the highway to find the trailhead. Starting in mixed forests of pine, juniper, and scrub, our trail climbs on switchbacks over a ridge into the ravine of intermittent Midge Creek, which we cross in a meadow after our first mile. Climbing again to another saddle, we cross Potter Creek close to its source and commence the final uphill push toward Potter Pass. After meeting a trail that comes up Potter Creek from Huntington Lake, we top out on Potter Pass at just under 9,000 feet. Though the abundance of forest cover around us reminds us how far we are below the alpine belt, our vista embraces a broad swath of High Sierra in the serrated peaks of the Ritter Range and Minarets, nearly 30 miles to the north.

At the pass we enter Kaiser Wilderness. Descending on a gravelly, winding path through meadows and forest, we turn left (west) at a junction near Round Meadow. Crossing a tiny creek amid a flowery meadow, where puttering bumblebees like to

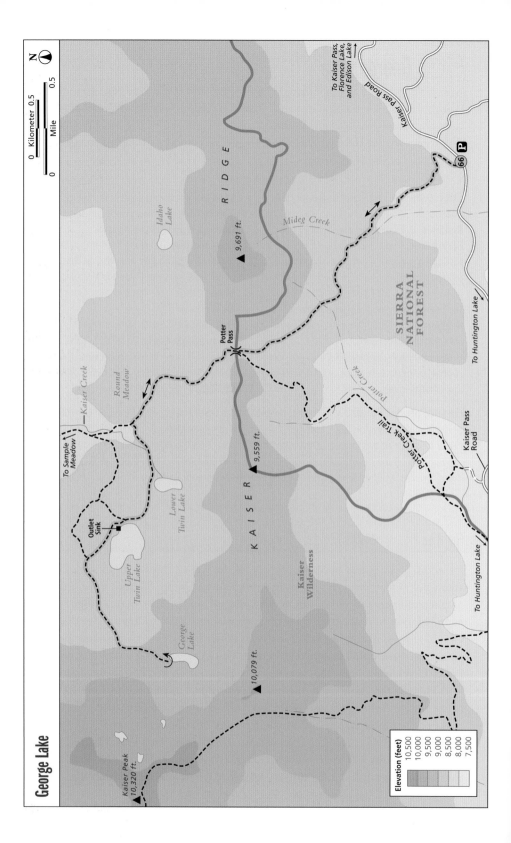

George Lake

N

0 Kilometer 0.5

0 Mile 0.5

RIDGE

Idaho Lake

▲ 9,691 ft.

Mideg Creek

Kaiser Pass Road

To Kaiser Pass, Florence Lake, and Edison Lake

66 P

To Huntington Lake

SIERRA NATIONAL FOREST

Potter Pass

Round Meadow

Kaiser Creek

To Sample Meadow

Outlet Sink

Upper Twin Lake

Lower Twin Lake

George Lake

Kaiser Peak 10,320 ft. ▲

▲ 10,079 ft.

▲ 9,559 ft.

KAISER

Kaiser Wilderness

Potter Creek Trail

Potter Creek

Kaiser Pass Road

To Huntington Lake

Elevation (feet)	
	10,500
	10,000
	9,500
	9,000
	8,500
	8,000
	7,500

hang out on warm days, we climb to the little basin where Lower Twin Lake reposes at 8,600 feet, swaddled in thick forest of aspen and conifer and backed on the south and west by granite ridges. There are many good campsites along the shore, and these are likely to be less popular than sites at the much larger Upper Twin Lake, a short and easy jaunt over a low ridge.

Only marginally different in elevation, Upper Twin does not drain into the lower lake, but both drain north into Kaiser Creek, which itself flows into the San Joaquin River. Backed by rising granite bluffs and embellished with an island, Upper Twin's handsome setting is still upstaged by its curious outlet stream, which no sooner leaves the northern shore when it disappears into a jumble of loose rocks, a glacial moraine deposited during the last ice age. It reemerges on the other side of the moraine, farther down the slope.

Our trail to George Lake continues from Upper Twin's farther (western) shore, climbing the steep slopes of Kaiser Peak, to gain about 400 feet of elevation in less than a mile. This extra effort is sufficient to encourage most visitors to walk no farther than the granite slabs above Upper Twin, so that George is typically the most serene, as well as the most beautiful, of the three lakes on our trail. With the rugged cliffs of Kaiser Peak as a backdrop, it also offers stupendous views from adjacent blocks of granite. Views reach more than 20 miles east to Mount Abbott and the other peaks of the Mono Divide, behind Lake Edison, and northeast to the Silver Divide.

Miles and Directions

- **0.0** Parking area.
- **2.0** Potter Pass.
- **2.9** Round Meadow junction; bear left (west).
- **3.3** Lower Twin Lake.
- **3.5** Junction at Upper Twin Lake; bear left (northwest).
- **3.9** Junction; bear left (southwest).
- **4.7** George Lake.
- **9.4** Arrive back at the parking area.

67 Florence Lake to Evolution Valley

Approaching by way of the rugged canyon of the San Joaquin River and surrounded by a host of jagged summits, this trail delves into the secluded heart of Kings Canyon's northern wilderness—the lush, green parkland of Evolution Valley.

Start: Florence Lake

Distance: 16.2 miles one-way; 32.4 miles out and back

Hiking time: A 4-night or longer backpack trip is recommended.

Difficulty: Strenuous, with more than 3,000 feet of elevation gained

Trail condition: The first 4.5 miles are confused by a medley of braided trails, though hikers are not likely to get lost. The remainder is a clearly marked singletrack path. There are some potentially hazardous stream fordings.

Seasons: June–Sept. Be wary of early season for high water and mosquitos.

Other trail users: Equestrians and pack trains are common. Hunters and dogs are allowed in the national forest but not the national park. Muir Trail Ranch uses a motorized vehicle for hauling gear.

Land status: John Muir Wilderness, Sierra National Forest, Kings Canyon National Park

Nearest towns: Florence Lake has a small store, Huntington Lake has some amenities, but Fresno is the nearest city.

Fees and permits: None for day hikers, but all overnight backpackers must obtain a wilderness permit from the ranger station (see "Finding the trailhead" below). Campfire permits are required for the national forest. No fires are allowed in Kings Canyon National Park above 10,000 feet (which is higher than any point on this trail). The ferry charges a fare.

Maps: Tom Harrison: *Mono Divide High Country.* USGS 7.5-minute quads: Florence Lake, Ward Mountain, Mount Darwin, Mount Henry.

Trail contacts: Sierra National Forest, 1600 Tollhouse Rd., Clovis, CA 93611; (559) 297-0706; www.fs.usda.gov/sierra. Kings Canyon National Park, 47050 Generals Hwy., Three Rivers, CA 93271-9700; (559) 565-3341; www.nps.gov/seki. Florence Lake Ferry and Store, www.florence-lake.com/FL-Ferry.html. Muir Trail Ranch, muirtrailranch.com.

Special considerations: The ferry makes several scheduled trips per day, conditions permitting. A radio on the eastern shore allows you to call for additional service. If you bypass the ferry and take the connector trail, you will add another 4 miles to your trip, in each direction. The late-season drop in the reservoir level may affect ferry service. The Muir Trail Ranch does not encourage visits from nonguests.

Finding the trailhead: The parking area for this trailhead is at Florence Lake. To get there from Fresno, drive 50 miles from central Clovis north on CA 168 to the end of that road on the east shore of Huntington Lake. Turn right (east) onto the Kaiser Pass Road (FR 80). The Eastwood Visitor Center is at this junction. Drive a bit more than 15 miles on the paved, mostly one-lane, winding road to the junction of the Florence Lake Road and the road to Lake Edison. (You will pass the High Sierra Ranger Station at Bosillo Creek along the way. Get your wilderness permit there.) At the junction turn right onto the Florence Lake Road and drive 6.5 miles to Florence Lake Resort, which offers a store and ferry service across the lake. Buy your ferry ticket at the store, but before hiking, move your car to the long-term parking lot about a quarter mile back from the store on the Florence Lake Road. Store entrance GPS: N37 16.580' / W118 58.437'

The Hike

The Florence Lake ferry ties off on the eastern shore, at an elevation of 7,350 feet. Trucks from the Muir Trail Ranch, a private guest resort, sometimes meet the boats to carry gear to or from the ranch. Heading uphill over granite slabs, our path is none-too-clearly marked by ducks, the fine views dominated by the pointed summit of Mount Shinn (11,020 feet). The route bears right as it climbs. It is amazing to think how the trucks negotiate this horrendous "road," though as a trail, it's easy enough. As you reach the top of the granite ridge, keep looking left (east) for the rock-lined footpath that takes us away from the road, making a slight descent across granite to more hospitable ground, softened with trees and meadows.

In the 3-mile walk from here to the western gate of the Muir Trail Ranch, the road and trail will intersect more times than anyone will care to count. The braiding is further complicated with bridle paths, anglers' paths, campers' paths, and other short-cuts. No one need get lost, however, so long as one keeps in mind that the two main trails are moving in the same general direction, that both converge at the western gate of the Muir Trail Ranch, and that our progress is always up-canyon with the San Joaquin River always on our right (although almost always out of sight).

The USGS map names Double Meadow and Blaney Meadow along our route, but they are not suitable landmarks, since it might not be clear where one begins and the other ends, depending on which track you are following. Suffice it to say that, after passing through sporadic lodgepole forests and meadows grazed by horses, you will cross Alder Creek. Thereafter, if you are on the trail, you will pass through Blaney Meadow, but if you are on the road, you will bypass it. In either case, the road and trail converge in pine woods at the small western gateway to the Muir Trail Ranch, 3.5 miles from the boat landing. A sign there notes that you may not camp or leave the trail for the next mile; that is, until you pass through the ranch's eastern gate. If you prefer to camp earlier than a mile, you could backtrack on the trail (the track closest to the river) about 0.2 mile to a packer camp in the woods next to Blaney Meadow.

Continuing onward through the ranch gate, you will pass a dirt drive and follow the line of a barbed-wire fence through the woods, crossing Sallie Keyes and Senger Creeks. The Muir Trail Ranch, called the Diamond D Ranch when it was established in the late 1800s, long predates the establishment of the John Muir Wilderness. Today it has about 200 acres on both sides of the river. Just before you get to the eastern gate, you will meet the junction leading to the ranch buildings. Take the public trail to the left, uphill, and through the eastern gate of the ranch back onto public property.

Beyond the gate, you will meet a spur trail forking right (south) toward a back-packer camp. You would also take this trail if you want to visit Blaney Hot Springs, a half mile's distance on the opposite side of the San Joaquin River. (The hot springs located on the Muir Trail Ranch property may be used only by paying guests.)

Continuing up-canyon from the ranch, we almost immediately pass a cutoff trail striking north toward the John Muir Trail (JMT). Stick with our southeast course along the heavily wooded floor of the San Joaquin's canyon, and the famous JMT condescends to join us at 6 miles, after wending its leisurely way down from Selden Pass and Sallie Keyes Lakes. From now on, our route and the JMT will be the same, a fairly gentle gradient largely screened from the San Joaquin River by dark woods. Periodic glimpses of the water reveal a river on its best behavior, calm and quiet. At 7 miles we pass a ranger patrol cabin named for John Muir.

The granite canyon walls close in as we approach the confluence of Piute Creek. The forest thins, and the scenery becomes more barren, rugged, and sublime. We cross the bridge over Piute Creek, stepping from John Muir Wilderness into Kings Canyon National Park, and passing some campsites amid the scrubby vegetation. Now the character of the San Joaquin changes to a more rambunctious mode, gaining speed in its race down-canyon. Confined between narrowing rocky walls, the river at times madly pummels itself into white froth, and at others slips swiftly into stealthier moods between gravel banks choked with willows. Our trail keeps pace from above, sometimes pushing through talus rock falls and sometimes blasted from solid rock. There are some nice campsites at Aspen Meadow. Crossing to the south bank on a bridge, we pass through a drift gate and ford a creek that drops down from the LeConte Divide. Passing many more fine campsites near the junction with the Goddard Canyon Trail, we again cross the South Fork of the San Joaquin River on a wooden bridge to dry Franklin Meadow.

Now we climb the eastern wall of the canyon on switchbacks edged by well-dressed stone blocks and landscaped with pines, junipers, and tiny aspens. On every north-facing leg of the switchback, we find ourselves approaching Evolution Creek as it dashes down our sheer wall, but we always veer away before reaching it. Then, on the south-facing legs of the zigzags, we find ourselves peering up rugged Goddard Canyon, where an old trail ascends to Hell for Sure Pass, which appears as a slot in the western ridge just this side of the last visible mountain.

The switchbacks end at the lower end of Evolution Valley, on the south bank of Evolution Creek. Looking across to the trail on the north bank, we are faced with the largest ford of the journey, a potentially perilous crossing in early season. Hikers attempting to find easier fords have worn use-trails along the banks, so be prepared to assess the season's offerings and choose the safest, because at this point we certainly don't want to turn back.

Among the most enchanting of Sierra vales, Evolution Valley forms a stately crescent some 5 miles long, through which the Whitney-bound JMT climbs a mere 600 feet in a grand procession through alternating stretches of meadows and woods. The valley's northern side is walled off by the rugged Glacier Divide. To the south the Hermit (12,360 feet) truly stands aloof. Fording small tributaries to Evolution Creek, we pass in succession through Evolution Meadow, parklike McClure Meadow (where we find a backcountry ranger station), and Colby Meadow, all with excellent campsites in the adjacent forest. The John Muir Trail, of course, goes on, but our hike ends here—at an elevation of about 7,700 feet—with an encouragement to make your

Florence Lake to Evolution Valley

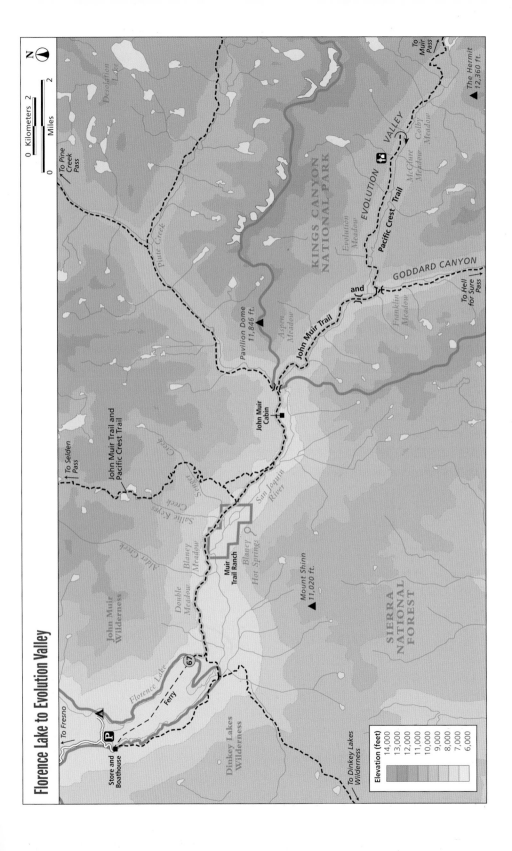

Elevation (feet)

14,000
13,000
12,000
11,000
10,000
9,000
8,000
7,000
6,000

Store and Boathouse

To Fresno

Florence Lake

Ferry

67

Dinkey Lakes Wilderness

To Dinkey Lakes Wilderness

John Muir Wilderness

Alder Creek

Double Meadow

Blaney Meadow

Sallie Keyes Creek

Senger Creek

Muir Trail Ranch

Blaney Hot Springs

Mount Shinn 11,020 ft.

SIERRA NATIONAL FOREST

San Joaquin River

John Muir Cabin

To Selden Pass

John Muir Trail and Pacific Crest Trail

Piute Creek

Pavilion Dome 11,846 ft.

To Pine Creek Pass

Desolation Lake

KINGS CANYON NATIONAL PARK

Aspen Meadow

John Muir Trail

Evolution Meadow

EVOLUTION VALLEY

McClure Meadow

Colby Meadow

Pacific Crest Trail

and

GODDARD CANYON

Franklin Meadow

To Hell for Sure Pass

To Muir Pass

The Hermit 12,360 ft.

N

0 Kilometers 2
0 Miles 2

camp and spend some time exploring one of the most magnificent of Sierra Nevada high-country valleys.

Miles and Directions

0.0   Ferry landing on Florence Lake's eastern shore.

0.5   Junction with trail to Florence Lake road head; bear left (east).

2.5   Alder Creek.

3.5   Muir Trail Ranch western boundary gate.

4.5   Muir Trail Ranch eastern boundary gate; spur trail to Blaney Hot Springs.

4.7   JMT trail cutoff junction; go right (southeast).

6.0   JMT trail junction; go right (southeast).

7.0   John Muir Cabin.

7.8   Bridge crossing of Piute Creek; bear right (east) at trail junction.

9.3   Aspen Meadow.

10.4   San Joaquin River bridge.

11.1   Ford of creek from LeConte Divide.

11.3   Bear left (north) at junction with the Goddard Canyon Trail and again cross the South Fork of the San Joaquin River on a wooden bridge (Goddard Creek bridge).

11.6   Bottom of switchbacks into Evolution Valley.

12.9   Ford of Evolution Creek.

13.1   Evolution Meadow.

15.3   McClure Meadow Ranger Station.

16.2   Colby Meadow.

32.4   Arrive back at the ferry landing.

68 Boole Tree

This short hike on the edge of Kings River Canyon loops through the logged remnants of what was once the largest grove of giant sequoias. Inexplicably spared the logger's ax, only the Boole Tree remains of the old giants, a lone behemoth thought to be the sixth-largest tree in the world.

Start: Boole Tree parking area, Giant Sequoia National Monument
Distance: 2.5-mile loop
Hiking time: About 1-2 hours
Difficulty: Moderate, with a gain and loss in elevation of about 750 feet
Trail condition: Good singletrack trail
Seasons: May through late Oct
Other trail users: Leashed dogs are allowed.
Land status: Giant Sequoia National Monument, Sequoia National Forest
Nearest towns: Grant Grove has food and lodging, Hume Lake has gasoline, but Fresno is the nearest town with all amenities.

Fees and permits: None, but entrance fee charged to enter park
Map: USGS 7.5-minute quad: Hume (**Note:** The trail is not marked on the map.)
Trail contacts: Giant Sequoia National Monument, Sequoia National Forest, 35860 E. Kings Canyon Rd., Dunlop CA 93621; (559) 338-2251; www.fs.fed.us/r5/sequoia/gsnm.html. Kings Canyon National Park, Grant Grove Visitor Center, (559) 565-4307.

Finding the trailhead: From Grant Grove Visitor Center in Kings Canyon National Park, drive north on CA 180 about 4.4 miles into the northern unit of Giant Sequoia National Monument, to an unpaved logging road (FR 13S55) on the left (northwest) side of the road. It is marked by a brown sign with white letters. Drive up the well-graded logging road, following the signs at every junction, 2.3 miles to Stump Meadow, where a group of blackened stumps recalls the fate of the Converse Grove, logged at the turn of the twentieth century. From Stump Meadow, drive 0.4 mile farther to the Boole Tree parking area. There is a toilet and sign-in board. Trailhead GPS: N36 49.330' / W118 57.650'

The Hike

Visitors who have seen an intact grove of giant sequoias will gain an eye-opening historical perspective with a short excursion to the Boole Tree, patriarch of the Converse Grove. Before it was logged, between 1892 and 1908, the Converse Grove was the largest giant sequoia grove in California—which is to say, the world. The Sanger Lumber Company, which cut the trees, lost money on the operation. Why the lumberjacks spared the Boole Tree, ironically naming it after their foreman, is not known. Presumably even they were impressed. Long claimed by the Forest Service to be the world's seventh-largest tree, the Boole Tree moved up the list in the winter of 2004–2005, after heavy snows toppled the upper half of the fire-weakened Washington Tree

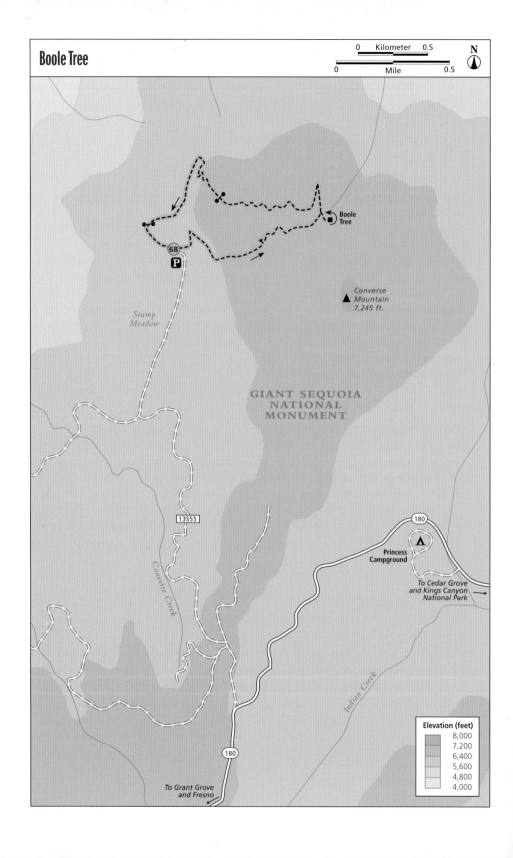

Boole Tree

0   Kilometer   0.5

0   Mile   0.5

N

Boole
Tree

68
P

Converse
Mountain
7,245 ft.

Stump
Meadow

GIANT SEQUOIA
NATIONAL
MONUMENT

13S55

180

Princess
Campground

To Cedar Grove
and Kings Canyon
National Park

Converse Creek

Indian Creek

180

To Grant Grove
and Fresno

Elevation (feet)

8,000
7,200
6,400
5,600
4,800
4,000

The cozy nook inside the Boole Tree has plenty of room for all.

in the Giant Forest of Sequoia National Park. The Boole Tree today is probably the sixth-largest tree in the world.

The two ends of the loop trail meet at the north end of the parking area, at an elevation of 6,250 feet. Take the right-hand (east) trail, going counterclockwise around the loop. We hike uphill over well-planned curves, through bracken ferns, manzanita, kit-kit-dizze, buckthorn, elderberry, pine, incense cedar, and red currant—the sort of plants that thrive where sun is plentiful, as in logged areas. Winding sinuously into the forest, we pass some cut stumps, a rill, a green pocket-size meadow, and a fallen sequoia broken and cut into pieces. Climbing now more steeply on wooden steps set in dirt, we crest a ridge at 6,750 feet, where we find many gargantuan stumps, all of them burned and inundated by montane chaparral plants.

Near an elephant-size boulder, we reach a junction marked BOOLE TREE. Turn right (east) and descend to a historical exhibit at a view point above the Boole Tree. Despite deep, burned clefts in the trunk—typical of giant sequoias—the tree is remarkably straight and proportional, though shockingly, nakedly out of proportion to the surrounding forest. It is this isolation from trees of a similar size that makes it seem much more massive, this austere solitude that makes it seem so grand. Going down to the tree, we walk around surveying its scars. On the lower side there are two "rooms" on each side of a great vertical scar, both of which are well cushioned and dry, should you care to crawl into them.

Returning to the junction, we turn right, taking the switchbacks to the top of the ridge and walking among boulders, shrubs, and small trees of the logged-over area. Passing through a gate, we make a zigzag descent down a slope rank with elderberry and red currant, both of which bear heavy fruits in September. Views to the north peer into the South Fork of the Kings River Canyon, arguably the deepest gorge in North America, with some 8,200 feet between the river and the top of Spanish Mountain, whose summit rises to 10,051 feet nearly 7 miles to the northeast. (Hells Canyon on the Oregon-Idaho border also reaches a depth of about 8,200 feet and is more commonly claimed to be the deepest gorge in North America. Statistics vary, depending, of course, on where measurements are taken. By comparison, the Grand Canyon is about 5,700 feet at its deepest.) Rounding the ridge, we complete the loop back at the parking area.

Miles and Directions

0.0 Parking area.
0.9 Boole Tree junction; bear right (east).
1.0 Boole Tree.
2.5 Arrive back at the parking area.

69 Yucca Point Trail

The wild confluence of the Middle Fork and South Fork of the Kings River lies at the bottom of the Sierra's deepest canyon, and is accessible only by this short and scenic footpath.

Start: Yucca Point trailhead, on CA 180 in Kings Canyon

Distance: 3.6 miles out and back

Hiking time: About 2 hours

Difficulty: If you carry water and avoid hot days, this trail's temperate gradient makes it a moderate hike, despite the 1,360-foot descent and ascent.

Trail condition: A well-graded, well-maintained, dirt singletrack trail all the way

Seasons: You could hike the trail all year, if you could get to it, but CA 180 closes typically from mid-Nov through early Apr. If you hike in the summer, early morning or evening are recommended.

Other trail users: Equestrians and dogs under control

Land status: Giant Sequoia National Monument, Sequoia National Forest

Nearest town: Fresno is the nearest town with all amenities, though gas and food are available nearby at Kings Canyon Resort and Hume Lake.

Fees and permits: There is a trail register, but no permit is required. The park charges an entrance fee for vehicles.

Maps: USGS 7.5-minute quads: Wren Peak, Hume

Trail contacts: See Hike 68.

Finding the trailhead: Drive north on CA 180 from Grant Grove Visitor Center in Kings Canyon National Park about 14 miles to the signed Yucca Point trailhead; look for it 1 mile beyond the Kings Canyon Lodge, on the left (west) side of the road. A Forest Service bulletin board marks the trailhead. Park off the road in a turnout. Trailhead GPS: N36 49.826' / W118 52.621'

The Hike

To know that the Kings River is (arguably) the deepest canyon in the United States gives a somewhat misleading impression of this trail's difficulty, and even of its grandeur. The summit of 10,051-foot Spanish Mountain rises more than 7,880 feet above the Kings River confluence, our destination. If this were one mighty vertical wall, it would be an impressive sight indeed, but spread as it is over a distance of 5 craggy miles, the depth of Kings Canyon does not boggle the senses so much as the intellect. You can't see the canyon rim from the river (though you can see it from the trailhead), but you still know that you're sitting at the bottom of a mighty deep hole.

Starting at the Forest Service sign-in board at 3,470 feet, our path sets off downhill through a small grove of oak and laurel before entering the chaparral. Dropping at a very steady, comfortable gradient, we walk through a mix of scrub oak, manzanita, redbud, poison oak, buckeye, and yucca, whose tall white stalks bloom from May through June. The terrain is dry, but to judge by the amount of bear scat encountered

The view from the Yucca Point Trail takes in one of the continent's deepest canyons, at the confluence of the Middle and South Forks of the Kings River.

on the path, there's obviously plenty to eat around here. The splash of Tenmile Creek occasionally rises to our ears.

As we round to the lower ridge of Yucca Point, we begin to enjoy fine views of a 4-mile sweep of the South Fork of the Kings River, as well as a window into the Middle Fork's canyon as it cuts downstream from the hidden bastion of Tehipite Valley. The two rivers are separated by the rugged Monarch Divide. On every plane the steep, rock-studded, chaparral-covered canyon walls sweep relentlessly downward in undulating diagonals, converging with an almost epic finality on the rivers' rocky banks. These mountains are not pretty in any conventional sense. They are primeval, hard-bitten, lean, and tough, but they don't seem to intimidate the plucky little Kings, which elbows its way through them with complete indifference.

After four long switchbacks down the north-facing canyon wall, we round the ridge to a sudden view of Tenmile Creek's surprise waterfall, draped like a skinny necktie carelessly tossed over the back of a wingback chair. A short spur trail goes down to its pools, a safer place for kids to splash than the main river below.

The trail bottoms out at the rocky confluence of the South Fork and Middle Fork, at an elevation of 2,250 feet. The Kings is a large river for the Sierra and would be a highly dangerous ford in any season. The valley floor appears surprisingly wide here, so that relatively minor details like Deer Ridge and Deer Canyon appear to dominate the landscape, although on the map they are mere footnotes to the larger canyon. Anglers should know that catch–and–release is official policy in this part of the canyon.

This is not the deepest part of Kings Canyon. That lies about 6 or 7 miles downstream, where the river bottoms out at about 8,200 feet below the summit of Spanish

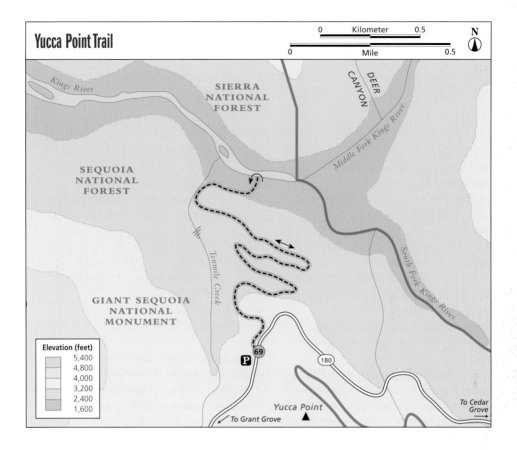

Mountain. It is somewhere downstream, then, that the contention of whether Hells Canyon or Kings Canyon is the deeper must be debated. Myself, I'll skip the debate and save my breath for the uphill return.

Miles and Directions

0.0 Yucca Point trailhead.

1.4 View of Tenmile Creek waterfall.

1.8 Kings River confluence.

3.6 Arrive back at the trailhead.

70 Mist Falls

This cataract on the upper gorge of the Kings River, a thundering spectacle in spring, still puts on a delightful water pageant even after the late summer's drought quells its roar.

Start: Roads End, Kings Canyon National Park
Distance: 8.4 miles out and back
Hiking time: About 4–5 hours
Difficulty: Moderate, with an elevation gain of about 1,000 feet, all in the last mile
Trail condition: Excellent singletrack trail, with some rock steps as you near the falls
Seasons: The trail should be open from late spring into Nov. Be aware that CA 180 typically opens in Apr and closes in early Nov, preventing you from driving to the trailhead.
Other trail users: No bikes or dogs are allowed, but you may meet equestrians and pack trains.
Land status: Kings Canyon National Park
Nearest towns: Fresno is the nearest city with all amenities, but Cedar Grove (open May–Oct) has food and lodging, and gas, food, and

lodging are available at Kings Canyon Resort on CA 180.
Fees and permits: None for day hikers. A wilderness permit is required for overnight use and available at the trailhead daily before 3:30 p.m., and at the Grant Grove. The park service charges a fee per wilderness permit obtained May 23–Sep 27, but they are free outside that period. Kings Canyon National Park charges an entrance fee per vehicle.
Maps: Tom Harrison: *Sequoia & Kings Canyon National Parks*. USGS 7.5-minute quad: The Sphinx.
Trail contacts: Kings Canyon National Park, 47050 Generals Hwy., Three Rivers, CA 93271-9700; (559) 565-3341; www.nps.gov/seki. Grant Grove Visitor Center; (559) 565-4307.

Finding the trailhead: Drive to the end of CA 180, Roads End, in Kings Canyon, about 34.5 miles from Grant Grove Visitor Center in Kings Canyon National Park. It has a wilderness-permit ranger station, potable water, and toilets. Trailhead GPS: N36 47.682' / W118 34.978'

The Hike

From the permit station (elevation 5,000 feet), we strike eastward on a dusty trail and almost immediately cross Copper Creek on a small bridge. (The name recalls a nearby copper mine worked by Napoleon Kanawyer, who later ran an early tourist camp on this site.) Plodding on level ground through cedars, pines, and patches of manzanita, we enjoy Kings Canyon's Yosemite-like walls and monuments of glacier-carved granite. Glancing backward, the canyon of Copper Creek cuts a surprisingly deep gorge in the wall beneath 8,800-foot North Dome, while the massive Grand Sentinel rises more than 3,300 feet above the valley floor on the southern wall.

Following the Kings River in an upstream direction, our trail is almost completely flat for the first 2 miles, when we dip slightly to meet a bosky junction with the Bubbs Creek Trail. Though you cannot see it for the trees, the hanging valley of

Framed by the U-shaped upper canyon of the Kings River, the Sphinx was carved by a glacier thousands of feet thick.

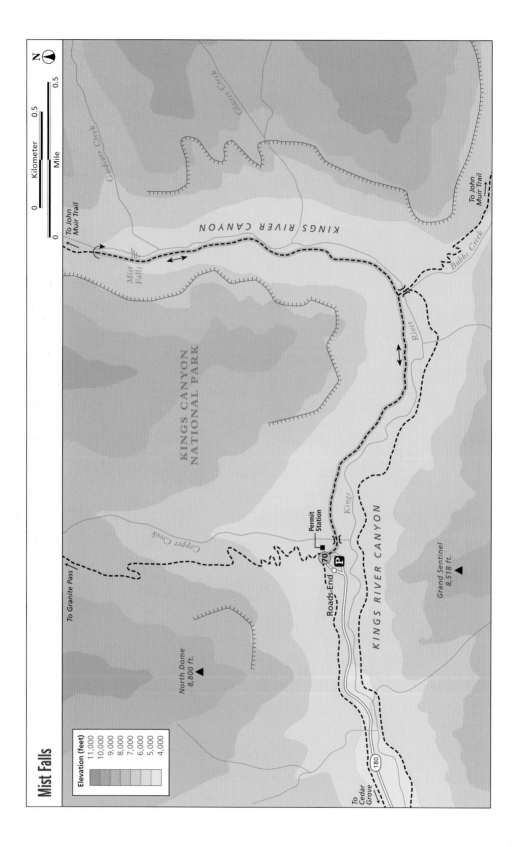

Mist Falls

Elevation (feet)
- 11,000
- 10,000
- 9,000
- 8,000
- 7,000
- 6,000
- 5,000
- 4,000

North Dome
8,800 ft.

To Granite Pass

Copper Creek

KINGS CANYON NATIONAL PARK

Gardiner Creek

Glacier Creek

To John Muir Trail

Mist Falls

KINGS RIVER CANYON

To John Muir Trail

Bubbs Creek

River

Kings

Permit Station

70

P

Roads-End

KINGS RIVER CANYON

Grand Sentinel
8,518 ft.

To Cedar Grove

180

N

Kilometer
0   0.5

Mile
0   0.5

Bubbs Creek is an old trans-Sierra route to the Owens Valley by way of Kearsarge Pass. We turn left (north) at this junction, making a short jog over a granite outcrop, from which we catch a fleeting glimpse of the Bubbs Creek Trail footbridge. We soon find ourselves in the narrower canyon of the upper Kings River, crowded with conifers, oaks, lush horsetails, and enormous boulders that pile up in gigantic talus aprons against the walls. The smaller, more companionable stream splashes merrily by our side, an audible sign that the canyon floor is beginning to rise.

As we gain height, it is impossible to ignore the spectacle growing behind us, where the obvious U-shape of the upper Kings Canyon frames the polished south wall of the main Kings Canyon. Scoured by ice, a weird, horned rock formation called the Sphinx rises nearly 4,000 feet above the valley, an impressive "textbook example" of the depth and dynamics of ice age glaciers.

The boulders along our trail grow larger and more unrelenting as we climb higher, constricting the river into a narrow granite gorge, where it foams and frenzies with pent-up rage. Peering down from one sheer slab on a whitewater chute choked with boulders and splintered logs, many a hiker must have wondered, "Is this Mist Falls?" Certainly it is part of a long series of rapids that includes Mist Falls. (John Muir described the upper Kings as "beating its way for 5 or 6 miles in one continuous chain of roaring, tossing, surging cascades and falls.")

But no, it is not Mist Falls. The National Park Service has dispelled all doubt by posting a sign at the foot of a particularly spectacular drop, 3.8 miles from Roads End, where the Kings River comes careening down a broad slab of granite to a 40-foot fall. Even if you climb the trail up the side of the falls, this is the spot to return to for a picnic, or simply to watch the water falling and (as Muir himself observed) "making marvelous mixtures with the downpouring sunbeams . . . and giving forth a great variety of wild mountain melody."

Miles and Directions

- **0.0** Permit station.
- **1.9** Trail junction near bridge to Bubbs Creek Trail; turn left (north).
- **3.8** Sign identifying Mist Falls.
- **4.2** Top of Mist Falls.
- **8.4** Arrive back at the permit station.

71 Deadman Canyon Backpack Trip

This semiloop backpack trip from Lodgepole to the Giant Forest delves through the backcountry of Kings Canyon and Sequoia National Parks, building by slow degrees to a grand climax of a High Sierra crossing at Elizabeth Pass, and winding down again with another gradual passage down the north wall of the Kaweah River. Glacier-carved cliffs and mountains, deep canyons, wildlife, and giant sequoias—this hike has it all.

Start: Lodgepole
Distance: 47.6 miles one-way
Hiking time: 5 days (4 nights)
Difficulty: Formidable, with more than 14,000 feet of elevation gained and lost overall
Seasons: June–Sept
Trail condition: Good, though the trail through Elizabeth Pass may be covered with snow
Other trail users: Equestrians permitted but no dogs or bikes
Land status: Sequoia and Kings Canyon National Parks
Nearest towns: Lodgepole has a store and cafe. Three Rivers is the nearest town.
Fees and permits: None for day hikers. Obtain a wilderness permit for overnight use at the Lodgepole Wilderness Office; the park service charges a fee per wilderness permit obtained May 23–Sep 27, but they are free outside that period. You will also need to pay the vehicle entrance fee to enter the national parks. No fires above 10,000 feet in Kings Canyon National Park or above 9,000 feet in Sequoia National Park.
Maps: Tom Harrison: *Sequoia & Kings Canyon National Parks.* USGS 7.5-minute quads: Lodgepole, Mount Silliman, Sphinx Lakes, Triple Divide Peak.
Trail contacts: Sequoia National Park, 47050 Generals Hwy., Three Rivers, CA 93271-9700; (559) 565-3341; www.nps.gov/seki

Finding the trailhead: From the Lodgepole Visitor Center in Sequoia National Park, drive 0.3 mile eastward, past the kiosk of Lodgepole Campground, and park next to the small nature center on the right (south) side of the road. Then walk up the road 0.1 mile to the automobile bridge across the Marble Fork of the Kaweah. Cross it and pass the signed trail to Tokopah Falls. Immediately beyond, the Twin Lakes Trail—our trailhead—begins on our right (east). Trailhead GPS: N36 36.360' / W118 43.379'

To get back to your starting point from Crescent Meadow trailhead, where this hike ends, simply take the free shuttle. If you still want a car at the end, drive from the Giant Forest Museum 1 mile south on the narrow Crescent Meadow Road. Turn left at the first junction, where a sign directs you toward Crescent Meadow, another 2 miles farther. Crescent Meadow Trailhead GPS: N36 33.286' / W118 44.932'

The Hike

From the Twin Lakes trailhead at Lodgepole (elevation 6,750 feet), our trail hooks around the campground perimeter and strikes a westbound course ascending the north wall of the Kaweah River's Marble Fork canyon. We can gauge our progress by checking up on Lodgepole through sporadic breaks in the wall of conifers and shrubs.

After a mile of steady climbing, we turn right (north) onto a flat stretch thickly clotted with lodgepole pine and red fir. A mile of easy rambling on forest duff brings us to a ford of Silliman Creek, where a sign admonishes us to stay out of the water because it is part of the park's water supply. Continuing uphill, we pass the flowery glade of Cahoon Meadow along its eastern edge, climbing a ravine to Cahoon Gap, a wooded saddle at 8,650 feet.

Our trail now descends about 250 feet of elevation to the banks of Clover Creek. We turn right at the junction with the JO Pass Trail, ford the stream, and commence a series of uphill switchbacks about 2 miles to the 9,500-foot shelf where Twin Lakes recline in the woods below Silliman Pass. There are popular campsites at both lakes.

The final climb starts without preamble on the eastern end of the lakes, zigzagging up through thick forest. Trees are even growing on the 10,200-foot brow of the Kings-Kaweah Divide at Silliman Pass, where the trail momentarily fades in gravel. If you walk a short distance up the knoll to the right (south), however, you can enjoy vast views east and north over the Kings River drainage. Below us we can pick out the namesake dome of Sugarloaf Valley, backed to the north by Sentinel Ridge, and beyond that a network of tributary canyons, including the great white cliff of Muro Blanco. Most spectacular of all is the Great Western Divide, to the east, surmounted by Mount Brewer (13,570 feet), named for the leader of the first survey party to map the area. William Brewer climbed it in June 1864 only to discover that the real Sierra Crest lay even farther to the east. "Such a landscape!" he wrote. "A hundred peaks in sight over thirteen thousand feet—many very sharp—deep canyons, cliffs in every direction almost rival Yosemite, sharp ridges inaccessible to man, on which human foot has never trod—all combined to produce a view of sublimity of which is rarely equaled, of which few are privileged to behold."

Crossing into Kings Canyon National Park at Silliman Pass, our trail winds down in full view of Mount Silliman (11,188 feet) to the south, as well as some dainty examples of natural flower gardens and miniature waterfalls. Reaching a wooded shelf, we pass the short entry paths to Beville Lake—popular with mosquitoes—and then larger Ranger Lake. The latter is the better camping place, with bear boxes and extensive granite terraces to raise your tent above most of the mosquitoes.

Leaving the lakes, our trail descends gradually northward, passing under Ball Dome and leveling out at the ford of Seville Lake's outlet stream in Belle Canyon. Turning right (northeast) at the junction, we follow the creek down to another junction at Camanche Meadow, where we turn right (east) again. Fording the creek that drains Williams Meadow, we hike down into Sugarloaf Valley. As the forest pulls back from dry meadows, the famous Sugarloaf soon pulls into view, a granite dome rising tusklike 1,000 feet above the valley floor. On the southwest corner of Sugarloaf, in woods on the edge of Sugarloaf Meadow, a small spur path on the left side of our trail leads to a comfortable packer camp, with creek, fire ring, bear box, and log seats.

The heavily forested 3-mile passage across Sugarloaf Valley would be easy hiking were it not for the fords of Sugarloaf and Ferguson Creeks, which are treacherous in early season. Apart from that, the trail is fairly level and soft on the feet. After Ferguson Creek we climb out of the valley over a dry moraine pushed up by ice age glaciers moving down Deadman and Cloud Canyons, whose combined drainages today form the Roaring River on the eastern side of the moraine. This is a swift, dangerous river at any time of year, but fortunately we do not have to ford it. Our path traces its rushing waters upstream to Scaffold Meadow, a strategic crossroads of Sierra byways. At this junction stands the Roaring River Ranger Station, staffed from June through September, unless the ranger is on patrol. A fine campsite here offers not only bear boxes but even the luxury of an outhouse, minus the house, with a toilet carved from an old stump, very sociably situated in a pasture beside the trail. A footbridge across Roaring River carries other trails toward the Kern River via Colby Pass and to Cedar Grove via Avalanche Pass—but our trail does not cross this bridge. Staying on the west bank of the Roaring River, we go upriver into Deadman Canyon.

As we begin the first temperate mile of Deadman Canyon, we begin to see signs that the hitherto prevalent forest cover is beginning to quaver. Independent Jeffrey pines and clumps of sagebrush—the harbingers of drier, rockier terrain—are growing more numerous. The canyon is narrowing, hemmed in on the left (east) by Glacier Ridge and on the right (west) by ridge spurs from the Tablelands.

After fording Deadman Canyon's creek (known as Copper Creek, for the mine at the head of Deadman Canyon), we hike through meadows on the eastern bank before arriving at the canyon's namesake, the grave of an Iberian sheepherder, Alfred Moniere. After taking sick here in 1887, probably of appendicitis, he died alone, while his partner sought help from distant Fresno. His timber monument is surrounded by avalanche-flattened trees. Closer to the creek, you can search the white-barked quaking aspen for old carvings made by bored sheepherders.

After leaving the grave to its lonely vigil, we again cross Copper Creek and pass a drift fence, an indication that this trail is popular among packers. As we climb higher, the canyon appears to deepen, especially as we enter Lower Ranger Meadow, about a mile above the ford, where the ridges have risen into respectable mountains. Hikers often meet herds of grazing horses. The boulders and woods along the east side of Lower and Middle Ranger Meadows shelter some old packer camps.

Passing through another stock gate, we make another ford of Copper Creek and climb a granite shelf to Upper Ranger Meadow, with an excellent packer camp in the trees overlooking Middle Ranger Meadow. From our final stretch of flat ground before the pass, we eye the canyon's looming headwalls, a glacial cirque that seems to offer no easy escape. It's hard to believe we are looking at Elizabeth Pass, the usually snowy low point on the right (southwestern) ridge, 2,000 feet higher than where we now stand.

Now begins the hardest climb of this trip. To recall the phraseology of a ranger once met at Lodgepole, Elizabeth Pass is "a real grunt"; that is, a climb of heroic proportions. Our trail takes off through fields of talus above the rushing creek, climbing to the top of a granite bluff and crossing the cascades to the opposite bank, a tricky ford when the water is high. The trail from here to the little meadow below the granite cirque is beautifully engineered with rock steps. As we turn uphill onto steep granite slabs above the meadow, however, the trail is sometimes hard to follow. The problem is snow, which sticks in patches to this northeast-facing slope often throughout the year. Keep in mind that you are aiming for the pass on the southwest ridge, and climb for that. Chances are good that you will at some point regain the trail, which climbs in broad switchbacks to the 11,400-foot pass, a narrow saddle in the Kings-Kaweah Divide.

There is a register box atop Elizabeth Pass. Behind us (northwest), we look down to Ranger Meadow, where Deadman Canyon makes a turn to disappear behind Glacier Ridge. Ahead (west), the rocky slopes of the Kaweah River drainage slip steeply away. It's a fine view, but the proximity of so many high ridges and peaks blocks our views of the Great Western Divide.

The 3,350-foot descent from Elizabeth Pass to Lone Pine Creek is tough on knees. We start down through talus on a set of tight, ambitiously engineered switchbacks, feeding thence onto long, sloping granite slabs interspersed with meadow and boulders. Ducks mark our route, which is not always easy to follow, but even when we lose it, we can often pick it up in the wide-open country by searching down the slope. Our trail descends to a lateral valley, crossing the outlet creek from Lonely Lake, whereupon we begin a series of merciless switchbacks through dry scrub down to the rocky floor of Lone Pine Creek's canyon, at about 8,050 feet. There we meet the trail to Tamarack Lake, which leads to some close campsites sheltered in the trees.

Just ahead on our trail lies another junction: Take the Over-the-Hill Trail to Bearpaw Meadow. We start by climbing through a subalpine world scoured by avalanches. Enjoy the fantastic views eastward to the Angel Wings and other polished granite domes and spires, because once we hit the crest, the forest closes in and we make a steep descent, well blinkered in forests of red fir. Arriving at Bearpaw High Sierra Camp, we find a ranger station and a canvas tent lodge that provides beds, showers, and meals to paying guests (who reserve the privilege months in advance). The Bearpaw Meadow Campground for backpackers has a water spigot, an outhouse, and bear boxes.

At Bearpaw Meadow, we pick up the famous High Sierra Trail back to Giant Forest, an 11.3-mile stretch that is engineered to keep the rise and fall to a minimum, while enjoying scenic views of Sugarbowl Dome, Little Blue Dome, Castle Rocks, and the Kaweah River gorge. There are campsites with bear boxes at Buck Creek, Nine Mile Creek, and Mehrten Creek. A pair of monumental sequoias marks our entry into the Giant Forest, where we meet the road head at Crescent Meadow.

Miles and Directions

0.0 Twin Lakes trailhead at Lodgepole.

1.2 Trail junction to Wuksachi Village; bear right (north).

4.1 Cahoon Gap.

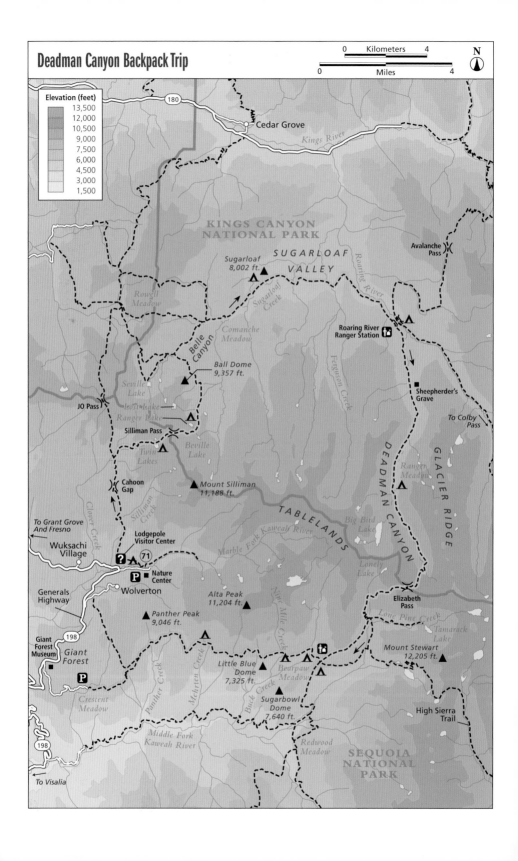

5.0 Junction with JO Pass Trail; bear right (northeast).

6.8 Twin Lakes.

7.9 Silliman Pass.

9.7 Beville Lake junction; bear left (north).

9.8 Ranger Lake junction; bear right (east).

13.0 Seville Lake junction; bear right (northeast).

14.7 Camanche Meadow junction; bear right (east).

17.9 Ford of Sugarloaf Creek.

19.3 Ford of Ferguson Creek.

22.1 Roaring River Ranger Station.

23.7 First Deadman Canyon creek ford.

24.6 Sheepherder's grave.

25.2 Second Deadman Canyon creek ford.

26.9 Lower Ranger Meadow.

30.5 Ford of creek above waterfall, upper Deadman Canyon.

31.7 Elizabeth Pass.

34.5 Junction with Tamarack Lake Trail; go right (south).

34.6 Over-the-Hill Trail junction; bear right (southwest).

36.5 Bearpaw Meadow junction; turn right (west) onto the High Sierra Trail.

36.6 Junction with Redwood Meadow Trail; keep right (west).

37.8 Buck Creek.

39.1 Nine Mile Creek.

42.0 Mehrten Creek.

47.6 Crescent Meadow.

72 Heather Lake via the Watchtower

Stupendous cliffs, views of the Tablelands, and a subalpine lake are three solid reasons to make this the day hike of choice for Giant Forest visitors who want a taste of the Sequoia high country.

Start: Wolverton parking area
Distance: 8.4 miles out and back
Hiking time: About 4 hours
Difficulty: Moderate, with an elevation gain of about 2,000 feet
Seasons: June–Oct
Trail condition: Excellent singletrack trail
Other trail users: Equestrians permitted but no dogs or bikes

Land status: Sequoia National Park
Nearest towns: Lodgepole has a store and cafe. Three Rivers is the nearest town.
Fees and permits: See Hike 71
Maps: Tom Harrison: *Mt. Whitney High Country*. USGS 7.5-minute quad: Lodgepole.
Trail contacts: Sequoia National Park, 47050 Generals Hwy., Three Rivers, CA 93271-9700; (559) 565-3341; www.nps.gov/seki

Finding the trailhead: Ride the free park shuttle. If you drive, the signposted Wolverton turnoff is on the east side of the Generals Highway (CA 198), about 3 miles south of the Wuksachi Village turnoff and 3 miles north of the Giant Forest Museum. After turning off toward Wolverton, drive 1.5 miles to the parking area. Trailhead GPS: N36 35.794' / W118 44.068'

The Hike

The Lakes Trail is the shortest and easiest path into the high country of Sequoia National Park from any road head in the Giant Forest area. Starting out at 7,000 feet, the trail climbs from a signpost on the north side of Wolverton's large parking lot. We quickly meet the trail coming up from Lodgepole and take the right (east) uphill fork. Steeper and dustier than most hikers like, the path is nonetheless well shaded and, after meeting Wolverton Creek in a meadow, well serenaded by babbling waters. Climbing about 800 feet in slightly less than 2 miles, we meet the Panther Gap Trail and turn left (north) toward the Watchtower.

Climbing steadily around the corner of the hill, we disregard the Hump Trail, which also goes to the lakes, but which is steeper and less scenic than the Watchtower route. Occasional boulders provide some rest but not a great deal of relief from the monotony of uphill walking through thick forest. Our efforts begin to pay off at 3 miles, however, when thinning forest and broadening horizons reward us with a view of the Watchtower, an 8,973-foot monolith that lords over the granite-clad Tokopah Valley. The river at the bottom is the Marble Fork of the Kaweah River, which tumbles from the high Tablelands down Tokopah Falls toward Lodgepole. Many hikers are so pleased with this prospect that they plunk themselves down and stir no farther up the trail, content to spend the rest of the day exploring the Tablelands and Tokopah Valley with a pair of binoculars.

Heather Lake via the Watchtower

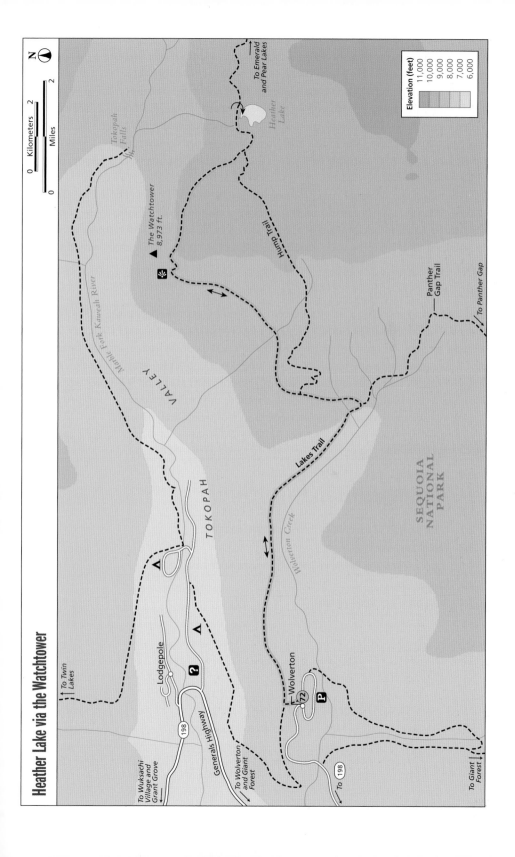

N

0 Kilometers 2
0 Miles 2

Elevation (feet)
11,000
10,000
9,000
8,000
7,000
6,000

To Twin Lakes

To Wuksachi Village and Grant Grove

Lodgepole

Generals Highway

198

To Wolverton and Giant Forest

Wolverton

72

P

To 198

To Giant Forest

TOKOPAH

VALLEY

Middle Fork Kaweah River

Tokopah Falls

The Watchtower 8,973 ft.

Heather Lake

To Emerald and Pear Lakes

Hump Trail

Panther Gap Trail

To Panther Gap

Lakes Trail

Wolverton Creek

SEQUOIA NATIONAL PARK

From here on, though, the Lakes Trail grows decidedly more interesting. Mounting the ridge behind the Watchtower on a couple of switchbacks, it then sets out across ledges dynamited on the rock face by the Civilian Conservation Corps in the 1930s. Curving upward with impressive views north across the floor of Tokopah Valley, nearly 2,000 feet below us, to the 11,000-foot crest around Mount Silliman, nearly 2,000 feet above, the trail is easily wide enough for summer hikers. The drop-off is risky if the trail is snowy or icy, in which case the aforementioned Hump Trail stands at the ready.

Rounding the mountain, we find ourselves in a wooded valley. The Hump Trail joins us from the right (south), and together we walk the final 0.2 mile to the shores of Heather Lake, at an elevation of about 9,300 feet. Where the outlet stream crosses the trail, turn left onto the rock slabs below the lake, where you can enjoy sensational views.

Options

You can visit a succession of other beautiful lakes by continuing up the Lakes Trail. Only 0.9 mile beyond the outlet of Heather Lake, we come to Emerald Lake, at 9,200 feet. By turning left (north) from where Emerald Lake's outlet stream crosses the trail and walking 0.2 mile downhill beside the creek, you could also visit Aster Lake. The Lakes Trail officially ends at Pear Lake, 9,510 feet in elevation and 1.8 miles beyond Heather. Many backpackers nevertheless continue onward from there to explore the Tablelands, where wide-open views are well suited for off-trail hiking.

Miles and Directions

0.0 Parking area.

0.1 Junction with trail to Lodgepole; bear right (east).

1.8 Junction with the Panther Gap Trail; bear left (north).

2.1 Lower junction with the Hump Trail; go straight (north).

3.2 Watchtower vista.

4.0 Upper junction with the Hump Trail; bear straight (southeast).

4.2 Heather Lake.

8.4 Arrive back at the parking area.

73 Giant Forest to Bearpaw Meadow

With near-constant views over the spectacular Kaweah Canyon, the High Sierra Trail leads from the Giant Forest to Bearpaw Meadow, a superb base camp for exploring the beautiful backcountry below the Great Western Divide.

Start: Crescent Meadow, High Sierra Trail sign
Distance: 11.3 miles one-way
Hiking time: About 8 hours walking time one-way, making for a 2-day round-trip
Difficulty: Strenuous as a 2-day round-trip but certainly easier if you slow the pace. Despite a net gain of only about 1,000 feet between Crescent Meadow and Bearpaw Meadow, the trail gains about 4,050 feet and loses about 2,950 feet overall.
Trail condition: Well-engineered, singletrack pack trail
Seasons: Mid-May through Oct

Other trail users: Equestrians and pack trains but no dogs or bikes
Land status: Sequoia National Park
Nearest towns: Lodgepole has a store, but Three Rivers is the nearest town.
Fees and permits: See Hike 71
Maps: Tom Harrison: *Mt. Whitney High Country.* USGS 7.5-minute quads: Lodgepole, Triple Divide Peak.
Trail contacts: Sequoia National Park, 47050 Generals Hwy., Three Rivers, CA 93271-9700; (559) 565-3341; www.nps.gov/seki

Finding the trailhead: Ride the free park shuttle. To reach the Crescent Meadow trailhead by vehicle from the Giant Forest Museum, drive 1 mile south on the narrow Crescent Meadow Road, turning left at the first junction, where a sign directs you toward Crescent Meadow, 2 miles farther. Some parking and outhouses are available, but there's no potable water. Trailhead GPS: N36 33.286' / W118 44.932'

The Hike

Bearpaw Meadow perches on a forested bench overlooking the castellated peaks and granite cliffs of remote River Valley and the Great Western Divide. Even hikers who shun heavy backpacks can enjoy a stay at Bearpaw, thanks to the Bearpaw High Sierra Camp, a canvas tent affair that provides beds, showers, and meals, including bag lunches for day hikers. (Reservations are required months in advance.) Backpackers can partake of the simpler amenities (piped water, outhouse, and steel bear boxes) of nearby Bearpaw Meadow Campground. Such luxuries allow greater time and leisure for unencumbered day hikes to remote glacier-scoured valleys, high-country lakes, and the secluded sequoia groves of the Great Western Divide.

As if that were not inducement enough to recommend this trip, the High Sierra Trail to Bearpaw is arguably the easiest route for its length and elevation anywhere in the rugged southern part of the range. Though our stretch of the High Sierra Trail to Bearpaw does rise and fall a bit, the worst is a 600-foot climb in the final mile—not bad at all for the Sierra Nevada. For backpackers who prefer to make the journey in two stages, there are three established backpack campsites (creek water, bear boxes, and flat ground) en route to Bearpaw at Mehrten Creek, Nine Mile Creek, and Buck Creek.

Colonel John White, an early superintendent of Sequoia and Kings Canyon National Parks, conceived the idea of the High Sierra Trail as a way of opening the backcountry to visitors. With federal funding and labor by the Civilian Conservation Corps, supervising ranger Guy Hopping pushed the trail westward from Crescent Meadow starting in 1928, dynamiting shelves on high contours along the north wall of the Kaweah Canyon. Our route starts at the official High Sierra Trail sign in the shade of Crescent Meadow (elevation 6,700 feet) by crossing two small bridges before branching off on the southernmost trail of the Giant Forest.

At a pair of monumental sequoias, we fork south and mount a low ridge to Eagle View, where gaping Kaweah Canyon drops 3,500 feet. This view sets the character of the High Sierra Trail as far as Buck Creek. Suspended on the south-facing slope of the canyon, midway between the river and the jagged ridge between Panther and Alta Peaks, the High Sierra Trail gathers sunshine most of the day, a boon when it comes to melting the snowpack by late spring but a bugbear on hot summer afternoons, especially if you're following a dusty pack train or troop of Boy Scouts.

In sight of Castle Rocks, towering above the southern walls of Kaweah Canyon, we cross some wide-open slopes of manzanita and black oak, all the while inhaling the scent of mountain misery, before delving into deep forests of white fir. Surmounting a pair of switchbacks—a thankfully scarce design feature on this trail—we round the canyon wall into a large bight, the basin of Panther Creek, which we traverse in a broad northerly arc after first pausing to sample a summer-ripened thimbleberry or two (and leaving the rest for the bears). The first tributary of Panther Creek has a little waterfall and space enough for one small tent. (Despite the easy contours of the trail itself, the canyon slope descends so steeply that flat ground sufficient even for a pitched tent is very hard to find.)

After passing several smaller forklets of Panther Creek, the trail reasserts its easterly course at Sevenmile Hill and rises modestly to its halfway point at Mehrten Creek. There you can find some plots of flat ground and a bear box atop the rocks to the left of the creek. After stepping across Mehrten, the route becomes more spectacular. With increasingly intimate views of the Great Western Divide, the route now alternates between stretches of soft forest duff and rocky shelves dynamited through exfoliating granite. Ahead, the bulbous domes of Little Blue and Sugarbowl appear through trees and disappear, repeatedly, growing larger by degrees as the trail winds in and out, until you finally pass them up at Nine Mile Creek (not named on the USGS maps but well known to park rangers), whose western bank harbors the finest campsite between Crescent and Bearpaw Meadows.

After descending to the bridge on Buck Creek, the largest stream yet crossed on our route, we immediately begin to climb out of Buck Canyon on switchbacks. The hike's biggest ascent hits just as our energy's most flagging. Console yourself that this is the final push. At the top of the ridge, you will find the Bearpaw Meadow

Giant Forest to Bearpaw Meadow; Bearpaw Meadow to Hamilton Lake, Tamarack Lake, and Redwood Meadow

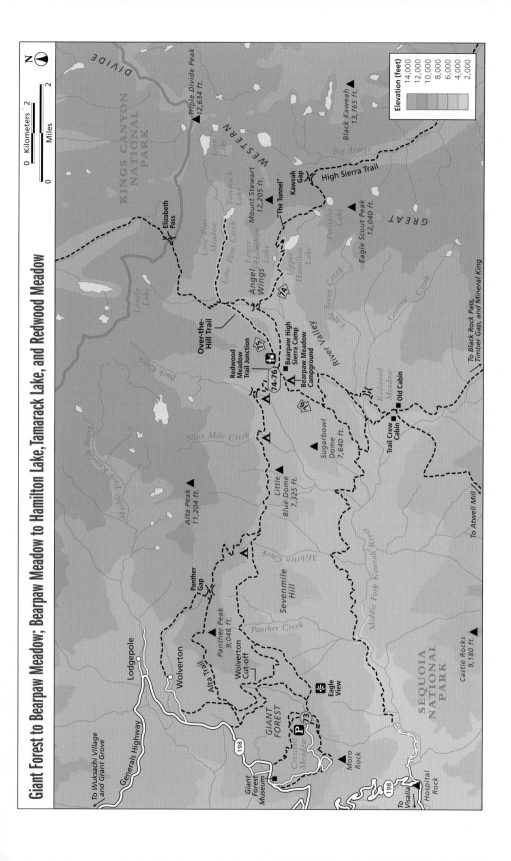

N

0 Kilometers 2
0 Miles 2

Elevation (feet)
14,000
12,000
10,000
8,000
6,000
4,000
2,000

To Wuksachi Village and Grant Grove

Lodgepole

Generals Highway

198

Giant Forest Museum

GIANT FOREST

Crescent Meadow

73

P

Moro Rock

198

To Visalia

Hospital Rock

Wolverton

Alta Trail

Wolverton Cut-off

Eagle View

Panther Peak 9,046 ft.

Panther Gap

Alta Peak 11,204 ft.

Middle Fork Kaweah River

Panther Creek

Sevenmile Hill

Melican Creek

Little Blue Dome 7,325 ft.

Nine Mile Creek

Sugarbowl Dome 7,640 ft.

Castle Rocks 9,180 ft.

SEQUOIA NATIONAL PARK

Middle Fork Kaweah River

To Atwell Mill

Trail Crew Cabin

Old Cabin

Redwood Meadow

To Black Rock Pass, Timber Gap, and Mineral King

Buck Creek

Redwood Meadow Trail Junction

74–76

15

Over-the-Hill Trail

Bearpaw High Sierra Camp

Bearpaw Meadow Campground

9L

74

River Valley

Lone Pine Meadow

Lone Pine Creek

Lonely Lake

Elizabeth Pass

Tamarack Lake

Angel Wings

Lower Hamilton Lake

Upper Hamilton Lake

Mount Stewart 12,205 ft.

"The Tunnel"

Precipice Lake

Eagle Scout Peak 12,040 ft.

Kaweah Gap

High Sierra Trail

Lion Lake

Big Arroyo

GREAT WESTERN DIVIDE

Triple Divide Peak 12,634 ft.

Black Kaweah 13,765 ft.

KINGS CANYON NATIONAL PARK

Middle Fork Kaweah River

Campground on the spur trail (the Redwood Meadow Trail) 0.2 mile to the right (south). The lodge itself lies 0.2 mile straight ahead (east), incorporating an A-frame ranger station, an older log cabin, a spigot dispensing untreated water, a scattering of tent cabins, and the main canvas dining hall with its rickety and thoroughly charming porch. One story claims the meadow was named for the discovery of a bear's paw nailed to a tree. Plenty of black bears reside there today, so use the bear boxes religiously.

Miles and Directions

0.0 Crescent Meadow.

0.8 Eagle View.

2.6 Junction of Wolverton Cutoff; keep straight (northeast).

5.6 Mehrten Creek campsite.

6.0 Junction with Alta Trail cutoff; keep straight (east).

8.5 Nine Mile Creek campsite.

9.7 Buck Creek campsite.

9.8 Buck Creek bridge.

11.1 Junction with Redwood Meadow Trail; bear right (south) to Bearpaw Meadow Campground or straight (east) to Bearpaw High Sierra Camp.

11.3 Bearpaw High Sierra Camp or (on a spur trail) Bearpaw Meadow Campground.

74 Bearpaw Meadow to Hamilton Lake

Scout this route from the porch of the Bearpaw Meadow High Sierra Camp, and you may find it hard to believe that any hiking trail can safely breach such sheer and polished cliffs. This path is a marvel of engineering, set in a perfect Sierra setting of glaciated canyons, granite cliffs, rivers, lakes, flower gardens, and waterfalls.

Start: Bearpaw Meadow Ranger Station
Distance: 7.6 miles out and back
Hiking time: About 6–7 hours
Difficulty: Moderately strenuous
Trail condition: Spectacular, occasionally exposed pack trail
Seasons: June through early Oct
Other trail users: Equestrians permitted but no dogs or bikes
Land status: Sequoia National Park

Nearest town: Ranger station and maintained camp at Bearpaw Meadow. Distant Lodgepole has basic amenities.
Fees and permits: See Hike 71
Maps: Tom Harrison: *Mt. Whitney High Country.* USGS 7.5-minute quad: Triple Divide Peak.
Trail contacts: Sequoia National Park, 47050 Generals Hwy., Three Rivers, CA 93271-9700; (559) 565-3341; www.nps.gov/seki

Finding the trailhead: This hike starts from the Bearpaw Meadow Ranger Station, which is an 11.3-mile walk from Crescent Meadow. (To reach the Crescent Meadow trailhead, see hike 73.) The ranger station sits beside the trail just above Bearpaw Meadow High Sierra Camp. Trailhead GPS: N36 33.557' / W118 37.149'

The Hike

From the Bearpaw Meadow Ranger Station, at an elevation of about 7,700 feet, the High Sierra Trail strikes eastward through woods toward the sheer brink of River Valley. This is an exciting stretch of trail. In places, only a thin line of ferns, buckthorn, chinquapin, and manzanita buffers the trail from lethal drop-offs of up to 1,000 feet. The ever-stunning background vista of fluted cliffs and rampant peaks vies with the exquisite foreground details of mountain scenery—a curtain of water hung on a cliff, a massive pine leaning over the verge, a riot of seeping gardens rank with wildflowers. Rounding one corner, we gain a spectacular view up-canyon to Mount Stewart and the Angel Wings.

While descending briefly toward the bridged crossing of Lone Pine Creek, we can see our trail across the canyon, mounting in switchbacks up the sheer wall. After passing a granite grotto with a trickling stream, we switchback down to a girder bridge built across a sheer-walled gorge. In the dizzying void 140 feet below the bridge, the powerful stream pours beneath an enormous boulder jammed between the walls of the gorge, around which an old steel bridge—built in 1957 and destroyed by an avalanche the following winter—is twisted like a paper clip. The present bridge was built in 1997.

As you climb the trail on the other side—chest-high with elderberry, ferns, thimbleberry, currant, and sage, and rife with scores of wildflower species—you can see

Lone Pine Creek above the bridge, pouring as a waterfall through a deep cleft. At the junction with the rocky Lone Pine Creek Trail, we turn right and begin a more sobering ascent toward Valhalla, sweeping upward in a couple of epic switchbacks through terrain so open and vast that you're largely distracted from the steepness of your climb. Turning eastward into Hamilton Creek canyon, the trail hairpins down to a bench from which you get a preview of a waterfall that you will shortly surmount and cross, fifty paces above its very brink.

Your continuing climb is inspired by the majesty of Angel Wings, rising more than 2,000 feet above the rock-bound valley. The peace and quiet are broken mainly by the muffled roar of cascading waters and the whistle of curious marmots. The trail climbs the rocks above Lower Hamilton Lake before leveling out in a wooded U-shaped valley. There, beyond the trees, Upper Hamilton Lake lounges at 8,235 feet, with a waterfall dashing down from the cliffs at its eastern end.

Options

From Hamilton Lake the High Sierra Trail continues its manic-but-perfectly-safe ascent to Kaweah Gap, 3.5 miles and 2,500 feet above Upper Hamilton Lake. It's a breathtaking climb, skirting sheer cliffs and sporting ever-closer views of the Great Western Divide. From the Divide, the trail descends partway down Big Arroyo before climbing again to the Chagoopa Plateau, on the western rim of the Kern River Canyon. After switchbacking down to the Kern River, the High Sierra Trail turns north, following the Kern upstream to Wallace Creek. It joins the John Muir Trail at the top of Wallace Creek and follows it to the top of Mount Whitney, 62 miles from Crescent Meadow. Visit www.nps.gov/seki/historyculture for more information.

Miles and Directions

0.0 Bearpaw Meadow Ranger Station.

1.6 Lone Pine Creek bridge.

1.8 Junction of Lone Pine Creek Trail; bear right (east).

3.1 Hamilton Creek crossing.

3.8 Upper Hamilton Lake.

7.6 Arrive back at the Bearpaw Meadow Ranger Station.

75 Bearpaw Meadow to Tamarack Lake

Hemmed within a glacier-scooped valley high in the west-facing wall of the Great Western Divide, Tamarack Lake offers wild solitude and magnificent scenery to day hikers from Bearpaw Meadow.

Start: Bearpaw Meadow (11.3 miles from the Crescent Meadow road head)
Distance: 8.4 miles out and back
Hiking time: About 6-7 hours
Difficulty: Strenuous, with a gross elevation gain of 2,300 feet
Trail condition: A clear trail until the final mile, when you need to follow ducks to avoid a confusion of streambeds
Seasons: Mid-June through mid-Oct
Other trail users: Equestrians permitted but no dogs or bikes

Land status: Sequoia National Park
Nearest towns: Ranger station and maintained camp at Bearpaw Meadow. Distant Lodgepole has basic amenities.
Fees and permits: See Hike 71
Maps: Tom Harrison: *Mt. Whitney High Country.* USGS 7.5-minute quad: Triple Divide Peak.
Trail contacts: Sequoia National Park, 47050 Generals Hwy., Three Rivers, CA 93271-9700; (559) 565-3341; www.nps.gov/seki

Finding the trailhead: This hike starts from the Bearpaw Meadow Ranger Station, which is an 11.3-mile walk from Crescent Meadow. (To reach the Crescent Meadow trailhead, see hike 73.) The ranger station sits beside the trail just above Bearpaw Meadow High Sierra Camp. Trailhead GPS: N36 33.557' / W118 37.149'

The Hike

The Over-the-Hill Trail leaves from an elevation of about 7,700 feet, immediately west of the Bearpaw High Sierra Camp. It climbs in businesslike fashion, steep and well blinkered in forests of red fir. As you crest and begin your descent into Lone Pine Valley, however, the forest thins, permitting fantastic views eastward to the Angel Wings and to unnamed polished granite domes and spires atop the western ridge of Eagle Scout Peak. By the time you reach tumbling Lone Pine Creek, the dense woodlands have been replaced by a subalpine world scoured by avalanches.

Turning east between the glacier-polished granite walls of Lone Pine Canyon, cross the shallow, gravelly flats scoured by the outlet creek from Lonely Lake, hidden more than 2,000 feet higher in the mountains to the north. The meadows beyond are strewn with huge boulders and daintier tufts of lupine, paintbrush, shooting star, and some scattered pines and firs. Within 0.5 mile you pass a sign nailed to a tree identifying Lone Pine Meadow, full of ferns and willows. By the end of your first mile in the canyon, you begin to ascend a granite bench that holds out promise of Tamarack Lake, but when you arrive you find another meadow backed by yet another granite bench topped by forest. As you cross this meadow, stay alert for the many rocky, seasonal streambeds that cross the trail, each of which looks suspiciously like the trail. If confused, look for the large stone ducks.

Crossing Lone Pine Creek on rocks, we begin our final 300-foot ascent to a ridge of lodgepole pines, also known as tamaracks, and find ourselves within sight of Tamarack Lake's heavily forested western shore. Excellent campsites (no fires allowed) stand near the inlet creek cascading down from Lion Lake to the eastern side of Tamarack. The sheer face of Mount Stewart (12,205 feet), rising some 3,000 feet above Tamarack's southern shore, harbors a small glacier. To the northwest, hulking Triple Divide Peak (12,634 feet) divides its snows between the Kaweah, Kern, and Kings Rivers.

Miles and Directions

0.0 Bearpaw Meadow Ranger Station.

0.1 Junction with Over-the-Hill Trail; bear right (north).

2.2 Junction with Elizabeth Pass Trail; bear left (north).

2.3 Junction with Tamarack Lake Trail; bear right (east).

3.7 Step-across ford of Lone Pine Creek.

4.2 Tamarack Lake.

8.4 Arrive back at the Bearpaw Meadow Ranger Station.

76 Bearpaw Meadow to Redwood Meadow

This out-and-back day hike descends from Bearpaw Meadow to a remote and wonderfully serene grove of giant sequoias.

Start: Bearpaw Meadow Ranger Station
Distance: 9.6 miles out and back
Hiking time: About 6 hours
Difficulty: Strenuous, with a gross elevation loss of 2,000 feet, all to be regained on the return trip
Trail condition: Excellent, sometimes steep forest path, with a ford of the Kaweah River
Seasons: July–Oct, though June is also good if the runoff is low enough to ford the Kaweah River
Other trail users: Equestrians permitted but no dogs or bikes
Land status: Sequoia National Park
Nearest towns: Ranger station and maintained camp at Bearpaw Meadow. Distant Lodgepole has basic amenities.

Fees and permits: See Hike 71
Maps: Tom Harrison: *Mt. Whitney High Country.* USGS 7.5-minute quads: Lodgepole, Triple Divide Peak.
Trail contacts: Sequoia National Park, 47050 Generals Hwy., Three Rivers, CA 93271-9700; (559) 565-3341; www.nps.gov/seki
Special considerations: Before leaving Bearpaw Meadow, inquire whether anyone there can advise you of the current water flow of the Kaweah River in River Valley. Attempt the ford only if your skill and experience are up to it. If you intend to explore the grove off-trail, bring a map and compass and know how to use them, for these woods are very dense and disorienting.

Finding the trailhead: This hike starts from the Bearpaw Meadow Ranger Station, which is an 11.3-mile walk from Crescent Meadow. (To reach the Crescent Meadow trailhead, see hike 73.) The ranger station sits beside the trail just above Bearpaw Meadow High Sierra Camp. Trailhead GPS: N36 33.557' / W118 37.149'

The Hike

From the Bearpaw Meadow Ranger Station (elevation 7,700 feet), hike down to the campground and continue downhill on the Redwood Meadow Trail. Heavily shaded by forest, the descent is steep and dusty, though there is one refreshing interlude as we skirt the tiny oasis of Little Bearpaw Meadow. Reaching the bottom at River Valley, the rushing Kaweah River parts the forests. There is no bridge, and hikers have to ford, so beware of periods of heavy runoff. It is usually manageable by July.

Once across, the trail attempts fairly successfully to follow contours southward along the wooded foot of the Great Western Divide, neither gaining nor losing much in elevation for the next 2.5 miles. This forest stroll is enlivened by two rambunctious creeks, Eagle Scout and Granite, the first a hop-across, the latter bridged. We dip slightly as we come into the Redwood Meadow Grove, where we meet a trail coming up from the lower Kaweah River. There are many campsites at hand, but water may not be readily available.

The centerpiece of the grove is Redwood Meadow. On the edge of the meadow stand two cabins, the larger built as a ranger station in 1938 and still used sporadically by trail crews. Massive sequoias loiter about the dooryard of the smaller cabin, dwarfing it. The drone of bees drifts over the meadow, rife with Bigelow sneezeweed, yarrow, corn lilies, and California coneflowers that grow chest-high by midsummer. Unencumbered by crowds or noises of civilization, it seems the kind of setting dreamed up in a fairy tale, an idyllic napping place on a balmy summer's afternoon.

The grove invites unhurried exploration. If you walk up the trail toward Timber Gap another mile south, you will enter a fine section of the grove, where giant sequoias stand in thick array. Many other massive specimens are west of the meadow, off-trail, but if you leave the path, be sure to keep your bearings and your wits, because this forest is very large, profuse, and disorienting.

Miles and Directions

0.0 Bearpaw Meadow Ranger Station.

0.3 Bearpaw Meadow Campground; continue downhill.

1.5 Little Bearpaw Meadow junction; bear left (east).

2.5 River Valley ford.

3.0 Junction of the Middle Fork and River Valley Trails; bear left (south).

3.4 Eagle Scout Creek crossing.

3.8 Granite Creek bridge.

4.7 Junction of the Middle Fork cutoff and River Valley Trails; bear left (south).

4.8 Redwood Meadow cabins.

9.6 Arrive back at the Bearpaw Meadow Ranger Station.

77 Kaweah River Trail

This multiday backpack trip up Kaweah Canyon offers inspiring views of the Great Western Divide and makes an ideal off-season excursion.

Start: Hospital Rock parking area (in late fall, winter, and early spring); Moro Creek parking area when the road opens for summer
Distance: 24.0 miles out and back from Hospital Rock
Hiking time: 2–3 days
Difficulty: Strenuous, with a gross elevation gain of nearly 4,500 feet
Trail condition: The trail is well maintained, but Moro, Panther, and Mehrten Creeks are not bridged and must be forded. This can be very dangerous during periods of heavy runoff during winter and spring.
Seasons: Apr–June is best for water displays but hardest for fords. Sept–Oct is best for fall

colors. July–Aug can be uncomfortably hot. Nevertheless, the trail is open year-round to hikers, so the time you choose to visit depends on your tolerance for local weather conditions.
Other trail users: Equestrians permitted but no dogs, bikes, or hunters
Land status: Sequoia National Park
Nearest town: Three Rivers
Fees and permits: See Hike 71
Maps: Tom Harrison: *Mt. Whitney High Country*. USGS 7.5-minute quads: Giant Forest, Lodgepole.
Trail contacts: Sequoia National Park, 47050 Generals Hwy., Three Rivers, CA 93271-9700; (559) 565-3341; www.nps.gov/seki

Finding the trailhead: During fall, winter, and early spring, park at Hospital Rock parking area about 5 miles east of the Ash Mountain Visitor Center on the Generals Highway (CA 198). Coming from the north on the Generals Highway, it lies about 10 miles south from the Giant Forest Museum, 14.5 miles from Lodgepole, and 16 miles from Wuksachi Village. Off-season trailhead GPS at Hospital Rock: N36 31.258' / W118 46.278'

During summer rangers open the road to the Moro Creek parking area, allowing drivers to shorten the hike by 1.7 miles (and a 550-foot elevation gain) by driving up the one-lane road across the Generals Highway, just east of the Hospital Rock parking lot. At the Buckeye Flat Campground junction (0.6 mile), take the left fork and drive 1.1 miles more over a bumpy dirt road to the Moro Creek parking area. Moro Creek Trailhead GPS: N36 31.656' / W118 45.070'

The Hike

Of the Sierra Nevada parks, Sequoia National Park preserves the greatest area of foothill terrain. This backpack trip along the Middle Fork Trail visits one of the most scenic foothill regions. In one glance from many sections of the trail, we can see the swath of life from the chaparral to alpine zones. The route is arguably at its most scenic when snow dusts the high country, making October and November premier months for a trip, but winter can also be an excellent time to go, weather permitting. Winter snow that does fall on the trail usually melts quickly at the lower elevations, and since the route described here does not hit 5,000 feet until its 10th mile, nor does it anywhere exceed 5,900 feet, the odds are good that you will be able to cover a lot of ground without bogging down in snowfields if you take a reliable weather forecast into consideration.

Starting from the Hospital Rock parking area (elevation 2,700 feet), cross the Generals Highway east to the narrow spur road that leads to Buckeye Flat Campground. (The metal gate will be closed between autumn and spring.) The one-lane paved roadway is carved from the steep hillside above the rushing Middle Fork of the Kaweah River. At this point the Kaweah Canyon is about 4,000 feet deep, yet wide enough to soak up sunshine for much of the day. In May and June, when hillside grasses are green and the wildflowers are in bloom, the flowering buckeye trees and candle-like stalks of white yucca stand out brilliantly even from a distance. When you reach the junction where the paved road drops to Buckeye Flat Camp, take the unpaved left fork toward Moro Creek, climbing mildly up a narrow sidehill road that leads to the Moro Creek parking area, a wide, dirt turnaround far above the river.

Passing signposts, we drop quickly to Moro Creek, which comes tumbling down from the Giant Forest just below Moro Rock. For such a minor drainage area, Moro makes a difficult ford in May and June. Now on a proper trail instead of a dirt road, we leave the trees to zigzag uphill to a ridge. Surveying the open canyon ahead, we spot our trail rounding the outside of chaparral-covered hillsides, dipping in and out of hidden ravines. Thick cushions of chaparral press in thick and high. Natural successor to the woodlands that burned in the Buckeye Fire of 1988, chaparral can be quite handsome in spring, when the buckbrush and deer brush bloom white, and in fall, when the chamise turns rust colored. Growing on burgundy-colored trunks to the size of small trees, the manzanitas are particularly impressive any time of year.

This high vegetation blocks our view of the Kaweah River and filters its roar to a sound like the surf, rising and falling as we move up the trail. A quarter mile beyond Moro Creek, we cross a second, unnamed creek. Hikers can hardly fail to notice the great rocks on both walls of the canyon. Bulbous Moro Rock balloons high up on the left (north) side. To the right (south), the massive granite turrets of Castle Rocks loom even higher above steep tributary canyons of the Kaweah. Ahead (east) we catch sight, from time to time, of distant Sugarbowl Dome, rising to 7,640 feet near Bearpaw Meadow.

As we pass beyond the burned zone, the foliage changes dramatically. Although grass and shrub still dominate the dry outer hillsides, the successive ravines between them fill with a profusion of riparian laurels, ferns, and oaks. Moss grows on shaded boulders. Poison oak, also, starts to become a problem.

We know we are approaching Panther Creek when the trail moves closer to the Kaweah River than it has been since we left Moro Creek. Though we are still a good 300 precipitous feet above it, fenced off only by a reassuring bank of trees, we can look down to its rapids at a point directly north of Castle Rocks. Rounding the corner into the next ravine—the ravine of Panther Creek—we can look down and see the fullest view of Panther Creek Falls that we will ever see from the trail. From this oblique angle, note how the creek flows southward over the first brink, hits a channel that deflects it eastward at right angles, and then drops out of sight.

The trail descends very steeply in 100 yards to Panther Creek, a rock-hopping ford at 3,900 feet elevation. You can find a good campsite and many excellent picnic

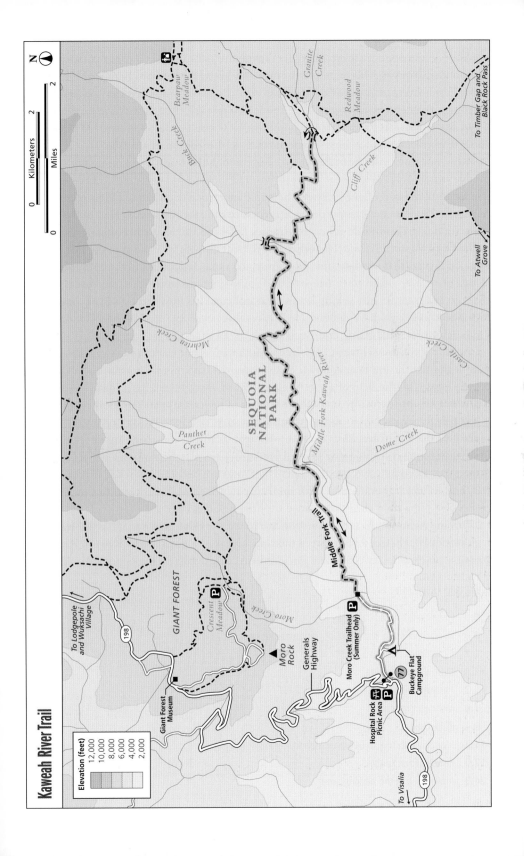

Kaweah River Trail

Elevation (feet)
12,000
10,000
8,000
6,000
4,000
2,000

N

0 — 2 Kilometers
0 — 2 Miles

To Timber Gap and Black Rock Pass

Granite Creek

Redwood Meadow

Bearpaw Meadow

Buck Creek

Cliff Creek

To Atwell Grove

Castle Creek

Mehrten Creek

SEQUOIA NATIONAL PARK

Middle Fork Kaweah River

Panther Creek

Dome Creek

Middle Fork Trail

GIANT FOREST

Crescent Meadow

Moro Creek

Moro Rock

Generals Highway

Giant Forest Museum

To Lodgepole and Wuksachi Village

198

Moro Creek Trailhead (Summer Only)

Hospital Rock Picnic Area

Buckeye Flat Campground

77

To Visalia

198

boulders on the opposite shore, amid the canyon live oaks, incense cedars, manzanitas, and ponderosa pines. The granite slabs near the lip of the falls are highly polished, making them very dangerous to approach too closely. In truth, we can see hardly anything of the elusive falls, which are about 200 feet tall, though we have excellent views of the Kaweah River's granite gorge and of Castle Rocks, well over 4,000 feet above. Do not attempt to climb down the cliffs to the bottom of the falls.

Now our route rises from Panther Creek through the forest, twisting tightly in a double switchback. We leave the Kaweah River far behind and never close ranks with it again until the end of our journey. The trail then relaxes to a routine cadence, gaining about 250 feet of elevation on each successive mile for the next 4. Half of that is spent rounding the outside of scrubby ridges far above the Kaweah, enjoying views of the Great Western Divide. The other half is spent dipping in and out of the heavily wooded ravines that separate one ridge from the next, delightful interludes through forests of incense cedar, wiry live oak, and spicy-smelling laurel trees that overarch the path and litter it with oblong leaves. Seasonal creeklets flow through many of the ravines, but only two have dependable streams that never dry up: Mehrten Creek, at 7 miles from Hospital Rock, and Buck Creek, at 9.4 miles.

As we approach Mehrten Creek's crossing, an excellent campsite lies on the east side of the trail in the ravine, down a very steep embankment. There is no bridge, but we cross with the help of a log. A bigger stream, Buck Creek has a sturdy bridge. There is a fine packer camp on the eastern bank of the creek, at an elevation of about 4,950 feet. Emerging from our northward deviation up Buck Creek's ravine, as we resume our eastward-trending climb up Kaweah Canyon, the changing vegetation once again reminds us that our gradual elevation gain may be slow, but it's definite. Poison oak, thankfully, has become rare. The forests are becoming thicker, darker. By the time we reach the junction with the Bearpaw Meadow Trail, white firs, incense cedars, and pines hold clear dominance over the broadleaf trees.

Turning right (south) at that junction, we round the ridge, topping out at our trail's high point of 5,900 feet. A short, steep hike quickly takes us down to the Kaweah River bridge, at an elevation of 5,500 feet. An excellent camp awaits on the opposite bank.

Miles and Directions

0.0   Hospital Rock parking area.

0.6   Road junction to Buckeye Flat Campground; bear left (east).

1.7   Moro Creek trailhead.

1.8   Moro Creek crossing.

4.3   Panther Creek Falls.

7.0   Mehrten Creek.

9.4   Buck Creek.

11.2   Junction with trail to Bearpaw Meadow; go right (south).

12.0   Kaweah River bridge.

24.0   Arrive back at the parking area.

78 Freeman Creek Trail

The pristine Freeman Creek Grove of giant sequoias is well removed from the tourist circuit, treating hikers to the thrill of discovery.

Start: Freeman Creek trailhead on the Great Western Divide, near Quaking Aspen
Distance: 8.6 miles out and back
Hiking time: About 4–5 hours
Difficulty: Moderately demanding, because of a 1,550-foot elevation loss and gain
Trail condition: Good, dusty, singletrack trail
Seasons: Apr through mid-Nov
Other trail users: Equestrians and hikers with dogs use this trail.
Land status: Giant Sequoia National Monument, Sequoia National Forest

Nearest towns: Ponderosa has a cafe and small store, but Springville is the nearest town with all amenities.
Fees and permits: None
Maps: Forest Service: *Sequoia National Forest* including Giant Sequoia National Monument. USGS 7.5-minute quads: Camp Nelson, Hockett Peak.
Trail contacts: Giant Sequoia National Monument, Sequoia National Forest, 1839 Newcomb St., Porterville, CA 93257; (559) 784-1500; www.fs.fed.us/r5/sequoia/gsnm.html

Finding the trailhead: Drive to Camp Nelson, about 30 miles from Porterville on CA 190. From the Camp Nelson turnoff, continue east on CA 190 9 miles to the junction with FR 21S50, on the left. Turn onto this road and drive north 0.5 mile to where a sign directs you right onto a dirt road, which immediately forks. Take the left (north) fork 0.2 mile farther to the unpaved parking area for the Freeman Creek Trail. Trailhead GPS: N36 07.807' / W118 32.393'

The Hike

A custom of travel boosters in the nineteenth century was to give every unusual tree or rock a name. In part this was to promote tourism, but it also appealed to the romantic Victorian imagination. Early California tourism left all the big trees at Calaveras, Wawona, and other celebrated groves not only with names but with signposts proclaiming those names. The Freeman Creek Grove missed this wave of tourism, just as it avoided the logging boom that decimated the once-sprawling Converse Grove. Today it is the largest pristine grove outside of a national park, and even though a road now leads to one corner of it, most of the grove's 1,425 acres are accessible only by walking.

That doesn't mean that individual trees haven't been named. A quick search of the literature turns up such old chestnuts of the Big Tree naming circuit as the Telescope Tree and the Ride-Through Tree, as well as the more distinctive Freeman Shaft, Goshawk Tree, President George H. W. Bush Tree, Loren's Tree, and the Freeman Stub. With the exception of the President Bush Tree, however, these trees are not labeled with signs. Each one's identity will be a mystery to anyone who visits without a guided tour. Hikers on the Freeman Creek Trail consequently have the pleasure not only of seeing the great trees in their natural state, but also of "discovering" them.

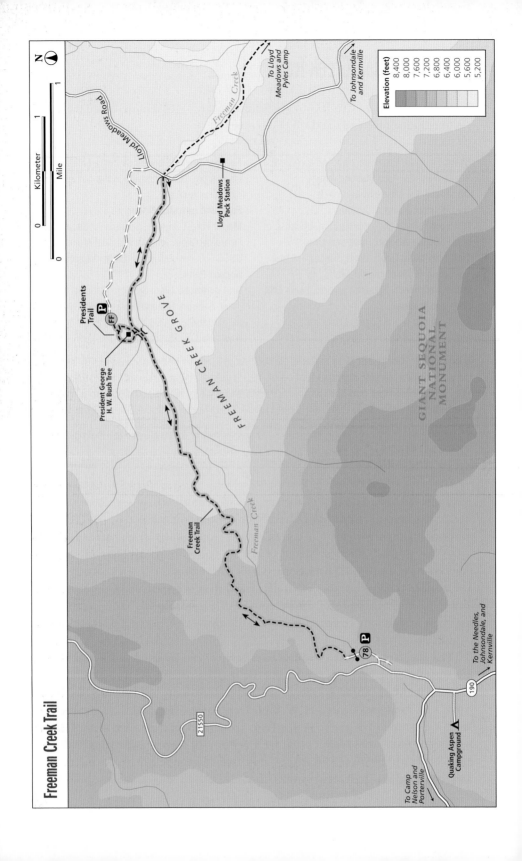
Freeman Creek Trail

Elevation (feet)
8,400
8,000
7,600
7,200
6,800
6,400
6,000
5,600
5,200

N

Kilometer
Mile

Lloyd Meadows Road

Freeman Creek

To Lloyd
Meadows and
Pyles Camp

To Johnsondale
and Kernville

Lloyd Meadows
Pack Station

Presidents
Trail

FF

President George
H. W. Bush Tree

FREEMAN CREEK GROVE

Freeman
Creek Trail

Freeman Creek

Freeman Creek

GIANT SEQUOIA
NATIONAL
MONUMENT

21S50

78

To the Needles,
Johnsondale, and
Kernville

190

Quaking Aspen
Campground

To Camp
Nelson and
Porterville

Along Freeman Creek grows the largest pristine grove of giant sequoias outside a national park.

And with more than a hundred trees greater than 15 feet in diameter, this impressive grove is well worth the discovery.

That is why, even though hikers can drive the very long road to the bottom of the grove near the Presidents Trail, you find some of us getting out of our vehicles up near 7,100 feet on the Great Western Divide, ready and willing to hike down to the 5,600-foot level and then back uphill again.

Straightforward and well maintained, the trail meets the first giant sequoias well within the first mile, and doles them out in generous helpings all along the way. Handsome, dignified, and well proportioned amid other large conifers and robust foliage, they are more majestic in this setting than when you find them fenced and surrounded by shutterbugs. Our trail also treats us to views of castellated Hermit Rock (8,465 feet), on a ridge 2.5 miles to the north.

The trail descends the ravine of Freeman Creek, which flows east into the broad, deep valley of the Kern River. After some switchbacks down the steepest slope, the gradient relaxes, and we enter the thickest part of the grove. Crossing a bridged feeder branch of Freeman Creek, we catch a glimpse of the President Bush Tree to the north, just beyond a trail junction marked by cut logs and a vertical slat sign. The Freeman

Creek Trail continues straight (east), but if you step between the logs to read the plaque in front of the Bush Tree, you will find yourself momentarily on the tamped-gravel Presidents Trail loop (Hike FF).

This part of the Freeman Creek Grove contains probably the youngest, and certainly the eastern-most, of all the giant sequoias in the Sierra Nevada. As the trail pushes eastward, the ground grows drier, flat and sandy, and a number of Forest Service trails and use-trails cross it, but ours remains the most prominent, obvious track. The paved Lloyd Meadows Road, adjacent to the Freeman Creek Bridge, makes a convenient landmark for a turnaround point, although the old trail crosses the road and continues 4.8 miles farther down to Forks of the Kern, and thence deeper into Golden Trout Wilderness.

Miles and Directions

- **0.0** Parking area.
- **1.0** Ford of small tributary.
- **3.3** Small bridge over small tributary of Freeman Creek.
- **3.4** View of President George H. W. Bush Tree at junction with Presidents Trail (GPS: N36 08.860/W118 30.449); keep straight (east).
- **4.3** Lloyd Meadows Road (GPS: N36 08.785/W118 29.455).
- **8.6** Arrive back at the parking area.

79 Needles Lookout

Until it burned in 2011, this fire tower provided one of the most thrilling hikes of the southern Sierra. Climbing a granite pinnacle on airy stairways and catwalk, hikers are treated to views overlooking the vast expanse of the Kern River drainage, even without the tower. By fall of 2014, the Forest Service plans to rebuild the tower on its original site, with the same spectacular "look and feel" as the original.

Start: Needle Rock parking area
Distance: 4.6 miles out and back
Hiking time: About 2-3 hours
Difficulty: Moderate, with an overall elevation gain and loss of about 500 feet
Seasons: May-Oct; check opening days and times with the Forest Service after the new tower opens.
Trail condition: Good singletrack trail. The metal stairway, at press time gated part-way up, is fenced and safe, but anyone afraid of heights may want to avoid it.
Other trail users: Equestrians and mountain bikers use the dirt trail, and dogs are welcome if under control.
Land status: Giant Sequoia National Monument, Sequoia National Forest
Nearest towns: Ponderosa has a small store, gasoline, cabins, and a cafe, but Porterville is the nearest large town.

Fees and permits: None
Maps: Forest Service: *Sequoia National Forest* including Giant Sequoia National Monument. USGS 7.5-minute quads: Sentinel Peak, Durrwood Creek.
Trail contacts: Giant Sequoia National Monument, Sequoia National Forest, 1839 Newcomb St., Porterville, CA 93257; (559) 784-1500; www.fs.fed.us/r5/sequoia/gsnm .html
Special considerations: Although the fire lookout burned in 2011, at press time the Forest Service hopes to rebuild by Fall 2014. Do not climb on the metal steps during lightning storms. No restroom or water is or ever will be available for visitors at the lookout.

Finding the trailhead: From the Western Divide Highway (CA 190) in Giant Sequoia National Monument, turn east at the signed junction of unpaved Needles Road (FR 21S05) and drive 2.8 miles to the parking area; this can be a very rough road, and it is unsuitable for low-clearance vehicles. The Needles Road junction is 0.7 mile south of the signed turnoff to Quaking Aspen Campground, or about 1 mile north of Ponderosa Lodge. (Do not make the easy mistake of taking Needlerock Road, which is south of Ponderosa.) Trailhead GPS: N36 07.195' / W118 30.502'

The Hike

The hike to this astonishing fire lookout—and especially the exhilarating climb up its spindly-looking stairway to the tip of its granite spire—was always great fun. Views from the top encompassed a vast extent of the Kern Plateau and Golden Trout Wilderness, clear to mountains along the boundary of Sequoia National Park. The station was staffed during the summer fire season, but you could visit the lookout even when

The Needles are every bit as spectacular when seen from below, as they are when seen from above, but less intimidating.

it was unstaffed. Even with the actual structure burned, it is still a worthwhile hike for the views of the Needles. Carry your own drinking water, as none is available anywhere along the trail.

Leaving from the northeast corner of the parking area (elevation 7,750 feet), our wide trail contours through conifers, manzanita, and chinquapin along the steep north side of Needles Ridge. The broad canyon of the Kern River gapes beyond the trees. Meeting the ridgetop in a timbered saddle, we zigzag eastward up the next rise. Before reaching this next summit, however, we cut left (north) and again contour around the hill to its eastern side. From this high point, we catch views of the precipitous dome where Needles Lookout stood, rising from the next and climactic high spot on Needles Ridge.

After descending to the next saddle—a spacious, flat, wooded piece of ground—we launch into our last series of switchbacks, mounting this final hillside through scrubby vegetation. Spurred by the proximity of looming granite slabs, we arrive in short order at the foot of the first flight of stairway to the Needles Lookout; we cannot see the summit from this point. The stairway, a metal frame with wooden steps, is fenced on the sides with wire mesh to prevent children and clumsy folks from slipping

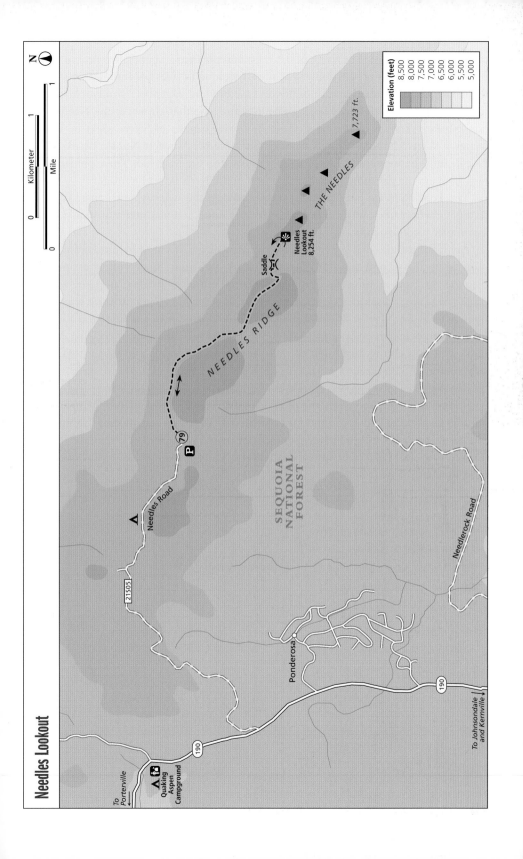

Needles Lookout

Elevation (feet)
8,500
8,000
7,500
7,000
6,500
6,000
5,500
5,000

N

0 Kilometer 1
0 Mile 1

THE NEEDLES

▲ 7,723 ft.

Saddle

NEEDLES RIDGE

Needles Lookout
8,254 ft.

79

P

Needles Road

21S05

SEQUOIA
NATIONAL
FOREST

Ponderosa

Needlerock Road

190

To Johnsondale
and Kernville

To
Porterville

Quaking Aspen
Campground

190

underneath the railings. The value of this precaution becomes abundantly clear as we mount this first flight up the dome's backside, watching its sides fall abruptly away to the left, to the right, and beneath us. If you have brought a climbers' handbook, you can identify some of the neighboring granitic spires together known as the Needles, but singularly known to climbers (those inveterate namers of Sierra rock) by the names of Wizard Needle, Warlock Needle, Witch Needle, Sorcerer Needle, Charlatan Needle, and Voodoo Dome. The lookout itself sat atop the Magician. These pinnacles rank high among the most challenging climbs of the Kern River Drainage.

The Forest Service has placed a gate partway up the stairway, restricting access to the higher portions, so I can only describe the route as it was, and as it should be again, after reconstruction:

Arriving atop the first spire, we cross its narrow crest of pitted granite, and then clamber up the second and third flights of stairs, each more spectacularly exposed than the last. Surmounting the third flight, we find ourselves standing atop one pinnacle gazing across a severely exposed crevasse to another, higher granite spire, whereupon perches the Needles Lookout itself, a frail-looking boxlike building protruding higher even than that apex of rock. Crossing the crevasse on a spindly-looking catwalk, we climb up the final flight of well-ventilated steps to the airy tower itself, at an elevation of 8,254 feet.

The tower and its approach stairways are sturdier than they appear from a distance. They have to be sturdy to withstand the storms that periodically slam into them, with winds unbroken by higher ground for miles around. Views are sensational. The sheer southern face of our spire falls away beneath our boots for more than a thousand feet. To the east, nearly 3,700 feet below us, the Kern River flows unheard at the bottom of its immense canyon.

Miles and Directions

- **0.0** Parking area (pit toilet available).
- **2.2** Base of metal stairway.
- **2.3** Turn around at a gate below the site of Needles Lookout.
- **4.6** Arrive back at parking area.

80 Johnsondale Bridge Hike

Johnsondale Bridge marks the southern edge of the largest roadless area in the Sierra Nevada. Prospects for backpackers are legion, even epic; but with an easy gradient and fine views of the Kern Canyon, this is a fun and rewarding trail even for a stroll of an hour or two.

Start: Johnsondale Bridge
Distance: 4.0 miles out and back
Hiking time: About 2 hours
Difficulty: Easy, with scant elevation gain or loss
Trail condition: Good singletrack trail
Seasons: Year-round, but Oct–May are prime
Other trail users: Dogs, equestrians, and bikes are allowed to use this trail.
Land status: Sequoia National Forest
Nearest town: Kernville

Fees and permits: Campfire permit required if pertinent
Maps: Forest Service: *Sequoia National Forest* including Giant Sequoia National Monument. USGS 7.5-minute quads: Fairview, Durrwood Creek.
Trail contacts: Sequoia National Forest, Cannell Meadow Ranger District, 105 Whitney Rd., Kernville, CA 93238; (760) 376-3781; www.fs .usda.gov/sequoia

Finding the trailhead: From Kernville, drive north on Sierra Way (CR SM99) about 20 miles to the Johnsondale Bridge. There is a large parking area on the west side of the bridge, at an elevation of about 3,760 feet. Trailhead GPS: N35 58.137' / W118 29.229'

The Hike

The old one-lane road to Kernville still crosses above the Kern River on its high steel bridge, parallel to the contemporary two-lane highway bridge. Even people who have no intention to hike will enjoy the view from the old bridge: of the deep, green river; the patient anglers; the rafters preparing to launch; and the receding canyon of the Kern River, which comes rolling down from its headwaters on the Kings-Kern Divide, some 58 river miles to the north.

We can also see our trail, a heavy-duty singletrack affair gouged through the crumbly metamorphic rock that forms the 800- to 900-foot-deep walls of this upper canyon. Descend the stairway on the eastern anchorage of the bridge, and head upstream past the Forest Service bulletin board. The slopes slip steeply to the Kern's green pools and white rapids. Keep an eye out for poison oak. Also, take time to enjoy the handsome views backward to the deck arch span of Johnsondale Bridge, and beyond that to the 2,000-foot-deep section of canyon where South Creek meets the Kern River. In fall the brilliant red blooms of the California hummingbird plant enliven the dry trailside.

After crossing over some mildly exposed rock ledges, the trail enters its woodsy phase. Oaks and pines close in; granite boulders make their appearance. We pass some

After descending on a stairway, the Johnsondale Bridge Trail turns upriver and follows the Kern River through its canyon.

campsites by the river—choice, except for their proximity to the road head. Before we hit our first mile, an old track that has been following us above the opposite bank ends suddenly at the open mouth of an old mine.

Beyond this point, harder walls of granite confine the gorge at the bottom of a much tighter V. The lower walls have been buffed and polished by the river to a rare state of smoothness. Many granite boulders and slabs along this stretch invite you to sit and enjoy a landscape that puts some in mind of the Merced Gorge above El Portal and below Yosemite.

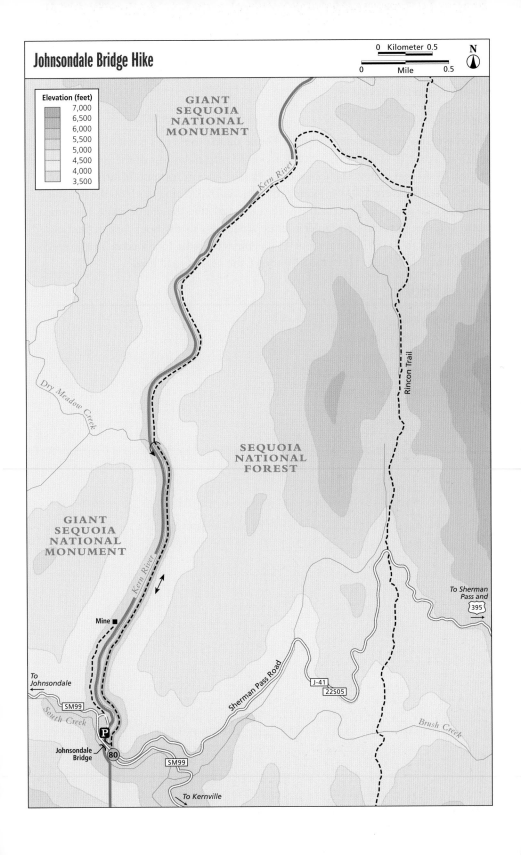

Johnsondale Bridge Hike

Elevation (feet)
7,000
6,500
6,000
5,500
5,000
4,500
4,000
3,500

0   Kilometer   0.5

0   Mile   0.5

N

GIANT
SEQUOIA
NATIONAL
MONUMENT

Kern River

Rincon Trail

Dry Meadow Creek

SEQUOIA
NATIONAL
FOREST

GIANT
SEQUOIA
NATIONAL
MONUMENT

Kern River

To Sherman
Pass and
395

Mine ■

To
Johnsondale

SM99

South Creek

Sherman Pass Road

J-41
22S05

Brush Creek

P

Johnsondale
Bridge

80

SM99

To Kernville

The turnaround point is up to you, but for the sake of a landmark, I chose the mouth of Dry Meadow Creek, which enters the Kern on the opposite bank 2 miles above Johnsondale Bridge.

Options

Hikers with an extra vehicle can hike a 7-mile shuttle route to a point on the Sherman Pass Road (J-41 and FR 22SO5), about 10 road miles east of the Johnsondale Bridge. To do that, follow the Johnsondale Bridge hike north until it turns east and climbs out of the Kern Canyon, joining the Rincon Trail. Going south on the Rincon Trail will take you to the Sherman Pass Road, completing the shuttle route. Heading north will take you through Golden Trout Wilderness to the boundary of Sequoia National Park in Kern Canyon, about 41 trail miles from the Johnsondale Bridge and some 20 trail miles from Horseshoe Meadows, the nearest road head.

Miles and Directions

- **0.0** Parking area.
- **0.1** Base of stairway on bridge.
- **0.8** View of mine across river.
- **2.0** Point opposite Dry Meadow Creek.
- **4.0** Arrive back at parking area.

81 Remington Ridge Trail to Lightner Peak

This hardy hike is best saved for off-season, when you can enjoy the distant views of the snowy high country, as well as the green, steep, rugged slopes of the lower ranges that surround Lightner Peak.

Start: Kern Canyon Road
Distance: 12.4 miles out and back
Hiking time: About 7 hours
Difficulty: Strenuous, with a 4,000-foot gain and loss in elevation
Trail condition: Dusty, occasionally steep, singletrack trail. Steep sections are rutted by bikes.
Seasons: Spring and fall are best to avoid snow and heat. Winter can be good on the lower slopes.
Other trail users: Equestrians, hikers with dogs, and mountain bikers all use this trail.

Land status: Sequoia National Forest, BLM
Nearest towns: Bodfish and Lake Isabella have all amenities.
Fees and permits: None
Maps: Forest Service: *Sequoia National Forest*. USGS 7.5-minute quads: Miracle Hot Springs, Breckenridge Mountain.
Trail contacts: Sequoia National Forest, Kern River Ranger District, 105 Whitney Rd., Kernville, CA 93238; (760) 376-3781; www.fs.usda.gov/recarea/sequoia/recarea.?recid=79571

Finding the trailhead: Take the Borel Road exit from California Highway 178, about 3.8 miles below its junction with CA 155, near Lake Isabella. Drive south, uphill on Borel 0.25 mile to the junction of Kern Canyon Road. Turn right (west) and drive 3.3 miles west to the signed trailhead on the left (south) side of the road. Park in one of the spacious turnouts, at an elevation just under 2,500 feet. Trailhead GPS: N35 34.541/W118 33.174.

The Hike

Squatting about midway along Hobo Ridge, Lightner Peak does not cut a particularly striking profile. The vistas from it are obscured by rocks and trees, and its 6,430-foot height makes it just another bump on the flanks of Breckenridge Mountain. The trail itself supplies all of the best views, as well as the good hiking that is its own justification.

Heading right (west) at the signposted trailhead on Kern Canyon Road, our trail climbs its first grassy ridge on several long switchbacks, a stately progression through oaks and boulders. Spur paths keep straying, but if you stick to the most obvious trail, you'll be fine. The roar of the freeway (CA 178) down the lower Kern Canyon fades as we surmount the first ridge at slightly over 2 miles.

Now we make a brief dip into a dry valley, set against the backdrop of our next ridge, which is clearly higher, steeper, and more rugged than the first. On the bottom of this shallow valley, we meet a primitive corral beside some motley oaks and Spanish bayonet. This rustic construction looks so decrepit, so redolent of old California,

The first 2 miles of the Remington Ridge Trail climb through oak woodland, with views down into the lower Kern River Canyon.

that one half-expects Zorro to come riding down the adjacent dirt track. That same track begins to climb our ridge but soon braids into separate paths; take the one that's signposted. Now climbing steeply, we pass some cactus and buckeye growing together on a rocky knoll.

In winter and early spring, the grass is green and the stalks of yucca bloom creamy white. In autumn the grass is tawny colored and the prevailing chaparral a motley drab, except for those slopes covered in mountain mahogany, which are then so laden with silken white tassels that they appear, when backlit, to be covered in rime frost. Coveys of quail, flushed from the brush by passing hikers, dart frantically for new cover.

As our trail tops the corner of the second ridge, we enter a scrubby forest of Piute cypress (a rare tree, related to the juniper), and broad views open up in new directions. The wooded summit of Lightner Peak rises toward the south on the back of Hobo Ridge. The big canyon to the east is Clear Creek, and beyond that are the Piute Mountains. Clear Creek was the site of a gold rush in the 1860s. Some 3,000 miners soon established a town, Havilah, which became the new seat of Kern County. Though it thrived for a decade, the gold faded, and Havilah declined. The richest

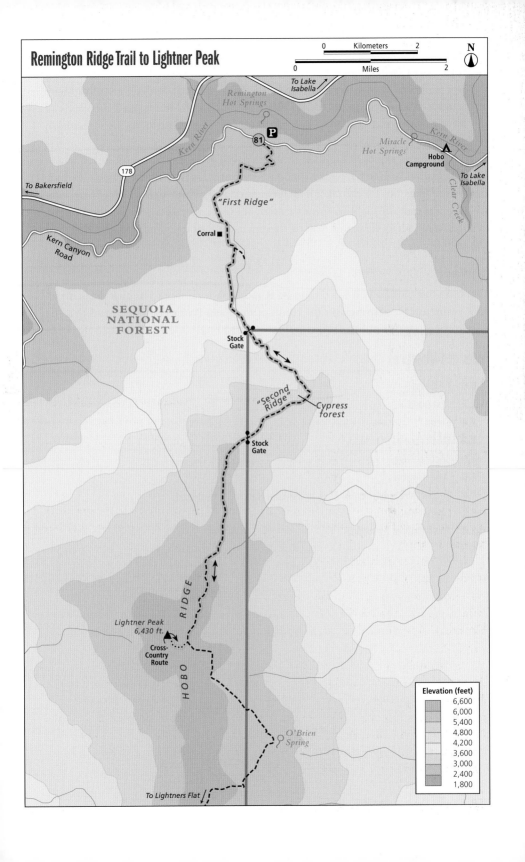

Remington Ridge Trail to Lightner Peak

0 — Kilometers — 2
0 — Miles — 2

N

To Lake Isabella

Remington Hot Springs

Kern River

P
81

Miracle Hot Springs

Kern River

Hobo Campground

To Lake Isabella

To Bakersfield

178

Clear Creek

"First Ridge"

Kern Canyon Road

Corral ■

SEQUOIA NATIONAL FOREST

Stock Gate

"Second Ridge"

Cypress forest

Stock Gate

HOBO RIDGE

Lightner Peak 6,430 ft.

Cross-Country Route

O'Brien Spring

To Lightners Flat

Elevation (feet)

	6,600
	6,000
	5,400
	4,800
	4,200
	3,600
	3,000
	2,400
	1,800

prospects filled the canyons on the side of the mountain where we now stand, the eastern flank of Hobo Ridge and Lightner Peak.

Our trail now swings westward, up to the back of Hobo Ridge. Views from here are at their best, reaching northeast over Lake Isabella to the rugged highlands of the Kern Plateau, and northwest beyond the lower Kern Canyon to the Greenhorn Mountains.

On the lower slopes of Lightner Peak, chaparral gives way to an oak forest, which turns yellow and red in fall before shedding its leaves. By now the best views are hidden by the trees, but for the sake of finality, after having come so far, a hiker may want to leave the trail on Lightner Peak's eastern shoulder to take a stab for the summit. A short, steep scramble brings you to the thick stand of trees and boulders that caps the high point.

Option

Opposite our trailhead on Kern Canyon Road, look for a short path that drops down to Remington Hot Springs, on the banks of the Kern River. Although primitive, the spring has a popular public following.

Miles and Directions

0.0 Trailhead.

2.2 First ridge.

2.4 Corral.

3.2 Stock gate to BLM land.

3.9 Second ridge.

4.0 Cypress grove.

4.4 Second stock gate; cross back to Sequoia National Forest land.

6.2 Lightner Peak.

12.4 Arrive back at trailhead.

Honorable Mentions

✕ Boyden Cavern

Although only 750 feet of this short hike actually happens underground, it is well worth your fee to see an example of a well-preserved Sierra cave. Tour guides lead visitors to examples of cave bacon and elaborate travertine features along walkways built during the Great Depression. The highlight is the undeveloped exit route along the creek, a narrow, twisting passage. The approach trail to the cave gate, though steep, is short and highly scenic in a wild way, with striking views to the Kings River and down the cliff-sided canyon. Contact: Giant Sequoia National Monument; www.fs .usda.gov/sequoia/. Trailhead GPS: N36 48.950' / W118 49.143'

Y Grant Grove

The General Grant tree is the world's second-largest living thing (second only to the General Sherman Tree, up the road in the Giant Forest), but the surrounding company of so many other giant sequoias really puts that gnarly old titan of tree in handsome perspective. One of the highlights of the short loop is the giant sequoia log with the trail laid out inside, end to end. It's one of the most memorable experiences

One of the highlights of the Grant Grove for kids (and adults) is the trail through the fallen sequoia log.

for children in the Sierra. Contact: Kings Canyon National Park; www.nps.gov/seki. Trailhead GPS: N36 44.821' / W118 58.384'

Z Muir Grove

Starting from the west end of Dorst Campground across the road from Group Site B, this easy 4.0-mile (round-trip) trail sets out from a forested sidehill above Dorst Creek. After crossing a seasonal feeder creek, we climb gently to a sunny little saddle, where we can spot the Muir Grove in profile at a distance, standing at ease atop the next ridge to the west. (The best view is from an obvious, low granite dome, reached by a short spur trail.) After another easygoing mile, puttering around the headwaters of the next ravine, the trail brings us back into the sun and face-to-face with the ancient outliers of the grove—great, strapping giants, positively flushed with vitality. The "usual suspects" found in most sequoia groves are all present here: the burned-out tree that you can walk through; the behemoth with a room for hide-and-seek; the fellow with the overdeveloped buttress; and, of course, the "monarch" of the grove—in this case, the Dalton Tree, one of the tallest of all sequoias. On the other hand, the most impressive thing about the Muir Grove really is the sense of solitude that comes from hiking to it, even if it's such a short distance from the road head. The turnoff to Dorst Campground is about 13 miles north of the Giant Forest Museum in Sequoia National Park on the Generals Highway. Contact: www.nps.gov/seki. Trailhead GPS: N36 38.070' / W118 48.966'

AA Moro Rock

Moro Rock provides one of the few points in the heavily forested western part of Sequoia National Park where you can gaze upon the spectacular Great Western Divide without hiking an hour or more. This granite dome rises so abruptly from the rim of Kaweah Canyon that from nearly every angle it looks unclimbable without technical gear. Not so, thanks to an exhilarating stairway built by the National Park Service in 1931, with iron handrails added two years later by the Civilian Conservation Corps. This marvelous stairway replaced a breezy wooden flight built in 1919, and is so unobtrusive that it was later entered on the National Register of Historic Places. Though spectacular, the path is safe for anyone who can negotiate steps—nearly 400 of them climbing about 300 vertical feet. The easy 0.3-mile route to the top makes imaginative use of the dome's natural clefts and shelves. Abrupt drop-offs are walled off with low parapets of cemented boulders, and benches are provided for resting and enjoying the stunning views. Our final stretch mounts the spine of the dome within a well-protected notch to the summit—a sheer, narrow, granite promontory. From behind protective railings, we can gaze down 4,000 feet to the Kaweah River, tracing its unglaciated V-shaped canyon westward into the San Joaquin Valley. Schematic maps identify the major summits and passes of the Great Western Divide, rising spectacularly to more than 12,000 feet at a distance of 12 miles, beeline, to the east.

Exposed Moro Rock and its steep stairway are not places to be in a lightning storm. If a storm threatens, stay away. Summer storms usually pass in a few minutes.

To get to Moro Rock from the Giant Forest Museum in Sequoia National Park, ride the free shuttle or drive 1 mile south on the Crescent Meadow Road from the Giant Forest Museum, turn right at the first junction, and follow the sign to the parking area another mile farther. Contact: Sequoia National Park; www.nps.gov/seki. Trailhead GPS: N36 32.815' / W118 45.928'

BB Tharps Log

By closing off one end of a fallen sequoia in the early 1860s, Hale Tharp made a roomy and serviceable cabin out of a single log. This easy 1.7-mile loop starts at

Crescent Meadow in the Giant Forest. Following the signposted, paved, wheelchair-accessible path to Log Meadow, we trace the edge of Crescent Meadow, buzzing with bees and bordered by the high-crowned columns of giant sequoias. Tharps Log lolls at the far end of Log Meadow, surrounded by ruddy-colored giant sequoias and a ground cover of chinquapin and ferns. The log itself is about 8 feet high at its walled-off entrance. Entering at the door, we find a fire-blackened hollow nearly 60 feet long, tapering to about 4 feet high at the far end. With a fireplace, hinged window, bed, table, and bench, it's as cozy as a hobbit house. John Muir, who stayed here for several days in 1875, described it as "sweet and fresh, weather proof, earthquake proof, likely to outlast the most durable stone castle, and commanding views of garden and grove grander far than the richest king ever enjoyed."

Return to the parking area via the north side of Crescent Meadow. The trail is dirt beyond Tharps Log, so wheelchair-bound travelers need to return the way they arrived.

To get to the Crescent Meadow trailhead, ride the shuttle or drive 1 mile south from the Giant Forest Museum on the narrow Crescent Meadow Road and turn left at the first junction, where a sign directs you toward Crescent Meadow, another 2 miles farther. Contact: Sequoia National Park; www.nps.gov/seki/index.htm. Trailhead GPS: N36 33.286' / W118 44.932'

CC   Nelson Trail

The Yaudanche Yokuts had a summer village here, but Milton Nelson's 1886 homestead was the start of the small resort community we know today as Camp Nelson. Once part of the Jordan Trail, which crossed the Sierra clear to the Owens Valley, the Nelson Trail follows the Middle Fork of the Tule River nearly 4 miles to CA 190 near Quaking Aspen Campground. Along the way, the McIntyre and Wheel Meadow groves crowd the narrow canyon bottom with giant sequoias. The many creek crossings might be tricky in spring. Camp Nelson is located on CA 190, about 30 miles east of Porterville. From the general store, drive 1.25 miles up paved Nelson Road, past Belknap Campground, to the last house of a small residential enclave, where you can park on an unpaved turnaround. Contact: Giant Sequoia National Monument, Sequoia National Forest, 1839 Newcomb St., Porterville, CA 93257; (559) 784-1500; www.fs.fed.us/r5/sequoia/gsnm.html. Trailhead GPS: N36 08.386' / W118 35.456'

DD   Dome Rock

This massive granite monolith along the Western Divide Highway (CA 190) makes an easy stroll: Just walk through the gate and follow the old road around to the top, a distance not more than a quarter mile. Your reward is a full view of the Needles to the north and a comprehensive vista over the broad Kern River Canyon, which was extensively burned in the McNally Fire of 2002. The face of the dome is a popular climbing wall, so take extreme care as you wander not to throw or kick anything over

The view from Dome Rock encompasses the Kern River, heavily burned by wildfire in 2002.

the edge. To get there from CA 190, turn east onto the signed, unpaved FR 21S70 (about 3.7 miles south of the entrance to Quaking Aspen Campground). Go left at the first junction, right at the second, and park in the dirt lot about 0.6 mile from the highway. Contact: Giant Sequoia National Monument, Sequoia National Forest, 1839 Newcomb St., Porterville, CA 93257; (559) 784-1500; www.fs.fed.us/r5/sequoia/gsnm.html. Parking area GPS: N36 04.069' / W118 31.933'

EE Trail of 100 Giants

Accessible for wheelchairs, this 1.0-mile self-guided loop trail is so flawlessly graded, paved with blacktop, and marked by interpretive signs that it feels more like a Lilliputian garden path than a track through wild woods. At an elevation of 6,150 feet, the grove is usually free of snow from May through October. A most marvelous sight is the Goose-Pen Tree, into which a fire has seared a narrow passage that curls around inside the tree to an interior room with a natural window. The passage is too small for many adults, but kids love it. Among the other 125 giants here are the Umbrella Tree, the False Bonsai, and the Quintet, a handsome grouping of five. (A tourist filmed two giant sequoia "twins" falling naturally onto this trail in September 2011, an incredible sight and sound that you can witness by searching "falling sequoia" on You Tube.) The trailhead parking area (fee) lies on the south side of CA 190 about 10 miles north of Johnsondale and 21 miles south of Camp Nelson. Contact: Giant Sequoia National Monument, Sequoia National Forest, 1839 Newcomb St., Porterville, CA 93257; (559) 784-1500; www.fs.fed.us/r5/sequoia/gsnm.html. Trailhead GPS: N35 58.614' / W118 35.777'

FF   Presidents Trail

Walkers who balk at the longer Freeman Creek Trail can cheat a little by driving to the Freeman Creek Grove of giant sequoias—a much longer road, but a much shorter walk. The trail, a 0.6-mile loop on packed sand, is smooth and well-graded for use with a wheelchair. Named for the senior President Bush on his 1992 visit (as a plaque notes), the Bush Tree is large, but by no means the largest tree of the Freeman Creek Grove. To see more of the giants, you would need to explore along the Freeman Creek Trail (Hike 78), which joins the Presidents Trail immediately south of the Bush Tree. From Kernville, drive north on the Kern River Highway about 25 miles, passing Johnsondale, to the paved Lloyd Meadows Road (Forest Road 22S82). Turn right and drive north 19 miles to the bridge across Freeman Creek. Just beyond, turn left onto an unpaved forest road and drive about 1 mile to the parking area. Contact: Giant Sequoia National Monument, Sequoia National Forest, 1839 Newcomb St., Porterville, CA 93257; (559) 784-1500; www.fs.fed.us/r5/sequoia/gsnm.html. Trailhead GPS: N36 08.970' / W118 30.350'

Eastern Sierra:
High Great Basin

The spectacular eastern face of the Sierra Nevada from the Nevada state line southward to the Volcanic Tableland, beyond Mammoth Lakes, juts up from high, rolling sage scrublands and piñon forests of the high Great Basin. Raked by strong winds and pocked by volcanism, this dramatic landscape has cold and snowy winters. Summer days can be hot, but evenings are typically cool. Mammoth Mountain, the 11,053-foot magnet for winter skiers and summer mountain bikers, is a volcano surrounded by many examples of volcanism—some ancient and extinct, and others very much alive. Among the more dramatic volcanic features are the geothermal fumaroles of Hot Creek in the Long Valley Caldera, the stark volcanic cones of Mono Craters on the shores of Mono Lake, and the famous basalt lava flow of Devils Postpile.

The region sparked frantic but short-lived silver and gold rushes in the nineteenth century. This is cattle country still, and large herds graze in the high country during summer. Many mining and ranching structures still survive in the canyons, valleys, and mountains of the Eastern Sierra, adding a colorful and historical burnish to many a hike.

Running north to south, US 395 connects the handful of population centers of Mono County with the rest of the state—tiny Coleville and Walker, the compact county seat of Bridgeport, handy Lee Vining on the shore of Mono Lake, the resort community of June Lakes, and the much larger year-round resort town of Mammoth Lakes. Snowplows keep US 395 open all year, but the only east–west routes across the Sierra Nevada into Mono County—Monitor Pass (CA 89), Sonora Pass (CA 108), and Tioga Pass (CA 120)—close from the first heavy snow of fall until late spring.

82 Snodgrass Creek to the Soda Cone

Aside from the obvious pleasure of hanging out with a creek called Snodgrass, the trailside views of rugged mountains, massive junipers, the Carson River canyon, broad, lush meadows, and a curious dome of white calcium capped by a bubbling spring are the real stars of this semiloop hike.

Start: Snodgrass Creek trailhead, Rodriguez Flat

Distance: 12.8 miles out and back

Hiking time: About 8 hours

Difficulty: Moderate overnighter or strenuous day hike

Trail condition: Decent singletrack trail mostly, but the detour to the top of the cone is off-trail. The ford and reford of Silver King Creek are tricky until late season.

Seasons: June–autumn; for fall colors, Sept–Oct is best

Other trail users: Equestrians, hikers with dogs permitted. Bikes prohibited. Hunters in fall.

Land status: Carson-Iceberg Wilderness, Humboldt-Toiyabe National Forest

Nearest towns: Gardnerville and Bridgeport have all amenities.

Fees and permits: None for day hikes. Wilderness permits are required for overnighters, and these double as campfire permits for stove or campfire; self-register at trailhead.

Maps: Forest Service: *Carson-Iceberg Wilderness.* USGS 7.5-minute quads: Coleville, Wolf Creek, Lost Cannon Peak.

Trail contacts: Humboldt-Toiyabe National Forest, Carson Ranger District Office, 1536 S. Carson St., Carson City, NV 89701; (775) 882-2766; www.fs.usda.gov/htnf

Finding the trailhead: From US 395, turn west onto Mill Canyon Road, about 7 miles south of the junction with CA 89 (Monitor Pass Road) and 16 miles from the junction with CA 108 (Sonora Pass Road). Proceed up the gorge 0.25 mile to a fork in the road. Turn right (west) on Golden Gate Road toward Rodriguez Flat. Driving on well-graded gravel, we cross Little Antelope Valley and start uphill, passing the stamp mill and ruins of the Golden Gate Mine. Ascending the mountainside on switchbacks, we ford a shallow creek twice. About 5.5 miles from US 395, we crest the ridge and arrive at a signed junction at Rodriguez Flat. Continue straight (west) a quarter mile to the next junction, where you take the right (west) fork and park just beyond, at the Snodgrass Creek trailhead. Trailhead GPS: N38 31.175' / W119 33.783'

The Hike

Starting from a high-country meadow, Snodgrass Creek and its namesake trail make for good companions on the jaunt down to Silver King Creek. The good cheer of its splashing carries to hikers' ears as they descend on the steady path through a forest that's green in summer and splotched with brilliant yellow in fall. Hitting the bottom at Silver King Creek, you will find a wide, sunlit bench for a large camp, though probably too sunny to enjoy on a warm day.

The obvious ford of Silver King Creek below the bench seems picked for horses and horse-drawn wagons, not humans afoot. You can find an easier ford a hundred

The summit of the Soda Cone looks like a thermal feature straight out of Yellowstone.

yards upstream, above where Snodgrass Creek flows into Silver King. At that point an island splits Silver King Creek, and a log reaches from the east shore to the island, leaving the other half of the creek much more manageable to ford.

Once across, our route heads initially upstream but soon turns with a vengeance toward the west, ascending a ridge on a gradient much steeper than what modern trail builders would design without switchbacks; I'll bet a cowboy on horseback built this trail. Relief comes as you near the top and the forest thins for the first time since the trailhead, opening up the beautiful country to more distant views of mountains and valleys. Closer at hand, large piles of rocks decorate the ridgetop, and sporadic, giant junipers corkscrew upward from their roots.

We bottom out in meadow with the unsavory name of Poison Flat. This is a clear reference to the high soda content of some streams in this area and rings like a harbinger of the Soda Cone to come. Turn right at the junction at the south end of the meadow, and follow the tree line northwest through mixed meadow and forest. We cross a barely perceptible divide and continue on through similar country with eyes peeled for some strange geological feature that warrants a name like Soda Cone.

That view does not arrive until a sudden change in the nature of the trail: as it begins to steepen dramatically, and the creek that's been growing slowly on the south

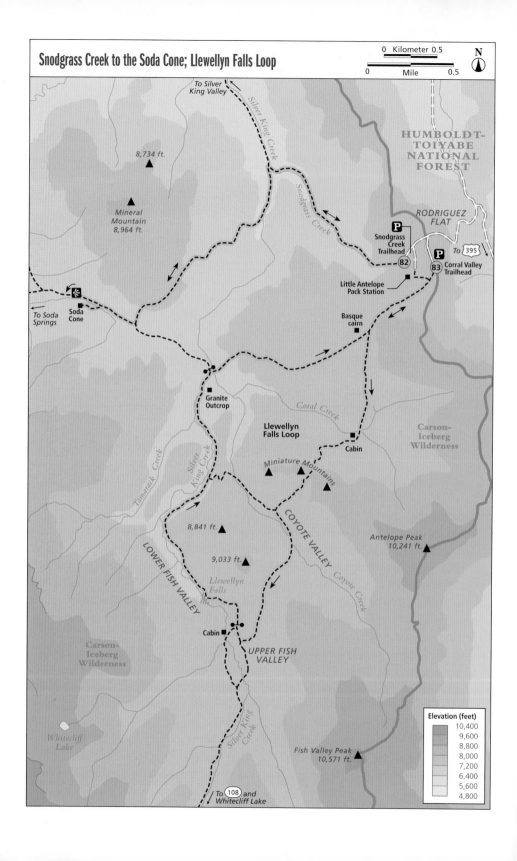

Snodgrass Creek to the Soda Cone; Llewellyn Falls Loop

0 Kilometer 0.5

0 Mile 0.5

N

To Silver
King Valley

Silver King Creek

Snodgrass Creek

8,734 ft.

Mineral
Mountain
8,964 ft.

HUMBOLDT-
TOIYABE
NATIONAL
FOREST

RODRIGUEZ
FLAT

P Snodgrass
Creek
Trailhead

82

To 395

P 83 Corral Valley
Trailhead

Little Antelope
Pack Station

To Soda
Springs

Soda
Cone

Basque
cairn

Coral Creek

Carson-
Iceberg
Wilderness

Granite
Outcrop

Llewellyn
Falls Loop

Cabin

Tamarack Creek

Silver King Creek

Miniature Mountains

COYOTE VALLEY

LOWER FISH VALLEY

8,841 ft.

9,033 ft.

Antelope Peak
10,241 ft.

Coyote Creek

Llewellyn
Falls

Cabin

UPPER FISH
VALLEY

Carson-
Iceberg
Wilderness

Whitecliff
Lake

Silver King Creek

Fish Valley Peak
10,571 ft.

Elevation (feet)
10,400
9,600
8,800
8,000
7,200
6,400
5,600
4,800

To 108 and
Whitecliff Lake

side of the meadow suddenly lurches downward, gouging out a substantially deep ravine. Meanwhile the vista to the west opens wider to embrace the canyon of the East Carson River. And then Soda Cone appears on the left, above the creek—an unmistakable hill-size, large, white dome. It's a startling sight, and you will be tempted to climb it, but don't climb it from this angle: The steep sides of the dome would be easily eroded.

Instead, after enjoying the sight of the dome in profile, backtrack about 0.1 mile to where the trail first started its sharper descent. As the valley begins to level out, look for a campsite on the right—a campsite with all the good things that a camper likes to have at hand: flat ground for a tent, large boulders for a table, shade trees, and a creek. At this point—though many nearby points will suffice if you don't identify the exact spot—step off the trail, cross the creek, climb to the low ridge, and follow that ridge (there is a use-trail) about 0.1 mile west. There you will encounter the top of Soda Cone, an even more startling sight than its profile. The summit of the dome is cracked open like the end of an egg, and there in the broken hollow bubbles a large blue pond of soda-charged spring water.

Miles and Directions

0.0 Snodgrass Creek trailhead.

2.6 Ford of Snodgrass Creek.

5.0 Junction with trail to Carson River; go right (west).

6.3 Trailside view point of Soda Cone; backtrack 0.1 mile to unnamed campsite.

6.4 From campsite, leave trail for short cross-country walk to Soda Cone.

6.5 Top of Soda Cone.

12.8 Arrive back at the trailhead.

83 Llewellyn Falls Loop

Undulating through a washboard-ridged corner of the Carson-Iceberg Wilderness, this loop hike traverses an exceptionally colorful palate of Eastern Sierra scenery, rich in wide-open vistas of meadow, sagebrush, and majestic mountains.

Start: Corral Valley trailhead, Rodriguez Flat
Distance: 13.2-mile lollipop loop
Hiking time: About 8 hours
Difficulty: Moderate overnighter or strenuous day hike with an overall gain and loss of 2,650 feet in elevation
Trail condition: Good singletrack trail. The two fords of Silver King Creek are tricky in early season.

Seasons: June–autumn; Sept–Oct best for fall colors
Other trail users: Equestrians and hikers with dogs permitted, but bikes are restricted. Hunters in fall.
For more information, see Hike 82

Finding the trailhead: From US 395, turn west onto Mill Canyon Road, about 7 miles south of the junction with CA 89 (Monitor Pass Road) and 16 miles from the junction with CA 108 (Sonora Pass Road). Proceed up the gorge 0.25 mile to a fork in the road. Turn right (west) on Golden Gate Road toward Rodriguez Flat. Driving on well-graded gravel, we cross Little Antelope Valley and start uphill, passing the stamp mill and ruins of the old Golden Gate Mine. Ascending the mountainside on switchbacks, we ford a shallow creek twice. About 5.5 miles from US 395, we crest the ridge and arrive at a signed junction at Rodriguez Flat. Our trail starts at the Corral Valley trailhead, to the left (south) 0.4 mile down a rocky, narrow, rough dirt road. Trailhead GPS: N38 31.014' / W119 33.401'

The Hike

What makes this route so special is not reaching the "goal" of Llewellyn Falls so much as enjoying its broader setting, the long approach and retreat over successive ridges, and the majestic views and ever-changing panoply of brilliant, varied Eastern Sierra landscapes. This hike is especially beautiful in autumn, when groves of quaking aspen are ablaze with yellow.

From the southwest edge of the Corral Valley trailhead parking area, at an elevation of 8,200 feet, our path almost immediately enters the Carson-Iceberg Wilderness. Here we meet a battery of signs informing us that fishing is not allowed in the drainages of Corral, Coyote, and Silver King Creeks above Llewellyn Falls—watersheds that we are now entering—to protect the world's only remaining native populations of Piute cutthroat trout. Passing a spur trail down to the stables, we make straight for the ridge crest through a forest of mostly lodgepole pine. Clearing the woods, we continue our ascent through sage, dwarfed aspens, and mule's ears, enjoying exalted views northwest to lush Silver King Valley and distant mountain ranges, and down to Rodriguez Flat below us. Almost all of what we see lies within the Carson River watershed, which drains east into the Great Basin.

Reaching a broad saddle covered with tawny sage-brush, views open westward toward the Sierra Crest. It's a landscape of strong horizontals, defined more by ridges than peaks, and by rolling sage flats more than valleys. Looking south to the next ridge—which we will shortly be crossing—we are particularly intrigued to see a grouping of odd, rocky "miniature mountains" protruding above the trees.

About the middle of our broad saddle, we reach a signed trail junction. To the right (west) we spy a surprising tower of rocks stacked about as high as a man can reach. This cairn was probably built by bored Basque sheepherders, who also get credit for many of the aspen carvings throughout the Sierra Nevada. Take a detour to investigate it if you like, but our path goes left at "Cairn" junction.

A bank of beautiful quaking aspens soon joins our stately descent into Corral Valley, broad and spacious cattle country, where dismantled fence lines attest to past grazing. After crossing the small creek on the valley floor, we find the ruins of a log cabin just inside the tree line.

Now we begin our day's second climb, gaining 500 feet of elevation to reach the high point of our trail, the 8,850-foot ridge between Corral and Coyote Valleys. This dry saddle is strangely beautiful. A castle-like prominence of granite rocks—one of those aforementioned "miniature mountains"—rears up now on our right

The large stacked rock monument along the Llewellan Falls Trail was apparently built by Basque sheepherders with time on their hands.

(west). A midget forest of scaly-barked, leathery-leafed mountain mahogany sprouts among weather-rounded boulders. Descending into the valley of Coyote Creek on switchbacks, we pass a gigantic Sierra juniper, the first of many of several feet in diameter along this trail. Bottoming out in the meadows of Coyote Valley, we step across its little creek and take a backward look at the jagged peaks that puncture the ridgetop.

Our third ridge, separating the Coyote Creek watershed from Fish Valley, entails less work than the second. After passing through an abandoned fence line near the top, we stop to admire Upper Fish Valley, sprawling under a vast sky uncrowded by the distant ridge that arcs between hatchet-faced Whitecliff Peak (10,833 feet) on the right (southwest), Wells Peak (10,833 feet) straight ahead (south), and Fish Valley Peak (10,571 feet) on the left (southeast). In autumn the groves of aspen lapping down the slopes toward the lush streamside pastures splotch the darker evergreens with yellow.

Walking down into Upper Fish Valley, we meet a junction on the edge of fenced meadows, beyond which we spy a patrol cabin in the woods. Turn right (north) and follow the Silver King Trail across the flat meadow and through a gate. (A spur trail departing near here leads across Silver King Creek and westward, but it is confused by a flurry of use-trails.) The sandy Silver King Trail now begins a gentle descent through pine forests, with the sound of Silver King Creek tumbling down its channel to the left (west). Decent campsites abound.

No sign points out Llewellyn Falls. To find it, look for the sign marking the boundary of the Piute Trout Management Area; a giant juniper stands nearby. At this point leave the trail and walk left (west) down the gravelly hill toward the noisy creek. You can hear the cascades about 100 yards upstream, where Silver King Creek makes an S-shaped descent through a shallow gorge banked by a weathered wall of orange-colored granite. It's very pretty but not significantly more so than a thousand other unnamed Sierra cascades.

Our return walk follows Silver King Creek downstream through narrowing canyons and stretches of forest alternating with meadows in Lower Fish Valley and Long Valley. Three miles below Llewellyn Falls, a low bluff of weathered granite deflects the creek, forcing our trail to cross to the other (west) side. This can be a hazardous ford when the water is running high. After crossing to the west bank, we follow the creek downstream for 0.2 mile to a gate near the junction to Poison Flat. Just beyond, we need to ford back across Silver King Creek to the east bank, near the confluence of Corral Valley Creek. From here the trail climbs steadily up through open sagebrush, 1,000 feet of elevation in about 2 miles. This can be hot going, but two massive trailside junipers (and a smaller one you can crouch under) provide welcome, shady rest stops. Regaining some fine, now-familiar views, we slowly level to the ridgetop and again meet the monumental rock cairn and its junction, where we keep straight (north) on the trail back to the Corral Valley trailhead.

Miles and Directions

0.0 Corral Valley trailhead.
0.1 Junction with trail to Little Antelope Pack Station; bear left (south) between the signs.
1.0 "Cairn" junction; bear left (south).
2.3 Corral Valley Creek ford.
3.2 Unnamed pass and high point.
4.3 Coyote Creek ford.
5.9 Upper Fish Valley junction; bear right (north).
6.7 Llewellyn Falls.
9.7 First ford of Silver King Creek.
9.9 Soda Springs junction; bear right (east) across second ford of Silver King Creek.
12.2 "Cairn" junction; bear left (north).
13.2 Arrive back at the trailhead.

84 Through the Roughs to Kirkwood Pass

From its long approach through majestic sagebrush flats to a mountain fastness behind a gateway gorge called "The Roughs," to its lofty climax vistas of Tower Peak and the Walker River country, this dramatic backpack route has the look and feel of an epic Western.

Start: Trailhead in Buckeye Campground
Distance: 22.4 miles out and back
Hiking time: 2 days or more recommended, with a camp above the Roughs
Difficulty: Strenuous, considering the distance and the elevation gain and loss of more than 2,880 feet, but unhurried backpackers can greatly moderate the exertion
Trail condition: Mostly singletrack trail, partly dirt road. With high water, the ford of Buckeye Creek may be difficult or impossible. The two junctions at the 3-mile mark and the main Buckeye Creek ford may require some scouting.
Seasons: June–Oct
Other trail users: Equestrians and dogs under firm control are welcome. Livestock graze alongside the trail. Mountain bikers use the dirt road but are excluded from Hoover Wilderness.

Land status: Hoover Wilderness and Humboldt-Toiyabe National Forest
Nearest town: Bridgeport
Fees and permits: Wilderness permit required for overnight use. Campfire permit required if using a stove or campfire. Bear canisters required.
Maps: Tom Harrison: *Hoover Wilderness.* National Geographic Trails Illustrated: *Yosemite NE.* USGS 7.5-minute quads: Twin Lakes, Buckeye Ridge, Tower Peak.
Trail contacts: Humboldt-Toiyabe National Forest, Bridgeport Ranger District, HC 62 Box 1000, Bridgeport, CA 93517; (760) 932-7070; www.fs.usda.gov/htnf

Finding the trailhead: From US 395 on the west end of Bridgeport, drive 7.2 miles on the Twin Lakes Road to the junction of Buckeye Road, by Doc and Al's Resort. Turn right and drive 2.8 miles on this unpaved road to the bridge across Buckeye Creek. Cross the bridge, turn left, and drive 0.6 mile to a second bridged crossing of Buckeye Creek. Around the next bend, you enter the campground on paved road. Keep straight, ignoring all turnoffs into the campground till you get to a single, small paring loop on the left (south) side of the road, about 0.5 mile from the last bridge. This is the parking area; it has a vault toilet and the signed trailhead. The elevation here is about 7,200 feet. Trailhead GPS: N38 14.142' / W119 20.888'

The Hike

There are many gorges like the Roughs in the Sierra Nevada, most of them unnamed. Why someone bothered to name the Roughs probably stems less from any outstanding roughness of the place than it does to history, and most likely has something to do with cattle ranching. After all, Buckeye Creek flows down into the grand ranching country of Bridgeport Valley, and herds still graze along its extensive summer pastures. The Roughs close off the upper end of those broad meadows.

The panorama of peaks along Buckeye Ridge cannot be seen from any road; they are reserved for hikers on the Buckeye Creek Trail.

The little path behind the signed trailhead takes you immediately back to the main campground road, where you turn left to a metal gate that marks a short stretch of private property. Do not loiter or stray. Go through the gate, shut it behind you, and follow it about 100 yards in a straight line to a second metal gate, where you cross back to Forest Service land.

Passing through a mixed forest cover of Jeffrey pine, sage, and aspen, our dusty dirt road soon begins to fade into more picturesque doubletrack. Rolling westward through now more distinct patchworks of aspen woodlot, sage flat, meadow, and forest, we sometimes meet grazing cattle. A nagging wind often blows through this country, but wind is so much a part of Great Basin life that visitors to the Eastern Sierra develop something almost like nostalgia for it.

As Buckeye Creek's valley bends around a corner at 2.5 miles, a grand panorama abruptly opens up—a column of peaks on the march down the south canyon wall, Buckeye Ridge, which we will follow clear through the Roughs.

But first, we must deal with an unmarked junction: Be alert for when our double-track enters a large, grassy (as opposed to sagebrush) meadow. As you enter, look to the left (south) for an unmarked singletrack path—that is our trail. It will become a very clear singletrack for the next mile, once you hit the trees on the south side of the meadow. (If you miss it, you'll know because the doubletrack fades into the increasingly wet meadow, adjacent to Buckeye Creek.)

Having safely found the singletrack trail just inside the forest on the southern edge of the meadow, we trace that meadow's edge westward for a mile, climbing to an elevated embankment with a majestic view of some rapids on Buckeye Creek as it races round a bend. Cutting down though mixed woodland and meadow, the trail braids and again peters out near the edge of Buckeye Creek. Assuming that water conditions permit, we will ford Buckeye Creek at this spot: a gravel-bottomed, quiet stretch on a quiet bend, with low turf banks. Looking to the opposite (northern) bank, you might even spot the post that marks where the trail resumes, but don't worry if you don't see it. Even if you were to ford in the wrong spot, you are still OK: Just walk northward, perpendicular to Buckeye Creek, and within 100 yards you will meet a dirt road running east–west, parallel to the creek. Turn left (south) and follow the road less than 100 yards to a stock gate, beyond which the road fades back into a singletrack trail. Go through the gate and close it behind you. The most confusing part of the trail has just ended.

From this gate to the beginning of the Roughs, a distance of nearly 3 miles, our route rolls right up the broad valley through undulating expanses of grass, sagebrush, and mule's ears, intermingled with conifer and aspen woods. We meet and hop across a sequence of four small creeks, the last in an aspen forest, and enter Hoover Wilderness. Emerging from the trees, we encounter a huge talus slide that has slammed into the middle of the valley, colliding there with a hard block of dark rock—the two massive heaps throwing a monkey wrench into a very freewheeling route, and forcing Buckeye Creek to pick its course down the rocks in a tumbling rush. At the head of the ravine, we can see a tributary waterfall pouring its own waters into the mix. This is the start of the Roughs.

Our trail passes over the Roughs on the north side, climbing first through the talus and surmounting a granite spur ridge that also tries to muscle into the fray. Frankly, the hiking trail through the Roughs is none too rough: We climb about 500 feet in elevation in 1 mile from the aspen-banked creek to the top of the granite spur ridge. Then we descend to the creek and follow it up inside its narrow granite gorge. None of this is taxing by Sierra standards, but you might think otherwise if you were driving a herd of cattle over it.

It sure is pretty, though. We get views of the glaciated U-shaped canyon ahead of us, with jagged profiles of Grouse and Center Mountains. We get close-ups of bright flower gardens sprouting from the granite-walled gorge, and of Buckeye Creek lulling through green dells against a forest backdrop. We know for sure that we are out of the Roughs when the canyon opens up into a broad, flat, forested valley, with plenty of room for campsites. This must have been some old mountain hunter's summer retreat, well watered and timbered, nestled snug below the high, barren ridges and mountains passes, yet secluded from below by the Roughs. There we meet a junction. One trail

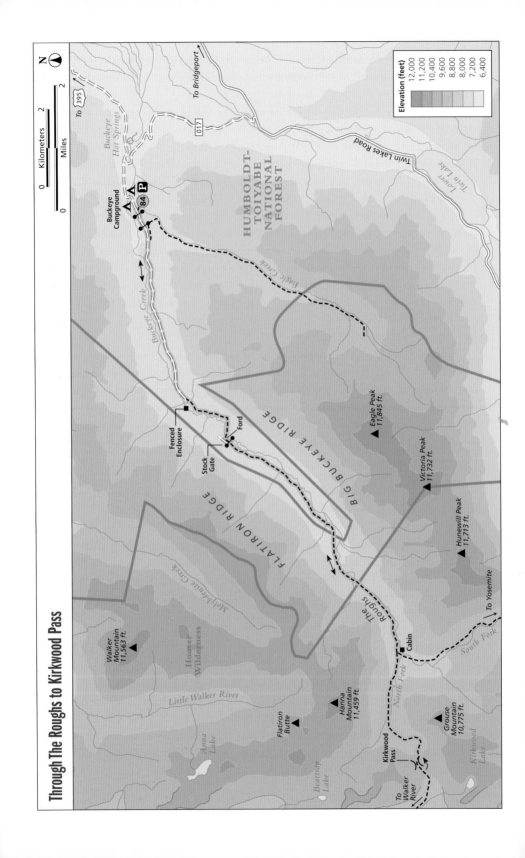

Through The Roughs to Kirkwood Pass

Elevation (feet)
12,000
11,200
10,400
9,600
8,800
8,000
7,200
6,400

To 395

To Bridgeport

017

Buckeye Hot Springs

Buckeye Campground

84

P

HUMBOLDT-
TOIYABE
NATIONAL
FOREST

Twin Lakes Road

Lower Twin Lake

Buckeye Creek

Eagle Creek

Eagle Peak
11,845 ft.

Victoria Peak
11,732 ft.

Hunewill Peak
11,713 ft.

BIG BUCKEYE RIDGE

FLATIRON RIDGE

Fenced Enclosure

Stock Gate

Ford

Molybdenite Creek

Hoover Wilderness

Walker Mountain
11,563 ft.

Little Walker River

Flatiron Butte

Hanna Mountain
11,459 ft.

The Roughs

North Fork

South Fork

Cabin

To Yosemite

Grouse Mountain
10,775 ft.

Kirkwood Pass

Kirkwood Lake

To Walker River

Beartrap Lake

Anna Lake

0   Kilometers   2

0   Miles   2

N

leads south over Buckeye Pass to Yosemite; if you walk just a few yards down the southbound trail, you will find a dilapidated log cabin, which is why I label this "Log Cabin junction" on the map.

The other trail goes west (right) to Walker River country, and this is our trail to Kirkwood Pass. After a brief meander through the wooded valley, the trail starts uphill adjacent to a small cascade of Buckeye Creek's North Fork; another cabin, now ruined, once stood above. As we climb, sometimes on switchbacks, the country quickly develops a more alpine feel, where forest, granite, and meadow interplay. We ford the North Fork of Buckeye Creek, bending south into the slot canyon that leads up to Kirkwood Pass. The final stretch breaks from the trees to a sudden, spectacular close-up vista of jagged Tower Peak, lording majestically over the lush, green canyons of the Walker River drainage. The boundary of Yosemite National Park starts on the ridge just half a mile south. Not many hikers come through here, probably because Kirkwood Pass is not labeled on the map, and yet the trail makes one of the most beautiful thoroughfares connecting the Sonora Pass Road with Yosemite. (The name of Kirkwood, itself, comes from the creek in the canyon just west of the pass and bears no connection to the more famous Kirkwood ski resort near Carson Pass.)

Miles and Directions

0.0   Trailhead parking area.

0.1   Go through metal gate.

0.3   Go through second metal gate.

0.4   Junction with Eagle Creek Trail; go straight (west).

2.5   "Grand panorama" of Buckeye Ridge.

3.0   Turn left (south) from dirt road onto unsigned singletrack trail at edge of meadow.

4.1   Ford of Buckeye Creek.

4.3   Stock gate.

6.7   Enter Hoover Wilderness.

6.9   Begin talus slope.

7.4   Cross creek above waterfall above the Roughs.

9.2   "Log cabin" junction; turn right (west).

10.2   Ford North Fork Buckeye Creek.

11.2   Kirkwood Pass.

22.4   Arrive back at the parking area.

Starting beneath the Sawtooth Ridge, the most stunning parapet of crags north of the Ritter Range, this trail breaches the Sierra's second-most-extensive roadless area, with stops along a string of exquisite lakes.

Start: Mono Village, Twin Lakes

Distance: 7.4 miles out and back for Barney Lake; 12.8 for Robinson Lake; 14.4 for Crown Lake

Hiking time: About 10 hours but 2 or more days are recommended

Difficulty: With 1,300 feet in elevation gained and then lost, Barney Lake is a moderate day hike. Robinson and Crown Lakes are strenuous, the latter gaining and losing more than 2,700 feet, and are more comfortable as overnighters.

Trail condition: Excellent, occasionally steep pack trail

Seasons: Late June through early Oct

Other trail users: Equestrians and hikers with dogs use the trail. No bikes are allowed in Yosemite or Hoover Wilderness.

Land status: Hoover Wilderness, Humboldt-Toiyabe National Forest

Nearest town: Bridgeport

Fees and permits: Wilderness permit required for overnighters. There's a fee to park overnight at Mono Village. Campfire permit required if using a stove or campfire.

Maps: Tom Harrison: *Hoover Wilderness. National Geographic Trails Illustrated: Yosemite NE.* USGS 7.5-minute quads: Buckeye Ridge, Matterhorn Peak.

Trail contacts: Humboldt-Toiyabe National Forest, Bridgeport Ranger District, HCR 1 Box 1000, Bridgeport, CA 93517; (760) 932-7070; www.fs.usda.gov/htnf

Finding the trailhead: From US 395 on the west end of Bridgeport, drive 13.5 miles on the Twin Lakes Road to the gate of Mono Village, on the west end of the upper lake. Go through the main entrance and turn hard left, driving past the cafe to the boat launch area. At the kiosk you must pay to park overnight near the marina.

Mono Village offers potable water, a store, cafe, lodging, toilets, and a campground, but it also presents a somewhat confusing gauntlet of roads and buildings for hikers seeking the trailhead. To be safe, inquire for the Barney Lake Trail at the kiosk. You will be directed west into the campground. After the campground ends, continue westward on a dirt road, passing around a cable gate that blocks public vehicular access. (Cable gate GPS: N38 08.818' / W119 22.926') After walking about 0.3 mile from the parking kiosk, you will meet a singletrack trail cutting west from the dirt road into the forest. This trailhead junction is signed BARNEY LAKE TRAIL. Trailhead GPS: N38 08.792' / W119 23.218'

The Hike

From the Barney Lake Trail junction (elevation 7,100 feet), the duff-covered forest path delves upstream, parallel to Robinson Creek, through dry forest of Jeffrey pine, juniper, cottonwood, and aspen, with spectacular views south to the glacier-carved crags and cirques of Sawtooth Ridge. Passing an informational display of Hoover Wilderness regulations, we begin to climb gently before we notch our first mile, crossing some small streams flowing from the northern ridges. As we climb, the conifers give way to even drier slopes of sagebrush, manzanita, mule's ears, mountain mahogany, rabbitbrush, and other scrubby plants, cobblestones, and boulders, interspersed with groves of aspen. Despite the heat and dust that pester late starters on this hike, this wide-open terrain offers some truly inspiring views of the mountains to the north, south, and west. Prominent among these, as we move up-canyon, are Hunewill and avalanche-carved Victoria Peaks to the north, and Kettle Peak (11,010 feet) to the south, above Little Slide Canyon.

We then commence a series of steep switchbacks up the canyon headwall, where dense clumps of aspen interweave with the montane chaparral. The dry slopes are occasionally watered by small creeklets, enriching the inventory of dry-slope wildflowers with more succulent riparian varieties. As the trail hooks south to follow the creek upstream, we ford a tributary that flows from Little Lake and the slopes of Hunewill Peak.

After mounting about 1,300 feet in elevation above our starting point at Twin Lakes, the trail levels in the forested approach to Barney Lake's northern shore. The view of the lake and its tree-lined beach, plunked down in a narrowing, glaciated gorge of granite, backed by mountains that rise between 2,000 and 3,000 feet above it, is quite striking. No camping is allowed.

Our trail climbs above the western shore over talus slopes, with fine views across the lake to the jagged spires of Kettle Peak. As we zigzag back down into Robinson Creek's inlet valley, crossing a tiny freshet not marked on USGS maps, we can look down to beaver ponds that have transformed forest into marsh. Descending briefly to cross Robinson Creek, we climb through lodgepole and red fir forest, recrossing Robinson Creek and promptly fording a tributary creek that flows from Peeler Lake. Now we begin a long series of steady but panoramic switchbacks up this tributary's canyon, climbing nearly 900 feet of elevation in 1 mile to a junction with the Peeler Lake Trail. Take the left (southeast) fork toward Crown Lake and Rock Island Pass.

Climbing more gradually over a small saddle, we drop slightly to the basin of Robinson Lakes and meet a rockslide of massive boulders, but cross through effortlessly on a rock-lined, crushed-gravel trail built by heroic trail builders. The first of the Robinson Lakes is a minute, rock-lined pool of exquisite clarity. The second is ringed by water grasses. The third and fourth alone reach sizes worthy to be called lakes. The trail passes between them, fording the creek that links them. There are good campsites both before and after the largest lake. Our final push takes us up Robinson Creek on switchbacks to Crown Lake, majestically reposing at the foot of ragged Crown Point (11,346 feet) on the west, and the massive buttress of Slide Mountain looming above its southern end. The lake is so narrowly confined by vertical granite walls that the best campsites lie below it along its outlet stream.

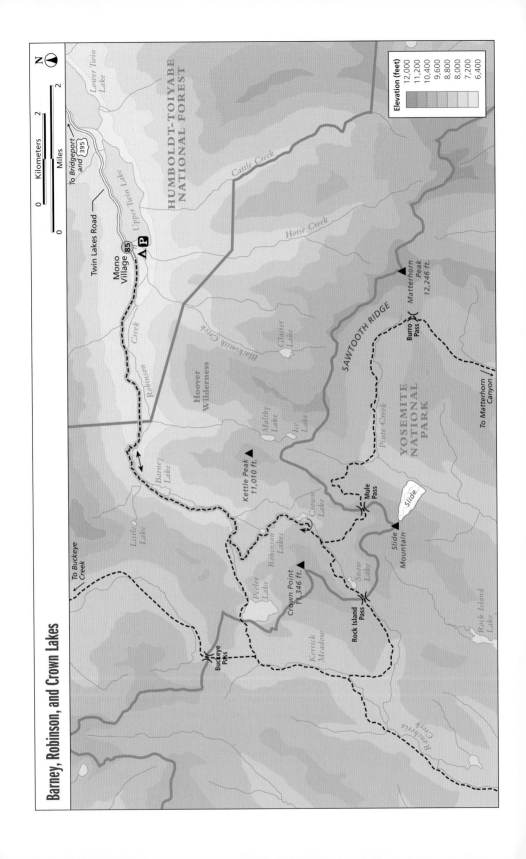

Barney, Robinson, and Crown Lakes

Elevation (feet)
12,000
11,200
10,400
9,600
8,800
8,000
7,200
6,400

N

0 Kilometers 2

0 Miles 2

To Bridgeport
and 395

Lower Twin
Lake

Upper Twin Lake

Twin Lakes Road

Mono
Village 85 ▲ P

HUMBOLDT-TOIYABE
NATIONAL FOREST

Cattle Creek

Horse Creek

Robinson Creek

Blacksmith Creek

Hoover
Wilderness

Glacier
Lake

SAWTOOTH RIDGE

Matterhorn
Peak
12,246 ft.

Burro
Pass

YOSEMITE
NATIONAL
PARK

To Matterhorn
Canyon

Barney
Lake

Kettle Peak
11,010 ft.

Maltby
Lake

Ice
Lake

Piute Creek

Mule Pass

Slide

To Buckeye
Creek

Little
Lake

Peeler
Lake

Robinson
Lakes

Crown
Lake

Snow
Lake

Slide
Mountain

Crown Point
11,346 ft.

Rock Island
Pass

Kerrick Meadow

Buckeye
Pass

Rancheria
Creek

Rock Island
Lake

Options

If you have a layover day at Crown Lake, take a rigorous day hike to see a natural marvel, Slide Canyon, in northern Yosemite. A hike of 4 miles one-way crosses Mule Pass into Yosemite National Park, where you can gain spectacular views of an enormous rockslide that fell from Slide Mountain in 1842, covering the canyon floor, burying Piute Creek, and even rolling a little way up the opposite wall of the canyon. Piute Creek flows underneath the talus. You can view the slide from the trail but will have to walk about a mile cross-country if you want to visit it.

Miles and Directions

0.0 Kiosk at parking area near marina. Follow campground and dirt road west.

0.3 Barney Lake trailhead. Leave the dirt road; go right (west) on the singletrack trail.

2.4 Hoover Wilderness boundary.

3.7 Barney Lake.

5.9 Peeler Lake junction; bear left (southwest).

6.4 Robinson Lakes.

7.2 Crown Lake.

14.4 Arrive back at parking area.

86 Virginia Lakes

Not many trails offer up such a profusion of alpine scenery in such a short jaunt as does this hike to a chain of High Sierra lakes.

Start: Big Virginia Lake
Distance: 3.0 miles out and back
Hiking time: About 2 hours
Difficulty: Moderate, with an overall gain and loss in elevation of about 560 feet
Trail condition: Good singletrack trail
Seasons: June through mid-Oct
Other trail users: Equestrians and dogs under owner's control are welcome. No bikes allowed.
Land status: Hoover Wilderness, Humboldt-Toiyabe National Forest
Nearest towns: Bridgeport or Lee Vining

Fees and permits: None for day hiking. If you plan to cross into Yosemite to camp, bear canisters are required.
Maps: Tom Harrison: *Hoover Wilderness. National Geographic Trails Illustrated: Yosemite NE.* USGS 7.5-minute quad: Dunderberg Peak.
Trail contacts: Humboldt-Toiyabe National Forest, Bridgeport Ranger District, HC 62 Box 1000, Bridgeport, CA 93517; (760) 932-7070; www.fs.usda.gov/htnf. Virginia Lakes Resort, HC 62 Box 1065, Bridgeport CA 93517-9602; (760) 647-6484; virginialakes resort.com.

Finding the trailhead: From Bridgeport, drive about 13 miles south on US 395 to Conway Summit, where you turn left (west) onto Virginia Lakes Road. (Conway Summit is about 12.5 miles north of Lee Vining on US 395.) Drive 6.25 miles to the end of Virginia Lakes Road, and park in the lot next to Big Virginia Lake. The trail starts behind the public restroom. Trailhead GPS: N38 02.877' / W119 15.813'

The Hike

Fed by a splashy cataract on its southern shore, Big Virginia Lake lies at an altitude of 9,805 feet, the second of a chain of lakes that sidle up a succession of glacier-carved terraces at the head of Virginia Creek canyon. The venerable Virginia Lakes Resort sits at the lowest level of the sequence, Little Virginia Lake. The goal of our route is to climb up the chain from Big Virginia to Blue, Cooney, and Frog Lakes.

We start by skirting the shore of Big Virginia Lake to the right (northwest), on one of its braided trails. Curving briefly east, our path joins with a larger trail, where we turn left (northwest) to walk up Virginia Creek, passing a marshy meadow and pond. At 0.5 mile we meet the outlet of Blue Lake, with a bracing view between the trees of jagged Dunderberg Peak (12,374 feet).

Now we launch into an uphill sweep around the talus headwall of Blue Lake, where the views really start to open up. Like Big Virginia Lake, Blue Lake also is fed by a cascade on its opposite shore, a classic feature of glacier-carved "staircase lakes" (known to geographers as "paternoster lakes" because they resemble a chain of rosary beads). Even more striking, Blue Lake cradles in the folds of metamorphic mountains so reddish and austere that they seem to forewarn of the impending Great Basin

This old cabin along the Virginia Lakes Trail is a reminder of one lone prospector who was still mining for gold here as late as the 1960s.

desert, which looms on the horizon, and where the waters of Virginia Creek are ultimately destined to sink.

There's nothing desertlike about our immediate surroundings, however. Climbing into a forest, we enter a willowy meadow and step across a creek that dashes down from unseen Moat Lake, sitting in a cirque below Dunderberg Peak and reached by an unmarked fishing trail that sneaks up from this meadow. After crossing another tiny, rock-lined creek, we approach a log cabin, propped up on one side, its roof covered in rocks. This cabin was occupied until the 1960s by a working gold miner named Cooney, still remembered down at the Virginia Lakes Resort for his love of pie.

In sight of its outlet stream pouring down from the next shelf, our trail mounts to the shore of Cooney Lake, its sunlit surface dazzling against the dark scree slopes of Black Mountain. Around the shore, lean rugs of meadow grasses, stunted pines, and short-cropped shrubbery attest to the hard winters and thin soils that give the alpine plant community its spare and stunning charisma.

Clambering up to the next shelf alongside Cooney Lake's inlet ravine, we cross the creek and arrive at Frog Lakes, clustered in a 10,370-foot glacial basin tucked against an arc of seemingly barren headwalls. Although this trail pushes westward across the boundary of Yosemite National Park, on the farthest ridge, hikers who go no farther than Frog Lakes can well appreciate, even in this short distance, how the

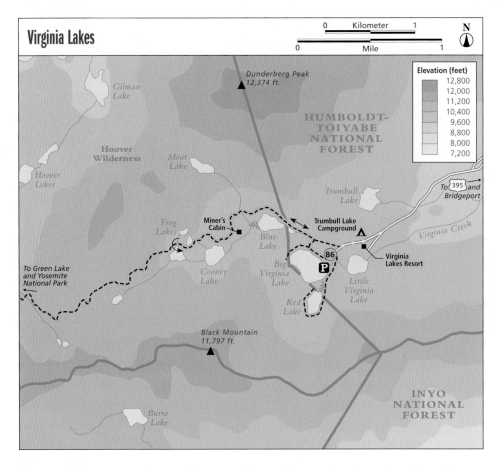

Virginia Lakes

change in life zones on the Sierra's eastern slope—from sagebrush scrub to the rocky alpine zone—is nothing short of marvelous.

Miles and Directions

0.0 Parking area.

0.2 Junction with main track; bear left (northwest).

0.5 Blue Lake; boundary of Hoover Wilderness.

0.8 Cross creek from Moat Lake.

1.0 Miner's cabin.

1.2 Cooney Lake.

1.4 First Frog Lake.

1.5 Turnaround point at last Frog Lake.

3.0 Arrive back at the parking area.

Local Attraction

Bodie State Historic Park; (760) 647-6445; www.parks.ca.gov/?page_id=509

87 Lundy to Lake Canyon

The remarkable old road to the May Lundy Mine now serves only as a footpath for hikers to explore the austere alpine scenery of Lake Canyon and the remains of one of the Eastern Sierra's more remote mining settlements.

Start: Lundy Lake
Distance: 6.8 miles out and back
Hiking time: About 4-5 hours
Difficulty: Moderately strenuous, with a gain and loss of about 1,900 feet in elevation
Trail condition: A steep, wide, old wagon road
Seasons: Late May through Oct
Other trail users: Equestrians and hikers with dogs. No bikes allowed in the Hoover Wilderness.

Land status: Hoover Wilderness, Inyo National Forest
Nearest town: Lee Vining
Fees and permits: None
Maps: Tom Harrison: *Hoover Wilderness*. USGS 7.5-minute quads: Lundy, Mt. Dana.
Trail contacts: Inyo National Forest, Mono Basin Scenic Area Visitor Center, US 395, Lee Vining, CA 93541; (760) 647-3044; www.fs .usda.gov/inyo

Finding the trailhead: From the Mono Basin Scenic Area Visitor Center north of Lee Vining, drive 6.4 miles north on US 395 and turn left (west) onto the Lundy Canyon Road. Drive 3.6 miles up the canyon to Lundy Dam Road, a bumpy dirt road that forks to the left. Drive 0.3 mile up this dirt road to the parking area by the dam. Trailhead GPS: N38 01.873' / W119 13.173'

The Hike

Lake Canyon is a hanging glacial valley that opens high on the southern wall of Lundy Canyon. After William Wasson discovered gold there in 1879, a boomtown ore-milling and transshipment center sprang up at the present site of the Lundy Resort at the west end of Lundy Lake, near a sawmill operated by local namesake, William Lundy. Mr. Lundy himself soon staked claim to a rich vein on the side of Mount Scowden, above Lake Canyon, which he developed and named after his daughter, May. In spite of its remote, forbidding location, the May Lundy Mine operated even through the long, bitter Sierra winters, producing $837,000 of gold from 1879 to 1888.

Our trail leaves from the south side of the dam on Lundy Lake, at an elevation of about 7,800 feet. After a short stretch along the shore through an aspen grove that turns flaming yellow in autumn, the trail cranks up to a steady, steep, and straight diagonal through a scrubby growth of currant, bitterbrush, and sage on Lundy Canyon's southern wall. Built in 1881 as a toll road to the May Lundy Mine, this path once provoked torrents of cusses from teamsters driving ore wagons down to the mills in Lundy Canyon. It is comparatively quiet these days. A little more than midway up this first diagonal of trail, we pass a hard-to-find, unsigned junction with a lateral shortcut to old Lundy, now a fishing resort.

The large ponds that we can see upstream from the resort were flooded by beaver dams on Mill Creek. Looming more than 3,000 feet above the surface of Lundy Lake,

Steep-walled Lundy Canyon has seen its share of avalanches in history.

the reddish, barbaric-looking metamorphic crags are severely eroded with avalanche chutes and bedecked with acres of rockslides on their lower slopes. Even higher above the head of Lundy Canyon, lighter-colored peaks of intrusive granite have pushed their way above these ruddy mountains of far more ancient metamorphic rock.

Reaching the mouth of Lake Canyon, from which the South Fork of Mill Creek debouches noisily down to the bottom of Lundy Canyon, our trail turns left (south) and proceeds upstream. Pine forests close in. Look sharp for some remnant poles from the Lundy-to-Bennettville telegraph line, completed in 1882. At a bit over 2 miles, we cross the South Fork on a culvert, traverse some willow and lodgepole flats, and begin another steep, straight ascent through a zone of rockslides toward a rugged bowl of mountains: Mount Scowden on the right (west), Gilcrest Peak on the left (east), and the Dore Cliffs on the Tioga Crest, straight ahead (south). All these mountains exceed 11,000 feet.

Our trail levels out in a wet meadow, with marshy Blue Lake on the left (east). The road then forks. The left branch goes about 0.2 mile to the site of Wasson, the town where the May Lundy's miners lived on the soggy shores of Crystal Lake. Wasson in 1882 sported three saloons, two boarding houses, a stamp mill, a laundry, and many cabins, but hardly anything is left. Most of the ruins on the site today date from an attempt in 1937 to rework the May Lundy's tailings. World War II and the federal regulation of gold prices closed down the works.

The right fork goes uphill, meeting Crystal Creek as it flows from the May Lundy Mine. Sealed with a gate, this entrance of the mine stands at about 9,600 feet. Railcar tracks emerging from the tunnel lead to the tops of enormous slag piles. From there we can look down upon Crystal Lake and to the flats where ruined buildings, boilers, and pieces of mining equipment are strewn about.

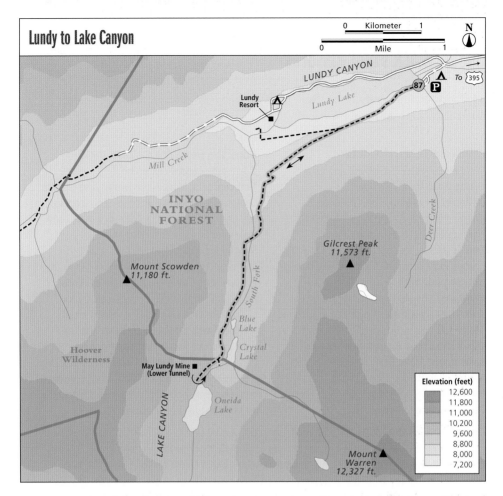

LUNDY CANYON

To 395

87

Lundy Lake

Lundy Resort

Mill Creek

INYO NATIONAL FOREST

South Fork

Gilcrest Peak
11,573 ft.

Deer Creek

Mount Scowden
11,180 ft.

Blue Lake

Crystal Lake

Hoover Wilderness

May Lundy Mine
(Lower Tunnel)

Oneida Lake

LAKE CANYON

Mount Warren
12,327 ft.

Elevation (feet)
12,600
11,800
11,000
10,200
9,600
8,800
8,000
7,200

Another 0.1 mile—in which we pass yet more cables, gears, and pieces of junk—brings us near the willowy shore of Oneida Lake. The wood and stone dam on its outlet stream diverted water for power to run the May Lundy's stamp mill. A trail built in 1882 once continued on from here over Dore Pass to Bennettville, but it was never an easy trail, and today has been partly obliterated by slides. While looking up-canyon at the relentless Tioga Crest, it is amazing to consider that twelve men and two mules hauled tons of mining equipment for the Bennettville mines (Hike 63) over this crest on sleds in 1882, using little more than manila rope, block, and tackle.

Miles and Directions

0.0 Parking area.

0.9 Unsigned junction of lateral trail to Lundy Resort; continue uphill (west).

2.1 Crossing of South Fork of Mill Creek.

3.0 Turnoff to site of May Lundy Mill and Wasson; bear right (southwest) up the hill.

3.3 May Lundy Mine.

3.4 Oneida Lake.

6.8 Arrive back at the parking area.

88 Black Point Fissures

This cross-country adventure explores a high-desert volcanic cone in search of bizarre box canyons in miniature.

Start: Black Point parking area
Distance: About 2.0 miles out and back
Hiking time: About 2–3 hours
Difficulty: Despite the short distance, the rugged ground and necessity of route finding make this a challenging hike.
Trail condition: There is no trail. This is a cross-country route over rock and sand and through thick sagebrush.
Seasons: Generally Mar–Nov, except on hot days. In mild years it is possible to hike during winter.
Other trail users: Foot travelers only
Land status: Mono Basin Scenic Area, Inyo National Forest
Nearest town: Lee Vining
Fees and permits: None

Maps: Tom Harrison: *Mono Lake.* USGS 7.5-minute quad: Negit Island.
Trail contacts: Mono Basin Scenic Area Visitor Center, Inyo National Forest, US 395, Lee Vining, CA 93541; (760) 647-3044; www.fs.usda.gov/inyo
Special considerations: Without a trail, this hike is an adventure. True, you are not likely to get seriously disoriented anywhere on Black Point, a hill surrounded by open country for miles around; but even still, if you are inexperienced with cross-country travel, this hike may not be for you. A compass might help but isn't necessary if you are observant and have a basic sense of direction. Wear long pants for bushwhacking, and bring water and a hat. And please don't fall into a fissure.

Finding the trailhead: From the Mono Basin Scenic Area Visitor Center north of Lee Vining, drive 4 miles north on US 395 and turn right (east) onto the Cemetery Road toward Mono Lake Park. The pavement ends after 1.3 miles at the cemetery, where Cemetery Road becomes well-graded gravel. Continue 1.2 miles to the signed turnoff to Black Point, where a right turn and drive of 2.6 miles over a washboard gravel road brings you to the parking area with a registration board, at an elevation of about 6,430 feet. (Two-wheel-drive automobiles should be able to negotiate this road.) Parking area registration board GPS: N38 01.624' / W119 05.087'

The Hike

No trail leads to the fissures, and this is but one of many ways to tackle this hike. The first thing to do is to get your bearings. From the parking lot, Black Point cone rises to the west, though you cannot see the summit from here. Likewise hidden behind Black Point cone to the west is the Sierra Crest, though you can see it trailing away toward the south. In the foreground to the south and east are the waters of Mono Lake. Black Negit Island rises from the lake toward the east, a handy landmark for our return trip. Take note of it.

Then head west, uphill behind the registration board, through cinders thickly overgrown with sagebrush. There are many use-trails, none clearly better than the next, so just keep upward, dodging sagebrush, your boots sinking comfortably, sometimes

A very tight squeeze in some places, the Black Point fissures form a natural maze on the southwest escarpment of a volcanic plateau.

frustratingly, in the sandy ash. Watch out for the rodent and reptile burrows. Black Point is tiered with old beach terraces, so that as you ascend toward the horizon, you surmount it only to discover a second tier, and later a third, in the process losing sight of your parked car (which is why it's handy to take note of the relative position of Negit Island, for reference on your return trip).

As you gain elevation, you also soon gain sight of Black Point's summit, capped with hard, ochre-colored basalt rock. Aim for it. As you rise higher, stark, stupendous vistas expand southward over Mono Lake, eastward into the Great Basin desert, and

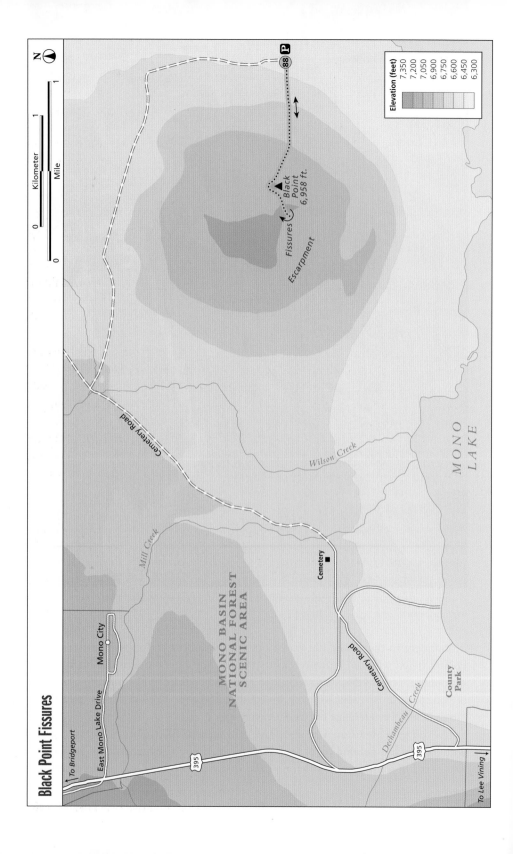

Black Point Fissures

Elevation (feet)
7,350
7,200
7,050
6,900
6,750
6,600
6,450
6,300

N

0   Kilometer   1
0   Mile   1

To Bridgeport

East Mono Lake Drive

Mono City

Mill Creek

Cemetery Road

MONO BASIN
NATIONAL FOREST
SCENIC AREA

Cemetery

Wilson Creek

Cemetery Road

Dechambeau Creek

County Park

395

To Lee Vining

395

Fissures

Escarpment

Black Point
6,958 ft.

88

P

M O N O
L A K E

west and southwest along the rugged crest of the Sierra Nevada. Shadows and bursts of light from ever-changing cloud formations play dramatically across the landscape.

When you arrive at the edge of the summit cap, it is not necessary to climb to the top. Make your way along the edge of the rock cap—either on it or in the sage—to the opposite (western) side, the side closest to the Sierra Crest. From this point you are looking down a gentle slope to a plateau that ends in an escarpment between 0.25 and 0.5 mile ahead. The fissures cut through this plateau, with their mouths at the escarpment.

Walk across the plateau roughly southwest, toward Mount Warren, the tall reddish peak immediately left (south) of what appears from this angle to be the biggest canyon in the Sierra wall, Lundy Canyon. (If you use a compass, the bearing is about 230 degrees.) You will soon begin to encounter the network of fissures, some merely ill-formed depressions in the dirt and others up to 50 feet deep and 2 to 3 feet wide. Watch your step, as the ground is often crumbly and there are no rails. You will not be able to climb into the fissures in most places, but their openings in the escarpment offer easy entry. While making your way to the escarpment, you may have to shift directions and even backtrack to avoid a gaping fissure.

At the escarpment's edge, climb down the slope a few feet and search left or right for the mouth of a fissure. Upon entering, you will find the walls are barely wider than your shoulders in places and are coated with tufa, a form of limestone. To walk through such otherworldly formations—so deep, pinched, twisted, and silent—is bizarre. Please damage nothing.

Black Point cone is a rarity among volcanoes, in that it formed underwater yet lies fully exposed today. The fissures are thought by some geologists to have formed as the volcano cooled some 13,000 years ago, underwater, when Mono Lake was much higher than it is today.

Miles and Directions

0.0 Parking area.
0.6 East side of summit cap.
0.7 West side of summit cap.
1.0 Mouth of fissures.
2.0 Arrive back at the parking area.

89 Panum Crater

In full view of the towering Sierra Crest, this hike around the rim of a textbook crater surveys one of the most enthralling, resplendent, surreal landscapes in the American West. Go when the shadows are long, during the lengthy afternoon or morning hours farthest from noon, or on any cloudy day (when lightning's not threatening), to enjoy the extraordinary spectacle of shifting light that can cast a mountain, spire, or sagebrush plain momentarily into deep shadow, and seconds later highlight it with a burst of brilliant sunlight.

Start: Panum Crater parking area
Distance: 2.0 miles round-trip
Hiking time: About 1-2 hours
Difficulty: Though steep and rocky, the route is short and easy.
Trail condition: Sandy, occasionally steep, but easy-to-follow path

Seasons: Generally Mar–Dec, except on hot summer afternoons or in lightning storms. In some mild winters it is possible to hike on snow-free days even Dec–Mar. Some people enjoy snowshoeing here.
For more information, see Hike 88
Note: Collecting anything, including rocks, is forbidden.

Finding the trailhead: From the Mono Basin Scenic Area Visitor Center (north of Lee Vining on US 395), drive 6.2 miles south on US 395 and turn left (east) onto CA 120 toward Benton. Drive 3.2 miles and turn left (north) onto a graded dirt road where a sign points to Panum Crater, then continue 0.8 mile to the parking area. Trailhead GPS: N37 55.544' / W119 02.922'

The Hike

The Mono Craters have been called the youngest mountains in North America. This northernmost of the Mono Craters upsurged from its volcanic vent about 600 years ago. Panum Crater rises from the southern shore of Mono Lake, a near-circle about half a mile in diameter, fantastic in appearance. Detached from the encircling pumice crater by a deep moat, the volcanic plug rises in the middle to an elevation of more than 7,000 feet, a bastion of glinting obsidian jutting somewhat higher than the rim.

From the parking area (elevation 6,800 feet), walk uphill between two posts to the rim of the crater. There a sign offers a choice between the Rim Trail and the Plug Trail. If time is short, do the plug, but if you have time, do both. The plug is that mountainous rock formation in the center of the crater. Its steep talus slopes and jagged parapets, ridges, and spires rise dramatically above the volcanic moat, strangely spiked in a few odd places with massive Jeffrey pines. To get there, turn left, walking clockwise around the rim for 0.2 mile to a second junction—"Plug Junction," I will call it. From there, turn right and zigzag to the top. There, at a spire of low-grade obsidian, the maintained trail splits into two informal trails, which themselves split into others, soon leaving you pretty much on your own to explore. The surface of the plug is amazingly jumbled with ridges, ravines, and sharp rocks. If rocks were candy,

Standing on the outer rim of Panum Crater, you can look across the "moat" to an obsidian cone that has risen in the middle.

this would be a candy factory. It is not hard to find fascinating chunks of deceptively light pumice rocks and crags of glassy obsidian, not to mention the small, black, rounded volcanic projectiles known as Pele's Tears. Even more amazing are the number of pines, chipmunks, ravens, and lizards that survive in this seeming wasteland.

Returning to the rim at Plug Junction, continue your clockwise circuit around the crater—though if you insist on walking widdershins, no harm done. Either way, clockwise or counter, the sandy path follows a clear circle round the rim, rising to high points on the north and west sides and returning to the parking area path junction after 1.4 miles. The views change constantly, taking in Mono Craters, Banner Peak, and the Minarets to the south; South Tufa, Mono Lake, Black Point, and the islands of Paoha and Negit to the north; and Mount Dana, Lee Vining, and Bloody Canyon to the west. A threadbare carpet of sagebrush, bitterbrush, desert peach, and rabbitbrush barely softens the surface of crater and moat, a feeding ground for grasshoppers and other insects, as well as for the birds, rodents, and reptiles that feed upon them. Among the most amazing insects is the hawk moth, as big and as noisy as a hummingbird. You might see it hovering amid the yellow rabbitbrush blooms of late summer, sipping nectar with its curled proboscis. No matter how often you come,

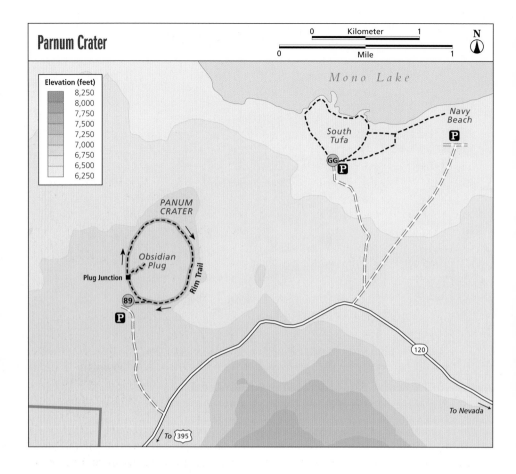

the lighting and clouds play different moods, most of them in exhilarating shades of grave sublimity.

Miles and Directions

0.0 Parking area.

0.1 Trail sign on crater rim; go left (clockwise).

0.3 Plug Junction; go right.

0.4 Summit of plug. Explore at your leisure.

0.7 Return to Plug Junction; go right to complete circuit of crater rim.

1.9 Return to trail sign; start down the Rim Trail.

2.0 Arrive back at the parking area.

90 Up Dragons Back to Seven Lakes Point

This exciting lollipop loop climbs to a sheer volcanic ridge with superlative vistas over the Mammoth Lakes basin.

Start: Lower campground at Twin Lakes
Distance: 3.7-mile lollipop loop
Hiking time: About 2-3 hours
Difficulty: Demanding, with an elevation gain of about 1,700 feet
Trail condition: Steep hiking, occasionally over exposed, crumbly pumice slopes
Seasons: June through mid-Oct
Other trail users: You might meet hikers with leashed dogs, but equestrians should confine themselves to the "easy" trail.

Land status: Inyo National Forest
Nearest town: Mammoth Lakes
Fees and permits: None
Maps: Tom Harrison: *Mammoth High Country.* Forest Service: *Mammoth Trails.* USGS 7.5-minute quad: Crystal Crag.
Trail contacts: Inyo National Forest, Mammoth Visitor Center, Highway 203 (as you enter town from US 395), Mammoth Lakes, CA 93546; (760) 924-5500; www.fs.usda.gov/inyo

Finding the trailhead: Take the free Lakes Basin Trolley. If you drive from the Mammoth Visitor Center, drive west (toward Mammoth Mountain) on Main Street. After 1.4 miles you will hit a major intersection where Main Street, Minaret Road, and Lake Mary Road all meet. Go straight through the intersection onto Lake Mary Road. Continue on that road for 2.9 miles, leaving the town of Mammoth Lake and turning right (southwest) at the second turnoff to the Twin Lakes Loop. Drive 0.4 mile to the Twin Lakes store and turn left (southwest) there onto the road to the lower campground. Drive 0.3 mile across the bridge into the campground, following the one-way road to a narrow dirt track that leads to private property just after campsite 36. Park on the wide spot of that dirt road, allowing room for cars to pass. (There is room for only about four parked cars, so if it is full, drive back to the Twin Lakes store and park there.) The trailhead begins immediately behind campsite 31, at an elevation of about 8,600 feet. Trailhead GPS: N37 36.916' / W119 00.674'

The Hike

Despite the dubious condition of some stretches of trail, this route in the end proves to be one of the most unusual, panoramic, and enjoyable hikes in the region. Its appeal stems partly from the slippery lip of the Bottomless Pit, partly from the ticklish stretch of crumbling trail below the Dragons Back, and partly from the airy scramble up the Dragons Back itself, with views literally to die for. The rest of the trail, the bulk of it spent going up and down switchbacks, is mainly businesslike. But such is the general rule of hiking: You pay for your rewards.

So step up to the base of the steep hill behind campsite 31. Our trail starts on the stone steps to the right, spurning the well-worn use-trail that lurches straight up the slope. Kicking up thick dust, we slog uphill on a steep diagonal and then zigzag back and forth among large red firs and lodgepole pines. Toward the top we spy a cabin in the woods above us, and shortly thereafter level out near a gulch that divides our forested ridge from the much drier, higher slope of Mammoth Mountain, whereon lies our destination.

As we tackle the mountain, our switchbacks turn to pumice gravel, and the forest gives way to sporadic Jeffrey pines and healthy scrub—manzanita, sage, rabbitbrush, bitterbrush, and currant. Like most chaparral, it provides rich feeding ground and homes for scores of flitting birds. Passing outcrops of lava, we start to appreciate the extraordinary vista of the Mammoth Lakes basin that is starting to spread below us.

Then the trail levels out, once again in thickening woods, and rounds a contour to the Bottomless Pit, whose funnel-shaped mouth, nearly 100 feet in diameter, gapes like a colossal ant-lion trap on the right (northeast) side of the trail. Approaching the gravelly brim with caution, we can peer down about 150 feet to the bottom, where a natural tunnel drains out whatever runnels of water might fall into it, eroding it even deeper. This bottom tunnel is known as "Hole in the Wall" to skiers approaching it in winter from the lower end.

The trail forks immediately beyond the pit, and a sign offers us a choice between the "easy" trail (left) and the "more demanding" trail (right). In this case, "easy" means longer, less steep, and not so spectacular. "More demanding" means shorter, steeper, and more exposed to the elements, but also more panoramic and certainly more fun. The route described below ascends the "more demanding" and descends the "easy" trail. To gauge if you feel up to the more demanding trail, ask yourself whether it was hard to approach the edge of the Bottomless Pit. If that made you quake in your boots, the more demanding trail might give you heart palpitations. But if you exercise a bit of care and common sense, you'll have no problems.

Bearing right (north) at this junction on the more demanding trail, we climb steeply and emerge from the woods at a gully choked with pumice gravel, tilting down to an edge whence it drops more precipitously some 600 feet to the valley floor. To be fair, this slope is not so slippery as greased ball bearings, but neither is it so reassuring as a solid, well-swept granite ledge. A slip is risky, although you'd probably not slide far, but it would be an unpleasant climb back up the slope. As it is, the trail has a tough enough time sticking to it, and is shakily "secured" in places by pieces of timber hammered into the sand with metal spikes.

After negotiating this gravelly slope, we begin to mount more steeply on loose rocks. The toylike valley floor, virtually underfoot, makes us all the more mindful of our footing. We emerge on the narrow, windswept, craggy tip of the Dragons Back, marked by a Forest Service sign. After taking in the impressive view, we turn west to zigzag up the narrow, lava-spiked spine of Dragons Back. With extensive vistas falling away behind and on both sides, this is an inspiring climb, though short—we arrive at Seven Lakes Point before we even break a sweat. At an elevation of 9,800 feet, this is not the highest point on our trail, but it offers the widest vista. The name comes from its inventory of lakes sighted: George, Mary, Mamie, Horseshoe, the pair of Twin Lakes, and TJ. On the horizon nearly 40 miles northeast you can see Boundary Peak (13,143 feet), highest point in Nevada and the northernmost summit of the White Mountains.

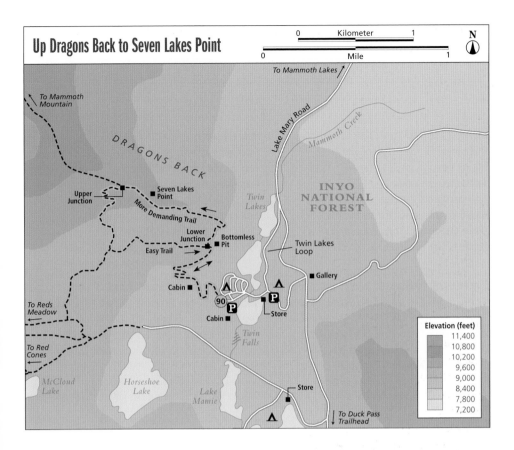

Up Dragons Back to Seven Lakes Point

Rather than descend the Dragons Back, we return by the "easy" trail, gently ascending on gravelly pumice from Seven Lakes Point through woods, to level out at a signed junction. The path to the right ascends Mammoth Mountain. We turn left (west), switchbacking down to our earlier junction beside the Bottomless Pit, and thence by our original route back to the car.

Miles and Directions

0.0 Trailhead at Twin Lakes Campground.

0.8 Bottomless Pit junction; bear right (north) up "more demanding" trail.

1.1 Bottom of Dragons Back.

1.5 Seven Lakes Point.

1.7 Upper junction; bear left (west).

2.3 Junction with McCloud Lake trail; bear left (east).

2.9 Return to Bottomless Pit junction; bear right (east).

3.7 Arrive back at the trailhead.

91 Duck Lake

This large, grand, austere mountain lake is close enough for a day hike from Mammoth Lakes, but far enough that it still offers solitude to those who want it.

Start: End of Coldwater Creek Campground
Distance: 8.8 miles out and back
Hiking time: About 9-10 hours
Difficulty: Strenuous
Trail condition: Good single-track trail.
Seasons: Late June through mid-Oct
Other trail users: Dogs, equestrians
Land status: Inyo National Forest, John Muir Wilderness

Nearest town: Mammoth Lakes
Fees and permits: None for day use. Wilderness permit for overnight use.
Maps: Tom Harrison: *Mammoth High Country*. USGS 7.5-minute quad: Bloody Mountain.
Trail contacts: Inyo National Forest, Mammoth Visitor Center, Highway 203 (as you enter town from US 395), Mammoth Lakes, CA 93546; (760) 924-5500; www.fs.usda.gov/inyo

Finding the trailhead: Take the free Lakes Basin Trolley. To drive from the Mammoth Visitor Center, head west (toward Mammoth Mountain) on Main Street. After 1.4 miles you will hit a major intersection where Main Street, Minaret Road, and Lake Mary Road all meet. Go straight through the intersection onto Lake Mary Road. Continue on that road for 2.9 miles, leaving the town of Mammoth Lake and turning left (south) on the road to the Coldwater Creek Campground. Drive to the end of the road and park at an elevation of about 9,125 feet. Trailhead GPS: N37 35.465' / W118 59.344'

The Hike

Like the devil himself, the duck was a frequent inspiration for the coiners of Sierra Nevada nomenclature. The namer of this particular Duck Lake, however, must have possessed a profoundly impoverished imagination. To a hiker rounding over the top of the also underwhelmingly named Duck Pass, the scene of overwhelming grandeur that unfolds below—the dark, majestic mountains, the cold, blue, reflective expanses of water, the vast, windswept barrens higher than timberline—will seem far better fitted to the Mephistophelean themes of Wagnerian opera than to a preening fowl that waddles and quacks.

But what's in a name? If you like your Sierra scenery sublime, then Duck Lake is your oyster.

As with many special destinations in the Sierra Nevada, we start with switchbacks through woods. Not until after we've passed Arrowhead Lake, reached by a spur trail but glimpsed from our trail through the forest, do the trees begin to thin substantially enough for us to begin to enjoy continuous views of the mountains around us, including the magnificent Mammoth Crest, which we must surmount to reach Duck Lake.

Climbing steadily, we pass close to Skelton Lake in its rocky basin, a high rockbound Sierra Lake worthy to be a destination in its own right. We reach our first

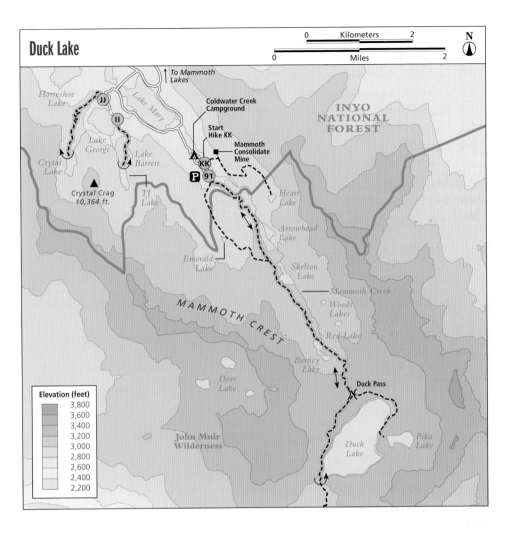

Kilometers

Miles

INYO NATIONAL FOREST

To Mammoth Lakes

Coldwater Creek Campground

Horseshoe Lake

Lake Mary

Start Hike KK

Mammoth Consolidate Mine

Lake George

Lake Barrett

Crystal Lake

KK

91

Crystal Crag 10,364 ft.

TJ Lake

Heart Lake

Arrowhead Lake

Emerald Lake

Skelton Lake

Mammoth Creek

Woods Lakes

M A M M O T H   C R E S T

Red Lake

Barney Lake

Deer Lake

Duck Pass

Elevation (feet)

3,800
3,600
3,400
3,200
3,000
2,800
2,600
2,400
2,200

John Muir Wilderness

Duck Lake

Pika Lake

1,000-foot milestone (elevation gained) just before scaring up the cluster of smaller lakes that include Red and Barney, electric under bright-blue skies, but possessed of that barren, still-born quality of beauty that so coolly complements the gray Sierra granite. Beyond Barney the trail climbs more steeply up the headwall cirque to the crest, engineered in places with the blocky steps and rustic masonry so redolent of High Sierra trail construction.

As we mount the saddle of the Mammoth Crest, passing through a rocky notch at 10,800-foot Duck Pass, the lake jumps into startling view, big, cold, and windy even on a sunny day. It lies only 300 feet below, but the trail that works its way down to the outlet stream takes a good, long time to get there, so large is the scale of these waters. Camping is not allowed along the shore of this lake or immediately near its outlet stream.

Miles and Directions

0.0 Trailhead at Coldwater Creek Campground.

0.8 Arrowhead Lake junction; keep straight (south).

1.3 Emerald Lake junction; take left fork (south).

1.4 Skelton Lake.

2.4 Barney Lake.

3.3 Duck Pass, followed by junction to east end of Duck Lake; keep right (southwest).

4.1 Duck Lake shore.

4.4 Duck Lake outlet stream.

8.8 Arrive back at Coldwater Creek Campground.

92 Minaret Summit Ridge

This dirt road ramble atop the Great Western Divide provides astonishing vistas of the Minarets and surrounding canyons and mountains of the Mammoth region.

Start: Minaret Vista
Distance: 4.4 miles out and back
Hiking time: About 2 hours
Difficulty: Moderate, with an elevation gain and loss of nearly 1,000 feet
Trail condition: Mostly steep, broad dirt road
Seasons: Late June through mid-Oct
Other trail users: Dogs, equestrians, mountain bikes, and 4-wheel-drive vehicles use the road.

Land status: Inyo National Forest
Nearest town: Mammoth Lakes
Fees and permits: None
Maps: Tom Harrison: *Mammoth High Country.* USGS 7.5-minute quad: Mammoth Mountain.
Trail contacts: Inyo National Forest, Mammoth Visitor Center, Highway 203 (as you enter town from US 395), Mammoth Lakes, CA 93546; (760) 924-5500; www.fs.usda.gov/inyo

Finding the trailhead: From the Mammoth Visitor Center, drive west (toward Mammoth Mountain) on Main Street. After 1.4 miles you will hit a major intersection where Main Street, Minaret Road, and Lake Mary Road all meet. Turn right (north) onto Minaret Road (CA 203) and drive about 5.5 miles to Minaret Summit. On the ridge, turn right toward Minaret Vista and drive 0.3 mile to the parking circle. Trailhead GPS: N37 39.409' / W119 03.661'

The Hike

The view from Minaret Vista is one of the finest obtainable from a roadway in the Sierra Nevada. Leaving the car to walk up the ridge greatly improves upon it.

The trailhead is not marked by a sign. From the parking area (elevation of 9,265 feet), walk behind the toilets to a picnic table and down the wide pumice gravel path to a dirt road. Note the spot for when you return.

Turn left and walk north up that dirt road, which makes a steady ascent through lodgepole pines, dry-land shrubs, and grasses. When the road forks, take either fork, for they rejoin after a couple hundred yards of steep ascent. At about 0.5 mile the road levels out into a pumice flat but soon begins to climb again. Walk until you wish to turn around. The high point just south of Deadman Pass, a stiff climb about 2.2 miles from the car, is a purely arbitrary goal, though one with a 360-degree view.

Comprising mostly pumice gravel with copses of windswept pines, the terrain is wide open. To the south, Mammoth Mountain rises naked of snow in summer, bearing the scars of its ski runs, lifts, and buildings, and yet it is a most extraordinary reflector of afternoon light. On the eastern horizon, you can see the White Mountains. To the west we have unobstructed views of the Minarets, Banner Peak (12,945 feet), and Mount Ritter (13,157 feet), a row of jagged stone teeth that, scaled down, would do credit to an alligator's jaw. In front of them lies a jumble of lesser ridges and deep gorges, most prominently the canyon of the upper San Joaquin River. We

Minaret Summit Ridge; Shadow and Ediza Lakes

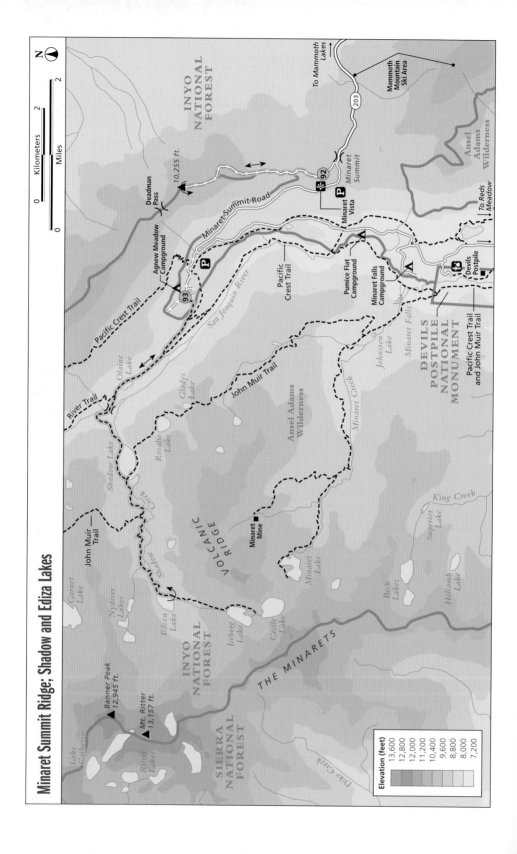

Elevation (feet)
13,600
12,800
12,000
11,200
10,400
9,600
8,800
8,000
7,200

N

Kilometers
0   1   2

Miles
0   1   2

INYO NATIONAL FOREST

Deadman Pass

10,255 ft.

Minaret Summit Road

To Mammoth Lakes

203

92

Minaret Summit

Minaret Vista

P

To Reds Meadow

Pacific Crest Trail

Agnew Meadow Campground

P

93

San Joaquin River

Pumice Flat Campground

Minaret Falls Campground

Minaret Falls

Devils Postpile

DEVILS POSTPILE NATIONAL MONUMENT

Pacific Crest Trail and John Muir Trail

Johnston Lake

Minaret Creek

Ansel Adams Wilderness

Ansel Adams Wilderness

Mammoth Mountain Ski Area

King Creek

Superior Lake

Beck Lakes

Holcomb Lake

Minaret Lake

Minaret Mine

Cecile Lake

THE MINARETS

Iceberg Lake

Ediza Lake

Nydiver Lakes

Garnet Lake

Shadow Creek

VOLCANIC RIDGE

John Muir Trail

Rosalie Lake

Shadow Lake

Gladys Lake

Olaine Lake

River Trail

John Muir Trail

Pacific Crest Trail

Lake Catherine

Ritter Lakes

Banner Peak 12,945 ft.

Mt. Ritter 13,157 ft.

INYO NATIONAL FOREST

SIERRA NATIONAL FOREST

Dike Creek

Dawn comes to Minaret Summit Ridge in a fog.

can follow its river passage downstream to the rolling foothills on the west side of the range. The Minarets are the most imposing ridge here, but they are not the Sierra Crest. Actually, we are standing on the Sierra Crest, and our dirt road also marks the boundary between Mono and Madera Counties.

The scene is especially awesome at sunset, when the Ritter Range is backlit, stark against skies at first multihued and then darkening. Hazy beams shine down Shadow Creek's canyon, briefly lighting up pockets of the lowlands. Pointed rays of light shoot up from the pointed Minarets. Closer at hand, but just as extraordinary, are the shadows on our own ridge just before sunset. Every plant and rock, and even separate blades of grasses and pebbles, are meticulously delineated in long shadows, growing longer with each passing minute, until they stretch taller than any of us. Our own shadows grow long likewise, brushing the meadows a hundred feet away. Sunrise here can also be awesome, mainly for watching the shadow of our ridge crawl up from the San Joaquin, though morning photographers will want some clouds to lend dramatic lighting to the front-lit Minarets.

Miles and Directions

0.0 Parking area.

0.1 Dirt road; go left (north, uphill).

2.2 Summit of hill south of Deadman Pass.

4.4 Arrive back at the parking area.

93 Shadow and Ediza Lakes

In a region of exceptionally stunning lakes, Shadow and Ediza are two of the loveliest. Both harbor views of the Ritter Range that are among the finest mountain landscapes in the Sierra Nevada.

Start: Agnew Meadow
Distance: 6.4 miles to Shadow Lake; 12.6 miles round-trip to Ediza Lake
Hiking time: About 4 hours for Shadow Lake; 7–8 hours for Ediza (although 2 days is preferable)
Difficulty: An overall elevation gain of about 1,700 feet makes this a challenging hike to Ediza. Shadow Lake is more moderate.
Trail condition: Excellent well-signed trail
Seasons: Late June through mid-Oct
Other trail users: Equestrians and leashed dogs allowed. Bikes are not allowed in the Ansel Adams Wilderness.
Land status: Ansel Adams Wilderness, Inyo National Forest

Nearest town: Mammoth Lakes
Fees and permits: Day hikers do not require any trail fees or permits, but there is a fee to ride the shuttle or to drive over Minaret Summit. Overnighters should obtain a wilderness permit. No camping is allowed between Shadow Lake and Ediza Lake's creek crossing, or on the south side of Ediza Lake. No campfires. Bear canisters required for overnighters.
Maps: Tom Harrison: *Mammoth High Country.* USGS 7.5-minute quads: Mammoth Mountain, Mount Ritter.
Trail contacts: Inyo National Forest, Mammoth Visitor Center, Highway 203 (as you enter town from US 395), Mammoth Lakes, CA 93546; (760) 924-5500; www.fs.usda.gov/inyo

Finding the trailhead: From Memorial Day to Labor Day, private cars are prohibited from driving to Agnew Meadow, unless drivers have campground or resort reservations or arrive outside shuttle operational hours. Ride the shuttle bus (fee) from Mammoth Mountain Ski Resort to the Agnew Meadow turnoff.

If you arrive outside the summer season, you can drive to the trailhead. From the Mammoth Visitor Center, drive west (toward Mammoth Mountain) on Main Street. After 1.4 miles you will hit a major intersection where Main Street, Minaret Road, and Lake Mary Road all meet. Turn right (north) onto Minaret Road (CA 203) and drive about 5.5 miles to Minaret Summit, where you leave the Great Basin, cross the Great Western Divide, and pay an entrance fee at the ranger kiosk. From there, continue downhill on a paved one-lane road 2.6 miles to the Agnew Meadow turnoff, on the right (north). Turn right and drive about 0.7 mile, past the stables to the farthest parking area on the edge of Agnew Meadow, at an elevation of about 8,300 feet. The signed trailhead is on the south side of the parking lot. Trailhead GPS: N37 40.912' / W119 05.168'

The Hike

A few trails and bridle paths converge at Agnew Meadow; look for the signpost to Shadow Lake. Crossing over a little creeklet, we meet an unsigned junction and turn right, walking alongside a meadow to a junction near an open view over the San Joaquin River. Here we turn right and walk on a slight gradient down through rocky scrub toward the river. Upon reaching the valley floor, we rejoin the trees for another long stretch of level walking. Placid, reedy, mosquito-infested Olaine Lake makes a brief appearance on our left (west) in a dark, cluttered forest. Another flat spell in the woods brings us, 2.3 miles from the start of the trail, to a bridged crossing of the rushing San Joaquin River.

Although we now commence the uphill portion of our hike, we also break from the trees and start to enjoy some amazing scenery, which more than compensates for the extra labor. With backward vistas of Mammoth Mountain, we switchback up Shadow Canyon, Shadow Creek cascading down the gorge to our left. The trail enters this gorge in a steep, exposed section cut from rock containing bands of

No Sierra tree is more graceful than the aspen, which grows profusely in the eastern canyons.

extraordinary green and violet metamorphic rock and some veins of quartz. Attaining the notch at the top of the gorge, we are slapped with a full-frontal view of the awesome Ritter Range, with enchanting Shadow Lake stretching away from our feet.

Winding along its charming north shore, the trail passes many inviting picnic spots, but no camping is allowed at Shadow Lake. At the head of the lake we follow its cascading inlet stream up to a junction, where the John Muir Trail (JMT) heads south across a bridge. We go right (west) up the JMT but part company 0.6 mile later at a creek-side junction, when we take the left (west) fork toward Ediza Lake.

Rolling through green meadows, conifer forests, and rocky outcrops, our trail rises by gradual degrees up the valley of Shadow Creek in view of Volcanic Ridge to the south. Some stretches have been finessed through rocky benches by the vigorous application of picks, shovels, and maybe a surgical stick or two of dynamite. The best of company, frolicsome Shadow Creek entertains us with music and assorted pretty little tricks, including a very clever cascade around an island of polished granite.

Somewhat less amusing is the tricky ford near Ediza Lake. Even in late season our rock-hopping entails a decent sense of balance, but an early-season crossing could be risky. After crossing Shadow Creek the trail delves straight into the woods at right angles to the creek, before rejoining it at the granite bench that dams Ediza Lake. Climbing a few steps cut in the rock, we pass through a narrow gully and emerge to the stunning scene of pristine lake and mountains. Except for the heavily forested northern shore, where camping is allowed, the lake is ringed by rocky meadows. The fascinating views of Ritter, Banner, and the Minarets change wonderfully as we walk along the shore.

Ediza Lake is known for a sad footnote in Sierra Nevada lore. It was the last campsite of Walter A. Starr Jr., climber and author of the first guide to the John Muir Trail, still known as *Starr's Guide*. He was 30 when he fell while climbing solo in the Minarets in August of 1933. His disappearance launched a massive search by some of the best Sierra mountaineers of his day, including Norman Clyde, who found and interred Starr's body on a ledge of Michael Minaret. The episode is described in Clyde's essay, "The Search for Walter Starr."

Miles and Directions

0.0 Parking area.

0.5 Junction with southbound cutoff to San Joaquin River; bear right (northwest).

1.1 Junction with southbound river trail; go upstream to the right (north).

1.8 Olaine Lake.

2.1 Junction with River Trail; bear left (northwest).

2.3 Bridge over San Joaquin River.

3.2 Shadow Lake outlet.

3.7 Junction with John Muir Trail above Shadow Lake; bear right (west).

4.3 Upper junction with John Muir Trail; bear left (west).

5.8 Shadow Creek ford.

6.0 Outlet of Ediza Lake.

6.3 Inlet creek of Ediza Lake.

12.6 Arrive back at the parking area.

94 Rainbow Falls via Devils Postpile

The Sierra Nevada is justly famed for its fancy work with rocks and water, but few examples are more wonderful than this natural stone cliff of remarkable mathematical regularity, and the graceful waterfall that lives just down the river.

Start: Devils Postpile parking area
Distance: 3.9 miles one-way
Hiking time: About 3 hours
Difficulty: Moderate, with scant elevation change
Trail condition: Good trails but with many intersections. Fortunately, the signs are clear.
Seasons: May–June best for water displays, though July–Oct is also pleasant
Other trail users: This trail is very popular. Equestrians are common. No bikes. Dogs are not allowed in the national monument but may use the trails of Inyo National Forest.

Land status: Devils Postpile National Monument, Ansel Adams Wilderness, Inyo National Forest
Nearest town: Mammoth Lakes
Fees and permits: Day hikers do not require any trail fees or permits, but there is a fee to ride the shuttle or to drive over Minaret Summit. Overnighters should obtain a wilderness permit.
Maps: USGS 7.5-minute quads: Mammoth Mountain, Crystal Crag
Trail contacts: Devils Postpile National Monument, PO Box 3999, Mammoth Lakes, CA 93546; (760) 934-2289; www.nps.gov/depo

Finding the trailhead: From Memorial Day to Labor Day, private cars are prohibited from driving to the vicinity of Devils Postpile National Monument, unless drivers have campground or resort reservations or arrive outside shuttle operational hours. During summer ride the shuttle bus (fee) from Mammoth Mountain Ski Resort to Devils Postpile.

If you arrive outside the summer season, you can drive to the monument. From the Mammoth Visitor Center, drive west (toward Mammoth Mountain) on Main Street. After 1.4 miles you will hit a major intersection where Main Street, Minaret Road, and Lake Mary Road all meet. Turn right (north) onto Minaret Road (CA 203) and drive about 5.5 miles to Minaret Summit, where you leave the Great Basin and cross the Great Western Divide. From there, continue downhill on a paved road (Minaret Summit Road, which is only one lane for the first 2.6 miles) nearly 7 miles to the Devils Postpile park headquarters. Park in the day-use lot. Trailhead GPS: N37 37.798' / W119 05.086'

Note: If you drive and park at Devils Postpile, your obvious need to walk back to your car will add 1.5 miles to your hike.

The Hike

The Sierra Nevada has many examples of the kind of geological phenomenon seen in Devils Postpile—lava flows of columnar basalt, a sight much more awesome in the rock than on the page. Judging by all the accents you will hear on this trail, people really do come from all over the world to see it—so arrive early in the day.

From the small ranger station beside the day-use parking lot (elevation 7,600 feet), the signed path runs parallel to the San Joaquin River through a pretty, willow-bordered meadow in a broad, flat valley. Rising slightly as we pass into a lodgepole forest, we soon meet the Postpile itself and a trail fork that climbs to its top. We will take that very trail, but first you will want to get a better look at the front of the Devils Postpile. The palisades are formed of regular basalt columns, the remains of a 600,000-year-old lava flow that cooled quickly under the ground, shrinking and fracturing in a regular pattern. Although the formation was originally 600 feet thick, glaciers sheered the present formation down so that individual columns stand no more than 60 feet tall. Some columnar sections are warped and others are broken, hence the wide talus apron.

Returning to the aforementioned fork to the top of the formation, climb the log steps for a "dorsal" view of the columns. They are surprisingly regular in shape, of mostly six to eight sides and 20 to 30 inches across, fitted and polished like a parquet tile floor.

The glacier-polished roof of Devils Postpile resembles a tile floor.

After inspecting the column tops, we proceed to Rainbow Falls by walking across the top of the Devils Postpile and rejoining the dusty trail on the other side. Our path loosely follows the monument's eastern boundary through deep forest. From here on out we will be passing a gauntlet of junctions and trails that would be confusing to describe. Fortunately, they are well signposted and easy to follow with the accompanying map. The two most noteworthy landmarks are the crossing of shallow Reds Creek and the four-way junction of the John Muir Trail, at 1.4 miles. (A brief detour west from that junction goes to the arched bridge across the San Joaquin River, a pleasant spot for a picnic.) Continuing south, we pass through a forest burned in September 1992 by the Rainbow Fire, which stopped short of Rainbow Falls.

Crossing the unmarked boundary of Ansel Adams Wilderness, we step across Boundary Creek and approach the waterfall from upriver. Our first view is therefore downriver, over its brink—a view that gives us no indication of the waterfall's height or shape. All is shortly revealed, however, as we pass by the first and second view points toward the top of a steep stone stairway with cable railings. We descend impressive bluffs of brown basalt, tinged with orange lichen and tufts of green foliage. At the head of the gorge, the San Joaquin River crashes 101 feet between dark-brown volcanic cliffs that frame the rising mists that generate its namesake rainbows. Though the water slips the brink in perfect symmetry, a ledge midway down the falls throws the entire display beautifully off balance.

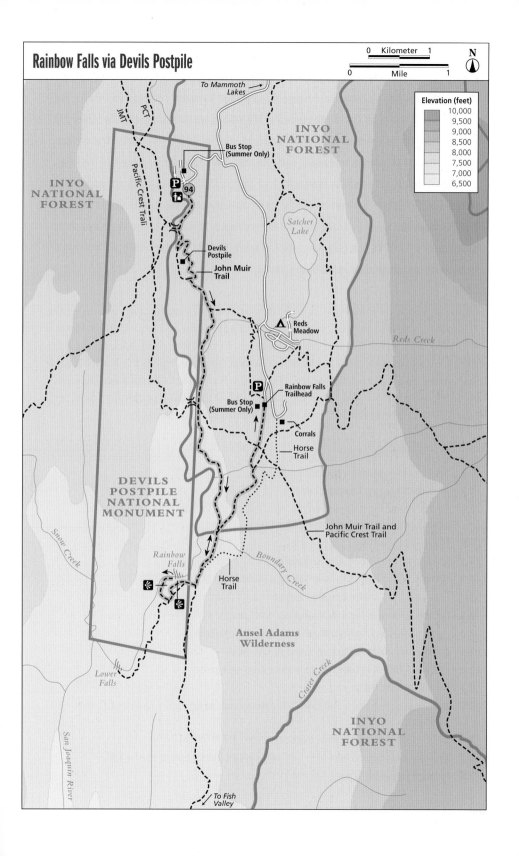

Rainbow Falls via Devils Postpile

0 Kilometer 1

0 Mile 1

N

To Mammoth
Lakes

JMT

PCT

Pacific Crest Trail

INYO
NATIONAL
FOREST

Bus Stop
(Summer Only)

P

94

INYO
NATIONAL
FOREST

Satcher
Lake

Devils
Postpile

John Muir
Trail

Reds
Meadow

Reds Creek

P

Rainbow Falls
Trailhead

Bus Stop
(Summer Only)

Corrals

Horse
Trail

DEVILS
POSTPILE
NATIONAL
MONUMENT

John Muir Trail and
Pacific Crest Trail

Snow Creek

Rainbow
Falls

Horse
Trail

Boundary Creek

Ansel Adams
Wilderness

Crater Creek

INYO
NATIONAL
FOREST

Lower
Falls

San Joaquin River

To Fish
Valley

Elevation (feet)

10,000
9,500
9,000
8,500
8,000
7,500
7,000
6,500

PUBLIC TRANSPORT AT MAMMOTH LAKES

Mammoth Lakes has an extensive system of free public transport, summer and winter. The main transport hub is on Canyon Boulevard at The Village, on the corner of Main Street and Minaret Road. The Town Trolley hauls visitors around town, while the Lakes Basin Trolley Shuttles heads south to provide trailheads, campgrounds, and lodges around most of the lakes. Mammoth Mountain is served by Mammoth Area Shuttle (MAS) buses, which are equipped to carry bikes. A separate bus service (fee) goes from Mammoth Mountain to Devils Postpile, Reds Meadow, and other trailheads west of Minaret Vista. Mammoth Lakes also connects to Yosemite by the YARTS bus (see Yosemite Transport, p. 284). Contact: www.visitmammoth.com/about-mammoth/transportation/summer/

Hikers who rode the shuttle from Mammoth can pick up the return shuttle from the Rainbow Falls parking area, which is only 1.2 miles from Rainbow Falls (as opposed to 2.7 miles back to the Devils Postpile trailhead). To get there, climb back up the stairs, visit the second and first view points in reverse order, pass the trail to the Reds Meadow horse corrals, and (in brief) follow the signs to the Rainbow Falls trailhead. The signed route is clear on the ground, following an easy uphill gradient through the forest, with fleeting views of the gondola terminus atop Mammoth Mountain.

Miles and Directions

0.0 Devils Postpile parking area and visitor center.

0.2 Junction to river; go straight (south).

0.4 Junction to the top of Devils Postpile; after viewing the formation from the front (just ahead), return to this junction and ascend.

0.5 Top of Devils Postpile.

0.7 Junction with main trail; turn left (south).

0.9 First junction to Reds Meadow; bear right (south) toward Rainbow Falls.

1.4 Four-way junction with John Muir Trail; go straight (south).

2.1 Second junction to Reds Meadow; bear right (south).

2.3 Horse trail junction to Reds Meadow corrals; go right (south).

2.4 Junction with pack trail to Fish Valley; go right (west).

2.6 Junction with trail to Lower Rainbow Falls; keep right (west).

2.7 Foot of Rainbow Falls.

3.2 Junction with foot trail to Rainbow Falls parking area; go right (northeast) toward Reds Meadow.

3.6 Junction with foot trail to Reds Meadow corrals; go left (north).

3.7 Four-way junction with John Muir Trail; keep straight (north) toward parking lot.

3.9 Rainbow Falls parking area.

Honorable Mentions

GG   South Tufa Trail

The most popular trail on Mono Lake meanders a little more than a mile through rock pinnacles called tufa towers. These grotesque, whitish limestone formations took shape under the surface of Mono Lake, where freshwater springs flowed into its alkaline waters, generating deposits of calcium carbonate. The towers were exposed when Los Angeles began diverting Mono Lake's inlet streams for its water supply in 1941. The retreat was reversed in a 1994 agreement with Los Angeles. As more water again flows into Mono Lake, the rising water level will force rangers to move this path back.

The tufa towers sprout like fantastic stalagmites from the alkaline flats. Their convoluted twisted spires, natural cavities, bulbous knobs, and continuously shifting shadows provide uninterrupted variety to patient photographers. These fragile formations are estimated to be between 200 and 900 years old. Dip your hand into the water, which feels strangely greasy. Clouds of alkali flies swarm about. From spring to fall the lake itself teems with trillions of tiny brine shrimp. These, in turn, attract hoards of birds that feed on them, making Mono Lake one of the crucial stops along the Pacific Flyway and a mecca for birders. Among the eighty species of migratory birds

A group of hikers sets out for the tufa towers at Mono Lake.

are some 50,000 California gulls that nest on the lake's islands, tens of thousands of phalaropes that stop off twice yearly en route between Canada and South America, and more than a million eared grebes.

The native Kuzedika people ate the shelled pupae of the alkali fly and traded them, dried, with other tribes over the Mono Trail. Among their trading partners there were the Yokuts, who called the Kuzedika "fly eaters," or *Monache*, from which we get the name of Mono. Ranger-led walks sometimes let visitors try this salty (and somewhat caviar-like) "delicacy."

If you wish to swim in Mono Lake, a good place is nearby Navy Beach, a 0.7-mile walk from the South Tufa parking area, though you can also drive. The water, a thousand times as alkaline and three times as salty as seawater, is surprisingly buoyant, but it will sting your eyes and any cuts. To get to the South Tufa parking area, drive 6.2 miles south on US 395 from the Mono Basin Scenic Area Visitor Center, turn left (east) onto CA 120 and drive 4.8 miles toward Benton, then turn left (north) onto the graded gravel road marked with a sign for the South Tufa Reserve. When the gravel road forks after 0.1 mile, turn left (northwest) and drive 0.9 mile to the South Tufa parking area (fee). Contact: Mono Basin Scenic Area Visitor Center, US 395, Lee Vining, CA 93541; (760) 647-3044; www.fs.usda.gov/inyo. (See the map for Hike 89, Panum Crater.) Trailhead GPS: N37 56.332' / W119 01.622'

HH   Hot Creek Gorge

One of the largest geothermal springs outside of Yellowstone, the boiling springs that heat Hot Creek are themselves heated by pools of magma 5 to 8 miles beneath the Long Valley Caldera. From the rim of the shallow gorge, the scene is enthralling. It smells of sulfur. The popping sound of percolating water emerges from steaming hollows in the ground and from bubbling Hot Creek itself. Scores of boiling springs congregate on both banks, their scalding waters trickling into Hot Creek, while other springs well up in the streambed itself, making swimming dangerous. That does not stop local swimmers from entering the creek during the day (it is illegal at night!), but heed the many signs and barriers that mark the scalding springs. Countless swimmers have been scalded over the years nonetheless, and some have died.

The braided trails that head upstream along the creek are actually anglers' paths. Tracing the bank between crumbly walls of consolidated volcanic ash, the trail follows the creek upstream into a cool-water zone, famous as a trout stream. (Barbless hooks and catch-and-release policies are strictly enforced.) The pocked volcanic walls of the gorge provide cavities for spiders' webs and swallows' nests. Photographers will find this area most beautiful in late afternoon light, when long shadows add intrigue to sagebrush flats, although the backdrop of the Sierra Crest and the steaming springs are also striking at dawn. To get there from US 395, exit at the Hot Creek Hatchery Road, about 3 miles southeast of Mammoth. Follow the signs toward the Hot Creek Geological Area, a little over 4 miles from US 395, partially on unpaved road. Contact: Mammoth Visitor Center, Highway 203 (as you enter town from US 395),

The steam rising from Hot Creek is a testament to the live magma deep below the Mammoth area.

Mammoth Lakes, CA 93546; (760) 924-5500; www.fs.usda.gov/inyo. Trailhead GPS: N37 39.663' / W118 49.651'

|| Barrett and TJ Lakes

TJ is one of the easiest of the Mammoth Lakes to reach on foot. With only 1.8 miles round-trip, it provides isolation from cars and cabins, and a superb vista of the Mammoth Crest. Starting at the south side of the Lake George parking area (9,050 feet), follow the gravel road south along its shore, passing below a campground, to the outlet creek. Crossing on a wooden bridge, we turn right and follow the shoreline to a steep rocky slope, where a sign points us uphill toward forest-bound Lake Barrett. Traversing Barrett's gravelly west shore, we mount over a low ridge and descend to the soggy swale of TJ's outlet creek. TJ Lake lies just ahead, cupped in a deep basin with a thickly forested ridge on the east and a high granite shelf on the west. Above all soar the granitic 10,364-foot monolith of Crystal Crag and the even greater parapets of the Mammoth Crest. Contact: Inyo National Forest, Mammoth Visitor Center, Highway 203 (as you enter town from US 395), Mammoth Lakes, CA 93546; (760) 924-5500; www.fs.usda.gov/inyo. (See the map for Hike 91, Duck Lake.) Trailhead GPS: N37 36.167' / W119 00.623'

JJ Crystal Lake

Cupped in a bowl between the Mammoth Crest and Crystal Crag (10,364 feet), Crystal Lake requires a 2.6-mile out-and-back hike with an elevation gain of 650 feet—harder than TJ Lake (Hike II) but paying greater scenic dividends. From the north end of the Lake George parking lot (9,050 feet), the signed trail sets out through a pine and fir forest shorn of ground cover, like campground dirt. Worse, it keeps such tiresome company with the road to Woods Resort, not to mention an ugly bunch of shortcuts, that by the time it leaves them in the dust, we are almost grateful to bear up with what at first promises to be a tedious set of switchbacks. Fortunately, they quickly redeem themselves, for the eastern bends on several of the switchbacks bring us repeatedly to increasingly superb views embracing ever greater expanses of the Mammoth Lakes basin, its blue lakes, green forests, and red mountains. These mountains take their color from metamorphic rocks, which are among the oldest in the Sierra, as well as from lava, which are among the youngest. After 1 mile we meet a signed junction and turn left (south). Surmounting a wooded crest, we saunter easily down into Crystal Lake's basin to the lake's outlet creek. Few places in Mammoth offer a closer or more spectacular platform for viewing the Mammoth Crest, an imposing, wall-like ridge of granite that separates the Mammoth Basin from the watershed of the San Joaquin River. Contact: Mammoth Visitor Center, Highway 203 (as you enter town from US 395), Mammoth Lakes, CA 93546; (760) 924-5500; www.fs.usda.gov/inyo. (See the map for Hike 91, Duck Lake.) Trailhead GPS: N37 36.233' / W119 00.679'

KK Mammoth Consolidated Mine

Like most Eastern Sierra towns, Mammoth Lakes was founded by mining. Although Red Mountain above Lake Mary was worked in the 1870s, the present ruins of the Mammoth Consolidated Mine enjoyed their last hurrah during the Great Depression. A short walk from Coldwater Creek Campground brings visitors to a well-preserved ghost settlement, rusted but still impressive mining equipment, and a gated mine spectacularly situated with front porch views to the rugged Mammoth Crest. Not least remarkable is what may arguably be the best preserved two-holer outhouse this side of the Ozarks. Contact: Inyo National Forest, Mammoth Visitor Center, Highway 203 (as you enter town from US 395), Mammoth Lakes, CA 93546; (760) 924-5500; www.fs.usda.gov/inyo. (See the map for Hike 91, Duck Lake.) Trailhead GPS: N37 35.518' / W118 59.379'

Eastern Sierra: Owens Valley

The Owens Valley is the deepest valley in the Western Hemisphere. The floor at Lone Pine lies more than 2 miles beneath the Sierra Crest on the west, and nearly as deep beneath the crests of the White and Inyo Mountains on the east. A part of the Great Basin, the Owens Valley is a block of land that has slipped down into the earth's crust between two parallel faults, a feature known to geologists as a graben. How deeply it has dropped in relation to the Sierra Crest is even more amazing than what now meets the eye. Geologists estimate that the valley's bedrock is buried under another 10,000 feet of rock washed down from the Sierra Nevada since the great uplift of 5 million years ago. In other words, the Owens Valley was once more than twice as deep as it is today.

The scenery along the Sierra escarpment is spectacular. Basking in the rain shadow of the Sierra Nevada, the Owens Valley is dry and desertlike, though crossed by many creeks that pour down from Sierra canyons and through the sagebrush-covered foothills, long riparian "oases" of cottonwood and willow that turn green in spring and golden in autumn. Ascending any of these eastern canyons provides some of the most spectacular and most grueling hikes in the Sierra Nevada. Inyo National Forest and the Bureau of Land Management (BLM) administer most of the public lands in the area. US 395 links the four main towns of the Owens Valley—Bishop, Big Pine, Independence, and Lone Pine—which all make excellent bases of operation for outdoor activities of all sorts, including hiking.

The White Mountains are separate from the Sierra Nevada but are included in this chapter because they harbor splendid trails with fantastic views of the Sierra Nevada. Another extremely interesting reason to visit the White Mountains is that they provide a living picture of what the ancestral Sierra Nevada may have looked like 5 million years ago. The older, geologically similar, but more slowly eroded White Mountains also have an uplifted granitic core, but the sedimentary and metamorphic "ancestral" range that lies on top is still quite extensive.

95 Little Lakes Valley to Gem Lakes

With the spectacular peaks of the Sierra Crest on constant display and a procession of lakes to vie for your attention, this out-and-back hike into the John Muir Wilderness offers majestic scenery for relatively moderate effort and is consequently popular.

Start: Mosquito Flat
Distance: 7.0 miles out and back, but there are many other lakes closer to Gem, allowing many shorter routes
Hiking time: About 4 hours
Difficulty: With an overall elevation gain of about 800 feet, this hike requires moderate effort.
Trail condition: Good singletrack trail
Seasons: Late June through Oct
Other trail users: Equestrians and hikers with dogs
Land status: Inyo National Forest, John Muir Wilderness

Nearest towns: Toms Place has food and lodging, Bishop all other amenities.
Fees and permits: None for day use. Wilderness permit required for overnighters. Campfires prohibited.
Maps: Tom Harrison: *Mono Divide High Country*. USGS 7.5-minute quads: Mount Morgan, Mount Abbot.
Trail contacts: Inyo National Forest, White Mountain Ranger Station, 798 N. Main St., Bishop, CA 93514; (760) 873-2500; www.fs .usda.gov/inyo

Finding the trailhead: From US 395, exit west onto Rock Creek Road at Toms Place, about 15 miles south of the Mammoth Lakes turnoff and 24 miles north of Bishop. The paved two-lane Rock Creek Road leads west about 9 miles up Rock Creek Canyon to Rock Creek Stables, whereupon it turns to a one-lane paved road for the remaining 1.6 miles. We pass many picnic areas with overflow parking on this one-lane road, but the main parking area is right at Mosquito Flat, at the end of the road. Trailhead GPS: N37 26.084' / W118 44.848'

The Hike

The highest paved road head in the Sierra Nevada, Mosquito Flat (elevation 10,250 feet) allows for some of the least demanding access to spectacular alpine trails in the entire range. Since our trail follows the route of an old road to the Pine Creek Tungsten Mine, gradients are easy. For these reasons, Little Lakes Valley can get crowded on summer weekends.

Our trail starts us off heading slightly uphill, with Rock Creek rushing past in the willows on our right. Within the first few hundred feet, the 13,000-foot ridge above Little Lakes Valley makes its first appearance, for this is one hike where almost nothing is withheld from the start. Dilettantes can champion their favorite lake or dispute which angle best suits a given peak, but the fact remains, whether you go to the first lake or the last lake in Little Lakes Basin, you're going to see all the best mountains.

Passing the John Muir Wilderness boundary, we walk past Mack Lake, barely noticeable down in its deep ravine, unless we make the effort to look for it. After

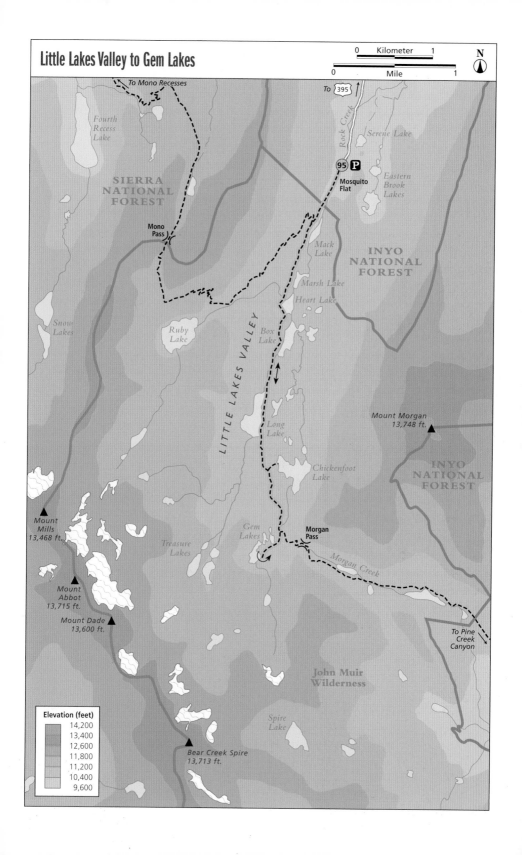

Little Lakes Valley to Gem Lakes

To Mono Recesses

To 395

Rock Creek

Serene Lake

95 P

Mosquito
Flat

Eastern
Brook
Lakes

Fourth
Recess
Lake

SIERRA
NATIONAL
FOREST

INYO
NATIONAL
FOREST

Mono
Pass

Mack
Lake

Marsh Lake

Heart Lake

Snow
Lakes

Ruby
Lake

Box
Lake

LITTLE LAKES VALLEY

Long
Lake

Mount Morgan
13,748 ft.

INYO
NATIONAL
FOREST

Chickenfoot
Lake

Mount
Mills
13,468 ft.

Treasure
Lakes

Gem
Lakes

Morgan
Pass

Morgan Creek

Mount
Abbot
13,715 ft.

Mount Dade
13,600 ft.

To Pine
Creek
Canyon

John Muir
Wilderness

Spire
Lake

Bear Creek Spire
13,713 ft.

Elevation (feet)

| 14,200 |
| 13,400 |
| 12,600 |
| 11,800 |
| 11,200 |
| 10,400 |
| 9,600 |

passing the signed trail junction to Mono Pass (keep left), we climb to a small rise for a splendid view of sprawling Little Lakes Valley, lying at a depth of 3,000 feet beneath its surrounding peaks. Among the most impressive summits are Mount Morgan (13,748 feet) to the left (southeast) and the impressive trio to the right (west): Mount Mills (13,468 feet), Mount Abbot (13,715 feet), and Mount Dade (about 13,600 feet). The Matterhorn-shaped Bear Creek Spire rises to 13,713 feet almost due south, directly above Gem Lakes.

As we hike onward, the lakes flow past in beautiful succession. Descending easily to within hailing distance of Marsh Lake, we cross wildflower meadows to an inlet stream flowing into Heart Lake, swelling full beneath Mount Morgan. Following Heart's shoreline through more meadows, we soon meet Box Lake. Crossing Rock Creek, we rise slightly to meet ravishing Long Lake and pass between its eastern shore and a granite cliff.

Again the path starts uphill—still at an easy gradient—toward Morgan Pass. We pass the junction to Chickenfoot Lake and descend to the outlet stream from Gem Lakes, where we pause at our final junction. Before turning right, look up at the rocky slopes to Morgan Pass, clearly steeper than anything we've encountered on this hike, and yet a modest climb to reach a pass in excess of 11,000 feet.

Turning right at the junction toward Gem Lakes, we head upstream across the meadows to the first of three, a marshy little thing. The second is even smaller, but the third, sitting smartly beneath a bluff, is a bona fide lake.

Miles and Directions

0.0 Parking area.

0.5 Junction to Mono Pass; bear left (south).

1.2 Heart Lake.

1.6 Box Lake.

2.1 Long Lake.

3.0 Chickenfoot Lake trail junction; bear right (south).

3.3 Gem Lakes junction; bear right (south).

3.5 Largest of Gem Lakes.

7.0 Arrive back at the parking area.

96 Lower Rock Creek Canyon

A lushly wooded creek, rich with bird life, makes for good company on this leisurely point-to-point hike through high-desert-like mountain scenery.

Start: Lower Rock Creek bridge on Sherwin Grade Road
Distance: 4.7 miles one-way/shuttle
Hiking time: About 2 hours
Difficulty: Gradually dropping a total of about 1,400 feet in elevation, this is a moderate hike.
Trail condition: Excellent singletrack trail, lined by rocks for much of the route
Seasons: This trail can generally be hiked Mar–Nov, but late Oct is best for fall colors, and Apr–June is best for wildflowers. The canyon is also a popular snowshoeing and ski-touring route in winter.

Other trail users: The trail is very popular among mountain bikers, so be especially wary on blind turns. Equestrians and hikers with dogs may use the trail.
Land status: Inyo National Forest and BLM
Nearest town: Bishop
Fees and permits: None required. This is a day-use area.
Maps: USGS 7.5-minute quads: Toms Place, Casa Diablo Mountain, Rovana
Trail contacts: Inyo National Forest, White Mountain Ranger Station, 798 N. Main St., Bishop, CA 93514; (760) 873-2500; www.fs .usda.gov/inyo

Finding the trailhead: This hike is set up to require a two-car shuttle. The finish is at the old Paradise Lodge, now a private residence. To get there, drive north from Bishop (11.9 miles from the intersection of US 395 and US 6 in Bishop) and exit left (west) at Gorge Road. Immediately beyond US 395 is the junction with Lower Rock Creek Road; turn right (north). The parking area at Paradise is 3 miles up the road. Ending trailhead GPS: N37 28.826' / W118 36.178'

The starting trailhead is about 5 miles farther up Sherwin Grade Road to the next bridge crossing at Lower Rock Creek. Park in the turnout. A road sign there indicates that it is a day-use area only. The trail heads downstream from the east side of the road. Trailhead GPS: N37 31.432' / W118 38.115'

The Hike

When the leaves of the aspens, willows, and cottonwoods turn bright yellow, the east side of the Sierra Nevada is celebrated for its fall colors. Probably no single canyon in the upper Owens Valley is more cherished by local residents for its fall colors than Lower Rock Creek Canyon. Besides these brilliant autumnal displays, the canyon also offers spring wildflowers, good fishing, great bird watching, and a unique hike alongside a "linear oasis" that winds down through the volcanic tablelands of the upper Owens Valley.

From our road head at an elevation of 6,150 feet, our trail winds downhill between steep canyon walls over dry, sandy soil overgrown with rabbitbrush and sage. In striking contrast immediately to our left, a luxurious conglomeration of willows, aspens, and strapping Jeffrey pines encumbers Rock Creek within an unbroken wall

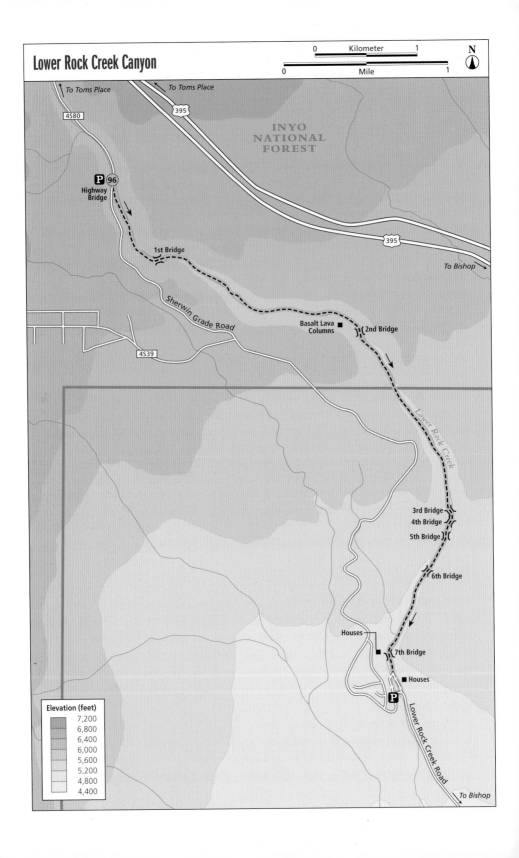

Lower Rock Creek Canyon

0   Kilometer   1

0   Mile   1

N

To Toms Place

To Toms Place

4S80

395

INYO
NATIONAL
FOREST

P 96
Highway
Bridge

395

To Bishop

1st Bridge

Sherwin Grade Road

Basalt Lava
Columns

2nd Bridge

4S39

Lower Rock Creek

3rd Bridge
4th Bridge
5th Bridge

6th Bridge

Houses

7th Bridge

Houses

P

Lower Rock Creek Road

Elevation (feet)

7,200
6,800
6,400
6,000
5,600
5,200
4,800
4,400

To Bishop

of foliage. In late October the broadleaf trees turn a brilliant yellow, sometimes pushing orange, while the shorter clumps of wild rose blaze red.

From the bridge crossing to the eastern bank, we can look up and down Rock Creek, cool and dark, laid out in its shady tunnel of trees and rushes. Among the migratory birds attracted to its flowing waters are the American goldfinch, Wilson's warbler, mountain chickadee, rufous-sided towhee, and Clark's nutcracker. You can sometimes spot American dippers diving to the bottom in search of waterborne insects.

As we descend the eastern bank, losing sight of the road, the canyon turns wilder and more rugged. In its rush toward the lower ground of the Owens Valley, Rock Creek—which originates among the 13,000-foot summits above the Little Lakes Valley, a little more than 10 miles to the west as a bird flies—cuts through hundreds of feet of Bishop Tuff, an extensive and deep lava flow poured into the upper Owens Valley from the Long Valley Caldera. The canyon at this point is about 600 feet deep. In places the higher levels of its walls are lined with sheer palisades of rock, basalt columns similar to those seen at Devils Postpile. Over the centuries these formations have shed tons of talus, building up broad aprons between the creek and canyon wall, and forcing our trail occasionally to climb up and over them in order to continue its downstream course. And yet, the canyon bottom remains consistently fertile, the catchment of all the water and particles of soil that cannot stick to the steep, barren walls.

Crossing and recrossing between Rock Creek's banks on bridges, but always keeping in close cahoots with the stream, we descend steadily for nearly 4 miles before reaching a southwest bend in the river's course, where pyramidal Mount Tom (13,652 feet) pops into view, framed between the V-shaped canyon walls. This signals that the canyon's mouth is near. We start to notice signs of civilization: a power pole, houses on the ridge, the trailhead sign, and, at last, a dirt road. Passing a local power station, we cross the creek a final time and walk down to Paradise through a congress of new houses built along the lower creek.

Miles and Directions

- **0.0** Lower Rock Creek bridge.
- **0.6** First bridge.
- **2.4** Second bridge.
- **3.6** Third bridge.
- **3.7** Fourth bridge.
- **3.8** Fifth bridge.
- **4.0** Sixth bridge.
- **4.4** Seventh bridge.
- **4.7** Lower Rock Creek Road.

97 Muir Pass via Bishop Pass

This arduous trek leads to some of the most stunning and remote mountain vistas in the southern Sierra, scores of alpine lakes, deep canyons, and an unusual bungalow atop Muir Pass.

Start: South Lake
Distance: 38.6 miles out and back
Hiking time: 5 or more days
Difficulty: With a total elevation gain and loss of more than 9,000 feet, this is a formidable trip.
Trail condition: Excellent singletrack trail with occasional exposure. Be prepared to ford creeks and find your way through patches of snow at any time of year.
Seasons: Late June through early Oct
Other trail users: Equestrians permitted but no dogs, hunters, or bikes
Land status: Kings Canyon National Park, John Muir Wilderness, Inyo National Forest

Nearest town: Bishop
Fees and permits: Wildness permit required for overnighters. No campfires permitted above 10,000 feet. Bear canisters required for backpackers.
Maps: Tom Harrison: *Mono Divide High Country, Kings Canyon High Country*. USGS 7.5-minute quads: Mount Thompson, North Palisade.
Trail contacts: Inyo National Forest, White Mountain Ranger Station, 798 N. Main St., Bishop, CA 93514; (760) 873-2500; www.fs .usda.gov/inyo

Finding the trailhead: From US 395 in the center of Bishop, turn west at the junction of CA 168 (West Line Street). Drive a little more than 15 miles to the signed junction of the road to South Lake. Turn left and drive about 7 miles to the end of the road, a trailhead parking area to the east of and above South Lake. Trailhead GPS: N37 10.156' / W118 33.952'

The Hike

From an elevation of about 9,750 feet, our trail climbs on a solid bed of stones in full sight of a crest so craggy, so lofty, so audaciously spectacular, that it makes us think twice—maybe even three times—about whether we really want to walk over it.

Yes . . . we do. So onward we push, passing up junctions to several closer lakes, crossing meadow and stream and mounting switchbacks amid seasonal wildflowers. After a gain of 900 feet in the first 2 miles, we level out and cross the outlet stream of Long Lake, stopping beneath Chocolate Peak (11,658 feet) for a welcome breather. With spectacular views southward to Mount Goode (13,085 feet), whose eastern ridge dips down to Bishop Pass, you may want to consider making your first camp here if you started hiking late in the day, or if you are as yet not accustomed to the thin air of Long Lake's 10,750-foot elevation.

When ready, we follow the eastern shore of Long Lake, hop over its inlet stream, and switchback up to the next shelf, where we cross another stream and pass some glacier-carved tarns. Long before we cross the outlet stream from Saddlerock Lake, we begin to notice how the more luxuriant forest cover has bowed down before the little

South Lake looks its best when fall turns the foliage yellow.

grassy tufts and temporal flowers of the alpine regions. The increasing desolation of the rocky tundra, though starkly beautiful, provokes some powerful empathy for the soul who named the mountains to our left (east) the Inconsolable Range.

Passing Bishop Lake at a distance (the lake is accessed by an unmarked use-trail), we begin our final push toward Bishop Pass, on switchbacks where stunted whitebark pines eke scant nourishment from nutrient-famished soils. Snows linger late on this northern exposure, making each step even more exhausting. Our efforts pay off as we top out at Bishop Pass (11,972 feet) and stop to marvel at the views. Looking backward (north), down the slot we've just ascended, we see a parade of lakes dropping over distance toward the semiarid Owens Valley. Turning ahead (south), we see the Dusy Basin and the plunging contours of the Kings River country, containing some of the deepest canyons on the continent. To our left (east), Mount Agassiz (13,891 feet) stands like a portal gatepost to Kings Canyon National Park, whose boundary is marked by a sign in Bishop Pass—a boundary, incidentally, that also marks our crossing from Inyo to Fresno Counties.

Now we begin our 3,300-foot descent into LeConte Canyon. The crest of the Black Divide rises across the great chasm to the west, its darker metamorphic rocks vertically displaced but not pushed aside by the granite batholiths during the Sierra uplift of 5 million years ago. To the south the unnamed lakes of Dusy Basin, backed by Columbine Peak (12,652 feet), offer some exposed campsites.

Better sites with timber exist in a hanging valley below Dusy Basin, following a grueling set of switchbacks and two crossings of Dusy Branch. After enjoying the briefest

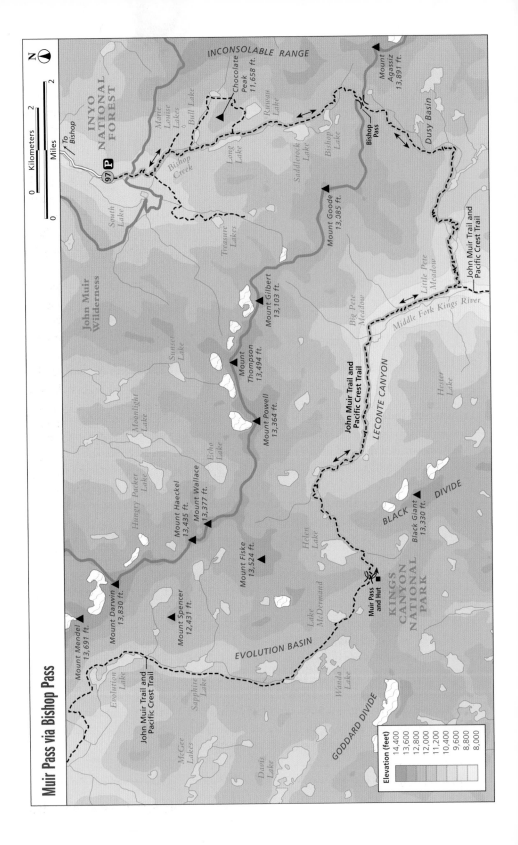

Muir Pass via Bishop Pass

INCONSOLABLE RANGE

Mount Agassiz
13,891 ft.

Chocolate Peak
11,658 ft.

INYO NATIONAL FOREST

To Bishop

Marie Louise Lakes

Bull Lake

Ruwau Lake

Bishop Creek

Long Lake

Bishop Lake

Bishop Pass

Dusy Basin

97

South Lake

Treasure Lakes

Saddlerock Lake

Mount Goode
13,085 ft.

John Muir Wilderness

Sunset Lake

Mount Gilbert
13,103 ft.

Little Pete Meadow

John Muir Trail and Pacific Crest Trail

Moonlight Lake

Mount Thompson
13,494 ft.

Big Pete Meadow

Middle Fork Kings River

Hungry Packer Lake

Echo Lake

Mount Powell
13,364 ft.

John Muir Trail and Pacific Crest Trail

LECONTE CANYON

Hester Lake

Mount Haeckel
13,435 ft.

Mount Wallace
13,377 ft.

Helen Lake

Mount Mendel
13,691 ft.

Mount Darwin
13,830 ft.

Mount Fiske
13,524 ft.

BLACK DIVIDE

Black Giant
13,330 ft.

John Muir Trail and Pacific Crest Trail

Mount Spencer
12,431 ft.

Lake McDermand

Muir Pass and Hut

KINGS NATIONAL PARK

Evolution Lake

Sapphire Lake

EVOLUTION BASIN

McGee Lakes

Davis Lake

Wanda Lake

GODDARD DIVIDE

Elevation (feet)
14,400
13,600
12,800
12,000
11,200
10,400
9,600
8,800
8,000

N

0 Kilometers 2

0 Miles 2

respite from switchbacks on our walk through this hanging valley, we resume our relentless zigzag drop to the floor of LeConte Canyon, where we meet the John Muir and Pacific Crest Trails at a junction near a wilderness ranger station at about 8,500 feet.

After our lean passage over Bishop Pass, the lush meadows and forests along the Middle Fork of the Kings River, which flows through this U-shaped valley of high granite walls, seem like very fat country indeed. Good campsites abound as we walk upstream through conifer forest to the flat, drier expanses of Little Pete Meadow.

Our trail then begins to gear up for its epic climb out of LeConte Canyon, gently at first to Big Pete Meadow, where the canyon bends 90 degrees to the left (west), and then more steeply as we push upward over dynamited sections of sheer granite. Behind us the great glacier-carved canyon gapes wide, like the letter *U* that has been stretched too wide at the top. This is one of the most spectacular sections of the John Muir Trail, but don't let the scenery distract you from your footing.

Climbing relentlessly through rock, we swerve north to avoid a ridge sweeping down from the Black Giant (13,330 feet). Repeatedly crossing and recrossing our narrowing stream, we watch the lodgepole copses give way to meager colonies of stunted whitebark pine, and thence to alpine tundra as we surmount the narrow gorge to reach the chilly shores of Helen Lake at 11,595 feet.

The final assault on Muir Pass is usually snow covered until late in the season, and in some years the snow doesn't melt at all. At 11,955 feet, Muir Pass occupies a rocky saddle in the Goddard Divide. To the west we can see Wanda Lake. This seems appropriate, since Wanda and Helen—the two lakes that flank Muir Pass—were Muir's daughters.

The most curious feature of Muir Pass is the round stone hut, built by the Sierra Club and Forest Service for snowbound travelers and dedicated in 1933 to John Muir. This apparent hybrid of an igloo and a beehive—though cold, dank, and often surrounded by snow—seems to attract its share of lodgers even in fine weather, mainly for the novelty of it.

Miles and Directions

0.0 South Lake parking area.

0.8 Junction of Treasure Lakes Trail; bear left (southeast).

1.4 Junction of Marie Louise Lakes trail; bear right (south).

1.8 Junction of Bull Lake Trail; bear right (south).

2.0 Long Lake.

2.6 Junction of Ruwau Lake Trail; bear right (south).

3.6 Saddlerock Lake.

5.3 Bishop Pass.

11.6 Junction with JMT and PCT in LeConte Canyon; bear right (north).

13.3 Big Pete Meadow.

18.2 Helen Lake.

19.3 Muir Pass.

38.6 Arrive back at the parking area.

98 The Little Loop from Glacier Lodge

Most mountain hikes on the east side of the Sierra Nevada are steep, long, and difficult. Here, in the heart of one of the most spectacular mountain canyons and in full view of the Palisade Crest and its glaciers, is an easy walk that even children can manage.

Start: Day-use parking area before the bridge near the end of Glacier Lodge Road

Distance: 1.8 miles round-trip

Hiking Time: About 1 hour

Difficulty: Easy, despite 400 feet elevation gained and lost

Trail condition: Part singletrack and part dirt road, this loop encounters some unmarked junctions, but it is easy to stay on track.

Seasons: June–Oct

Other trail users: Equestrians and hikers with dogs may use the trail.

Land status: Inyo National Forest

Nearest town: Big Pine

Fees and permits: None

Maps: Tom Harrison: *The Palisades Trail Map.* USGS 7.5-minute quads: Split Mountain, Coyote Flat.

Trail contacts: Inyo National Forest, 351 Pacu Ln., Suite 200, Bishop, CA 93514; (760) 873-2400; www.fs.usda.gov/inyo

Finding the trailhead: From US 395 in downtown Big Pine, drive west on two-lane, paved Glacier Lodge Road for 10.7 miles to the day-use parking area at the end of the road. There are picnic tables and pit toilets at the parking lot. No overnight parking is allowed. Trailhead GPS: N37 07.520' / W118 26.259'

The Hike

Big Pine Creek is one of those gargantuan, raw-boned clefts in the eastern Sierra wall, opening from the high desert of the Great Basin with all the promise of desolate mountains. Upon driving up the road, however, we quickly find ourselves in forests, with a dashing creek for company. The glaciated, U-shaped valley lies 4,000 feet below the Palisade Crest, and is so wide and open that it seems quite parklike. The landmark resort of Glacier Lodge, which stood for decades on the south side of Big Pine Creek, burned down in spring 1998. The tiny Glacier Lodge Store and post office (GPS: N37 07.435' / W118 26.217') now anchors the settlement of summer homes.

Starting from the road's end, where a gate regulates vehicular access to several residential cabins, we set out upstream through pines and cottonwoods, from an elevation of 7,800 feet. Near the bosky confluence of Big Pine Creek's north and south forks, we cross the road to the last cabin and mount on a switchback to a bridged crossing of the North Fork. Dashing down through forest cover, the stream here is known as First Falls.

Across the bridge, we turn uphill at a junction, steeply zigzagging up the rushing North Fork through delightful pockets of aspen, Jeffrey pine, mountain mahogany,

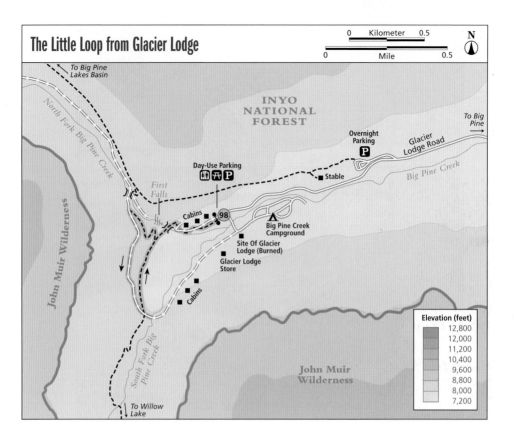

The Little Loop from Glacier Lodge

Kilometer 0 0.5

Mile 0 0.5

N

To Big Pine Lakes Basin

North Fork Big Pine Creek

INYO NATIONAL FOREST

John Muir Wilderness

Overnight Parking P

To Big Pine →

Glacier Lodge Road

Day-Use Parking P

Big Pine Creek

First Falls

Stable

Cabins 98

Big Pine Creek Campground

Site Of Glacier Lodge (Burned)

Glacier Lodge Store

Cabins

South Fork Big Pine Creek

John Muir Wilderness

Elevation (feet)
12,800
12,000
11,200
10,400
9,600
8,800
8,000
7,200

To Willow Lake

sage, and seasonal wildflowers. Though steep, the climbing ends abruptly at a dirt road, where we turn left.

Old dirt roads make the most evocative of tracks through sagebrush hills, reminding at least some of us of old Western movies. Layers of ridges provide backdrops to the flood-scoured valley of the South Fork, culminating in the Palisade Crest, between 3 and 4 miles distant. The high point of that ridge is the Middle Palisade (14,040 feet), which nurses the Middle Palisade Glacier, the second largest in the Sierra, after the Palisade Glacier, out of sight just to the right. This quintessential alpine scene is the same that drew famed mountaineer Norman Clyde to spend some twenty winters as a caretaker at Glacier Lodge.

Descending the road through sagebrush, we pass our return trail (the South Fork Trail) for now to walk down to the South Fork of Big Pine Creek. The valley floor is chock full of boulders and cobbles, the vestiges of hefty spring runoffs that periodically wash over the banks, leaving jumbled rocks and shrubs or (in years of heavy overflow) denuded tufts of vegetation.

In late-season times of low water, consider fording this creek (see "Option," below); otherwise, turn around here. Backtrack up the dirt road about 200 yards to where the South Fork Trail crosses the road, and take the

First Falls keeps up a lively flow till late in the summer season.

branch that goes to the right (east). Walk to the bridge by First Falls, which we crossed earlier, and return to your car the way you came.

Option

If the South Fork of Big Pine Creek is shallow and slow enough for your party to ford safely, consider taking off your shoes and doing that. The dirt road on the opposite bank leads past summer cabins 0.7 mile down to the site of Glacier Lodge, where you can cross Big Pine Creek on the road bridge back to your car.

Miles and Directions

0.0 Day-use parking area.

0.3 Footbridge over North Fork of Big Pine Creek (GPS: N37 07.487' / W118 26.500').

0.4 Junction after bridge; bear right (northwest).

0.6 Meet dirt road; turn left (south).

1.1 South Fork of Big Pine Creek; turn around here (GPS: N37 07.206' / W118 26.595').

1.2 Junction with return trail; bear right (northeast).

1.8 Arrive back at the day-use parking area.

99 Big Pine Lakes Basin

This out-and-back day hike or overnight backpack trip visits two of the Big Pine Lakes, resplendent in their mountain basin hemmed in by the 14,000-foot Palisade Crest, home to the Sierra Nevada's largest glacier.

Start: Overnight parking area near the end of Glacier Lodge Road

Distance: 9.6 miles out and back

Hiking time: About 6–7 hours, but the basin makes a better backpack trip of 2 or 3 days

Difficulty: Strenuous, with a gross elevation gain and loss of 2,500 feet

Trail condition: Good singletrack trail

Seasons: June–Sept

For more information, see Hike 98.

Finding the trailhead: From US 395 in downtown Big Pine, drive west on two-lane, paved Glacier Lodge Road for 10 miles, where you turn right (north) into the long-term parking area for backpackers (elevation 7,700 feet). If you drive past the stable, you have gone too far. Trailhead GPS: N37 07.691' / W118 25.667'.

The Hike

Start early on this trip, for the trail kicks off with nearly 2 miles of steady climbing up a dry, sandy sagebrush slope, only fleetingly dotted with Jeffrey pines. Afternoon temperatures can grow uncomfortably warm, at which times the tantalizing views up the South Fork of Big Pine Creek to the Palisade Crest and the Middle Palisade Glacier will make the long haul seem all the longer.

Meeting a signed spur trail, we have the option of descending to a bridge for water if we need it. If you don't need the water, stay on the upper trail. There's no use losing altitude that we only have to regain later.

As we approach the rocky head of the canyon, we can see the North Fork of Big Pine Creek pouring down the rocks in the guise of Second Falls. Despite the passage of ancient glaciers through this canyon, this is not one of your white, clean-edged waterfalls that drops so neatly from a hanging valley. Instead, Second Falls gushes in somewhat hectic disarray all over the rocks, but we admire it nonetheless for that.

A lower trail from the bridge meets up with us at a four-way junction, where another, rather poorly maintained path rises to Logging Flat and the Baker Creek drainage. We, however, continue straight, toward the right (north) side of the waterfall, climbing the rocky wall on a couple of switchbacks that take us into a narrow, reddish-walled ravine shared with the North Fork's cascades. Passing the John Muir Wilderness sign, we climb over the rim into a wooded valley known by the Tolkienesque name of Cienega Mirth. Since *cienega* is Spanish for "swampy place," its whole meaning perhaps hits close to "Jovial Fen." The gladdening sound of the creek notwithstanding, the surrounding valley seems more on the dry side, with woods of Jeffrey pine and lodgepole pine interspersed with flats of manzanita and other scrub.

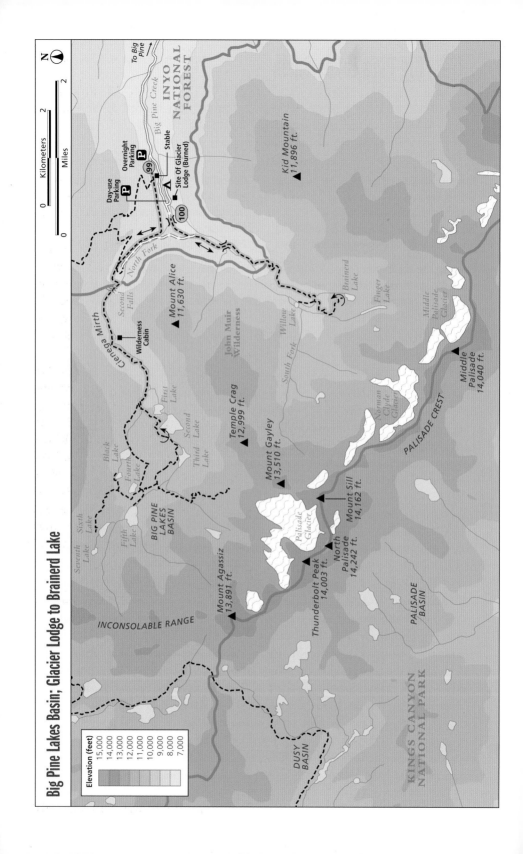

Big Pine Lakes Basin: Glacier Lodge to Brainerd Lake

Elevation (feet)
- 15,000
- 14,000
- 13,000
- 12,000
- 11,000
- 10,000
- 9,000
- 8,000
- 7,000

N

Kilometers
0   1   2

Miles
0   1   2

To Big Pine

Big Pine Creek

INYO NATIONAL FOREST

Overnight Parking

Day-use Parking

99

Stable

Site Of Glacier Lodge (Burned)

100

North Fork

Second Falls

Mount Alice 11,630 ft.

Cienega Mirth

Wilderness Cabin

First Lake

Black Lake

Fourth Lake

Second Lake

Third Lake

Fifth Lake

Sixth Lake

Seventh Lake

BIG PINE LAKES BASIN

Mount Agassiz 13,891 ft.

INCONSOLABLE RANGE

Palisade Glacier

Thunderbolt Peak 14,003 ft.

North Palisade 14,242 ft.

Mount Sill 14,162 ft.

Mount Gayley 13,510 ft.

Temple Crag 12,999 ft.

JOHN MUIR WILDERNESS

South Fork

Willow Lake

Norman Clyde Glacier

PALISADE CREST

Middle Palisade Glacier

Middle Palisade 14,040 ft.

Brainerd Lake

Finger Lake

Kid Mountain 11,896 ft.

PALISADE BASIN

KINGS CANYON NATIONAL PARK

DUSY BASIN

At 2.7 miles we pass a short detour that leads to the Big Pine Creek Wilderness Ranger Station, a handsome stone cabin visible from the trail on the edge of the creek. It was built in 1925 as a vacation lodge by actor Lon Chaney, who specialized in playing werewolves and other monsters, a thought that may or may not quicken our resolve to return before nightfall.

The forest thins beyond the cabin as we climb out of Cienega Mirth on rocky slopes overgrown with scrub. We soon become aware of rising mountaintops ahead, especially the broken front of Temple Crag (12,999 feet) on the left (south). As we rise farther into the Big Pine Lakes basin, larger summits slide over the horizon—the 13,000-foot ridge of the Inconsolable Range, its southern end terminating at Mount Agassiz (13,891 feet).

After crossing and recrossing the creek, you zigzag to a junction. Turn left (south) to cross the North Fork creek yet again, and climb within the next mile to views of First and Second Lakes, both of which bear the strange, milky, turquoise hue of "glacier milk," meltwater from glaciers containing granules ground from the rocks beneath it. The source is the spectacular Palisade Glacier, the largest active glacier south of the Cascades, which hangs spectacularly beneath North Palisade. An obvious use-trail leads to campsites near Second Lake.

Take some time to look around this corner of the Big Pine Lakes Basin, and to climb the trail above Second Lake for different points of view of the astounding scenery. South of Mount Agassiz, the Sierra Crest crescendos to the 14,000-foot ridge of the Palisades, containing the northernmost of the Sierra's 14,000-foot peaks—no fewer than five of them standing in a line less than 1.5 miles long: Thunderbolt Peak (14,003 feet), Starlight Peak (about 14,200 feet), North Palisade (14,242 feet), Polemonium Peak (about 14,200 feet), and Mount Sill (14,162 feet). In fact, the Palisade Crest does not stop there, for it reaches yet another notable zenith in Middle Palisade (14,040 feet), out of sight about 2 miles southeast of Mount Sill, above the drainage of the South Fork of Big Pine Creek. This formidable armory of peaks effectively closes off the basin to all proper trails, except for the one on which we came and now return.

Miles and Directions

0.0 Overnight parking area.

0.9 Junction to lower trail; bear right (west).

1.7 Four-way junction; continue straight (northwest).

2.7 Ranger patrol cabin (Lon Chaney's house).

4.2 Junction with basin loop trail; bear left (south).

4.4 Hillside above First Lake.

4.8 Inlet creek above Second Lake.

9.6 Arrive back at the overnight parking area.

100 Glacier Lodge to Brainerd Lake

Sheltered below the jagged crest of the Palisades, the Sierra's largest collection of glaciers provides a magnificent alpine backdrop to this rugged Eastern Sierra canyon.

Start: Day-use parking area before the bridge near the end of Glacier Lodge Road
Distance: 8.4 miles out and back
Hiking time: About 5–6 hours
Difficulty: Moderately demanding, with an overall elevation gain and loss of about 2,700 feet
Trail condition: Good singletrack trail
Seasons: June–Sept
Other trail users: Equestrians and hikers with dogs use trail. No bikes.

Land status: Inyo National Forest, John Muir Wilderness
Nearest town: Big Pine
Fees and permits: Day hikers do not need a wilderness permit, but overnighters do. Campfire permit required if using a stove or campfire.
Maps: Tom Harrison: *The Palisades Trail Map.* USGS 7.5-minute quad: Split Mountain.
Trail contacts: Inyo National Forest, 351 Pacu Ln., Suite 200, Bishop, CA 93514; (760) 873-2400; www.fs.usda.gov/inyo

Finding the trailhead: From US 395 in downtown Big Pine, drive west on two-lane, paved Glacier Lodge Road for 10.7 miles to the end of the road on the north side of Big Pine Creek. (If you cross the bridge to the site of Glacier Lodge, you've driven too far.) Park in the day-use parking area. There are picnic tables and pit toilets. No overnight parking is allowed. Trailhead GPS: N37 07.521' / W118 26.223'

The Hike

Starting from the road's end at an elevation of 7,800 feet, walk upstream past several residential cabins. After the last cabin, mount on a switchback to a bridged crossing of the North Fork at First Falls. Across the bridge, our trail contours around the hillside (bypassing an uphill junction) to a dirt road. From there, we jog left briefly to the signposted junction with the South Fork of Big Pine Creek trail at 0.7 mile.

The South Fork canyon makes a handsome transition between the deserts of the high Great Basin and the jagged alpine teeth of the Palisade Crest. Pungent sagebrush carpets the ground, spiked with pines, mountain mahoganies, and even some daring little beavertail cacti, while cottonwoods and aspens hug Big Pine Creek, all within ready sight of the Palisade glaciers. In August, blue elderberry trees dangle bunches of seedy, tart fruit, but red Sierra gooseberries make far sweeter trailside snacks.

At 1.2 miles we cross the South Fork of Big Pine Creek on a sturdy bridge of split logs, planed flat. From the broad upper basin, we have a fine full view of the South Fork valley's granite headwalls and their talus aprons, sporadically reclaimed by ranks of sturdy evergreens. Climbing gently to these boulder slopes, we cross the signposted margin of John Muir Wilderness and begin our switchbacking climb up the north-facing headwall, enjoying the views down-canyon clear to the cabins near our road head.

Topping the first headwall on a granite ridge amid a scattering of lightning-blasted pines, the Palisade Crest reappears, larger than life and radiant with light reflected from the Middle Palisade Glacier. One of the most jagged, stirring landscapes of the Sierra Nevada, the Palisade Crest looks the way all mountains would look if kindergarteners were in charge of drawing up the plans. As we hike farther, the rocks and granite crags in the foreground shift aside to permit new perspectives of this awe-inspiring ridge, especially its looming northern wall, which culminates in 14,162-foot Mount Sill.

We drop into a valley, where the forest closes in. Passing the turnoff to Willow Lake (which is well advanced in its

The mighty Palisade Crest, with the largest glaciers in the Sierra Nevada, rise grandly above the upper reaches of the South Fork of Big Pine Creek.

transition to a marsh), we hop across the outlet stream from Brainerd Lake and commence the climb up the second headwall of the South Fork canyon. Skirting the noisy outlet ravine from Finger Lake, our trail passes a small, unnamed, granite-bound lakelet before mounting to splendid Brainerd Lake, coddled in its high granite basin below an amphitheater of peaks around the crest of the 14,040-foot Middle Palisade.

Miles and Directions

- **0.0** Day-use parking area.
- **0.3** Footbridge over North Fork of Big Pine Creek (GPS: N37 07.487' / W118 26.500').
- **0.4** Junction after bridge; bear left (south).
- **0.6** Junction with dirt road; turn left (south).
- **0.7** Junction with South Fork trail; turn right (southwest).
- **1.2** Bridge across South Fork of Big Pine Creek.
- **1.6** Enter John Muir Wilderness.
- **2.8** Top of first headwall.
- **3.2** Junction with Willow Lake trail; bear left (south).
- **3.4** Cross Brainerd Lake's creek.
- **3.9** Unnamed lakelet.
- **4.2** Brainerd Lake.
- **8.4** Arrive back at the day-use parking area.

101 Methuselah National Recreation Trail

Fantastic for their tortured shapes and longevity, the bristlecone pines that dwell in the harsh White Mountains are the world's oldest living things. This loop hike visits a grove where the oldest of them all still lives.

Start: Schulman Grove Visitor Center
Distance: 4.2-mile loop
Hiking time: About 2 hours
Difficulty: Moderate, despite an elevation gain and loss of more than 800 feet
Trail condition: Excellent singletrack trail
Seasons: Late May through early Nov
Other trail users: Leashed dogs are welcome. No hunting or bikes are allowed on the trail.
Land status: Inyo National Forest, Ancient Bristlecone Pine Forest
Nearest town: Big Pine
Fees and permits: The Forest Service charges a fee to enter the Ancient Bristlecone Pine

Forest, payable the visitor center at Schulman Grove. No campfires permitted.
Map: USGS 7.5-minute quad: Mount Blanco.
Trail contacts: Inyo National Forest, White Mountain Public Lands Information Center, 798 N. Main St., Bishop, CA 93514; www.fs.usda.gov/recarea/inyo/recreation/recarea/?recid=40292. InterAgency Visitor Center (intersection of US 395 and CA 136, south of Lone Pine), PO Box R, Lone Pine, CA 93545; (760) 876-6222; www.fs.usda.gov/recarea/inyo/recarea/%3frecid=20698.

Finding the trailhead: To reach the trailhead parking area at Schulman Grove, go to the junction of US 395 and CA 168, on the northern edge of Big Pine. Turn east onto CA 168 and drive about 13 miles east to Cedar Flat, an undeveloped area of the White Mountains. Turn left (north) at the signed road junction of White Mountain Road, drive 10 miles up the winding, paved, two-lane mountain road to the Schulman Grove parking area. No water is available. Trailhead GPS: N37 23.129' / W118 10.681'

The Hike

Although not in the Sierra Nevada, this White Mountain hike is close to the Owens Valley and features spectacular views of the Sierra, and so it seems fair game for any hiker in the region. There is also the added attraction of walking through a forest that contains probably the oldest living thing on earth, a bristlecone pine (*Pinus longaeva*) known as Methuselah. Scientists have estimated its age to be close to 5,000 years old. Although the exact tree is not identified in an effort to discourage vandalism, it is both humbling and exhilarating to walk among living groves that were old when the Great Wall of China was being built.

Stop by the visitor center at the Shulman Grove, where you park, to learn how scientists date these ancient bristlecones. Signs also explain how to identify them, a matter mainly of distinguishing them from limber pines, the only other pine that can grow in the harsh, arid heights favored by the bristlecone.

The Methuselah Trail starts at the wooden porch outside the visitor center, at an elevation of 10,050 feet. A trail booklet, linking text to numbered posts, guides hikers to various points of interest along the trail. Some benches are occasionally provided.

Turning right at the first junction, we ascend a steep hillside through a bristlecone forest above the dry canyon of the South Fork of Birch Creek. Climbing to a ridge at 0.5 mile, we enjoy our first extensive view on the trail, looking east over the bristlecone groves to the distant desert ranges and basins of the Death Valley region. On an easy gradient, we now traverse a ravine to the second ridge, where we can look down to the Methuselah Grove on the dry slopes below us.

Rather than descend directly to the Methuselah Grove, the trail takes a gentler roundabout course, crossing over to yet a third ridge, which offers the most extensive views from our trail, and one of the most comprehensive views on the continent. To the southwest the line of the Sierra Crest marches southward down the Owens Valley, a wall containing some of the highest mountains in the contiguous United States. To the southeast the distant Last Chance Range fences off the northern end of Death Valley, lowest point in the Western Hemisphere. This view, sweeping from west to east, encompasses an elevation difference of close to 14,000 feet. Closer to the foreground, the dry expanses of the Inyo and White Mountains, and the desert playa in the valley below us, provide a desolate yet utterly enchanting scene.

Now we begin our descent to the Methuselah Grove, switchbacking down a dry ridge studded with gnarly mountain mahogany trees. As we enter the grove, we find the weather-beaten pines mostly of modest stature, though their stark, contorted shapes certainly project an ancient image. Unlike the giant sequoia, the bristlecone grows very slowly, adding perhaps an inch in radius every century. The wood consequently is very dense and hard. To conserve energy in the sparse soil, parts of the tree actually die, while other parts continue to live. Their age boggles the mind. Take some time to reflect that some of these trees, living now, were alive before the Great Pyramid at Giza was built. Methuselah itself (which, as noted above, is not identified) was already 2,400 years old when Julius Caesar conquered Gaul. Scientists have found pieces of deadwood in these groves that were alive more than 11,000 years ago—that is, since before the world's first urban civilizations developed in Mesopotamia. Small wonder that the Forest Service strictly enforces that you stay on the trail, not pick up any pieces of wood, and build no campfires.

After leaving the Methuselah Grove, our return trail roughly parallels our earlier efforts, only at a lower elevation, undulating between ravine and ridge spur. Throughout the next mile we meet many more striking examples of ancient trees, including, at about 3 miles, a large grove of bristlecone pines between 3,000 and 4,000 years old. At about 3.5 miles, we begin to ascend our ridge back to the visitor center on switchbacks through a thickening forest. Reaching a bench at a final overlook, we walk back to the parking area on a more leisurely gradient.

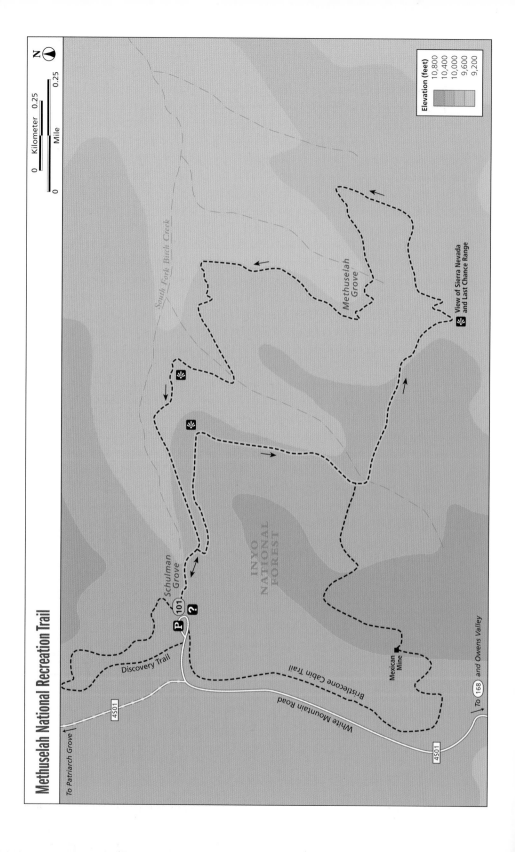

Methuselah National Recreation Trail

To Patriarch Grove

4501

Discovery Trail

Schulman Grove

P

101

?

INYO
NATIONAL
FOREST

White Mountain Road

Bristlecone Cabin Trail

Mexican Mine

4501

To 168 and Owens Valley

South Fork Birch Creek

Methuselah Grove

View of Sierra Nevada
and Last Chance Range

N

Kilometer   0   0.25

Mile   0   0.25

Elevation (feet)
10,800
10,400
10,000
9,600
9,200

Miles and Directions

0.0 Parking area.

0.1 Junction; bear right (south).

0.8 Junction with trail to Mexican Mine; bear left (south).

1.5 View of Last Chance Range and Sierra Nevada.

2.4 Methuselah Grove.

4.2 Arrive back at the parking area.

102 White Mountain Peak

At 14,246 feet above sea level, California's third-highest peak offers the most extensive views of the Sierra Nevada and surrounding Great Basin of any spot on earth. White Mountain Peak does not require a permit and is an easier climb than its far more popular rival, Mount Whitney, the only other California "fourteener" with a maintained trail to its summit.

Start: Locked gate near the end of White Mountain Road

Distance: 15.0 miles out and back

Hiking time: About 8–9 hours

Difficulty: Strenuous because of high altitude and an overall gain and loss in elevation of more than 3,000 feet

Trail condition: Rocky dirt road the entire way

Seasons: Mid-June through Oct. Avoid in stormy weather, which can occur throughout summer.

Other trail users: Dogs under control are welcome.

Land status: Inyo National Forest

Nearest town: Big Pine

Fees and permits: None

Maps: USGS 7.5-minute quads: Mount Barcroft, Juniper Mountain, White Mountain Peak

Trail contacts: Inyo National Forest, White Mountain Public Lands Information Center, 798 N. Main St., Bishop, CA 93514; www.fs.usda.gov/recarea/inyo/recreation/recarea/?recid=40292

Special considerations: You should be acclimated to high altitudes before attempting this hike. There is no reliable water. Start early because thunderheads tend to build in the afternoon, and this is an exposed route the entire distance. Bring warm, wind-resistant clothing. You also might want to bring a broad-scale map to help identify distant landmarks, from Tioga Pass south to below Lone Pine and eastward far into Nevada. The staff at the White Mountain Research Station can lend assistance in an emergency, but please do not bother them with requests that are within your power to fulfill with a reasonable measure of foresight (e.g., lack of water or food, inadequate clothing, exhaustion, or impending darkness). To get an early start, many hikers spend the night camped in or beside their vehicles at the locked gate, at an elevation of 11,680 feet; campfires are not permitted. Because of the fragile ground cover and lack of any facilities there, however, the Forest Service strongly encourages hikers instead to camp at the Grandview Campground, 5.2 miles up White Mountain Road from its junction with CA 168, at an elevation of 8,600 feet.

Finding the trailhead: From the junction of US 395 and CA 168, on the northern edge of Big Pine, drive east on CA 168 about 13 miles to Cedar Flat, an undeveloped area of the White Mountains about 1.3 miles before you reach Westguard Pass. Turn left (north) at the signed road junction of White Mountain Road. Drive 10 miles up the winding, paved, two-lane mountain road to the Schulman Grove turnoff. Beyond there, White Mountain Road is unpaved but wide and generally suitable for two-wheel drive. Drive 16.4 miles to where the road is closed by a metal gate, and park to the side. Trailhead GPS: N37 33.479' / W118 14.182'

Dawn on the White Mountain Peak Trail reveals the neighboring Sierra Nevada flush with light.

The Hike

Beyond the locked gate (elevation 11,680 feet), the dirt road climbs steeply through a tundra-like world of grasses, low ground covers, stones, and lichens. The English have a good word for this type of landscape—heath—by which they mean a wasteland, unproductive except as meager forage for sheep. (And sure enough, a herd of desert bighorn do frequent this trail.) Biologists prefer the term alpine fell-field. Whatever you call it, it's a vast landscape—treeless, wind-blasted, exposed to the elements, and domed by the biggest sky this side of Montana. To the south and east, range upon desert range recede into the distance. To the west the great wall of the Sierra Nevada stretches from horizon to horizon; and yet, from our own lofty point of view, it appears less mighty than it does from the Owens Valley floor.

At 2 miles our road passes through the middle of an outpost of the University of California: the White Mountain Research Station, aka the Barcroft Lab. Resident scientists study high-altitude physiology, arctic flora and fauna, astrophysics, and geology. Its motley collection of sheds, storage trailers, working vehicles, barking dogs, a sheep paddock, and other bits and pieces, gathered about a central Quonset hut, give this place the atmosphere of some half-familiar locale from a 1950s science-fiction movie.

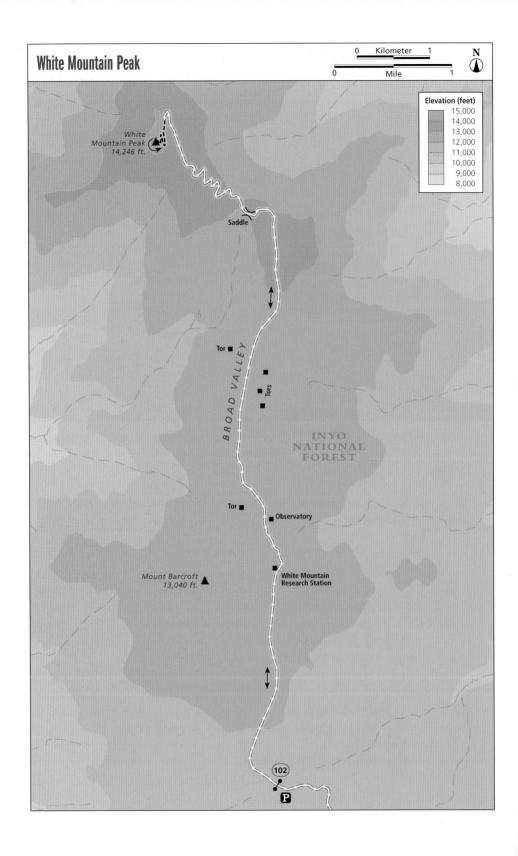

Climbing the low ridge behind the main station to the astronomical observatory, our first view of White Mountain Peak is a stunner. Its sharp summit rises abruptly from a low, broad valley. Bizarre, isolated heaps of rocks jut upward from this ridge and from the wide plain below, like a crop of Neolithic burial mounds. The English have a good word for these too—they call them tors. Our lonely road, as it rolls down into that broad valley between the tors, would not seem out of place on some forlorn English moor.

If the wind is blowing as you climb the low ridge up the north side of the valley, you will be glad you brought a windbreaker, watch cap, and wool sweater. We gain a small breather while dropping briefly to a saddle between the ridge and the barren peak, which looms just ahead, larger than life. We can see our road sweeping upward in broad, well-graded switchbacks that climb the steep mountainside through fields of dark scree.

On this final 2-mile stretch to the summit, each switchback brings vistas more dramatic than the last. Huge green circles appear on the floor of Deep Springs Valley, to the east, produced by irrigation systems that revolve around a central pivot. More "crop circles" and field patterns appear in the Hammil Valley, to the west, and around the "oasis" of Bishop in the Owens Valley. Boundary Peak, Nevada's highest at 13,143 feet, juts up from the northernmost end of the White Mountain range, whose western escarpment drops abruptly away in a sequence of deep canyons.

The 14,246-foot summit of White Mountain Peak is capped with a stone hut, another scientific outpost of the University of California. It's closed to the public, but the walls provide a welcome windbreak, enabling you to sit with a map and binoculars for an hour or two, though mindful of the weather. A good map reader can easily pick out scores of Sierra Nevada summits and canyons along well over 100 miles of its eastern escarpment. Even if you don't read maps, it's an awesome sight.

Miles and Directions

- **0.0** Locked gate.
- **2.0** White Mountain Research Station.
- **2.5** Observatory on ridge with first view of White Mountain Peak.
- **5.5** Saddle below White Mountain Peak.
- **7.5** Summit of White Mountain Peak.
- **15.0** Arrive back at the gate.

103 Whitney Portal Natural Arch

This cross-country adventure leads to what is arguably the most spectacular wind-carved arch in the Alabama Hills, perched on a ridge with superlative views of the Whitney Crest. Although it requires some cross-country walking, it's a fun challenge for veteran hikers who take care to observe their route and surroundings.

Start: Whitney Portal Road

Distance: About 1.4 miles, depending on your route

Hiking time: About 2 hours

Difficulty: Moderate, with negligible change in elevation

Trail condition: We start and end on an established singletrack trail, but depart from it to walk cross-country to the arch, mainly by direct sight and common sense. Footing is rocky. Be prepared for some basic boulder-scrambling on the ridge.

Seasons: Year-round, depending on local weather conditions. May is best for wildflowers.

Other trail users: Hikers with dogs, equestrians. The trail from the trailhead is open to motorized bikes, but they are restricted from cross-country travel.

Land status: Alabama Hills Recreation Lands, BLM

Nearest town: Lone Pine

Fees and permits: None

Map: USGS 7.5-minute quad: Mt. Langley

Trail contacts: Alabama Hills Recreation Area, BLM, www.blm.gov/ca/st/en/fo/bishop/scenic_byways/alabamas.html. Eastern Sierra InterAgency Visitor Center (intersection of US 395 and CA 136, south of Lone Pine), PO Box R, Lone Pine, CA 93545; (760) 876-6222; www.fs.usda.gov/recarea/inyo/recarea/%3frecid=20698.

Finding the trailhead: From US 395 in the center of Lone Pine, drive west up Whitney Portal Road 5.2 miles, past Cuffe Guest Ranch, and turn right (north) onto an unmarked dirt road (turn-off GPS: N36 35.685' / W118 09.158') that goes about 100 yards to a wire fence. Park there. The trail starts through the open gateway in a wire fence, at an elevation of about 5,150 feet. Trailhead GPS: N36 35.725' / W118 09.182'

The Hike

One of the most dramatic scenes in the western United States is the view of the Sierra Crest from the Alabama Hills. The mountains—including Mount Whitney, highest in the continental United States—rise nearly 2 vertical miles above the fantastically weathered hills at their base. The fantastic boulder piles and weathered granite of the Alabama Hills have set the stage for scores of films, including *Gunga Din* (where they served as a stand-in for the Himalayas), *Star Trek, Gladiator, Django Unchained, Tremors, Maverick, How the West Was Won*, and *Nevada Smith*, as well as the *Lone Ranger* TV series and scores of other Westerns. Dirt roads and primitive tracks crisscross the hills, many manageable by ordinary two-wheel-drive vehicles. The BLM manages 30,000 acres of the rugged landscape as the Alabama Hills Recreation Area, and visitors who want to drive to visit celebrated settings for movie and TV shows can find maps aplenty, but hikers will find few dedicated hiking trails. (One of them, the Alabama Hills Natural Arches Trail, is described as Hike MM). The wide-open landscape makes for easy and enjoyable cross-country exploration from any road.

An established trail starts at the parking area, and we will follow it part of the way. From the trailhead gate, you look downhill to Lone Pine Creek. Despite the hulking presence of Lone Pine Mountain and the Whitney Crest, the landscape immediately surrounding us is desert—sagebrush is the dominant plant—but Lone Pine Creek is a startling contrast, a lush, linear oasis some hundred feet wide and many miles long, choked with willows, cottonwoods, aspens, and gigantic sagebrush. If you linger with a pair of binoculars on this hillside above the creek, especially in the evening and early morning, you should be able to enjoy a rich display of bird and animal life.

Plunked down at the foot of the highest section of the Sierra Crest, the photogenic Alabama Hills have starred in hundreds of films, advertisements, and TV shows.

After crossing the footbridge across Lone Pine Creek, the established trail plows up the shallow, sandy ridge to the left. Before going farther, stop and get your bearings so you can easily find this bridge on your cross-country return: The Alabama Hills lie north beyond that first little ridge, while the Sierra escarpment rises dramatically to the west. Note also how two fence lines converge on the bridge from the west and the north, funneling us back to the stream crossing—an important point on our return trip. Hit that "funnel" and you will be funneled back to the bridge.

Then walk westward up the established trail. You will pass the end of the fence line and then, at 0.4 mile from the start, meet a busted but firmly planted yellow signpost. This is a good spot to leave the trail, but first spot the arch for your target destination: It is perched on the crest of the nearest ridge of the Alabama Hills, smoothly rounded like the eye of a needle with sky showing through the hole. You may have to search carefully, because it appears quite small from this distance.

The plan now, quite simply, is to walk cross-country to the arch. Initially you need to walk downhill to a dry wash at the base of our destination ridge. Bottoming out in

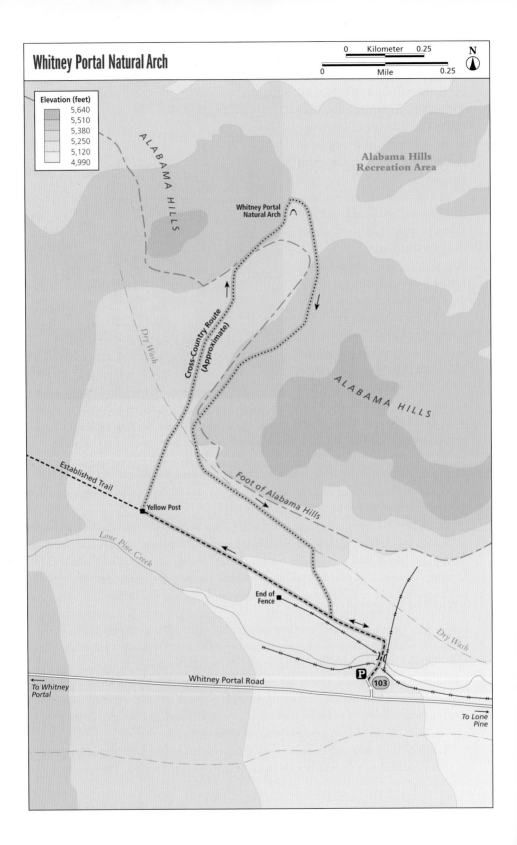

the wash, with the arch in sight, climb steeply up toward the ridge over granite sand and rock, hiking through sagebrush and taking special care to avoid the occasional cholla cactus, whose vicious barbs hook everything that brushes it and are very painful and difficult to remove. Soon we are surrounded by a fantastic jumble of orange-tinted boulders, rounded and weathered into globes, fins, and hoodoos.

The views from the arch are intensely dramatic. To the west we see the Whitney Portal Road zigzagging up the front of the massive escarpment, with Mount Whitney (14,505 feet) plainly visible above, the highest point in the contiguous United States—although Lone Pine Peak (12,944 feet) appears to be much larger from here because it is closer. Photographers can spend hours here studying the constantly changing shadows that play across the rounded, weathered Alabama Hills and the serrated peaks of the Sierra escarpment. Take some time to explore the rocky ridge around the arch, where thousands of intriguing shapes and crevices will stir the imagination and challenge the rock climber in all of us. You may find other, smaller arches as well.

When time comes to return, you could return the same way. Or you could also try this different, more direct approach: Descend the ridge to the dry wash, then follow its natural "flow" downhill to the left. As you descend the wash, you may note an isolated clump of large boulders, one of which has a small hole carved through it by the wind and rain—yet another natural arch. Although every hiker will walk a different path, keep an eye out to the south for the sandy ridge and the fence line beyond it. Making your way to that sandy ridge, you will find our original established trail, which will take us back to the bridge and the parking area.

Miles and Directions

- **0.0** Trailhead gateway (GPS: N36 35.725' / W118 09.182').
- **0.1** Bridge over Lone Pine Creek.
- **0.3** Fence line on left ends (GPS: N36 35.875' / W118 09.371').
- **0.4** Yellow signpost (GPS: N36 35.918' / W118 09.469'); identify natural arch to north, and walk to it.
- **0.8** Whitney Portal Natural Arch (GPS: N36 36.142' / W118 09.344').
- **1.4** Arrive back at the parking area.

Local Attraction

Movie fans will want to look through Lone Pine Film History Museum (www.lone pinefilmhistorymuseum.org), a fun way to learn more about Hollywood's long celluloid obsession with the Alabama Hills. The museum, on Main Street at the south end of Lone Pine, also sponsors the annual Lone Pine Film Festival in October.

104 Mount Whitney Trail to Lone Pine Lake

Perched on a shelf with awesome views down a heavily glaciated canyon that gives name to Whitney Portal, Lone Pine Lake makes an excellent consolation prize for the hiker who does not have a permit to climb Mount Whitney.

Start: Whitney Portal
Distance: 5.6 miles out and back
Hiking time: About 3 hours
Difficulty: Strenuous, with an elevation gain and loss of about 1,750 feet
Trail condition: Excellent singletrack trail
Seasons: June through early Oct
Other trail users: Hikers and equestrians only
Land status: Inyo National Forest, John Muir Wilderness
Nearest towns: Lone Pine, though Whitney Portal has a small store and cafe
Fees and permits: None required for hikers going no farther than Lone Pine Lake. Day hikers going beyond require a day-use permit, obtained from the Mount Whitney Ranger

Station in Lone Pine. Overnight hikers require a wilderness permit. Hikers bound for the top of Mount Whitney are controlled by a strict quota system and need to reserve a space far in advance.
Maps: Tom Harrison: *Mount Whitney High Country*. USGS 7.5-minute quads: Mount Whitney, Mount Langley.
Trail contacts: Inyo National Forest, Mount Whitney Ranger Station, 640 S. Main St., Lone Pine, CA 93545; (760) 876-6200; www .fs.usda.gov/inyo. InterAgency Visitor Center (intersection of US 395 and CA 136, south of Lone Pine), PO Box R, Lone Pine, CA 93545; (760) 876-6222; www.fs.usda.gov/recarea/ inyo/recarea/%3frecid=20698.

Finding the trailhead: From US 395 in the center of Lone Pine, drive west up Whitney Portal Road 12 miles to the end of the road. Whitney Portal has campgrounds, picnic areas, toilets, potable water, and a small store (open summers only). The parking spaces fill early in summer, especially on weekends. Signs farther back on the Whitney Portal Road point out overflow parking areas. Trailhead GPS: N36 35.219' / W118 14.408'

The Hike

Because so many hikers want to climb Mount Whitney—at 14,505 feet the highest point in the contiguous United States—the Whitney Portal trailhead is one of the most heavily used and strictly regulated in the Sierra Nevada. With its stringent quota system, hikers submit their requests for a permit months in advance, and many are disappointed.

Since you do not need a permit to hike to Lone Pine Lake, it makes a convenient destination for hikers who want a taste of this famous trail but who have not reserved a place for a long jaunt. As far as destinations go, the multitude of switchbacks might seem a steep price to pay to reach what is, admittedly, a pretty but ordinary lake. But factor in the fantastic views of Mount Whitney on the way up, the glacier-carved canyon of Whitney Portal, the leisurely pace permitted by the shorter distance, and

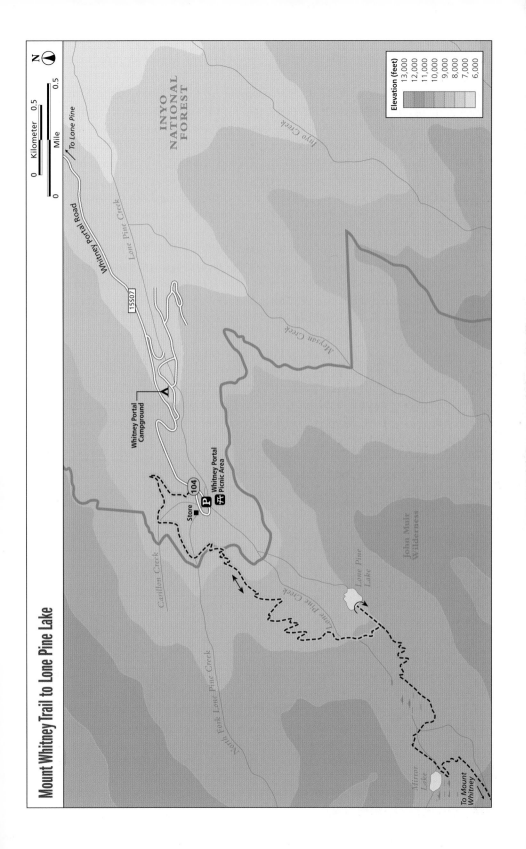

Mount Whitney Trail to Lone Pine Lake

INYO NATIONAL FOREST

John Muir Wilderness

Whitney Portal Campground

Whitney Portal Picnic Area

Store

Whitney Portal Road

Lone Pine Creek

Carillon Creek

North Fork Lone Pine Creek

Meysan Creek

Inyo Creek

Lone Pine Lake

Mirror Lake

To Lone Pine

To Mount Whitney

15507

104

N

0   Kilometer   0.5

0   Mile   0.5

Elevation (feet)

13,000
12,000
11,000
10,000
9,000
8,000
7,000
6,000

the freedom from dealing with backpacks and quotas, and Lone Pine Lake makes a very rewarding day hike.

Prepared for a bit of work, then, we start on the right (north) side of the Whitney Portal parking area (elevation 8,350 feet), passing between a battery of signs. The heavy conifer forests quickly thin as we contour toward the northern wall of the Whitney Portal canyon. Reversing directions at a switchback, we begin to mount steadily up the southern exposure of the canyon through manzanita, mountain mahogany, chinquapin, foxtail pine, and Jeffrey pine—sunny slopes that can grow hot in summer, but which stay relatively free of ice and snow throughout the spring and autumn swing seasons. Framed by granite buttresses, Mount Whitney looms on the high western horizon.

At just over half a mile, we hop across modest Carillon Creek, which some climbers mistake for the main route up Whitney's east face; a sign sets them right. The climber's intended spur is the North Fork of Lone Pine Creek, a larger stream that crosses the trail around the corner. Crossing on rocks, we pass directly into the John Muir Wilderness. We also lose sight of Mount Whitney.

Now the switchbacks begin in earnest, a steady and even gradient that carries us back and forth and ever upward, hedged in a rocky chute between Lone Pine Creek and the sheer walls of the canyon. Looking back, the desert landscapes of the lower Owens Valley and the Inyo Mountains are framed in the V-notch of Whitney Portal.

After zigzagging up 1,000 feet in 1.5 miles, the trail cuts a diagonal onto a heavily forested bench above Whitney Portal. We cross Lone Pine Creek on a series of logs that keep us from turning its wet, grassy banks into a mud hole. Climbing easily through the forest, we arrive at the high point of our trail, the Lone Pine Lake junction. Turn left (northeast), and less than a minute's walk brings us into view of Lone Pine Lake, slightly below us, sitting like a round saucer on the edge of the shelf above Whitney Portal.

Miles and Directions

0.0 Whitney Portal parking area.

0.6 Step across Carillon Creek.

0.9 Ford North Fork of Lone Pine Creek.

2.6 Log bridge over Lone Pine Creek.

2.7 Junction; bear left (northeast).

2.8 Lone Pine Lake.

5.6 Arrive back at the parking area.

Honorable Mentions

LL   Owens River Gorge

This easy out-and-back walk descends into a high-desert gorge cut into the plateau at the northern end of the Owens Valley. The plateau is made of tuft, welded volcanic cinders that were blown out over millennia in eruptions of the Long Valley Caldera. Our route is a steep, paved, 1.3-mile access road to a powerhouse owned by Los Angeles, which is closed to vehicles except for maintenance trucks. Nearly 500 feet deep in places, the sheer walls of the gorge display layers of rock—brown, yellow, pink, and white—and even some volcanic columns in the mode of Devils Postpile. The network of use-trails along the riverbanks and climbers' bolts in the rocks above attest to the popularity of the gorge among anglers and climbers. To get there from Bishop (junction of US 6 and US 395 at the north end of Main Street), drive northbound on US 395 nearly 12 miles to the Gorge Road. Turn right and drive 0.7 mile to the first junction, then turn left and continue 3.3 miles north to the turnoff to the Middle Gorge Powerhouse. Turn right and park 0.25 mile ahead in a turnoff near the locked gate. The views of the Sierra Crest from here are spectacular. Contact: Eastern Sierra InterAgency Visitor Center (see Hike 104). Trailhead GPS: N37 29.506' / W118 33.798'

MM   Alabama Hills Natural Arches Trail

If you find yourself in the Lone Pine area with time enough only for one short hike, this is the one. One of only two official hiking trails in the Alabama Hills, this 1.0-mile loop would be worth it only for the views of the boulders and the mighty Sierra Crest. Yet it is also blessed with a score, more or less, of wind-carved arches, most of them small but some of them, like Mobius Arch, large and lovely to behold. To get there, drive a bit more than 2.6 miles up Whitney Portal Road, turn right on unpaved Movie Flat Road, and drive 1.5 miles to a three-way junction. Turn right and park in the parking area that you immediately see on your left. Contact: See Hike 103. Trailhead GPS: N36 36.685' / W118 07.484'

NN   Pinyon Pine Loop

This short and sunny nature trail loops through a piñon-juniper woodland on the lower flanks of the White Mountains. Suspended above the desert at an elevation of about 7,700 feet, the trail looks eastward over a succession of desert basins and ranges of the Great Basin, clear to the Last Chance Range on the edge of Death Valley, the lowest point in the Western Hemisphere. The hardy trees and picturesque rock outcrops make a scene as handsome as any landscaped desert garden. Signage points out the piñon pine, which produces the largest and most nutritious of pine nuts, one item

Mobius Arch is a favorite among photographers.

of the traditional Piute diet that is popularly eaten today. Aficionados still gather the cones green and roast them so they open to expose the nuts, which are then shelled and eaten whole, or parched for future use, or pounded into cakes. The nuts are extraordinarily rich in fats and protein, 1 pound yielding up to 3,000 calories! The trail begins at the Pinyon Picnic Area on White Mountain Road, 3.3 miles from the junction of CA 168 at Cedar Flat, which itself is 13 miles east of US 395 in Big Pine. Contact: See Hike 102. Trailhead GPS: N37 18.868' / W118 10.863'

⊙⊙ Patriarch Grove of Bristlecone Pines

The world's largest bristlecone pine, the Patriarch Tree, grows at 11,300 feet elevation on the eastern slopes of Sheep Mountain, in the White Mountains. Measuring some 37 feet in circumference at its fluted base and spreading into a brace of stubby trunk-lets, the Patriarch looks more like a grotesque pipe organ than your standard, garden-variety pine tree. Many other bristlecones—some stark, some handsome, all highly photogenic—grow along the 0.5-mile Timberline Ancients Nature Trail. The adjacent 0.5-mile Cottonwood Basin Overlook Trail loops eastward for views down into a well-watered, granite-walled canyon, a startling contrast to the parched limestone-studded elevations where the bristlecones live. To get there from the junction of US

395 in Big Pine, drive 13 miles east on CA 168 to Cedar Flat, where you turn left onto White Mountain Road. Drive 10 miles to the Schulman Grove Visitor Center, where the pavement ends. Continue another 11.9 miles farther on White Mountain Road to the signed junction with the narrow 1-mile spur road to the Patriarch Grove. Contact: See Hike 101. Trailhead GPS: N37 31.659' / W118 11.880'

PP Fossil Falls

In the middle of a desert lava field beneath the soaring Sierra crest, a flood from the ancient Owens River carved this gorge from the volcanic mesa. By climbing along the lip of the gorge, pitted by the flood to resemble Swiss cheese, you can find a trove of bizarre, stupendous views. The canyon is only 0.25 mile from the parking area, on the east side of Highway 395 about 40 miles south of Lone Pine. Contact: Eastern Sierra InterAgency Visitor Center (intersection of US 395 and CA 136, south of Lone Pine), PO Box R, Lone Pine, CA 93545; (760) 876-6222; www.blm.gov/ca/st/en/fo/ridgecrest/fossil.html. Trailhead GPS: N35 58.305' / W117 54.638'

About the Author

A freelance writer and independent publisher who lives in the East Bay region of the San Francisco Bay Area, Barry Parr also teaches English and journalism at Livermore High School. He spends as much time in the Sierra Nevada as he can, but it is far too big to see all of it in any single lifetime.

HELP US KEEP THIS GUIDE UP TO DATE

Every effort has been made by the author and editors to make this guide as accurate and useful as possible. However, many things can change after a guide is published—trails are rerouted, regulations change, techniques evolve, facilities come under new management, and so on.

We would appreciate hearing from you concerning your experiences with this guide and how you feel it could be improved and kept up to date. While we may not be able to respond to all comments and suggestions, we'll take them to heart, and we'll also make certain to share them with the author. Please send your comments and suggestions to the following address:

Globe Pequot Press
Reader Response/Editorial Department
PO Box 480
Guilford, CT 06437

Or you may e-mail us at: editorial@GlobePequot.com

Thanks for your input, and happy trails!

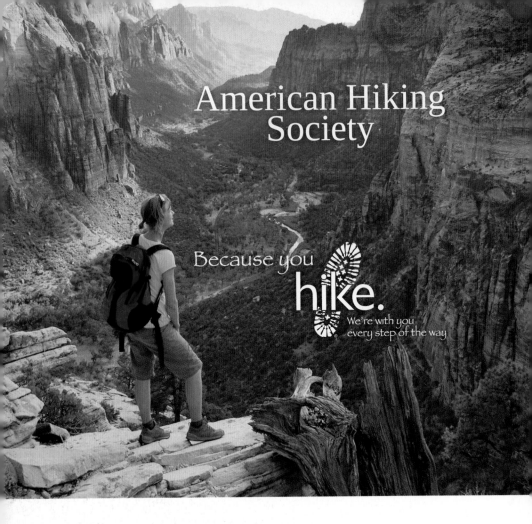